REAL MATERIALISM

Real Materialism

and other essays

GALEN STRAWSON

CLARENDON PRESS · OXFORD

OXFORD
UNIVERSITY PRESS

Great Clarendon Street, Oxford OX2 6DP

Oxford University Press is a department of the University of Oxford.
It furthers the University's objective of excellence in research, scholarship,
and education by publishing worldwide in

Oxford New York

Auckland Cape Town Dar es Salaam Hong Kong Karachi
Kuala Lumpur Madrid Melbourne Mexico City Nairobi
New Delhi Shanghai Taipei Toronto

With offices in

Argentina Austria Brazil Chile Czech Republic France Greece
Guatemala Hungary Italy Japan Poland Portugal Singapore
South Korea Switzerland Thailand Turkey Ukraine Vietnam

Oxford is a registered trade mark of Oxford University Press
in the UK and in certain other countries

Published in the United States
by Oxford University Press Inc., New York

British Library Cataloguing in Publication Data

Data available

Library of Congress Cataloging in Publication Data

Strawson, Galen.
Real materialism and other essays / Galen Strawson.
p. cm.
Includes bibliographical references (p.   ) and index.
ISBN-13: 978–0–19–926742–2
ISBN-13: 978–0–19–926743–9
1. Philosophy, Modern—21st century. I. Title.
B805.S77 2008
146'.3—dc22
2008000198

Typeset by Laserwords Private Limited, Chennai, India
Printed in Great Britain
on acid-free paper by
CPI Antony Rowe, Chippenham, Wiltshire

ISBN 978–0–19–926742–2
ISBN 978–0–19–926743–9 (Pbk.)

1 3 5 7 9 10 8 6 4 2

To my father P. F. Strawson
il miglior fabbro

Preface

The original versions of these essays were first published in the following places. Essay 1, 'Real Materialism' (2003), in *Chomsky and his Critics* edited by L. Antony & N. Hornstein (Oxford: Blackwell), pp. 49–88. Essay 2, 'Realistic Monism: Why Physicalism entails Panpsychism' (2006), in *Consciousness and its Place in Nature* edited by A. Freeman (Thorverton: Imprint Academic) pp. 3–31. Essay 3, 'Can We know the Nature of Reality?' (2002, originally called 'Knowledge of the World') in *Philosophical Issues* 12 pp. 146–75. Essay 4, 'Red and "Red"' (1989), in *Synthese* 78: 193–232. Essay 5, 'Self, Body, and Experience' (1999), in *Proceedings of the Aristotelian Society* 73 pp. 308–31. Essay 6, 'What is the Relation Between an Experience, the Subject of the Experience, and the Content of the Experience?' (2003), in *Philosophical Issues* 13 pp. 279–315. Essay 7, 'Against Narrativity' (2004), in *Ratio* 16 pp. 428–52. Essay 8, 'Episodic Ethics' (2007), in *Narrative and Understanding Persons* edited by D. Hutto (Cambridge: Cambridge University Press). Essay 9, 'Mental Ballistics: the Involuntariness of Spontaneity' (2003), in *Proceedings of the Aristotelian Society* 103 pp. 227–56. Essay 10, 'Intentionality and Experience: Terminological Preliminaries' (2005), in *Phenomenology and Philosophy of Mind*, edited by David Smith & Amie Thomasson (Oxford: Oxford University Press), pp. 41–66. Essay 11, 'Real Intentionality 3' (2008), in *Teorema* 27 (this is the final version of 'Real Intentionality' (2004), in *Phenomenology and the Cognitive Sciences* 3 pp. 287–313, and 'Real Intentionality 2' (2005), in *Synthesis Philosophica* 20 pp. 279–97). Essay 12, 'On the Inevitability of Freedom' (1986), in *American Philosophical Quarterly* 23 pp. 393–400. Essay 13, 'The Impossibility of Moral Responsibility' (1994), in *Philosophical Studies* 75 pp. 5–24. Essay 14, 'Consciousness, Free Will, and the Unimportance of Determinism' (1989), in *Inquiry* 32 pp. 3–27. Essay 15, 'Free Agents' (2004), in *Philosophical Quarterly* 32 pp. 371–402. Essay 16, 'Realism and Causation' (1987), in *Philosophical Quarterly* 37 pp. 253–77. Essay 17, 'The Contingent Reality of Natural Necessity' (1991), in *Analysis* 51 pp. 209–13. Essay 18, 'David Hume: Objects and Power' (2000), in *The New Hume Debate*, edited by R. Read and K. Richman (London: Routledge), pp. 31–51. Essay 19, 'Epistemology, Semantics, Ontology, and David Hume' (2000), in *Facta Philosophica* 2, pp. 113–31.

When I cite a work in this book I give the date of first publication, or occasionally the date of composition, while the page reference is to the edition listed in the bibliography. Although I usually cite standard editions of texts, the translations are sometimes different from those found in the standard edition. In quoting Descartes, for example, I cite the Cottingham, Stoothoof, Murdoch, and Kenny edition, but draw also on Clarke's translations and my own. In the case of Kant, I refer to Kemp Smith's translation but draw also on Pluhar and the advice of friends.

References to Hume's *Treatise* give the Selby-Bigge page reference followed by the Norton page reference or paragraph number (e.g. '218/144' or '218/1.4.3.56'). References to Hume's *Enquiry* give the Selby-Bigge page reference followed similarly by the Beauchamp page reference or paragraph number.

I am most grateful to my son Thomas Strawson for help with the compilation of the index. I am equally grateful to Peter Momtchiloff, at the Oxford University Press, for his help and encouragement, and to Nadiah Al-Ammar, Angela Anstey-Holroyd, and Christine Ranft, for their work in the final stages.

Contents

Introduction

Philosophy is world-wisdom; its problem is the world.

Schopenhauer (1819: 2.187)

Almost all the controversies of philosophy arise only from misunderstandings between philosophers.

Descartes (1646: 3.281)

1

Philosophy is one of the great sciences of reality. It has the same goal as natural science. Both seek to give true accounts, or the best accounts possible, of how things are in reality. They standardly employ very different methods. Philosophy, unlike natural science, usually works at finding good ways of characterizing how things are without engaging in much empirical or a posteriori investigation of the world. It has a vast field of exercise. Many striking and unobvious facts about the nature of reality can be established a priori, facts about the structure of self-consciousness, for example, or the possibility of free will, or the nature of intentional action, or the viability of the view that there is a fundamental metaphysical distinction between objects and their properties.

That some matters of fact are a priori (an infinite number) doesn't mean that they're not real matters of fact.[1] They're as much facts about reality as the fact that the sun shines.[2] Nor is an account of the nature of reality simply an account of what actually exists. It's equally an account of what could exist, of what is possible. To know the structure of reality is to know what is possible, and to know what is possible given what. This, accordingly, is a large part of the business of philosophy, as it is of physics, cosmology, mathematics and logic.

Philosophy, like physics, has its own distinctive domain, but it isn't isolated from natural science or empirical investigation. Good philosophy stays close to the science of its day and is continuous with it in certain respects. Philosophers regularly carry out empirical research on one of the most remarkable features of reality—conscious experience—by engaging in mental self-examination.[3] Here their work overlaps

---

At various points in this introduction I draw on material in the papers that follow.

[1] I don't use the expression 'matters of fact' in the same way as Hume (1748: 25–6/4.1).

[2] 'Logic is ... about the real world', as Prior remarked (c.1967: 45).

[3] 'Empirical' doesn't imply 'publicly observable or checkable', although the two terms have often been pushed together. 'Empirical' covers anything given in experience.

with scientific psychology, although many recent experimental psychologists have neglected the information delivered by such research on the grounds that it isn't susceptible of precise quantitative treatment.

Common sense is fundamental in philosophy, but it doesn't follow that views taken to be part of common sense outside philosophy must prevail within it.[4] There's no more reason to think that this is a condition on good philosophy than it is on good science, which is constantly overturning common-sense views of the world. Common sense isn't a matter of a body of opinions, although some opinions are a matter of common sense. It's something one uses—a way of approaching things—and it's typically common sense, exercised within philosophy or science, that leads to the abandonment of opinions held to be part of common sense outside philosophy—such as the idea that colour-as-we-experience-it is an objective property of objects.[5] If we call the body of opinions that are held to be part of common sense outside philosophy 'Common Sense' we may say that in philosophy as in science, common sense regularly leads to the rejection of Common Sense. So too, many of the most dramatic departures from common sense within philosophy take the form of holding on at all costs to parts of Common Sense. It's ordinary factotum common sense that needs to operate in philosophy, and the fact that it can lead to conclusions far from Common Sense is itself a matter of common sense, for it's a matter of common sense that 'when you have eliminated the impossible, whatever remains, however improbable, must be the truth'.[6] William James says that 'metaphysics means nothing but an unusually obstinate effort to think clearly',[7] and proper obstinacy is, again, just an attitude of steady common sense in the face of the data.

Fear is probably the greatest enemy of common sense—philosophers often reach a point where they can't face the truth—but Nietzsche picks up on another, perhaps hardly less important, when he speaks of 'philosophers . . . with . . . their vice of contradiction, of innovation at any price', a trait that we may reasonably trace back to sexual selection.[8] Descartes concurs, remarking that when it comes to speculative matters the scholar will take the more pride in his views 'the further they are from common sense . . ., since he will have had to use so much more skill and ingenuity in trying to render them plausible'.[9] In mitigation, it should be said that although common sense is fundamental in philosophy it isn't everything. Sometimes its job is to keep thinking on track when it has started out from strange and counterintuitive premises, or when it is exploring strange possibilities: 'nothing is more important for teaching us to understand the concepts we have than constructing fictitious ones'.[10]

---

[4] Nor does this follow from the fact that in philosophy as in life, many of 'the aspects of things that are most important for us are hidden because of their simplicity and familiarity' (Wittgenstein 1953: §129).

[5] See Essay 4. Philosophers will find a way to take the expression 'colour-as-we-experience-it' that allows them to say that colour-as-we-experience-it is indeed a quality in the objects themselves, but the sense in which it isn't is very plain.

[6] Sherlock Holmes in Conan Doyle 1890.   [7] 1890: 1.144.

[8] Nietzsche 1885–8: 98.   [9] Descartes 1637: 115.

[10] Wittgenstein 1914–51 (1948): 74.

It's often said that argument is the heart of philosophy, and especially of analytic philosophy, but I'm sure that's not true, if argument is thought of as primarily a matter of formally arrayed premises and conclusions. Argument in this sense is the handmaiden of philosophy, an underlabourer (the head underlabourer), to be summoned as necessary. All arguments have premises, after all, and not all premises can be argued for on pain of never getting started. The fundamental philosophical activity, I think, is a kind of open, investigative dwelling on ideas. It may well make use of formal argument, but it need not, and it is at its heart an essentially looser matter of redescribing things, putting them in other ways, spreading them out descriptively, telling stories that articulate and animate them. These are the instruments and the experiments of philosophy. It is, as a science, a suasive art, a mixture of plain speaking and the 'arduous invention which is the very eye of research'.[11] Tight argument can be very fine, but it constantly degrades the quality of philosophical debate, scholasticizing it and pushing it into unimportant minutiae and fantasy. It obstructs vision if overdone, and it invites overdoing. There's nothing quite like formal argument for losing the philosophical plot. William James made the fundamental criticism a century ago when he observed that 'the abuse of technicality is seen in the infrequency with which, in philosophical literature, metaphysical questions are discussed directly and on their own merits'.[12] Descartes is right as usual when he writes that 'those who have never studied judge much more reliably and clearly about salient matters than those who have spent all their time in the Schools'.[13] It's a further point that logic and argument operate wholly within the realm of discursive thought, and that we can see a priori, within philosophy, that discursive thought and the metaphysics it standardly presupposes aren't adequate to the characterization of reality.[14]

I greatly enjoy coming across early expressions of views I think correct, especially if they're not widely known, and a number of these pieces incorporate newly added quotations (they're otherwise very little revised). The older philosophers very often put the issues we discuss today much more clearly and directly, and I find it hard not to quote them.[15] It's nice to find Joseph Priestley making the fundamental mind-body 'supervenience' claim in 1778,[16] and depressing to see philosophers making long-corrected mistakes over and over again in reputable printed places. It's sad and sometimes annoying,[17] and sometimes funny, to see philosophers falling into the happy trap of thinking that they have come up with something new, fiercely ignorant of the real history of the tradition in which they work and often little helped by much that is written under the heading of history of philosophy. (I speak as a past and no doubt future victim.) In this respect philosophy can't compare with science, logic and mathematics; but there are well known reasons why this isn't all a bad thing. First among them is the fact that philosophy is a practice and a discipline as much as it is a

---

[11] George Eliot 1871–2: ch. 16.   [12] 1909: 15.   [13] Descartes 1618–28: 1.16.
[14] See e.g. p. 73 below. See also James 1909, for some interesting (if slightly new-age sounding) support.
[15] We do discuss the same issues—but differently dressed and increasingly scholasticized in the pejorative sense.
[16] See pp. 46–7 below.   [17] It depends on the degree of self-importance.

body of doctrine, and that there are mistakes that have to be re-experienced by philosophers from generation to generation in the process of achieving understanding.[18]

In discussion groups, the rôle of distinguished older members often seems to be to speak first, after the paper has been delivered, in order to point out that the hot theory put forward by the younger member is really no different from what so-and-so said *n* years ago.[19] The young party is blithely confident that the old body just doesn't get it, and the young party is often right, inasmuch as the old body isn't entangled in the details of the new terminology, but the younger body is almost certainly wrong in the larger scheme of things.[20] I'm sure everything I'm saying here has been said before, including this.[21] But this comment too needs to be qualified, by Pascal's reply to the charge that there was nothing original in his work:

Let no one say that I have said nothing new: the organization of the subject matter is new. When we play tennis, we both play with the same ball, but one of us places it better.[22]

One reason why philosophy can seem so unappreciative of its history is internal to the nature of the discipline. Some philosophy 'has constantly to be done over again',

[18] ' "How great a philosopher is Reid? The answer is best conveyed by a story concerning Roderick Chisholm, [who] received a telephone call from a man saying that he was a busy man but had time to read one serious book in philosophy and wanted to do so. He said that he was not interested in entertainment but simply wanted to read a book with a greater amount of truth than any alternative. Chisholm, wishing to reflect on the matter, said the man should call back the next day, and he would give him his advice. The next day Chisholm recommended that the caller study Reid. It was a sound judgement" [Lehrer 1989: 1]. Maybe it was a sound judgement, but it was a terrible idea. Chisholm should have told the man that he had the wrong approach, and that he should read several books or none—perhaps Descartes, Locke, Berkeley, and Hume, and then Reid. The latter may well have been right to say that "it is genius, and not the want of it, that . . . fills [philosophy] with error and false theory", but he was quite wrong to say that genius thereby "adulterates" the subject. Philosophical understanding has a very strange dynamic, and makes progress only by means of the errors (it is not an adequate word) of genius. This is something Reid would probably have been the first to acknowledge: he owed his own philosophical achievement to the impact which Hume's "errors" were able to make on him given the enormous impact that Berkeley's "errors" had already made on him' (Strawson 1990: 15).

[19] *n* can be as large as 3,000.

[20] A. J. Ayer was particularly good at this, in the discussion group called 'Freddie's Group' after him. After his death my father took up something of the same rôle, although without any of Ayer's (not unenjoyable) exasperation. On the general question of influence, all professional philosophers, even the youngest, have a rich past of reading and listening and teaching in the course of which they often come across an idea, fail to see the point of it, fail to understand it fully or think it plain wrong and forget it, while remaining sensitized to it in such a way that it is more ready to hand in the mind when their own thoughts later lead them that way. But it may just as often happen that one has the idea in question simply because it lies in the logic of one's current train of thought, without any significant causal link to a past encounter.

[21] 'Everything has been said before, but since nobody listens we have to keep going back and beginning all over again' (André Gide, 1891). A good example is the present-day discussion of perception, which makes enjoyable use of new experimental-psychological results but hasn't surpassed the outstanding eighteenth-century debate in any fundamental respect (it has on the whole fallen short of it). The last fifty years of debate about the 'mind-body problem' have been greatly inferior to the seventeenth- and eighteenth-century debate (see Essay 1).

[22] *c.*1640–1662, §575; this is why introductions to philosophy can make important contributions. 'One might as well say that I've used old words', Pascal continued, for 'just as the same words constitute different thoughts by being differently arranged, so too the same thoughts constitute a different body of work by being differently arranged.'

as P. F. Strawson remarks in the course of making his well-known distinction between 'descriptive' and 'revisionary' metaphysics.[23] A different point concerns individuals rather than their times. It seems one never really understands an idea until one has had it oneself in some active, involved way that essentially outstrips off-the-page understanding. One consequence of this is that many, when they really grasp an idea, tend to experience it as new and somehow their own. And they're right in a way. It is one-self alone who has had the idea now and *in vivo* in one's own thinking, and there is in this sense a great deal of genuine private originality in the profession.[24] This, however, tends to lead to an illusion of Originality—greatly strengthened by the fact that one has probably added some small personal twist to the idea or employed a different terminology (to which one has become rather attached) to express it. Many derive great pleasure from a sense of new discovery, creation and independence, and this tilts the landscape of judgement. Some of us are intensely proprietorial creatures, strongly governed by the territorial instinct, the appropriative urge and the accompanying 'anxiety of influence'.[25]

None of this can be changed in human nature, and some of it may be needed. The free-will problem will always be recapitulated by each student philosopher in a way that involves considerable emotion, and an accompanying sense of individual ownership of the problem, and there's certainly nothing wrong with that. But present-day analytic philosophers badly need to know more about their intellectual ancestors, and to keep them alive by quotation on the pages of new work. No one should let the need to feel original undercut the thrill of belonging to a powerful, beautiful and ancient tradition. It's extremely moving to see thinkers dealing with the same difficulties and grasping the same abstract truths across the centuries, even as (nearly) everything has to be done over again. That apart, it can save a great deal of time. Some think no age or culture can really understand another because the differences—of

---

[23] 'There is a massive core of human thinking which has no history—or none recorded in histories of thought; there are categories and concepts which, in their most fundamental character, change not at all. Obviously these are not specialities of the most refined thinking. They are the commonplaces of the least refined thinking; and are yet the indispensable core of the conceptual equipment of the most sophisticated human beings. It is with these, their interconnexions, and the structure that they form, that a descriptive metaphysics will be primarily concerned.

Metaphysics has a long and distinguished history, and it is consequently unlikely that there are any new truths to be discovered in descriptive metaphysics. But this does not mean that the task of descriptive metaphysics has been, or can be, done once for all. It has constantly to be done over again. If there are no new truths to be discovered, there are old truths to be rediscovered. For though the central subject-matter of descriptive metaphysics does not change, the critical and analytical idiom of philosophy changes constantly. Permanent relationships are described in an impermanent idiom, which reflects both the age's climate of thought and the individual philosopher's personal style of thinking. No philosopher understands his predecessors until he has re-thought their thought in his own contemporary terms; and it is characteristic of the very greatest philosophers, like Kant and Aristotle, that they, more than any others, repay this effort of re-thinking' (P. F. Strawson 1959: 10–11).

[24] Grote 'can think of nothing more noxious for students than to get into the habit of saying to themselves about their ordinary philosophic thought, Oh, somebody must have thought it all before' (1865: 130).

[25] Most strikingly described, in the case of literature, by Nicholson Baker (1991). One often sees acknowledgements of others in early drafts of a piece of work drop out in later drafts in spite of the fact that they remain as apposite as ever.

idiom, presupposition, 'episteme'—are always too deep, but this idea is as silly in the history of ideas as it is in anthropology.

2

'So far as I know, the existence of . . . states of consciousness . . . has never been doubted by any critic, however sceptical in other respects he may have been. That we have *cogitations* of some sort is the *inconcussum* in a world most of whose other facts have at some time tottered in the breath of philosophic doubt.'[26] This was William James's view in 1890, and he was as far I know correct—that up to that point, no philosophers had actually denied the existence of consciousness or conscious experience, although they had denied almost everything else. It was only in the twentieth century that some philosophers took the final step and denied the existence of conscious experience, which I'll call 'experience' for short.[27]

This is surely the strangest thing that has ever happened in the whole history of human thought, not just in the whole history of philosophy.[28] It shows in a very pure way that the power of human credulity is unlimited, that the capacity of human minds to be gripped by theory, by faith, is truly unbounded. I wish it hadn't fallen to philosophy to expose the deepest irrationality of the human mind, but there's no escaping the fact. Next to the denial of the existence of experience, every known religious belief is only a little less sensible than the belief that grass is green. 'Nothing can be imagined which is too strange or incredible to have been said by some philosopher', as Descartes says,[29] but the denial of the existence of experience suggests that he was more right than he could have imagined.

There are psychiatric patients suffering from Cotard's delusion who sincerely believe they don't exist. It is, however, possible to give a rather plausible explanation of this pathological phenomenon, if only in general terms,[30] whereas no explanation of the same general sort seems available in the case of those who deny the existence of experience.[31] Their case deserves careful attention from anyone seeking a general theory of the mechanisms of delusion in human beings, for any such general theory must

---

[26] James 1890: 1.185. The *inconcussum* is the unknockable-out thing. He uses the word 'cogitation' or 'thought' in the wide Cartesian sense to cover all kinds of conscious mental episodes or 'states of consciousness' (see e.g. 1890: 1.186, 224).

[27] In 1904 James published a piece provocatively entitled 'Does Consciousness Exist?'. He was not, though, an early advocate of the silliest view ever put forward. His title is misleading, to put it mildly, for his central thesis in this essay is (in the words of the title of his next essay) that the world is 'A World of Pure Experience', and his opening proposal is that 'we start from the supposition that there is only one primal stuff or material in the world, a stuff of which everything is composed, and [that] we call that stuff "pure experience" ' (1904: 3). His objection is to the idea that consciousness is an 'entity' that is in any sense an isolable factor in experience.

[28] No Buddhist school, however nihilistic its language, has ever gone this far.

[29] 1637: 1.118.

[30] See e.g. Gerrans 2000: 112: 'The Cotard delusion, in its extreme form, is a rationalization of a feeling of disembodiment based on global suppression of affect resulting from extreme depression.'

[31] That said (and putting aside the effects of fashion) it is perhaps a serious empirical hypothesis that the most committed deniers of the existence of experience have in common certain sorts of psychological pain experienced in early life that they have dealt with in a way that made it possible

recognize the fact that people whom we do not consider to be psychologically unwell can sincerely (or so it seems) hold a view whose falsity is inescapably proved to them every second of their waking life, simply because it follows from some other view or views that they are utterly unprepared to give up (in this they are like sufferers from Capgras's delusion who are certain that someone very close to them is an impostor).

What could this other view be, in the present case? In the philosophy of mind it usually goes under the name of 'physicalism' or 'materialism', the view that everything mental—and indeed everything that concretely exists—is physical.[32] Physicalism about the mind is usually understood to be the same thing as 'naturalism' about the mind, and in these papers—essays—I accept this equation of naturalism with physicalism. I also accept that physicalism/naturalism is true. But I don't for a moment think that it has the consequence that there's no such thing as experience. This is because I'm a *realistic* physicalist, a *real* physicalist, a *realistic* or *real* naturalist, and one can't be one of those if one denies the existence of the entirely natural phenomenon whose existence is more certain than the existence of anything else: experience. Full recognition of the reality of experience is the obligatory starting point for any remotely realistic version of physicalism because it's the obligatory starting point for any remotely realistic theory of what there is. It's the obligatory starting point for any theory that can legitimately claim to be naturalistic because experience is itself the fundamental given natural fact.

It's also the only certainly known natural fact, according to one classical high standard of certainty that has an unshakably important place in philosophy (even if it must be sparingly used). This makes it all the more bewildering to find philosophers arguing from physicalism or naturalism to the non-existence of experience; for the foot, in fact, is in the other boot. If we call experience 'E', the correct argument can be expressed as follows.

[1] If there exists something other than E that we as naturalists take to be a natural phenomenon, e.g. physical-stuff-conceived-as-something-that-is-in-its-intrinsic-nature-wholly-non-experiential (call it 'NE'), and which is such that we find it hard to understand how E exists as it does if NE exists, then NE must be a problem for naturalism; but not E.

We are in this case in no position to say, as naturalists,

[2] NE certainly exists, as a matter of natural fact, and it's most unclear, given NE and the evidently intensely intimate relation between NE and E, how E is possible (and perhaps E is not possible).

We are in a position to say

[3] *If* NE exists, as a matter of natural fact, then it is most unclear how E is possible, given the intensely intimate relation between NE and E.

for them to be attracted to such a denial. The cases of the behaviourists Skinner and Watson are instructive.

[32] Many build 'concretism'—the view that no non-concrete or 'abstract' entities (e.g. numbers) are part of reality—into physicalism, and accordingly take physicalism to be the view that everything that exists is physical. It does not follow from this that all truths are truths about physical matters.

But then we must contrapose (roughly speaking) and go on to say

[4] Well, E certainly exists, as matter of certain natural fact, so it is most unclear how NE is possible, given the intensely intimate relation between NE and E; and we have in fact no good reason to believe NE is actual.

This is the correct conclusion. The truth is that we don't really have any good reason to believe that anything like NE exists in nature, although nearly everyone takes its existence for granted.[33]

My use of the words 'physicalism' and 'materialism' is non-standard relative to their use in the last fifty years or so, because many philosophers in this period have used them—and still use them—in such a way that it follows from the truth of physicalism or materialism that there's no such thing as experience. This is, however, a very recent use. None of the many and great materialists of past times held this view. Their view, as materialists, was (in Locke's words) that matter might think, i.e. that experience itself, conscious experience conceived of in a wholly realistic, non-reductionist way, might be a wholly physical phenomenon.[34] It was only in the twentieth century—the silliest of all the centuries, philosophically speaking (for all its achievements)—that 'materialism' and 'physicalism' came to have this extraordinary meaning (though never for all), in a way that allowed the debate about physicalism to become completely unreal.

It's hard to imagine a more anti-naturalist doctrine than naturalism as currently defined, given that it denies the existence of—treats as *super*natural—the fundamentally given natural fact: (conscious) experience. Some define naturalism primarily in a methodological way, as the doctrine that all valid enquiry into the nature of things must proceed in accord with the methods of the natural sciences, and believe that they can extract from this the conclusion that naturalism can take no account of experience (although it is the fundamental given natural fact) and indeed that experience doesn't exist. It takes a very rigid and peculiar definition of the methods of the natural sciences to achieve this result, in fact, for many experimental psychologists deal in the phenomena of experience in a fully realist manner. Still, some have persisted in the rigid definition of naturalism, and gone on to embrace—with some passion—the silliest view ever held by any human being.

Twentieth-century philosophy followed an extraordinary fashion, then, especially in its second half, and especially in the philosophy of mind. But no sensible philosophers ever took it seriously, even for a moment. They suffered radical eyebrow-elevation when people started talking about the 'hard' problem of consciousness (a) as if there were an easy problem of consciousness[35] and (b) as if the problem of consciousness had somehow slipped off the agenda in philosophy. These philosophers knew as

---

[33] See further Essay 2.   [34] On Locke's view see further p. 39 n83 (Essay 1).

[35] This was part of the implication of the phrase as popularized by Chalmers, but it involved a shift in the standard philosophical meaning of the word 'consciousness'. The *mind-body* problem does have an easy part, from the materialist point of view, but it's not part of the traditional problem of *consciousness*. See Strawson 1994: 93–6.

well as Descartes, Locke, Leibniz[36] and a host of others that the problem of consciousness was the hard part of the mind-body problem (given the standard conception of the nature of the physical) and continued to discuss it fruitfully throughout the crazy years.

3

I've given the issue of physicalism (in the philosophy of mind) special mention in this introduction, because it's a constant theme of these papers.[37] I'll now say a little more about their content and origins. Looking back, I see a strong degree of developmental coherence. Sidetracks turn out to be things that I needed to work out given existing concerns. I had no idea that this was so, although I expect it's true of nearly everyone.

I took up philosophy in 1972 in my fourth and final year at Cambridge University after two years of Islamic Studies and a year of Social and Political Science. My intention was to go back to social and political science after having acquired a better idea of its foundations, but that intention expired in the pleasure and often painful fascination of doing philosophy. I sat the Cambridge University Moral Sciences Part II exam in May 1973 after less than six months' study of the subject,[38] and knew almost nothing about it when I began on a DPhil at Oxford in October 1974 (having in the intervening period lived in Paris, worked on a building site and in television, and got married). After about a year my supervisor Derek Parfit advised me to switch from the DPhil to the BPhil in order to acquire some grounding in the subject. I followed this good advice and took the BPhil exam in 1977—but still without having read any Locke, nor indeed any significant amount of Hume, nor any moral philosophy. In the BPhil exam I answered at length a question about the difference between being the same person and being the same man without having any idea that the question contained a reference to Locke's famous discussion of personal identity.

At this time I had a wife, a daughter, a mortgage and no money. We moved to Paris for a year. My wife worked as a *capésienne* schoolteacher, I attended the Ecole normale supérieure as an *auditeur libre* and French government scholar, joining Jacques Derrida's Groupe de Recherche pour l'Enseignement de la Philosophie and his seminar for Yale students in Paris and trying (with no success) to understand what he was talking about. In June 1978 we returned to England and I took a temporary job as an editorial assistant at the *Times Literary Supplement* under John Gross, reading and marking up proofs, editing copy, and, later on (when the job prolonged itself), commissioning reviews. From 1978 to 1986 I worked two to three days a week at the

---

[36] For Leibniz's famous story of the mill see p. 401 below.

[37] See in particular Essays 1 and 2. I repeat the point in many of the other papers, which were written as self-standing pieces, because I have to explain my use of the terms 'physicalism' and 'naturalism'.

[38] I returned late to Cambridge for my final year, having contracted hepatitis in the Middle East in the preceding summer, and learnt what I could in a short time under the sure direction of Philip Pettit, David Papineau and Timothy Smiley. I think I had about a dozen supervisions in all.

Times Literary Supplement office, commuting from Oxford to London forty-six weeks a year, and from 1979 onwards I also taught full-time at Oxford, holding a series of temporary college lecturerships, wrote numerous book reviews for a number of different papers and magazines (something I found very difficult), and tried to finish my DPhil thesis on free will. I applied for all the many junior research fellowships and other research posts on offer in Oxford during this period but was uniformly unsuccessful, as I was also in applying for permanent teaching jobs—until 1987, when with a shiny first book in hand I had the good fortune to be elected Fellow and Tutor in Philosophy at Jesus College.

For these reasons and others, including the birth of my son Tom, I didn't publish any work of philosophy until 1986, when I was thirty-four. These papers are a selection of those I've published since then. Philosophers often write papers and work them into a book, but I've gone the other way. Most of these papers develop themes either from my DPhil thesis and subsequent book *Freedom and Belief* (1986) or from *The Secret Connexion* (1989) and *Mental Reality* (1994). I'm struck now by the fact that I've written almost exclusively about the things I wanted to write about when I was an undergraduate in a state of high excitement. The feeling of excitement remains the same thirty-five years later. I find philosophy a profoundly concrete, sensual activity.[39] The world of ideas is as solid as the world of seas and mountains, or more so. One can no more change its topography than one can move Oxford closer to London, although one can discover new views or discover that one has got the topography wrong, or that many people have for many years. Ideas seem as embodied, in the world of ideas, with its views and obstructions and vastness, as we do in our material world. They seem tangible, with specific savours, aesthetic properties, emotional tones, curves, surfaces, insides, hidden places, structure, geometry, dark passages, shining corners, auras, force fields and combinatorial chemistry.

I've been almost uniformly unsuccessful in submitting papers to journals. Almost all my early work was published only in book form. Only three of the papers in this book (4, 12, and 16) made it through the process of anonymous peer review.[40] All the others are commissions of one sort or another. My publication record with *Mind* is particularly distinguished: six submissions between about 1985 to 2000, six rejections, including Essays 1, 4, 16 and papers that were eventually published as parts of books, such as 'The Weather Watchers', which became chapter 9 of *Mental Reality*, and a paper of which I was particularly fond (it became §§1.4 and 1.7 of *Mental Reality*), which received the most dismissive criticism of all. This may or may not be disheartening to younger philosophers, depending on their view of the rejected work and their finances. I was in any case lucky to get a job in the UK, where there is no tenure process, near the beginning of my publishing career. This freed me from dependence on the process of learned-journal peer review, a process that probably

---

[39] In some sense of 'sensual' given which the intellectual can be sensual. Mention of *The Critique of Pure Reason* always causes in me the same physiological reaction as hungry thought about food.

[40] Of these only Essay 12 (my first submission) had a straight passage. Essays 4 and 16 were rejected and re-rejected in their present form before finding a peer-reviewed berth.

works reasonably well in knocking out papers below a certain level of basic competence, but seems otherwise close to random.

The first two papers, 'Real Materialism' and 'Realistic Monism: Why Physicalism entails Panpsychism', take forward the discussion of the 'mind-body problem' in chapters 3 and 4 of *Mental Reality*. The discussion in *Mental Reality* arose in turn from problems encountered when writing a DPhil in the late 1970s, problems with the standard opposition between mental and physical that led me increasingly to abandon the terms 'mental' and 'physical' in favour of a distinction between the mental and the non-mental (or the experiential and the non-experiential).[41] Both these papers terminate in the claim that if you're a materialist or physicalist in the philosophy of mind, if you want to call yourself a materialist or a physicalist, then you should be prepared to be a panpsychist physicalist (a view already adopted in *Mental Reality*, but rather covertly).

The next, somewhat overwrought paper, 'Can we Know the Nature of Reality as It is In Itself?', is a revision of a paper first published under the title 'Knowledge of the World', itself a pruning and elaboration of chapter 7 and Appendix B of *The Secret Connexion*. I argue that there's nothing wrong with the much-criticized phrase 'reality as it is in itself', and that it's often very useful although strictly speaking redundant. I then argue that there's no reason in principle why one couldn't attain to some knowledge of the nature of that part of concrete reality (as it is in itself) that is other than the part that consists of one's own conscious experience, whose nature I take it that one does know as is in itself, at least in certain respects, simply because 'the having of it is the knowing'.[42] At the same time I grant that one could never know that one had done so, and that there are also considerable difficulties in the whole idea.

I also defend the irrefutability of scepticism, arguing that the determination to refute scepticism is one of the great sources of philosophical error. Many philosophers have thought that a good philosophical theory should provide an answer to scepticism, but this is the reverse of the truth. Acknowledgement of the irrefutability of scepticism (so far as claims to knowledge of the ultimate nature of reality other than one's own conscious experience are concerned) is an essential part of a realist attitude to the world, and therefore of any defensible philosophical attitude to the world. Realism broadly construed—the view that something other than one's own conscious experience is real and that this reality has some intrinsic or ultimate nature—is effectively inescapable,[43] and with it comes the irrefutability of scepticism. It follows that any theory which on its own terms provides an answer to scepticism with respect to knowledge claims about the ultimate nature of mind-independent reality (more precisely, reality independent of one's own experience) is ipso facto refuted.

To think that scepticism must be defeated is to take it too seriously. It is to accord it too much force. To acknowledge that it is irrefutable is to keep it in proportion. In this sense Kant is wrong to say that 'it remains a scandal to philosophy and to human

---

[41] See e.g. *Freedom and Belief*, ch. 9 §1.

[42] pp. 25, 41 below (Essay 1). I develop the point in Strawson 2006b: 250–6, responding to queries raised by Goff (2006).

[43] Berkeley counts as a realist by this fundamental measure, as he should.

reason in general that the existence of things outside us . . . must be accepted merely on *faith*, and that if anyone thinks good to doubt their existence, we are unable to counter his doubts by any satisfactory proof',[44] and Heidegger is right (although not for the right reasons) to say in reply that 'the "scandal of philosophy" is not that this proof has yet to be given, but that such proofs are expected and attempted again and again'.[45] It is not a virtue of Wittgensteinian accounts of the nature of language and thought that they build the falsity of scepticism about other minds into the very meaning of terms for mental states and occurrences; it is, rather, a proof of their inadequacy. The price they pay—severing words like 'pain' from what they actually mean or refer to—is so high that it constitutes a spectacular if covert capitulation to scepticism.

The fourth paper, 'Red and "Red"', has its origins not in a book, but in an undergraduate project to write a paper called 'Red, Square, and In Pain'.[46] It argues that words for colour properties are essentially words for phenomenal properties, i.e. properties whose whole and essential nature can be and is fully revealed in sensory experience.[47] It defends and endorses the well known colour-spectrum-inversion thought-experiment, according to which (in its most dramatic version) it's possible that the experience you think of as red-experience is qualitatively just like the experience I think of as green-experience although we agree fully in language about which things are red and which things are green. It considers the consequence for language: that if we take a word like 'red' to be essentially a word for a phenomenal property, as it seems we should, then it doesn't seem that it can name any *particular* phenomenal property. This paper already has a somewhat historical air because of the way in which it focuses on questions about language. It was the first paper I read to 'Freddie's Group', an Oxford discussion group presided over by A. J. Ayer which I had recently joined. I remember the sympathetic manner in which Donald Davidson, then a temporary member, phrased his criticisms.

The fifth paper, 'Self, Body, and Experience', was a contribution to an enjoyable symposium at the Aristotelian Society and Mind Association Joint Session in 1999 at which Sydney Shoemaker was the first speaker and Greg McCulloch the combative commentator. The paper has its origins in a paper written for Ralph Walker in 1976 when studying for the BPhil, and abridges a much longer piece, 'The Grounds of Self-Consciousness', which I wrote in 1995 after being asked to give the final lecture on 'The Self' in the 1996 Wolfson College Lecture Series 'From Soul to Self'. Writing this paper left me empty, although the later parts flowed effortlessly.[48] One reason for this may have been that the paper argued directly against the neo-Kantian framework of discussion of self-consciousness established by my father in his books *Individuals* (1959) and *The Bounds of Sense* (1966) and widely endorsed in the Oxford

---

[44] 1781–7: Bxxxix n.   [45] 1927: 249.

[46] Ch. 8 of *Mental Reality* ('Pain and "Pain"') attempts to carry out the third part of this project. It strikes me now that the second ('Square') part of the project turned into Essay 3.

[47] Mark Johnston (1992) calls this position 'Revelation' and is followed in this by Frank Jackson (1998) and others (e.g. Stoljar 2006).

[48] It is now Part Three of *Selves: An Essay in Revisionary Metaphysics*, one of two fission products of an abandoned book called *The Self*.

philosophical community to which I had no sense of belonging although I was at that time a Fellow of Jesus College.

The next paper, 'What is the Relation between an Experience, the Subject of the Experience, and the Content of the Experience?' grew out of work on the abandoned book *The Self*, largely completed in 1998, after a wonderful year of writing as a Leverhulme Trust Senior Research Fellow, but unfinished for lack of time.[49] This is another paper that flowed out, for better or worse. It argues that if one starts from a currently unusual but not unnatural 'thin' or 'live' understanding of the notion of the subject of experience, according to which a subject of experience exists *sensu stricto* only when there is experience that it is the subject (or haver) of, then the right answer to the title question is 'identity'.[50] This, of course, is a piece of extreme revisionary metaphysics, and I am therefore the more happy to report that my father, renowned as a descriptive metaphysician who regarded revisionary metaphysics with considerable suspicion, told me that he thought the conclusion was probably right—if one chose to do philosophy that way at all.

When I went back to this paper in preparing this collection I found many errors of numbering, notation, typography and thought. The fundamental drift and spirit of the paper are clear in spite of its errors (it was published to a deadline before I had had time to finish it properly), but I've revised it thoroughly for this collection in an attempt at greater clarity.

§7 of the paper is concerned with the object/property distinction. I argue in Cartesian terminology for the Cartesian view (I didn't then know it to be such) that there is no 'real distinction' between an object and its properties or propertiedness, no sense in which the object and its properties or propertiedness are metaphysically distinct, although we can make a valid 'conceptual' distinction or 'distinction of reason' between them. This was my first encounter with the 'problem of universals', and I have revised this section for two reasons. First, I no longer think that there is any respect in which ordinary thought (as opposed to philosophy) makes an error about the nature of the object/property relation. Second, I no longer think it's rhetorically helpful to defend any version of the claim that there is a sense in which objects can be said to be 'collections' of properties, however carefully the claim is qualified.[51]

The next two papers, 'Against Narrativity' and 'Episodic Ethics', expand on the themes of a Wolfson College lecture on 'The Sense of the Self' delivered in 1996.[52] These too were once parts of *The Self*, and I hope that their descendants will one day appear in a distinct book called *Life in Time*. 'Against Narrativity' begins by introducing a distinction between 'Diachronic' and 'Episodic' personalities. When people think about themselves they often figure themselves as something whose identity and persistence conditions are not necessarily the same as the identity and persistence

[49] *The Self* grew in turn from ch. 9 of *Freedom and Belief*, 'Self-Consciousness', and its Appendix, 'The Sense of Self', together with ch. 5 of *Mental Reality*.

[50] I say unusual, but it is in fact Descartes's conception of the subject of experience, and Hume's, and Fichte's, and I think Spinoza's, and Leibniz's. . . .

[51] On this point I have benefited from discussions with Philip Goff.   [52] Strawson 1999c.

conditions of the human being that they know themselves to be when considered as a whole. More particularly, people often figure themselves specifically as a self or 'inner mental someone', rather than as a whole human being, and to be *Diachronic* is to experience oneself, so figured, as something that was there in the (further) past and will be there in the (further) future, something that has relatively long-term diachronic continuity, something that persists over a long stretch of time—perhaps for life. To be Episodic is to lack this perspective. It is to have little or no sense that the self that one experiences oneself to be was there in the (further) past and will be there in the (further) future, although one is perfectly well aware that one has long-term continuity considered as a whole human being.

I then introduce a further distinction between 'Narrative' and 'non-Narrative types'. To be Narrative is, roughly, to have a tendency to apprehend one's life as constituting a story or having a story-like development of some sort, and also, no doubt, to have some sort of investment (positive or negative) in this way of apprehending it. To be *non-Narrative* is to have no such tendency or investment.

With these distinctions in hand, I argue against two theses that are currently widely accepted in the humanities: a descriptive empirical thesis which I call the 'psychological Narrativity thesis', according to which all ordinary, normal human beings see or live or experience their life as a narrative or story of some sort, or at least as a collection of stories, and a normative thesis which I call the 'ethical Narrativity thesis', according to which such an outlook on one's life is a good thing, essential to living well, essential to true or full personhood.

It seems plausible that psychological Narrativity presupposes Diachronicity (although this can be challenged), and this leads some to think that an Episodic person can't live a good life. Some think that being Episodic rules out leading a good life even if one can live a good life and develop fully as a person independently of being properly moral. 'Episodic ethics' argues against both these opinions.

The next paper, 'Mental Ballistics: the Involuntariness of Spontaneity', is a recasting and expansion of material largely omitted from my DPhil thesis and *Freedom and Belief*, supplemented by a good number of quotations picked up over the years. It argues that there's a fundamental respect in which reason, thought and judgement neither are nor can be a matter of action. Nor can they be said to be a matter of spontaneity in anything other than Kant's original sense of the term according to which the freedom of true spontaneity is in fact wholly a matter of necessity, of being determined by reason. Rimbaud is the poet of the point when he writes that

it's false to say: I think. One ought to say 'it thinks [in] me . . . for *I* is an other. . . . It's obvious to me that I am a spectator at the unfolding of my thought: I watch it, I listen to it[53]

but you certainly don't have to be a genius to agree with him.

The tenth and eleventh papers, 'Intentionality and Experience: Terminological Preliminaries' and its sister paper 'Real Intentionality 3', try to advance the position adopted in chapter 7 of *Mental Reality* according to which all genuinely intentional

---

[53] 1871: 249, 250.

states are conscious or experiential states.[54] Both stress the point that the phenomenological character of our experiences is not just a matter of sensory character but also of cognitive character, so that we need a *cognitive phenomenology* as well as a sensory phenomenology. Both grew out of a long and rather rickety paper prepared for the 2002 NEH Summer Institute on Intentionality and Consciousness held in Santa Cruz. 'Intentionality and Experience' laments the extraordinary terminological wreckage that has recently been visited on large parts of the philosophy of mind as the flight from 'psychologism' in the theory of meaning has (utterly predictably) returned like a boomerang to produce an anti-psychologistic psychology, or rather an anti-psychological psychology—an anti-psychology psychology.

Both papers repeat a proposal from *Mental Reality* which is I think important but unlikely to achieve adequate recognition in the current philosophical, cognitive-psychological and experimental-psychological climate of thought. This is the proposal that when we engage in phenomenology, and consider experience, we need a more general category than the category of a *sensory modality*—even when we blithely stretch the meaning of 'sensory' to cover all affective or emotional matters, all matters of mood. We need the general category of an *experiential modality*. We can then subsume the sensory modalities under this general category while leaving a clear place for a distinct experiential modality: the experiential modality of conscious thought. Having done this, we need to be very clear that (find no difficulty in the idea that) the particular form of the experiential modality of conscious thought that is found in creatures like ourselves is something that has evolved naturally—just as the particular forms of the sensory modalities that are found in creatures like ourselves have evolved naturally. Any realistic physicalist who believes in the theory of evolution by natural selection must believe that this has happened, because the existence of the experiential modality of conscious thought is an evident fact (as I try to show in these two papers).

Perhaps nothing like the fully developed human form of the experiential modality of conscious thought can evolve until sensory modalities like ours are already well evolved. Perhaps the former grow out of the latter, or on top of them, in some way.[55] It may well be that the former cannot exist in nature independently of the latter. These are interesting (and old) questions, but they are questions of detail none of which impugn the point that the existence of the experiential modality of conscious thought—its concrete reality—is an unbudgeable natural fact. Nor do they cast any doubt on the idea that the experiential modality of conscious thought is a distinct experiential modality, as distinct from each of the sensory modalities as they are from each other.

The free-will papers, 'On the Inevitability of Freedom', 'On the Impossibility of (Ultimate) Moral Responsibility' and 'Consciousness, Free Will, and the Unimportance of Determinism', overlap considerably. They develop some of the themes of

---

[54] 'Real intentionality 3' is so-called because it's the finished version of a paper—'Real intentionality'—that was published uncompleted to a deadline in 2004, and published again, still unfinished, in 2006.

[55] Or perhaps the latter are already seeded with the former in some way. There are various reasons to suspect the idea of pure or mere sensation, given the entanglement of sensation and cognition in perception.

Freedom and Belief, in which I argue that there is a fundamental 'strong' sense of the word 'free' given which we neither are nor can be free agents in such a way as to be truly or ultimately responsible for what we do. It strikes me now that 'On the Inevitability of Freedom' deals with the problem posed by Harry Frankfurt's famous paper 'Alternate Possibilities and Moral Responsibility', a paper which I somehow managed to be ignorant of at the time. 'Consciousness, Free Will, and the Unimportance of Determinism' is a contribution to a set of papers that discuss Ted Honderich's book *A Theory of Determinism* (Oxford University Press, 1990). 'Free Agents' is a recent attempt to compress the core of Part III of *Freedom and Belief* — penetrated, understandably, by very few readers — into a single more accessible paper.

What is this so-called 'ultimate' responsibility? One dramatic way to characterize it is by reference to the story of heaven and hell: ultimate moral responsibility is responsibility of such a kind that, if we have it, it makes sense to propose that it could be just to punish some of us with torment in hell and reward others with bliss in heaven. It makes sense because what we do is absolutely up to us. I say 'makes sense' because one doesn't have to believe in the story of heaven and hell in order to understand the notion of ultimate responsibility that it is used to illustrate. Nor does one have to believe in the story of heaven and hell in order to believe in ultimate responsibility (many atheists have believed in it). One doesn't have to have heard of the story at all, and there's another equally good if less colourful way to characterize the notion of ultimate responsibility, although it takes a little more thought: ultimate responsibility exists if and only if punishment and reward can be fair without having any pragmatic justification.[56]

The next paper, 'Realism and Causation', expounds the causal realism that forms the background to the discussion of Hume in *The Secret Connexion*. In that book I argue directly against the view, then orthodox (although not universal) in philosophy, that Hume did not merely hold the epistemological view that all we can *know* of causation is regular succession or constant conjunction, but also held the outright ontological view that such regular succession is quite definitely all there *is* to causation in the world and was, in addition, right to do so.

One of the strange things about this orthodoxy, back in the day, was that although the philosophical community tended to take the correctness of the regularity theory for granted when discussing other things, they were considerably less likely to do so when causation was itself their main topic of discussion: a respectable number of philosophers always had their doubts about the regularity theory. By far the oddest thing, though, was the way in which the regularity theory of causation had by then come completely apart from the phenomenalism about physical objects with which it had so intimately co-evolved. The regularity theory made a lot of sense in partnership with phenomenalism, and really only in that partnership,[57] and yet it

---

[56] See p. 361 below.

[57] Given his idealism, Berkeley was quite right to hold a regularity theory about the nature of causation considered as a phenomenon that exists in the physical world. It is instructive to compare the phenomenon of causation as it exists in cartoon worlds, discussed in Strawson 1989b: Appendix A.

somehow persisted after the phenomenalism had been largely abandoned. The standard and extraordinary position at that time was a combination of realism about physical objects and radical anti-realism about the causal relations that held between them. On this view it was not only the case that the order of the world was a complete, fully objective, constant and enormous fluke; it was also the case that we knew this to be so.

The next paper, 'The Contingent Reality of Natural Necessity', responds briefly to an objection to *The Secret Connexion*, put by Nicholas Everitt, that has nothing essentially to do with Hume. It makes a suggestion about how best to convey the character of a non-regularity theory of causation. Like its predecessor, it presupposes a view of time as something that (so to say) really passes and flows. Neither paper addresses an issue of which I was then unaware: the issue of whether the distinction between regularity and non-regularity views of causation survives in a 'four-dimensionalist' or 'block-universe' view of reality.

The next two papers, 'Epistemology, Semantics, Ontology, and David Hume' and 'David Hume: Objects and Power', seek, overlappingly, to strengthen the case in favour of the 'sceptical realist' interpretation of Hume offered in *The Secret Connexion*, an interpretation originally so named and championed by John Wright in his 1983 book *The Sceptical Realism of David Hume* in the face of an almost perfect consensus of disagreement. These papers are contributions to what came to be known as 'the Hume wars', in which Kenneth Winkler fired the first retaliatory salvo against the so-called 'New Hume' (who was really none other than Hume himself).[58] For a time the Hume establishment did its best to ignore the sceptical realist interpretation, along with Edward Craig's outstanding (and essentially more moderate) account of 'One Way to Read Hume' in his book *The Mind of God and the Works of Man*. Things have moved on since then, and many members of the old establishment seem now to have accepted the main idea behind the sceptical realist interpretation while pretending, to varying degrees, that they never really thought otherwise. Don Garrett was never, perhaps, a full member of the old establishment, but he is now the doyen of Hume studies, and a useful measure of the distance that has been covered since the publication of Wright's book in 1983 is provided by the following quotation from Garrett's rightly admired book *Cognition and Commitment in Hume's Philosophy* (1997):

Hume is not forbidden by his empiricist principles from postulating the existence of unperceived deterministic mechanisms that would underlie the propensities of perceptions to appear in particular ways. He is forbidden by his principles only from trying to specify the nature of those mechanisms [in a way that goes] beyond what experience can warrant.[59]

This is an observation that would have left pre-'New Hume' Humeans gasping.

One of the most striking things about the resistance to the sceptical realist reading of Hume has been the way in which commentators have newly defended their existing view while refusing to address directly the objections it faces from the sceptical

---

[58] Winkler 1991.　　[59] Garrett 1997: 171.

realist reading. The issue of Hume's two definitions of cause provides an example. After stating that

the ideas which we form concerning [the relation of cause and effect are] so imperfect . . . that it is impossible to give any just definition of cause, except what is drawn from something extraneous and foreign to it

Hume gives his two famous definitions and immediately reiterates the point that they are imperfect, observing that 'we cannot remedy this inconvenience, or attain any more perfect definition, which may point out that circumstance in the cause, which gives it a connexion with its effect'.[60] The sceptical realist point here is that this by itself refutes the view that Hume held that there was nothing more to causation 'in the objects', or in reality, than regularity, for if causation in the objects were just regular succession or constant conjunction, then there would be no inconvenience or imperfection in the first definition at all, and in giving the first definition we could hardly be said to be in the position of finding it 'impossible to give any just definition of cause, except what is drawn from something extraneous and foreign to it'. The challenge to members of the old orthodoxy—it has not been faced, as far as I know—is simply to explain why this does not definitively and forever refute their view.[61]

---

[60] 1748: 76/7.29.
[61] See pp. 434–6 below. See also the discussion of the use of the word 'definition' in the eighteenth century on p. 436.

1

Real Materialism

'Trinculo might have been referring to modern physics in the words, "This is the tune of our catch, played by the picture of Nobody".'

Eddington (1928: 292)

Love like Matter is much
  Odder than we thought.

Auden (1940, 'Heavy Date')

1 INTRODUCTION

Materialism is the view that every real, concrete[1] phenomenon[2] in the universe is physical. It is a view about the actual universe, and for the purposes of this paper I am going to assume that it is true.

It has been characterized in other ways. David Lewis once defined it as 'metaphysics built to endorse the truth and descriptive completeness of physics more or less as we know it',[3] and this cannot be faulted as a terminological decision. But it seems unwise to burden materialism—the view that every real concrete phenomenon in the universe is *physical*—with a commitment to the descriptive completeness of *physics* more or less as we know it. There may be physical phenomena which physics (and any non-revolutionary extension of it) cannot describe, and of which it has no inkling, either

---

This paper is an attempt to elaborate on 'Agnostic materialism' (Strawson 1994: 43–105); trailers appeared in Strawson 1998 and 1999b. Since writing it I have come across several expressions of similar views and have added a considerable number of quotations. When I cite a work I give the date of first publication, or occasionally the date of composition, while the page reference is to the edition listed in the bibliography.

[1] By 'concrete' I simply mean 'not abstract'. It is natural to think that any really existing thing is *ipso facto* concrete, non-abstract, in which case 'concrete' is redundant. But some philosophers like to say that numbers (for example) are real things—objects that really exist, but are abstract.

[2] I use 'phenomenon' as a completely general word for any sort of existent that carries no implication as to ontological category (the trouble with the perfectly general word 'entity' is that it is now standardly understood to refer specifically to things or substances); and suppress its meaning of *appearance*.

Note that someone who agrees that physical phenomena are all there are but finds no logical incoherence in the idea that physical things could be put together in such a way as to give rise to non-physical things can define materialism as the view that every real, concrete phenomenon that there is *or could be* in the universe is physical.

[3] 1986: x.

descriptive or referential.[4] Physics is one thing, the physical is another. 'Physical' is a natural-kind term—it is the ultimate natural-kind term[5]—and no sensible person thinks that physics has nailed all the essential properties of the physical. Current physics is profoundly beautiful and useful, but it is in a state of chronic internal tension.[6] It may be added, with Russell and others, that although physics appears to tell us a great deal about certain of the general structural or mathematical characteristics of the physical, it fails to give us any further insight into the nature of whatever it is that has these structural or mathematical characteristics—apart from making it plain that it is utterly bizarre relative to our ordinary conception of it.

It is unclear exactly what this last remark amounts to (is it being suggested that physics is failing to do something it could do?), but it already amounts to something very important when it comes to what is known as the 'mind–body problem'. Many take this to be the problem of how mental phenomena can be physical phenomena *given what we already know about the nature of the physical.* But those who think this are already lost. For the fact is that we have *no* good reason to think that we know anything about the physical that gives us any reason to find any problem in the idea that mental phenomena are physical phenomena. If we consider the nature of our knowledge of the physical, we realize that 'no problem of irreconcilability arises'.[7] Joseph Priestley saw this very clearly over two hundred years ago, and he was not the first. Noam Chomsky reached essentially the same conclusion over thirty years ago, and he was not the last.[8] Most present-day philosophers take no notice of it and waste a lot of time as a result: much of the present debate about the 'mind–body' problem is beside the point.

2   TERMINOLOGY

I am going to use the plural-accepting, count-noun form of the word 'experience'[9] for talking of experienc*es* as things (events) that may (and presumably do) have non-experiential being as well as experiential being. And I am going to reserve the adjective 'experiential' and the plural-lacking form of the noun 'experience' for talking about the qualitative character that experienc*es* have for those who have them as they have them, where this qualitative character is considered wholly independently of

---

   [4] Physics is trivially referentially complete, according to materialism, in so far as its object of study is the universe, i.e. the whole of concrete reality. There may nevertheless be specific, smaller-scale phenomena of which physicists have no descriptive or referential inkling.

   [5] Failure to recognize this simple point, long after the existence of natural-kind terms has been generally acknowledged, is one of the more disastrous legacies of positivism. (Compare the survival of the 'regularity theory of causation' after the abandonment of phenomenalism.)

   [6] I have in mind the old quarrel between general relativity theory and quantum mechanics, but there is also turmoil in cosmology.

   [7] Eddington 1928: 260.

   [8] Chomsky 1968: 6–8, 98; 1988: 142–7; 1994 passim; 1995: 1–10; 1996: 38–45; 1998: 437–41; compare Crane and Mellor 1990.

   [9] The words 'experience' and 'experiential' were capitalized in the originally published version of this paper, and I have removed this as unnecessary.

everything else. The phenomenon of experiential[10] qualitative character is part of what exists—it is part of reality, whatever its ontological category—and it is important to have some unequivocal way of referring to it and only to it.

One could express this terminological proposal by saying that 'experiential phenomena' and 'experience' (plural-lacking form) refer in a general way to: that part of reality which one is left with when, continuing to live and think and feel as one does, one engages in an old sceptical thought experiment and imagines that the 'external world', including one's own body, does not exist. They refer to the part or aspect of reality one has to do with when one considers experiences specifically and solely in respect of the experiential qualitative character they have for those who have them as they have them, and puts aside the fact that they may also be correctly describable in such non-experiential terms as 'a 70–20–30 Hertz coding triplet across the neurons of area V4'.[11]

3   REALISTIC MATERIALISM

Realistic materialists—realistic anybodys—must grant that experiential phenomena are real, concrete phenomena, for nothing in this life is more certain.[12] They must therefore hold that they are physical phenomena. It may sound odd to use the word 'concrete' to characterize the qualitative character of experiences of colour, gusts of depression, thoughts about diophantine equations, and so on, but it isn't, because 'concrete' simply means 'not abstract'.[13] For most purposes one may take 'concrete' to be coextensive with 'possessed of spatiotemporal existence', although this will be directly question-begging in some contexts.[14]

It may also sound odd to use 'physical' to characterize mental phenomena like experiential phenomena: many materialists talk about the mental and the physical as if they were opposed categories. But this, *on their own view*, is like talking about cows and animals as if they were opposed categories. For every concrete phenomenon in the universe is physical, according to materialists. So all mental phenomena, including experiential phenomena, are physical phenomena, according to materialists: just as all cows are animals.

So what are materialists doing when they talk, as they so often do, as if the mental and the physical were entirely different? What they may mean to do is to distinguish, within the realm of the physical, which is the only realm there is, according to them,

---

[10] 'Qualitative' has to be qualified by 'experiential' because experiences also have non-experiential qualitative character, according to materialists (every non-relational property of a thing contributes to its qualitative character). Having made the point, I will either bracket 'experiential' or follow common practice and omit it.

[11] Churchland 1995: 202. Obviously 'correctly describable' does not entail 'fully describable'. Note that one also puts aside the fact that they can be correctly described in such non-experiential terms as 'a perception of the Eiffel Tower'.

[12] I make no distinction between 'materialism' and 'physicalism'.

[13] If 'immaterial souls' existed, they would of course be concrete phenomena.

[14] Experiential phenomena would be concrete phenomena even if space and time were not really real—were somehow mere forms of experience.

between the mental and the non-mental, or between the experiential and the non-experiential; to distinguish, that is, between mental (or experiential) features of the physical, and non-mental (or non-experiential) features of the physical.[15]

It is this difference that is in question when it comes to the 'mind-body' problem; materialists who persist in talking in terms of the difference between the mental and the physical perpetuate the terms of the dualism they reject in a way that is inconsistent with their own view. I use the words 'mental' and 'non-mental' where many use the words 'mental' and 'physical' simply because I assume, as a (wholly conventional) materialist, that every real concrete phenomenon is physical, and find myself obliged to put things in this way.[16]

There is tremendous resistance to abandoning the old mental/physical terminology in favor of the mental/non-mental, experiential/non-experiential terminology, although the latter seems to be exactly what is required. Many think the old terminology is harmless, and a few are not misled by it: they consistently use 'physical' to mean 'non-mental physical'. But it sets up the wrong frame of thought from the start, and I suspect that those who are never misled by it are members of a small minority.

When I say that the mental, and in particular the experiential, is physical, and endorse the view that 'experience is really just neurons firing', I mean something completely different from what some materialists have apparently meant by saying such things. I don't mean that all aspects of what is going on, in the case of conscious experience, can be described by current physics, or some non-revolutionary extension of it. Such a view amounts to radical 'eliminativism' with respect to consciousness,[17] and is mad. My claim is different. It is that the experiential (considered just as such)[18]—the feature of reality we have to do with when we consider experiences specifically and solely in respect of the experiential character they have for those who have them as they have them—that 'just is' is physical. No one who disagrees with this is a remotely realistic materialist.

When aspiring materialists consider the living brain, in discussion of the 'mind-body problem', they often slide into supposing that the word 'brain' somehow refers only to the brain-as-revealed-by-current-physics. But this is a mistake, for it refers just as it says, to the living brain, i.e. the living brain as a whole, the brain in its total physical existence and activity. Realistic—real—materialists must agree that the total physical existence and activity of the brain of an ordinary, living person, considered over time, is *constituted* by experiential phenomena (if only in part) in every sense in which it is constituted (in part) by non-experiential phenomena characterizable by physics. A real (realistic) materialist cannot think that there is something still left

---

[15] One needs to distinguish between mental and experiential phenomena because although all experiential phenomena are mental, not all mental phenomena are experiential, on the ordinary view of things: certain *dispositional* states—beliefs, preferences, and so on—are mental phenomena although they have no experiential character. There are also powerful reasons for saying that there are *occurrent* mental phenomena that are non-experiential.

[16] See Chomsky 1968: 98.

[17] Some readers doubt this, but it follows from the fact that current physics contains no predicates for experiential phenomena at all, and that no non-revolutionary extension of it could do so.

[18] The parenthesis is redundant given the definition of 'experiential' in §2.

to say about experiential phenomena, once everything that there is to say about the physical brain has been said.

4 MATERIALISM FURTHER DEFINED

Materialism, then, is the view that every real concrete phenomenon is physical in every respect, but a little more needs to be said, for experiential phenomena— together with the subject of experience, assuming that that is something extra—are the only real, concrete phenomena that we can know with certainty to exist,[19] and as it stands this definition of materialism doesn't even rule out idealism—the view that mental phenomena are the only real phenomena and have no non-mental being— from qualifying as a form of materialism! Now there is a sense in which this consequence of the definition is salutary (see e.g. §§14–15 below), but it would none the less be silly to call an idealist view 'materialism'. Russell is right to say that 'the truth about physical objects *must* be strange',[20] but it is reasonable to take materialism to be committed to the existence of non-experiential being in the universe, in addition to experiential being, and I shall do so in what follows.

It is also reasonable to take materialism to involve the claim that *every* existing concrete phenomenon has non-mental, non-experiential being, whether or not it also has mental or experiential being. Applied to mental phenomena, then, materialism claims that each particular mental phenomenon essentially has non-mental being, in addition to mental being. This is, I think, the standard view.[21]

I will assume, then, that all realistic materialists take it that there is both mental and experiential being and non-mental, non-experiential being. Must all realistic *monists* also take it that there is non-mental, non-experiential being? Many would say Yes, on the grounds that it is not remotely realistic to suppose either that there is, or might be, no non-mental or non-experiential being at all. But the question of what it is to be (metaphysically) realistic is far harder here than it is when it is merely the existence of experience that is in question. For the purposes of this paper I will *assume* that any realistic position does take it that there is non-mental or non-experiential being in addition to mental and experiential being, for this assumption accords with ordinary conceptions, and my main argument does not require me to challenge it. But it is at best an assumption. Idealists, of course, reject the assumption that realistic monism requires acknowledgement of non-mental, non-experiential phenomena, and I will enter a number of reservations along the way.[22]

---

[19] Unless the existence of experiential phenomena of kinds that we know to exist entails the existence of non-experiential phenomena. See n22 below.

[20] 1912: 19.

[21] In the case of experiences, it amounts to saying that they are not just experiential phenomena, although experiential phenomena are of course part of what constitutes their existence. Note that to distinguish between mental being and non-mental being is not to claim to know how to draw a sharp line between them. The starting situation is simply this: we know there is mental being, and we assume, as materialists, that this is not all there is.

[22] Elsewhere (1994: 134–4) I argue that there could not be experiential or experiential content phenomena of the sort with which we are familiar unless there were also non-experiential phenomena;

It is clumsy to oscillate between 'mental' and 'experiential', or constantly double them up, and in the next few sections I will run the discussion in terms of the mental/non-mental distinction (such as it is). This said, all my *examples* of mental phenomena will be experiential phenomena, for they suffice to make the relevant point and are, in the present context, what matter most.

It may be added that the reference of the term 'experiential' is much clearer than that of the essentially contestable term 'mental', and that the latter may in the end deserve the treatment proposed for the term 'physical' in §15 below. Nevertheless it seems best to begin in this way.[23]

I will quote Russell—post-1926 Russell—frequently when discussing materialism, for my views converge with his in certain respects, and he has been wrongly ignored in recent discussion.[24] He was still inclined to call himself a 'neutral monist' at that time, but he is equally well read as a thoroughgoing materialist.[25] He rejects materialism in name, pointing out that 'matter has become as ghostly as anything in a spiritualist séance'—it has, he says, disappeared 'as a "thing"' and has been 'replaced by emanations from a locality'[26]—, but he grants that 'those who would formerly have been materialists can still adopt a philosophy which comes to much the same thing. They can say that the type of causation dealt with in physics is fundamental, and that all events are subject to physical laws'.[27] And this, in effect, is what he does himself.[28]

and if it is true (1) that a subject of experience cannot itself be a wholly experiential phenomenon (ibid. p. 144), and (2) that 'experience is impossible without an experiencer' (Frege 1918: 27), then the conclusion that the existence of experience entails the existence of non-experiential phenomena is guaranteed. The argument stalls, however, if one substitutes 'mental' for 'experiential', if only because of the vagueness of the term 'mental' (ibid. pp. 140–2 and ch. 6).

[23] I discuss the difference between 'experiential' and 'mental', and the vagueness of 'mental', in Strawson 1994 (see e.g. pp. 136–44 and ch. 6). Here I am trying to avoid the issue as far as possible.

[24] Largely, perhaps, because of the looseness of his use of the word 'see', and the reactive excesses (which led to exegetical insensitivity) of the first wave of twentieth-century 'direct realists'. See, however, Lockwood 1981.

[25] See e.g. Russell 1927b: 110, 119, 123, 126, 170. I do not understand everything Russell says and may misrepresent him. I aim to take what I think is right from his views without attempting exegesis, and I will sometimes detour from the main argument in Russellian directions.

[26] 1927b: 78, 84. N. R. Hanson spoke similarly of the 'dematerialization' of matter, and Priestley (1777) made essentially the same point. See also Lange 1865.

[27] 1927b: 126–27.

[28] In his introduction to Lange's *History of Materialism*, Russell notes that 'physics is not materialistic in the old sense, since it no longer assumes matter as permanent substance' (1925: xix), and he may have the following passage from Lange in mind: 'We have in our own days so accustomed ourselves to the abstract notion of forces, or rather to a notion hovering in a mystic obscurity between abstraction and concrete comprehension, that we no longer find any difficulty in making one particle of matter act upon another without immediate contact. We may, indeed, imagine that in the proposition, "No force without matter", we have uttered something very Materialistic, while all the time we calmly allow particles of matter to act upon each other through void space without any material link. From such ideas the great mathematicians and physicists of the seventeenth century were far removed. They were all in so far still genuine Materialists in the sense of ancient Materialism, that they made immediate contact a condition of influence. The collision of atoms or the attraction by hook shaped particles, a mere modification of collision, were the type of all Mechanism and the whole movement of science tended towards Mechanism' (1865: 1.308, quoted in Chomsky, 1996: 44).

5 'MENTAL' AND 'NON-MENTAL'

It may seem odd to take 'mental' as the basic positive term when characterizing materialism. But one is not a thoroughgoing materialist if one finds it so. For all materialists hold that every concrete phenomenon in the universe is physical, and they are neither sensible nor realistic if they have any inclination to deny the concrete reality of mental phenomena like experiential phenomena.[29] It follows that they have, so far, no reason to find it odd or biased to take 'mental' rather than 'non-mental' as the basic term.

—Surely it would be better, even so, to start with some positive term 'T' for the non-mental physical, and then define a negative term, 'non-T', to cover the mental physical; or use a pair of independently positive terms?

There are two good reasons for taking 'mental' as the basic positive term, one terminological, the other philosophical. The terminological reason is simply that we do not have a convenient positive term for the non-mental (obviously we can't use 'physical', and there is no other natural candidate). The philosophical reason is very old: it is that we have direct acquaintance with—know—fundamental features of the mental nature of (physical) reality just in having experience in the way we do, in a way that has no parallel in the case of any non-mental features of (physical)[30] reality. We do not have to stand back from experiences and take them as objects of knowledge by means of some further mental operation, in order for there to be acquaintance and knowing of this sort: the having is the knowing.[31]

This point has often been questioned, but it remains immovable. Russell may exaggerate when he says that 'we know *nothing* about the intrinsic quality of physical events except when these are mental events that we directly experience',[32] or that 'as regards the world in general, both physical and mental, *everything* that we know of its intrinsic character is derived from the mental side',[33] for it is arguable that the spacetime character of the world is part of its intrinsic character, and, further, that we may have some knowledge of this spacetime character. I don't think he exaggerates much, however. He is onto something important, and the epistemological asymmetry between claims to knowledge of experiential being and claims to knowledge of non-experiential being is undeniable, however unfashionable.

---

[29] This is so even if 'eliminativism' about other candidate mental phenomena—dispositional phenomena like preferences, beliefs, and so on—is worth serious discussion.

[30] The word 'physical' is bracketed because it is redundant, here as elsewhere. See §14.

[31] Compare Shoemaker's idea (rather differently applied) that many mental states and goings on are 'constitutively self-intimating' (1990). See also Maxwell 1978: 392, 396.

[32] 1956: 153; my emphasis.

[33] 1927a: 402; my emphasis. See Lockwood 1989: 159: 'Consciousness . . . provides us with a kind of "window" on to our brains, making possible a transparent grasp of a tiny corner of material reality that is in general opaque to us . . . . The qualities of which we are immediately aware, in consciousness, precisely *are* some at least of the intrinsic qualities of the states and processes that go to make up the material world—more specifically, states and processes within our own brains. This was Russell's suggestion.'

The asymmetry claim that concerns me is not the claim that all epistemic contact with concrete reality involves experience, and that we are inevitably a further step away from the thing with which we are in contact when it is a non-experiential phenomenon. It is, rather, the claim that we are acquainted with reality *as it is in itself,* in certain respects, in having experience as we do. This second claim revolts against the tendency of much current epistemology and philosophy of mind, but there is no reason why it should trouble thoughtful materialists, and I will offer a brief defence of it in §13. Here it is worth noting that it is fully compatible with the view that there may also be fundamental things we don't know about matter considered in its experiential being.[34]

6   ASIDE: 'AS IT IS IN ITSELF'

Does one need to defend the phrase 'as it is in itself', when one uses it in philosophy? I fear one does, for some think (incoherently) that it is somehow incoherent. Still, it is easy to defend. The supposition that reality is in fact a certain way, whatever we can manage to know or say about it, is obviously true. To be is to be somehow or other. Nothing can exist or be real without being a certain way at any given time.[35] And the way something is just is how it is in itself. This point is not threatened by the suggestion that our best models of the behaviour of things like photons credit them with properties that seem incompatible to us—wave-like properties and particle-like properties, for example. What we learn from this is just that this is how photons affect us, given their intrinsic nature—given how they are in themselves, and how we are in ourselves. We acquire no reason to think (incoherently) that photons do not have some intrinsic nature at any given time. Whatever claim anyone makes about the nature of reality—including the claim that it has apparently incompatible properties—just is a claim about the way it is. This applies as much to the Everett 'many-worlds' theory of reality as to any other.

Some think that what we learn from quantum theory is that there is, objectively, no particular way that an electron or a photon is, at a given time. They confuse an epistemological point about undecidability with a metaphysical claim about the nature of things. The problem is not just that such a claim is unverifiable. The problem is that it is incoherent. For whatever the electron's or photon's weirdness (its weirdness to us: nothing is intrinsically weird), its being thus weird just is the way it is.

So we may talk without reservation of reality as it is in itself. Such talk involves no (allegedly dubious) metaphysics of the Kantian kind. Its propriety derives entirely

---

[34] Not only facts about experience in sense modalities we lack, or (e.g.) about the brightness-saturation-hue complexity of seemingly simple colour-experience, but also, perhaps, murkier facts about its composition, and also, perhaps, about the 'hidden nature of consciousness' postulated by McGinn 1990: chs 3 and 4.

[35] If you are worried about the concept—or reality—of time, drop the last four words.

and sufficiently from the thought that if a thing exists, it is a certain way. For the way it is just is how it is in itself.

7 STRUCTURE AND STRUCTURED

So much, for the moment, for our theoretical conception of the mental: it has some securely anchored, positive descriptive content, and we can know that this is so; for whatever the best general account of the mental, it includes experiential phenomena in its scope; and experiential phenomena are not only indubitably real; they are also phenomena part of whose intrinsic nature just is their experiential character; and their experiential character is something with which we are directly acquainted, however hard we may find the task of describing it in words. This is so even if we can make mistakes about the nature of our experiences, and even if we can do so even when we consider them merely in respect of their (experiential) qualitative character.[36] It is so even if we differ dramatically among ourselves in the qualitative character of our experiences, in ways we cannot know about.

Our theoretical conception of the mental, then, has clear and secure descriptive content. (Don't ask for it to be put further into words; the anchoring is sufficiently described in the last paragraph.) Our theoretical conception of the non-mental, by contrast, remains, so far, a wholly negative concept. It has, as yet, no positive descriptive content.

Can anything be done about this? On one reading, Russell thinks not: the science of physics is our fundamental way of attempting to investigate the non-mental being of physical reality, and it cannot help us. 'Physics is mathematical', he says, 'not because we know so much about the physical world, but because we know so little: it is only its mathematical properties that we can discover. For the rest, our knowledge is negative.' 'We know nothing about the intrinsic quality of physical events except when these are mental events that we directly experience.' On this view, neither physics nor ordinary experience of physical objects give us any sort of knowledge of the intrinsic nature of non-mental reality.[37]

Is Russell right? Something needs to be said about his use of the word 'intrinsic'. It is potentially misleading, and it helps to consider other ways in which he puts the point. Thus he talks regularly of the 'abstractness' of physics. The knowledge it gives is, he says, 'purely formal'. It reveals the abstract 'structure' of physical phenomena while saying nothing about their 'quality'.[38]

---

[36] See e.g. Dennett 1991a: ch. 11.

[37] Russell 1927b: 125, 1956: 153. Lockwood 1989: ch. 10 contains some illuminating pages on Russell and a useful historical note on versions of the idea that precede Russell's. See also Maxwell 1978, whose Russellian approach is treated sympathetically in Chalmers 1996: 153–4 (and see index), and Chalmers 1997: 405–6. Jeremy Butterfield and Bas van Fraassen have pointed out to me the link here to John Worrall's 'structural realism'; see e.g. Worrall 1989 and Ladyman 1998.

[38] 1927a: 392, 382, 388.

I am not sure that the distinction between structure and quality is clear, or fundamental in such a way that it holds 'all the way down',[39] but (putting that doubt aside) it seems that the fundamental distinction that Russell has in mind can be expressed by saying that it is a distinction between *how X is structurally disposed* and *what X is apart from (over and above) its structural disposition*.[40] Physics gives the structure, but not the structure-transcendent nature, of the thing that has the structure. If we say that truths about how X is structurally disposed have purely *structure-specifying* content, while truths about what X is over and above its structural disposition also have *structure-transcendent* content, or, more simply, *non-structural* content, then we may say that 'non-structural' covers everything that Russell has in mind when he talks of the 'intrinsic' nature of things.[41]

One might dramatize Russell's idea by saying that physics can be thought of as a formal system which remains, in a peculiar sense, an *uninterpreted* formal system, even though we know that it *applies* to something=x—reality, the universe—and even though it is elaborated specifically in causal response to x. On this 'Ramseyfied' view, we may suppose that the universe has features that are *structurally isomorphic* to the structures delineated in the equations of physics, but we have no account of the non-structural nature of the thing that has the structure(s) in question.[42]

So we are (to pursue the metaphor) in the peculiar position of having a known, concrete *application* (and so, in one sense, an *interpretation*) for a formal system, without that application constituting a *model* (in the sense of model-theoretic semantics) that can confer positive descriptive meaning on its terms. In being the

---

[39] Structure is a matter of quality because a thing's qualitative character, exhaustively considered, is a matter of *all* aspects of how it is, and its structural character is an aspect of how it is. The converse claim—that quality (in spacetime) is in some sense a matter of structure—sounds a bit mystical, but it can on further reflection begin to seem hard to rebut, even when one maintains, as one must, a sharp distinction between epistemology and metaphysics. (The distinction between form and content may seem more robust, but may also succumb.)

[40] It seems (subject to the doubt expressed in the last footnote) that this distinction must be a real one—that if there is structure, there must be something structured. Only extreme positivistic irresponsibility, or failure to 'realize what an abstract affair form [or structure] really is'. Russell 1927a: 392, can make this seem questionable.

[41] At one point Russell also takes it that position in spacetime is an intrinsic property of things. Considering the relation between a perception and the object it is a perception of, he remarks that 'we cannot say whether or not it resembles the object in any intrinsic respect, except that both it and the object are brief events in space-time' (1927b: 118).

[42] When thinking of structural isomorphism, it is helpful to consider a version of an old example: the structural isomorphism between (1) sound waves produced by an orchestra playing Sibelius's 'Valse Triste' that are registered as (2) vibrations of a condenser plate in a microphone and sent as (3) electrical signals to a recording device that stores them as (4) pits on the surface of a compact disk that is then read as (5) digital information by a machine that transmits this information in the form of (6) radio waves to (7) a receiver that puts it through (8) an amplifier to (9) speakers that give rise to (10) sound waves that give rise to (11) electrical impulses in the auditory nerve that give rise to (12) neural occurrences in the auditory cortex and elsewhere that are conscious auditory experiences. There is a structural description that captures the respect in which all these phenomena are the same (assuming no significant loss of information even at the stage of conscious hearing). The abstract character of this description is revealed precisely by the fact that this is what it does: capture the respect in which all these substantially different phenomena are—structurally—the same. Compare Wittgenstein 1922: 4.0141.

subject matter of physics, the universe provides it with a merely referential model or object, of which it gives a merely structure-specifying description. Physics is *about* the physical, and may give a correct abstract representation of its structural disposition as far as it goes; but it does not and cannot tell us anything about what the physical actually is, over and above the fact that it exemplifies a certain formal structure.[43]

8 THE NON-MENTAL—SPACE

Back now to the question whether physics can endow our general theoretical conception of the non-mental with any positive descriptive (not merely referential) content. Russell in 1927 thinks not. I disagree because correct structural description of a thing is already description of a feature of its intrinsic nature. But this disagreement is merely terminological, and the real question is this: Can one go any further than structure-specifying content, when attempting to give a satisfactory theoretical characterization of the non-mental? Again, Russell in 1927 thinks not. It seems to me, however, that we may be able to go a little further. For I think that our ordinary conception of space may get something fundamental right about the nature of reality as it is in itself, and hence about the intrinsic nature of reality—something that survives even after the finite-but-unbounded curved gravity-constituting spacetime of relativity theory (or the ten- or eleven- or twelve-dimensional spacetime of one of the leading versions of string theory) has been granted to be closer to the truth.

I am tempted to hold up my hands, like G. E. Moore, and to consider, not my hands, but the space—by which I mean only the spatial extension[44]—between them, and to say: 'This is space (spatial extension), and it is real, and I know its nature, in some very fundamental respect, whatever else I do not know about it or anything else (e.g. the fact that it is an aspect of spacetime).' On this view the ordinary concept of space, or indeed the concept of spacetime, in which (I claim) a fundamental feature of our ordinary conception of space survives, has correct non-structural descriptive content. It does not relate only to 'what we may call the causal skeleton of the world',[45] if to say this is to say that it does not capture any aspect of the non-structural nature of the world. It has non-structural content, and can transmit this content to our more general conception of the non-mental.[46]

Russellians may object as follows 'This line of thought is profoundly natural, but it depends on a fundamentally false imagining. It involves the conflation of 'objective'

---

[43] In 1928, a year after the publication of *The Analysis of Matter*, Max Newman published a conclusive objection to the pure form of this view, as Russell immediately acknowledged (1967–9: 413–14). See Demopoulos and Friedman 1985.

[44] I am not at all concerned with the 'substantivalist' versus 'relationalist' debate about the nature of space.

[45] Russell 1927a: 391.

[46] Cf. Hirsch 1986: 251–4. I will not here consider the 'direct realist' view that we may have some real insight into the non-mental nature of force, say, or causation, as a result of experiencing pushes and pulls and so on in the way we do.

spatial extension, spatial extension 'as it is in itself' (where this is taken as a merely referential, structural-equivalence-class specifying term with no pretension to non-structural content) with the phenomenological space (or spaces) associated with perception. It involves an almost irresistible but entirely fatal failure to 'realize what an abstract affair form really is'.[47] All those, like yourself, who think that it is viable are 'guilty, unconsciously and in spite of explicit disavowals, of *a confusion in their imaginative picture*' of reality.[48]

In reply I think that some who take this line may be suffering from excessive empiricism. They take it that the notion of spatial extension—or indeed shape—that we possess is essentially informed by the character of our sensory experiences, and in this I think they are mistaken. It may well be true that sensory experiences of specific kinds are necessary for the acquisition of concepts like SHAPE or SPACE, in the case of beings like ourselves.[49] Such concepts can nevertheless float free of the different possible sensory bases of their acquisition and subsequent deployment, without *ipso facto* becoming 'merely' formal or structure-specifying in character. It is easy to see that grasp of the content of SHAPE (say) does not require essential reference to any specific sensory experience. It suffices to point out that exactly the same concept of shape—that is, *the* concept of shape, for there is only one—can plausibly be supposed to be fully masterable by two different creatures A and B on the basis of sensory experiences in entirely different sensory modalities familiar to us—sight and touch.[50] One has to endorse a rather crude form of meaning-empiricism or concept-empiricism to suppose that A and B do not—cannot—have the same concept, as they do geometry together. A concept is not a faint copy or transform of a sensory experience. It is, precisely, a concept.

That's one point. Another, crucial in this context, is that the concept of shape or space that A and B have in common is not an entirely abstract or purely formal concept, as the supporters of Russell seem to suggest. There is more to A and B sharing the specific concept SHAPE or SPACE than there is to their sharing mastery of the principles of an uninterpreted formal system that is in fact suitable for the expression of shape configurations or spatial relations although they know it only as an uninterpreted formal system. It is precisely because pure form is such a *very* 'abstract affair', as Russell says, that the concept of shape or space that A and B can have in common in spite of their different sensory experiences cannot be supposed to be a matter of pure form. To think that it is a matter of pure form is to miss out precisely their grasp of the *spatiality* of space—of that which makes their grasp of the concept of space more than grasp of (say) an abstract metric. The concept has non-structural content.

It is true that this content is abstract in one sense: it is abstract relative to all the particularities of sensation, in a way that is sufficiently indicated by reference to the fact that different creatures can acquire it (the very same concept) on the basis of

---

[47] Russell 1927a: 392. One could say that it is this point that Newman turns back against Russell (see n43).

[48] Russell 1927a: 382; my emphasis.   [49] I use small capitals for names of concepts.

[50] One may contrast the case of a congenitally blind person with the hypothetical case of a fully sighted person congenitally paralysed and devoid of tactile or any other somatosensory sensation—before thinking of superintelligent echolocating bats and aliens with other sensory modalities.

experience in entirely different sensory modalities. It is indeed, and essentially, a *non-sensory* concept.[51] But it is not purely abstract in Russell's sense, because (to repeat) it involves grasp of the spatiality—rather than what one might call the mere abstract dimensionality— of space.[52] Spatiality is not abstract dimensionality: the nature of abstract dimensionality can be fully captured by a purely mathematical representation; the nature of spatiality cannot. One can give a purely mathematical representation of the dimensionality of space, but it won't distinguish *space* from any other possible three-dimensional 'space', e.g. the emotional state-space of a species that have just three emotions, love, anger, and despair.

Obviously questions arise about the precise nature of the non-structural content of concepts like SHAPE and SPACE, about what it is, exactly, to grasp the spatiality of space, given that SHAPE and SPACE may be fully shared by A, B, superbats, and others. But in the present context I am inclined just to hold up my hands again.[53]

Russellians may be unimpressed. Michael Lockwood, in particular, is sympathetic to the idea that knowledge of spacetime structure is not knowledge of any feature of the 'intrinsic' or non-structural nature of reality. In doing physics, Lockwood says, we may grasp the abstract structure exemplified by space while having 'no conception of its content: i.e. what it is, concretely, that fleshes out this structure. (For all we know, on this view, Henry More and Newton may be right in equating space with God's sensorium!)'[54]

But I am prepared to grant this. I am prepared to grant that we cannot rule out the possibility that space is God's sensorium,[55] or something even more unknown, and that there is therefore a sense in which we may have no idea of what it is that 'fleshes out' the abstract structure exemplified by space. For it may still be true that one grasps something fundamental about the non-structural nature of space in thinking of it as having, precisely, spatiality, rather than mere abstract dimensionality. If space is God's sensorium, so be it: God's sensorium may really have the property of spatiality. Between a fat-free, purely mathematical and thus wholly abstract representation of the structure of space and a partly structure-transcending conception of space as God's sensorium (or some such) lies a third option: an ostensibly less rich

---

[51] See Evans 1980: 269–71; McGinn 1983: 126.

[52] Even if no finite sensory-intellectual being can possess SHAPE or SPACE without having, or without at least having grasp of the nature of, some form of sensory experience, it does not follow that specification of the content of the concept it possesses necessarily involves reference to any features of sensory experience.

[53] If empiricists press me further I will offer (a) the suggestion that sensory modalities that differ qualitatively at first order (i.e. in the way that sight and touch do) may be said to be crucially similar at second order in as much as they are 'intrinsically spatial' in character, (b) the speculation that this similarity can itself be understood as a kind of similarity of (experiential) *qualitative* character, (c) the acknowledgement that it may be that one must be capable of experience in some 'intrinsically spatial' sensory modality or other (even if only in imagination) in order to possess SHAPE or SPACE, (d) the reservation that even if a *non-conceptual* experiential modality must be in play, it is not obvious that this must be a *sensory* modality. This, however, is too simple (I discuss the question further in Essay 3).

[54] Personal communication. Eddington agrees: 'We know nothing about the intrinsic nature of space' (1928: 51–2).

[55] After setting aside the problem of evil.

but still structure-transcending conception of space as specifically spatial (hands held up) in its dimensionality. Some may think this a fine point, but it is (I take it) a huge step away from Russell's claim that we know *nothing* about the intrinsic quality of non-mental events.[56]

I am not claiming that we do know something about the non-structural nature of space, only that we may (I hold up my hands, I move them apart—but my sense of the vulnerability of this claim has increased since I wrote this paper in 1997). This claim allows, as it should, that there may well be more to space than we can know. SPACE, like PHYSICAL, is a natural-kind concept, and there are some atrociously good reasons for thinking that there is more to space than we know or can fully understand. In addition to the (already weighty) points that physical space is non-Euclidean, and is itself something that is literally expanding,[57] and the non-locality results,[58] and questions about the nature of the vacuum, and widespread agreement that 'there is no good a priori reason why space should be a continuum',[59] I for one still can't fully understand how space and time can be interdependent in the way that they demonstrably are. We are also told on very good authority that gravity is really just a matter of the 'curvature' of space, and that string theory is an immensely promising theory of matter (especially after the 'second superstring revolution' and the growth of M-theory, and especially when it comes to understanding gravity) that entails that there are at least ten spatial dimensions . . .

These points reopen the connection to the mind–body problem. For as they pile up, one can't reputably hold on to the old, powerful-seeming Cartesian intuition that there is a 'deep repugnance' or incompatibility between the nature of conscious experience and the nature of spatial extension—the intuition that 'the mental and the spatial are mutually exclusive categories'.[60] We have direct acquaintance with fundamental features of conscious experience—experiential features—just in having it; but we really have no good reason to think that we know enough about the nature of space—or rather, about the nature of matter-in-space-considered-in-so-far-as-it-has-non-mental-being—to be able to assert that there is any repugnance.[61] And if

---

[56] 'We know nothing about the intrinsic quality of physical events except when these are mental events that we directly experience' (1956: 153). Perhaps Russell takes this distancing step himself in his 1928 reply to Newman (see n43): 'It was quite clear to me, as I read your article, that I had not really intended to say what in fact I did say, that *nothing* is known about the physical world [the non-mental world as opposed to the mental world, in my terminology] except its structure. I had always assumed that there might be co-punctuality between percepts and non-percepts, and even that one could pass by a finite number of steps from one event to another compresent with it, from one end of the universe to the other . . . spaciotemporal continuity of percepts and non-percepts was so axiomatic in my thought that I failed to notice that my statements appeared to deny it' (1967–9: 413).

[57] In such a way that the correct answer to the question 'Where was the Big Bang taking place at the first moment in which it made sense to say that it was taking place anywhere?' is 'Right here', wherever you are.

[58] Bell 1996; for an informal illustration see Lockwood 1996: 163–4.

[59] Isham and Butterfield 2000.   [60] McGinn 1995: 221.

[61] Foster 1982a: ch. 5 and McGinn 1995 give forceful presentations of the repugnance intuition. At one point McGinn makes the funky suggestion that consciousness might be a manifestation of the non-spatial nature of pre-Big Bang reality (223–4). I think he moves in a better direction

conscious experience is in time, as almost everyone agrees, then it is in spacetime, given the way in which space and time are demonstrably interdependent—in which case it is in space in every sense in which it is in time.

Note that it follows that even if our notion of space can confer some non-structural content on our best theoretical conception of the non-mental, it cannot confer any content that is guaranteed to distinguish it from any fully articulated theoretical conception of the mental, although we still intuitively feel it to fit with the former conception in a way in which we don't feel it to fit with the latter.[62]

9   THE NON-MENTAL—SPIN, MASS, AND CHARGE

I have proposed that our theoretical conception of the non-mental may be able to acquire some non-structural content from its first lieutenant, the concept of space. Can it acquire any more? Well, I think that our more particular spatial concepts of shape, size, position, distance, and local motion (I raise my hands and bring them together) *may* also get something right about reality as it is in itself, and so contribute to the non-structural content of our general theoretical conception of the non-mental; I think Locke may be essentially right in his view that some of our ideas of primary qualities correctly represent how things are in themselves, although his account needs recasting.[63] It may also be that our ordinary conception of time gets something right about the nature of reality (both experiential and non-experiential)—even if we need to conceive time as part of spacetime in order to think about it properly. I just don't know.[64]

Going on from space, time, extension, shape, position, distance, and motion, in the attempt to give a positive characterization of the non-mental, one may want to mention properties like spin, mass, charge, gravitational attraction, 'colour' and 'flavour' (in the quantum-theoretic sense). But one will have to bear in mind that our grasp of these things—any grasp of them over and above that which is conveyed by their intimate relation to concepts of space and time—is expressed merely in equations;[65] and the truth in Russell's remark that physics is mathematical not because we know so much about the physical world, but because we

---

when he shifts to the very different claim that 'consciousness tests the adequacy of our spatial understanding. It marks the place of deep lack of knowledge about space' (230).

[62] I am grateful to Mark Sainsbury for encouraging me to make this point more explicit.

[63] Locke's talk of 'resemblance' between primary qualities and ideas of primary qualities is unfortunate in as much as it suggests a (mere) picturing relation, and Russell, 1927a: 385, holds that Locke is definitely wrong.

[64] Perhaps it gets something right in an Augustinian sense, according to which we can be said to know what time is even though we find we don't know what to say when someone asks us what it is.

[65] Unless some 'direct realist' account of our understanding of force is defensible. See n48. Note, though, that no sensible direct realist view can suppose that we derive understanding of the nature of force directly from the merely *sensory* character of experiences of pushes, pulls, and so on; that would be like thinking that we can get some real insight into the nature of electricity from the qualitative character that experiences of electric shocks have for us (compare Evans 1980: 270). Somehow, the sensory experiences would have to be the basis of an abstract, essentially cognitive, general, non-sensory concept of force.

know so little. So although I like to think that concepts of space and time carry non-structural content, I do not think this can be true of any of these other concepts considered independently of their relations to concepts of space and time. Here Russell is right: we know nothing of the non-mental non-structural nature of—for example—electrical phenomena apart from their spacetime structure; all we have are equations.[66]

But even if knowledge of spacetime structure is all we have, in the way of non-structural knowledge of the nature of the non-mental, it makes a huge difference to the case. Consider the difference between a characterization of the forces of electrical attraction and repulsion in which their spatial character (the way they decrease with increasing distance) is given a purely mathematical, abstract-dimensional interpretation, and one in which it is given a genuinely spatial interpretation. Consider any account of anything in which time relations have a merely mathematical abstract representation, and one in which the temporality of time is somehow represented.

10   HENS' EGGS

I want now to give a further characterization of what it is to be a genuine materialist. But I must first answer an objection that occurs to many.

—It seems to follow, from your claim that we have no knowledge of the non-structural, intrinsic or as we may say *N-intrinsic* nature of things, that we cannot know that there are tables and chairs and hens and hens' eggs and 'that hens' eggs are generally laid by hens'.[67] But this is a chair I'm sitting in, and it's made of wood, and this is a hen, and this is a hen's egg, and this hen laid it. These are all facts I know, and they are N-intrinsic facts—ultimate, absolute truths—about the nature of reality. They must be included in any true and full account of the history of the universe.

My reply to this objection is similar to Moore's a hundred years ago. I agree that we know many such truths, but I take it, as a materialist, that hens are wholly made of the fundamental constituents of matter that physics discusses, and that when we consider our knowledge of these fundamental constituents we encounter the crucial and entirely general sense in which we know nothing about the fundamental N-intrinsic nature of matter. As far as I can see, this ignorance is entirely compatible with the sense in which we do have knowledge of the N-intrinsic of reality in knowing that there are hens, and what hens are, and what wood is, and so on. And this compatibility is no more surprising than the fact that I can know that this is a statue without knowing what it is made of.

—But we know what hens are made of—carbon, hydrogen, and oxygen, mostly—and we know what carbon, hydrogen, and oxygen are made of—electrons and quarks with

[66] The word 'non-mental' is not redundant in the last sentence, for it seems very plausible to suppose that consciousness is an electrical phenomenon, whatever else it is; in which case it may be said that we do have some knowledge of the non-structural nature of electrical phenomena just in having conscious experience.

[67] Moore 1905–6: 64.

various characteristics. Physics gives us knowledge of the properties of these things. If you think that it fails to give us any knowledge of their ultimate, N-intrinsic nature that's because you think that a thing is more than its properties. But that's just bad old metaphysics. A thing is not in any sense more than its properties.

I agree that there is an irredeemably difficult but inescapable sense in which it is true to say that a thing is not more than its properties—I agree that 'in their relation to the object, the properties are not in fact subordinated to it, but are the way of existing of the object itself'[68]—but the present claim is not that a concrete phenomenon must be more than its properties, but that it must be more than its purely formal or structural properties. If you say that this is more bad metaphysics, a yearning for lumpen stuff, our disagreement will be plain. My reply will be that you have evidently forgotten 'what an abstract affair form really is'. A concrete phenomenon must be more than its purely formal or structural properties, because these, considered just as such, have a purely abstract mathematical representation, and are, concretely, nothing—nothing at all. It is true that we get out of the realm of the purely abstract when we add in spatiotemporal properties, on my account, but a thing's non-structural properties can't consist only in its spatiotemporal properties—at least so long as space-time is conceived merely as a dimensional manifold with no physical or substantial nature.[69]

Here, then, we return to the point that—the sense in which—we have no knowledge of the N-intrinsic nature of things in spite of the sense in which it is true to say that we know what hens and hens' eggs are.

11 TRUE MATERIALISM

I have suggested that our general theoretical conception of the mental has substantial non-structural descriptive content, because we have acquaintance with fundamental features of the mental nature of reality just in having experience in the way we do. Our general theoretical conception of the non-mental has substantial structure-specifying content, and I have suggested, with some hesitation, that it may also have crucial and correct *non*-structural content deriving from spatiotemporal concepts. Apart from this, though, it is arguable (subject to note 46) that we know nothing about the intrinsic or non-structural nature of non-mental reality.

With this in place, we may ask what is to be a genuine materialist. The first thing to do is to intone once more that realistic or real materialism entails full acknowledgement of the reality of experiential phenomena: they are as real as rocks, hence wholly physical, strictly on a par with anything that is correctly characterized by physics.[70] They are part of fundamental reality, whatever is or is not the case.

---

[68] Kant 1781: A414/B441. I have substituted 'object' and 'property' for 'substance' and 'accident' respectively.

[69] For the importance of this qualification, see n122 below.

[70] 'As characterized by physics' is a necessary qualification; see the remarks about 'brain' on p. 22 above.

It follows that current physics, considered as a general account of the general nature of the physical, is like *Othello* without Desdemona: it contains only predicates for non-experiential being, so it cannot characterize experiential being at all (recall the definition in §2). It cannot characterize a fundamental feature of reality at all.

No one who doubts this is a true materialist. Partly for this reason, I think that genuine, reflective endorsement of materialism is a considerable achievement for anyone who has had a standard modern Western education. Materialism must at first provoke a feeling of deep bewilderment in anyone contemplating the question 'What is the nature of the physical?' The occurrence of such a feeling is diagnostic of real engagement with the materialist hypothesis, real engagement with the thought that experiential phenomena are physical phenomena just like extension phenomena and electrical phenomena in so far as they are correctly characterized by physics (or indeed common sense). I think Russell is profoundly right when he says that most are 'guilty, unconsciously and in spite of explicit disavowals, of a confusion in their imaginative picture of matter'.

I suspect that some will be unable to shake off the confusion, although Locke made the crucial move long ago. Some may say that modern science has changed the situation radically since Locke's time. It has—but only in so far as it has massively reinforced Locke's point.

Perhaps I am generalizing illegitimately from my own experience, revealing my own inadequacy rather than the inadequacy of recent discussion of the 'mind–body' problem, but I don't think so. Genuine materialism requires concerted meditative effort. Russell recommends 'long reflection'.[71] If one hasn't felt a kind of vertigo of astonishment, when facing the thought, obligatory for all materialists, that consciousness is a wholly physical phenomenon in every respect, including every experiential respect—a sense of having been precipitated into a completely new confrontation with the utter strangeness of the physical (the real) relative to all existing common-sense and scientific conceptions of it—, then one hasn't begun to be a thoughtful materialist. One hasn't got to the starting line.[72]

Some may find that this feeling recurs each time they concentrate on the mind-body problem. Others may increasingly think themselves—quietistically, apophatically, pragmatically, intuitively—into the unknownness of the (non-mental) physical in such a way that they no longer experience the fact that mental and non-mental phenomena are equally physical as involving any clash. At this point 'methodological naturalism'—the methodological attitude to scientific enquiry into the phenomena of mind recommended by Chomsky—will become truly natural for them, as well as correct.[73] I think it is creeping over me. But recidivism is to be expected: the powerfully open state of mind required by true materialism is hard to achieve as a natural

---

[71] 1927b: 112.

[72] The only alternative, I think, is that one has a very rare and beautiful intellect.

[73] See Chomsky 1994; 1995: 1–10. Chomsky is a clear example of someone who is, methodologically, a true materialist in my sense. I am not sure that he would accept the title, however; he avoids the term 'materialist' because of the point made by Lange in n26 above, which I try to counter on pp. 48–9 below.

attitude to the world. It involves a profound reseating of one's intuitive theoretical understanding of nature.[74]

I say 'intuitive theoretical understanding of nature', but it isn't as if there is any other kind. For (briefly) what we think of as real understanding of a natural phenomenon is always at bottom just a certain kind of *feeling*, and it is always and necessarily relative to other things one just takes for granted, finds intuitive, feels comfortable with. This is as true in science as it is in common life. I feel I fully understand why this tower casts this shadow in this sunlight, given what I take for granted about the world (I simply do not ask why light should do *that*, of all things, when it hits stone). I may also feel I understand—see—why this billiard ball does *this* when struck in this way by that billiard ball. But in this case there is already a more accessible sense in which I don't really *understand* what is going on, and it is an old point that if I were to ask for and receive an explanation, in terms of impact and energy transfer, this would inevitably invite further questions about the nature of impact and energy transfer, starting a series of questions and answers that would have to end with a reply that was not an explanation but rather had the form 'Well, that's just the way things are.'[75]

The true materialist outlook may become natural for some, then, but many will find they can maintain it only for relatively short periods of time. It is not a small thing. To achieve it is to have evacuated one's natural and gripping common-sense ± science-based conception of the nature of the physical of every element that makes it seem puzzling that experiential phenomena are physical. I think it is to be at ease with the idea that consciousness is a form of matter.[76]

It can help to perform special acts of concentration—focusing one's thought on one's brain and trying to hold fully in mind the idea that one's experience as one does so is part of the physical being of the brain (part of the physical being of the brain that one may be said to be acquainted with as it is in itself, at least in part, because its being as it is for one as one has it just is what it is in itself, at least in part). It is worth trying to sustain this—it is part of doing philosophy—, forcing one's thought back to the confrontation when it slips. At first one may simply encounter the curious phenomenological character of the act of concentration, but it is useful to go on—to engage, for example, in silent, understanding-engaging subvocalizations of such thoughts as 'I am now thinking about my brain, and am thinking that this experience I am now having of this very thinking—and this subvocalization—is part of the physical activity and being of my brain.' It is also useful to look at others, including young children, as they experience the world, and to think of the common-or-garden matter that is in their heads (hydrogen, oxygen, carbon, iron, potassium,

---

[74] In fact one doesn't have to be a materialist to hold that no defensible conception of the physical contains any element that gives one positive reason to doubt that experiential phenomena are physical. One can hold this even if committed to dualism.

[75] See e.g. van Fraassen 1980: ch. 5; Strawson 1994: 84–93.

[76] I think that it requires realization that this claim is inadequately expressed by saying 'consciousness is a property of matter', or even 'consciousness is a physical property of matter', given the almost irresistible incentives to metaphysical misunderstanding that are—I argue elsewhere—already built into the word 'property'.

sodium, and so on). It is useful to listen to music, and focus on the thought that one's auditory experience is a form of matter.[77]

12   KNOWLEDGE OF IGNORANCE

Finding it deeply puzzling how something could be physical is not the same as finding something that one takes to be physical deeply puzzling. It is often said that quantum theory is deeply counterintuitive—in its description of the wave-like and particle-like behaviour of fundamental particles, for example—but no one seems to find it puzzling to suppose that it deals wholly with physical phenomena.[78]

The main reason for this seems to be as follows: WAVE and PARTICLE engage smoothly with standard physics concepts of shape, size, position, motion, and so on. There is, so far, a clear sense in which the two concepts are *theoretically homogeneous*, or at least non-heterogeneous; they operate on the same, single conceptual playing field of physics.[79] But when we try to integrate conscious-experience terms with the terms of physics (and common-sense physics), we find that they entirely lack any such felt theoretical homogeneity, or non-heterogeneity. To this extent, they force constantly renewed bewilderment—in a way quite different from the way in which quantum-mechanical phenomena do—on materialists who like to think they have *some* sort of coherent, theoretically unified understanding of the overall nature of the physical, however general that understanding may be, and however incomplete in its details.

But this is the central mistake: to think that one has some sort of theoretically uni-fied understanding of the overall nature of the physical. Once one realizes that this cannot be true, if materialism is true, things change.[80] It begins to look as if there is actually *less* difficulty in the suggestion that physical phenomena have both experi-ential and non-experiential being than in the suggestion that photons (for example) behave both like particles and waves. For in the case of experiential terms and non-experiential terms there is no direct clash of concepts of the sort that occurs in the case of the wave-particle duality. Being a wave is incompatible with being a particle,

---

[77] Perhaps intuitive materialism is not always an achievement, and comes easily, and without positive error, in certain Eastern schools of thought. The requirement that there be no positive error of conception is, however, important.

[78] Some may object that there is a compelling description of quantum-mechanical phenomena that completely eliminates the air of mystery attaching to wave-particle duality (see e.g. Deutsch 1997: ch. 2); but it does so at the cost of another large strangeness, because it requires one to accept Everett's many-worlds hypothesis; and although it may be that this is what one should do, I will continue to use the case of wave-particle duality as an example for the purposes of discussion. (I will also put aside the view that the real intuitive difficulty resides in the phenomenon of superposition rather than in the wave-particle duality.)

[79] I try to give more content to the idea of theoretical homogeneity in Strawson 1994: 88–93. Note that one can have a sense that a group of terms is theoretically homogeneous, or at least not problematically heterogeneous, without feeling that one *understands* the phenomena these terms are used to describe.

[80] Although there are plenty of deep puzzles in physics even when mind is put to one side.

but there is nothing in the possession of non-experiential being that we know to be intrinsically inimical to the possession of experiential being: we simply do not know enough about the nature of non-experiential being to have any good reason to suppose that this might be so. Thus the experiential terms and the non-experiential terms do not in fact *actively clash*, as the wave and particle terms do. Rather, they fail to connect or engage. One is making progress as a materialist when one has lost all sense of an active clash. It has no scientific or philosophical justification. As Russell says, 'the physical [sc non-mental] world is only known as regards certain abstract features of its space-time structure—features which, because of their abstractness, do not suffice to show whether the physical world is, or is not, different in intrinsic character from the world of mind'.[81]

Arnauld made the essential point in 1641, in his comments on Descartes's *Meditations*, and he was not the first.[82] Locke in 1689 'did not apprehend that there was any real inconsistency between the known properties of body, and those that have generally been referred to mind'.[83] Algarotti observes in 1737 that

we are as yet but Children in this vast Universe, and are very far from having a compleat Idea of Matter; we are utterly unable to pronounce what Properties are agreeable to it, and what are not,[84]

and Hume in 1739 shows a very clear understanding of the point.[85] Priestley in 1777 argues, with unanswerable force, and by appeal to a scientific conception of the physical that (in essence) still holds good today, 'that we have *no reason* to suppose that there are in man two substances so distinct from each other as have been represented'.[86] Kant concurs in 1781, although his special terms of debate preclude him from agreeing directly with Priestley's further materialist claim that 'mind . . . is not a substance distinct from the body, but the result of corporeal organization'; that 'in man [thought] is a property of the nervous system, or rather of the brain'; that

---

[81] 1948: 240; see also 247.

[82] In Descartes 1641: 2.141–3. Lange (1865) discusses many precursors.

[83] Priestley 1777–82: 115. Locke doesn't fully carry through his point that our ignorance of the nature of the physical means that we lack any good reason to doubt that consciousness is wholly physical; for at one point he says that 'matter . . . is evidently in its own nature void of sense and thought' (1689: 4.3.6; see also 2.10.5). But he also says that we 'possibly shall never be able to know whether any material being thinks, or no', and holds that an omnipotent being could give 'some systems of matter, fitly disposed, a power to perceive and think' (4.3.6.). The force of the second quotation is less than one might suppose: it does not conclusively establish that Locke thought that God could make matter have such a power *intrinsically* or in and of itself—i.e. without any special wizardry. But Locke's correspondence with Stillingfleet strongly suggests that his considered view is that our ignorance of the nature of the matter is in the end too great for us to have any good reason to claim that matter could not have the power of thought in and of itself (1696–9: 459–62).

[84] 1737: 2.194.   [85] 1739–40: 246–8.

[86] 1777–82: 219. Priestley observes, correctly, that there is no evidence for absolute solidity: 'I . . . define . . . matter . . . to be a substance possessed of the property of *extension*, and of *powers of attraction and repulsion*. And since it has never yet been asserted, that the powers of *sensation* and *thought* are incompatible with these (solidity, or impenetrability only, having been thought to be repugnant to them), I therefore maintain that we have no reason to suppose that there are in man two substances so distinct from each other as have been represented.'

'sensation and thought do necessarily result from the organization of the brain'.[87] The quality of the mind-body debate is in many ways lower today than at any other time in the last three hundred years.

Substance dualism may have looked like a plausible response to the mind-body problem in Descartes's time, for classical *mechanistic* materialism, according to which the physical world consists entirely of small, solid, intrinsically inert particles in motion, was then the dominant view, and Leibniz's famous image of the mill seemed hard to counter.[88] But the strict mechanist understanding of the physical world was fatally undermined by 1687, when Newton published his *Principia*.[89] Since then we have had no good scientific reason to think that mind is not physical. And even before Newton, in the high days of 'contact mechanics', there were no *philosophically* respectable grounds for claiming that mind is not physical. The mechanists or 'Cartesians', as Hume calls them, made a wholly unjustifiable move: they 'established it as a principle that we are *perfectly acquainted* with the essence of matter'.[90] That is, they not only assumed that their fundamental theory of matter was sound as far as it went; they also assumed that it went all the way—that it was complete. It is the second of these two false assumptions that causes most trouble, for even if the Cartesians had been right that all physical change is a matter of the motion, contact, and impact of solid particles, they still would not have been justified in claiming that this fact was definitely—knowably—incompatible with some of it also being a matter of conscious goings on. Many today make exactly the same sort of mistake.

13   THE REALITY OF APPEARANCE

I have claimed that thoughtful materialism requires draining one's conception of the non-experiential physical of any element that, in a puzzling world, makes it seem especially puzzling that the experiential is physical. Many philosophers—all those legions who tried, for most of the twentieth century, to reduce the mental to the

---

[87] Kant 1781: A358–60; Priestley 1777–82: 220, 244, 303. John Toland in 1704 'obviously regards thought as a phenomenon which is an inherent accompaniment of the material movements in the nervous system' (Lange 1865: 1.329).

[88] 'We must admit that perception, and whatever depends on it, cannot be explained on mechanical principles, i.e. by shapes and movements. If we pretend that that there is a machine [e.g. a brain] whose structure makes it think, sense and have perception, then we can conceive it enlarged, . . . so that we can go inside it as into a mill. Suppose that we do: then if we inspect the interior we shall find there nothing but parts which push one another, and never anything which could explain a perception. Thus, perception must be sought in simple substances, not in what is composite or in machines' (Leibniz 1720: 150 [*Monadology* §17]).

[89] Locke saw this pretty clearly after reading Newton (see e.g. Locke 1689: 2.23.24, 4.3.29; 1696–9: 467–8). Chomsky (1995: 4) quotes tellingly from Leibniz and Huygens, who condemned Newton for abandoning sound 'mechanical principles' and reverting to mystical 'sympathies and antipathies' and 'inexplicable qualities'.

[90] Hume 1739–40: 159; my emphasis.

non-mental in some way—think this is the wrong way round. They think we have to drain our conception of the experiential of any element that produces special puzzlement, leaving our existing conception of the non-experiential physical in place. But no substantial draining can be done on the experiential side. In having experience in the way we do, we are directly acquainted with certain features of the ultimate nature of reality, as Russell and others have remarked—whether or not we can put what we know into words in any theoretically tractable way. And this is so whatever it is best to say about any non-experiential (e.g. dispositional) aspects of the mental that there may be. We may certainly hope to *develop* our understanding of the nature of the experiential; but we can do this only by adding to what we already know of it by direct acquaintance:

—But in having experience we only have access to an appearance of how things are and are not cognizant, in the mere having of the experience, of how anything is in itself.[91]

The reply is immediate. Here, how things appear or seem is how they really are: the reality that is at present in question just is the appearing or seeming. In the case of any experiential episode E there may be something X of which it is true to say that in undergoing E we only have access to an appearance of X, and not to how X is in itself. But serious materialists must hold that E itself, the event of being-appeared-to, with all the qualitative character that it has, is itself part of physical reality. They cannot say that it too is just an appearance, and not part of how things are, on pain of infinite regress. They must grant that it is itself a reality, and a reality with which we must, in plausibility, be allowed to have some sort of direct acquaintance. As Russell says, we must 'treat "seeming" with respect'.[92]

At this point some may try to adapt Ryle-type arguments for the 'systematic elusiveness of the "I"' to the present case.[93] They may argue that anything that can count as *knowledge* of experience involves an operation of taking experience as an object that necessarily precludes apprehending it in such a way that one can be said to have access to how it is in itself, rather than merely to an appearance of it. Now I suspect that this ancient form of argument is invalid even in its original application, where it is used to argue that the putative mental subject of experience can never directly apprehend itself.[94] But even if this is not so it has no valid application to the present case—to things like pain and colour-experience. The way a colour-experience is experientially, for the subject of experience that has it, is part of its essential nature—its ultimate reality—as a physical phenomenon. When we claim (with Russell) that to have an experience is *eo ipso* to be acquainted with certain of the intrinsic features of reality, we do not have to suppose that this acquaintance involves standing back from the experience reflectively and examining it by means of a further, distinct experience. It doesn't. This picture is too cognitivist (or perhaps too German-Idealist). The having is the knowing.

---

[91] See Dennett 1991a: 365–6, and the reply in Strawson 1994: 51–2.   [92] 1927b: 101.
[93] Ryle 1949: 186–9. The idea is an old one.   [94] I argue for this in Strawson 1999a: §10.

14   THE RADIANCE OF REALITY

I have argued that the first thing that one needs to do, when it comes to the mind–body problem, is to reflect on one's ignorance: one's ignorance of the non-experiential. One's intuitive theoretical attitude to the nature of the non-experiential needs to evolve until any sense that there is an active clash between experiential terms and non-experiential terms has disappeared, leaving only the awareness that they fail to connect in a way that brings a sense of intuitive understanding. This awareness ought not to be merely a matter of book learning.

At this point at least two paths open up for materialists. The first goes deeper into reflection on the nature of understanding in physics. Proceeding down this path, one encounters one's sense that at least some of the terms of physics (both common-sense and scientific) connect up with one another in a way that justifies a feeling of intuitive understanding of at least some of what goes on in the world. One is then asked to examine (possibly at length) the question of what exactly one supposes this to amount to. Does it really amount to anything very solid? Is it more than a certain kind of feeling one is disposed to get (either innately or as a result of training) when considering some but not other co-occurrences of features in the world? What exactly is its significance?[95]

Well, one probably has to go down this path, as a materialist, returning to the questions raised on p. 37. But I will choose another, which has a sunnier aspect. Here one confronts the deep puzzlement one still feels when one considers experiential properties and non-experiential properties and fails to see how they coexist, and, also, one's persisting feeling that this puzzlement has, in a puzzling world, a very special if not unique status.

The question is whether one can do anything about this. I think the answer is Yes. I think physics can help us—it has already helped us a great deal—by diluting or undermining features of our natural conception of the physical that make non-experiential phenomena appear *toto coelo* different from experiential phenomena.

The basic point is simple, and can be elaborated as follows. At first, perhaps, one takes it that matter is simply solid stuff, uniform, non-particulate: Scandinavian cheese. Then, perhaps, one learns that it is composed of distinct atoms—particles that cohere more or less closely together to make up objects, but that have empty space (to put it simplistically but intelligibly) between them. Then, perhaps, one learns that these atoms are themselves made up of tiny, separate particles, and full of empty space themselves.[96] One learns that a physical object like the earth or a person is almost all empty space. One learns that matter is not at all what one thought.

Now one may accept this while holding on to the idea that matter is at root solid and dense. For this picture retains the idea that there are particles of matter:

[95] See, again, van Fraassen 1980: ch. 5.
[96] As in the old quantum-theory model of the atom, *c.*1910–24. The standard way to convey the amount of empty space inside an atom is to say that if the nucleus is imagined to be as big as a 1 mm pinhead, then the nearest electrons—themselves much smaller than the nucleus—are 100 metres away.

minuscule grainy bits of ultimate stuff that are in themselves perfectly solid (in Locke's phrase), 'continuum-dense'. And one may say that only these, strictly speaking, are matter: matter as such. But it is more than two hundred years since Priestley (citing Boscovich) observed that there is no positive observational or theoretical reason to suppose that the fundamental constituents of matter have any perfectly solid central part.[97]

In spite of this, a fairly robust conception of truly solid particles survived all the way into pre-1925 quantum mechanics. It suffered its most dramatic blow only in modern (1925 on) quantum mechanics, in which neither the nucleus nor the electrons of an atom are straight-up solid objects, and are much more naturally thought of as fields. It may be said that the basic idea of the grainy particle survives even here, at least in as much as the nucleus and its components are still fairly well localized within a small central region inside the atom (albeit with small 'tails' that go out to infinity), and in as much as the probability of finding one of the (far less localized) electrons is significant only within a volume that is normally considered to be the dimensions of the atom. But this commitment to the localization of particles does not in itself amount to any sort of commitment to continuum-dense solidity, but only to fields and repulsive forces that grow stronger without any clear limit when one travels in certain directions (i.e. towards the centre of the field associated with a particle). And whatever is left of the picture of ultimate grainy bits is further etiolated in quantum field theory, in which the notion of the field more fully overrides the picture of grainy particles.[98] In this theory it becomes very hard to treat 'bound' systems like atoms at all. As for what I've been calling 'empty space'—the supposed vacuum—, it is understood to be simply the lowest energy state of fields like the electron, proton, and photon fields. It turns out to be something which 'has structure and can get squeezed, and can do work'.[99]

It may be said that quantum field theory is complicated and ill-understood, but there is a clear sense in which grainy, inert bits of matter, naively conceived, are already lost to us independently of quantum field theory, given only the fact that matter is a form of energy, and interconvertible with it. This fact of interconvertibility is widely known, however little it is understood, and it seems to me that it further, and utterly, confounds any understanding of matter that takes it to be in any obvious way incompatible with consciousness. To put it dramatically: physics thinks of matter considered in its non-experiential being as a thing of spacetime-located forces, energy, fields, and it can also seem rather natural to conceive of consciousness (i.e. matter apprehended in its experiential being) as a spacetime-located form or

[97] See also Foster 1982a: 67–72, and Harré and Madden 1975: ch. 9.

[98] 'In the modern theory of elementary particles known as the Standard Model, a theory that has been well verified experimentally, the fundamental components of nature are a few dozen kinds of field' (Weinberg 1997: 20). We continue to talk in terms of particles because the quantization of the field, whereby each different (normal) mode of vibration of the field is associated with a discrete ladder of energy levels, automatically gives rise to particle-like phenomena so far as observation is concerned.

[99] Harvey Brown, personal communication; see Saunders and Brown 1991. Perhaps Descartes was right, deep down, in his theory of the plenum.

manifestation of energy, as a kind of force, and even, perhaps, as a kind of field.[100] We may still think the two things are deeply heterogeneous, but we have no good reason to believe this.[101] We just don't know enough about the nature of matter considered in its non-experiential being; and doubtless there are things we don't know about matter considered in its experiential being. Those who think speculations like this are enjoyable but not really serious haven't really begun on the task of being a materialist; they haven't understood the strangeness of the physical and the extent of our ignorance. It is a long time since Russell argued that 'from the standpoint of philosophy the distinction between physical and mental is superficial and unreal', and it seems that physics can back philosophy on this question.[102] In fact—and it had to come back to this—we really don't know enough to say that there is any non-mental being. All the appearances of a non-mental world may just be the way that physical phenomena—in themselves entirely mental phenomena—appear to us; the appearance being another mental phenomenon.[103]

Whatever you think of this last proposal, lumpish, inert matter, dense or corpuscled, stuff that seems essentially alien to the phenomenon of consciousness, has given way to fields of energy, essentially active diaphanous process-stuff that—intuitively—seems far less unlike the process of consciousness. When Nagel speaks of the 'squishy brain', when McGinn speaks of 'brain "gook"' and asks how 'technicolour phenomenology . . . can . . . arise from soggy grey matter', when the neurophysiologist Susan Greenfield describes the brain as a 'sludgy mass', they vividly and usefully express part of the 'imaginative . . . confusion' in the ordinary idea of matter.[104] But physics comes to our aid: there is a clear sense in which the best description of the nature of the non-experiential *in non-technical, common-sense terms* comes from physics. For what, expressed in common-sense terms, does physics find in the volume of spacetime occupied by a brain? Not a sludgy mass, but an astonishingly (to us) insubstantial-seeming play of energy, an ethereally radiant vibrancy.

---

[100] Compare Maxwell 1978: 399; James 1890: 1.147 n. It is arguable that Schopenhauer holds something close to this view.

[101] Using this very wording, Kant, 1781–7: B427–8, remarks that the 'heterogeneity' of mind and body is merely assumed and not known.

[102] Russell 1927a: 402.

[103] Richard Price is consistently outclassed by Priestley in their *Free Discussion of the Doctrine of Materialism*, but he gets this point exactly right: 'if . . . it comes out that [Priestley's] account of matter does not answer to the common ideas of matter, [and] is not *solid* extension, but something *not solid* that exists in space, it agrees so far with spirit', or mind (Priestley and Price 1778: 54; Price held that spirit was not only located in space but might also be extended). This is a rather good description of how things have come out, in physics. The account of matter given by current physics does not 'answer to the common ideas of matter'; it does not take matter to be 'solid extension', but rather 'something not solid that exists in space'. So far, then, it agrees with our understanding of mind or consciousness, although the agreement can only be negative, given that we have no non-mathematical grasp of the non-structural nature of the non-experiential being of matter—apart (perhaps) from our grasp of its spacetime structure.

[104] Nagel 1998: 338; McGinn 1991: 1, 100; Greenfield BBC 21 June 1997. In spite of these quotations I think that all three of these writers are fundamentally on the right track when it comes to the mind-body problem.

It finds, in other words, a physical object; which, thus far examined, is like any other. Examined further, this particular physical object turns out to have a vast further set of remarkable properties: all the sweeping sheets and scudding clouds and trains of intraneuronal and interneuronal electrochemical activity which physics (in conjunction with neurophysiology) apprehends as a further level of extraordinarily complex intensities of movement and (non-experiential) organization existing in an *n*-dimensional realm that we call spacetime although its nature is bewilderingly different from anything we ordinarily have in mind in thinking in terms of space and time.

All this being so, do we have any good reason to think that we know anything about the non-mental physical (assuming it exists) that licenses surprise—even the very mildest surprise—at the thought that the experiential is physical? I do not think so. Brains are special, but they are not strange. The ghost in the machine is special, but it is certainly in the machine, and the machine, like the rest of the physical world, is already a bit of a ghost—as ghostly, in Russell's view, 'as anything in a spiritualist séance'.[105]

So when David Lewis says that 'the most formidable opposition to any form of mind-body identity comes from the friends of qualia'[106] there is no reason to agree. The main opposition to (realistic) mind–body identity comes, paradoxically, from its most passionate proponents, who are so strongly inclined to think they know more about the nature of the non-mental physical than they do. Lewis exemplifies the great mistake in his well-known summary account of his position in the philosophy of mind: 'Remember', he says, 'that the physical nature of ordinary matter under mild conditions is very well understood.'[107] But there is no reason to believe this, and every reason to disbelieve it. 'What knowledge have we of the nature of atoms that renders it at all incongruous that they should constitute a thinking [experiencing] object?', asks Eddington, who took the existence of experiential phenomena 'qualia' for granted: 'science has nothing to say as to the intrinsic nature of the atom.' The atom, so far as we know anything about it,

is, like everything else in physics, a schedule of pointer readings [on instrument dials]. The schedule is, we agree, attached to some unknown background. Why not then attach it to something of a spiritual nature of which a prominent characteristic is *thought*. It seems rather *silly* to prefer to attach it to something of a so-called 'concrete' nature inconsistent with thought, and then to wonder where the thought comes from. We have dismissed all preconception as to the background of our pointer readings, and for the most part can discover nothing as to its nature. But in one case—namely, for the pointer readings of my own brain—I have an insight which is not limited to the evidence of the pointer readings. That insight shows that they are attached to a background of consciousness.[108]

The point is still negative. It may destroy one common source of puzzlement, but it doesn't offer any sort of positive account of the relation between the play of energy non-experientially conceived and the play of energy experientially apprehended, and

---

[105] 1927b: 78.   [106] Lewis 1999: 5; qualia are experiential phenomena.
[107] Lewis 1994: 412.   [108] Eddington 1928: 259–60; my emphasis on 'silly'.

some may find it no help at all. Others may say that it is a positive mistake to think that it is especially helpful, on the grounds that there is in the end no more difficulty in the thought that the existence of matter naively and grossly conceived involves the existence of consciousness than there is in the thought that matter quantum-mechanically conceived does so.[109]

We can grant them their objection for their own consumption (they are likely to be fairly sophisticated philosophers). Many others—not excluding philosophers—are likely to find the negative point rather useful, and I will conclude this section by relating it to three currently popular issues.

(1) Eliminativism. Consider any philosopher who has ever been tempted, even momentarily, by the 'eliminativist' suggestion that one has to question the reality of the experiential in some way in order to be a thoroughgoing materialist. It is an extraordinary suggestion,[110] and what is most striking about it in the present context is that it constitutes the most perfect demonstration in the history of philosophy of the grip of the very thing that it seeks to reject: dualist thinking. The eliminativists make the same initial mistake as Descartes—the mistake of assuming that they understand more about the nature of the physical than they do—but their subjugation to dualist thinking is far deeper than Descartes.[111] They are so certain that the physical excludes the experiential that they are prepared to deny the reality of the experiential in some (admittedly unclear) way—to make the most ridiculous claim ever made in philosophy—in order to retain the physical. (The mistake of thinking one may have grasped the essential nature of the physical is perhaps forgivable in the early seventeenth century, but not now.)

(2) The hard part of the mind-body problem. It can be seriously misleading to talk of 'the hard part of the mind-body problem',[112] or 'the hard problem',[113] for this suggests that the problem is clearly posed. It is not, as Chomsky has observed. One might say that it is not sufficiently well defined for us to be able to say that it is hard; for although we have a clear and substantial positive fix on the non-structural nature of experiential reality, we have no substantial positive fix on the non-structural nature of non-experiential reality, apart, perhaps, from its spatiotemporal characteristics. To this extent we have no good reason to think that the mind-body problem is a

---

[109] They will find Russell's line of thought equally unnecessary as a way of reaching a conclusion they already fully accept: 'having realised the abstractness of what physics has to say, we no longer have any difficulty in fitting the visual sensation into the causal series. It used to be thought "mysterious" that purely physical [i.e. non-mental] phenomena should end in something mental. That was because people thought they knew a lot about physical phenomena, and were sure they differed in quality from mental phenomena. We now realise that we know nothing of the intrinsic quality of physical phenomena except when they happen to be sensations, and that therefore there is no reason to be surprised that some are sensations, or to suppose that the others are totally unlike sensations' (1927b: 117).

[110] It seems considerably more implausible than Xenocrates' suggestion that the soul is a self-moving number (see Aristotle *De Anima* 408b–409a).

[111] In fact it is not clear that Descartes does make this mistake, although it is clear that some eliminativists do. Descartes was for a long time seen as a dangerous source of materialist views, and there are some reasons for thinking that his official dualism was motivated partly by the desire to stave off persecution by religious authorities.

[112] Strawson 1989: 80, 1994: 93; compare McGinn 1989: 1.   [113] Chalmers 1995: 200.

harder problem than the problem posed for our understanding by the peculiarities of quantum physics, or indeed—as Chomsky might say—by the phenomenon of motion. The problem is the nature of the physical, and in particular, perhaps, of the non-mental physical.

(3) Zombies. It is, finally, a mistake to think that we can know that 'zombies' could exist—where zombies are understood to be creatures that have no experiential properties although they are *perfect physical duplicates* (PPDs) of experiencing human beings.[114] The argument that PPD-zombies could exist proceeds from two premises: [1] it is conceivable that PPD-zombies exist, [2] if something is conceivable, then it is possible. The argument is plainly valid, and (unlike many) I have no great problem with [2]. The problem is that we can't know [1] to be true, and have no reason to think it is. To be a genuine materialist is precisely to hold that [1] is false, and while materialism cannot be known to be true, it cannot be refuted a priori, as it could be if [1] could be known to be true. PHYSICAL is a natural-kind concept, and since we know that there is much that we do not know about the nature of the physical, we cannot claim to know that a experienceless PPD—a perfect physical duplicate, no less—of a currently experiencing human being is even conceivable, and could possibly exist. One needs to be very careful how one embeds natural-kind terms in 'it is conceivable that' contexts.[115]

It is worth adding that anyone who holds that it is as a matter of *physical* fact impossible for a PPD of an actual, living normally experiencing human being to have no experience must hold that PPD-zombies are *metaphysically* (if not *logically*) impossible. Physical impossibility entails metaphysical impossibility in this case, because the question is precisely what is possible given the actual nature of the physical.

15 REALISTIC MONISM

In §1 I pointed out that the word 'physical', as used by genuine materialists, entails 'real and concrete': given that one is restricting one's attention to concrete phenomena, as we are doing here, to say something is a physical phenomenon is simply to say that it is a real phenomenon. But then why bother to use 'physical'?[116] It has become an entirely empty or vacuous term, in so far as it is supposed to mean anything more than 'real'. So why not simply use 'real'? And why bother with 'real', given that we are talking about whatever (concretely) exists, whatever it is? It is redundant. All one strictly needs, to mark the distinctions centrally at issue in the unfortunately named 'mind–body problem', are 'mental' and 'non-mental', 'experiential'

---

[114] I don't know where these zombies come from—but they may be Australian. Ten years or so ago philosophical zombies were far more plausible creatures: they were defined to be *outwardly* and *behaviourally* indistinguishable from human beings while having unknown (possibly non-biological) insides, and were, accordingly, of considerable interest to functionalists and behaviourists.

[115] It is worth noting that a perfect physical duplicate of an actual human being would also have to be governed by the same physical laws.

[116] Compare Crane and Mellor 1990.

and 'non-experiential'.[117] One can simply declare oneself to be a *experiential-and-non-experiential* monist: one who registers the indubitable reality of experiential phenomena and takes it that there are also non-experiential phenomena.

I nominated this position for the title 'realistic monism', having explicitly assumed (p. 23) that any realistic position must take it that there is non-experiential being. Now this assumption can be backed by an argument that seems quite strong—(1) experience (experiential content) certainly exists, (2) experience (experiential content) is impossible without a subject of experience, (3) a subject of experience cannot itself be an entirely experiential (experiential-content) phenomenon, so (4) the existence of experience (experiential content) entails the existence of non-experiential phenomena.[118] But one can have no deep confidence in the correctness of the assumption if one accepts the general principles of ignorance defended in this paper, and this argument for it invites the reply that even if a subject of experience must have non-experiential being relative to its own experience, its non-experiential being may be the experience of some other, lower-order, subject or group of subjects, and so on down. I am not sure this reply is cogent, in fact, or that premiss (3) is solid,[119] but I propose to leave the assumption as an assumption: one cannot really know what is 'realistic', at this point.

—You say we can do without the word 'physical'. But if one can do without 'physical', then 'materialist', used so diligently in this paper, is just as superfluous—vacuous. You have already stated (note 12) that you make no distinction between materialism and physicalism, and the word 'materialist' is deeply compromised by its history.

History is two-faced, and I think that 'materialist'—an adjective formed from the natural-kind term 'matter'—can be harmlessly and even illuminatingly retained.[120] What, after all, is matter? As a materialist, I take it that it is whatever we are actually talking about when we talk about concrete reality. I fix the reference of the term 'matter' in this way—giving a chair a kick, perhaps—independently of any reference to theories. I can be certain that there is such a thing as matter, as a realistic materialist monist—one who takes it that experience is wholly material in nature—because I can be certain that there is such a thing as concrete reality: experience, at the very least. What a materialist may still wish to add to this is the insistence that nothing can count as matter unless it has some sort of non-experiential being (see §4); together with the working presumption that current physics is genuinely reality-representing in certain ways, even if any correctness of representation is only a matter

---

[117] According to the view presented in Strawson 1994: 162–75, the latter pair suffice on their own.

[118] As remarked in note 22, I do not think that there is any clear parallel argument for the claim that non-*mental* being must exist if experience exists, because the term 'mental' is too unclear for such an argument to be constructed. Nor do I know how someone like Bradley would respond to this argument.

[119] I address this question in Essay 6.

[120] Here at last, it seems, I may differ from Chomsky—but only, I think, on a point of terminology. (Obviously 'physical' can also be retained in so far as it is synonymous with 'material'.)

of the holding of certain relations of structural correspondence between the nature of matter and the equations of physics.

In so far as I am a realistic materialist monist, then, I presume that physics's best account of the structure of reality is genuinely reality-representing in substantive ways, and that the term 'materialist' is in good order. I sail close to the wind—by which I mean the charge of vacuousness, and the charge that it may be hard to distinguish my position from idealism—in my use of the word 'matter' because that is exactly what one has to do at this point. Kicking another chair, I grant that the term 'materialist' has travelled far from some of its past uses, but there is no good reason to think that its meaning is especially tied to its past uses rather than to the current understanding of matter.[121] And there is a sense in which its past use makes it particularly well worth retaining: it makes the claim that the present position is materialist vivid by prompting resistance that turns out to be groundless when the position is properly understood.[122]

That is all I have to say about the word 'materialist', and some will probably think that I would do better to call myself a 'neutral monist', or just a 'monist'.[123] But what about 'monist'? There is serious unclarity in this notion. Monists hold that there is, in spite of all the variety in the world, a fundamental sense in which there is only one basic kind of stuff or being. But questions about how many kinds of stuff or being there are are answerable only relative to a particular point of view or interest; and what point of view is so privileged that it allows one to say that it is an absolute metaphysical fact that there is only one kind stuff or being in reality? Materialists call themselves monists because they think that all things are of one kind—the physical kind. But many of them also hold that there is more than one kind of fundamental particle, and this claim, taken literally, entails that there isn't after all any one basic kind of

---

[121] There is, in particular, no good reason to think that it is especially tied to the seventeenth-century conception of matter as something passive and inert. The conception of matter as essentially energy-involving, or at least as something to which motion is intrinsic, is already present in the work of Democritus and Epicurus.

[122] I should add that I take it that spacetime itself is material (it is a disputed question). In quantum field theory, reality consists of spacetime and a collection of fields defined on spacetime; what we think of as material objects are emergent (in the non-spooky sense) features of these fields. But spacetime is not a merely passive container, for according to general relativity the action-reaction principle applies as between spacetime and matter (this is the phenomenon Pullman, 1998: 351, usefully calls 'the vacuum-matter complementarity, or . . . the virtual-material duality of particles'). Moreover, the gravitational field, unlike the other fields, is not distinct from spacetime itself. Rather, the gravitational field, within a given region, just is the spacetime geometry of that region. The structural relations it involves are physical or material because they are spatiotemporal (they are not merely abstract-dimensional). Note also that energy can be stored and propagated within the gravitational field, and hence within the spacetime fabric itself, which again suggests that spacetime is substantial and hence—given materialism—material, in a way that Newtonian space and time, say, are not. (My thanks to Michael Lockwood and Harvey Brown for discussion of this matter.)

[123] Neutral monism is not an option on the present view, because we know that experience like ours is part of reality, whatever else is or is not the case, and we know its nature—its 'ultimate' nature, if you like—in having it; whatever else is or is not the case. It cannot be supposed to be merely an appearance of something that is in itself quite unlike experience.

being out of which everything is constituted. For it is the claim that these particles are themselves, in their diversity, the ultimate constituents of reality; in which case there is kind-plurality or stuff-plurality right at the bottom of things.

—But these particles are nevertheless all *physical*, and in that sense of one kind.

To say that they can be classed together as single-substanced in this way is question-begging until it is backed by a positive theoretical account of why it is correct to say that they are all ultimately (constituted) of one kind (of substance). To claim that their causal interaction sufficiently proves their same-substancehood is to beg the question in another way, on the terms of the classical debate, for classical substance-dualists simply deny that causal interaction entails same-substancehood. The claim that they are all spatiotemporally located also begs the question. For how does this prove same substancehood?

It may be replied that all the particles are just different forms of the same stuff —energy. And it may be added that the so-called fundamental particles—quarks and leptons—are not strictly speaking fundamental, and are in fact all consti-tuted of just one kind of thing: superstrings. And these monist approaches deserve investigation—to be conducted with an appropriately respectful attitude to pan-psychism.[124] But one can overleap them by simply rejecting the terms of the classical debate: one can take causal interaction to be a sufficient condition of same-substancehood.

I think that this is the right dialectical move in the present context, if one wants to retain any version of the terminology of substance. Dualists who postulate two dis-tinct substances while holding that they interact causally not only face the old prob-lem of how to give an honest account of this interaction. They also face the (far more difficult) problem of justifying the claim that there are two substances. As far as I can see, *the only justification that has ever been attempted* has consisted in an appeal to the *intuition* that the mental or the experiential is utterly different in nature from matter. But this intuition lacks any remotely respectable theoretical support, if the argument of this paper is even roughly right. The truth is that dualism has nothing in its favour—to think that it has does is simply to reveal that one thinks one knows more about the nature of things than one does—and it has Occam's razor (that blunt sharp instrument) against it. This is not to rule out the theoretical possibility that sub-stance dualism—or pluralism—is in fact the best view to take about our universe for reasons of which we know nothing.[125] The fact remains that the objection to dual-ism just given remains decisive when dualism is considered specifically as a theoretical response to the 'mind-body problem'.

—But why persist with 'monist'? You might as well call yourself a 'neutral pluralist', for all the difference it makes, and 'monist' carries bad baggage. Why not simply call

---

[124] See e.g. Seager 1995. Note that panpsychism does *not* require one to believe that tables and chairs are subjects of experience.

[125] There may be phenomena in the universe that cannot interact causally given their nature (rather than their position in spacetime), or that do so only on the first Thursday of every seventh century, in a highly peculiar way.

yourself a 'non-committal naturalist', or, with Chomsky, a 'methodological naturalist'? Or a '?-ist'?[126]

This section stirs up large questions, but I'm not too troubled. In some moods I am prepared to call myself an experiential-and-non-experiential ?-ist and think no more about the word 'monist'; there is no decidable issue here, as the old decriers of metaphysics (e.g. Locke, Hume, Kant) knew. At the moment, though, the physics idea (the ancient idea) that everything is made of the same ultimate stuff—that the deep diversity of the universe is a matter of different states or arrangements of the same fundamental *ens* or *entia*—that 'in the whole universe there is only one substance differently modified'[127]—seems to me as compelling as it is remarkable, and I choose to register my attraction to it with the word 'monism'.[128]

---

[126] Sebastian Gardner proposed that I am a '?-ist' in 1990 (see Strawson 1994: 105). It is hard to find satisfactory names, and Grover Maxwell, who holds essentially the same position as I do, calls himself a 'nonmaterialist physicalist' (1978: 365).

[127] La Mettrie, 1747: 39.

[128] The theme of this paper is continued in the next. I am especially grateful to Noam Chomsky, Michael Lockwood and Undo Uus for the leads they have given me. I would also like to thank Lucy Allais, Harvey Brown, Jeremy Butterfield, Arthur Collins, Tim Crane, Mark Greenberg, Isaac Levi, Barry Loewer, Brian McLaughlin, Philip Pettit, Mark Sainsbury, Simon Saunders, Stephen Schiffer, Peter Unger, Bas van Fraassen, and audiences at the University of Birmingham, CUNY Graduate Center, and Columbia University in 1997 and 1998.

2

Realistic Monism: Why Physicalism Entails Panpsychism

1 PHYSICALISM

I take physicalism[1] to be the view that every real, concrete phenomenon in the universe is . . . physical. It is a view about the actual universe, and I am going to assume that it is true. For the purposes of this paper I will equate 'concrete' with 'spatiotemporally (or at least temporally) located', and I will use 'phenomenon' as a completely general word for any sort of existent. Plainly all mental goings on are concrete phenomena.[2]

What does physicalism involve? What is it, really, to be a physicalist? What is it to be a *realistic* physicalist, or, more simply, a *real* physicalist? Well, one thing is absolutely clear. You're certainly not a realistic physicalist, you're not a real physicalist, if you deny the existence of the phenomenon whose existence is more certain than the existence of anything else: experience, 'consciousness', conscious experience, 'phenomenology', experiential 'what-it's-likeness', feeling, sensation, explicit conscious thought as we have it and know it at almost every waking moment. Many words are used to denote this necessarily occurrent (essentially non-dispositional) phenomenon, and in this paper I will use the terms 'experience', 'experiential phenomena', and 'experientiality' to refer to it.

Full recognition of the reality of experience, then, is the obligatory starting point for any remotely realistic version of physicalism. This is because it is the obligatory starting point for any remotely realistic (indeed any non-self-defeating) theory of what there is. It is the obligatory starting point for any theory that can legitimately claim to be 'naturalistic' because experience is itself the fundamental given natural fact; it is a very old point that there is nothing more certain than the existence of experience.

This paper develops parts of 'Agnostic materialism' (Strawson 1994: 43–105, especially 59–62, 72, 75–7) and Essay 1 and inherits their debt to Nagel 1974.

[1] I have replaced the word 'materialism' by 'physicalism' and speak of 'physical stuff' instead of 'matter' because 'matter' is now specially associated with mass although energy is just as much in question, as indeed is anything else that can be said to be physical, e.g. spacetime itself—or whatever underlies the appearance of spacetime.

[2] More strictly, 'concrete' means 'not abstract' in the standard philosophical sense of 'abstract', given which some philosophers hold that abstract objects—e.g. numbers, or concepts—exist and are real objects in every sense in which concrete objects are. I take 'spatiotemporal' to be the adjective formed from 'spacetime', not from the conjunction of space and time.

It follows that real physicalism can have nothing to do with *physicṣalism*, the view—the faith—that the nature or essence of all concrete reality can in principle be fully captured in the terms of *physics*. Real physicalism cannot have anything to do with physicṣalism unless it is supposed—obviously falsely—that the terms of physics can fully capture the nature or essence of experience.[3] It is unfortunate that 'physicalism' is today standardly used to mean physicṣalism because it obliges me to speak of 'real physicalism' when really I only mean 'physicalism'—realistic physicalism.

Real physicalism, then, must accept that experiential phenomena are physical phenomena. But how can experiential phenomena be physical phenomena? Many take this claim to be profoundly problematic (this is the 'mind–body problem'). This is usually because they think they know a lot about the nature of the physical. They take the idea that the experiential is physical to be profoundly problematic *given what we know about the nature of the physical*. But they have already made a large and fatal mistake. This is because we have no good reason to think that we know anything about the physical that gives us any reason to find any problem in the idea that experiential phenomena are physical phenomena. If we reflect for a moment on the nature of our knowledge of the physical, and of the experiential, we realize, with Eddington, that 'no problem of irreconcilability arises'.[4]

A very large mistake. It is perhaps Descartes's, or perhaps rather 'Descartes's', greatest mistake,[5] and it is funny that in the past fifty years it has been the most fervent revilers of the great Descartes, the true father of modern materialism, who have made the mistake with most intensity. Some of them—Dennett is a prime example—are so in thrall to the fundamental intuition of dualism, the intuition that the experiential and the physical are utterly and irreconcilably different, that they are prepared to deny the existence of experience, more or less (c)overtly, because they are committed to 'physicalism', that is, physicṣalism.[6]

---

[3] For a standard argument that this is impossible in principle, see e.g. Strawson 1994: 62–5.

[4] Eddington 1928: 260; the thought was not new. In the background stood Arnauld 1641; Locke 1689; Hume 1739–40; Priestley 1777; and many others—see Essay 1: §12. Kant makes the point very clearly, on his own special terms. See e.g. 1781–7: A358–60, A380, and B427–8, where he remarks that the 'heterogeneity' of mind and body is merely 'assumed' and not known.

[5] I think that, in his hidden philosophical heart, he did not make it (he is certainly not a 'substance dualist' as this expression is currently understood; see Clarke 2003). Arnauld saw the problem clearly, and Hume (1739–40: 159/1.3.14.8) diagnosed the mistake definitively in two lines, with specific reference to the Cartesians, but the twentieth century—philosophical division—wasn't listening.

[6] Dennett conceals this move by *looking-glassing* the word 'consciousness' (his term for experience) and then insisting that he does believe that consciousness exists (to looking-glass a term is to use a term in such a way that whatever one means by it, it excludes what the term means—see Essay 10). As far as I can understand them, Dretske, Tye, Lycan, and Rey are among those who do the same. It seems that they still dream of giving a reductive analysis of the experiential in non-experiential terms. This, however, amounts to denying the existence of experience, because the nature of (real) experience can no more be specified in wholly non-experiential terms than the nature of the (real) non-experiential can be specified in wholly experiential terms. In the normal case, of course, reductive identification of X with Y is not denial of the existence of X. The reductive claim is 'X exists, but it is really just this (Y)'. In the case of experience, however, to say that it exists but is really just something whose nature can be fully specified in wholly non-experiential, functional terms is to deny its existence. 'But what is this supposed thing you say we're denying?'

'They are prepared to deny the existence of experience.' At this we should stop and wonder. I think we should feel very sober, and a little afraid, at the power of human credulity, the capacity of human minds to be gripped by theory, by faith. For this particular denial is the strangest thing that has ever happened in the whole history of human thought, not just the whole history of philosophy. It falls, unfortunately, to philosophy, not religion, to reveal the deepest woo-woo of the human mind. I find this grievous, but, next to this denial, every known religious belief is only a little less sensible than the belief that grass is green.[7]

Realistic physicalists, then, grant that experiential phenomena are real concrete phenomena—for nothing in life is more certain—and that experiential phenomena are therefore physical phenomena. It can sound odd at first to use 'physical' to characterize mental phenomena like experiential phenomena,[8] and many philosophers who call themselves materialists or physicalists continue to use the terms of ordinary everyday language, that treat the mental and the physical as opposed categories.

---

say the deniers. It's the thing to which the right reply to the question 'What is it?' is, as ever, the (Louis) Armstrong–Block reply 'If you gotta ask, you ain't never gonna get to know' (Block 1978). It's the thing whose deniers say that there is no non-question-begging account of, to which the experiential realist's correct reply is: 'It's question-begging for you to say that there must be an account of it that's non-question-begging in your terms.' Such an exchange shows that we have reached the end of argument, a point further illustrated by the fact that reductive idealists can make exactly the same 'You have no non-question-begging account' objection to reductive physicalists that reductive physicalists make to realists about experience: 'By taking it for granted that the physical is something that can (only) be specified in non-mental terms, you (reductive physicalists) simply beg the question against reductive idealists.' It's striking that the realist notion of the physical that present-day physicalists appeal to was thought to be either without warrant or unintelligible by many of the leading philosophers of the twentieth century. Many were in effect reductive idealists about the physical, and Quine famously compared belief in physical objects to belief in the gods of Homer (1951: 44).

[7] Dennett has suggested that 'there is no such thing [as] . . . phenomenology' and that any appearance of phenomenology is, somehow, wholly the product of some cognitive faculty, the 'judgment module' or 'semantic intent module' that does not itself involve any phenomenology. '*There seems to be phenomenology*,' he concedes, 'but it does *not* follow from this undeniable, universally attested fact that *there really is* phenomenology' (1991b: 365–6). It is unclear what Dennett means by 'phenomenology', but whatever he means this move fails immediately if it is taken as an objection to the present claim that we can be certain both that there is experience and that we can't be radically in error about its nature. It fails for the simple reason that for there to seem to be rich phenomenology or experience just is for there to be such phenomenology or experience. To say that its apparently sensory aspects (say) are in some sense illusory because they are not the product of sensory mechanisms in the way we suppose, but are somehow generated by merely cognitive processes, is just to put forward a surprising hypothesis about part of the *mechanism* of this rich seeming that we call experience or consciousness. It is in no way to put in question its existence or reality. Whatever the process by which the seeming arises, the end result of the process is, as even Dennett agrees, at least this: that it *seems* as if one is having phenomenally rich experience of Beethoven's eighth quartet or an Indian wedding. And if there is this seeming, then, once again, there just is phenomenology or experience (adapted from Strawson 1994: 51–2).

In denying that experience can be physical, Dennett and his kind find themselves at one with many religious believers. This seems at first ironic, but the two camps are deeply united by the fact that both have unshakable faith in something that lacks any warrant in experience. That said, the religious believers are in infinitely better shape, epistemologically, than the Dennettians.

[8] For purposes of argument I make the standard assumption that while all experiential phenomena are mental phenomena, the converse is not true.

It is, however, precisely physicalists (real physicalists) who cannot talk this way, for it is, on their own view, exactly like talking about cows and animals as if they were opposed categories. Why? Because every concrete phenomenon is physical, according to them. So all mental (experiential) phenomena are physical phenomena, according to them; just as all cows are animals. So when physicalists—real ones—talk as if the mental (experiential) and the physical were entirely different all they can really mean to be doing is to distinguish, within the realm of the physical, which is the only realm there is, according to them, between mental (experiential) features of the physical, and non-mental (non-experiential) features of the physical.

As a real physicalist, then, I hold that the mental/experiential is physical, and I am happy to say, along with many other physicalists, that experience is 'really just neurons firing', at least in the case of biological organisms like ourselves. But when I say these words I mean something completely different from what many physicalists have apparently meant by them. I certainly don't mean that all characteristics of what is going on, in the case of experience, can be described by physics and neurophysiology or any non-revolutionary extensions of them. That idea is crazy. It amounts to radical 'eliminativism' with respect to experience, and it is not a form of real physicalism at all.[9] My claim is different. It is that experiential phenomena 'just are' physical, so that there is a lot more to neurons than physics and neurophysiology record (or can record). No one who disagrees with this is a real physicalist, in my terms.

In Essay 1 I considered some objections to the claim that the position I have just outlined can really be called a physicalist position. I did my best to answer them and ended concessively, allowing that one might better call the position 'experiential-and-non-experiential monism' rather than 'real physicalism'. It is, in any case, the position of someone who (a) fully acknowledges the evident fact that there is experiential being in reality, (b) takes it that there is also non-experiential being in reality, and (c) is attached to the 'monist' idea that there is, in some fundamental sense, only one kind of stuff in the universe.

The objectors then picked on the word 'monist', and I considered a further concession. You can call my position 'experiential-and-non-experiential ?-ism', if you like, and opt out of the monism-dualism-pluralism oppositions of classical metaphysics. Perhaps you can simply call it '?-ism'.[10] But then you will have to allow that the existence of experiential being at least is certain, and is not put in question by the '?'—so that it would be better to call it 'experiential ?-ism'. And if you then want to insist, in line with all standard conceptions of the physical, that non-experiential being also exists, then you will also need to signal the fact that the non-experiential is not put in question by the '?'. In which case you may as well go back to calling the position 'experiential-and-non-experiential ?-ism'.

---

[9] This follows from the fact that current physics contains no predicates for experiential phenomena, and that no non-revolutionary extension of it (no currently conceivable extension of it—see n3) could do so.

[10] A suggestion made by Sebastian Gardner, nearly twenty years ago.

I persist in thinking that 'physicalism', 'real physicalism', is a good name for my position in the current context of debate, but it's time to admit that in my understanding real physicalism doesn't even rule out panpsychism—which I take to be the view that the existence of every real concrete thing involves experiential being, even if it also involves non-experiential being. If this seems a little colourful then it's time to read Locke on substance again.[11]

Surely I've pushed myself over the edge? How can I say that 'physicalism' is an acceptable name for my position? Because I take 'physical' to be a natural-kind term whose reference I can sufficiently indicate by drawing attention to tables and chairs and—as a realistic physicalist—experiential phenomena.[12] The physical is whatever general kind of thing we are considering when we consider things like tables and chairs and experiential phenomena. It includes everything that concretely exists in the universe. If everything that concretely exists is intrinsically experience-involving, well, that is what the physical turns out to be; it is what energy (another name for physical stuff) turns out to be. This view does not stand out as particularly strange against the background of present-day science, and is in no way incompatible with it.

I don't *define* the physical as concrete reality, as concrete-reality-whatever-it-is; obviously I can't rule out the possibility that there could be other non-physical (and indeed non-spatiotemporal) forms of concrete reality. I simply fix the reference of the term 'physical' by pointing at certain items and invoking the notion of a general kind of stuff. It is true that there is a sense in which this makes my use of the term vacuous, for, relative to our universe, 'physical stuff' is now equivalent to 'real and concrete stuff', and cannot be anything to do with the term 'physical' that is used to mark out a position in what is usually taken to be a substantive debate about the ultimate nature of concrete reality (physicalism vs immaterialism vs dualism vs pluralism vs . . .). But that is fine by me. If it's back to Carnap, so be it.[13]

Have I gone too far? It seems to me that to go this far is exactly the right thing to do at this point in the debate. It's worth it if it helps us to get back to a proper (realistic) openmindedness. But anyone who prefers to call my position 'realistic monism' instead of 'real physicalism' should feel free to do so.[14]

2 'IT SEEMS RATHER SILLY . . . '

This may all seem a little giddy, so I will now rein things in a little by making three conventional substantive assumptions about the physical for purposes of argument,

---

[11] Locke 1689: 2.23 and 4.3.6.

[12] It's striking that analytic philosophers and psychologists have talked so much about natural-kind terms but have failed to see that 'physical' is a paradigmatic example of such a term in every sense in which 'gold' is.

[13] See Carnap 1950.

[14] It is less certain that there is non-experiential stuff than that there is experiential stuff, and in most ears 'real physicalism' signals commitment to the existence of non-experiential stuff in a way that 'realistic monism' does not.

using the term 'ultimate' to denote a fundamental physical entity, an ultimate constituent of reality, a particle, field, string, brane, simple, whatever:

[1] there is a plurality of ultimates (whether or not there is a plurality of types of ultimates)[15]

[2] everything physical (everything physical that there is or could be) is constituted out of
ultimates of the sort we actually have in our universe

[3] the universe is spatiotemporal in its fundamental nature.[16]

I do not, however, think that I need these assumptions in order to show that something akin to panpsychism is not merely one possible form of realistic physicalism,
real physicalism, but the only possible form, and, hence, the only possible form of
physicalism *tout court*. Eddington is one of those who saw this clearly, and I am now
going to join forces with him and ask you to be as tolerant of his terminological loose-
nesses and oddities as I hope you will be of my appeals to intuition.[17]

One thing we know about physical stuff, given that (real) physicalism is true, is
that when you put it together in the way in which it is put together in brains like
ours, it regularly constitutes—is, literally is—experience like ours. Another thing
we know about it, let us grant, is everything (true) that physics tells us. But what is
this second kind of knowledge like? Well, there is a fundamental sense in which it is
'abstract', 'purely formal', merely a matter of 'structure', in Russell's words.[18] This is a
well established but often overlooked point.[19] 'Physics is mathematical', Russell says,
'not because we know so much about the physical world'—and here he means the
non-mental, non-experiential world, in my terms, because he is using 'mental' and
'physical' conventionally as opposed terms—

but because we know so little: it is only its mathematical properties that we can discover. For
the rest, our knowledge is negative.... The physical world is only known as regards certain
abstract features of its space-time structure—features which, because of their abstractness, do
not suffice to show whether the physical world is, or is not, different in intrinsic character from
the world of mind.[20]

---

[15] I believe that cosmology raises serious doubts about (Leibnizian) [1]. A powerful rival
(Spinozistic) view is that there is at bottom just one thing or substance, e.g. spacetime, or whatever
underlies all spacetime appearances. But [1] does not beg any important questions. If anything, it
makes things more difficult for me.

[16] This is in doubt in present-day physics and cosmology, for 'rumors of spacetime's impend-
ing departure from deep physical law are not born of zany theorizing. Instead, this idea is
strongly suggested by a number of well-reasoned considerations' (Greene 2004: 472; see also
473–91). Note that if temporality goes, i.e. not just spacetime as we currently understand it
but temporality in any form, then experience also goes, given that experience requires time.
One of the fine consequences of this is that there has never been any suffering. But no
theory of reality can be right that has the consequence that there has never been any suffering.

[17] I came upon Eddington's book *The Nature of the Physical World* in a holiday house in Scotland
in 1999.

[18] 1927a: 392, 382; 1956: 153; 1927b: 125.

[19] It takes time to assimilate it fully. It cannot be simply read off the page.

[20] 1948: 240; see also 247. Russell's overall view is that 'we know nothing about the intrinsic
quality of physical events except when these are mental events that we directly experience' (1956:
153), and that 'as regards the world in general, both physical and mental, everything that we know

Eddington puts it as follows. 'Our knowledge of the nature of the objects treated in physics consists solely of readings of pointers [on instrument dials] and other indicators'. This being so, he asks, 'what knowledge have we of the nature of atoms that renders it at all incongruous that they should constitute a thinking object?' Absolutely none, he rightly replies: 'science has nothing to say as to the intrinsic nature of the atom'. The atom, so far as physics tells us anything about it,

is, like everything else in physics, a schedule of pointer readings [on instrument dials]. The schedule is, we agree, attached to some unknown background. Why not then attach it to something of a spiritual [i.e. mental] nature of which a prominent characteristic is *thought* [=experience, consciousness]. It seems rather *silly* to prefer to attach it to something of a so-called 'concrete' nature inconsistent with thought, and then to wonder where the thought comes from. We have dismissed all preconception as to the background of our pointer readings, and for the most part can discover nothing as to its nature. But in one case—namely, for the pointer readings of my own brain—I have an insight which is not limited to the evidence of the pointer readings. That insight shows that they are attached to a background of consciousness

in which case

I may expect that the background of other pointer readings in physics is *of a nature continuous with that revealed to me in this way,*

even while

I do not suppose that it always has the more specialized attributes of consciousness.

What is certain is that

in regard to my one piece of insight into the background no problem of irreconcilability arises; I have no other knowledge of the background with which to reconcile it . . . . *There is nothing to prevent the assemblage of atoms constituting a brain from being of itself a thinking [conscious, experiencing] object in virtue of that nature which physics leaves undetermined and undeterminable.* If we must embed our schedule of indicator readings in some kind of background, at least let us accept the only hint we have received as to the significance of the background—namely, that it has a nature capable of manifesting itself as mental activity.[21]

This all seems intensely sensible and Occamical. Eddington's notion of silliness is extremely powerful. Why then—on what conceivable grounds—do so many physicalists simply assume that the physical, in itself, is an essentially and wholly non-experiential phenomenon?

of its intrinsic character is derived from the mental side' (1927a: 402). See Lockwood 1981, 1989, and Essay 1.

[21] Eddington 1928: 258–60; my emphasis on 'silly'. It is remarkable that this line of thought (so well understood by Russell, Whitehead, Eddington, Broad, Feigl, and many others, and equally, in a number of slightly different guises, by Spinoza, Locke, Hume, Kant, Priestley, and many others) disappeared almost completely from the philosophical mainstream in the wake of Smart's 1959 paper 'Sensations and brain processes', although it was well represented by Chomsky (see e.g. Chomsky 1968, 1995). At this point analytical philosophy acquired hyperdualist intuitions even as it proclaimed its monism. With a few honourable exceptions it out-Descartesed Descartes (or 'Descartes') in its certainty that we know enough about the physical to know that the experiential cannot be physical.

I write this and think 'Do they really?', and this rapid inner question is not rhetorical or aggressive, meaning 'They must be pretty stupid if they really think, and think they know, that physical stuff is, in itself, and through and through, an essentially non-experiential phenomenon.' It is, rather, part of a feeling that I must be wrong. I must be doing what philosophers are famous for doing—setting up strawman opponents who do not really exist while erasing awareness of my real audience, who will protest that of course they aren't so foolish as to claim to know that physical stuff is, in itself, in its root nature, a wholly non-experiential phenomenon.

My next thought, however, is that I am not wrong. It looks as if many—perhaps most—of those who call themselves physicalists or materialists really are committed to the thesis that

[NE] physical stuff is, in itself, in its fundamental nature, something wholly and utterly non-experiential.

I think they take it, for a start, that ultimates are in themselves wholly and essentially non-experiential phenomena. And they are hardly going out on a limb in endorsing NE, for it seems to be accepted by the vast majority of human beings. I do not, however, see how physicalists can leave this commitment unquestioned, if they are remotely realistic in their physicalism, if, that is, they really do subscribe to the defining thesis of real physicalism that

[RP] experience is a real concrete phenomenon and every real concrete phenomenon is physical.

For if they are real physicalists they cannot deny that when you put physical stuff together in the way in which it is put together in brains like ours it constitutes—is—experience like ours; all by itself. All by itself: there is on their own physicalist view nothing else, nothing non-physical, involved.

The puzzle, for me, is that I'm sure that some at least of those who call themselves physicalists are realistic physicalists—real realists about experiential phenomena. And yet they do I think subscribe to NE—even when they are prepared to admit with Eddington that physical stuff has, in itself, 'a nature capable of manifesting itself as mental activity', that is, as experience or consciousness.

3 EMERGENCE

Is this a possible position? Can one hold RP and NE together? I don't think so, but one defence goes like this:

Experiential phenomena are *emergent* phenomena. Consciousness properties, experience properties, are emergent properties of wholly and utterly non-conscious, non-experiential phenomena. Physical stuff *in itself*, in its basic nature, is indeed a wholly non-conscious, non-experiential phenomenon. Nevertheless when parts of it combine in certain ways, experiential phenomena 'emerge'. Ultimates in themselves are wholly non-conscious, non-experiential phenomena. Nevertheless, when they combine in certain ways, experiential phenomena 'emerge'.

Does this conception of emergence make sense? I think that it is very, very hard to understand what it is supposed to involve. I think that it is incoherent, in fact, and that this general way of talking of emergence has acquired an air of plausibility (or at least possibility) for some simply because it has been appealed to many times in the face of a seeming mystery.[22] In order to discuss it I am going to take it that any position that combines RP with NE must invoke some notion of emergence, whether or not it chooses to use the word. I will start on familiar ground.

Liquidity is often proposed as a translucent example of an emergent phenomenon, and the facts seem straightforward. Liquidity is not a characteristic of individual H_2O molecules. Nor is it a characteristic of the ultimates of which H_2O molecules are composed. And yet when you put many H_2O molecules together they constitute a liquid (at certain temperatures, at least), they constitute something liquid. So liquidity is a truly emergent property of certain groups of H_2O molecules. It is not there at the bottom of things, and then it is there.

When heat is applied evenly to the bottom of a tray filled with a thin sheet of viscous oil, it transforms the smooth surface of the oil into an array of hexagonal cells of moving fluid called Bénard convection cells.[23] This is another popular example of an emergent phenomenon. There are many chemical and physical systems in which patterns of this sort arise simply from the routine workings of basic physical laws, and such patterns are called 'emergent'.

This is all delightful and true. But can we hope to understand the alleged emergence of experiential phenomena from non-experiential phenomena by reference to such models? I don't think so. The emergent character of liquidity relative to its non-liquid constituents does indeed seem shiningly easy to grasp. We can easily make intuitive sense of the idea that certain sorts of molecules are so constituted that they don't bind together in a tight lattice but slide past or off each other (in accordance with van de Waals molecular interaction laws) in a way that gives rise to—is—the phenomenon of liquidity. So too, with Bénard convection cells we can easily make sense of the idea that physical laws relating to surface tension, viscosity, and other forces governing the motion of molecules give rise to hexagonal patterns on the surface of a fluid-like oil when it is heated. In both these cases we move in a small set of conceptually homogeneous shape-size-mass-charge-number-position-motion-involving physics notions with no sense of puzzlement. Using the notion of reduction in a familiar loose way, we can say that the phenomena of liquidity reduce without remainder to shape-size-mass-charge-etc. phenomena—I'll call these 'P' phenomena for short, and assume for now that they are, in themselves, utterly non-experiential phenomena. We can see that the phenomenon of liquidity arises naturally out of, is *wholly dependent on*, phenomena that do not in themselves involve liquidity at all. We can with only a little work suppress our initial tendency to confuse liquidity as it appears to sensory experience (how, we may think, could *this* arise from individual

[22] Compare the way in which the word 'immaterial' comes to seem to have some positive descriptive meaning although it quite explicitly has none. For a recent helpful taxonomy of types of emergence, see van Gulick 2001; see also Broad 1925 and McLaughlin 1992.

[23] Velarde and Normand 1980.

non-liquid molecules?) with the physical phenomenon of liquidity considered just as such, and see clearly that it is just and wholly a matter of P phenomena.

This notion of total dependence looks useful. It seems plain that there must be a fundamental sense in which any emergent phenomenon, say Y, is wholly dependent on that which it emerges from, say X. It seems, in fact, that this must be true by definition of 'emergent'; for if there is not this total dependence then it will not be true after all, not true without qualification, to say that Y is emergent from X. For in this case at least some part or aspect of Y will have to hail from somewhere else and will therefore not be emergent from X. Plainly this is not how it is with liquidity.[24]

It is the dependence requirement that causes the problem when it comes to relating the supposedly emergent phenomena of experience to the supposedly wholly non-experiential phenomena from which they supposedly emerge. For it now seems that if experiential phenomena—colour-experiences, for example—really are somehow (wholly) dependent on non-experiential phenomena, as they must be if they are to be truly emergent from them, that is, emergent from them and from them alone, then there must (to quote myself in a former century) be

a correct way of describing things . . . given which one can relate [the experiential phenomenon of] color-experience, considered just as such, to the non-experiential phenomena on which it is supposed to depend, in such a way that the dependence is as intelligible as the dependence of the liquidity of water on the interaction properties of individual molecules. The alternative, after all, is that there should be total dependence that is not intelligible or explicable in any possible physics, dependence that must be unintelligible and inexplicable even to God, as it were.[25]

I wouldn't put it this way now. The notions of explicability and intelligibility are in origin epistemological, and are potentially misleading because the present claim is not epistemological. It is not, for example, touched by the reply that there is a sense in which all *causal* dependence relations, at least, are ultimately unintelligible to us, even those that seem most intuitively understandable. For although there is a sense in which this is true, in as much all our explanations of concrete phenomena come to an end in things that are simply given, contingent, not further explicable, it has no bearing here. 'Intelligible to God' isn't really an epistemological notion at all, it's

---

[24] Here, then, I reject the commonly embraced but little examined and seemingly wholly mystical notion of emergence that van Gulick (2001) calls 'Radical Kind Emergence' and defines as follows: 'the whole has features that are both [a] different in kind from those had by the parts, and [b] of a kind whose nature is not necessitated by the features of its parts, their mode of combination and the law-like regularities governing the features of its parts.' (Liquidity, in van Gulick's scheme, is by contrast a case of 'Modest Kind Emergence': it is simply that 'the whole has features that are different in kind from those of its parts (or alternatively that could be had by its parts). For example, a piece of cloth might be purple in hue even though none of the molecules that make up its surface could be said to be purple.')

Some hold out for mystico-magical emergence by saying that liquidity is only a resultant phenomenon, not truly emergent, a truly emergent phenomenon being precisely one that does not perspicuously 'reduce' to what it emerges from in the way that the liquid phenomena reduce to non-liquid phenomena. Mystery, however, should be used sparingly. It should not be used to try to solve a problem of reconcilability that turns out on close examination not to exist.

[25] 1994: 69.

just a way of expressing the idea that there must be something about the nature of the emerged-from (and nothing else) in virtue of which the emerger emerges as it does and is what it is.

You can get liquidity from non-liquid molecules as easily as you can get a cricket team from eleven things that are not cricket teams. In God's physics, it would have to be just as plain how you get experiential phenomena from wholly non-experiential phenomena. But this is what boggles the human mind. We have, once again, no difficulty with the idea that liquid phenomena (which are wholly P phenomena) are emergent properties of wholly non-liquid phenomena (which are wholly P phenomena). But when we return to the case of experience, and look for an analogy of the right size or momentousness, as it were, it seems that we can't make do with things like liquidity, where we move wholly within a completely conceptually homogeneous (non-heterogeneous) set of notions. We need an analogy on a wholly different scale if we are to get any imaginative grip on the supposed move from the non-experiential to the experiential.

What might be an analogy of the right size? Suppose someone—I will call him pseudo-Boscovich, at the risk of offending historians of science—proposes that all ultimates, all real, concrete ultimates, are, in truth, wholly unextended entities: that this is the truth about their being; that there is *no* sense in which they themselves are extended; that they are real concrete entities, but are nonetheless true-mathematical-point entities. And suppose pseudo-Boscovich goes on to say that when collections of these entities stand in certain (real, concrete, natural) relations, they give rise to or constitute truly, genuinely extended concrete entities; real, concrete extension being in this sense an *emergent property* of phenomena that are, although by hypothesis real and concrete, wholly unextended.

Well, I think this suggestion should be rejected as absurd. But the suggestion that when non-experiential phenomena stand in certain (real, natural, concrete non-experiential) relations they *ipso facto* instantiate or constitute experiential phenomena, experience being an emergent property of wholly and utterly non-experiential phenomena, seems exactly on a par. That's why I offer unextended-to-extended emergence as an analogy, a destructive analogy that proposes something impossible and thereby challenges the possibility of the thing it is offered as an analogy for. You can (to use the letter favoured by the German idealists when either stating or rejecting the law of non-contradiction) get A from non-A for some substitutions for A, such as liquidity, but not all.

—My poor friend. The idea that collections of concrete entities that are truly, genuinely unextended can give rise to or constitute concrete entities that are truly, genuinely extended is actually scientific orthodoxy, on one widely received view of what ultimates are. It's an excellent candidate for being an analogy of the right size.

But this won't do. It won't do when one is being metaphysically straight, not *metaphysically* instrumentalist, or positivist, or operationalist, or phenomenalist, or radical-empiricist, or verificationist, or neo-verificationist or otherwise anti-realist or Protagorean (alas for the twentieth century, in which all these epistemological notions somehow got metaphysicalized). If one is being metaphysically straight, the intuition that nothing (concrete, spatiotemporal) can exist at a mathematical point, because there just isn't any room, is rock solid.[26] It may be added that anything that has, or is well understood as, a field, or that has any sort of attractive or repulsive being or energy, or any area of influence or influencability, *ipso facto* has extension—extension is part of its being—and that although there are plenty of ultimates that have no charge in what physicists call 'the standard model', there are I believe none that are not associated with a field.[27] So if the idea of unextended-to-extended emergence is offered as an analogy for non-experiential-to-experiential emergence, I don't think it can help.

I'll take this a little further. Suppose someone proposes that there are real, concrete, intrinsically, irreducibly and wholly *non-spatial* phenomena ('wholly non-S phenomena'), and that when they stand in certain wholly non-spatial relations they give rise to or constitute real, concrete, intrinsically and irreducibly spatial phenomena, ('S phenomena'), these being emergent features of wholly non-S phenomena. Those who claim to find no difficulty in the idea that genuinely unextended concrete entities can give rise to or constitute genuinely extended concrete entities may like to consider this case separately, because they presumably take it that their putative mathematical-point entities are at least spatial entities, at least in the sense of being spatially located. My hope is that even if they think they can make sense of the emergence of the extended from the unextended, they won't think this about the more radical case of the emergence of the spatial from the non-spatial.

But what do I know about this? Almost nothing. With this kind of speculation 'we are got into fairy land', as Hume says, or rather I am, and any impossibility claim on my part, or indeed anyone else's, may seem rash.[28] And some may now propose that the 'Big Bang' is precisely a case in which S phenomena are indeed emergent features of wholly non-S phenomena.

Don't believe it, I say, falling back on the *argumentum a visceris*. S phenomena, real, concrete, intrinsically and irreducibly spatial phenomena (bear in mind that we are seeking an analogy for experiential phenomena that we know to be real, concrete, intrinsically and irreducibly experiential) *can't* be emergent properties of wholly non-S phenomena. This is a case where you can't get A from non-A. The spatial/non-spatial case may look like an analogy of the right size for the experiential/non-experiential case, but all it turns up, I suggest, is impossibility. If there is any sense in which S phenomena can be said to emerge from wholly non-S phenomena, then they must fall back into the category of mere appearance, and they are then (by definition,

---

[26] Do not be cowed by physicists or philosophers of physics. (It seems intuitively obvious, by the grace of mathematics, that to introduce real, concrete entities that are infinitely small and therefore metaphysically impossible into one's theory will lead to infinite largenesses popping up in protest elsewhere in one's equations. And so it came to pass.)

[27] As I understand it, every particle in the standard model feels a force, even the photon (i.e. photon-photon forces, mediated by—virtual—pair creation/annihilation processes for the sources of the photon). This sort of point no longer seems required, however, in string theory (M-theory or brane theory), given that all the ultimates of M-theory have extension.

[28] 1748: 72. It is quite plain, in any case, that people can think (or think they think) anything.

see above) not S phenomena at all. Experiential phenomena, however, cannot do this. They cannot be mere appearance, if only because all appearance depends on their existence.[29] If it were to turn out that real S-phenomena can after all emerge from wholly non-S phenomena, all that would follow would be that the spatial case did not after all constitute an analogy of the right size. The experiential/non-experiential divide, assuming that it exists at all, is the most fundamental divide in nature (the only way it can fail to exist is for there to be nothing non-experiential in nature).[30]

The claim, at least, is plain, and I'll repeat it. If it really is true that Y is emergent from X then it must be the case that Y is in some sense wholly dependent on X and X alone, so that all features of Y trace intelligibly back to X (where 'intelligible' is a metaphysical rather than an epistemic notion). *Emergence can't be brute.* It is built into the heart of the notion of emergence that emergence cannot be brute in the sense of there being absolutely no reason in the nature of things why the emerging thing is as it is (so that it is unintelligible even to God). For any feature Y of anything that is correctly considered to be emergent from X, there must be something about X and X alone in virtue of which Y emerges, and which is sufficient for Y.

I'm prepared to allow for argument that an ultimate's possession of its fundamental properties could be brute in the sense of there being no reason for it in the nature of things, so long as it is agreed that *emergence* cannot be brute. One problem is that brute emergence is by definition a miracle every time it occurs, for it is true by hypothesis that in brute emergence there is absolutely nothing about X, the emerged-from, in virtue of which Y, the emerger, emerges from it. And this means that it is also a contradiction in terms, given the standard assumption that the emergence of Y from X entails the 'supervenience' of Y on X,[31] because it then turns out to be a strictly law-like miracle. But a miracle is by definition a violation of a law of nature![32] If someone says he chooses to use the word 'emergence' in such a way that the notion of brute emergence is not incoherent, I will know that he is a member of the Humpty Dumpty army and be very careful with him.

How did the notion of brute emergence ever gain currency? By one of the most lethal processes of theory formation, or term formation, that there is. The notion of brute emergence marks a position that seemingly has to exist if one accepts both RP (or, more simply, the reality of experience) and NE. And since many are irredeemably committed to both RP and NE, the notion of brute emergence comes to feel substantial to them by a kind of reflected, holographical energy. It has to be there, given these

---

[29] See n7. One current view of the 'Big Bang' is that it occurred everywhere in an already existing infinite space.

[30] The viscera are not unsophisticated organs. They can refuse the getting of A from non-A for some substitutions for A even while they have no difficulty with the strangest quantum strangenesses (see e.g. Essay 1: 38–9).

[31] The supervenience thesis states that if Y is supervenient on X then whenever you have an X-type phenomenon you must also have a Y-type phenomenon.

[32] This is Hume's definition of a miracle (I'm assuming that there is no *deus ex machina*). It is often said that this definition requires an absolute, non-statistical notion of a law of nature, but this is not so (see Mackie 1982: ch. 4).

unquestioned premisses, so it is felt to be real. The whole process is underwritten by the wild radical-empiricism-inspired metaphysical irresponsibilities of the twentieth century that still linger on (to put it mildly) today and have led many, via a gross misunderstanding of Hume, to think that there is nothing intrinsic to a cause in virtue of which it has the effect it does.[33]

I'll say it again. For Y truly to *emerge* from X is for Y to arise from or out of X or be given in or with Y *given how X is*. Y must arise out of or be given in X in some essentially non-arbitrary and indeed wholly non-arbitrary way. X has to have something—indeed everything—to do with it. That's what emerging is (that's how liquidity arises out of non-liquid phenomena). It is essentially an in-virtue-of relation. It cannot be brute. Otherwise it will be intelligible to suppose that existence can emerge from (come out of, develop out of) non-existence, or even that concrete phenomena can emerge from wholly abstract phenomena. Brutality rules out nothing.[34] If emergence can be brute, then it is fully intelligible to suppose that non-physical soul-stuff can arise out of physical stuff—in which case we can't rule out the possibility of Cartesian egos *even if we are physicalists*. I'm not even sure we can rule out the possibility of a negative number emerging from the addition of certain positive numbers. We will certainly have to view with equanimity all violations of existing laws of (non-experiential) physics, dross turning adventitiously into gold, particles decaying into other particles whose joint charge differs from that of the original particle.

Returning to the case of experience, Occam cuts in again, with truly devastating effect. Given the undeniable reality of experience, he says, why on earth (our current location) commit oneself to NE? Why insist that physical stuff in itself, in its basic nature, is essentially non-experiential, thereby taking on

[a] a commitment to something—wholly and essentially non-experiential stuff—for which there is *absolutely no evidence whatever*

along with

[b] the wholly unnecessary (and incoherent) burden of brute emergence

otherwise known as magic? That, in Eddington's terms, is silly.

---

[33] Here I make the common assumption that it is legitimate to segment the world into causes and effects. Hume's wholly correct, strictly epistemological claim—that so far as we consider things a priori 'any thing may produce any thing'—came to be read as the metaphysical claim that anything may produce anything. For a discussion of this error see e.g. Craig 1987: ch. 2 and Essay 18 below. It is worth noting that the epistemological restriction is usually explicitly stated in Hume's *Treatise*, in spite of his youthful liking for dramatic abbreviation: 'I have inferr'd from these principles, that *to consider the matter a priori*, any thing may produce any thing, and that we shall never discover a reason, why any object may or may not be the cause of any other, however great, or however little the resemblance may be betwixt them' (T247); '*for ought we can determine by the mere ideas*, any thing may be the cause or effect of any thing' (T249–50; my emphasis). Brute emergence does indeed license the non-Humean, ontological version of 'any thing may produce any thing'.

[34] Even if a universe could just come into existence when nothing existed, it certainly couldn't emerge from non-existence in the relevant sense of 'emerge'. *Ex nihilo nihil fit*, whatever anyone says (Nobel Prize winners included).

—What about the emergence of life? A hundred years ago it seemed obvious to many so-called 'vitalists' that *life* could not emerge from utterly lifeless matter (from P phenomena), just as it seems obvious to you now that *experience* could not emerge from utterly non-experiential matter (from P phenomena). Today, however, no one seriously doubts that life emerged from matter that involved no life at all. The problem of life, that seemed insuperable, simply dissolved. Why should it not be the same with consciousness, a hundred years from now?

This very tired objection is always made in discussions of this sort, and the first thing to note is that one cannot draw a parallel between the perceived problem of life and the perceived problem of experience in this way, arguing that the second problem will dissolve just as the first did, unless one considers life completely apart from experience. So let us call life considered completely apart from experience 'life*'. My reply is then brief. Life* reduces, experience doesn't. Take away experience from life and it (life*) reduces smoothly to P phenomena. Our theory of the basic mechanisms of life reduces to physics via chemistry. Suppose we have a machine that can duplicate any object by a process of rapid atom-by-atom assembly, and we duplicate a child. We can explain its life* functions in exquisite detail in the terms of current sciences of physics, chemistry, and biology. We cannot explain its experience at all in these terms.

One of the odd things about the supposed problem of life* is that although it was popular at the end of the nineteenth century it would not have been thought very impressive in the seventeenth and eighteenth centuries. The problem of *experience* seemed as acute then as it does today, but many found little difficulty in the idea that animals including human beings were—except in so far as they had experience—simply physical machines.[35] It should be added that many were quite unmoved by the problem of life* even when it was at the height of its popularity, but found the problem of experience as acute as their seventeenth- and eighteenth-century predecessors and twentieth and twenty-first century successors.[36]

4 'PROTO-EXPERIENTIAL'

Some may insist again that they find nothing intolerable in the idea that (spatial) S-phenomena can be emergent properties of something wholly non-S, and they may add that they feel the same about the experiential emerging from the wholly non-experiential.

What should one do? Encourage them, first, to see—to allow—that if S phenomena can be emergent properties of wholly non-S phenomena then the stuff emerged-from, the non-spatial whatever-it-is, must at the very least be somehow *intrinsically suited* to constituting spatial phenomena, on their view; it must be 'proto-spatial' in that sense.

[35] Many also took it that experience, too, was just a physical phenomenon, although we could not understand how. Joseph Priestley made the point that we know nothing about the physical that gives us reason to think that the experiential is not physical with its full force in 1777; Locke had already made it, somewhat circumspectly, in the 1690s, as had the 'a-posteriori physicalist' Regius, forty years earlier (1647: 294–5).

[36] See e.g. James 1890, and references there.

—Quite so. And exactly the same may be true of experiential phenomena. Experiential phenomena can indeed emerge from wholly and utterly non-experiential phenomena. This is possible because these non-experiential phenomena are intrinsically suited to constituting experiential phenomena in certain circumstances, and are 'proto-experiential' in that sense, although ultimately non-experiential in themselves.

This doesn't escape the problem, it merely changes the terms. 'Proto-experiential' now means 'intrinsically suited to constituting certain sorts of experiential phenomena in certain circumstances', and clearly—necessarily—for X to be intrinsically suited to or for constituting Y in certain circumstances is for there to be something about X's nature *in virtue of which* X is so suited.[37] If there is no such in-virtue-of-ness, no such intrinsic suitability, then any supposed emergence is left brute, in which case it is not emergence at all, it is magic, and everything is permitted, including, presumably, the emergence of the (ontological) concrete from the (ontological) abstract. If on the other hand there is such intrinsic suitability, as there must be if there is to be emergence, how can this be possessed by wholly, utterly, through-and-through non-experiential phenomena? (This is the unargued intuition again. Bear in mind that the intuition that the non-experiential could not emerge from the wholly experiential is exactly parallel and unargued.) If you take the word 'proto-experiential' to mean 'not actually experiential, but just what is needed for experience', then the gap is unbridged.[38] If you take it to mean 'already intrinsically (occurrently) experiential, although very different, qualitatively, from the experience whose realizing ground we are supposing it be', you have conceded the fundamental point.

—You're waving your arms around. H_2O molecules are, precisely, 'proto-liquid', and are at the same time, in themselves, wholly and utterly non-liquid.

To offer the liquidity analogy is to see its inadequacy. Liquidity is a P phenomenon that reduces without remainder to other P phenomena. Analysed in terms of P properties, liquid bodies of water and H_2O molecules have exactly the same sorts of properties, and they are made of exactly the same stuff (ultimates). This is not the case when it comes to experiential phenomena and non-experiential phenomena, for it is built into our starting point, set by NE, that they do not have the same sorts of

---

[37] It's not clear what the import of the phrase 'in certain circumstances' is, but the circumstances must presumably themselves be wholly non-spatial and non-experiential, and they cannot in any case make any contribution to the spatiality or the experientiality if it is to emerge wholly and only from the wholly non-spatial and non-experiential phenomena that are being taken to be distinct from the circumstances in which they find themselves.

[38] Compare Chalmers's (1997) use of 'protophenomenal'. Chalmers is a realist about experience but he gives central place to an idea that rules out real physicalism: the idea that there could be creatures that have no experiential properties although they are 'perfect physical duplicates' of experiencing human beings. These creatures, *Australian zombies*, have done a lot of damage in recent discussion, blotting out classical philosophical zombies, who are outwardly and behaviourally indistinguishable from human beings but with unknown and possibly non-biological insides. Chalmers holds that Australian zombies are a real possibility, but this is not something that can be shown, if only because there is a great deal we do not know about the physical, and it is fabulously implausible to suppose that an atom-for-atom, state-for-state duplicate of an experiencing human being could be produced and not have experience (note that one cannot produce an atom-for-atom, state-for-state duplicate of one of us while varying the laws of nature).

properties at all in this sense. The analogy is not of the right size or kind. What we need, to put it now in terms of P properties, is, precisely, an analogy that could give us some idea of how (natural, intrinsic, non-conventional) non-P properties could emerge from P properties—and of how things with only P properties could be proto-non-P phenomena.[39]

It may be said that the analogy can still help indirectly, by pointing to a version of 'neutral monism'. The central idea of neutral monism is that there is a fundamental, correct way of conceiving things—let us say that it involves conceiving of them in terms of 'Z' properties—given which all concrete phenomena, experiential and non-experiential, are on a par in all being equally Z phenomena. They are on a par in just the same way as the way in which, according to NE physicalism, all concrete phenomena are on a par in being P phenomena. The claim is then that if one duly conceives all concrete phenomena as Z phenomena, thereby acknowledging their fundamental uniformity, [i] the emergence of experiential phenomena from non-experiential phenomena is as unsurprising as [ii] the emergence of liquid phenomena from non-liquid phenomena is when one conceives things in terms of P phenomena. For both non-experiential P phenomena and experiential phenomena are Z phenomena, so really all we find is the emergence of Z phenomena from Z phenomena.

This proposal, however, merely confirms the current position. For what we do, when we give a satisfactory account of how liquidity emerges from non-liquidity, is show that there aren't really any new properties involved at all. Carrying this over to the experiential case, we get the claim that what happens, when experientiality emerges from non-experientiality, is that there aren't really any new properties involved at all. This, however, means that there were experiential properties all along; which is precisely the present claim. One cannot oppose it by appealing to 'neutral monism' in any version that holds that really only the Z properties are ultimately real, if this involves the view that experiential and non-experiential properties are at bottom only appearances or seemings. Such a view is incoherent, because experience—appearance, if you like—cannot itself be only appearance, that is, not really real, because there must be experience for there to be appearance (see note 7).

Some may reject 'intrinsically suited to *constituting* Y' as a gloss on 'proto-X'. In place of 'constituting' they may want to substitute 'giving rise to' or 'producing', and this may for a moment seem to open up some great new leeway for the idea of radical emergence. The idea will be that X remains *in itself* wholly and utterly non-experiential, but *gives rise to* something wholly ontologically distinct from itself, i.e. Y. But real physicalists can't make this substitution. For everything real and concrete is physical, on their view, and experiential phenomena are real and concrete, on their

---

[39] Objections to [a] standard physicalism and [b] the rejection of radical emergence sometimes advert to the fact that conventional phenomena—phenomena essentially involving conventions—may plausibly be said to arise from wholly and utterly non-conventional phenomena. There is, however, no difficulty in the idea that all concretely existing conventional phenomena are wholly physical phenomena, and the emergence of conventional phenomena from non-conventional phenomena is easily explicable in general terms by real physicalism, which acknowledges, of course, the existence of experiential phenomena.

view, and none of them will I think want to throw away the conservation principles and say that brand new physical stuff (mass/energy) is produced or given rise to when experiences are emergent from the non-experiential, i.e. all the time, as we and other animals live our lives. That is magic again, and I am assured that nothing like this happens with liquidity and Bénard convection cells.

Quite independently of these examples, and the laws of physics, the relevant metaphysical notion of emergence is I think *essentially* conservative in the sense of the conservation principles.

5   MICROPSYCHISM

I have been trying to see what can be done for those who want to combine NE and RP and (therefore) hold that the experiential may emerge from the wholly and utterly non-experiential. I looked for other examples of emergence, in case they could help us understand the possibility, at least, of such a thing, but examples like liquidity seemed wholly inadequate, not the right size. I then looked for cases of emergence that promised to be of the right size, but they seemed to describe impossibilities and so backfire, suggesting that there really could not be any such thing as radical non-experiential-to-experiential emergence.

That is what I believe: experiential phenomena cannot be emergent from wholly non-experiential phenomena. The intuition that drives people to dualism (and eliminativism, and all other crazy attempts at wholesale mental-to-non-mental reduction) is correct in holding that you can't get experiential phenomena from P phenomena, that is, shape-size-mass-charge-etc. phenomena, or, more carefully now—for we can no longer assume that P phenomena as defined really are wholly non-experiential phenomena—from *non-experiential* features of shape-size-mass-charge-etc. phenomena. So if experience like ours (or mouse experience, or sea snail experience) emerges from something that is not experience like ours (or mouse experience, or sea snail experience), then that something must already be experiential in some sense or other. It must already be somehow experiential in its essential and fundamental nature, however primitively or strangely or (to us) incomprehensibly; whether or not it is also non-experiential in its essential nature, as conventional physicalism supposes.

Assuming, then, that there is a plurality of physical ultimates, some of them at least must be intrinsically experiential, intrinsically experience-involving. Otherwise we're back at brutality, magic passage across the experiential/non-experiential divide, something that, *ex hypothesi*, not even God can understand, something for which there is no reason at all as a matter of ultimate metaphysical fact, something that is, therefore, objectively a matter of pure chance every time it occurs, although it is at the same time perfectly law-like.[40]

---

[40] Note again that this is not a version of the merely epistemological point that all concrete connection (e.g. causal connection) is ultimately unintelligible to us (ultimately 'epistemologically brute' for us).

I conclude that real physicalists must give up NE.[41] Real physicalists must accept that at least some ultimates are intrinsically experience-involving.[42] They must at least embrace *micropsychism*. Given that everything concrete is physical, and that everything physical is constituted out of physical ultimates, and that experience is part of concrete reality, it seems the only reasonable position, more than just an 'inference to the best explanation'. Which is not to say that it is easy to accept in the current intellectual climate.

Micropsychism is not yet panpsychism, for as things stand realistic physicalists can conjecture that only some types of ultimates are intrinsically experiential.[43] But they must allow that panpsychism may be true, and the big step has already been taken with micropsychism, the admission that at least some ultimates must be experiential. 'And were the inmost essence of things laid open to us'[44] I think that the idea that some but not all physical ultimates are experiential might look like the idea that some but not all physical ultimates are spatiotemporal (on the assumption that space-time is indeed a fundamental feature of reality). I would bet a lot against there being such radical heterogeneity at the very bottom of things. In fact (to disagree with my earlier self) it is hard to see why this view would not count as a form of dualism.[45] So I'm going to assume, for the rest of this paper at least, that micropsychism is panpsychism.

So now I can say that physicalism, that is, real physicalism, entails panexperientialism or panpsychism. It entails panpsychism given the impossibility of 'radical' emergence. All physical stuff is energy, in one form or another, and all energy, I trow, is an experience-involving phenomenon. This sounded crazy to me for a long time, but I am quite used to it, now that I know that there is no alternative short of 'substance dualism', a view for which (as Arnauld saw) there has never been any good argument. Real physicalism, realistic physicalism, entails panpsychism, and whatever problems are raised by this fact are problems a real physicalist must face.

They seem very large, these problems (so long as we hold on to the view that there is indeed non-experiential reality). To begin with, 'experience is impossible without an experiencer', a subject of experience.[46] So we have, with Leibniz, and right at the start, a rather large number of subjects of experience on our hands—if, that is, there are as many ultimates as we ordinarily suppose. I believe that this is not, in fact, a serious problem, however many ultimates there are,[47] but we will also need to apply

---

[41] Part of being realistic, evidently, is that one does not treat experience as objectively miraculous every time it occurs.

[42] The most ingenious attempt to get round this that I know of is Broad's—see Broad 1925: ch. 14 and McLaughlin 1992—but it does not, in the end, work.

[43] They may for example propose (after assuming that the notion of charge has application to ultimates) that only those with electric charge are intrinsically experiential.

[44] Echoing Philo, who speaks for Hume in his *Dialogues*: 'And were the inmost essence of things laid open to us, we should then discover a scene, of which, at present, we can have no idea. Instead of admiring the order of natural beings, we should clearly see, that it was absolutely impossible for them, in the smallest article, ever to admit of any other disposition' (1779: 174–5).

[45] 1994: 77.

[46] Frege 1918: 27. No sensible Buddhist rejects such a claim, properly understood.

[47] For reasons I lay out in Strawson 2003b.

our minds to the question whether the class of subjects of experience contains only ultimates, on the one hand, and things like ourselves and other whole animals, on the other hand, or whether there are other subjects in between, such as living cells. Panpsychism certainly does not require one to hold the view that things like stones and tables are subjects of experience—this receives no support from the current line of thought—but we will need to address James's objection to the idea that many subjects of experience can somehow constitute a single 'larger' subject of experience.[48] In general, we will have to wonder how macroexperientiality arises from microexperientiality, where by microexperientiality I mean the experientiality of ultimates relative to which all evolved experientiality is macroexperientiality.[49]

We also have to wonder how the solution to the 'problem of mental causation' is going to drop out of all this. We know, though, that different arrangements of a few types of fundamental ultimates give rise to entities (everything in the universe) whose *non*-experiential properties seem remarkably different from the non-experiential properties of those fundamental ultimates, and we have no good reason not to expect the same to hold true on the experiential side. It may be added that there is no more difficulty in the idea that the experiential quality of microexperientiality is unimaginable by us than there is in the idea that there may exist sensory modalities (qualitatively) unimaginable by us.

It is at this point, when we consider the difference between macroexperiential and microexperiential phenomena, that the notion of emergence begins to recover some respectability in its application to the case of experience. For it seems that we can now embrace the analogy with liquidity after all, whose pedagogic value previously seemed to lie precisely in its inadequacy. For we can take it that human or sea snail experientiality emerges from experientiality that is not of the human or sea snail type, just as the shape-size-mass-charge-etc. phenomenon of liquidity emerges from shape-size-mass-charge-etc. phenomena that do not involve liquidity. Human experience or sea snail

---

[48] James 1890: vol. 1, ch. 6. The following fine passage precedes his statement of the objection: 'We need to try every possible mode of conceiving the dawn of consciousness so that it may not appear equivalent to the irruption into the universe of a new nature, non-existent until then. Merely to call the consciousness 'nascent' will not serve our turn. It is true that the word signifies not yet quite born, and so seems to form a sort of bridge between existence and nonentity. But that is a verbal quibble. The fact is that discontinuity comes in if a new nature comes in at all. The quantity of the latter is quite immaterial. The girl in 'Midshipman Easy' could not excuse the illegitimacy of her child by saying, 'it was a very small one'. And Consciousness, however small, is an illegitimate birth in any philosophy that starts without it, and yet professes to explain all facts by continuous evolution. If evolution is to work smoothly, consciousness in some shape must have been present at the very origin of things. Accordingly we find that the more clear-sighted evolutionary philosophers are beginning to posit it there. Each atom of the nebula, they suppose, must have had an aboriginal atom of consciousness linked with it; and, just as the material atoms have formed bodies and brains by massing themselves together, so the mental atoms, by an analogous process of aggregation, have fused into those larger consciousnesses which we know in ourselves and suppose to exist in our fellow-animals' (1890: 1.148–9).

[49] As Nick White reminded me, we certainly don't have to suppose that microexperientiality is somehow weak or thin or blurry (this is perhaps how some people imagine the most primitive Leibnizian monads). It can be as vivid as an experience of bright red or an electric shock (both of which are 'confused' and 'indistinct' in Leibniz's terms). Compare Rosenberg 2005: ch. 5.

experience (if any) is an emergent property of structures of ultimates whose individual experientiality no more resembles human or sea snail experientiality than an electron resembles a molecule, a neuron, a brain, or a human being. Once upon a time there was relatively unorganized matter, with both experiential and non-experiential fundamental features. It organized into increasingly complex forms, both experiential and non-experiential, by many processes including evolution by natural selection. And just as there was spectacular enlargement and fine-tuning of non-experiential forms (the bodies of living things), so too there was spectacular enlargement and fine-tuning of experiential forms.[50]

This is not to advance our detailed understanding in any way. Nor is it to say that we can ever hope to achieve, in the experiential case, the sort of feeling of understanding that we achieve in the liquid case.[51] The present proposal is made at a very high level of generality (which is not a virtue); it merely recommends a general framework of thought in which there need be no more sense of a radically unintelligible transition in the case of experientiality than there is in the case of liquidity. It has nothing to offer to scientific test.

One can I think do further work on this general framework, by working on one's general metaphysics. The object/process/property/state/event cluster of distinctions is unexceptionable in everyday life but it is hopelessly superficial from the point of view of science and metaphysics, and one needs to acquire a vivid sense that this is so. One needs a vivid sense of the respect in which (given the spatiotemporal framework) every object is a process; one needs to abandon the idea that there is any sharp or categorial distinction between an object and its propertiedness.[52] One needs to grasp fully the point that 'property dualism', applied to intrinsic, non-relational properties, is strictly incoherent (or just a way of saying that there are two very different kinds of properties) in so far as it purports to be genuinely distinct from substance dualism, because there is nothing more to a thing's being than its intrinsic, non-relational propertiedness.

We are as inescapably committed to the discursive, subject-predicate form of experience as we are to the spatiotemporal form of experience, but the principal and unmistakable lesson of the endlessness of the debate about the relation between objects and their propertiedness is that discursive thought is not adequate to the nature of reality: we can see that it doesn't get things right although we can't help persisting with it. There is in the nature of the case a limited amount that we can do with such insights, for they are, precisely, insights into how our understanding falls short of reality, but their general lesson—that the nature of reality is in fundamental respects beyond discursive grasp—needs always to be borne in mind.

---

[50] The heart of experience, perhaps, is electromagnetism in some or all its forms; electromagnetism being just one expression of some single force whose being is intrinsically experiential, whatever else it is or is not. (I do not, unfortunately, foresee any kind of scientific research programme.)

[51] Feelings of understanding are just that; they are essentially subjective things with no metaphysical consequences.

[52] See e.g. Essay 6: following Nagarjuna, Nietzsche, James, Ramsey, and many others.

I have argued that there are limits on how different X and Y can be (can be intelligibly supposed to be) if it is true that Y emerges from X. You can get A from non-A for some substitutions for A but not all. The extended, I have proposed, can't emerge from the intrinsically wholly non-extended (except on pain of being a mere appearance and so not really real). The spatial can't emerge from the intrinsically wholly non-spatial (except on the same pain). The experiential can't emerge from the intrinsically wholly non-experiential, and it doesn't have the option of being a mere appearance. You can make chalk from cheese, or water from wine, because if you go down to the subatomic level they are both the same stuff, but you can't make experience from something wholly non-experiential. You might as well suppose—to say it once again—that the (ontologically) concrete can emerge from the (ontologically) abstract.[53] I admit I have nothing more to say if you question this 'can't', but I have some extremely powerful indirect support from Occam's razor and Eddington's notion of silliness.

I finish up, indeed, in the same position as Eddington. 'To put the conclusion crudely', he says, 'the stuff of the world is mind-stuff'—something whose nature is 'not altogether foreign to the feelings in our consciousness'. 'Having granted this', he continues,

the mental activity of the part of the world constituting ourselves *occasions no surprise*; it is known to us by direct self-knowledge, and we do not explain it away as something other than we know it to be—or, rather, it knows itself to be. It is the physical aspects [i.e. non-mental aspects] of the world that we have to explain.[54]

Something along these general panpsychist—or at least micropsychist—lines seems to me to be the most parsimonious, plausible and indeed 'hard-nosed' position that any physicalist who is remotely realistic about the nature of reality can take up in the present state of our knowledge.[55]

---

[53] Objection: the comparison is false because the experiential and the non-experiential are two categories within the concrete. Reply: the concrete and the abstract are two categories within the real.

[54] 1928: 276–7. 'Mind-stuff' is William James's term: 'The theory of "mind-stuff" is the theory that our mental states . . . are composite in structure, made up of smaller [mental] states conjoined. This hypothesis has outward advantages which make it almost irresistibly attractive to the intellect, and yet it is inwardly quite unintelligible' (1890: 1.145).

[55] I am grateful to participants in the 2002 University of London one-day conference on consciousness, and, since then, to audiences at the University of Reading, Copenhagen University, University of California at Irvine, Trinity College Dublin, and Columbia University, including in particular Nick White, Alva Noë, Bill Lyons and David Albert. I am especially grateful to members of the 2002 Konstanz Workshop on 'Real materialism' for their constructive scepticism. (This paper first appeared in the *Journal of Consciousness Studies* 13, 2006, with replies by Carruthers and Schecter, Coleman, Goff, Jackson, Lycan, Macpherson, McGinn, Papineau, Rey, Rosenthal, Seager, Simons, Skrbina, Smart, Stapp, Stoljar, and C. Wilson, and a reply to the replies.)

3

Can we Know the Nature of Reality as It is In Itself?

1 THE PROBLEM

Can we apprehend the nature of reality? Can we apprehend the nature of concrete reality? Can we apprehend the nature of concrete reality 'as it is in itself'? Can we apprehend the nature of *non-mental* concrete reality as it is in itself? This last is my question.[1]

Some say Yes, many say No. Against Kant, Bradley, and a huge crew of empiricists, positivists, anti-realists, and miserable post-modernists, I think there is no insuperable difficulty in the answer Yes—no difficulty of principle in the idea that finite beings like ourselves may be able to apprehend the nature of reality as it is in itself, at least in certain respects. To this extent I am with Descartes and Locke.

Put differently, the question is whether any *representation* of the nature of reality can render or represent it as it is in itself in any respect. There is certainly difficulty in this idea, but one of the most important things about the difficulty is what it is not. It is not that there is any deep difficulty in the claim that

[A] something is real—reality, no less—and this reality has some intrinsic or ultimate nature.

Of course something is real, and of course it has some nature. And whatever nature it has just is its intrinsic or ultimate nature. There is nothing wrong with using these words, even when they add little or nothing.

Nor is there any deep difficulty in the supposition that

[B] there may be features of reality that are completely inaccessible and unintelligible to us.

This paper is an adaptation of 'Knowledge of the World', published in *Philosophical Topics* 12, 2002, which grew out of ch. 7 and Appendix B of Strawson 1989b. Re-reading it I realize that its Kantian terms of debate are very distant from those currently in vogue, in a way that I have tried to clarify. Most importantly, perhaps, a concept is understood here as something that does not derive any of its representational content from its referent (compare the discussion of cognitive phenomenology in Essays 10 and 11).

[1] It is close to the old question 'Can we know the nature of the *mind-independent, external* world?', but the words in italics cause unnecessary problems. Some hold that there is abstract reality (for example mathematical reality) as well as concrete reality (the universe) but in this paper I will take 'reality' to refer only to concrete reality.

Barest common sense—not to mention a minimum degree of modesty—requires us
to grant the truth of [B].[2]

If there is a difficulty it is not with [A] or [B], it is with the claim that

[C] there could be a representation of the nature of reality available to finite beings that captured the nature of reality as it is in itself, at least in some respect.

[A], the fact that there is a certain way things are, does not entail [C] that it is possible to represent how things are in themselves—not so long as we are concerned with
finite beings like ourselves.

In this paper I will concentrate on [C], but I will first make a couple of points about
[A]. [B] is a topic for another time, but it should not need to be a topic at all.

2   NATURALIZING THE NOUMENAL: 'AS IT IS IN ITSELF'

[A], the supposition that reality is in fact a certain way, whatever we can manage
to know or say about it, is obviously true. Some have denied it; every position has
its defenders; the closet mysticism of some quantum theorists and other anti-realist
extremists should not be underestimated. But not all positions are worth arguing against. [A] is obvious. Nothing can exist or be real without being a certain way at any
given time.[3] If this is metaphysics, thank heavens for metaphysics. To be is to be
somehow or other.

Suppose our best models of the behaviour of things like photons credit them with
properties that seem incompatible to us—for example wave-like properties and particle-like properties. This does not threaten the truth of [A]. What we learn is simply
that this is how photons affect us, given their intrinsic nature, and ours. It does not
provide us with any reason to think that photons do not have some intrinsic nature at
any given time. Whatever claim anyone makes about the nature of reality—including
the claim that it has apparently incompatible properties—just is a claim about the
way it is. This remark applies as much to the Everett 'many-worlds' theory of reality
as it does to any other.

Some think that what we learn from quantum theory is precisely that there is, objectively, no particular way that an electron or a photon is, at a given time. They confuse an epistemological point about undecidability with a metaphysical claim about
the nature of things. The problem is not just that such a claim is unverifiable, the
problem is that it is incoherent. For whatever the electron's or photon's weirdness (its
weirdness-to-us, that is, for nothing is intrinsically weird), its being thus weird just is
the way it is.

So we may *naturalize the noumenon*: we may talk without reservation of reality as
it is in itself. Such talk involves no odd metaphysics; its propriety derives entirely and
sufficiently from the thought that if a thing exists, it is a certain way.

---

[2] A number of 'anti-realist' philosophers reject [B], sometimes on the extraordinary ground that
it is incoherent. The idea, roughly, is that no phrase like 'features of reality' can really succeed in
denoting anything that is posited as completely inaccessible and unintelligible to us.

[3] If one is worried about the concept—or reality—of time, one can drop the last four words.

Some may still think the phrase 'as it is in itself' disreputable. Anyone who still doubts its honesty should consider the account of it just given. For we all agree that something (reality, no less) exists, and all that is added here is that if something exists then it is a certain way. And the way it is just is—of course—how it is in itself. The notion of how things are in themselves is an entirely innocent and indispensable notion in any sensible philosophy, as Kant was well aware.

It may be thought that there is a special problem with the idea that conscious mental reality is always a certain way for any given conscious being—Louis, for example—at any given moment. But there is no special problem; the case is the same. For whatever happens mentally, with Louis, at any given time, things will just be a certain way, mentally, with Louis, at that time. It may well be that no one can give a definitive account of how things are mentally with Louis; not even—sometimes least of all—Louis. But this epistemological point is irrelevant to the ontological-metaphysical point that things are a certain determinate way, mentally, for Louis, at any given time.

Understood in this way the phrase 'as it is in itself' contributes nothing except emphasis, but it is often extremely helpful, and I will use it freely.[4]

3 CONSCIOUS EXPERIENCE

—It's obvious that the answer to your opening question is Yes. It's obvious that an account or apprehension of the nature of reality available to finite beings with a specific sensory-intellectual constitution can constitute or contain a correct representation or apprehension of the nature of reality as it is in itself, in certain respects. For conscious experience is itself part of concrete reality. More particularly, the phenomenon of conscious experience's having a certain *experiential-qualitative* character for whoever or whatever has the experience—call this phenomenon E—is a richly featured part of reality, as much part of concrete reality as anything else, including anything that may be held to 'realize' E and yet be in some way other than or ontologically over and above E. E is accordingly something that must be included in any full account of the general nature of reality, and we can indeed be said to know it as it is in itself, at least in certain respects, simply because our having it as we do is our knowing it: the having is the knowing. Consider pain. It may have non-experiential being, in some sense, in addition to having experiential qualitative being, and there may be respects in which we are not able to grasp the nature of that non-experiential being (considered as it is in itself). But we know the nature of part of concrete reality (considered as it is in itself) just in feeling the pain as we do, whatever else is or is not going on. One's own conscious experience is a part of reality for which the gap between reality and its apprehension does not open up when one considers the question of one's acquaintance with it.

---

[4] 'As it is in itself' can also be used to distinguish the 'intrinsic' properties of a thing from its 'relational' properties. (The existence of the universe involves the instantiation of relational properties just as surely as it involves the instantiation of intrinsic properties, and there is a way instantiations of relational properties are in themselves just as surely as there is a way instantiations of intrinsic properties are in themselves.)

I think this claim about conscious experience is correct, although it needs some defence, and although recent philosophical fashion may make it hard for some to see. Nothing in what follows depends on accepting it, though, and I am going to put the case of conscious experience aside. I have assumed that there is such a thing as non-mental concrete reality, and I am going to restrict my attention to the question of whether one can have any grasp or knowledge of the nature of non-mental concrete reality as it is in itself.[5]

4   A PARADOX?

In setting out the main argument I will use '*x*', in honour of Kant's 'transcendental object=x',[6] to denote either some particular part of (concrete non-mental) reality, considered as it is in itself, or (concrete non-mental) reality in general, considered as it is in itself. As remarked, 'as it is in itself' adds nothing, strictly speaking, but it is often useful as a reminder of what is at issue.[7]

It seems very plausible—to begin—that

[1] One can form a representation of *x*, and a fortiori a correct representation of *x*, only if one is affected by *x*.

One must be in some sort of *contact* with *x*.[8]

It is also arguable, however, that one can form a correct representation of *x* only if one is *not* affected by it, or rather—less paradoxically—that

[2] One can attain a correct representation of the nature of *x* only if the representation one forms of *x* does not essentially involve elements whose representational content depends essentially on the particular way in which one is affected by *x*.[9]

The standard Kantian presumption is that the content of one's *representation* of *x*, by which I mean the content that one's representation has considered as a mental particular in its own right, i.e. completely independently of any external, non-mental, concrete object or referent that it may have, does always essentially involve elements whose content depends essentially on the particular way in which one is affected by *x*; so that if [2] is right, correct representation of the nature of *x* is not—is never— possible.

---

[5] Strictly speaking it might be better to make the cut between *experiential* concrete reality and *non-experiential* concrete reality rather than between mental and non-mental reality, for many take it that there is non-experiential reality that is nonetheless part of mental reality.

[6] Kant 1781: A109. When I cite a work I give the original publication date; the page reference is to the edition listed in the bibliography.

[7] '*x*' can always be expanded to '*x* as it is in itself'.

[8] Scientists on a hydrogen-and-oxygen stocked but waterless planet may postulate the existence of water and correctly predict its properties, on the terms of their science, without ever having been in any contact with it. They have, however, been in contact with the constituents of water, and are merely contemplating different arrangements of them. They may also work out the nature of zinc in their zincless universe, having a good command of the periodic table; but, first, zinc is not part of *x*, in their universe, so the case is not relevant; second, and on the other hand, they have been in contact with the constituents of zinc.

[9] The two occurrences of 'essentially' make this a little heavy. I'll eliminate one in due course.

In the next section I will give an argument for [2]. First, though, a question arises about whether the putative correct-representation-engendering affection or contact must be sensory, at least in part.

The notions of affection and contact are highly general. One can be in contact with a thing A via a written or spoken description. This involves sensory experience of sounds or shapes, but not of A itself. Direct alteration of one's neuronal connections by neuroscientists in contact with A who operate with a view to inducing correct beliefs about A may also constitute a form of contact with A that suffices to furnish one with a representation of A without one's having any sensory experience of A, and there may be other, stranger possibilities. On the whole, though, I will take it that any putative correct-representation-engendering contact with x will always involve sensory affection by x, directly or indirectly. I will also take it that the notion of wholly non-conceptual sensory content—merely or purely phenomenal sensory content—is in good order for purposes of philosophical analysis of the nature of experience. Finally, let me repeat that by 'representational content' I mean content that a representation has considered as a vehicle or medium of representation and so considered completely independently of its actual concrete object or referent—of whatever it actually represents. On this natural and traditional use a veridical perception and a qualitatively identical hallucination have exactly the same representational content. Later on I will make room for the directly opposed (!) new use of the expression, according to which the content of a representation is just what it is a representation of and has nothing to do with its character as a vehicle of representation, by allowing that a representation may have referential content as well as non-referential positively descriptive or positively characterizational content.

5 AN ARGUMENT

Recast in terms of sensory affection, [2] becomes

[2] One can attain a correct representation of the nature of x only if the putatively reality-representing content of one's representation of x does not essentially involve elements whose content depends essentially on the particular way in which one is sensorily affected by x.[10]

The argument for [2] runs as follows:

[2.1] If an experiencing being B is sensorily affected by x, then how B is sensorily affected by x is necessarily a function not only of how x is, but also of how B is.

[2.2] It is always possible that there should be two experiencing beings B and C who differ in their natures in such a way that they differ significantly or dramatically in the way they are sensorily affected by x, even when they are functioning normally given the kinds of being they are.

[2.3] Suppose that there are two such beings B and C. One cannot say that B-type beings are right or correct in the way they are sensorily affected by x, while C-type beings are wrong or

---

[10] 'x' functions both as a name for a type of feature and also as a name for particular tokens of that type, as required.

incorrect, given that both are functioning normally given the kinds of being they are. There is, plainly, no such thing as *the correct* way of being sensorily affected by *x*—the single universally correct way. Instead one can talk only of how B-type beings are (normally) sensorily affected by *x*, how C-type beings are sensorily affected by *x*, and so on. One cannot even say that one way of being sensorily affected is closer to being correct than another. Nor can one speak of roughly the correct way of being sensorily affected.

So [?]

[2.4] If a representation one forms of *x* essentially involves elements whose putatively reality-representing content depends essentially on the particular way in which one is sensorily affected by *x*, it cannot constitute a correct representation of the nature of *x*.

It cannot be a correct representation of any feature of the nature of reality as it is in itself.

Does [2.4] follow from [2.1]–[2.3]? I will consider this question shortly. First, though, note that many would continue the argument by accepting [2.4], asserting its antecedent as applied to finite beings, and detaching the corresponding consequent as follows:

[2.5] All representations of *x* available to finite beings do essentially involve elements whose content depends essentially on the particular way in which those beings are sensorily affected by *x*.

This would then allow them to conclude

[2.6] Finite beings cannot attain to any correct representation of the nature of *x*—of concrete, non-mental reality-as-it-is-in-itself.

Does [2.4] follow from [2.1]–[2.3]? It is not obvious that it does, and the first thing that requires comment is the phrase 'essentially involves'. It allows for the possibility that some elements of a representation may be inessential, and it may be objected that this is not a real possibility: 'Every representation essentially involves whatever elements it involves, for the trivial reason that it is the particular representation it is in virtue of the particular elements it involves.'

This is true but irrelevant. The issue is whether the content of a representational element can be essential or inessential to a representation in one specific respect: in respect of the representation's correctness—where its correctness is a matter of its representing some feature of a thing's nature considered as it is in itself. Consider a simple case: if in the normal course of things you wish to form a representation of a cube, and form a visual representation of a red cube, the red element in the representation is inessential. Blue would have done just as well, and a person blind from birth may form a representation of a cube that is not visual at all.

The phrase 'depends essentially' also requires comment. To say that the content of a representational element depends essentially on a particular way of being sensorily affected is to say that this content cannot be made available by anything else. Access to it not only depends on having been sensorily affected in some way or other; it also depends on having been sensorily affected in some particular way—in some particular sense modality or modalities.

It seems clear that this dependence can be essential only if this content either is itself, or essentially involves, an instance of a particular type of sensory content.[11]

A colour-involving representation is an obvious candidate for being a representation with content that depends essentially on a particular—visual—way of being sensorily affected.[12] And a representation of triangularity is, I take it, an example of a representation with content that does not depend essentially on a particular way of being sensorily affected. It may be that no finite creature can have a notion of triangularity without having had some sensory experience or other, but the sensory experience may be either visual or tactile or echolocatory or who knows what else. If so, the representation of triangularity does not depend essentially on any particular one of these ways of being sensorily affected.

Suppose all this is granted. Do [2.1]–[2.3] entail [2.4]?

Well, let x be the triangularity of some particular object (I assume—hereby—that triangularity may be and at any rate could be a feature of reality as it is in itself).[13] And now suppose [2.4] is false. Suppose, that is, that

[i] a being B has formed a correct representation R of x

and

[ii] R's being correct in this respect essentially involves R's containing a certain representational element E;

suppose, in other words, that E cannot be altered or replaced by any other representational element without R ceasing to be correct in the respect in question.[14] Suppose further that

[iii] the ability to have E-type representations depends essentially on the ability to have a particular type of sensory experience;

suppose, that is, one cannot have E-type representations unless one can have such sensory experience.

Suppositions [i]–[iii] amount to the claim that [2.4] is false. That is, they amount to the claim that R can be a correct representation of x although it essentially involves elements that depend essentially on a particular way of being sensorily affected. So the question is this: is their joint truth ruled out by [2.1]–[2.3]?

No. The first thing to say, perhaps, is that the argument equivocates on the word 'correct'. It is certainly true that there is no single correct way of being sensorily

---

[11] Sensory experience induced by brain tinkering involves sensory affection on the present understanding of the term, as does the auditory and visual experience of a 'brain in a vat' without eyes or ears, or a creature in whom such experiences arise with no external cause at all. It is the qualitative-experiential content of the experience that matters, not the process by which it comes to exist (it may take place wholly in the imagination).

[12] What does 'visual' cover? I consider some complications in §11.

[13] I choose to discuss TRIANGULAR rather than SQUARE because I am not sure what consequences the theory of relativity has for the view that squareness is an objective property of anything, and take it that triangularity (or pyramidicity) may be an objective or non-frame-relative property even if squareness (or cubicity) is not. This is merely to advertise my ignorance.

[14] Change of colour would not matter in the present case.

affected, given the way that the word 'correct' is used in [2.1]–[2.3]. Given this use there are as many 'correct' ways of being affected by x as there are species whose normal members are differently affected by x. But it doesn't follow that no way of being sensorily affected is intrinsically better than any other, so far as the attempt to form a correct representation of x is concerned. Nor do [2.1]–[2.3] actually manage to rule out the possibility directly rejected by [2.4]—the possibility that one particular way of being sensorily affected may in fact be essential to forming a correct representation of the nature of x.

I will take these points in turn. As for the first, it seems plausible that some ways of being sensorily affected are intrinsically more useful or reality-revealing than others. Suppose B and C are placed in front of a triangle and that both are sensorily affected by light reflected from it. Suppose B has the same basic visual experience that you have when you look at a triangle of that sort, and that C has the sort of experience you have when you hear G-flat played on a clarinet. It seems intrinsically more useful to have B-type experience than C-type experience, given the shape-content of the B-type experience, if one is trying to find out how things are.

—This is not obvious, for the usefulness of any sensory input, and the extent to which it is reality-revealing, depend entirely on what one makes of it and can do with it. The B-type being might apprehend its visual intake as a baby does, while the C-type being might automatically infer complex spatial information from differences in the volume, pitch, and timbre of the sound it hears.

True, but this reply won't deal with every case. Consider D, who is like C in responding to light waves with auditory experience, but whose hearing is so primitive that the sounds it hears differ only in pitch, never in loudness or timbre. In this case, it seems, D's way of being sensorily affected by reality is intrinsically less informative than C's or B's. And if this is right, we can make sense of the comparative claim that one way of being sensorily affected may be intrinsically better than another, so far as the attempt to form a correct representation of the nature of x is concerned.

As for the second point: it is true that [2.1]–[2.3] do not entail [2.4], but [2.4] is none the less correct. It is correct in denying that any one particular way of being sensorily affected could be essential to forming a correct representation of the nature of x (some feature of concrete, non-mental reality as it is in itself). How could some way of being sensorily affected be essential to forming a correct representation of x in such a way that no other way would do *however the representational elements that derived from it were interpreted by the subject*? The answer seems clear. This could not be: any way of being sensorily affected that systematically had the same degree of structural complexity as the supposedly essential way could deliver experience that could possibly be interpreted by its subject in such a way as to yield the same information as the information yielded by the experience delivered by the supposedly essential way. Quite generally, it cannot be the sensory content as such that matters when we consider representations that purport to represent x. It must be how it is interpreted that matters.

6   INTELLECTUAL INTUITION

Kant's notion of 'intellectual intuition' is sometimes dismissed as a foolish obscurity, but it is of great interest here because it is precisely an attempt to characterize a kind of knowledge-of-x-involving *relation* with x (some feature of concrete, non-mental reality as it is in itself) that does not involve being *affected* by x. It is motivated precisely by an awareness of the force of the thought that if one's potentially knowledge-of-x-involving relation to x essentially involves one's being sensorily affected by x then there is an immoveable sense in which one can only ever hope to attain to knowledge of an *appearance* of x, and hence (so the thought goes) never to knowledge of x.[15] Descartes, of course, is an example of someone who rejects this idea, arguing in his 'Second Meditation' that one can attain to knowledge of the essential nature of x (for example a lump of wax) even if one starts from an essentially-sensation-involving contact with it.

In fact Kant's thought seems more general than this. It seems that one can drop the qualification 'sensorily' to give

if one's potentially knowledge-of-x-involving relation to x essentially involves one's being *affected* by x in any way at all then there is an immoveable sense in which one can only ever hope to attain to knowledge of an *appearance* of x, and hence never to knowledge of x (as it is in itself).[16]

The point of intellectual intuition is that it does away with all affection. As a possible example, Kant offers the knowledge-involving relation that a divine creator would stand in to its works—call them 'x'—in being their creator or originator.[17] If the relation holds, x is somehow fully specified and grasped in its creator's intellect, and therefore completely known, without the knowledge resulting in any way from x's being a thing that 'stands over against' the subject as something which affects it in some particular way. There is thus no indirectness or mediatedness of apprehension of a kind that seems to be necessarily involved in any affection-dependent representation of x. Nor is there any sort of *partiality of perspective* of the kind that is necessarily involved in any sensation-involving experience of x and that might also be thought to threaten the possibility of knowledge or correct representation of the nature of x.

---

[15] It is natural to use 'knowledge' rather than 'correct representation' in this section on intellectual intuition although I am not at all concerned with questions of justification.

[16] 'Nothing which emerges from *any* affecting relation can count as knowledge or awareness of the affecting thing as it is in itself. Therefore there can be no knowledge or awareness of things which exist *independently* of that knowledge or awareness and of which that knowledge or awareness is consequently an effect. More exactly, there can be no knowledge of such things as they are in themselves, but only as they appear—only of their appearances' (Strawson 1966: 238–9; see also 249–56, 264–5).

[17] See Kant 1781–7: B72, A248–256/B307–312; see also Stump and Kretzmann 1996. It is arguable that the model of a creator's relation to its own works is less interesting as a model of intellectual intuition than 'pure' omniscience.

Equipped with intellectual intuition one may be supposed to attain directly to the 'absolute conception of reality', in Bernard Williams's phrase, or to the view 'from nowhere', in Nagel's and Merleau-Ponty's phrase—the view from no particular perspective.[18] Kant concedes that we 'cannot comprehend even the possibility' of such intellectual intuition, in the sense of having a positive conception of what it might be like, but insists that the idea is free from contradiction.[19]

Partiality of perspective that stems merely from the fact that finite beings always occupy a particular place in spacetime doesn't raise a deep problem for the idea that they might attain a correct general theoretical representation of the nature of *x* (at least in certain respects). One can readily generalize away from specificities of spatiotemporal location. It is the particularities of perspective imposed on us by our most basic sensory-intellectual equipment—by the fundamental conceptual categories and sensory modalities that we happen to have—that are presumed to pose the problem. Kant argues that while we ourselves are inescapably committed to a spatiotemporal way of experiencing things, a spatiotemporal 'form of sensibility', other finite rational creatures capable of 'objective experience' may possibly differ radically in their fundamental forms of sensibility.[20] He also holds—and in this he is joined by a number of present-day thinkers—that reality as it is in itself is not spatial (or not in anything remotely like the way we suppose) and not temporal either (or not in anything remotely like the way we suppose); and this of course bolsters his view that we can never attain to knowledge of the nature of *x* (as it is in itself).

Does he also think that finite rational creatures could differ in their most fundamental intellectual equipment (the 'pure concepts of the understanding', the categories considered independently of their attunement to some particular form of sensibility)? Is he gesturing at the possibility that there may be other finite creatures capable of objective experience whose intelligence does not involve the fundamental forms of judgement (A70/B95) and is wholly non-discursive, wholly non-conceptual, when he writes that 'other forms of understanding than the discursive forms of thought, or of knowledge through concepts, even if they should be possible, we cannot render in any way conceivable and comprehensible to ourselves'?[21] It is far from clear, for here he may well be thinking only of the possibility of intellectual intuition. Does he nonetheless think that the particularity of our fundamental *intellectual* equipment (considered wholly independently of our sensory equipment) is, in addition to the particularity of our sensory equipment, a potential or knowably fatal bar to correct representation of *x*? One might expect him to say this, given his constant striving for maximum generality, but the question is not pressing for Kant because correct representation of *x* is already ruled out by the fact that the operation of our

[18] 'The house itself . . . is the house seen from nowhere. But what do these words mean? Is not to see always to see from somewhere?' (Merleau-Ponty 1945: 67). See also Nagel 1986: ch. 2; Williams 1978: 65–8, 245–9.

[19] Kant 1781–7: B307, A254/B310; he takes the same line about human freedom.

[20] See e.g. A27/B43, B72. Here 'objective experience' means experience that has, for the experiencer, the character of being experience of an objective order of things that exists independently of the experiencer's experience of it.

[21] A230/B283.

fundamental conceptual equipment—its very existence in us as a set of categories—is primordially conditioned by the form of our sensibility. The same will be true, and necessarily so, for any possible finite, rational, 'discursive' creature,[22] and this is already sufficient, in Kant's book, to show that we can only ever attain to knowledge of how x appears to us, not to knowledge of the nature of x.[23]

On the whole it seems that Kant doesn't think that anything other than pure-concepts-of-the-understanding-based categories could structure *discursive* objective experience. He speaks of 'this peculiarity of our understanding, that it can produce *a priori* unity of apperception [hence objective experience] solely by means of the categories, and only by such and so many', and remarks that it is 'as little capable of further explanation as why we have just these and no other functions of judgement, or why space and time are the only forms of our possible intuition'. But to say that something is not capable of further explanation is not to say that it could be otherwise.[24]

The purpose of this brief section, in any case, is to suggest that in introducing the idea of intellectual intuition Kant is trying precisely to characterize what knowledge or correct representation of the nature of x (of reality as it is in itself) would have to be like. A necessary condition of such knowledge or correct representation, for any being B, is that

knowledge of x has to flow from B's being in *relation* with x without B's being *affected* by x in such a way that B can only be said to have access to an *appearance* of x.

7   SENSATION AND CORRECT REPRESENTATION

Can we (or any finite beings) fulfil this Kantian necessary condition? I don't see why not. I see no difficulty of principle in the idea that we may be able to be in cognitive relation with x—with reality as it is in itself or some feature of it—without being affected by it in such a way that we can only be said to have access to an appearance of it.

In §5 I stressed the point that there can be no such thing as the right way of being sensorily affected by x. B-type beings may be in a far better position to elaborate a practically useful theoretical account of x than C-type beings, given the differences in their characteristic ways of being affected by reality, and this may be so even if B-type and C-type are equal with respect to intellectual capacities, but still there is and can

---

[22] This is the lesson of the 'Schematism'. Kant certainly does not think that one cannot meaningfully apply the categories to reality as it is in itself (as many have supposed). He thinks only that one cannot do this in such a way as to acquire knowledge of any sort. See e.g. B166 n: 'in our *thinking* the categories are not limited by the conditions of our sensible intuition, but have an unbounded realm'.

[23] In Kant's scheme differences of *sensory modality* are superficial as compared with differences of *forms of sensibility*. The spatial form of sensibility doesn't have to involve the sensory modality of vision; it may involve only touch, or echolocation, or who knows what else. In this way forms of sensibility offer a higher-order classification of types of sensory modalities, and creatures with entirely different sensory modalities can clearly share the same fundamental forms of sensibility.

[24] B145; this passage was brought to my attention by Wayne Waxman.

be no such thing as the right way of being sensorily affected by x, either in general or when it comes to the question of whether one can form a correct representation of x. Nor is any one way of being sensorily affected by x closer to being right than any other. One might as well claim that the decimal system is closer to being the right way of representing the nature of numbers than the binary system.

Let 'x' now denote some particular feature of reality considered as it is in itself, and consider the following expanded restatement of [2.4]:

[2.4.1] If specification of the non-referent derived (*NR*) or positively descriptively character-izational (*PDC*) content of any representation R of x available to finite beings necessarily involves reference to features of how the beings are sensorily affected by x, in such a way that the content of R is not fully graspable by beings who do not or cannot have experience with those sensory-affection features, then there can be no such thing as a correct PDC representa-tion of x, so far as any finite being is concerned.

As with [2.4], so with [2.4.1]: some philosophers may accept [2.4.1] and its ante-cedent and detach the consequent, concluding that there can be no such thing as a correct PDC representation of x, so far as any finite being is concerned. Their con-clusion is not just the unremarkable conclusion that one could never know for sure that one had attained a correct representation of the nature of x. It is the Kantian conclusion that it is demonstrably impossible for a finite, essentially sensory being to attain to such a representation.

[2.4.1] raises a number of questions. The most important of them, I think, is whether one can deny its antecedent. Perhaps the NR or PDC content of a finite being's representation of the nature of x can be radically independent of its sensory experience in certain vital respects, even if its sensory experience is genetically speak-ing indispensable to its achieving any representation of the nature of x at all.

Let me stress again that my concern is with PDC or NR content: content that is reality-representing in some way that goes essentially beyond being reality-representing merely in referring to or being about x. This concern is captured, in effect, in the phrase 'know the nature of', but it is worth underlining. If NR con-tent were not our concern the possibility of grasp or correct representation of aspects of x would seem easily secured, for it is widely accepted that even if we are in fact quite profoundly wrong or ignorant about certain features of the nature of mercury and electrons, say, we can nonetheless refer to these things and talk about them, if indeed they exist, and on this view statements like 'atoms of mercury contain elec-trons' may qualify as fully correct representations of x even though formulated by us in our human terms and even if we have a hugely imperfect grasp of the nature of what we are talking about. As soon as one grants that such natural-kind concepts can reach out referentially to x (reality as it is in itself) despite the limits and particular-ities of our sensory-intellectual apparatus, vast tracts of claims of science and com-mon sense—*cats like cream, some human beings like gold*—are irresistible candidates for being correct representations of x: for our concepts of natural kinds give us a magic-bullet referential link to x.

8   EMPIRICISM?

Can one reasonably deny the antecedent of [2.4.1]? Consider the following claim:

[2.4.2] In order to give good sense to the notion of a being B's achieving a correct representation of *x* we are obliged to suppose that B's representation of the nature of *x* is intellectually
abstract in some way. There must be some fundamental respect in which B can be correctly
said to abstract, in its mode of representation of *x*, from all features of how it is (sensorily)
affected by *x*.[25]

Is this a help? I think it is. The (Cartesian) suggestion is that a being can form an
intellectual conception of *x*, partly as a result of being sensorily affected by *x*, in such
a way that its conception of *x* is in some strong sense independent of the particular
quality of the (sensory) affection which is, for it, a condition of the possibility of its
formation of the conception.

   'As a result of' is intentionally imprecise. An old question arises: what is the relation between the (non-referential) content of the sensory affection and the (non-
referential) content of the intellectual conception? Is there some straightforward sense
in which the content of the sensory affection is the source or 'original'—even more
vaguely, the inspiration—of the content of the intellectual conception? Or is the
sensory affection best thought of as a kind of trigger for (the unfurling of) the intellectual conception, rather than as a source of its content?

   Empiricists maintain, with varying degrees of ingenuity, that the content of our
conceptions of the nature of reality is ultimately derived from, and is therefore ultimately reducible to, the sensory content of our experience. Rationalists deny this,
and there is certainly something staggeringly implausible about the classical empiricist
programme.[26] I think the theory of evolution may be able to effect a full reconcili-
ation between rationalism and a kind of empiricism, but that is a topic for another
time.[27] My present concern is with the idea that the NR or PDC content of concepts
of certain features of (non-mental, concrete) reality may in some way radically tran-
scend any origins that they may have in the sensory content of our experience, for it
appears that this is a condition on knowledge of the nature of reality as it is in itself.

9   I-CONCEPTS AND S-CONCEPTS

From here on I feel I am not fully in control of this topic. I hope that what I have to
say may be useful in spite of this. The central thought was expressed in [2.4.1] and

---

[25] This is, in effect, the contrapositive of [2.4.1].
[26] 'Everybody's a Rationalist in the long run' (Fodor 1981: 315). For his development of this
view, see Fodor 1996. See also McGinn 1983: 126.
[27] For the basic idea see Strawson 1989b: 247–50. See also William James's profound thoughts
on this matter 1890: 2. 617–40.

it can be rephrased as a partial definition of a *sensory-element-transcendent* concept or *intellectual* concept or *I-concept* for short:

If a concept C is an I-concept, specification of the PDC or NR content of C does not involve any essential reference to any particular type of sensory content S in such a way that the content of C is fully graspable only by beings who have access to S.

This may be shortened to

If C is an I-concept, specification of the PDC or NR content of C does not involve reference to any particular type of sensory content.

A concept is an essentially *sensory-element-involving* or *S-concept* just in case it is not an I-concept: just in case specification of its content does essentially involve reference to some particular type of sensory content. I take it that the distinction is exhaustive as well as exclusive, and that the converse of the partial definition is obvious, so that one can advance to the stronger claim that a concept is an I-concept *if and only if* specification of its content does not involve reference to any particular type of sensory content. This allows room for the idea that one must have experience of or acquaintance with some sensory content or other in order to have any given I-concept, although it does not endorse it.

How does the distinction between I-concepts and S-concepts divide up the realm of concepts? One suggestion is that there are no I-concepts, strictly speaking. This is what empiricists—or at least 'concept-empiricists'—are supposed to suppose. A slightly less extreme suggestion is that there are no I-concepts when one considers concepts of straightforwardly physical properties of reality, rather than considering intuitively more abstract concepts like JUSTICE, BEAUTY, IMPLICATION, HERE, and $\sqrt{-1}$.[28]

But perhaps this is the wrong way round. Perhaps there are no S-concepts—or very few. Concepts, after all, are concepts. (Here again it is important to remember that we are assuming that concepts essentially have PDC, NR content as well as merely referential content, for in the current philosophical climate this idea has become almost invisible.) They are paradigmatically intellectual phenomena, not sensory phenomena. Perhaps the only S-concepts are concepts like COLOUR (or RED), TASTE (or SWEET), and so on; or, more narrowly, concepts like RED-AS-SEEN (SWEETNESS-AS-TASTED); or, more narrowly still, RED-AS-SEEN-by-B-AT-t (and so on). Perhaps DOG, WATER, and TRAIN are I-concepts, as well as MOTHER, PRESIDENT, and APARTHEID. Perhaps this is so even though 'S-concept' certainly does not stand for 'purely sensory' concept (whatever that might mean) but only for 'essentially-sensory-element-involving' concept. A creature's sensory-intellectual constitution may be such that it has to have sensory experience of a certain kind in order to acquire use of a certain concept, as already remarked, and we may assume, at least for the purposes of argument, that this is true of all of us and all our concepts, but it doesn't follow that all

----

[28] I use small capitals for names of concepts.

our concepts are S-concepts.[29] Sensory experience may be an essential part of what triggers or fosters the acquisition of a concept without being a source of its content in such a way that specifying its content involves reference to any part of the sensory content of the triggering experience; and this may be so even when the triggering or activating or fostering relation between the content of the experience and the content of the concept is non-accidental or non-brute in the way that we intuitively suppose it to be, whether we are considering DOG or TRIANGLE or CAUSE.

This notion of non-accidentality is of enormous importance (and difficulty) in any general account of concept acquisition, and it is extremely hard to know exactly what it amounts to. It seems that accidentality can be fairly clearly characterized: there is no logical difficulty in the idea that a creature might be so constituted that a certain experience—a stroboscope flashing forty-seven times a second—was a mere or brute ON switch for a concept—DODECAGON—in such a way that no intelligible contentual relation held between the two.[30] To this extent, we can give a clear negative characterization of non-accidentality. But it is far less clear how to go on to a positive account—one which would, crucially, allow us to say something about differing *degrees* of non-accidentality.[31]

This, however, is not my present concern. I am considering the possibility of knowledge or correct representation of (concrete, non-mental) reality as it is in itself, and I am simply going to assume that sensory experience can be a contributory factor in our coming to possess concepts without *ipso facto* being a source of their content in such a way that full specification of their content will always involve reference to the sensory content of some experience or experiences. I am simply going to assume, in other words, that we have I-concepts, and acquire them in the course of our experience, this being so even if 'experience' is understood to be something that is always and essentially sensation-involving. It seems clear that this is how things go even in the case of intuitively more abstract concepts like USEFULNESS or IMPLICATION or JUSTICE, for example.[32] But my current interest is not in I-concepts of this sort. I am interested in the less obvious idea that basic concepts of concrete physical reality like SHAPE (TRIANGULARITY), EXTENSION, POSITION, MOTION, HARDNESS or SOLIDITY—may also be I-concepts.

[29] 'There can be no doubt that all our knowledge begins with experience . . . . But although all our knowledge begins with experience, it does not follow that it all arises out of experience' (Kant 1781–7: B1).
[30] The present notion of accidentality only concerns the relation between the content of the concept and the content of the triggering experience; the stroboscope-DODECAGON connection could of course be non-accidental evolutionarily speaking.
[31] A form of experience can be both non-accidental and inessential, relative to the acquisition of a concept: both the congenitally blind being and the congenitally non-tactile and asomatosensory being can acquire the concept TRIANGLE. On the general question of non-accidentality approached from an informationalist position, see Fodor 1998: ch. 6. See also, again, William James: 1890: 2.617–40.
[32] Concepts like these can be acquired only from experience that already has conceptual content as well as sensory content, but this is not an objection to the present point.

I will call such basic concepts of physical reality *P-concepts*. My question is whether such P-concepts can be I-concepts, considered specifically as things that have positively descriptive, not merely referential content. And—to narrow things further—I am principally concerned with P-concepts that feature in ordinary thought, rather than with those that are taken as basic in physics. I want to consider the idea that everyday P-concepts like SHAPE or TRIANGLE are I-concepts, for it is P-concepts like these, with their observational air, that are most likely to be thought to be S-concepts.

The point of considering the proposal that P-concepts are I-concepts is the same as before: to try to remove an obstacle (radical empiricist, positivist, Kantian, antirealist, post-modernist, whatever) to the idea that we may be able to grasp something about the nature of (concrete) reality as it is in itself. The question is whether the descriptive (not merely referential) content of the concepts can be supposed to correctly represent reality as it is in itself in any respect.

I will begin with some loosening-up comments about a patently more abstract I-concept, and about some putative S-concepts.

10   AN I-CONCEPT

We come to be able to deploy USEFULNESS on the basis of our experience, but very different forms of experience—Martian, pre-Christian Abyssinian, twentieth-century Japanese—can lead to its acquisition. The content of USEFULNESS is, surely, independent of the experiential details of its many individual acquisitions, and a fortiori of the sensory-experiential details of these acquisitions. Hence its specification does not involve essential reference to any particular type of sensory affection. It is an I-concept.

—But perhaps each individual's concept of usefulness is somehow constitutively saturated with features—including sensory features, however vague their presence—of the experiences which led to its acquisition (yours involved Swiss Army penknives, mine involved wheels); not to mention features of the experiences in which it has subsequently been active.

On this view, each person's concept of usefulness is likely to be different from everyone else's, in greater or lesser degree, both within and across cultures. But there is no reason to believe this; it has no phenomenological or behavioural support, and Wittgensteinian arguments that equate concept-possession with language mastery move heavily against it, especially when we consider members of a single language-community who have acquired the concept in very different ways. Wittgensteinian arguments are doubtful things, and I will question an application of this one in the next section, but the idea that cultural differences may lead to significantly different concepts of usefulness, rather than to different views about what is useful, does not I believe survive unprejudiced reflection.[33]

---

[33] Suppose we have two expressions, 'useful' and 'beautiful', where a New Guinea language has only one. It doesn't follow that we don't have the same concept of usefulness, rather than (say)

11 S-CONCEPTS

Among the prime candidates for being S-concepts are concepts like RED, which raise famous and instructive difficulties.

Some, like myself, think that colour properties are essentially *phenomenal* properties, i.e. properties whose whole and essential nature can be fully revealed in sensory experience given only the qualitative (experiential) character that that experience has. Others think colour properties are not phenomenal properties, and are best thought of as powers or dispositional properties of objects. On this familiar view, for an object to be red is for it to be disposed to cause certain sorts of experiences in creatures like ourselves in certain conditions. Members of a third group agree with members of the second group that colours are not phenomenal properties, but think that 'red' is best thought of as a name for whatever 'categorical' properties—for example molecular-structure properties—'underlie' the dispositional properties just mentioned.

The second and third views are not worth distinguishing for present purposes. The important disagreement is over whether or not colour properties are phenomenal properties. I take it that they are. I think that colour concepts like RED are *essentially* concepts of properties whose whole and essential nature can be fully revealed in sensory experience, given only the qualitative experiential character that that experience has, and that the same goes for colour words like 'red', *mutatis mutandis*.

This view is certainly correct according to common sense, but it is little more than a terminological decision in philosophy, for the philosophical discussion of colour has taken on a life of its own, and it is far from being unproblematic. Consider the word 'red'. If we take it that it is essentially a word for a phenomenal property, then the problem is that it does not seem that it can name any *particular* phenomenal quality. For it seems very plausible—it is an old idea, which I take it to be correct—that creatures who have mastery of the word 'red', and who apply the word on the basis of experience that they take to be experience of red, and who fully agree in language on what things are red, may nonetheless have radically qualitatively different sensory experiences when they look at things they agree to be red.[34] But then it is hard to resist the conclusion that 'red' cannot be supposed to name any one particular phenomenal quality. But if this is so, and if shared mastery of the word 'red' amounts to shared possession of the concept RED (as Wittgensteinians suppose), it seems clear that specification of the content of RED does not require reference to any particular type of sensory content—*phenomenal red* as you think you know it now, for example. In which case RED is an I-concept. The argument quickly generalizes to all

different views about what is useful. It doesn't even follow that we have different views about what is useful: the most accurate thing to say about the New Guinea language may well be that there are two words which are homonyms (it would be a simple mistake about language use and understanding to think that there will necessarily be some sort of semantic seepage from one to the other). And even if it were granted that we had different concepts, the fundamental point would remain: there would be no reason to think that specification of the content of the concepts involved any essential reference to sensory elements.

[34] See e.g. Locke 1689–1700: 2.32.14–15.

other concepts of phenomenal qualities, with the striking consequence that they are all I-concepts.

The argument is too quick, whatever you think of the conclusion. Consider the following four positions. First, P1, the extreme behaviourist view that a creature—for example a robot or 'zombie'—can possess RED even if it is incapable of any sort of conscious experience at all (it has sensors that detect and distinguish the light-reflection properties of objects, and is able to acquire colour vocabulary on that basis).

Less extreme is P2, the view that mastery of colour concepts must be tied to experience of *some* type of sensory content, but that the sensory content in question needn't be *visual* content as we know it. It may be some form of auditory experience; it may involve some sort of exquisitely refined echoic content, or it may be something unimaginable by us. (Note that I am assuming that the general qualitative character of experience we agree to call 'visual' is fundamentally the same for all of us even if we differ strikingly in respect of the colour quality of the experiences we have when exposed to identical light stimuli. I am assuming, in other words, that 'visual' names a particular *general qualitative type* of sensory content. It does not merely name a particular *functional type* of sensory content which can be roughly characterized as follows: sensory content that results from a creature's sense organs receiving light reflected or emitted from objects in such a way that the creature is in a position to master colour vocabulary directly on that basis.)

It follows from P1 that RED is an I-concept, and also from P2, given the present account of I-concepts. A third view is a restriction of the second: P3 states that mastery of colour concepts is essentially linked to specifically *visual* sensory content as just (qualitatively rather than functionally) defined. According to P3 you and I may both fully possess RED even though your red-experience is qualitatively the same as my green-experience and vice versa. What matters is that we both have genuinely visual sensory content (in the qualitative-type sense just sketched), master colour vocabulary on that basis, and take colour properties to be directly revealed in visual sensory content.

A fourth view, P4, dismisses all these complications and insists that RED is indeed the concept of one particular phenomenal quality—you know, phenomenal red, *RED*! According to P4, RED is a red-blooded S-concept: specification of its content involves essential reference to one very particular type of sensory content, *RED!*, and RED is fully graspable only by a being who is acquainted with that type of sensory content.

I don't, however, think one can ignore all the old complications, as P4 suggests. Even untutored thought tends to wonder whether we all experience colour in the same way. P4 may seem attractive, but it really is too simple. And P1 can be rejected outright. I favour P3, in spite of its paradoxical air—it says that RED is the concept of a phenomenal property whose whole and essential nature can be directly revealed in visual sensory content *even though it is not the concept of any one particular phenomenal property*—, on the grounds that it effects the best compromise between common sense and adequate acknowledgement of the philosophical complications.

—But if you accept P3, you cannot say that P2 is indefensible. For P2 differs from P3 only in that it relativizes the notion of visual experience in the way P3 relativizes the notion of red-experience.

True. I think P2 is defensible. I favour P3, but P2 is an interesting position. It can't be disproved.

Does P3 treat RED as an I-concept or an S-concept? It treats RED as an S-concept, for it states that specification of the content of RED does involve essential reference to a particular type of sensory content—visual content understood to be a particular general *qualitative* type of sensory content, not merely a particular *functional* type—in such a way that it is fully graspable only by beings who are acquainted with that type of sensory content. P3 does not, however, treat RED as what one might call a *first-level* S-concept, in the way that P4 proposes to do: it does not require reference to *RED!*, phenomenal redness as naively conceived (it takes it that there is no such single thing as phenomenal redness naively conceived). Instead it treats RED as a *second-level* S concept. By which I mean only that there is no essential reference to the phenomenal character of phenomenal redness as naively conceived in the specification of its content. Instead there is essential reference to the phenomenal character of specifically visual experience. It is true that this reference to the phenomenal character of specifically visual experience doesn't distinguish red from blue, or indeed RED from BLUE, but this is just as it should be, on the present view.[35]

P3 may seem very strained, so it is worth pointing out that it respects the intuition behind P4 as far as possible. It makes the smallest change to P4 that is compatible with allowing that two people can both have the concept RED even if the colour-experience one of them has on looking at a ripe tomato is qualitatively the same as the colour-experience that the other has on looking at well-watered grass. If Nida-Rümelin is right, this difference in colour-experience is actually found among human beings whom we firmly believe to possess the concept RED. But the change to P4 would be necessary even if this were not so.[36]

On my view, then, RED may be supposed to be an S-concept, and the argument for this view generalizes to all other concepts of sensory qualities.[37] They are not, however, S-concepts as naively conceived. They are second-level S-concepts, and there are no first-level S concepts—no concepts specification of whose content requires reference to particular phenomenal qualities naively conceived. As for DOG, SUBWAY, and so on, they are clearly I-concepts, on this view: you do not need to have experience in any particular sensory modality in order to possess them, even if you must have experience in some sensory modality or other.[38]

---

[35] I count black, white and grey among the colours, and take it that all visual experience is essentially colour experience (thanks to Brian McLaughlin).

[36] Nida-Rümelin 1996 estimates that 14 out of every 10,000 males may differ from other people in this way.

[37] Pain raises a curious issue. See Strawson 1994: 247–50.

[38] Might SENSATION, EXPERIENCE, and CONSCIOUSNESS count as third-level S-concepts, on this account? They certainly seem to be concepts that one cannot fully grasp unless one is acquainted with sensation, experience, and consciousness—and not simply because one cannot be said to grasp

Two final comments on colour. First, we are driven to this conclusion by the colour-spectrum inversion thought experiment, and although the use of the thought-experiment is valid and cannot be ignored, it is open to someone to say that if all human beings who are capable of the same sorts of colour discriminations do *in fact* have the same sort of colour-experience when looking at ripe tomatoes, then RED—the human concept—can after all be taken to be a first-level S-concept. I think that this suggestion is worth recording, although it faces very serious (I believe overwhelming) difficulties.[39]

The second and connected comment is this. There is pressure to say that the—*the*—concept RED cannot be the concept of any particular phenomenal quality only if one assumes that we all share a common, single concept of red as well as a common, single word for red. Many, Wittgensteinians and others, take it as axiomatic that a common word entails a common concept, but it is not clear why one should agree with this. Perhaps the concept-name 'RED', as used here, is deceptive in so far as it affects to be the name of a single shared concept. Perhaps the best thing to say is that each of us has a private *concept* of red that essentially incorporates a particular sensory-phenomenal colour-element in its content, and that it is on this basis that we participate successfully in a common linguistic practice involving a single *word* 'red'.[40]

On this view, words are one thing, concepts are another. The word 'red' is not tied to any one single concept, *the* concept RED, for there is no such thing. Instead, 'red' is the common, public linguistic correlate of a whole group of simple S concepts, x's RED, y's RED, and so on, which are indeed all first-level S concepts.

Does it matter which side one takes in this debate, in the case of colour concepts? I'm not sure that it does. Perhaps one can take both sides. I have opted for position P3 above, according to which colour concepts are taken to be shared second-level

any concept at all unless one has acquaintance with these things—and perhaps one can express things as follows:

Level	Type of affection	Sub-type
1	Visual	colour-experience, (visual) shape-experience . . .
2	Sensory	Visual, auditory, gustatory (defined as qualitative types not functional types)
3	Experiential affection in general	Sensory, emotional, propositional, intellectual-intuition-involving (?)

Adding level 3 allows one to integrate the thought that SENSATION is an S-concept into the existing scheme of things; it presupposes—reasonably, I think—that the idea of non-sensory experiential affection is intelligible. It is a further question how this scheme might cope with Kantian forms of sensibility, but I will leave it here.

[39] See e.g. Strawson 1994: 246–7. I have drawn on Essay 4 throughout this section.

[40] Back to the 'beetle in the box'—and not in a way that Wittgenstein (1953: §293) would clearly have to reject. Note that there are also certain constraints on possession of colour concepts that flow from the similarity and difference relations between different colours (see McLaughlin 2003).

S-concepts, but I have no strong objection to the privatized version of P4 just described, according to which they are taken to be private first-level S-concepts.[41]

12   ARE P-CONCEPTS I-CONCEPTS?

The central question of this paper, in any case, is whether it is possible for finite creatures like ourselves to grasp or correctly represent the nature of (concrete nonmental) reality as it is in itself, and I will now return to this question in the form that it assumed at the end of §9:

Are P-concepts—SHAPE (TRIANGULAR), SIZE, EXTENSION, MOTION, SOLIDITY, POSITION—I-concepts? Could they be?

The first issue that arises, given the preceding section, is whether a privatizing move of the sort considered in the case of RED can be extended, not only to DOG or indeed USEFULNESS, but also to P-concepts like SHAPE, in such a way as to reintroduce the possibility of arguing that they are S-concepts after all, each with its local, private, person-relative content (tactile elements for the congenitally blind person's concept of shape, visual elements for the non-tactile and asomatosensory person's concept of shape, and so on).

The privatizing move can be made with P-concepts as with concepts like RED, but not, I think, with any theoretical peacefulness. Consider SHAPE. It seems so clear that different creatures can come to have the concept of shape we possess—*the* concept of shape, for there is only one—on the basis of very different sensory experiences; so that superintelligent bats (for example) could on the basis of their echolocation experiences acquire and subsequently deploy exactly the same concept of shape as we acquire and deploy on the basis of visual and tactile experiences. In fact, it suffices to note that exactly the same concept of SHAPE can plausibly be supposed to be fully masterable by two different creatures B and C on the basis of sensory experiences in entirely different sensory modalities familiar to us—sight and touch—in order to illustrate the sense in which the concept of SHAPE floats free of the sensory elements in the different possible bases of its acquisition and subsequent deployment. One has to endorse a rather crude form of meaning-empiricism or concept-empiricism to suppose that B and C do not—cannot—have the same concept, as they do geometry together, even when the focus is on PDC, NR content. A concept, after all, is not a faint copy or transform of a sensory experience; it is a concept. Here, then, I explicitly reject the privatizing move.

I choose to concentrate on concepts like SHAPE, and on more particular concepts of shape like TRIANGULAR, because the claim that P-concepts are I-concepts may seem considerably harder to believe in their case than in the case of ELECTRICITY, say, or SOLIDITY. In the case of ELECTRICITY it is relatively easy to see that its content does not involve any particular sensory elements (one might as well suppose that its content,

---

[41] Just as each of us has a Chomskyan I-language (Chomsky 1986), so too each of us has an I-scheme, an internal individual conceptual scheme.

or some part of its content, can be given in the sensory content of an experience of an electric shock).[42] In the case of SOLIDITY it is at first harder to see this, but it is something that one should learn as an undergraduate in philosophy.[43] In the case of TRIANGULAR it seems more counterintuitive (in spite of the fact that TRIANGULAR is a member of one of the few classes of concepts that seem to be open to exhaustive verbal definition), for TRIANGULAR is the concept of a property that we tend to think of as (capable of) being directly and fully presented to us in sensory experience.

One general obstacle to allowing that concepts like TRIANGULAR are I-concepts is that sensory content can sometimes seem to be quite generally pervasive of the content of thought, especially when one has been raised in an empiricism-dominated philosophical culture. One may later come to doubt this idea, but it can still seem very hard to deny in the case of the concepts like TRIANGULAR. And yet it seems that the antidote is simple, once one has rejected the privatizing move: all one has to do, as remarked, is to consider the point that congenitally blind and congenitally non-tactile and asomatosensory beings may both have the—*the*—concept TRIANGULAR. The same argument can be adapted to work for MOTION, EXTENSION, and so on. Even if we suppose that all processes of conscious thought in human beings do in some way inevitably involve or implicate occurrent sensory content (this seems to be clearly false, but let us grant it for the sake of argument) nothing follows about the content of *concepts*, for we are given no reason to think that these occurrent sensory contents are an essential part of what makes these processes entertainings of specific conceptual contents, and the view that congenitally blind and congenitally unfeeling human beings and superintelligent non-human echolocators may all have the concept SHAPE (EXTENSION, and so on) remains as compelling as ever.

13   CONCEPTS WITHOUT INTUITIONS?

I assumed earlier that sensory experience is necessary for the *acquisition* of any concept in the case of finite beings like ourselves.[44] It follows that sensory experience is necessary for the acquisition of all P-concepts even if P-concepts are I-concepts.[45] But this is, so far, quite a weak claim. As it stands, it allows that one might continue to possess an acquired concept while losing any sort of capacity for sensory experience, and a natural stronger suggestion is that possession of I-concepts (including all P-concepts, on the present account) at any time may require possession of capacities for certain sorts of sensory experience at that time.

Is this true? Well, it too has weaker and stronger forms. We may take the limiting case of possession of a capacity for a certain sort of sensory experience to be possession

---

[42] See Evans 1980: 270.

[43] Hume makes the point that our concept of solidity is sensory-element-transcending in the *Treatise* (1739–40: 229–31/150–2). Reid makes it in a very accessible manner in §2 of his *Inquiry* (1764: 61–4). See also Mackie 1976: 24–6.

[44] The assumption begs no questions because it can only make things more difficult for me.

[45] I take it that this is compatible with the deep respects in which our predisposition to acquire P-concepts is innate (see e.g. Spelke 1994).

of a capacity for a certain sort of sensory imagining. This allows one to say, plausibly, that one can possess the concepts SHAPE and TRIANGULAR even if one has lost (or perhaps never had) sight and tactile-somatosensory feeling, so long as one retains a capacity to imagine seen or felt shape. But now suppose that one has also lost the capacity to imagine seen or felt shape. Can one still possess the concept?

I don't know. Here we encounter the difficulties addressed by Kant in his discussion of pure imagination and pure intuition. But even if No were the right answer it wouldn't follow that sensory content derived from visual or tactile experience is constitutive of the content of our shape concepts in such a way that these concepts are not I-concepts. One can answer No while still holding that SHAPE, TRIANGULAR, MOTION, EXTENSION, and so on are all-out I-concepts, P-concepts whose content radically, and in some way entirely, transcends the content of our sensory experience. An account of the conditions of *possession* of such a concept must be sharply distinguished from an account of the *content* of the concept.

All these things being so, it is not only possible that we may fully share P-concepts with other beings who have radically different sensory equipment. It is also possible—crucially for the present argument—that some at least of our P-concepts may have a place in a correct representation of *x* in spite of all the particularities of the specifically human idiom of reality representation; and that this is so even though the P-concepts are being considered specifically in respect of their PDC or NR content.

Neither of these possibilities is available on the view according to which the PDC or NR content of our concepts is not ultimately independent of our sensory experience. The first is obviously unavailable: if our P-concepts really are essentially informed by our sensory peculiarities then we can't fully share them with creatures that have radically different sensory equipment. The second is unavailable given the truth of [2.4.1], endorsed on p. 86: given that no representation can correctly represent any feature of *x* if its representation of that feature essentially involves sensory elements. If, however, the claim that our P-concepts are I-concepts is correct, it undercuts [2.5], which led from [2.1]-[2.4], which are true, to [2.6], the claim we are trying to block: the claim that no account or apprehension of *x*, on the part of a finite sensory-intellectual creature, can ever be supposed to constitute a correct representation of (any feature of) *x*.

14   A SPECULATION

I have argued that there is no reason in principle why we cannot attain to a correct and descriptively (characterizationally) substantive representation of certain aspects of the nature of *x*. (Those who take this to be obvious may think I am wasting their time, but many take it to be obviously and provably false.) I want now to consider a simple Kantian speculation that doesn't undercut the preceding argument in any way, but may be thought to throw a heavy dampener on it.

Perhaps *x* is indeed far, far stranger than we suppose. Perhaps an appropriate analogy for the overall experiential relation in which we and other very different beings of types B and C stand to *x* is provided by the case of three physical creatures who have exactly the same patterns of electrical impulses transmitted to their brains (these impulses play the role of the concrete non-mental reality that affects us), but react to them in very different ways. In the first the impulses produce colour experience, in the second they produce auditory experience, in the third they produce smell experience. Perhaps the differences between our overall (not merely sensory) sensory-intellectual apprehension of reality and those of the B-type and C-type beings are as great as the qualitative differences between these three modes of sensory experience. Perhaps we and they are entities constituted of some unintelligible substance receiving the same input from one common thing, but experiencing things in inconceivably different and utterly incommensurable ways.

If this analogy is in fact appropriate to our actual situation, then, in spite of the apparent sophistication of our theories of reality, the nature of x is as inaccessible for us and the B-type and C-type beings as any conception of the nature of electrical impulse is for beings whose only possible mental states are just uninterpreted colour experiences or sound experiences or smell and taste experiences.

We cannot know that the analogy is not appropriate. And so it seems that even if we can and do in fact grasp—know—something about the nature of x, we can never know that we do.

Well, this conclusion is correct, whether or not it is warranted by the considerations that deliver it: acknowledgement of the irrefutability of scepticism, so far as claims to knowledge of the ultimate nature of (non-conscious features of) things are concerned, is an essential part of a realist attitude to the world, and indeed of any defensible philosophical attitude to the world. Many philosophers have taken it that it is a prerequisite of a good philosophical theory that it should provide an answer to scepticism, but this is the reverse of the truth. Realism itself is inescapable, at least in the form summarized in [A] and [B] at the beginning of this paper, and with realism comes the irrefutability of scepticism. Any theory which on its own terms provides an answer to scepticism—scepticism with respect to knowledge claims about the ultimate nature of reality—is *ipso facto* refuted.

15   WHAT CAN WE KNOW?

I have argued against Kant and others that there is no insuperable difficulty of principle in the idea that finite sensory-intellectual creatures like ourselves can have descriptively substantive (rather than merely referential) knowledge of x, the nature of reality as it is in itself. But how much do we actually have? I don't know, but I will indicate two areas—mathematics and space—where I think we may be cottoning on, at least in certain respects, to x.

Consider Eddington's description of the achievements of physical theory:

Something unknown is doing we don't know what—that is what our theory amounts to. It does not sound a particularly illuminating theory. I have read something like it elsewhere . . .

... the slithy toves
Did gyre and gimble in the wabe.

There is the same suggestion of activity. There is the same indefiniteness as to the nature of the activity and of what it is that it is doing. And yet from so unpromising a beginning we really do get somewhere. We bring into order a host of apparently unrelated phenomena; we make predictions, and our predictions come off. The reason—the sole reason—for this progress is that our description is not limited to unknown agents, executing unknown activities, but *numbers* are scattered freely in the description. To contemplate electrons circulating in the atom carries us no further; but by contemplating eight circulating electrons in one atom and seven circulating atoms in another we begin to realise the difference between oxygen and nitrogen. Eight slithy toves gyre and gimble in the oxygen wabe; seven in nitrogen . . . .[46]

I think this is an essentially correct account of how things stand in physics, but it does not have the consequence that we know nothing about the nature of reality as it is in itself. Up to this point I have left NUMBER off the list of P-concepts, but it must now be reinstated, accompanied by the crucial claim that number knowledge, mathematical knowledge, is genuinely descriptive of, genuinely characterizational of, the nature of reality.

This claim may give some people pause, but I think it is evident on reflection. I think there are eight oranges in front of me. And I think I may well be getting something right about x, no less, in taking it that there are eight things in the offing, at least according to one objectively valid principle of counting things,[47] however wrong I am about the nature of space, time, and matter and, therefore, oranges (and the offing). And I cannot here be supposed to be *merely referring* to things, in using the term 'eight', without giving any sort of descriptively substantive account of *how things are*. Perhaps there is some great sense in which Parmenides is right that all is one. It is today a respectable hypothesis that there is (as Spinoza supposed) only one substance, spacetime, all fundamental particles being 'rips' in spacetime (or 'spacetimematter'). Even so, my bet is that eightness—number in general—is a real and ultimate property of concrete non-mental reality as it is in itself, and that we possess a great deal of mathematically expressible, NR-contentful descriptively substantive knowledge of x. A lot of us think we know that gravitational attraction between two objects a and b decreases as a function of the square of the distance between them, and if we are right, then again we have some very substantial and not merely referential descriptive or characterizational knowledge of an aspect of the nature of reality as it is in itself, even if the referring expressions 'gravitational attraction', 'a', 'b', and even 'distance' pick out entities that we are, given our grasp of the nature of spacetime, and matter, in some ways hopelessly wrong about.

This claim to knowledge of the nature of x may seem very thin, even if it is allowed. It may be asked whether we have any non-mathematical knowledge of the nature of concrete, non-mental reality as it is in itself? I am inclined to believe that we do, for I

---

[46] 1928: 291.
[47] Another might pick up on the number of fundamental particles constituting the oranges.

think we may also possess some non-referentially substantive knowledge of the nature of space—of the spatial properties of x—even if we can never know that we do.[48] These, though, are questions for another occasion.

This may still seem rather exiguous; sceptics about the possibility of knowledge of x may even feel that their essential point has been conceded. But this is certainly not true if their point is the point of principle—the claim that it is in principle impossible for finite beings to know the nature of x. And when it comes to conscious mental reality—that great (and perhaps universal—see Essay 2) part of concrete reality that was put aside in §3. although it is the only part of whose existence we are certain—we know a great deal about the nature of reality as it is in itself.[49]

---

[48] Russell disagrees, at least at one point in his career (see e.g. Russell 1927a, 1927b), as does Lockwood (1989), and I am now (in 2007) much less sure. Eddington disarmingly suggests that we know what time is—'I do not see how the essence of "becoming" can be much different from what it appears to us to be' (1928: 95)—but intuition fails me here.

[49] I am especially grateful to Lucy Allais and Mark Greenberg for their comments, and to Quassim Cassam, Brian McLaughlin and Ernie Sosa. I also learnt from audiences in London, Oxford, and NYU.

4

Red and 'Red'

This is a paper about the meaning of the word 'red', but its general conclusions should apply equally, *mutatis mutandis*, to words for sounds, tastes, and smells. Many of the arguments are familiar in general form, and one of the aims of the paper is simply to clarify the existing debate. But I hope that it also introduces some new elements.

1

Four useful expressions require immediate introduction: 'ordinarily colour-sighted', 'colour-experience', 'phenomenal quality', and 'qualitative character'. I take it that to say that a man is *ordinarily colour-sighted* is *not* to say that he has colour-experiences of a certain particular qualitative character when he looks at certain things, but only that he is able to make the full range of colour *discriminations* that most people can make. In fact the necessity of understanding the expression 'ordinarily colour-sighted' in this way is a consequence of the argument that follows.

Let *a* be such an ordinarily colour-sighted man. When he looks at a bright red British pillar box in ordinary daylight, and at some particular time, he has some *colour-experience* (the case of 'absent qualia' will be considered in §8). I will say that, in having that colour-experience, he has experience of some *phenomenal quality*: for his colour-experience has, of course, a certain *qualitative character*, specifically qua a colour-experience; and I shall suppose that to say that his colour-experience is an experience *of* a certain phenomenal quality is just one way of characterizing the fact that it has a certain qualitative character, specifically qua a colour-experience (just as it has a certain qualitative character specifically qua a shape-experience).

The expression 'phenomenal quality' deserves further comment. First, though, I wish to fend off an objection. There may still be some, verificationists or their sophisticated descendants, who will want to object that the main argument of this paper depends on certain suppositions that are, as they may say, 'meaningless' or spurious—in particular, the supposition that two people looking together at objects could agree in all their colour-judgements while differing in their colour-experiences. I intend to take it for granted that this supposition is not meaningless or spurious, even if nothing can ever count as good evidence for, let alone as proof of, its truth. It may be noted, though, that the *intelligibility* of the supposition follows directly from three claims that nearly all philosophers accept (once the caveats and qualifications are over):[1]

(1) that other people exist, and have minds, and experiences;

(2) that experiences characteristically have a certain qualitative character (or sensational content);

(3) that people who look at a thing in order to judge its colour standardly judge as they do because of the qualitative character of the experience they then have, and, in particular, because of its qualitative character specifically qua colour-experience.[2]

Not everyone will be satisfied by this—and some may feel that it gives rise to another objection: what is this *qualitative character* that is so confidently invoked?[3] Most, however, will agree that the notion of the qualitative character of colour-experience can reasonably be taken for granted. And for present purposes, a sufficient reply to those who disagree is simply as follows. Consider your present visual experience. Look at the bookshelf. (Get out some of the brightest books.) There you have it.[4]

It is no part of the present claim that the qualitative character (or sensational content) of a sensory experience is some kind of pure-given, uncontaminated by belief, pro-attitude, or expectation. Nor can the content of experience always be sorted out neatly into a sensory, qualitative-character component, and a conceptual component. It is, certainly, taken for granted that the qualitative character of one's colour-experience is in some way importantly independent of—in such a way that it is not merely a function of—one's judgement-dispositions or other behavioural dispositions. (Thus it seems reasonable to suppose that the *basic structure* of an ordinary person's colour vision will be the same at three months and at thirty years, independently of his or her acquisition of conceptual skills.) But there is no denial that discriminatory sensitivity can be much refined by experience, or that 'phenomenology is

---

[1] To say that the supposition is *intelligible* is not to deny that what is supposed might conceivably be shown to be impossible, at least in the case of colour vision of human complexity, because of some unobvious facts about the structure of 'colour-space'.
     To claim (i) that two genuinely distinct possibilities cannot have been distinguished when there is *ex hypothesi* no possibility of any evidence ever becoming available (to us, this side of heaven) which might decide the question, is apparently to accept (ii) that Berkeley and Locke were not really describing distinct possibilities in their account of the nature of reality. Assuming that (something like) Berkeley's account is at least coherent, I take the falsity of (ii) as a sufficient reason for denying (i); though Carnap, for one, was disposed to accept (ii) (Carnap, 1967). To assent to (i) is arguably to succumb to what one could call the *mysticism* of empiricism—to lose one's grip on the vital (realist) distinction between what may be the case, and what may be known, or warrantably asserted, to be the case.

[2] Standardly: this is not to say that their expectations, views about shape, lighting, etc. never affect their colour judgements—or indeed their colour-experiences.

[3] See Dennett 1988, for doubts about this confidence. Given that Dennett does not actually deny the fact of the qualitative character of experience (he appeals to it constantly in his argument), the general drift of his paper may be seen as supporting the conclusion of the present paper.

[4] Some doubts about this natural strategy are registered and put aside in §8.

conceptually driven' in many fundamental respects. The present point remains unaffected by such facts, important though they are.[5]

So much for qualitative character. Before moving to the main argument in §2, it is worth making a few further (essentially routine) comments on the expression 'phenomenal quality', which is defined in terms of qualitative character.

It follows from what has already been said that the expression 'experience *of* a certain phenomenal quality' should not be taken to imply that the experienced phenomenal quality is something that exists independently of *a* and his mind, something that is objectively 'out there' and of which he becomes aware: for, after all, *a* may be the only person in the world whose colour-experience, upon looking at the pillar box (in these lighting circumstances), has exactly the qualitative character that his colour-experience has now. To speak of his colour-experience as experience *of* a certain phenomenal quality is simply a way of expressing the fact that it has a certain qualitative character (specifically qua colour-experience).

It is true that the naturalness of talking about colour-experiences in this way (talking about them as experiences *of* phenomenal qualities) derives largely from the fact that when we see an object and see it to have a certain phenomenal-quality colour, it is, for us, as if the phenomenal-quality colour were an entirely mind-independent objective quality of the object—a phenomenal quality of the object, as we may naturally say. But one can perfectly well deny that such experienced phenomenal qualities are entirely mind-independent qualities *of objects* while continuing to express the fact that an experience has a certain qualitative character by saying that it is experience *of* a certain phenomenal quality.

Suppose one looks at an object *o*, and has a colour-experience *e*. I (hereby) assume that it is wrong to suppose that the phenomenal-quality colour that *o* appears to be, as one looks at it, is an entirely mind-independent quality of *o*.[6] But even when phenomenal qualities are treated as essentially mind-dependent in this way, they can still be treated as fully *real*. They can, after all, be named. Imagine a book containing 250 full-page colour samples on numbered pages (numbered on the back). One can name the phenomenal qualities that certain experiences are experiences of, specifically in so far as they are colour-experiences, as follows: phenomenal quality 'Q_{c-1}' is the phenomenal quality that *a* has experience of, now at time *t*, when looking at page 1 of this book, just in so far as the experience *a* then has is specifically a colour-experience; phenomenal quality 'Q_{c-2}' is the phenomenal quality *a* has experience of, now at t_1, when looking at page 2 . . . ; and so on. It can be simply true that these are names for distinct phenomenal qualities, names that we can perfectly well use, and understand to be names for distinct phenomenal qualities, even though we cannot know for sure

---

[5] And by Dennett's interesting strictures on the concept of 'qualia' (1988). When doubts recur, one should look at the brightly coloured books, because all that is meant here by saying that colour-experience has a certain qualitative character is revealed when one looks at the books (the look of the printed page will do, but it is less persuasive when one is under the influence of philosophy). The point is simply untouched by such thoughts as that our colour-experiences could conceivably change systematically every ten seconds in such a way that we did not notice it, given compensating changes in memory.

[6] This assumption is very widely held, and will be supported at various points in what follows.

what the phenomenal qualities they name are like, qua phenomenal qualities, because we are not a.[7]

On the present view, then, talk of phenomenal qualities is reducible to talk about experiences and the qualitative character of experiences, at least in the case of those phenomenal qualities that experiences are experiences of specifically in so far as they are colour-experiences—or indeed sound, taste, or smell experiences.[8] Notice that it is not said that the phenomenal quality Q_{c-1} is itself a property of the experience e. It is not itself a property of e any more than it is a property of the object, o, that e is an experience of. To say that e is an experience of Q_{c-1} is simply to say something about the qualitative character (or sensational content) of e. And although e is both an experience of o and an experience of Q_{c-1}, Q_{c-1} is not a property of o either. What is true is that o has a property reference to which helps to explain the fact that a's experience e of o is an experience of Q_{c-1}: the property (possibly further describable) of being such as to cause a to have experience of Q_{c-1} when looking at o.[9]

All this is familiar enough. The upshot is that there is nothing wrong with talking about particular phenomenal qualities when talking about colours (sounds, etc.) as long as it is clearly understood that reference to such phenomenal qualities cannot in the final analysis be detached from reference to experiences, and to particular

---

[7] If one has been led to doubt this (e.g. by Dennett, op cit., §3), the thing to do is to try it out on oneself. It involves no assumption about constancy over time in a's colour-experience dispositions, colour-judgement dispositions, or (colour-recognition-related) memory dispositions.

[8] Concentrating on 'secondary' qualities, I avoid vexed questions about the relations between primary qualities and experience—questions, for example, about the relations between (i) the shapes of physical objects and (ii) the phenomenal qualities that experiences are experiences of specifically in so far as they are shape-experiences. Obviously, experiences are experiences of particular phenomenal qualities in so far as they have a shape-involving qualitative character to just the same extent that they are experiences of particular phenomenal qualities in so far as they have a colour-involving qualitative character.

[9] If one is determined to say that Q_{c-1} is a property of something (some thing), rather than merely understanding talk of phenomenal qualities as a way of talking about the qualitative character of experiences, then one has to introduce a realm of propertied phenomena that are somehow involved in experiences of objects but are themselves neither experiences nor objects. This can, perhaps, be done: it seems that one can (to take the visual case) perfectly well attribute phenomenal qualities to areas of a's visual field, when he has e. But it is not necessary.

So far as shape-experience is concerned, none of the above rules out the legitimacy of saying something like the following. Suppose a is 'ordinarily shape-sighted'—that is, his (vision-based) shaped-discrimination capacities are (humanly) normal. When a looks at an object o (in normal circumstances), and has as a result a visual experience e of o which is, among other things, a shape-experience, and is, specifically in being a shape-experience, experience of a certain phenomenal quality Q_{sh-1}, then *a has veridical experience of* the *actual shape* of o; where 'the actual shape of o' denotes, of course, an entirely mind-independent property of o. To say this is certainly not to make any simple *resemblance* claim. For on this account, *whatever* angle a looks at a plate from, the experience he has specifically in so far as he has a shape-experience can correctly be said to be veridical experience of the shape of the plate (given normal circumstances), whether or not he *realizes* that it is experience of a plate or even of a plate-shaped object—and whether or not there could possibly be a significant systematic qualitative difference in the quality of shape-experience for 'ordinarily shape-sighted' people (the notion of such systematic difference is of course far more doubtful here than in the case of colour; connectedly, the phenomenology of shape-experience is strongly 'conceptually driven').

experiencers. Such phenomenal qualities remain fully real for all that. For a particular individual's having an experience *e* is as real an occurrence as any other occurrence in nature; and *e*'s property of having a certain qualitative character specifically in so far as it is a colour-experience (sound-experience, etc.)—that is, its character of being experience of a particular phenomenal quality specifically in so far as it is a colour-experience (sound-experience, etc.)—is in turn a fully real property that it has, however resistant to linguistic description it may be.

2

What does 'red' mean? Imagine a simple scene. Pillar box P is in front of us. *That*, we say, is red. (We may suppose that when we do this, we just know that we are talking about colour, and not, say, about shape or size.)[10] And we are right. P is red. But what exactly has been said? Despite all that Wittgenstein wrote, one may be strongly inclined to think that at least *part* of the meaning of the word 'red' is (to use an intentionally slightly ungainly expression) that it *carries reference* to a certain particular phenomenal quality: that quality—call it 'Q_{c-1}'—that one is oneself experiencing now, looking at P. What could be more natural, than to think that the word 'red' is a word for a particular phenomenal quality? In fact, however, reference to Q_{c-1} plays no part at all in an adequate account of the meaning of the word 'red'. Nor does reference to any other particular phenomenal quality. Why not? Simply because of the much discussed possibility that people may have different colour-experiences, different experiences of presented phenomenal quality, when they all look together at a single pillar box in normal and uniform lighting conditions—and even while they all agree that the pillar box is red.

Wittgenstein is often appealed to by those who wish to cast doubt on this possibility. This is curious in a way, because his well-known story about a group of people each of whom possesses a private box in which he, or she, keeps a beetle that the others cannot inspect provides a dramatic illustration of exactly the possibility that is doubted.[11] If one takes the beetle—the thing in the private (mental) box—to be, not a sensation of pain, but a particular colour-experience, then the story fits the present case exactly: as the group looks at the pillar box, each member of it has his or her own colour-experience, and, according to the story, their colour-experiences may differ, although they—and we—cannot know that this is so.

Wittgenstein drew certain conclusions about the meaning of the word 'pain' from this story, some of which are valid for the word 'red'. The main point is familiar, but it is worth stating.

[10] We may suppose, that is, that any problems associated with the idea of indicating a certain property, as being possessed by some object in the vicinity, are not at issue.
[11] Wittgenstein (1953: §293). I will assume familiarity with this section of Wittgenstein's book in what follows. The present invocation of Wittgenstein's name may seem misguided to some, but the validity of the ideas is of course independent of their attribution to Wittgenstein.

To make things vivid, suppose that the colour-experiences of the members of the group do differ, as they look together at P, although the members of the group are all ordinarily colour-sighted in the sense defined in §1. (I will consider Wittgenstein's suggestion that one of them may have an 'empty box' in note 13.) Suppose next that lighting conditions are constant, and that P has certain constant light-reflection-and-absorption-and/or-emission properties, or *L-properties*, for short. Suppose, finally, that the colour-experiences of the members of the group, who are all fully competent speakers of English, do not change from time to time, as they look at P.[12] Suppose that all these things are so. What remains true, in the terms of the beetle story, is that 'the thing in the box has no place in the language-game [the language-game for the word "red"] at all'. That is, more generally, facts about what particular colour-experiences speakers of English have when looking at things like pillar boxes are irrelevant to an adequate account of the meaning of the word 'red' in English. That is, the word 'red' carries no reference to any particular sort of colour-experience at all; but to say this is (given §1) in effect to say that it carries no reference to any particular phenomenal quality.[13]

The general point is again familiar. The members of the group certainly all know what the word means, all being competent speakers of English; and since they do not differ at all in what they are disposed to apply the word to, they can all correctly be said to mean the same thing by it. (They don't just agree about what objects it applies to; they agree that it applies to those objects precisely in respect of what they think of as those objects' colour properties.) The respects in which they *do* differ (i.e. their colour-experiences) are therefore entirely irrelevant to the meaning of the word. It follows that reference to particular sorts of colour-experiences—and, hence, particular phenomenal qualities—has no place *at all* in an adequate account of the meaning of the word 'red'. Similarly, since they all have different colour-experiences, in looking at P, there just is no phenomenal colour quality that P has, although P is indeed red; nor is there any phenomenal colour quality that *red* is.

---

[12] The point of this supposition is to put to one side Wittgenstein's remark that 'one might even imagine such a thing [the beetle, the colour-experience] constantly changing'.

[13] Wittgenstein's suggestion (op. cit. §293) that it wouldn't even matter if one of them had an empty box requires a comment. Here are two possible views about it (neither will please some Wittgensteinians). According to the first, the idea is that mastery of the word 'red' could possibly be attained even by one who had no experience at all when appropriately situated vis-à-vis P (the case can easily be restated to fit the word 'pain'). This view is indirectly considered further in §8, in a discussion of the idea that there might be a completely experienceless creature that was, in its behaviour, indistinguishable from an ordinary human being.

A second view is this: *ex hypothesi*, those with beetle-inhabited boxes confront different things, experientially speaking. But the fact that they confront different things doesn't affect their ability to master a common concept in a shared language. In fact it wouldn't even matter if one of them had an empty box. For this—the empty box, or the box's state of being empty—can also be seen as something confronted, experientially speaking, one positive datum among others. On this second view, then, 'empty box' doesn't stand simply for global experiencelessness, as it does on the first view. Instead it is just the limiting case in a range of possible experiences of the pillar box whose difference from person to person is no obstacle to their achieving complete similarity in respect of their mastery of the word 'red'.

3

Consider the way this point can be stated in the terms of the theory of evolution (its speculative division). Just as we differ markedly in eye colour, so we might differ markedly in colour-experience. Environmental pressures have operated to give most human beings similarly sophisticated *discriminatory* capacities vis-à -vis the different L-properties of objects; but it is very hard to imagine what kind of selective pressure there could have been on us not only to evolve a high level of *discriminatory* sensitivity vis-à -vis environmental differences, but also to evolve in such a way that those basic experiences of qualitative difference in which our similar discriminatory capacities are grounded should themselves be qualitatively similar for different people in similar situations. It may be a simple accident that they are thus similar; colour-experience-based discriminatory capacities may have evolved in just one way, and may therefore have a similar phenomenal-quality-experience basis in all ordinarily colour-sighted people. But it seems just as likely that these similar discriminatory capacities are not similarly based in similar phenomenal-quality experience, in different people. The fact that, if these differences in phenomenal-quality experience exist, they do not show up in language (the fact that three ordinary people who are looking at the pillar box and having different colour-experiences will all agree that the colour of the pillar box is red), which is often invoked as the basis for an argument that questions the very *intelligibility* of the idea that they could correctly be said to be having different colour-experiences, can equally well be invoked as supplementary support for the claim that these undeniably possible and very possibly actual differences would not give rise to difference in practical capacities, and so would not affect chances of survival—even when a capacity for linguistic communication with one's conspecifics has been 'selected for' by environmental pressures.

Of course, as remarked, all those human beings who are not colour blind *may* have colour-experiences that are roughly similar, qualitatively speaking, when looking at a pillar box. But, equally, they may not. And even if they do, the logical possibility of their not doing so, and, equally, of other alien and sighted creatures not doing so, remains untouched. And, as I shall try to show, this is what really matters.

In order to get a clearer picture of what is at issue, we may fix a standard of (subjective) colour-experience, by reference to an individual person's colour-experience, and three objects taken to be representative examples of objects coloured red, yellow, and blue. Let Claude Monet (M) be the person, and let a certain British pillar box (P), a certain New York taxi (T), and the inmost division of the French flag currently flying above the Elysée palace (F), be the three objects. We may say that the colours that Monet experiences when looking successively at P, T and F, are, successively, Monet-red (R), Monet-yellow (Y), and Monet-blue (B). Incorporating the reference to Monet (M) into a simple symbolism, we may say that Monet is M(R-Y-B) relative to P-T-F; and then we may say that to be M(R-Y-B) relative to P-T-F is to have 'Monet colour vision'.

Given this standard we can suppose, in a familiar way, that Renoir's colour-experience may be completely 'inverted' (either exactly, or roughly) relative to Monet's;

so that he sees Monet-green (G), Monet-purple/violet (V) and Monet-orange (O) respectively when looking at P, T and F respectively. Renoir is thus M(G-V-O) relative to P-T-F. Speaking in terms of Monet's colour vision, we may say that he sees the colour that is complementary to the colour that Monet sees, when they both look at the same object.

It seems that this could be a consequence of genetic differences between Monet and Renoir. For as far as the genetic determination of the nature of colour-experience is concerned, it seems that the following could be true: there could be two colour-experience-determining genes which are *alleles* of one another. That is, they are each equally capable of occupation of the same 'locus' of the relevant chromosome, to the exclusion of the other. (We could call them the RYB/PTF allele and the GVO/PTF allele.) Monet and Renoir could each have a different one of these alleles determining their colour-experiences. So might you and I. According to genetic theory, alleles are said to compete with each other for occupation of their common potential locus.[14] But it seems clear that nothing could favour the selection of one over the others, in the present case, since it is to be presumed that each gives rise to exactly the same discriminatory capabilities, and it is presumably only these capabilities, not any particular quality of colour-experience (Monet's, say), that have survival value. The point can be put as follows: *discriminatory* capacities are 'selected for' by environmental pressures, and have evolved accordingly. But these discriminatory capacities cannot only be realized in *physically* different ways; they can also be realized in—so to say—*phenomenally* different ways. Monet and Renoir may 'phenomenally realize' exactly the same discriminatory capacities in different ways.[15]

There may very well be different colour-experience-determining alleles in the human gene-pool, then. There may be just two, as in the case above. So the idea that we may *in fact* all have very similar experiences, qualitatively speaking, when looking at P, not only prompts the standard sceptical comment that even if this is so, we simply cannot know that it is. It is also open to the objection that there is no evolutionary advantage for us in our being similar in this way.

4

Before continuing the main argument, it is worth noting that the present total colour-spectrum inversion hypothesis requires that Renoir see Monet-black where Monet sees Monet-white: it requires that Renoir's experiences of relative lightness and darkness be inverted vis-à -vis Monet's just as his colour-experiences are, although they

---

[14] See, for example, Dawkins 1982: 283.

[15] A trait which causes animals to become especially alert in the presence of objects that reflect certain wavelengths of light may be 'naturally selected'. There is apparently good evidence that this is true of monkeys and red objects—i.e. objects that have certain L-properties, and that we call 'red' (Humphrey 1983). But here again there is no selective pressure on animals (human or otherwise) to evolve the same sort of phenomenal experience when they look at objects we call 'red'.

agree in all their judgements about what is lighter than what. This may be thought to create a difficulty.

Suppose, for simplicity, that we are like Monet. We have to suppose not only that black-and-white photographs look to Renoir a bit like photograph negatives look to us, but also that he, like us, finds his way easily about a room that he and we agree to be flooded with light, although his colour-and-lightness experience is in this case something like our experience in a room that is very dark.

It may be objected that we cannot plausibly be supposed to have the same difficulty finding our way about a room that we consider to be very light as people with Renoir vision would have in finding their way about a room that they (speaking from the Monet point of view) experienced as dark (it is only 'Monet-dark', of course; people with Renoir vision will call it 'light', just as we do).

I do not think this objection has much force, however. For, sticking to our own case, consider just how light a room would have to be, for us, if it were really colour-and-lightness inverted relative to a room that we found it hard to find our way about. It would presumably be so light that we could hardly distinguish objects (angles and edges, etc.) in it. Typically, there are strong contrasts in a very light room; these would be preserved in a colour-and-lightness-inverted room. And so it seems that despite the inverted nature of their colour-and-lightness experience relative to ours, people with Renoir vision would find their way about a room that we and they agreed to be very light as easily as we do.

No doubt there are various other difficulties here. I will not pursue them, however. Instead I will take it that Sydney Shoemaker is right to claim that difficulties of the sort discussed in this section do not appear to be of fundamental philosophical importance. As he says,

if spectrum inversion is to be possible, there must be a mapping which maps every determinate shade onto some determinate shade and at least some onto shades other than themselves, which preserves, for any normally sighted person, all the 'distance' and 'betweenness' relationships between the shades.... Even if our color experience is not invertible, it seems obviously possible that there should be creatures, otherwise very much like ourselves, whose color experience does have a structure that allows for such a mapping—creatures whose color experience *is* invertible. And the mere possibility of such creatures is sufficient to raise the philosophical problems the possibility of spectrum inversion has been seen as posing.[16]

It may be objected that in so far as the principal aim of this paper is to make a certain claim about our *actual* colour words, it does presuppose that some sort of colour-spectrum inversion—some sort of systematic difference in colour-experience among human beings who agree in all their colour judgements—is indeed possible given the nature of human colour vision. However this is not quite right, as will emerge in §6. It does not have to be possible for such systematic differences to obtain between different human beings. It will suffice if they can obtain between ordinarily colour-sighted human beings and any being that can learn a human language.

---

[16] Shoemaker 1982: 336. Cf. also McGinn 1982: 35, who considers the simple case in which two creatures have monochromatic vision but in two distinct colours.

It is worth noting that 'sound-space' is, in certain respects at least, much simpler than 'colour-space'. It seems that even if there were insoluble problems in the case of colour, two people *a* and *b* could agree in all their judgements about the pitch of sounds although *a* heard everything five tones higher than *b* (that is, intuitively, if *a* could *per impossibile* hear middle C 'through *b*'s ears', *a* would call it 'G above middle C'). Notice that this could be so even if both *a* and *b* had perfect pitch—the ability, that is, to state the pitch of any note just on hearing it. (All the present arguments about colour adapt to the case of sound pitch.)

It may be objected that the sound case is actually less good than the colour case. For it may be said—roughly—that even if we grant that there is some sense in which the 'raw, uninterpreted' sound received by *a* and *b* can be five tones apart, still their actual sound-*experience* will be a function of their interpretative attitude to the 'raw' sound. So the alleged difference in their experience will in effect disappear, rather as the dramatic difference between *a* and *b*, who are, we may suppose, *ex hypothesi* initially similarly sighted, will disappear as *b* gets used to spectacles or neurological tamperings that turn her experienced visual input upside down.

But however plausible this may seem in the shape-and-space-perception case, there seems to be no reason at all to abandon the intuition that it could just be a simple unknowable fact that *a*'s and *b*'s overall experiences of sounds were five tones apart. We may imagine that they were born with this difference (it would be very strange if human beings did not vary in this respect, given that they vary in every other respect), and have remained with it, just as they may have been born with the colour-spectrum inversion difference. It may be indeterminable whether or not this is so. The hypothesis may be without interest or testable consequences for psychology; but it may still be true, and the possibility of its truth is philosophically important.

5

At the end of §2 it was remarked that reference to particular phenomenal qualities, and to particular colour-experiences, has no place at all in an adequate account of what red is, or of the meaning of 'red'. Presumably anyone who can see that a pillar box is red (and who has mastered the colour vocabulary of a language) must have some colour-experience *or other* (a challenge to this will be considered in §8). But speakers of a common language need not have the same colour-experience as each other. This is an idea familiar from Locke, and, as I understand him, from Wittgenstein.[17] But it is not easy to be precise about what it involves, and about what it obliges us to say about the meaning of 'red'.

Perhaps one could say this: the word 'red' simply holds a more or less determinate place in a *linguistic system of differences*. But it does not hold this place in virtue of

---

[17] Locke 1689–1700: 2.32.15. Kant agrees: 'colours . . . cannot rightly be regarded as properties of things, but only as changes in the subject, changes which may, indeed, be different for different men' (1781–7: B45). It is not clear how this fits with Kant's 'empirical realism', however.

picking out (or 'carrying reference to') a particular phenomenal quality that exists, identifiably, in a *non*-linguistic system of phenomenal-quality differences (although we can describe what it would be to specify such a system, as remarked in §1). Rather the situation is this: the linguistic system of differences consists of a group of words—colour words—none of which carries any sort of reference to any particular phenomenal quality at all. Mastery of this linguistic system of differences is mastery of a common (public) system of differentiation which is ostensibly a system of objective-feature differentiation. It derives its possibility and its point from the fact that, in its own special way, it does indeed provide a representation—a kind of abstract map—of a real, objective structure of non-linguistic differences between physical objects: a structure of differences in L-properties. Each of us has genuine experience of this structure of differences in having colour-experiences. Equally, there is a sense in which we communicate about it, given that the overall structure of our discriminations of the differences (on the basis of our colour-experiences) is more or less the same. But when one says 'red' and, pointing at the pillar box, says, 'That colour, that is', one is wrong to think that one *means*—in any sense—that particular phenomenal quality that one then has experience of oneself, although it is certainly very natural to think this.

One could say that in so far as one does think this, it is because one is not only pointing outwards to the object, but also, covertly or implicitly, inwards to the phenomenal quality one is then experiencing. But in covertly 'pointing' inwards in this way to an experienced (privately experienced) phenomenal quality—one is not pointing to something which is such that reference to it is essential to any adequate account of the meaning of the word (the public word) 'red'; for our colour-experiences enter into the account of the meaning of the word 'red' only in the essentially more indirect way sketched.

The word 'red', then, does not pick out any one, particular phenomenal quality at all. But, it may be said, either it picks out a phenomenal quality or it picks out no quality at all. Hence it does not pick out any property at all.

One principled way of denying this odd-sounding conclusion—which involves identifying the property *red* with a certain L-property of objects—will be considered in §9. Here it may be stressed that even if the odd-sounding conclusion is correct, it remains true that the word 'red' is correctly applied to certain objects. It holds a determinate place in a (public) language, and does so specifically because objects have certain objective properties (L-properties); and, holding the place it does for the reason it does, it enables us to talk about, and plan and co-ordinate action in, the real world. These things are possible even if (even though) we are not affected by the world in such a way that we all have qualitatively similar experiences in similar situations. They are possible because—to rephrase—when we are in some particular visual-experience-inducing situation, our possibly different experiences of the distribution of colours, in the scene that confronts us, are *structurally isomorphic* even if they are qualitatively dissimilar in their character as colour experiences.

6

Can this account of 'red' be held to be correct if all fully colour-sighted human beings do in fact have the same colour-experience, qualitatively speaking, on seeing pillar box P in similar lighting conditions? Well, suppose they do; suppose they all have Monet colour vision; and suppose, for simplicity, that everyone speaks English and only English. Can one then say that 'red' does in fact carry reference to a particular phenomenal quality—the one that all human beings experience when they see a pillar box in ordinary light? No, because there may be Martians. Martians who do not have Monet colour vision but rather Renoir colour vision could arrive on earth and *learn English*. And it seems that when they had done so, there would not be anything they did not know about the meaning of the word 'red'.

Some may disagree. They may compare this case to the imaginary case of human beings born incapable of feeling pain: these people can learn to use the word 'pain' correctly, and yet it seems clear that there is something crucial that they do not know about pain, and, hence, about the meaning of the word 'pain'. Could one say the same about the Martians and the word 'red'? Well, suppose that they settle and breed and share our world and our language. Does the word 'red' still carry reference to a particular phenomenal quality, as time passes—human phenomenal red as opposed to Martian phenomenal red (i.e. Monet-green), as it were? Surely not. Suppose that they slowly displace us, and that we finally become extinct. Does the word 'red' slowly change its meaning, despite a rich practice of unbroken agreement about its proper application? Again, surely not.[18]

Consider another supposition. There are no Martians, and everyone has Monet colour vision except one person, Renoir. Renoir speaks the language as well as any of us, of course. Is he wrong about what 'red' means—in any way at all? Surely not. Some may wish to say that he is wrong. But what if his kind increases—until people with Renoir colour vision outnumber people with Monet colour vision. Does the meaning of the word 'red' change, either gradually, or abruptly? Surely not.

Perhaps there is a certain pull of intuition towards the view that it does change, which may prove irrepressible. But colour words are simply not vulnerable to this kind of change of meaning—precisely because they are not names (or predicates) for specific phenomenal qualities at all. The particular manner in which they are open to being learned or mastered, whether by Monet, Renoir, or Martians, shows that this is so. They are, rather, a set of abstract and in a sense *contentless* (phenomenally speaking contentless) 'difference-markers' that all those who have certain visual-experience-based—colour-experience-based—discriminatory capacities may learn to use fully correctly, and hence fully understand.[19] All those who learn to use colour words in

---

[18] Here some may feel the pull of an analogy with proper names: once 'red' meant—referred to—*this* phenomenal quality (Monet red), but now it refers to a different one (Monet green, or Martian red). Cf. Evans 1973.

[19] The claim that one must have visual experience, and indeed colour experience of the general sort that human beings ordinarily have, in order to know the meaning of colour words, is questioned in §8.

this way come to use them in the same way and with the same *meaning*, in the strongest sense of the phrase 'same meaning'. This is so whatever differences there are in their dispositions to have particular phenomenal-quality experiences (colour-experiences) in particular situations, although it is these dispositions which underlie their possession of the discriminatory capacities which they have in common, and which form the basis of their common ability to master the colour vocabulary of the common language that they speak. In the terms of Wittgenstein's beetle story: even if we do all have the same sort of experiential beetle in our private boxes when we see a thing we all agree to be red, this fact is irrelevant to the question of the meaning of the word 'red'.

The point can be made by reference to the notion of translation. Suppose that the phenomenon of convergent evolution produces two superficially very similar, but genetically very different language-speaking and fully colour-sighted groups of animals on opposite sides of a planet. Suppose that one group—the 'Germans'—has, uniformly, Monet colour vision, and that the other group—the 'Italians'—has, uniformly, Renoir colour vision; and that in one language '*rot*' is the colour word applied to things that have the same sort of L-properties as pillar boxes, while in the other language '*rosso*' is. Suppose next that they meet, and learn each other's languages. Then '*rosso*' is clearly the *correct* translation of '*rot*', and vice versa; these two words mean the same thing. These people *understand* each other. If so, '*rot*' and '*rosso*' cannot be supposed to carry reference to Monet's red and Monet's green respectively, as part of their respective meanings—even though it is *ex hypothesi* true that when the 'Italians' look at pillar boxes they see what Monet would call 'green' if he had the same (colour-)experience as they then had, and when the 'Germans' look at pillar boxes they see what Monet would call 'red', if he had the same (colour-)experience as they then had. The words '*rot*' and '*rosso*' cannot carry these different references, for they mean the same thing, and Monet's red and Monet's green are two very different things. They are two very different phenomenal qualities, named here by reference to Monet in the way laid down in §3.

Some may not be convinced. They may deny that '*rosso*' is clearly the correct translation of '*rot*', in this case. But to this the following reply seems decisive. Imagine that the two groups intermingle after meeting, 'Italians' settling among 'Germans' and vice versa, but that they cannot interbreed, and so retain their colour vision distinctness as non-interbreeding species. Time passes, and in the end many 'Italians' grow up speaking 'German' (and vice versa). It would be absurd to say that such 'German'-speaking 'Italians' are wrong about what '*rot*' means, or that they are wrong, as bilinguals, to think that '*rot*' means the same as '*rosso*'.

7

In this paper, conclusions about the proper account of the meaning of a word are drawn by reference to statements about what may come to be the case, or what may actually be the case, but unknowably so. This may be objected to. It may again be suggested that the truth about the meaning of the word 'red' depends partly on such

things as whether ordinarily colour-sighted people do as a matter of (again unknowable) contingent fact all have more or less the same colour-experiences in similar circumstances.[20] If they do, it may be said, then part of the meaning of the word 'red'
is indeed that it carries reference to a particular phenomenal quality. But this suggestion is open to many objections that have already been stated. Here one may add that
it also has the counter-intuitive consequence that we cannot know what the truth is
about the meaning of the word 'red'. We have to say 'It may mean this, or it may not;
we cannot be sure'. And this seems highly objectionable. The present line of argument is not open to such an objection. But then, it does have the arguably equally
objectionable consequence that nearly all English speakers are wrong about what 'red'
really means (even after they have accepted that there is a sense in which colours are
'not really in objects', being merely 'secondary qualities'), in so far as they naturally
take it to carry reference to some single, determinate phenomenal quality that all
ordinarily colour-sighted people have experience of when they look at things like pillar boxes. I think that this consequence must be accepted, however. Relations between
experience, language, and the world are more complicated than we ordinarily suppose. (Here I consider the complications that arise in the case of a single word, but
the general point has wide application.)

8

A question may now be raised about an alien being, *A*, that has, *ex hypothesi*, no visual
or colour-experience at all, but learns to use colour words on the basis of some entirely
non-visual, *non*-colour-experience-based sensitivity to the L-properties of objects.
Why deny that *A* too fully understands the meaning of the word 'red', given that it
agrees with the rest of us in all its judgements about the colours of objects, and, unlike
B, a man blind from birth, can apparently identify objects as red *directly*, without
making use of any knowledge about properties invariably associated with redness? (*B*
can know that something is red if he knows that it is blood, or a ripe tomato. But
in the absence of such information about properties invariably associated with being
red, he cannot identify anything as red on the basis of his sensory experience.)

It is instructive to compare *A* and *B*, the alien and the blind man. *B* can learn to
use the word 'red' correctly, of course.[21] And yet one is strongly inclined to say that
there is something crucial that he does not know about the meaning of the word.
One important reason why one is inclined to say this is probably that one tends, mistakenly, on the present view, to think of 'red' as carrying reference to a particular

[20] 'More or less' allows for differences of brightness and dullness; for the fact that *a*'s vision may
be uniformly slightly tinged with brown, relative to *b*'s, and so on. Such differences between human
beings almost certainly exist, and suffice to establish that specific colour words like 'Pillar Box Red
Standard Colour No. 12345' cannot be supposed to refer to some particular phenomenal quality.

[21] This is so although his ability to apply the word is of course limited, relative to ours; he is
not in a position to apply it correctly in all those situations in which ordinarily colour-sighted
people are.

phenomenal quality—that particular phenomenal quality that one sees oneself when looking at a pillar box in normal light; and this reason is entirely undermined when one sees that the word 'red' cannot be construed as a name for (as carrying reference to) a particular phenomenal quality at all. But even after granting this one may still plausibly insist that *B* does not fully (or really) understand the meaning of the word 'red', simply because he has no colour-experience at all, nor any real conception of what colour-experience is. And one could do the same in the case of *A*, the non-visual alien: one could say that *A*'s apparently perceptually direct ability to identify objects as red is really indirect. For the situation is this: objects that we call 'red' cause a certain sensation S_1 in *A*, given its *ex hypothesi* non-visual sensory modality; objects that we call 'yellow' cause a certain other such sensation S_2, and so on. And they cause these sensations because of the L-properties that they have. *A* cottons on to this pattern of association between its sensations and our colour words. It learns to use our colour vocabulary because a certain pattern of word usage fits exactly with a certain salient pattern of sensations that it has, and it finds these words useful in communication (as well as finding the sensations interesting in themselves, perhaps).

This description of how the alien learns to use colour words is very general, and as such it applies equally to human beings. The difference between the alien and a human being is this: the human being's pattern of sensations is a pattern of *visual, colour*-experiences, whereas the alien's pattern of sensations is a pattern of (to us mysterious) *ex hypothesi* non-visual sensations. It is simply this difference that leads most people to say that there is something crucial that the alien does not know about what it is for something to be red, and, hence, about the meaning of the word 'red'. This is so, they will say, even though the alien's ability to use the word fully matches our ability to use it, unlike the blind man's, and even though it is not the case that the word 'red' can be supposed to carry reference to a particular phenomenal quality.

Others may demur. They may say that the alien does fully understand the meaning of the word 'red', and that although its mysterious non-visual sensations are by hypo-thesis qualitatively speaking very unlike any human colour-experiences, the mere fact that these sensations make it possible for the alien to match us fully in our ability to make colour-judgements show that we must include them under the heading of colour-experiences.

Now those who say this agree with the central claim of this paper; for they agree that the word 'red' carries no reference to any one particular phenomenal quality of the sort we can be said to have experience of when we have human colour-experience. But they go further. For they claim (contrary to §6 above) that to experience that something is red one need not even have some visual experience *or other*, let alone some colour-experience or other (i.e. some experience that we would ordinarily call 'colour-experience').

The natural reply to this is simple: the alien does not fully understand the English word 'red', because one cannot possibly fully understand the word 'red' unless one has visual experience (or has at some time had visual experience, at least). For one cannot fully understand the word 'red' unless one knows what colour is *like*, and it is a necessary truth that the what-it-is-like-ness of colours is apprehended only in visual experience. And this is so even if (even though) colour words like 'red' cannot be supposed to pick out any one particular visual what-it-is-likeness.

This looks like an obvious move. But there are various other options. Some may be inclined simply to reject the alleged necessary connection between fully understanding the meaning of the word 'red' and having (or having had) visual experience, given the case for saying that the alien does fully understand the word. Others, alternatively, may accept the necessary connection between fully understanding the word 'red', and visual experience, and accordingly challenge the claim that the alien cannot be said to see, or have visual experience. For it has a capacity to detect objects and certain of their properties at a distance on the basis of a certain kind of sensitivity to its L-properties, and it can exercise the full English colour vocabulary (and, we may suppose, shape and size vocabulary) correctly and directly on the basis of this capacity; and it may be said that this is all that is crucial, so far as the question of what seeing is is concerned.

How, after all, can we know that half the human race is not in fact something like the alien, in respect of those sensations on the basis of which it detects objects and their features at a distance—so that what we call 'visual experience', and apply to sighted human beings generally, in fact covers two radically different sorts of experience? Here it has simply been assumed that all those whom we call ordinarily colour-sighted people are alike in respect of having what has been called 'human colour-experience': it has simply been assumed that they are alike in having sensory experience that is, qualitatively speaking, of a certain single *general* kind (which we call 'visual' experience), even if they do not have the same *particular* colour-experiences, qualitatively speaking, as they look together at a pillar box. But this assumption may be false.[22] Furthermore, if the Martians arrived on earth, and behaved exactly as if they could see in the way that we do (as is *ex hypothesi* the case with the alien, *A*), then we would naturally and reasonably be led to say that they saw, whatever the precise and unknowable nature of the sensory experiences which led them to behave in this way. The fact that this is so is a fact about the word 'see' as we currently have it. It appears to follow that it is reasonable to say that *A* can see, and has visual experience.

No doubt the suggestion about how the human race might see in two very different ways is not very convincing; but there is no need to pursue the point here. The issues it raises are I think clear enough, and I wish now to put them aside in order to concentrate on some further questions.

For this reason I will now make the following explicit commonsense assumptions:

(1) that one cannot fully understand the meaning of the word 'red' unless one has (or has had) *visual* experience;

---

[22] I don't suppose it is, but appeals to general similarity of physiology are arguably not decisive, so far as the attempt to deny that there could be such major differences of experience among different human beings is concerned; for the link between physiology and the very existence of sensory experience, let alone the particular nature of experience, is (and seems likely to remain) mysterious.

(2) that 'visual experience' is correctly taken to be the name of one particular general *type* of sensory experience, where the *nature* of the type of experience is understood to be *essentially qualitatively defined, at least in part;*[23]

(3) that all those human beings who seem able to see do in fact have such visual experience in common (though they may still differ as Monet, Renoir, and the colour-blind man do).

In the same way I assume:

(4) that '*colour*-experience' (as opposed e.g. to shape-experience) stands for one particular general qualitative characteristic of visual experience as just characterized;

(5) that all those human beings who qualify as ordinarily colour-sighted do in fact have the same *general* sort of colour-experience in common, even though they may still differ in having Monet or Renoir colour vision.

Assumptions (2)–(5) amount to explicitly assuming the truth of the common-sense view that all human beings who seem able to see, and to distinguish colours, are able to do so on the basis of having the same *general* sort of experience, qualitatively speaking. *That* sort of experience is what is now under discussion. What sort, exactly? Well, those of us who can see colours know what it is like to have this sort of experience—each from his or her own case. So they know what is being talked about, given the above assumptions.

The practical consequence of these assumptions is simply to limit consideration of the many possible differences between the experience of different beings to differences like the differences between beings with Monet colour vision and beings with Renoir colour vision; thereby omitting consideration of further possible differences, like the differences between Monet and the alien *A*. The crucial justification for making these assumptions is that the further possible differences only complicate the general issue, and do not change it fundamentally. (At various points, however, I will draw attention to the fact that these assumptions have been made. Dropping them leads to an even more radical version of the claim that 'red' cannot be supposed to pick out any particular phenomenal quality.)

I will also ignore those problems that can be raised by reference to the idea that there could logically possibly be a 'zombie', i.e. an entirely experienceless being *E* that was indistinguishable from an ordinary human being in all behavioural respects even

---

[23] In particular, it is not merely functionally or causally defined. Thus *visual experience* is experience which has a particular sort of general qualitative character. It cannot be fully defined in causal and functional terms, as experience which is (i) characteristically caused by the incidence of light upon light-sensitive sense organs, and which (ii) characteristically enables one to detect objects and certain of their properties at a distance, because these clauses fail to exclude the alien *A*. Indeed it seems that claims like (i) and (ii) do not even form part of the definition of 'visual experience', as currently understood. Certainly they form part of the definition of 'to see', or 'vision'. But they do not seem to be necessary to the definition of 'visual experience', because it is conceivable that a creature *C* could be so constituted that air-waves that cause auditory experiences in us caused colour- and shape-experiences in it. *C* would thus have *visual experience*, in the present sense, but would not be able to *see* in any sense. There are many other odd possibilities.

though it had no experience at all (even though there was nothing it was like to be it, experientially speaking).[24]

Here again at least two attitudes are possible: even if one is inclined to grant that the alien *A* can be said to see (despite the fact that the experiential basis of its ability to detect objects and certain of their properties at a distance, as a result of a certain kind of sensitivity to their L-properties, is non-visual, and is *ex hypothesi* qualitatively unlike the experiential basis of our own detection ability), one may still deny that *E* can be said to see, since its ability to detect objects and certain of their properties at a distance has (for it) no experiential basis at all. (Note that this may be so even if its ability is causally based on a certain sensitivity to their L-properties, as in the case of an experienceless machine equipped with photosensitive cells.)

If, alternatively, one adopts a certain sort of radically functionalist position, one may wish to claim (however implausibly) that *E* has to be credited with a genuine visual capacity given its capacity to detect objects and certain of their properties at a distance.[25]

9

Now consider a different supposition that may be thought to create difficulties for the present view of the meaning of 'red'. (It is likely to be advanced in direct opposition to the conclusion reached earlier that the word 'red' does not pick out any determinate property at all, either of objects, or of the content of experiences.)

It may be said—it has been said—that one can define 'red' in terms of the L-properties of objects; and that the true meaning of the word 'red', as applied to objects, is 'reflects light of wavelengths of between x and y, or z and w, or . . . nanometres, or emits light of wavelengths of between x and y, or z and w, or . . . nanometres.[26] This is offered as an a posteriori truth: we cannot be absolutely sure that it is true; we might always have counted the units wrongly, or we might conceivably be wrong about the whole physical transaction, the nature of light, and so on. But if it is true, then it is necessarily true (like the statement that platinum has atomic number 78).[27]

---

[24] Cf. §2 above, and Wittgenstein's remark (op cit., §293) that 'the thing in the box has no place in the language-game at all; not even as a *something*: for the box might even be empty'.

[25] Many positions are possible. Ordinarily, we accept both (i) that *experience* is necessary for vision and (ii) that no capacity to detect objects and certain of their properties at a distance can be called a visual capacity unless it is (unlike sonar, for example) essentially based on sensitivity to the L-properties of objects. But it seems that one could conceivably reject (i) and accept (ii). Again, one could accept (ii) while ruling out the suggestion that use of a 'tactile-visual substitution system' or 'TVSS' can count as a way of seeing—cf. Peacocke 1983: 15. Alternatively, one might accept (i), and reject (ii)—see Dawkins 1986: 33–5, for the suggestion that echolocating bats might reasonably be said to see.

[26] This is entirely schematic; the physics of colour is complicated and surprising (cf. Westphal, 1986: esp. 325–6), but not, I trust, in a way that matters here.

[27] Cf. Kripke 1972: 116–28. An alternative suggestion is that the word 'red' picks out whatever the physical ground(s) of the disposition to reflect or emit light of this wavelength is (are). I will not consider this alternative, because the differences between this suggestion and the suggestion discussed in the text are not of any present importance.

A natural response to a definition of this kind is to say that in excluding all reference to experience, or to phenomenal appearance (a pleonasm), it leaves out what is most essential to the meaning of 'red': for 'colours are visibilia or they are nothing'.[28] That is, in the present terms, any adequate account of the meaning of colour words must capture the fundamental point that, whatever else they are, colour words are words for properties whose essential nature as properties can be and is fully revealed in sensory (and indeed visual) experience, given only the qualitative character that sensory (visual) experience has. (Look at the brightly coloured books.) 'In the case of a quality like red, experiential facts are *constitutive* of the presence of the quality in question.... To grasp the concept of red [and, hence, the meaning of "red"] it is necessary to know what it is for something to look red, since this latter constitutes the satisfaction condition for an object's being red'; and such knowledge of what it is for something to look red is 'available only to someone who enjoys... certain kinds of experience'.[29]

On this view, if *a* is fully to understand the meaning of the word 'red', he must not only have (or once have had) (1) *visual* experience (cf. assumption (2) in §8); he must also have (or once have had) (2) *colour*-experience (cf. assumption (4) in §8). And even that is not enough. For he must also have (or once have had) what one could call (3) *red*-experience—experience of, specifically, red.

This last claim may look very surprising, given the argument so far. But in fact one must add something like (3) to (1) and (2), and this is so even though the phrase 'experience of red' does not name a particular qualitative experience. For (3) makes the point that in order to have acquired a fully-fledged understanding of the word 'red' in the first place, *a* must have been such that when he looked (in normal circumstances) at objects generally agreed to be red he had some colour-experience or other which, given its qualitative character as a colour-experience, enabled him to distinguish such objects reliably, in respect to their colour, from all other objects generally agreed to be not red.[30] (It points out that he must either still be like this, or must once have been like this.) It does *not* say that he must when looking at objects generally agreed to be red have had some one qualitatively specific colour-experience, i.e., '*the* experience of red'—that non-existent thing.[31]

In order to see the necessity of condition (3), consider two beings who fail to fulfil it: (i) an ordinarily colour-sighted being b_1 that lives in a yellow-(green)-blue world where, contingently, only two of the three primary colours are to be found (ordinarily

---

[28] P. F. Strawson 1979: 56.   [29] McGinn 1983: 8.

[30] So if *a* is 'red-green' colour blind as we say, he cannot be said to understand fully what 'red' means. This would be so even if, as a matter of unknowable fact, (a) all ordinarily colour-sighted people had Monet colour vision, and (b) *a* did in fact (and implausibly) experience all red and green objects, in respect of their colour, in exactly the way all ordinarily colour-sighted people experience things like pillar boxes.

[31] Nor does it rule out the possibility that he changes in a weekly cycle from Monet to Renoir vision without realizing that this is so, on account of matching changes in memory. For he can on this basis retain the right object-discriminating capacities. (To say this is to agree with Wittgenstein, although not perhaps in a way he would have approved of, that 'one might even imagine [the beetle in the box—the subjective colour-experience] constantly changing'.) I will not consider this sort of possibility further.

colour-sighted human beings would all agree it was a yellow-(green)-blue world, if transported there as observers); and (ii) a being b_2 that lives in our world and has yellow-(green)-blue vision, but not red vision, red being for it like grey is for us. b_2 can match us in yellow-(green)-blue identifications, but cannot distinguish red from grey, or light grey from pink. Clearly, b_1 and b_2 have (1) vision and (2) colour-experience, but they fail to fulfil condition (3) above, and so they do not have the concept of red, or know what 'red' means.[32]

10

This sort of response to the unqualified L-property-definition approach looks very strong. It seems clear that a person who knows all about wavelengths of light, but who has been blind from birth, or, better, has only black-and-white (or, generally, monochromatic) vision, does not really know what 'red' means. Such a person does not really possess the concept of red at all, although able to master the use of the word well enough. The same goes for the alien in §8. It is indeed a necessary truth that colours are directly apprehended only in visual experience, and that if you don't know what it is for something to *look* red, you don't know what red is.

However, even if we continue to assume that 'visual experience' does indeed name one particular, qualitatively distinctive mode of sensory experience (thereby ignoring the problems raised in §8, and then put to one side by means of assumption (2)), there is a difficulty with this response that should by now be familiar: it encourages (without necessitating) a number of presumptions. It encourages the presumption

[32] This may seem odd. For suppose once again (a) that all ordinarily colour-sighted human beings in fact have Monet colour vision; (b) that all inhabitants of the yellow-(green)-blue world have Renoir colour vision; (c) that b_2 also has Renoir colour vision. In this case, the beings on the yellow-(green)-blue world see it as Monet purple/violet-(red)-orange (i.e. they have experiences which are just like the sorts of colour-experiences we have when looking at things like violets, pillar boxes, and oranges). Similarly, b_2 sees our world as Monet purple-(red)-orange. Nevertheless it is true to say that b_2 cannot distinguish red from grey, or light grey from pink—even though we can, by referring to the Monet-based standard of subjective colour-experience, perfectly well say that what he cannot distinguish is Monet green from grey, or Monet light green from light grey. Do suppositions (a)–(c) force us to say that b_1 and b_2 do after all have the concept of red, although neither we nor they know it? No—to think this is to relapse once again into the view that the word 'red' picks out a determinate phenomenal quality. b_2 can be said to possess the concept of red (in a way that the congenitally blind man does not) only if he can (was once able to) apply the word 'red' correctly and directly on the basis of his visual experience (in ordinary lighting circumstances). And he can't (never could).

As for the inhabitants of the yellow-(green)-blue world: if we travel there, and enter into communication with them, then whatever words they use for the colours of objects we call 'yellow', 'green', and 'blue' will *mean* the same as our words 'yellow', 'green', and 'blue', even if their colour-experience of objects we call 'yellow', 'green', and 'blue' respectively is qualitatively just like our colour-experience of objects we call 'purple/violet', 'red', and 'orange' respectively. (This is like the case of the 'Germans' and the 'Italians'.) These creatures cannot be supposed to possess the concept of red, whatever the particular qualitative character of their colour-experiences. This may seem very implausible. But its apparent implausibility may exactly match its value as an illustration

(1) that (to put it bluntly) an object's *looking red* is its possessing a determinate phenomenal quality, this phenomenal quality being conceived to be a property of the object in the fullest sense;[33]

and

(2) that the *experience of something's looking red* is therefore similarly determinate in having a (more or less) fixed qualitative character.

Now entails the view

(3) that to say that *a* has an experience of something's looking red is to say that he has (more or less) the same experience (the same experience *qualitatively* speaking) as anyone else who is said to have an experience of something's looking red.

And the final stage of this line of thought, whether or not it is made explicit, is

(4) that it is because of the truth of what has just been said in (1)–(3) about *looking red* and *the experience of something's looking red* that these are notions that one can profitably (and indeed must) appeal to in one's analysis of the meaning of the word 'red'. They provide a fixed point, as it were, something determinate that ties the analysis of 'red' down to some single feature of objective or at least intersubjective reality.

This line of thought is completely at odds with the view developed in this paper. Yet it starts from the obviously sound idea that *some* sort of reference to experience, and to how things look, must enter into any adequate account of the meaning of colour words: L-properties are not enough.

There are two particular objections to it. Both are by now familiar. The first is that one cannot know that it is true that two people who are alike in that something now *looks red* to each of them are also alike in respect of the colour-experience they are having. (It is probably not true, even among human beings.) And if it is not true, then (1)–(3) are all indefensible. For it is at least a necessary condition of *looking red*'s (or indeed *red*'s) being a determinate phenomenal quality (of objects) that all ordinarily colour-sighted beings should be affected in (more or less) the same way in respect of colour-experience by pillar boxes. Only something of this sort can 'constitute the fact' of *red*'s or *looking red*'s being a determinate phenomenal quality. (The view that it is sufficient is rejected in §6.)

The second objection is that whether or not ordinary colour-sighted people do have qualitatively similar colour-experience in similar situations, it is neither necessary nor correct to incorporate the view that they do in one's analysis of 'red'. Certainly, if a being has full mastery of the concept of red, then there must be (or have

---

of the oddity, the semantic abstractness, the phenomenal contentlessness, of colour words and concepts (see further §11).

[33] For purposes of discussion I here admit this natural use of the phrase 'phenomenal quality', which corresponds to the ordinary non-philosophical view of objects as mind-independently coloured; the complication that underlies this natural use is set out in §13: although colour words are phenomenal-quality words, and although to talk of phenomenal qualities is just to talk in a certain way of the qualitative character of experience, nevertheless colour words are correctly applied to objects.

been) some particular sort of (visual and indeed colour-) experience which constitutes (or constituted) a thing's looking, specifically, red to it.[34] But, once again, the particular qualitative character of its (visual and indeed colour-) experience of something's looking red needn't be (have been) the same—even roughly—as mine or yours. There is just no such thing as *the* experience of something's looking red, where this is conceived as something which has some one particular qualitative character as an experience.

There is of course an interpersonally applicable notion of *something's looking red*; for *x*, *y*, and *z* can undeniably agree, and be right, about what looks red and what does not. But, once again, we cannot suppose this notion of something's looking red to be characterizable by reference to any one particular phenomenal-quality experience. (Nor, therefore, can we suppose the concept of red *tout court* to be so characterizable.) Indeed it will now be argued that we cannot even suppose the notion of something's looking red to be characterizable independently of reference to the notion of possession of *linguistic abilities*; or, in particular, independently of reference to grasp of the meaning of the word 'red' or some word meaning the same as 'red'.[35]

This claim looks very odd. It seems clearly right to say that animals without linguistic abilities can have colour-experience that is just like our own. Furthermore, it seems that there could have been such animals even if no creatures with linguistic abilities had ever evolved. But the argument for the claim may be worth considering. For although it is in one sense trivially true, given its chosen terms, and in another sense highly implausible, it may yet dramatize the special nature of words like 'red'—and thus some central complexities of the relations between mind, language, and reality—in a helpful way.

11

Colour-experience precedes and is independent of language mastery. Animals have it. It is very curious to claim that no sense can be given to the general notion of something's looking red or blue independently of reference to language, and to the notion of creatures possessed of mastery of the use of words like 'red' and 'blue'. It looks like a *reductio* of the basis of the claim. But the key point is familiar.

Suppose that something—P—now looks red both to me and to you, and that we know that this is so, in the ordinary sense of 'know': here we are, sane and sober, we

---

[34] Here I am once again ignoring the issues about the nature of visual and colour-experience put to one side by explicit assumption in §8. Clearly, dropping the assumptions in §8 simply multiplies the objections to the idea that 'red' picks out some particular phenomenal property. I am also ignoring the complicating possibility that a being may acquire and retain mastery of the concept of red even though its colour-experience is changing from day to day—either detectably or undetectably (see n31).

[35] I am ignoring problems that arise from the much discussed difficulties of translating colour words.

both speak good English, we agree that P looks red, we agree in all our other colour judgements, and so on.

We know, then, that we *resemble* each other in this respect—in respect of possessing the property of being such that P *looks red* to each of us. But what exactly does this resemblance—call it 'R1'—consist in? It seems that one cannot give an adequate account of it without reference to our linguistic abilities and dispositions. For it seems that the *only* way in which we necessarily exactly resemble each other, in both being such that something now looks red to each of us, is that as we each have whatever colour-experience we do have, we resemble each other in both being in some state which is such that we are disposed to *say* or *judge* that P is or looks red (and hence also to act in non-linguistic ways that show that we judge that P is or looks red). Call this resemblance 'R2'. But if one cannot give an account of what it is for two beings to *resemble* each other in both being such that something looks red to them (an account of R1) without reference to R2, then it seems that one cannot give an account of what it is for something to *look red* without reference to R2.

The idea behind this is again familiar. (1) Although it is true that we *may* also resemble each other—call this resemblance 'R3'—in having qualitatively similar colour-experience in this situation, (i) this is not something we can know to be so (you may be Renoir, I may be Monet), (ii), more importantly, it has been argued at length that it simply does not matter whether or not we do so resemble each other. But (2) it does not seem that any *other* resemblance between us (any resemblance other than R2 or R3) could possibly be essential, so far as our complete (R1-) resemblance in respect of the fact that P looks red to each of us is concerned. So (3) R2 is essential to R1, since R3 is not. It appears to follow that languageless beings cannot be said to be such that things look red to them; for they cannot resemble us in respect of having this property unless they resemble us in respect of R2, which they cannot do.

Someone will say: if the colour-experience of all fully colour-sighted human beings is in fact qualitatively speaking very similar, and if there are languageless animals whose colour-experience is, in fact, qualitatively speaking just (or very) like that of human beings, then it is just obviously true to say of those animals that things look red or blue to them in just the way they do to us, although they have no language—and even if we can never know that it is true.

Reasonable though this sounds, the old objection recurs: we are unable to know that human colour-experience *is* qualitatively speaking similar from person to person, and we are not justified in supposing (roughly) that the phrase 'the state of being such that something looks red to one' names some single, determinate experiential state S_1 which possesses some particular qualitative character specifically qua colour-experience-involving state.[36] If we could suppose this, and could (roughly) equate 'being such that P looks red to one' with 'being in S_1 on account of looking at P',

---

[36] Cf. §§6–7, where it was argued that even if we could know this we would not be justified in supposing that this phrase named a determinate experiential state, given Martians, and the mere possibility of future divergence in human colour-experience.

then we could indeed say that P may (unknowably) look red to animals, just as it does to us; for animals might, like us, unknowably be in S_1 when looking at P.[37] But we cannot suppose this. For you and I may (sincerely) agree that P looks red, genuinely resembling each other in being such that P looks red to each of us, while you are in S_1 and I am in a qualitatively different state S_2. And so it seems that we can say that P looks red to both of us only because we agree or are disposed to agree in language that it is red.[38] To suppose that unknowable but possible similarity of colour-experience is what really matters is to accept that no two people can ever know that something looks red or blue to both of them, despite the evident fact of their agreement about its colour. It is to treat colour words as names for private and incommunicable sensations. It is to misunderstand the nature and logic of colour words.[39]

It looks, then, as if our agreeing or being able to agree in language that P and F are red and blue respectively is *essential* to the possibility of our being similar in our possession of the property of being such that P and F look red and blue to us; for as far as colour-experience goes, we may not be similar at all. It appears to follow that P and F can be said to look red and blue to the languageless animal as they do to us only if the animal can agree linguistically that they are red and blue. For only in this way can it *fulfil the requisite similarity condition*, and so correctly be said to have the *same property* as we do—the property of being such that P and F look red and blue to it. But the animal is, *ex hypothesi*, languageless.

Imagine a history of the universe in which we do not come to exist, and in which there are no linguistic beings, but in which there are animals—rather like ring-tailed lemurs, say—that have the same discriminatory capacities vis-à -vis the L-properties of objects as we do. There is no type of colour-experiential state S_1 which is such that if they have it, on looking at certain objects of type O, we can say that O-objects *look red* to them; for there is no type of colour-experiential state which is either necessary or sufficient for being such that something looks red to one. Even if they did all have the same colour-experiences, on looking at objects with L-properties like those of P, there would be no point to saying that those objects *looked red* to them. This notion would not get any grip in their universe (or in our account of it), in the absence of the phenomenon of linguistic agreement that things looked red, since it cannot be grounded by reference to any particular colour-experiential state.

None of this is going to stop people talking of things looking red to monkeys, say, if monkeys have a discernibly regular reaction to all those things we call 'red'. And it may yet be said that a sufficient condition for a languageless being to be such that something looks red to it can be stated roughly as follows: something looks red to it if (a) it is looking at an object that reflects or emits light that has a wavelength of between x and y or. . . ., nanometres (see §8), and (b) it has the same sorts of

---

[37] Here as elsewhere I presuppose normal lighting conditions. (There is no need here to consider the fact that a white object seen in red light (e.g.) can correctly be said to look white to one even though there is also a sense in which it may be causing the same colour-experiential state in one that a pink object seen in normal light may cause in one.)

[38] We can correctly be said to be so disposed, now, even if we would have to have learnt (part at least of) a common language before we could actually so agree.

[39] This sort of position is traditionally associated with Locke; but see n49.

vision-dependent discriminatory capacities, in respect of the L-properties of objects, as ordinarily colour-sighted human beings. This suggestion is no doubt sensible enough; but the main point of the argument of this section remains untouched.

Similarly, a child's present (or future) mastery of colour vocabulary may be held to give good grounds for saying that things looked (look) red and blue to it, as they do to us, before it had (has) learnt to speak. There is no need to object to this, given the present argument. What matters is simply the way in which possible differences in colour-experience (in two beings who agree on what things are red) raise a problem about what can ground the judgement that two beings resemble each other in being such that something looks red to both of them.[40]

1 2

The L-property-definition approach to the meaning of 'red' considered in §9 prompted a series of linked objections.

(1) It ignores the fact that 'colours are visibilia or they are nothing' (§9): 'red' does not just pick out a certain L-property of objects, nor does it pick out the physical ground (or grounds) of any such property. (If it did, both the non-visual alien and the blind man discussed in §8 could know as well as we do what red is, and what 'red' means.)

(2) Connectedly, it ignores the fact that reference to experience has to enter into any adequate account of the meaning of 'red' (§9): it ignores the sense in which it is true that 'experiential facts are *constitutive* of the presence of . . . a quality like red'.

(3) In §11 an argument was presented for the claim that reference to language-ability is also necessary in an account of the meaning of 'looks red': to look red is not to look any particular way; one has to analyse 'to look red' partly in terms of 'to be called (or adjudged) "red" '. If valid, this argument should have consequences for an adequate account of the meaning of 'is red', given that, for any object *o*, '*o* is red if and only if *o* looks red (in normal circumstances)' is a conceptual or a priori truth.[41]

In order to assess these objections further, it is worth briefly considering the relations between (i) '*o* is red'; (ii) '*o* looks red'; and (iii) '*x* is such that something looks red to *x*'. Perhaps the whole puzzle about 'red' can be stated in terms of the connections between the properties attributed by these expressions.

---

[40] Perhaps it should be noted that the idea that systematic differences in the colour-experiences of beings who agree in all their colour judgements might be undiscoverable plays no essential part in the present argument. On the contrary: if it were discoverable that people who agreed completely in all their colour judgements could differ in their colour-experiences, this would just provide further support for the present view.

[41] Cf. McGinn 1983: 20. The relations between 'is red' and 'looks red' are also discussed in Peacocke, op cit., 28–44.

(iii) is clearly an experiential property of experiencing beings. (i) is ostensibly a non-experiential property of objects. (ii) is also ostensibly a non-experiential property of objects; but we cannot analyse ostensibly non-experiential property (i) by reference to ostensibly non-experiential property (ii) without reference to experiential property (iii). For we cannot understand the notion of *o*'s possessing the property (ii) of looking red apart from the notion of *o*'s possessing the property of looking red *to someone*—that is, apart from introducing reference to the notion of beings that have or can have the experiential property (iii) of being such that *o* looks red to them.

But it is not only the case that we must move from talking of ostensibly non-experiential properties to talking of an experiential property (from (i) and (ii) to (iii)), when trying to give an account of the meaning of 'red'. What is also true is that this experiential property (iii)—the property of *being such that something looks red to one*—is itself no more available as a primitive notion which is in no need of further analysis, and which is therefore an unproblematic starting point for analysis of 'red', than (ii)—the property of *looking red*. For, once again, the expression 'being such that something looks red to one' does not pick out any qualitatively speaking single or determinate experiential state: the colour-experiences of two beings about whom it is a given fact that they both have the property of being such that something now looks red to them, may for all we know be different. And it seems that the only way in which we can capture the respect in which they are definitely similar, in both being such that something looks red to them, is by reference to the fact that they are both reliably disposed to *call* the thing in question 'red' in some language.[42]

The situation is then this:

(I)   One promising line of departure, in the analysis of 'red', or (i) '*o* is red', involves reference to (ii) '*o* looks red'.

(II) Analysis of (ii) involves reference to (iii) '*x* is such that *o* looks red to *x*'.

(III) Analysis of (iii) apparently involves reference to (iv) '*x* is such that *x* is disposed to call *o* "red".'[43]

This may now look like a blatant circularity: trying to analyse the word 'red', one refers in (iv) to the very same word. But there is no circularity. For at stage III, the word 'red' is not itself used. Instead reference is made *to* its use, and to the crucial notion of mastery of its use, and it—the word 'red'—is merely mentioned, in order for that reference to be made. Indeed it is only at stage III that the (apparently benign) circularity that *does* affect analyses of 'red' that retain essential reference to subjective experience and the looks of things—analyses, e.g., that claim (as at stage I) that to *be* red is (simply) to *look* red (in ordinary light)—disappears. For it is only

---

[42] As remarked at the end of §11, one may then establish a derivative sense in which things may be said to look red to languageless animals if those animals have the same (vision-based—see §8) *discriminatory* capacities vis-à-vis the L-properties of objects as ordinarily colour-sighted human beings.

[43] Or at least—see the preceding note—'*x* is such that *x* has the same sort of vision-based discriminatory capacities vis-à-vis the L-properties of objects as some *y* who is disposed to call *o* "red" in some language (in normal circumstances etc.)'. Even if this is acceptable, the reference to language is ineliminable; as it is not in the case of a word like 'gold', say.

at stage III that the phrase 'looks red', which contains a *use* of the word 'red', is eliminated—being further analysed by reference to the notion of mastery of the *word* 'red' (here the word 'red' is mentioned, not used).[44]

It may yet be objected that the analytic sequence is no good, because it can be summarized as follows.

(1) To be red is to look red (in ordinary light, etc.).
(2) To look red (in ordinary light, etc.) is to be called 'red'.

But (1) and (2) together entail

(3) To be red is to be called 'red'.

And so it looks as if we may be obliged to say (a) that a thing is red because it is called 'red', rather than saying (b) that it is called 'red' because it is red. And this is unacceptable.

We can reject this suggestion, however (though it contains an important element of truth about the logic of colour words). We are not in fact obliged to make the first 'because' claim, (a). We are not obliged to make a 'because' claim at all; the 'is' of (3) does not license the 'because' either of (a) or of (b).

Still, we may regard it as essential to any adequate account of the meaning of the word 'red' that it permit us to assert something like (b), the second 'because' claim, and to uphold the common-sense view that a thing is called 'red' because it is red. And it may be asked what grounds have we got left for saying this.

Well, in order to assert something like (b) we need some single, non-linguistic, objective, and publicly available feature or set of features (call it F) that can be invoked in order to explain the existence of the phenomenon of our common response to certain objects—our common response (call it R) of saying or judging that the things in question are red. There must be a true statement of the form 'R because of F'. One suggestion that has been considered is that F can be: the objective phenomenal quality of *looking red*. But we have seen that this cannot be right: 'looking red' does not pick out any single, determinate, non-linguistic, 'objective phenomenal quality' F of objects (cf. note 33) that can be invoked to explain R, our common linguistic response to them.

What else might F be? It seems that there is nothing relevant left, in the way of non-linguistic, objective, publicly available properties of objects that can explain R, except their L-properties (or those basic, structural, physical properties in virtue of which they have the L-properties that they do have). So we seem to be forced back to the L-property approach to the definition of 'red' after all, although we have already found reason to reject this approach, because it eliminates any sort of reference to experience from the account of the meaning of the word 'red'.

We now seem to be in danger of being forced to oscillate between two unsatisfactory views. But this is not so—there is no deep difficulty here. Differences in the L-properties of objects are indeed the objective-feature basis, F, that makes possible our

---

[44] This analytic sequence would terminate with (IV) an account of what is involved in a being's acquiring and having mastery of the word 'red'.

acquisition of responses like R, and indeed our whole language of colour. And, taking F in this way, we can perfectly well say 'Part of the explanation of common response R is the existence of objective, non-linguistic feature F'. But we do not, in saying this, have to say, incorrectly, that explicit reference to L-properties enters essentially into any adequate account of the meaning of the word 'red'.

13

To summarize and conclude. Take English colour words. Together they form a linguistic system of differences. These linguistic differences (i.e. the colour words themselves) correspond to real non-linguistic differences, being learnt in specific response to them, and these non-linguistic differences are in fact differences in the L-properties of objects. But colour words are not words for particular L-properties. For they are, essentially, *phenomenal-quality words*, and as such they would *mean* the same as they actually do now, in English, even if the colour-experiences we actually have were produced by different L-properties of objects than the ones they actually are produced by. (If the L-properties of all British-pillar-box-coloured things and all New-York-taxi-coloured things changed overnight, and yet they continued to produce the colour-experiences in us that they actually do produce (given that we too had changed) it would clearly be wrong to say that the *meaning* of the words 'red' and 'yellow' had changed.)

Particular colour words, then, are (of course) phenomenal-quality words. That is, (1), there is (as remarked in §9) a fundamental sense in which colour words are *words for properties which are of such a kind that their whole and essential nature as properties can be and is fully revealed in sensory, phenomenal-quality experience, given only the qualitative character that that sensory experience has.*[45] But, (2), because of actual or possible differences in those phenomenal-quality experiences on the basis of which different fully competent users of colour words initially master and subsequently apply colour words, particular colour words cannot correctly be said to be words that pick out *particular* phenomenal qualities. And so it is that they, like other 'secondary-quality' words, are phenomenal-quality words, but *phenomenally speaking contentless phenomenal-quality words*—words for no particular phenomenal quality. This is the crux of the matter.

At the same time, (3), colour words are (without qualification) correctly applied to objects—*although* colour words are words for properties which are of such a kind that their whole and essential nature as properties can be and is fully revealed in sensory, phenomenal-quality experience, given only the qualitative character that that sensory experience has, and *although* to talk of phenomenal qualities is, on the present terms, just to talk in a certain way of the qualitative character of experience.

---

[45] To talk in this way of the qualitative character of sensory experience is not to deny any of the respects in which 'phenomenology may be conceptually driven'. See §1.

Keeping these three points in balance can be a delicate matter, because (3) and (1)—namely the fact that colour words are (a) correctly and without qualification applied to objects, and are (b) phenomenal-quality words in the present sense—must continually prompt one to think that objects do after all have (mind-independent) phenomenal qualities of the sort that colour words are words for. But awareness of (2) can help to maintain the balance: the possibility that different fully competent users of colour words may have systematically different colour-experiences, when looking together at objects, sufficiently indicates the sense in which the phenomenal qualities they then have experience of are not mind-independent qualities of objects.[46]

Note that, suitably adjusted, (1) and (2) hold equally well for the general word 'pain'.[47] In the case of both 'red' and 'pain', the philosophical task is, very roughly, to reconcile Locke and Wittgenstein: one must, first, have a proper respect for the fact, and facts, of private experience, and acknowledge the element of truth in the doctrine of the 'incommunicability of (private experiential) content'. At the same time, one must pay due attention to the consequences of the fact that words like 'red' and 'pain' are words in a public language that are learnt in a social context, and are, furthermore, learnt in such a way that they can be fully mastered and understood by different people despite possible differences in the character of their experience.[48]

14

One reaction to the preceding may be this. 'I know what *I* mean by "red". I mean *that* colour [Here one points at a British pillar box, apprehending it specifically as being a certain colour; and the overall character of one's experience is of course that it is an experience of looking at an object that has, as one of its fully objective or mind-independent properties, the property of having a certain colour—the colour red]. Furthermore, nothing is ever going to convince me that there is no sense in which it is true to say that it is part of the meaning of the word "red" that it picks out *that* particular quality [gesturing at the pillar box] as opposed to *that* one [gesturing at well watered grass] or *that* one [gesturing at the inmost section of the French flag]. I grant that the supposition about Monet and Renoir is an intelligible one, and that it could

[46] There are of course independent grounds for adopting a Lockean or 'scientific realist' account of the nature of colour.

[47] (2) may be thought to apply less naturally to more particular plain words like 'stabbing pain' than it does to particular colour words.

[48] So that in so far as one talks about the content (or meaning) of *words*, rather than about the content of *experiences*, there is no incommunicability of content *at all*. (Thus: although the word 'pain' is indeed, and fundamentally, a word for experiences or inner sensations, it is not tied to the experiences or inner sensations in such a way that any incommunicability of content regarding our experiences results in any sort of incommunicability of content afflicting our use of the word 'pain'.)

conceivably be true. But one thing is certain. Whatever *you* may mean by "red", I mean *that*.'

I have no answer to this view except the preceding arguments.[49,50]

---

[49] How Lockean are they in spirit? Locke famously considers the possibility that things might be 'so ordered, that *the same object should produce in several Mens' Minds different* Ideas at the same time; *v.g.* if the *Idea*, that a *Violet* produced in one Man's Mind by his eyes, were the same that a *Marigold* produced in another Man's, and *vice versa*' (1689–1700: 2.32.15).

Clearly, a question arises as to how this squares with the rest of his theory. For his official view is that a man uses words 'as marks for the *Ideas* within his own Mind' (3.1.1.); and that '*Words in their primary or immediate Signification, stand for nothing, but the* Ideas *in the Mind of him that uses them*' (3.2.2.). So I may signify or mean one thing by 'red', and Renoir another thing. On this view, (A), each of us uses the word 'red' to pick out a particular phenomenal quality. And even if we do in fact signify or mean the same thing, we cannot know that we do, and may not. We are therefore faced with the 'incommunicability of content': our colour words have specific phenomenal-quality content, for us as we use them, but this content is incommunicable. And since the point of language is '*To make known* one Man's Thoughts or *Ideas* to another' (3.10.23), language is a serviceable but distinctly imperfect tool for communication.

However—when Locke discusses the possibility of the blue/yellow colour-spectrum displacement he does not endorse the view that words signify ideas or images in their users' minds. Instead he appears to favour the view (B) that colour words are not really words for phenomenal qualities at all, let alone words for ideas. Rather they pick out those unknown properties of objects in virtue of whose possession objects appear to us as they do, in respect of colouredness: 'the Name *Blue* [de]notes properly nothing, but that Mark of Distinction, that is in a *Violet*, discernible only by our Eyes, **whatever it consists in**' (2.32.14; my emphasis marked by bold typeface). He goes on to remark that the man in his colour-spectrum displacement case, who sees blue for yellow and vice versa, 'would be able as regularly to distinguish Things for his Use by those Appearances, and **understand**, and signify those distinctions marked by the Names *Blue* and *Yellow*, as if the . . . *Ideas* in his Mind . . . were exactly the same, with the *Ideas* in other Men's Minds' (2.32.15). So he would *understand the meanings of colour words as well as everyone else*. His colour-spectrum displacement relative to everyone else would not entail any falsity or inadequacy either in his colour *experience* or in his use of colour *words*: 'neither the *Ideas* . . . nor the Names would be at all confounded, or any *Falsehood* be in either' (ibid.). Here Locke is much closer to Wittgenstein. (Perhaps he would have found the tension in his position—the tension between (A) and (B)—satisfactorily resolved by the present conclusion.)

[50] I would like to thank Jennifer Hornsby and Hazel Rossotti for their criticisms, and John McDowell for his sceptical encouragement.

5

Self, Body, and Experience

ABSTRACT What are the grounds of self-consciousness? I consider 29 proposals and reject 22, including a number of proposals that experience of
body (or bodies) is necessary for self-consciousness. A popular strategy in
debates of this sort is to argue that one cannot be said to have some concept
c (e.g. the concept ONESELF, necessary for self-consciousness) unless one has
a need or a use for c given the character of one's experience considered independently of the character that it has given that one possesses c. I suggest
that such arguments are invalid.

What is the relation between the self and the body? I think it is a straightforward
part-whole relation—if selves exist at all—but I want to consider a different question: What is the relation between *experience* of self and *experience* of body? Or rather:
What is the relation between *self-consciousness* and experience of body? Or more precisely: What is the relation between self-consciousness and *experience that has the character of being experience of body*? Kant, Strawson, Evans, Cassam and others think the
former thing requires the latter. I agree with Wundt that this is so in the human case,
but I don't think it need be so in every case. I accept Shoemaker's general position in
'Self, Body, and Coincidence'—I am as much a 'friend of the body' as he is—and
want to offer different reasons why the current 'enthusiasm for the body', as he calls
it, is philosophically unbalanced.[1]

I assume that materialism is true—that every thing and event in the universe
is physical—and that the 'mind-body problem' is not the problem of the relation
between the mental and the physical (since by assumption everything is physical)
but, rather, the problem of the relation between the mental and the (concrete) non-
mental.[2] So the general form of the question that concerns me is: What is the relation
between self-consciousness and *experience of (concrete) non-mental being*? But I will
often use the simpler word 'body' to refer to (concrete) non-mental being.[3]

---

[1] Shoemaker 1999: 287; Kant 1781–7; Strawson 1966; Evans 1982; Cassam 1997; Wundt
1874 (cf. James 1890: 1.303).

[2] 'Concrete': some say that numbers exist and are non-mental, but they are 'abstract' objects, if
so, and not of concern here.

[3] Obviously all mental phenomena are concrete in the current sense. The distinction between
the mental and the non-mental is not very clear, but it will do for present purposes, and I will often
take the word 'concrete' as read.

1　SELF-CONSCIOUSNESS

The first thing to do is to define self-consciousness. I understand it in a strong sense as the capacity to be explicitly aware of oneself *as oneself*; the capacity to think of oneself, thought of as oneself, as being some way or other. More simply, it is possession of the concept (ONE)SELF or (MY)SELF.[4] As is well known, possession of this concept allows one to think about that which is in fact oneself in a certain way that is unlike any other way: not as the child of Y and Z, or the thing visible in the mirror, but just as—oneself.[5]

'Explicitly' is vague, but the idea is this: if a being is self-conscious, it must be capable of awareness of its states as its own that is explicit in something very like the way in which a being's awareness of its states as its own can be explicit when it is able to entertain the thought that they are its own in a conscious, occurrent, linguistic form of thought. 'Very like': self-conscious thought may not require linguistic ability as we know it, but it seems it must involve language-*like* thought, at least. For it must take place in a medium of thought that has the resources for the expression of thoughts correctly characterizable as involving an explicit conception of something *as myself*, or *as my own* (this being a characterization of their 'notional' content). And this conceiving of something *as* oneself, or *as* one's own, seems necessarily to involve representation that is abstract, in a clear sense. It cannot be literally pictured, it cannot possibly be represented in some merely sensory mode. It is abstract in such a way that linguistically articulated thought is our only clear model of what it might be like.

2　THE CORE

If this is self-consciousness, what are its conditions? I will propose three Core conditions without argument. I will then consider several versions of the *Others thesis* (according to which self-consciousness requires some sense of other subjects) and the *Body thesis* (according to which it requires some awareness of body). The Body thesis incorporates the *Embodiment thesis* (according to which one must have some awareness of embodiment) and is sometimes developed as the *Ordered World thesis* (according to which one must have some sense of oneself as located in an ordered world). I will record 29 proposed conditions of self-consciousness and reject 22. I state them all, to give the geography of the debate, but do not argue fully for all my acceptances and rejections and whizz through the first 24 in order to get to the main argument in §8.[6] 'S'—a physical being that has experiences of various sorts, and is actively self-conscious in the sense that it actually has thoughts of the form 'I am *F* ' or 'My *F* is *G* '—is my candidate for the position of minimal self-conscious subject.

---

[4] I use small capitals for names of concepts.　　　[5] Cf. e.g. Castañeda 1966; Perry 1979.
[6] This paper summarizes a longer paper called 'The Grounds of Self-Consciousness'.

The three Core conditions are as follows. If one is self-conscious

[1] one must possess the concept (ONE)SELF
[2] one must possess some conception of the subject of experience
[3] one must possess some conception of experience.

I take it that it follows that

[1'] one must in some manner possess the concept of what is not-self
[2'] one must in some manner possess a conception of what is not a subject of experience
[3'] one must in some manner possess a conception of what is not experience.

[1] has a guaranteed place because it merely repeats the definition of self-consciousness, [3] follows from [2], and most find [2] intuitively plausible.[7] But if someone thinks the Core is too rich and can be cut down, good. My aim is to argue that many popular claims about the conditions of self-consciousness are too strong even if one accepts the Core.

3   THE OTHERS THESIS

It may seem to follow from [1'] and [2] that self-consciousness not only requires possession of conceptions of *not-self* and *subject of experience*. It also requires possession of a conception of that which is both not-self and a subject. So that

[4] one must possess the concept of other subjects.

This, however, is not obvious. The most that follows from [1'] and [2] — if not from [2] alone — is that self-consciousness requires

[5] possession of the ability (conceptual resources) to form and entertain the concept of other subjects,

and some would say that even this is questionable. I am inclined to accept [5], but it does not entail [4]. Nor does it seem as if any stronger version of the Others thesis can be established. For even if [4] is true, as well as [1'] and [2], it does not follow that

[6] one must have explicitly had the thought that there might be other subjects, at some time.

Still less, that

[7] one must actually believe that there are other subjects (or at least that there have been).

Still less, that

[8] one must have experience that has the character of being experience of interaction with other subjects.

Still less, that

[9] one must have actual experience of interaction with other subjects.

---

[7] I think, in fact, that it needs argument. I attempt this in Strawson 1986: 154–60, and try to do better in 'The Grounds of Self-Consciousness'.

Our own early acquisition of self-consciousness is closely tied in with our coeval (or earlier) and automatic presumption that we are surrounded by other subjects, but this is a fact about human development and does not apply to S. It may be claimed that S's conception of itself will be peculiarly strengthless, in so far as it exists at all, but there is no good reason to believe this. Given that S's sense of itself as a subject exists, it may continue to be sharply defined for it by its struggle to attain its goals in a recalcitrant and inanimate environment. And struggle is not necessary. S's sense of itself as subject may be clear even if it spends all its time peacably on logic and mathematics, or in having smell and sound experiences.

I will give the main argument for this in §8. For the moment, note that it does not even seem to be true that human self-consciousness depends essentially on possession of the idea of other subjects. One could surely forget, on a fauna-free desert island, that other subjects exist, while retaining a robust and ordinarily unreflective use of 'I'. We often have no thought of others when we think, and it is hard to see why the belief that other subjects of experience exist would have to continue to be present in the background in some way in order for one to have a normal use of 'I' in thought. And if even a human being can be self-conscious while having no thought or memory of other subjects, it is all the more clear that S (the minimal self-conscious subject) can be self-conscious with no thought of others, even if it has to have the conceptual resources to entertain the idea of others.[8]

4   THE BODY THESIS

Kant argues that one can't be self-conscious unless one also has (or has had) some experience and concept of *body*: or, more generally, of (concrete) *non-mental being* (1781–7: B275–279). Many agree, endorsing the Body thesis, which in its simplest form states that

[10] one must have experience of body (or concrete non-mental being),

but is best revised to

[11] one must have experience that has the character of being experience of body (or concrete non-mental being),[9]

because it isn't a metaphysically assertive thesis about what there must be in reality, in addition to experience of a certain sort, and about what that experience must be experience of 'relationally' speaking. It is, rather, a thesis about what sort of structure or character experience must have, considered without reference to its causes, if it is to be the experience of a self-conscious being.[10]

---

[8] I disagree here with Strawson 1959: 99 ff., though see his note on p. 99.

[9] This is the most that would be established by Kant's so-called Refutation of Idealism if it were valid, which it is not.

[10] If everything that has mental being also has non-mental being, then it may be said that all experience of mental being is experience of non-mental being, relationally speaking. See Essay 1: 23.

Many philosophers understand 'experience' as it occurs in [11] in such a way that [11] entails

[12] one must possess a concept of body (or concrete non-mental being),

but rats and cats presumably have experience that has the character of being experience of body, so it is worth distinguishing [11] from [12].

5 THE EMBODIMENT THESIS

Many go further than Kant and endorse a more specific version of the Body thesis. To the claim that one must have experience of body they add the claim that one must be aware or conceive of oneself as embodied or as having non-mental being, if one is to be self-conscious. I disagree. I take it (as a materialist) that S has non-mental being, but think that S may be self-conscious even if it has no such awareness or conception of itself.

The Embodiment thesis states that

[13] one must be aware of oneself as being embodied (as having concrete non-mental being).

It has been widely endorsed, and has interesting variants, such as

[14] one must be aware of oneself as embodied by means of external sense organs of some kind

and

[15] interoceptive experience of oneself as embodied is indispensable (or central).[11]

It is usually taken for granted that a single body is in question, but it is not clear that this is necessary, and one can distinguish the Embodiment thesis from the *Single Embodiment* thesis:

[16] one must be aware of oneself as singly embodied.

I doubt that this would be true even if some form of the Embodiment thesis were true, but I will assume that a single body is in question for purposes of discussion.

The Embodiment thesis can be weakened in the same way as the Body thesis, for it is not true that one must be aware of oneself as embodied. It is enough that one should have experience as of being embodied, whether or not veridical. So the Embodiment thesis becomes

[17] one must have experience that has the character of being experience of (single) embodiment.

Many philosophers understand 'experience' as it occurs in [17] in such a way that [17] entails

[18] one must conceive of oneself as (singly) embodied,

---

[11] One can always replace 'embodied' by 'having concrete non-mental being' and make a weakening move like the move from [10] to [11].

but cats and rats may presumably have experience that has the character of being experience of being (singly) embodied without having any such conception, so we may distinguish [17] from [18].[12]

I have no doubt that the Embodiment thesis is false, but the basic thought that has motivated many to accept it is I believe a good one. At bottom, perhaps, it is prompted by the very general *Self as Thing* thesis

[19] one cannot think of oneself in the distinctively self-conscious way unless one experiences or conceives of oneself as a thing in some suitably robust sense.

I think [19] is true, when 'as a thing' is interpreted in an appropriately liberal way.[13] I do not, however, think that it entails any Embodiment thesis—for reasons still to come.

6   THE SUBJECTIVE/OBJECTIVE THESIS

The Embodiment thesis is one of the principal tributaries of the Body thesis. The Ordered World thesis is another. I will state it in a familiar strong way and note some weakenings. First, though, I need to record the *Subjective/Objective* thesis that

[20] one must be able to make a distinction between the way things are subjectively and the way things are objectively—between the way things are and the way one experiences them to be

because it is acceptance of [20] that leads many to think that some version of the Ordered World thesis must be true.

[20] may be misleading, for one can grasp the subjective/objective distinction even if constituted or situated in such a way that one never actually has any thought like 'This is how things are experienced to be, but how they are experienced to be is distinct from how they are.' One may take it that objective reality consists entirely in one's existing and having the experiences one does; or one may simply have no thought that it does not. So it seems better to restate [20] as

[21] one must have a grasp of the distinction between the way things are and the way one experiences them to be

for one can have a grasp of this distinction even if nothing in one's experience invites the thought that how things are experienced either is or might be different from how they are. To judge that how things are is in no way different from how one experiences them to be is precisely to exercise grasp of the distinction.

Is [21] true? One argument for it runs as follows. [a] Self-consciousness requires [b] possession of the notion of the subject of experience, which requires [c] possession

---

[12] Cassam 1997 argues that [18] is too strong, although a version of [17] is correct.
[13] I discuss this in Strawson 1999: §9. Kant 1781–7 makes the point well in his discussion of the First Paralogism.

of the notion of experience, which requires [d] grasp of the notion that experience is experience of something other than itself, which requires [e] grasp of the notion that there is something that is not experience, which requires [f] grasp of the notion that how things are experienced to be is distinct from (not all there is to) how things are.

I think there are at least two false steps here, but I will note only that the notion of experience is not in fact intrinsically relational in the way supposed. Experience necessarily has experiential content, but it needn't be experience of something that exists independently of experience, and even if it is it needn't be supposed to be.

Objection: 'Self-consciousness requires (a) a sense of oneself and (b) a sense of oneself *as* subject. This entails (c) a sense of oneself as distinct, as subject, from the content of one's experiences, that is, from how things are experienced to be. And this amounts to (d) some grasp of the Subjective/Objective distinction.' Reply: This argument operates with too limited a notion of the content of experience. In the self-conscious case, the subject, considered as such, is part of what is presented in experience: the 'how things are experienced to be' includes the subject, and we still lack a reason to think that a self-conscious being must grasp the subjective/objective distinction.

'But if the subject, grasped as such, is presented to itself in experience, it must be aware that it is dealing with a representation of a thing that is not the thing itself. So it must after all grasp the distinction between what is and what is experienced—between the way things are and the way it experiences them to be.' Reply: Why should the subject be that reflective? Thinking of itself, it may never think it is dealing with a representation of a thing that is not the thing itself (compare our unreflective encounters with tables and chairs). It is hard to see why one cannot be self-present or 'constitutively self-intimating'[14] in self-consciousness in such a way that one's sense of oneself as subject in the living moment of experience does not involve or even presuppose any grasp of any such division into representation and represented. One may simply take it that what is experienced—including, in reflective moments, oneself as experiencer, and the fact that one is is experiencing things—is what is.

'But sensory experiences like colour or sound experiences are already and necessarily experiences that have the character of being experience of concrete non-mental being.' Reply. They may be apprehended merely as differently qualitied ways of experiencing, in so far as they are reflected on at all.[15]

So I take it that [21] is false. Should I at least concede that

[22] one must have the conceptual resources to come to grasp the distinction between the way things are and the way one experiences them to be, if one is self-conscious?

[14] Cpf. Shoemaker 1990: ix; Rosenthal 1986: 470; and Strawson 1999: §10.

[15] I pass over complexities in the notion of 'having the character of being experience of non-mental being'. Note that even if some version of this objection were sound it would not follow

I cannot at present see that the logic of self-consciousness demands that one must have this capacity.[16]

7   THE ORDERED WORLD THESIS

The Ordered World thesis is developed from the Subjective/Objective thesis as follows. If one is to grasp the distinction between how things are and how they are experienced to be then

[23] one must conceive of oneself as located in a world that exhibits a certain degree of order and regularity of which one is aware (one must have experience that has the character of being experience of such location).

The ordered world in question is initially modelled on the world of persisting bodies in space with which we take ourselves to be familiar, but it is standardly granted that it need not be just like this. The root idea is that one must trace an experiential 'route' through a 'space' or 'dimension' of some kind 'containing' 'entities' of some kind, and that these entities must be experienced as possessing an order and variety sufficiently similar (what is sufficient invites and resists precise specification) to the order and variety exhibited by objects in space as experienced by us.[17]

It seems to me that the Ordered World thesis is not entailed by the Subjective/Objective thesis even if the latter is true,[18] and is in any case false, even when it is separated from any version of the Embodiment thesis and stripped down to the (*Mere*) *Point of View* thesis that

[24] one must at least experience oneself as having a point of view in an ordered world of objects of some sort.[19]

I will now try to say why in more general terms.

---

that anything close to a standard Body thesis is true. Cf.—for one thing—Strawson's reply to Evans (1980: 277 ff).

[16] Note that S can think 'My experiences went A, B, C, but they might have gone A, C, B' without any grasp of the thought that how things are is or might be different from how they are experienced to be.

[17] Strawson, 1959: ch. 2, gives a striking description of of a non-spatial ordered 'world', and later develops a more explicitly Kantian version of the Ordered World thesis (1966: 82–112). Kant himself endorses [11], and more specifically [23] or [24], because he thinks it states a necessary condition of having a sense that there is a real or 'objective' time-order, which he takes to be a necessary condition of self-consciousness. However, he gives us no good reason to believe this (he offers a need argument of the sort to be rejected in §8), or for doubting that S's sense of the passing of time and of itself as persisting through time may simply be intrinsic to its experience of succeeding states of consciousness.

[18] Why should a capacity to distinguish between how things are objectively and how they are subjectively require any sort of order in experience at all, let alone experience that has the character of being experience of an order of things distinct from one's experiences?

[19] Strawson, 1995: 417 (cf. Cassam 1997: 44ff) seems to endorse the coherence of [24].

8   THE NEED ARGUMENT

I have proposed that one can be self-conscious without any thought of the possibility of other subjects and without any sense of embodiment or of body in general. Many will object that one can have no *need* or *use* for the concept (ONE)SELF (or I) in such a case, and that if one has no need for it—if there is no work for it to do in the articulation of one's experience—then one cannot really be said to have it at all. In which case one cannot really be said to be self-conscious.

King Lear gives the first answer: 'O reason not the need'. We can possess things, including contentful concepts, that we do not need or use; it seems it is only some unhappy version of verificationism that militates against this idea.

Second answer. S does have a use for the concept of self just in so far as S naturally uses it to think self-conscious thoughts about itself, as we do. And given that S does think in this way, S needs the concept. S needs it to think in the distinctive way that it makes possible. There is no further external or antecedent source of the need. But why should there be?

'Because one cannot really be said to have some fundamental concept C unless one has a need or a use for C given the character of one's experience—the character of one's experience *considered independently of the fact that one possesses* C.'

This is the mistake. If I have concepts of various animals, but no knowledge of horses, and encounter horses, it seems plausible to say that I subsequently have a need and a use for the concept HORSE in ordering my experience; and (waiving various complications that tell in my favour) there seems to be a clear sense in which this is so because of the character that my experience has considered independently of the character that it has specifically because I possess HORSE. So too for RED, and so on. But to say that it holds good of such empirical concepts is not to say it holds good generally. Suppose I think up the idea of a centaur. Suppose I think up the idea of a triangle by a stroke of artistic genius, living in a world where everything is—and appears—smoothly curved. Here I may create a genuine use for CENTAUR or TRIANGLE that does not exist antecedently to my thinking it up.

I think it useful to say that once I have done this I have a *need* for the concept. I have a need for it given the conceptual space I now inhabit. This may be thought perverse, because it considers the limiting case in which my need for C is not independent of the fact that I possess C. Some, accordingly, may prefer to say only that I have a use for C. I think, however, that it is telling to say that one also creates a need, even though one doesn't need C to do anything other than think in the way it makes possible. One is now so disposed, mentally, that certain thoughts can occur to one, and one needs C in order to have those thoughts.

What about the concept I or (MY)SELF? It is not like HORSE, or CENTAUR, but the elements of disanalogy do not matter. Suppose I am just created thinking in the distinctively self-conscious way. Or suppose I am a creature innately disposed to come to think in the distinctively self-conscious way even if my experience is very limited.

Then I have (or come to have) a genuine use for (MY)SELF even if nothing in my experience considered independently of my possession of (MY)SELF encourages its deployment. And now that I have it I need it. I need it to think in the distinctively self-conscious way in which I just do think. The possession of the concept can itself be (and arguably must be) what makes the difference—the experiential cut—that gives it its function or use. Once the concept (MY)SELF is deployed, the world divides for me into I and not-I. The concept has, thenceforth, a use and a proper application. I have a need for it because I tend to think in the distinctively self-conscious way and cannot think in the distinctively self-conscious way without it. And although possession of (MY)SELF (trivially) requires possession of some conception of not-I, it does not follow that I must have any thought of other subjects, as the Others thesis claims. In the limiting case, it seems that my experiences, naturally apprehended by me as phenomena that stand over against me, the subject, can suffice as the not-I.

These objections to the need argument suggest that there are no valid arguments for the claim that one cannot possess the concept (MY)SELF unless one's experience has a certain character considered independently of the fact that one possesses the concept. If the objections are sound, a whole swathe of theses lose their purchase: all those, like the various versions of the Body thesis, that make claims about what the *concept-of-(one)self-independent* character of experience must be like if one is to be self-conscious.

I think they are all false. I find no incoherence in the idea of a self-conscious creature that (1) has all sorts of absorbing experiences, and thinks 'I am happy', 'I am *F*-ing', 'I am *G*-ing', although it does not take itself to be embodied or located in any sort of ordered world, or *B-realized*, for short. Or in the idea of a self-conscious creature that (1) has experiences and (2) naturally thinks of them *as* experiences, although it does not take itself to be B-realized. Don't ask how it came to be this way. To think this matters is to misunderstand the issue. My reply will be that it may just so think of them, however disordered they are—that it may be a matter of innate disposition.

Nor do I find any incoherence in the idea of a self-conscious creature that (1) has experiences and not only (2) thinks of its experiences as experiences, but also (3) thinks of them as experiences of something other than itself, although it does not take itself to be B-realized (it may think of its experiences in this way even if they appear utterly random in character). Or in the idea of a self-conscious creature that, in addition to (1) and (2), and perhaps (3), also (4) thinks of its experiences *themselves* as something other than itself, the subject considered as such, although it has no sense that it is B-realized, nor any sense that its experiences have any order or regularity.[20] For it may just so think of them, however disordered they are. How might this be? The case is the same. Possession of the concept of what is not-self doesn't depend on possession of the concept of non-mental existence: in the limiting case my experiences themselves, apprehended as phenomena that are distinct from (not identical with) me, the subject, can suffice as the not-self.

---

[20] (4) entails (1) and (2) but not (3). I consider the case in which the subject does not fulfil (3).

If I am right, a whole tradition of argument collapses. All its claims about unobvious incoherence come to nothing, because they depend on the need argument, which has no valid form. Furthermore: although I have claimed that possession of a concept c can be the source of a need for c without anything in experience-considered-independently-of-possession-of-c inviting deployment of c, it is arguable that there is a fundamental sense in which only the possession of c can be a source of a need for it. Those who argue that self-consciousness requires (for example) experience that has the character of being experience of other subjects are led to talk of experience inviting or favouring deployment of the concept (ONE)SELF, or creating a natural need for it. But perhaps there is a more fundamental sense in which it is only the possession of the concept that gives it a needed use, because only the possession of a concept really opens up the scene of thought and experience in which it finds such a use.

9 EMPIRICALLY APPLICABLE CRITERIA OF IDENTITY

Let me change the idiom: there does not seem to be any incoherence in the idea that a creature may be self-conscious although it entirely lacks any 'empirically applicable criteria of identity' for itself and for things of the kind it takes itself to belong to, of the sort paradigmatically supplied by our ability to be aware of ourselves as embodied and located in an ordered world of bodies.[21] Many disagree, endorsing the *Empirical Criteria* thesis, according to which

[25] one cannot have a genuine self-conscious thought about oneself unless one is in possession of such empirically applicable criteria of subject-identity.

This is standardly taken to be the thesis that one must oneself be able—or at least must have been able—to apply such criteria of identity in practice. But this seems unnecessary even if some version of [25] is true. The fundamental proposal is about a self-conscious being's conceptual resources and thought-dispositions, not about its evidential situation, and it seems it could have the conceptual resources specified by the Empirical Criteria thesis even if it were constitutionally incapable of any actual application of the criteria in question. It would, for example, be enough if it were innately determined to have some conception of itself as B-realized. It would not matter if it were in fact an immaterial soul with no sense organs, for it would in this case possess empirically applicable criteria of identity even though it was not in a position to apply them to itself, and even though they were incorrect. It would have the required conceptual competence—a picture that did the right sort of thought-structuring work—even though it was mistaken.

I think the Empirical Criteria thesis is false even when this point has been registered. I support S, who thinks of itself as just: a self, a presence, an experiencer. S has no thought or experience of B-realization or of body in general. It is just a fact that S naturally and automatically thinks of itself as a single thing. It cannot give any account of why this way of thinking is justified. The question has not arisen for

21 Cf. Strawson 1966: 167. All quotations from Strawson in this section are from pp. 164–7.

it—this is just how things are for it. The field of its experience is divided or structured by this habit of thought. It has no empirical criteria of subject-identity, but it does not need any. It is not as if it has to put the way it experiences things to the test. It is not as if the character of its experience has to make the I/not-I distinction useful for it for reasons independent of the fact that it already thinks in this way. For there it always is for itself: the subject of experience, available to be thought about in a way that is familiar to us all. In apprehending itself as the subject, S apprehends itself as something that is distinguishable from its experiences and their content, whatever their content is. These stand over against it as what is not-self, not the subject. It is quite unclear that anything more is required.

We may imagine that S recapitulates part of Descartes's *cogito* argument, thinking 'I know that I exist; the question is, what is this "I" that I know? I do not know. But whatever I suppose, and whatever the truth is, for all that I am still something.' S's reasoning here is as unexceptionable as Descartes's, and is not open to Lichtenberg's famous but mistaken objection that Descartes should at this stage in his argument have said only 'there is thinking' or 'it is thinking'.[22]

S, then, is a physical being, something for which empirically applicable criteria of identity are available, although not to it. And the thing that S is thinking of (relationally speaking) is certainly itself. So why is it widely supposed that S's apparent self-conscious thought of itself cannot be genuine unless it possesses, in some form, empirical criteria of identity for itself? One reason why this is puzzling is that it is generally agreed that thinking of oneself simply as a mental presence or subject is a genuine way of thinking of oneself, one that is in fact available to all of us. Strawson makes the point. When human subjects of experience use 'I' to ascribe a state of consciousness to themselves they typically do so without making any 'use whatever of any . . . empirically applicable . . . criteria of identity'. 'It would make no sense', he says, for such a subject 'to say: *This* inner experience is occurring, but is it occurring to *me*?' There is in such cases 'nothing that one can . . . encounter or recall in the field of inner experience such that there can be any question of one's applying [empirically applicable] criteria of subject-identity to determine whether the . . . experience belongs to oneself—or to someone else'.

This is right, but Strawson does not take this fact to support the view I am defending. Instead he identifies it as the 'the fact that lies at the heart of the Cartesian illusion'. When 'I' is used by a subject in this way to ascribe an experience to itself, he says, there is indeed no 'need or . . . possibility of this use being justified by empirical criteria of subject-identity'. How is such a use still possible—valid and properly contentful? Because, he says, 'even in such a use, the links with [empirical] criteria [of

---

[22] Cf. Descartes 1641: 18. Lichtenberg's objection is mistaken if applied at this point because the 'I think', as asserted by Descartes (or S) here, does not presuppose any opinion about the ultimate nature of the phenomenon picked out by 'I'. Descartes uses 'I' simply because our thought about ourselves naturally and inevitably occurs for us in terms of 'I', and he is right to do so. He uses 'I' as a referential term that picks out an undeniable reality, whatever else is true of that reality, and explicitly says that he might for all he knows be something that has non-mental being as well as mental being—even something that is more like a process or a property than a self-subsistent substance.

subject-identity] are not in practice severed'. They are not severed in the human case, with which he is principally concerned, because one's use of 'I' is in practice securely underwritten by one's possession of empirical criteria of identity for oneself which are in turn grounded in one's experience of oneself as embodied and located in an ordered spatiotemporal world.

Strawson proposes, then, that the experience of criterionless self-ascription of experiences gives rise to an illusion in human beings, 'the illusion of a purely inner and yet subject-referring use for "I" '. But even if the claim that this is an illusion is true in our case,[23] it does not follow that it is impossible for any self-conscious creature to refer to itself unless it possesses empirical criteria for itself of the paradigmatic sort. In fact, as it stands, Strawson's observation provides very strong support for the view that it is indeed possible for a creature to refer to itself without possessing such criteria. For if we can think about ourselves in such a way that there is 'no question' of our applying empirical criteria of subject-identity when we do so (we may also be in a sensory isolation tank, but it is not important), why can't S always do so?

Some may reply that our ability to think of ourselves in this way at any given time depends essentially on the presence of the 'somatic field' of awareness, conceived of as some sort of permanent background awareness of embodiment. But even if this is true of us it does not undercut the present suggestion, and it points clearly to another possibility: if a background somatic field of awareness can be so important for self-consciousness, then presumably a background *psychic* or mental field of awareness, featuring structures of mood, emotion, character, preferences, and knowledge, can serve the same function.

It may now be said that one must experience B-realization at some time in order to come to be such that one can engage in criterionless self-ascription of experiences in the first place. The reply is the same: if such experience can give rise to the ability to engage in self-ascription of experiences without any concurrent awareness of B-realization, then this ability can exist while lacking this particular aetiology. It can, for example, be supposed to be innately given; the aetiology can't be what matters.

The aetiology can't be what matters. But it may now be said that memory or awareness of embodiment (or something relevantly equivalent) must always be somehow *actively present*, if only implicitly, when a being engages in what appears to be criterionless self-ascription of experiences. But how might this (very unclear) claim be proved? The phenomenological facts seem to be as Strawson says: there need be no trace of any thought or experience of oneself as embodied, or as a thing of a kind for which there are empirical criteria of identity, in the experience of oneself as a subject that one may have when ascribing experiences to oneself. One can seem to oneself to have all the solidity of a genuine referent just by virtue of one's experience of oneself as a subject, a mental presence with certain properties. And if it can be like this for us on occasion, it can presumably be like this all the time for some other kind of being. Once again, a being may simply be innately disposed to experience things in this way. The habit of self-reference doesn't need any further or external grounding.

---

[23] I believe it is false.

10   BOUNDING THE SELF

Perhaps the key thought behind the Empirical Criteria thesis is the *Self-Identifiability* thesis

[26]   if one is genuinely self-conscious one must be able to identify something as oneself.

This seems trivially true at one end of the spectrum of readings of the word 'identify', where it amounts to nothing more than the claim that one must (a) be able to fix on oneself in thought in such a way as to be the actual target of one's own thoughts, and (b) be able to think of oneself *as* oneself. At the other end of the spectrum, however, where the word 'identify' has powerful connections with the notions of being able to pick something out, establish its identity, reidentify it at a later time, and so on, it seems false. It is generally agreed that there can be criterionless self-conscious self-ascription of properties, and I have already argued that there are no good grounds for saying that a being cannot engage in such self-ascription of properties unless it possesses empirical criteria of subject-identity.

A general version of the question that leads people to endorse the Empirical Criteria thesis can be put like this: What must be true if one is to be able to put a line or boundary round oneself in thought, in such a way that one can really be said to take oneself as an object of thought? Does S really have the resources to do this, without possessing any empirical criteria of subject-identity?[24]

Yes. The line is sufficiently drawn, the boundary sufficiently demarcated, just so long as something presents or is conceptually figured as self, in self-conscious thought. If this always requires that something also presents as not-self, so be it: one's experiences that come upon one, the subject, and that are naturally conceived of as distinct from oneself, are already sufficient to fill this role. What reason is there to think that the line defining oneself cannot be primitive in the sense that it is just given, unquestioned, built into the structure—the cognitive phenomenal character[25]—of one's conscious self-conscious thought, having no further possible expression for one and no independent justification or corroboration? This, in fact, is how it is in our case, when we engage in criterionless self-conscious self-ascription of experiences, and there is (once again) no good reason to suppose that the basic structure our thought then has depends essentially on the kinds of developmental antecedents that it has in the human case. The aetiology can't be what matters.

Perhaps we can re-express the fundamental thought that attracts philosophers to the Empirical Criteria thesis in the *External Figuration* thesis

[27]   if one is self-conscious there must be some source of one's grasp of oneself as an individual something—some model or experiential corroboration or figuration of oneself as an individual something—external to and independent of any experience of oneself as

---

[24]   I owe this version of the question to Quassim Cassam.

[25]   On this crucial notion see e.g. Essay 10: §6 and Essay 11: §4. See also Ayers 1991: ch. 31; James 1890: ch. 12; Pitt: 2004.

an individual something that one may have simply in grasping or experiencing oneself as the mental subject.

But I can see no reason to accept this. Why must a self-conscious being be able to figure or put a thought-boundary round itself, in a way that demarcates it as an individual thing, in some frame other than the frame involved in its experience of itself merely as a mental phenomenon or subject? Some think this is necessary because they link thought essentially to language, and hold a mistaken view about the constraints that the role of language in public communication places on the possible content of thought. But this line of thought is bad at the best of times and hopelessly out of place here. Others appeal to the Kantian thought that concepts require 'sensible intuitions' and are 'empty' without them (cf. Kant 1781–7: A51/B75). On this view, one can't exercise the concept (ONE)SELF at all unless there is some 'intuition' or sensory experience, or at least some non-conceptual element in one's mental contents, for the concept to lambada with; and this requires something like the Figuration thesis.

But why does it require the Figuration thesis? We may grant that one cannot be said to have a concept at all unless the concept in question has some genuine *application-occasions*. It does not follow that the Figuration thesis is true. S can have a rich source of application-occasions for the concept of (it)self simply in having explicitly self-conscious thoughts in the way that it is innately disposed to do, and without any capacity for any sense-like self-presentation: without any capacity for any presentation of itself in any mode other than whatever is necessarily involved in self-conscious thought of a kind that we can have a sense of by reference to our own experience of criterionless self-ascription of experiences. When I consider the way in which S can feature in its own experience when it thinks self-consciously I wonder whether there is any better or more solid way in which anything can ever feature in anything's experience. A natural bias has it that we are essentially better placed in our thought about tables or human bodies than S can ever be when it thinks of itself, given its lack of any sense of concrete non-mental being. But this view confuses perceived material solidity, or something like it, with referential solidity.

Am I begging the question? Surely not. The question is whether one can make sense of the idea that S is self-conscious (perhaps innately, and from the first moment of its existence) after having explicitly *assumed* that S lacks any (external) figuration of itself in the present sense. Having made this assumption, I offer various descriptions of how things are for S, with its limited experiential resources. The burden of argument is on those who deny that they make sense. Given that S's self-apprehension must involve some non-conceptual element, the point is then that non-conceptual experience is not restricted to sensory forms of experience (interoceptive or exteroceptive) as ordinarily understood. S must be given to itself in experience in some way; we may say that it must be given in some 'experiential modality' or other. But it may be so given (and there is perhaps no way in which it can be more robustly given) in an experiential modality that is not a sensory modality. It may be so given just by being aware of itself as the mental subject.

11   THE CRITERIA THESIS

One way to put the point is to say that the use of the word 'empirical' in the Empirical Criteria thesis

[25]   a self-conscious being must be in possession of empirical criteria of subject-identity.

is either redundant or mistaken. Whenever we and S have any experience, and a fortiori when we experience ourselves as subjects in self-conscious thought, this is a matter of empirical experience. But this is not to say that it is a matter of experience of anything publicly observable: a long tradition in which 'empirical' and 'publicly observable' have been coextensively applied has led to their confusion. It is a confusion because the private aspects of the content of experience are as much a matter of empirical content as any other aspects. So if the supporters of the Empirical Criteria thesis are demanding public criteria of identity, they are misusing the word 'empirical', and should distinguish the Empirical Criteria thesis from the *Public Criteria* thesis

[28]   if one is self-conscious, and can genuinely think of oneself as oneself, one must possess public criteria of subject-identity.

They must then decide whether they want to endorse this thesis, which I take to be false, and distinguish it in turn from the less specific and more fundamental *Criteria* thesis

[29]   if one is self-conscious, and can genuinely think of oneself as oneself, one must possess criteria of subject-identity.

I think there is a respect in which [29] is true, and part of the correct analysis of the conditions of active self-consciousness, along with [1]–[3], [5], [19], and the first, anodyne reading of [26]. But it depends on how one understands 'criterion'. Confusion arises from the fact that it can be employed either with epistemological or conceptual-logical stress. When the stress is epistemological the main beat of the Criteria thesis falls on the idea that a self-conscious being must be in possession of some way of *finding out* that something is a subject of experience within the total field of its experience, some *rule for judgement* or *method* for distinguishing that which is a subject from that which is not. When the stress is conceptual-logical, by contrast, the beat falls more simply—on the idea that a self-conscious being must possess an *adequate conception* of what it is to be a subject: a grasp of what is criterial (as we naturally say, using the word with this stress) for being a subject. The mistake is to think that possession of criteria understood epistemologically in the above way is necessary for possession of criteria conceptually-logically understood. The mistake goes deep and has old and twisted empiricist roots.

I think the Criteria thesis is true when the stress is conceptual-logical.[26] Is it true when the stress is epistemological? It seems to me that the answer is No or Not

---

[26]   It amounts, in effect, to [2] on p. 133 above.

Applicable: nothing can really count as S's possessing—let alone applying—a certain rule or method for distinguishing, within the total field of its experience, that which is itself (or a subject) from that which is not. The distinction is always already[27] given in experience in such a way that there is no room for anything that could constitute either the possession or the application of a method for making the distinction.

12   EVANS'S 'I'

I now encounter a new set of opponents, who agree that it can *seem* that a subject like S is thinking in a fully self-conscious way, but insist that things cannot be as they seem. Evans, for example, endorses a form of the Ordered World thesis as a condition on successful or genuine I-thought, claiming that a being cannot think of itself as 'I' if it cannot think of itself as (or identify itself with) 'an element in the objective order' located at a particular place which it can think of as 'here' (1982: 254). He grants that a being may continue to have *apparent* I-thoughts when it can no longer identify itself with an element in the objective order, but holds that in this case 'its 'I'—its habitual mode of thought about itself—is simply inadequate for this situation. (It forces the subject to think in ways which are no longer appropriate)' (p. 255).

It seems possible, he writes,

to envisage organisms whose control centre is outside the body, and connected to it by communication links. . . . An organism of this kind could have an Idea of itself like our own, but . . . would be unable to cope with the situation that would arise when the control centre survived the destruction of the body it controlled. Thinking like us, the subject would of course have to regard itself as somewhere, but in this case it would not make any sense to identify a particular place in the world it thought of as *here*. The place occupied by the control centre is certainly not the subject's *here*; and even if we counterfactually suppose the control centre re-equipped with a body, there is no particular place where that body would have to be. Because its 'here' picks out no place, there is no bit of matter, no persisting thing, which the subject's Idea of itself permits us to regard as what it identifies as itself. Here, then, we have a very clear situation in which a subject of thought could not think of itself as 'I'; its 'I'—its habitual mode of thought about itself—is simply inadequate for this situation. (pp. 254–5)

He thinks this sort of inadequacy can also afflict us in more ordinary situations: 'our ordinary thoughts about ourselves are liable to many different kinds of failings, and . . . the Cartesian assumption that such thoughts are always guaranteed to have an object cannot be sustained' (p. 249).

The above passage makes a powerful case for the opposite conclusion, however. It makes it vivid that 'I' succeeds in hitting its mark—the I, the subject that indubitably exists, whatever its ultimate nature—even when there is no bit of matter or other persisting thing that the subject can identify as itself. It shows, in effect, that a subject's apparent 'I'-thoughts that lack nothing experientially speaking (cf. note 25) always

[27] This phrase, made fashionable by Heidegger and Derrida, occurs in *The Critique* of *Pure Reason* (A346/B404).

have an object. It seems to me, in fact, that such thoughts always have the object they are thought to have, however many false beliefs the subject has about its nature; and that even if such thoughts could (somehow) fail to have an object, they would still have an object in situations in which Evans denies that they can. (A more direct objection to Evans's case runs as follows. Suppose the subject thinks 'I'm in big trouble, wherever I am,' or 'I don't know where I am, or how much of me is left intact, but I'm in big trouble wherever I am'. In this case there seems to be no good reason to think that 'the control centre is certainly not the subject's *here*'.)

Evans considers another case, in which one has a 'quasi-memory' (cf. Shoemaker 1970): an apparent memory of perceiving a certain past event E that derives directly (by some peculiar mechanism) from someone else's perception of that event. One thinks, in the present, 'I perceived E', or 'I perceived E in 1990'; but in fact it was C, not oneself, who perceived E. Evans claims that one's I-thought has no object in this case, because one is bringing 'both present-tense . . . and past-tense . . . information to bear upon [one's current] self-conscious reflections, and there is no one thing from which both kinds of information derive[s]'. He compares the case to one in which one is looking at one cup and feeling another. One falsely supposes that there is just one cup, and thinks 'this cup is well made' (pp. 249–50).

The case of the cups is good, but the comparison is unhelpful. The occurrence of 'I' in the thought 'I perceived E (in 1990)' (or, generally, 'I was *F*') is guaranteed a reference because it unfailingly cleaves to one thing, oneself as present at the time of the thought. It concerns oneself thought of as a thing that exists now and that existed in the past and is false precisely because one did not perceive E in the past. It does not involve any confusion about who or what the subject of the thought is, even though it involves a mistake. Evans claims that 'it is of the essence of an "I"-Idea that it effects an identification that spans past and present' (p. 246), but even if this is granted[28] it still does not undercut the view that one's apparent I-thought has an object in the case in question, and has, indeed, the object that one takes it to have—oneself. Even if it is of the essence of an 'I'-Idea to effect an identification that spans past and present, it remains true that one's quasi-memory concerns only oneself—oneself as one is now, thought of, if only implicitly, as temporally extended and as existing both now and in 1990. This fact effortlessly trumps any facts about the actual source of the quasi-memory, and Evans's cases give us no reason to doubt that when a being appears to have an I-thought—where 'appears' means that the basic phenomenology of I-thought is in place—it really does have an I-thought: always.

13 CONCLUSION

I have argued that if one is self-conscious, one must possess [1] the concept (ONE)SELF, and have [2]–[3] some conception of experience and of a subject of experience; one must it seems possess [5] the conceptual resources to form and entertain the concept

---

[28] It is hard to see why there could not be a self-conscious being that had no significant sense or conception of the past.

of other subjects; one must be able [19] to think of oneself as a thing or entity in some suitably robust sense; one must be able [26] to identify something as oneself (in the weak sense of 'identify'), and one must possess [29] criteria of subject-identity (where 'criteria' is understood in its conceptual-logical sense). But that is all. If this makes me a Cartesian, then that is what I am. If 'Cartesian' is a stigma, as Shoemaker suggests (p. 287), it is not the only stigma that is an honour. We have good reason to reject parts of Descartes's view of the mind—his substance dualism, his view that the mind is self-transparent, and so on—but he is still much closer to the truth about mind than many twentieth-century philosophers.[29]

[29] My thanks to Paul Snowdon for comments on this paper, and to Ralph Walker for comments on its (1976) original. The final revision was carried out with the help of a British Academy Leverhulme Trust Research Fellowship.

6

What is the Relation Between an Experience, the Subject of the Experience, and the Content of the Experience?

'Eventually meditators... come to see that the perceiver is only the subject side of a momentary experience, an aspect of the perception or thought itself.'

Eleanor Rosch (1997: 193)[1]

1 INTRODUCTION

Materialism or physicalism—I use the terms interchangeably—is the view that every real, concrete[2] phenomenon[3] in the universe is physical. It is a view about the actual universe, and in this paper I will assume that it is true.[4]

Consider Louis, a representative human being. Louis is part of physical reality. Everything about him is a wholly physical phenomenon, including, of course, his conscious experience, and the experiential qualitative[5] character that it has for him as he has it.[6]

The original version of this paper was published to a deadline before it was finished. There were many errors of numbering, notation and thought (resulting principally from insufficiently considered insertions of new passages to fix problems) and I have significantly revised it in an attempt to reduce their number.

[1] When I cite a work I give the date of its completion or first publication, while the page reference is to the edition listed in the bibliography.

[2] By 'concrete' I simply mean 'not abstract'. It is natural to think that any really existing thing is concrete, in which case the word is redundant, but some like to say that numbers (for example) are real things—objects that really exist but are 'abstract'.

[3] I use 'phenomenon' as a general word for any sort of existent, suppressing its meaning of *appearance*.

[4] See further Essay 1. Someone who agrees that physical phenomena are all there are but finds no logical incoherence in the idea that physical things could be put together in such a way as to give rise to non-physical things can define materialism as the view that every real, concrete phenomenon that there is *or could be* in the universe is physical. See McLaughlin 2002: 146.

[5] I qualify 'qualitative' by 'experiential' because every (non-relational) property of a thing contributes to its qualitative character, and the standard materialist assumption is that experiences have non-experiential non-relational properties as well as experiential properties.

[6] Serious materialism, *real* or *realistic* materialism, is wholly realist about consciousness, phenomenology, 'what-it's-likeness'—whatever you prefer to call it. I set out this position in Essay 1.

Let us call the part of reality that consists of Louis the *Louis-reality*—the *L-reality* for short. The notion of the L-reality is rough, for as a concrete physical being Louis is enmeshed in wide-reaching physical interactions, but it is serviceable none the less.[7]

Consider one of Louis's experiences, and suppose for simplicity that it is a sharply delimited, uninterrupted, two-second-long episode lasting from t_1 to t_2 and preceded and followed by a period of complete unconsciousness on Louis's part. Call this event of *experience* '*e*', call the *subject* of this experience '*s*', and call the overall experiential *content* of this experience '*c*', where by 'content' I mean, non-standardly, concretely occurring experiential content that is, furthermore, 'narrow' content, purely 'internal' content, 'phenomenological' content—whatever you want to call the thing whose existence is the most certain of all things and which includes conscious entertainings of thoughts as much as sensory contents.[8] My question is

What is the relation between *e*, *s*, and *c*?

I call the subject of *e* '*s*' rather than 'Louis' in order not to beg any questions. It may seem obvious that *s* = Louis, but there are different views of what subjects of experience are, and of what Louis is, and some combinations of these views have the consequence that *s* is no more identical with Louis than Louis is identical with his left hand.

It helps to start with some general truths about the relations between experience, subject, and content, such as 'There cannot be an experience without experiential content', 'There cannot be an experience without a subject'. These, I take it, are necessary truths, true without possible exception. If we take 'Ex', 'Sx', and 'Cx' to stand for 'x is an experience', 'x is a subject of experience', and 'x is an experiential content' respectively, we can express them as

(1) $[\exists x Ex \Rightarrow \exists y Cy]$

where '$\Rightarrow$' has modal force, strong as you like, and

(2) $[\exists x Ex \Rightarrow \exists y Sy]$

which I will call the *Subject Thesis*.

Introducing 'Oxy' to stand for 'x is the content Of y', one can tighten (1) to

{1} $\forall x[Ex \Rightarrow \exists y[Cy \wedge Oyx]]$.

Letting 'O*xy' stand for 'x is the subject (i.e. haver) Of y', one can tighten (2) to

{2} $\forall x[Ex \Rightarrow \exists y[Sy \wedge O^*yx]]$.

---

[7] Louis is constitutively entangled with the quantum vacuum, and is not neatly separable out as a single portion of reality. There are at any given time many millions of neutrinos passing through the spatial volume bounded by the surface of Louis's skin that are not, I take it, part of Louis. The same goes for much of the content of his intestinal tract (and I'm told that ninety per cent of the cells that make up what we think of as Louis's body are microbial cells that do not carry Louis's DNA).

[8] It is very important to acknowledge that there is cognitive phenomenology as well as sensory phenomenology: experience of thought, of understanding mathematics, a metaphor, and so on. See e.g. James 1890: 1.245–246, Strawson 1994: 5–13, Essay 10 (§6), Essay 11 (§4).

Some have proposed that the Subject Thesis is false, but this view is surely crazy, on its most natural reading. It is 'an obvious conceptual truth that an experiencing is necessarily an experiencing by a subject of experience, and involves that subject as intimately as a branch-bending involves a branch';[9] 'an experience is impossible without an experiencer'.[10] This is not a 'grammatical illusion', as some have proposed, but an inconcussible metaphysical truth. There cannot be experience without a subject of experience simply because experience is necessarily experience *for*—for someone-or-something. Experience necessarily involves experiential 'what-it-is-likeness', and experiential what-it-is-likeness is necessarily what-it-is-likeness *for* someone-or-something. Whatever the full story about the substantial *nature* of this experiencing something, its *existence* cannot be denied.

Descartes gets this exactly right in his *Second Meditation*, remarking that he can know that he exists as thinker or subject however wrong he is about his substantial nature. As he explicitly says, he might for all he knows at this point in his argument be nothing more than his body.[11]

The Cartesian point is secure even if individual-substance-suggesting noun phrases like 'experiencer', 'subject of experience', or 'someone-or-something' are felt to be misleading. Nothing in Buddhism challenges it, when it is understood as it is here. One could put the point paradoxically by saying that if *per impossibile* there could be intense pain-experience without any subject of that experience, mere experience without any experiencer, there would be no point in stopping it, because no one would be suffering.

(1) and (2) are true, then, obviously true.[12] And so also, no doubt, are

(3) $[\exists x Cx \Rightarrow \exists y Ey]$

(4) $[\exists x Cx \Rightarrow \exists y Sy]$

and their tightenings

{3} $\forall x[Cx \Rightarrow \exists y[Ey \wedge Oxy]]$

{4} $\forall x[Cx \Rightarrow \exists y[Sy \wedge O^* yx]]$.

Evidently there can't be concretely occurring experiential content without there being an experience of some sort which the content is the content of. Equally evidently there can't be occurrent content without there being a subject of experience which is the subject that experiences the content. (4) is in effect a version of (2) and is in any case entailed by (2) and (3).

---

[9] Shoemaker 1986: 10.   [10] Frege 1918: 27.

[11] 1641: 18. This is why Lichtenberg's famous objection does not really tell against Descartes's use of 'I' in the Second Meditation. For at that stage his use of 'I' refers to something X which can be known to exist—to be something, not nothing—*whatever it is:* before any metaphysical speculation about what sort of entity it is (i.e. even if it is a property or a 'vapour' rather than a substance).

[12] Some think that Hume denies (2). This is wrong. At the end of §5 I will consider a challenge to (2) raised by the suggestion that the individual-substance-suggesting word 'subject' can be replaced by 'subjectivity'.

(3) and (4) can be questioned, on one reading, for it is arguable that there are occurrent but unexperienced experiential contents.[13] I will put this issue to one side, however, and take 'experiential content' to mean 'experienced content', so that (3) is trivial and (4) is certainly true given that (2) is. For the question that concerns me is not whether there is some sense in which experiential content can possibly exist without experience existing, but: *given* an experience, which must have content, and must have an experiencer (= (1) and (2)), what is the relation between that experience, its content, and its subject?

With (1)–(4) in place, two possible entailments remain

(5) $[\exists x S x \Rightarrow \exists y E y]$
(6) $[\exists x S x \Rightarrow \exists y C y]$[14]

and if either is true the other is,[15] but both are plainly false given the common understanding of the notion of a subject, according to which a subject can exist at a given time without any experience existing at that time. There is, however, a crucial way of conceiving of subjects which has the consequence that (5) and (6) are true, and I will set it out in the next section. I think it is extremely important to have this way of understanding subjects to hand when considering the metaphysics of consciousness.

First, though, let me simplify my terminology, and replace (1)-(6) and their tightenings by

(1) $[E \Rightarrow C]$
(2) $[E \Rightarrow S]$
(3) $[C \Rightarrow E]$
(4) $[C \Rightarrow S]$
(5) $[S \Rightarrow E]$
(6) $[S \Rightarrow C]$.

Thus (4) $[C \Rightarrow S]$ states that there cannot be experiential content without there being a subject of experience who is the subject or experiencer of that experiential content. (1)-(4) are as trivial as ever, and I will now defend (5) and (6) which, conjoined with (1) and (3), give $[S \Leftrightarrow C]$ and $[S \Leftrightarrow E]$ and so

(7) $[E \Leftrightarrow S \Leftrightarrow C]$.[16]

2 SUBJECTS OF EXPERIENCE—THICK, TRADITIONAL, THIN (LIVE)

Many find it natural to say that human beings and other animals *considered as a whole* are subjects of experience. I'll call this the *thick* conception of the subject. It's taken

---

[13] See e.g. Lockwood 1989: 162–168, Strawson 1994: 170 n.
[14] Duly accompanied by {5} $\forall x[Sx \Rightarrow \exists y[Ey \wedge O^*xy]]$ and {6} $\forall x[Sx \Rightarrow \exists y[Cy \wedge Oxy]]$.
[15] If (5) is true then (6) is, by (5) and (1); if (6) is true then (5) is, by (6) and (3).
[16] I omit the brackets required by the convention that every two-place operator brings a pair of brackets.

for granted by experimental psychologists and most analytic philosophers, who may not easily see (or remember) that it is neither mandatory nor particularly natural.

In spite of this orthodoxy, many think that the subject properly or strictly speaking is some sort of inner mental thing or presence, 'the self', or some such: a persisting something that is essentially distinct from, not identical with, the persisting human being considered as a whole. This conception of the subject has for long periods been dominant in philosophy, and I will call it the *traditional inner* conception. It comes extremely naturally to us, given the character of our experience of ourselves; it is not a covert product of philosophical or religious speculation, or a rare (or 'Western') eccentricity, as some body-stressing philosophers suppose. 'No matter how my brain works . . . , one single fact remains . . . I am aware of a self that looks out at the world from somewhere inside my skull . . . this is . . . the central datum with which every theory of consciousness has to grapple.'[17]

Some who favour the thick conception of the subject accept that the traditional inner conception is widespread, but think it mistaken, pernicious, and in some way anti-materialist. I agree with them that it is mistaken in so far as it posits a *genuinely persisting* inner subject distinct from the persisting human being, but it is certainly not anti-materialist, as will emerge.

So far, then, we have two conceptions of the subject:

[i] the *thick* whole-creature conception dominant in present-day analytic philosophy and experimental psychology

and

[ii] the *traditional inner* conception according to which a subject of experience is an inner thing or presence of some sort.

I take it that [i] and [ii] both build in the assumption that a subject may and standardly does continue to exist even when it is not having any experience: whether you think that human subjects are whole human beings or whether you think they are inner mental somethings you are likely to allow that they can continue to exist during periods of complete unconsciousness or experiencelessness—in periods of dreamless sleep, say.

It is this that creates the need for a third conception of the subject

[iii] the *thin* conception according to which a subject of experience does not and cannot exist at any given time unless it is having experience at that time.

The thin conception stands opposed to both [i] and [ii] precisely because they both build in the assumption that a subject can be said to exist in the absence of any experience.

—Why shouldn't they? It seems overwhelmingly natural.

Perhaps it does. But to limit oneself to [i] and [ii] is to run the risk of begging a central question. Here I face a problem of exposition, because many philosophers are so

[17] Trefil 1997: 181.

accustomed to [i] and/or [ii], and to the idea that they exhaust the options, that they cannot take [iii] seriously. And yet [iii] simply makes a place for a natural use of the term 'subject' according to which it is a necessary truth, no less, that

there cannot be a subject *of experience*, at any given time, unless some *experience* exists for it to be a subject *of*, at that time.

The thin conception of the subject requires that the subject be 'live', so to say, in order to exist at all (I will use 'thin' and 'live' interchangeably). This is sufficient to establish

(5) [S ⇒ E]

and (5) conjoined with (1) entails

(6) [S ⇒ C].

This gives the full house of (1)–(6) which we can as noted write as

(7) [E ⇔ S ⇔ C].

As it stands, [iii] does not specify that the thin subject be an *inner* thing, relative to the whole human being, so let me make this explicit, altering [iii] to

[iii] the *thin* conception according to which a subject of experience is an inner thing of some sort that does not and cannot exist at any given time unless it is having experience at that time.

As a materialist I take the subject to be inner in a robust spatial sense because the physical goings on that wholly constitute its existence consist entirely of parts of a brain in a certain state of activation.

—Look, I can form [iv] the thin conception of an *eater* according to which an eater doesn't and can't exist at any given time unless it's eating at that time. But a (possibly fat) thin eater is just one of those silly putative objects (or 'objects') that some metaphysicians like to play with. It's of no real interest or use in philosophy, and your thin subjects seem just as silly.[18]

That remains to be seen. It's true that [iii] is formally similar to [iv]. [iii] can't by itself do the work of showing that the thin conception of the subject (unlike the thin conception of an eater) cuts reality at the joints in an important or fundamental way. I hope this will be done in the next section.

The thin conception of the subject is hardly new. Descartes accepts [iii] in its first formulation. He holds that the soul or subject cannot exist in the absence of experience or consciousness. In fact he holds that the subject is in some sense wholly constituted of experience or consciousness. I think he may be right about this, but for the wrong reasons. (His view is entangled with his dualism, but I think he may be right even if materialism is true.)

---

[18] Thanks to John Broome, who was more courteous. It's in the spirit of such spurious object-generation that one could equally well define a happy thin eater in this way: an eater that doesn't and can't exist at any given time unless it's eating and happy at that time. And so on.

Hume also accepts [iii]: 'when my perceptions are remov'd for any time, as by sound sleep', he writes, 'so long am I insensible of *myself*, and may truly be said not to exist'. He holds that there is no self or subject at all when there is no experience, although there is certainly a self or subject when there is experience.[19]

How does all this apply to Louis—to the L-reality? Those who favour [i] find one subject in the L-reality. The same goes, no doubt, for those who favour [ii].[20] But those who favour [iii], and who believe that human life regularly involves periods of complete experiencelessness (periods of dreamless sleep, for example), must find many subjects in the L-reality considered over time.[21] Some will say that this consequence counts strongly against [iii], but I think this is mere terminological habit or prejudice.

However that may be, I will be concerned only with thin subjects from now on, and only with human thin subjects, unless I specify otherwise. Nothing I say will challenge any of the many true things that have been said about subjects of experience by those who favour the thick use of 'subject'.

Are thin subjects persons? If you wish. In philosophy, the sense of the word 'person' is not fixed independently of theory. Certainly longevity is not decisive: if a creature qualitatively identical to me during three seconds of my life exists for just three seconds, that creature is certainly a person and deserves all the consideration due to any of us. And there may be creatures who live lives as complex as ours in three seconds. Thin subjects have been defined as inner things of some sort, but this doesn't decide the issue against their being persons. Some think it evident that human persons cannot be anything other than human beings considered as a whole, but Henry James's phrasing is very natural when he writes, of one of his early books,

I think of... the masterpiece in question... as the work of quite another person than myself... a rich relation, say, who... suffers me still to claim a shy fourth cousinship.[22]

James knows perfectly well that he is the same *human being* as the author of that book, but he does not feel he is the same *person* as the author of that book.

Are thin subjects things that can be said to speak English and know French and algebra? Certainly, in every sense in which you can be said to know these things at any given time.

Are we thin subjects? In one respect, of course, we are thick subjects, human beings considered as a whole. In this respect we are, in being subjects, things that can yawn and scratch. In another respect, though, we are in being subjects of experience no more whole human beings than hands or hearts: we are—literally—inner things, thin subjects, no more things that can yawn or scratch than eyebrows or thoughts. Once again there is nothing anti-materialist about this view.[23]

[19] 1739–40: 252/1.4.6.3. For a discussion of Hume's chronically misunderstood position on personal identity and the self, see Strawson 2001 and *The Evident Connexion*.
[20] Louis has not had a cerebral commisurotomy, is not suffering from dissociative identity disorder, and so on.
[21] It is an unsettled empirical question whether there are any periods of complete experiencelessness during a normal human life, after the experiential quickening in the womb.
[22] 1915: 562–3.　　[23] I discuss these questions at greater length in Part 7 of *Selves*.

—But 'What then am *I*?'[24] Am I two different sort of things, a thin subject and a thick subject? This is ridiculous. Who—or what—speaks when Louis says 'I'?

My answer is that 'I' is not univocal. We move naturally between conceiving of ourselves primarily as a human being and primarily as some sort of inner subject (we do not of course naturally conceive of ourselves as a *thin* subject). Sometimes we mean to refer to the one, sometimes to the other; sometimes our semantic intention hovers between both, sometimes it embraces both.[25]

3   TERMS AND ASSUMPTIONS

To introduce the notion of a thin subject is, so far, simply to introduce a certain way of talking about something whose existence is not in question. It is to draw a theoretical line around a certain aspect or 'portion' of concrete reality and to choose to give it a certain name. The way of talking may be disliked or thought unhelpful. Attachments to linguistic and theoretical habits can be as intense as attachment to dietary prohibitions, and can give rise to a conviction that other ways of talking are intrinsically wrong. But the phenomenon I refer to in speaking of thin/live subjects is indisputably real and utterly commonplace.

It's true that the inclination to think of the inner subject (or self) as a persisting thing is basic in ordinary thought. It is, no doubt, one manifestation of the fact that human beings have a deep, innate, highly general (and often thoroughly sensible) tendency to posit and think in terms of persisting things, long-term continuants, when faced with sequences of items (e.g. appearances) that resemble each other in certain respects although they are numerically distinct.[26] But it has no special weight when it comes to metaphysics.

The existence of thin/live subjects is not an assumption, then. It is, so far, a terminological ruling. 'Thin/live subject' picks out whatever aspect or portion of reality constitutes the existence of a subject of experience when it is defined as an inner thing that does not and cannot exist when there is no experience for it to be the subject of. The question is whether this use of 'subject' can survive and thrive given the other energies contained in the word.

I am making certain assumptions: I've assumed that materialism or physicalism is true, and I'm now going to assume that human live subjects are short-lived entities. I'm going to take it that the human process of consciousness is non-continuous in a certain way. I believe, in fact, that it is non-continuous in such a way that there are many thin subjects of experience in the L-reality in any normal waking day (others,

---

[24] As Descartes asked (1641: 18).

[25] See Strawson 1999: 515, and *Selves* §7.2 for a defence of this view. With regard to the inner reference, I claim that we take ourselves to be referring to a persisting subject, but that since there is no such thing we refer in fact to the current thin/live subject, or the series of such subjects—in so far as we refer to a subject at all.

[26] See Hume 1739–40 (for the case of objects in general see 201–4/1.4.2.29–35; for the case of self or subject in particular see 259ff/1.4.6.15–22. For important recent improvements on the idea see e.g. Spelke 1994, 1996.

perhaps, believe that it is continuous in the case of any waking day but interrupted at night).

An outright temporal gap in consciousness in the L-reality is obviously sufficient for non-continuity, but it is not necessary, on the present view: one experientially unitary period of experience or 'pulse' of thought (in William James's terminology) may succeed another in a temporally seamless way and yet count as a discontinuity for the purposes of counting subjects.[27]

Let me also register my view that subjects of experience are happily thought of as *objects*,[28] even when they are thinly understood, as here. If one is going to talk of objects at all in one's metaphysics, then it is I think not hard to show that live subjects have at least as good a claim to be called objects as anything else. For whatever objects are, they are, given materialism, physical *unities* of a certain sort, and there are I think no more indisputable, objective, natural, theory-independent physical unities than thin subjects of experience.[29]

That said, I think that matter is best thought of as what one might call 'process-stuff', and that all physical objects are best thought of as processes, even if the converse is not true. And I take it this to be true on a three-dimensionalist or 3D view of objects as much as on a four-dimensionalist or 4D view (it doesn't matter if you're not familiar with this distinction).[30] We have continually to combat a deep and misleading *staticism* in our thought about matter and objects.[31] Matter is essentially *dynamic*: essentially in time and essentially changeful.[32] All reality is process, as Whitehead was moved to observe by his study of twentieth-century physics, and as Heracleitus proposed long ago. Perhaps we would do better to call matter 'time-matter', or 'matter-in-time', so that we never for a moment forget its temporality. We think of matter as essentially extended, but we tend to think only of extension in space—something that can, we intuitively feel, be given to us as a whole at an instant. But space and time are interdependent. They are aspects of spacetime, and all concrete spatial extension is extension in spacetime.[33]

It follows from this interdependence alone, I think, that there is no *metaphysically weighty* distinction between objects and processes given which objects are not truly said to be processes, although there is for many purposes a perfectly *respectable* distinction to be made between them. But even if relativity theory is false there is no metaphysically defensible conception of a physical object—a 'spatio-temporal

---

[27] It may have very similar or radically different content.

[28] I prefer not to use the philosopher's count-noun 'substance', although I think it can be understood in a non-misleading way.

[29] For a brief defence see Strawson 1999; for a more sustained defence see *Selves* §§6.13–14. The thin eaters cannot compete.

[30] It is arguable that it is more obviously true on a 3D view than on some versions of the 4D view which see time as 'spacelike'; but 'process' is a time word that has application on any view that is realist about time, and the 4D view is realist about time. (The adversarial character of the 3D/4D debate is a waste of time; for some outstanding mediation, see Jackson 1994: 96–103.)

[31] I defend this idea in Essay 16 (§4) and Strawson 1999 (§§15–16).

[32] I am taking 'dynamic' to be equivalent to 'in time and changing', although some realists about time might precisely wish to question the aptness of the words 'dynamic' and 'changing'.

[33] This is not a distinctively 4D claim (should anyone's terminological habits make it seem so).

continuant', as philosophers say—that allows one to distinguish validly between objects and processes by saying that the latter are essentially dynamic or changeful phenomena in some way in which the former are not. The source of the idea that there might be some metaphysically deep distinction between objects and processes lies in everyday habits of thought that are ordinarily harmless and useful but seriously disabling—almost perfectly unhelpful—in certain theoretical contexts. I think philosophers continue to be very severely hampered by these habits of thought even when they have fully agreed and, as they think, deeply appreciated, that objects are entirely creatures of time, process-entities.

Here is an analogy that I should not use, because it has illustrative force only relative to the staticist picture I reject. Imagine a customized set of party lights. Switched on for two seconds, each light flashes in a pattern that depends on the other lights' state of activation. The object that corresponds to the subject *s*, in this analogy, is not the set of lights conceived as something you can put away in a box for next year (which we naturally think of as an object). Nor is it the set of lights considered as a few-seconds-long temporal slice of the thing that you can put away in a box for next year (a rather peculiar object, by our ordinary lights). The object that corresponds to *s* (*s* having *e*) in this analogy is: the-set-of-lights-in-the-process-of-flashing.

One might try to underline the idea by repeating that thin subjects are dynamic entities, but this already concedes too much to the staticism of ordinary thought about objects, because all physical objects are dynamic entities (there's an awful lot going on in a stone). The lights analogy draws what force it has from the contrast between the natural staticist picture of the set of lights and the 'dynamic' entity that consists of the set-of-lights-in-the-process-of-flashing-for-two-seconds, but really all objects are best conceived on the model of the set-of-lights-in-the-process-of-flashing-for-two-seconds—as essentially processual entities made of process-stuff.

I labour the point to establish its banality. I think there are areas of metaphysics in which it is crucial to cultivate the intuition of process in thinking about concrete reality.

—In that case, why bother with the solid staticist word 'object' at all, or the strongly substantial word 'subject'? Why not fall back into a world—or vocabulary—of Russellian 'events' or Whiteheadian 'occasions'?

First because there is no reason why one should not take the words 'object' and 'subject' with one into the processual outlook, realigning them to mean more clearly on their faces what they have meant (referentially speaking) all along. Second because there are positive reasons why one should take these words with one, rather than leaving them behind as specious rallying points for bad intuitions.

Certainly the brevity (by our lights) I attribute to human thin subjects should not count against their claim to be objects. W-particles and Z-particles presumably count as objects in almost any serious materialist metaphysics that countenances objects at all, and they are considerably more ephemeral entities than thin subjects.

Thin subjects certainly exist as defined, then, and are to be counted among the objects, on the present terms; objects being processes, wholly constituted out of time-matter, process-stuff. I take it, as a materialist, that all thin subjects are

entirely constituted out of process-stuff in the brain. This process-stuff is constantly being recruited—electrochemically corralled—into one transient subject-
constituting (and equally experience-constituting) *synergy* of process-stuff after
another. These synergies, these experiences, are I propose *intrinsically unified* phenomena, objective physical unities; and there is one subject to each. (It is a necessary
truth that an experience is unified at any given time, however complex it is, because it
is true by definition of 'an experience'—'experience' used as a count noun—that an
experience is experience had from a single subjective perspective. What I add here to
the necessary truth about necessary unity at a given time is the claim that individual
experiences can have diachronic unity, true unity across time, however fleeting they
are. See the Kantian point below.)

This, I propose, is what the conscious life of a human being consists in. My (empirical) bet is that these intrinsically unified episodes of experience, and hence these thin
subjects, last for a maximum of about two seconds, in the human case; with many
being much shorter.[34] I believe that there is always some sort of break of consciousness in any longer period of time, although this is not phenomenologically accessible
to most people in normal life.

What sort of break? There may be a straightforward temporal gap between one
experience-upsurging and the next, as already remarked. Alternatively, an experience-
upsurging with a new subject may follow its predecessor seamlessly (either picking up the baton of its predecessor's content or switching to something completely
new). We can also allow the possibility that a new experience can overlap its predecessor temporally, as one recruitment or neurons gathers pace and peaks in subject-
involving conscious experience before the previous one has died away to nothing (see
Figure 6.1).[35]

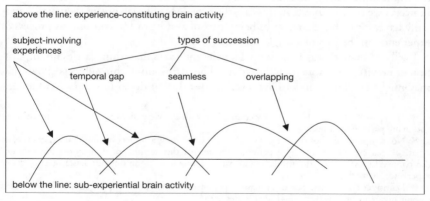

Figure 6.1.

[34] I am influenced by research by Pöppel and others (Pöppel 1978, Ruhnau 1995). I don't want
to rule out the possibility that the human mind can be trained to sustain longer periods of unified
experience. (Added 2007: for a revision of this view see *Selves* §5.8.)

[35] James agrees (1890: 1.401).

These experience-upsurgings are, I propose, primitive unities, 'indecomposable unities', in James's phrase,[36] and they essentially contain only one subject.[37] They are of course physical unities, on the present view, and they are, most strikingly, unities that we can know to exist and to be true unities, given that physicalism is true. For we know that thoughts—events of proposition-comprehension—occur.[38] And we know that they have (must have) distinguishable parts or elements, to be thoughts. And we know that these distinguishable parts must be held together (bound together in the sense of the 'binding problem') in the unity that is the comprehension of the proposition by a subject, if there is indeed to be a thought. So we know that there are actually existing concrete physical entities that realize a certain sort of unsurpassable unity, a 'logical' unity, in Kant's terms, the 'absolute . . . logical unity of the subject', the 'logical unity of any thought'.[39] One may put the point by saying that the unity necessarily involved in the comprehending entertaining of a thought, which is itself a concrete unity, as real and concrete a unity as any unity in nature, is itself a metaphysical unity of the highest order. This is so whatever else is involved in its existence, whether it be many neurons acting in concert, as we ordinarily suppose, or, in Kant's more neutral terms in his Second Paralogism, a 'collective unity of different substances acting together'. I take it that the same holds true of multimodally complex sensory experiences, although we do not have the special proof of unity that is available in the case of thoughts.

If overlap of the sort just imagined occurs in the L-reality then there are for a brief time two experiences-with-subjects in the L-reality. But neither of the two (thin) subjects that are numerically distinguishable at time *t*, on this view of experiences as successive neuronal recruitments, is aware of there being two subjects at *t*; nor is Louis the whole human being considered as a (thick) subject of experience aware of this at *t*. However we count subjects in this case the experience of each one of them will standardly have, for it, the character of being part of a more or less continuous process of experience on the part of a single subject.[40]

I will elaborate this as I go along. Here let me stress that 'thin' carries no implication of brevity, any more than 'live' does. The definition of thin subjects allows that they might last for hours or days, even if they do not do so in our case. One may

---

[36] James 1890: 1.371. This is wholly compatible with the view that they involve many neurons and many parts of neurons.

[37] No 'temporal slice' of the subject can be said to be itself a subject having that experience, or a part of that experience, or any experience. (Note that this account of things does not rule out the panpsychist view that the fundamental particles might in some difficult sense be subjects of experience themselves.)

[38] I consider the popular case of thought-experiences, but the point applies equally to a subject's having any experience with distinguishable elements.

[39] 1781–7: A356, A398. See also B407: 'that . . . the *I* of . . . thought . . . designates a logically simple subject—this lies already in the very concept of thought'.

[40] Standardly: some, like myself, often experience consciousness as gappy in everyday life—as if it were somehow continually restarting. See e.g. Strawson 1997.

even suppose, with Descartes, that human thin subjects may be immortal, sempi-ternal.

—But what is the relation of a thin subject to a human being? What is the relation between this putative thin subject *s* existing in the L-reality from time t_1 to t_2 and Louis the human being?

I take it to be a straightforward part-whole relation, like the relation between Louis the whole human being and one of his toes or transient blemishes. *s* is a spatiotempor-ally bounded piece of process-stuff which one may call p^s, Louis considered as a whole is a spatiotemporally bounded piece of process-stuff which one may call p^L, and p^s is ontically distinct from p^L in the way in which any (proper) part of an object that is itself correctly thought of as an object (a cell, a heart, a goose pimple) is ontically dis-tinct from the larger object of which it is a part. *s* is also *not* ontically distinct from Louis in any sense in which such a part of Louis is not ontically distinct from Louis.[41]

I assume in a standard physicalist way that p^s is wholly constituted of a plurality of fundamental entities in a certain state of activation—'particles' or 'strings' or 'fields' or 'physical simples' or *ultimates*, as I will call the ultimate constituents of reality, whatever they are—and I take it that its identity conditions as a piece of process-stuff are a strict function of its parts dynamically conceived: if one adds or subtracts a single ultimate or changes its state of dynamic activation in any way, one no longer has the same synergy or the same subject. (Staticist superficiality threatens even in the distinction between the ultimate and its state of activation, but it would take too long to rewrite everything in an appropriately dynamic idiom.)

I have said that *s* is identical with p^s: $[s = p^s]$. *s* is wholly constituted of the ulti-mates which wholly constitute *p*. It would, however, be a mistake to assume that this identity claim is a 'merely' constitutive identity claim—*if*, that is, one understands a constitutive identity claim (as many do) to be an identity claim that allows that the constituter can possibly exist in the absence of the constitutee, or conversely.[42] p^s and *s* are defined in an essentially temporal-dynamic way, as the very same pro-cess, and it appears to follow that a *simple* identity claim holds true of them: neither can exist without the other, any more than (what is in fact the same thing) something can exist without itself. *s* could not possibly have consisted of anything other than the particular synergy of process-stuff p^s and p^s could not possibly have existed without *s* existing. Or so I will maintain, in the face of objections that appeal to counterfactual speculation.

Assuming this is so, the same goes for *e* and *c*. An experience—a spatiotemporal patch of occurrent content—is a concrete existent. It therefore consists of—is—a

---

[41] Note how the notion of the thin subject can accommodate the powerful three-dimensionalist intuition that a person is fully present *right now*, in the ordinary loose sense of 'now' that allows a few seconds stretch, within a generally four-dimensionalist scheme.

[42] One popular example considers a statue and the lump of bronze out of which it is made. The lump can survive the melting down of the statue, and some loss of parts, and the statue can survive loss of parts and repair. See e.g. Wiggins 2001.

portion of process-stuff in the brain and is, as such, a candidate for being treated as an object: $[e = p^e]$ and $[c = p^c]$. Neither could possibly have consisted of any ultimate constituents other than the ones of which it does consist.

It may help to speak of a *t-portion* so that the essential temporality of the portion is always marked. But then it must be stressed that the t-portions of process-stuff with which we are concerned are things that have real or natural temporal boundaries and have nothing to do with the analytic metaphysicians' 'temporal parts'. Overall, I prefer to stick with plain 'portion'—having just explicitly cancelled the staticist force of the word.

Many may think that c is best understood as a property and not as a thing, and that the same goes for e (and indeed for s, relative to Louis the human being), but their candidacy for being thought of as particulars is sufficiently established for present purposes by the fact that we can legitimately think of their existence as consisting wholly in the existence of a certain portion of process-stuff. This suggestion may raise deep resistances. I think these stem from the inadequacy of the standard conception of the relation between an object and its properties which I will consider in §7.

This way of setting things up offends some common intuitions about the conditions under which something can be correctly said to remain the same thing, and I will later consider and reject some counterfactual-based objections to it.

I hope the word 'synergy' does some work against the staticist tendencies of our ordinary conception of objects. It is not wrong, nor even particularly unclear, to say simply that s (or e) consists of a piece or bit or segment or portion of process-stuff, for the essentially temporal, dynamic nature of what is in question has already been strongly marked by the term 'process-stuff'. But a piece of time-matter, process-stuff, could be dynamic in every part (every piece of physical process-stuff *is* dynamic in every part, every atom is in internal uproar) without being synergetic in any particularly interesting way, let alone synergetic in the way required for it to be a subject or an experience.[43] It is the *synergy* of process-stuff p^s that constitutes—is— s. One is not thinking accurately about the piece of process-stuff (involving 10^{12} ultimates, say) that wholly constitutes $s = p^s$ if one is thinking of it in any way that allows it to be some sort of further fact about it that it is synergetic in the way that it is.

Shifting from s to e (where the same points apply), I take the 'process-stuff' idiom to allow one, in talking of e ($= p^e$), to refer to a portion of reality—e—in an *extremely* specific way that excludes any and all process-stuff that is not *directly constitutive* of e, i.e. part of the being of e; and I take it that to do this is to exclude things like cell-wall-constituting ultimates, myelin-constituting ultimates, and so on (always assuming that nature in her astonishing ingenuity has not found a way to put even these things to work as directly consciousness-constituting elements) that may be supposed to be part of e on a more inclusive view of what an experience is. It is to e so conceived that the simple identity claim $[e = p^e]$ applies: the process-stuff picked out by 'p^e' involves only those ultimates that actually constitute or are the experiencing. The process-stuff idiom allows intensely fine-grained demarcations of portions of reality

---

[43] Mutual gravitational influence is already synergy, on one view. The physical synergy that is of particular interest in the present case is the sort of (macroscopic) thing studied by neurophysiologists.

(I hope the account of the relation between an object and its properties in §7 will clarify this). It allows one to separate off the process-stuff that directly constitutes *e* from everything else in the neuronal synergy that is a candidate for being constitutive of *e* on a blunter view of things which lets in cell-wall-constituting ultimates, and so on.[44]

4   WHAT IS THE RELATION BETWEEN e, s, AND c?

So much for preliminaries. Thin subjects certainly exist as defined. Human thin subjects certainly exist (I think they last for a maximum of about two seconds). I have suggested that, when we come to fundamental metaphysics, they have at least as good a claim to the title 'physical object' as anything else. They are not metaphysically silly, like the thin eaters. (They have nothing to do with the toy objects that analytic metaphysicians delight in.) Like all other physical objects they are essentially spatiotemporal, essentially dynamic entities. Like all other physical objects other than individual ultimates they are constituted of collections of ultimates. They are synergies of process-stuff of a certain very special sort, involving special macroelectrical goings on.

We may now repeat the question:

What is the relation between *e*, *s*, and *c*?

We have established that

(7) $[E \Leftrightarrow S \Leftrightarrow C]$

—that no experience can lack a subject or a content, that no content can occur without a subject and an experience, and that no subject can exist in the absence of an experience and (hence) a content. As it stands, though, this is a relatively weak claim, and I am going to put forward the stronger claim that no experience can have a subject or a content different from the one it does have, along with its natural companions (the claim that no subject can have an experience or an experiential content other than the one it does have, and the claim that no experiential content can be an experience other than the one it is or have a subject other than the one it does). Some of these claims are trivial—all of them are trivial on one natural reading of the claim that everything is what it is and not another thing—but others may seem less obvious.

5   THE SUBJECT THESIS: POLARITY

I introduced '*e*', '*s*', and '*c*' in §1 to refer to a particular experience of Louis's, the (thin) subject of that experience and its content (conceived of as before as something

---

[44] It doesn't matter if these examples are wrong. It is enough that there may be ultimates in the brain that are necessary for the existence of *e* although they are not directly constitutive of *e*. I will say a little more about this in §9.

occurrent), but I am now going to use them to refer quite generally to any particular individual experience occurring at a particular time $t_1 - t_2$, the subject of that experience, and the content of that experience. The claim to be considered, then, is the particularized version of (7), i.e.

[7] $[e \Leftrightarrow s \Leftrightarrow c]$

or, in other terms,

[7^p] $[p^e \Leftrightarrow p^s \Leftrightarrow p^c]$.

All of (1)–(6) can be particularized in the same way. '$\Leftrightarrow$' and '$\Rightarrow$' acquire a new use, linking objects rather than propositions, but this use is not hard to understand. The particularized version of

(5) $[S \Rightarrow E]$

for example, i.e.

[5] $[s \Rightarrow e]$,

states that *s* cannot possibly exist without *e* existing; *s* cannot possibly exist apart from *e*.

[7] has strong modal force, but ' $\Leftrightarrow$' is not very informative. If it is true it would be good to know more about what makes it true. It would be nice to know more about the metaphysics of the situation.

My first proposal is that we may and should move on from [1] and [2]—the obvious thesis that every experience has some experiential content, and the equally obvious Subject Thesis that experience has to be experience-*for* someone-or-something—to the thesis that an experience *consists* of a (thin) subject entertaining—having, living—a content. I propose to write this as

[8] $[e = s{:}c]$

where ':' has some kind of strong intimacy-intimating function whose force (over and above '$\Leftrightarrow$') remains to be determined. [8], then, is formed on the model of the general connection schema [7]. It replaces the first '$\Leftrightarrow$' in [7] by identity (an explanatory move) and the second by some as yet unspecified metaphysical intimacy (a potentially explanatory move).

One thing that seems helpful about [8] is that it gives expression to the idea that any experience comports a fundamental and irreducible *polarity*—the polarity of subject and content. I will now expound this idea, and say something further about the Subject Thesis. In order to do this I will abstract away from the non-experiential being of *e* in the way anticipated at the end of the §3 (for *e* certainly has non-experiential being according to standard materialism) and consider it only in its experiential being. I will call the object of enquiry that is delivered by this move e_e.

In fact I think one can pick out e_e not just as an object of thought or enquiry but as a physical object, a portion of reality that has (in fundamental metaphysics) at least as good a claim to that status as anything else. I think, in other words, that when one is picking out physical objects, in this particular area of reality, one can not only pick out the object that consists of those synergetic ultimates that are directly constitutive of *e*, and that have (as standard materialism supposes) both experiential and non-experiential being; one can also pick out, as a portion of reality that has an equally good a title to the description 'physical object', just the experiential being of *e*—i.e. e_e. But I do not need to consider this point further here.[45]

Given that e_e exists, what else *must* exist? Different metaphysical positions deliver different answers, but the Subject Thesis completely bypasses these disputes. It points out that one has to grant that a subject must exist, given that *e* exists, even when one considers only e_e, and before one has made any other assumptions about the nature of reality. Even when all one has assumed to exist is e_e one can already know—so it seems—that what exists given that e_e exists is *complex* in a certain respect. e_e may be complex in virtue of its content: it may be experience as of seeing a complicated array of different colours. But even if e_e is just uniform experience of green or a pure note[46] it seems that one is already in a position to assert (to know) that what exists, given that e_e exists, is and must be complex or plural in a certain respect. For e_e cannot possibly exist without the polarity of experiencer and experiential content. Where there is experiential content there is necessarily experienc*ing*, and where there is experiencing there is necessarily an experienc*er*—a subject of experience. This is the polarity that, so far, seems well expressed by the colon in [8].

Some may want to replace the individual-substance-suggesting word 'subject' by 'subjectivity', in spite of assurances that the Subject Thesis (in good *Second-Meditation* style) makes absolutely no claim whatever about the ultimate substantial nature of the subject, and certainly doesn't claim that the subject can be known to be something ontologically distinct from *e* (or indeed e_e). That's fine. I'm not prepared to allow the replacement of 'subject' by 'subjectivity' in the Subject Thesis unless it is allowed in return that 'subject' can also be correctly used, but this is surely only a matter of terminology,[47] and the basic point surely remains untouched: e_e must still involve *some* sort of irreducible complexity or polarity in involving the phenomenon of subjectivity, on the one hand, and the phenomenon of content, on the other.

Well, perhaps the point is not entirely untouched; perhaps it does not seem quite so luminously evident after the substitution of 'subjectivity' for 'subject'. That's fine, too, for in the end, I do not want it to be untouched. And to say that it is provable that any experience comports some sort of irreducible polarity, and that this can be

---

[45] This raises deep and important issues. I hope the discussion of the relation between an object and its properties in §7 will help to show how it can be so, for if one uses the standard object/property idiom it looks pretty dubious. For suppose one says that e_e is identical with a synergy of ultimates and conceives these ultimates as objects that 'have' 'properties' in the usual way. One may then feel obliged (as a standard materialist) to say that these ultimates have non-experiential properties. In which case one inevitably picks out something with non-experiential being in attempting to pick out e_e as a distinct physical object. In which case one cannot really pick e_e out at all, because it has, by definition, no non-experiential being.

[46] Putting aside brightness/saturation/hue and pitch/timbre/loudness complexity.

[47] Some Buddhists find it hard to accept, given time-honoured terminological habits, but I am struck by the claim of the great Buddhist scholar Edmund Conze 'that no passage in the Buddhist scriptures teaches that there is no self' or subject (1963: 242). Godehard Bruntrup tells me that this claim has been refuted, but it seems highly significant none the less.

known to be so even when one restricts oneself to e_e, is not yet to say that one can prove irreducible, full-on ontological *plurality a priori* from the mere existence of e_e.

—I don't know what you mean by 'full-on ontological plurality', and this is all wrong in any case. Experiential *content* is all that can be truly discerned when one restricts attention not just to e but to e_e. The subject of experience cannot be discerned. This is what Hume took such pains to show.

Hume did no such thing,[48] but let's leave him out of this. Even it were true that experiential content is all that can be *discerned* when one is restricted to e_e it would still be true that the subject can be known to *exist* if e_e is known to exist, for the same old reason: if there is an experience of pain, then there must be something, however unknown it is in any further respect, that feels the pain. There cannot be *just* experiential content—if to say this is in any way to suggest that there could possibly not also be a subject of experience.[49] Experience (once again) is necessarily experience-*for*. We must discern at least this much structure in the world if it contains an experience. This is the Subject Thesis. It does not depend on the traditional idea that an experience, being a *process* or *event*, necessarily requires some sort of *substance* that is in some way distinct from it, in which it can go on or occur. It holds good even if one proposes that there is nothing but process, 'pure process', indeed pure mental process, in the universe.

Some, given their terminological preferences, think that Buddhist meditation, or indeed any remotely successful practice of meditation, however secular, shows the noun-phrase 'subject of experience' to be irredeemably metaphysically excessive and to carry a heavy traditional-metaphysical-object-implying force. But there is no reason to accept this. It is only a terminological attachment, a verbal clinging. The reply is not just that objects are process-stuff. The principal reply is that the force of the word 'subject' in its present use is such that the existence of subjectivity *entails* the existence of a subject (certainly the notion of a subject carries no implication of long-term persistence).

Before I was interrupted (before Hume was misrepresented) I was proposing that we can know that reality is complex in a certain way even if all we know is that a given experience e exists—even when considering e just as e_e. Experience seems to involve an irreducible polarity, which seems, so far, well enough represented by the colon in [8] $[e = s{:}c]$. It is not, however, clear that we can know that this polarity involves some sort of genuine ontological plurality—a *real* distinction, as opposed to a merely *conceptual* distinction, in Descartes's terms. There is a real distinction between two phenomena, in his terms (so that genuine ontological plurality is in question), if and only if they can possibly 'exist apart', and a merely conceptual distinction between them if and only if they are conceptually distinct, like trilaterality and triangularity, but cannot possibly exist apart.[50] I am going to consider the suggestion that the actual subject s of any given actual experience e cannot possibly exist apart from the

---

[48] See Strawson 2001, and *The Evident Connexion*.
[49] Kant (1781–7) puts this well in the Paralogisms.
[50] I will use these terms in this sense throughout (see Descartes 1644: 1.213–15).

occurrent content c^{51} of e, even in thought. So I don't want to suggest that the allegedly irreducible subject-content polarity of experience proves its irreducible ontological plurality. Some may think that counterfactual speculation can easily pull them apart, but I am going to deny this.

—Well, is there or is there not irreducible ontological plurality?

This issue now has to be addressed. It is very difficult—it includes, for one thing, the perennial problems raised by the distinction between an object and its properties—but I will now begin on it.

$$6 \quad [e = s = c]?$$

The colon-designated relation is admittedly murky, but at least it seems clear that we cannot develop it into identity and say that

[9] $[e = s = c]$.

The subject cannot, surely, *be* the content. Even if there is some sense in which it is best to say that the subject of the experience is just the (necessary) subjectivity of the experience, still the subjectivity cannot, surely, obviously, *be* the content.

That remains to be seen. In the meantime, it may be suggested that the colon in [8] is too appositional, and too separatist, and perhaps also too egalitarian, suggesting full equality of ontological status across the double dots—so that there is no difference between *s:c* and *c:s*. In reply one can insist that the ':' is directional, as in its ordinary punctuational use, so that *s:c* and *c:s* are not the same, but it might perhaps be more graphic to write [8] as

[10] $[e = s(c)]$,

the curved brackets introducing a clear asymmetry and also representing the fact that c is essentially something *for s* and essentially *belongs* to *s*.

The embracing brackets might also be put to work to represent the idea that c is somehow involved in s in such a way that its being is at least partly *constitutive* of the being of s. On this view c is, as it were, the body or flesh of s, without which s (a thin subject) cannot exist, because it would then be nothing. s, we feel, cannot simply be the same as c, but s is nothing without c—not just utterly empty, but non-existent. s, on this view, cannot possibly exist apart from c.

—What if the *s:c* entity begins to exist but then c is cut short—after a millisecond—to be seamlessly replaced by $c^* \neq c$? Doesn't s then continue without c?

I am going to reject this proposal.

In the terms of §3, the existence of s is the existence of p^s, a synergy of process-stuff: $[s = p^s]$. And whatever else it is or is not, the existence of c, too, is, given materialism, nothing over and above the existence of some process-stuff which we may call

---

[51] In the originally published paper, 'E' appears in error in place of 'C'.

p^c: $[c = p^c]$.[52] The question is then this: what is the relation between p^s and p^c? What is the relation between the process-stuff that is (wholly constitutive of) the being of s and the process-stuff that is (wholly constitutive of) the being of c.

—This is really hard to follow—it looks as if the real achievement of the colon and the curly brackets is simply to dramatize our uncertainty about the metaphysics of the relation between s and c. The meaning of '=', by contrast, is very clear.

I agree. '=' has an agreeable clarity. It would be nice to have more of it. Perhaps [9], the triple identity, is not as crazy as it sounds. If it is incoherent, it may be worth examining where and how it hits incoherence.

The central strangeness is the identification of s and c. How can the subject possibly be the content? How indeed? But perhaps the intense intuition that s cannot be the same as c feeds off some elision or blurring of the difference between qualitative-identity considerations and numerical-identity considerations; or between type identity and token identity; or between contents considered as abstract particulars and contents considered as concrete, occurrent particulars; or perhaps it is fuelled by a false picture of the relation between an object and its properties. I think one needs to bring the question 'What is it, actually, for concrete, occurrent, live, experiential content to exist?' before one's mind again and again, in order to put the idea to the test.

In order to do this I need first to consider an ancient problem about the relation between objects and their properties. It sits at the centre of the present difficulty, blinking like a slow loris.

7   OBJECTS AND THEIR PROPERTIES

Objects have properties, we say. There are, indisputably, objects; and, indisputably, they have properties. Our habit of thinking in terms of the object/property distinction[53] is ineluctable, and it is perfectly correct, in its everyday way. But ordinary language is not a good guide to metaphysical truth, and when we repeat the observation in philosophy—*Objects Have Properties*—I think we are at great risk of error, the error of thinking that there is a fundamental categorial distinction between objects and their properties (we compound the error if we think such a distinction is fundamental to ordinary thought). This is a point that will obviously be important if one takes s to be an *object* (as I do) and is inclined to think of c as essentially on the *property* side of things; for this immediately makes the proposal that $[s = c]$ look like a Class A category mistake.[54]

[52] To some this may seem an odder claim than the claim that $[s = p^s]$. I hope the discussion of the object/property distinction in §7 will make it less unpalatable.

[53] Also known as the distinction between particulars and universals, between the particular and the general, between individuals and universals, and so on.

[54] Some may think that s, too, a thin/live subject, is best thought of as a property of something else, a human being considered as a whole, but I take s to be as good an example of an object as can be found (see note 30).

The truth about the relation between objects and their properties eludes sharp formulation. Millennia of vehement philosophical disagreement testify to this fact. But I think it's possible to express the truth about it in a philosophically respectable fashion, and that the key is not to say too much. (I think my profound ignorance of the traditional debate gives me a head start.)

In setting out the issue I'll consider only concrete phenomena, although the basic idea has general application. So my concern with properties will be only with concretely existing properties, concrete propertiedness, and only with intrinsic, natural (non-conventional) properties of objects.[55] I'll use the word 'property' as it is used with no knowledge of philosophy—I'm offering this as a working definition of 'property'—although I think that this crucial use may have become inaccessible to some philosophers. I could try to convey the point about being concerned only with concretely existing properties by saying that I'll be concerned only with 'property-instantiations' or 'property-concretions', but these terms are already problematic inasmuch as they imply a contrast with properties considered as universals considered as abstract objects.

What is at issue, then, is the relation between a particular concrete object and its properties, i.e. its whole actual qualitative being.[56] And the proposal is that one has already gone fatally wrong if one thinks that there is any sort of ontologically weighty distinction to be drawn according to which there is the object, on the one (concrete ontological) hand, and the properties of the object, on the other (concrete ontological) hand: according to which one can distinguish between the existence or being of the object, at any given time, and its nature, at that time—between the thatness of the object and the whatness or howness of the object, at any given time. One of the deep agents of confusion in this matter is counterfactual thinking, which I'll come to shortly.

Plainly objects without properties are impossible. There can no more be objects without properties than there can be closed plane rectilinear figures that have three angles without having three sides. 'Bare particulars'—objects thought of as concretely existing things that do of course *have* properties but are *in themselves* entirely independent of properties—are incoherent. To be is necessarily to be somehow or other, i.e. to be some way or other, to have some nature or other, i.e. to have (actual, concrete) properties.

Rebounding from the obvious incoherence of bare particulars, it may seem that the only other option is to conceive of objects as nothing but collections or 'bundles' of properties (property-concretions). But this option seems no better. Mere bundles of properties seem as bad as bare particulars. Why accept properties without objects after having rejected objects without properties?

But this is not what we are asked to do, in the second case. The claim isn't that there can be concrete instantiations of properties without concrete objects. It is,

---

[55] I am taking the general propriety of such notions for granted. For some recent discussion, see Lewis & Langton 1996 and the ensuing debate in *Philosophy and Phenomenological Research* 2001: 347–403.

[56] 'Qualitative' has nothing in particular to do with experience—my teapot has many qualities.

rather, and to repeat, that concrete objects are nothing but concrete instantiations of properties. However this strange this claim sounds, it is not the claim that there can be concrete instantiations of properties without concrete objects; that is no more true than it's true that there can be concrete objects without concrete instantiations of properties.

It still sounds intolerably peculiar, though, and it is not in the end a helpful thing to say.[57] What is helpful, I think, is to compare the point that there can no more be concrete instantiations of properties without concrete objects than there can be concrete objects without concrete instantiations of properties with the point that there can no more be dispositional properties without categorical properties than there can be categorical properties without dispositional properties.[58] And we can add to this the much stronger point that there is in the case of any object, considered at any time, no *real* distinction in Descartes's sense (see p. 168 above) between its dispositional properties and its categorical properties, although there is no doubt a perfectly workable *conceptual distinction* between them, again in Descartes's sense: there is no real distinction between them because nothing can possibly have the categorical being that it has and not have the dispositional being that it has, and nothing can possibly have the dispositional being that it has and not have the categorical being that it has.[59]

Transferring this underappreciated point back to the case of objects and properties, we may say, again with Descartes, that there is equally no real distinction between an object and its properties, although there is no doubt a useful and workable conceptual distinction between them. (These two points together set one well on the way to acquiring a plausible metaphysics.)

This may seem plainly false. We find it extremely natural to engage in 'counterfactual' thought: we're constantly thinking or hoping or fearing that actual objects may be or could be other than they are, or that they might or could have been other than they were, and this can presumably nourish the idea that there is after all a real distinction between an object and its properties. So perhaps ordinary thought does harbour a tendency to metaphysical error after all (when it comes to the question of the relation between an object and its properties), in being so laden with counterfactual thinking?

No. The legitimacy of counterfactual speculation makes no difference to the crucial sense in which there is no real distinction between an object and its properties, as I will shortly argue, and it does not lead ordinary thought astray.

---

[57] I said it in Strawson 2003 and the first edition of Strawson 2006b, and am grateful to Philip Goff for persuading me to give it up.

[58] The two points are at bottom deeply related.

[59] See further Strawson 2008. Quick thoughts about the 'multiple realizability' of certain functional properties may spark the idea that two things can be dispositionally identical without being categorically identical, and this may lead to the idea that a thing's categorical properties could be changed without its dispositional properties being changed; but a moment's more thought reveals that this cannot be so. Many philosophical thought-experiments assume that a thing can be thought to retain its identity across different nomic environments. It is not clear that this makes sense, but even if it does it is superficial to think that its fundamental dispositions will change; for these fundamental dispositions will include the disposition to behave in way A in nomic environment 1, the disposition to behave in way B in nomic environment 2, and so on.

What is the best way to express the object/property relation? When Kant says that

in their relation to substance, accidents [or properties] are not really subordinated to it, but are the mode of existing of the substance itself

I think he gets the matter exactly right.[60] Nothing more needs to be said. Consider an object in front of you. There is no ontological subordination of the object's properties to the object itself. There is no existential inequality or priority of any sort, no ontological dependence of either on the other, no independence of either from the other. (The counterfactuals are coming.)

There is, in other terms, no ontological subordination of the total *qualitative* being of the object to the object *an Sich*, 'in itself', no ontological subordination of its nature to its existence. It seems just right to put the point by saying—again—that the distinction between the actual being of a thing or object or particular, considered at any given time, and its actual properties, at that time, is a merely conceptual distinction (like the distinction between triangularity and trilaterality) rather than a real (ontological) distinction. We can as Armstrong says '*distinguish* the particularity of a particular from its properties', but

the two 'factors' are too intimately together to speak of a *relation* between them. The thisness and the nature are incapable of existing apart from each other. Bare particulars are vicious abstractions . . . from what may be called states of affairs: this-of-a-certain-nature.[61]

We can 'distinguish the particularity of a particular from its properties', we can make this *conceptual* distinction, but we can't really 'speak of a relation', a real relation, a *real* distinction, 'between them'. This is precisely the view of Descartes, Spinoza, Leibniz, Kant, me, and no doubt many others. It's worth adding that we can replace 'states of affairs' with 'objects' in the quotation from Armstrong as the prime examples of 'this-of-a-certain-nature' entities. This is to give a good characterization of the ordinary notion of an object, the notion that we need. (One can then go on to allow that states of affairs, too, are 'this-of-a-certain-nature' entities.)

Nagarjuna talks in the same vein of the complete codependence of things and their attributes.[62] Nietzsche is admirably brief—'A thing = its qualities',[63] and P. F. Strawson's use of the suggestive phrase 'non-relational tie' can profitably be extended from a logico-linguistic application (to grammatical subject-terms and predicate-terms) to a straightforwardly metaphysical application (to objects and their properties).[64]

---

[60] Kant 1781–7, A414/B441. It's important that 'mode of existing' cannot just mean 'the particular way a substance is', where the substance is thought to be somehow independently existent relative to its mode of existing; for that would be to take accidents or properties to be somehow 'subordinate' after all. (I'm assuming that here 'accident' means effectively the same as 'property-instance'.)

[61] 1980: 109–110. Armstrong puts things this way for well-known dialectical reasons to do with stopping 'Bradley's regress' (see Loux 2002: 39–40), but I take it that there are completely independent metaphysical reasons for saying it.

[62] *c*.50 CE: chapter V (1995: 14–15, see commentary pp. 149–152).

[63] 1885–8: 73; see also pp. 88, 110, 104–5.

[64] Strawson 1959: 167–178. 'Tie', though, is not a very good word for this non-relational mutual metaphysical involvement.

I believe it should be. One should—must—accept the 'non-relational' conception of the relation (!) between an object and its intrinsic properties, if one is going to retain words like 'object' and 'property' in one's metaphysics at all. This is entirely compatible with claiming that an object's properties—including its intrinsic or non-relational properties—may and do change through time, while it remains the same object.

—But we also want to be able to say that an object would have been the very object it is, at *t*, even if its properties had been different, at *t*. We think that the (actual) object could have existed apart from some at least of its (actual) properties.

True—but nothing here forbids this way of talking about the non-actual. To see this, all one needs to do is to lose any tendency to slip, even in one's underthought, from the evident fact

(i) that there are contexts in which it is entirely natural to take it that (some at least of) an object's properties might have been different from what they are while it remained the same object

to the entirely mistaken idea

(ii) that an object has—must have—*some* form or mode of being independently of its having the properties it does have.

—But we also want to be able to say that an object would still be the object it is even if (some at least of) its properties were other than they are in fact.

True. This is how our ordinary notions work. But present-tense counterfactual talk is no more problematic than past-tense. In itself it's innocent, because it doesn't in any way license a shift from (i) to (ii). To think that it does is to build a whole metaphysics of object and property into counterfactual thought, a metaphysics that it does not contain or license as it stands, and that is simply incorrect, on the present view.

—You're wrong; ordinary counterfactual talk does in fact involve a commitment to something like (ii).

I disagree, but I have no special wish to defend ordinary thought, and it doesn't really matter if you're right. If you're right, all that follows is that ordinary thought does after all harbour a deep, inbuilt metaphysical error, when it comes to the question of the object/property relation. So be it: the adequacy of ordinary thought and talk to represent reality is already in the dock in many courts, and already stands condemned on many counts. Appeal to it can't by itself ground any argument that the current Cartesian proposal is incorrect. Those who wish to reject the current proposal will have to produce independent (non-linguistic) metaphysical arguments in support of their view.

Although I don't think our ordinary understanding of counterfactuals is a vector for metaphysical error, there is a related claim that does seem to be true: that when human beings philosophize about the object/property relation, certain features of language naturally lead them to think that (ii) is true.[65] I don't think Ramsey exaggerates when he says that 'the whole theory of universals is due to mistaking...a characteristic of language...for a fundamental characteristic of reality'.[66] He agrees with Nietzsche, who writes that

language is built in terms of the most naïve prejudices... we read disharmonies and problems into things because we *think only* in the form of language—thus believing in the 'eternal truth' of 'reason' (e.g. subject, predicate, etc.)

That we have a right to *distinguish* between subject and predicate—...that is our strongest belief; in fact, at bottom, even the belief in cause and effect itself, in *conditio* and *conditionatum*, is merely an individual case of the first and general belief, our primeval belief in subject and predicate.... Might not this belief in the concept of subject and predicate be a great stupidity?[67]

I think these are powerful and dramatic ways to put the point. (It may be that Nietzsche is claiming that metaphysical error is indeed endemic in ordinary thought; but perhaps he is only pointing to the innocent grounds in ordinary thought of the distinctively philosophical error.) For all that, the best thing to do, I think, is simply to keep Kant's phrase in mind:

in their relation to the object, the properties are not in fact subordinated to it, but are the mode of existing of the object itself.[68]

This is another of those points at which philosophy requires a form of contemplation, something more than theoretical assent; cultivation of a shift in intuitions, acquisition of the ability to sustain a different *continuo* in place in the background of thought, at least for a time.

There is in any case no real problem of universals and particulars—a realization which can be uncomfortable at first, if one has been exposed to the philosophical debate, but which settles out and matures powerfully. One looks at any ordinary object and it is deeply mysterious how there can be thought to be a problem.[69]

---

[65] It may also lead them to think its converse is true: the idea (iii) that properties have—must have—*some* form or mode of being that is independent of the being of the objects that have them.

[66] Ramsey 1925: 60.

[67] 1885–8: 110, 104–5. 'The separation of "doing" from the "doer", of what happens from a something that makes it happen, of process from something that is not process but is enduring, substance, thing, body, soul, etc.—the attempt to grasp what happens as a kind of displacement and repositioning of what "is", of what persists: that ancient mythology set down the belief in "cause and effect" once this belief had found a fixed form in the grammatical functions of language' (ibid., p. 88). With regard to the last two quotations, note that Nietzsche firmly believes in causation in the sense of natural necessity; what he is objecting to is the substantivalist separatism of talk of individual causes and effects: 'The unalterable sequence of certain phenomena does not prove a "law" but a power relation between two or several forces. To say: "But precisely this relation remains the same!" means nothing more than: "One and the same force cannot be a different force as well"' (ibid., p. 88).

[68] I have substituted 'object' and 'property' for 'substance' and 'accident' respectively.

[69] In discussing the 'mind–body problem' it seems to me best to replace talk of a thing's properties with talk of its being wherever possible.

8 $[e \Leftrightarrow s \Leftrightarrow c]$?

I have proposed that

[8] $[e = s{:}c]$

and I have floated the idea that [8] might be true because

[9] $[e = s = c]$.

But [9] seems as absurd as ever, and it may now be wondered whether even the much weaker

[7] $[e \Leftrightarrow s \Leftrightarrow c]$

has been established. So I will take a step backwards and consider the components of [7], i.e. [1]–[6].

We can begin with an old slogan: ideas (contents, experiences) are 'logically private'. This secures both

[2] $[e \Rightarrow s]$

and

[4] $[c \Rightarrow s]$.

If *e* did *per impossibile* have a different subject it could not be *e*—it could not be the experience it is. There is a simple and immovable sense in which the identity of a particular experience is essentially tied to the subject whose experience it is. I cannot—logically—have your experience, nor can you have mine. Suppose you and I are 'consciousness functions' active in a single brain and suppose you and I are having qualitatively identical experiences because we are both related to (partly constituted of) the same portion of brain activity. Even then there are two experiences numerically speaking, yours and mine.

The same holds for [4]. This particular bit of occurrent, living, experiential content could not have had a different subject from the subject for whom it is experiential content. You and I may be consciousness functions active in a single brain and having qualitatively identical experiences in being related to (partly constituted of) the same bit of brain activity. Even so there are two distinct occurrences of experiential content, numerically speaking, if you and I are indeed two distinct subjects. There is yours and there is mine. One could conceivably exist without the other—if you and I are indeed two distinct subjects.

Given the similarity of the points I have made about [2] and [4] it may seem odd to distinguish *e* and *c* at all. True—but one has to do so as soon as one allows that the total existence of an experience involves the existence of a subject and an experiential content, and holds (so very naturally) that the subject is distinct from the content. For then one has to grant that the occurrent content is not identical with the experience. The only way to reject the distinction between *e* and *c* is to reject the distinction between them and *s*, and that is to accept [9].

To [2] and [4] we can add

[3] $[c \Rightarrow e]$.

This particular event of actually occurring experiential content, this particular bit of synergetic process-stuff p^c, couldn't have been the content of some patch of experience other than e. Perhaps the very same ultimates that are caught up in p^c could have been caught up in some other content-occurrence at some time other than $t_1 - t_2$.[70] Perhaps they could have been caught up in a content-occurrence qualitatively identical to p^c, every one of them in just the same (dynamic) relative position as before. Even so, this synergetic process wouldn't have been c—or e; it would have been a completely different entity.

The next component of [7]

[1] $[e \Rightarrow c]$

may seem no less secure. For surely this very experience couldn't have had a different content and still been the experience it is?

—Yes it could. e occurred, and it actually had content c, and it's true that it could not have come into existence at all without its existence involving the existence of content right from the very start. Still, as soon as e has come into existence (in a necessarily content-involving way) we can get a referential grip on it that allows us to consider the possibility that its content might have been different from what it actually was, without its actually ceasing to exist. The same goes for the other two remaining components of [7],

[5] $[s \rightarrow e]$

and

[6] $[s \rightarrow c]$

and we may as well take the three together. s existed, and it actually had experience e, and it could not have come into existence at all (by definition of a thin subject) without its existence involving the existence of experience from the very start. But once it has come into existence (necessarily already having experience of some sort) we can get an identifying fix on it which allows us to suppose that its experience might thereafter have been different from what it was in fact, so that [5] is false—which is to suppose that the actual occurrent content of its experience might thereafter have been different from what it was, so that [6] is false.

Suppose s and c begin to exist together at time t_1, in the L-reality, as of course they do and must, only for c to be cut short after 10 milliseconds, at $t_{1.1}$ and seamlessly replaced by $c^* \neq c$, which lasts until t_2? Surely in this case s continues with c^* and without c? President Mandela would have continued to exist throughout April 27, 1994 if he had eaten a different breakfast from the one he did eat. So too s would have

---

[70] Waiving the thought that it's not possible for the 'virtual-particle' ultimates that are part of what constitutes p^c at t_1 to t_2 to exist at any other time (it seems that it's not even logically possible, given the definition of 'virtual particle').

continued to exist—apart from c—in the case just described. Essentially the same sort of point holds even when we allow that

[8] $[e = s:c]$

or if you prefer

[10] $[e = s(c)]$.

We can suppose that the $s{:}c$ or $s(c)$ entity begins to exist, but that c is then cut short—after a millisecond—to be seamlessly replaced by $c^* \neq c$. In this case s continues without c.

In sum, an experience could possibly have had a content other than the content it does have, a thin subject could have had experience different from the experience it actually does have—experience with different occurrent content from the content it actually does have.

It is precisely these sorts of counterfactual proposals that are blocked on the present view. This is not the point made on p. 174. That was the point that the naturalness and legitimacy of counterfactual speculation do not touch the fact that there is no real distinction between an object and its properties. This is the specific claim that e, s and c are counterfactually invariable *relative to each other*—that

[7] $[e \Leftrightarrow s \Leftrightarrow c]$.

We can speculate counterfactually about e, s and c as much as we like so long as we don't try to hold any one of them constant while varying any of the others. It may be thought that I need to argue for this claim, but it's guaranteed, given the way I've introduced terms. The present task is not to defend a factual claim that stands in need of argument. It is, rather, to try to work out what must be the case given that [7] is correct.

9 $[e = s = c]$

Experiences are real. They concretely exist, whatever their ultimate ontological category. It follows[71] that thin subjects are real and concretely exist, whatever their ultimate ontological category. It follows equally that actually occurring phenomenological content[72] is real and concretely exists, whatever its ultimate ontological category.[73]

We can take it, then, that the terms 'e', 's' and 'c' pick out genuine portions of reality—using the term 'portion' very generously, so that it has application even if we think that the terms 'e', 's' and 'c' are best thought of as picking out properties of particulars rather than particulars—although we should now, after §7, be profoundly wary of this traditional categorial distinction. And we can take materialism alone to

---

[71] By definition of 'thin subject'.   [72] Internalistically understood.

[73] There is no conflict here with the assumption that materialism is true, for the existence of phenomenological content is—obviously—fully acknowledged by any serious or realistic version of materialism.

license the view that each of *e, s* and *c* is identical with a spatiotemporally bounded piece of process-stuff—p^e, p^s and p^c respectively.[74]

I have ruled that the identity of a piece of process-stuff is a strict function of its constituent ultimates (its constituent ultimate process-parts), so that if one meddles in any way with any constituent ultimate of p^s (or p^e or p^c) one no longer has p^s (or p^e or p^c). It follows that if the three identity claims $[s = p^s]$, $[e = p^e]$ and $[c = p^c]$ are simple identity claims (as opposed to constitutive identity claims as characterized on p. 163), as I have supposed they are, then *e, s* and *c* cannot survive any change at all under counterfactual speculation, let alone change relative to each other. To this extent, my picture is secure. But this is hardly interesting. A more interesting question—given that *e, s* and *c* exist, and that $[s = p^s]$, $[e = p^e]$ and $[c = p^c]$—concerns the relations between p^s, p^e, and p^c. What would a plausible account of their relations look like?

It would be very surprising if '*e*', '*s*' and '*c*' all picked out portions of process-stuff with no overlapping parts at all. As referential terms, they surely overlap in what they pick out. But how much? Well,

[8] $[e = s{:}c]$

and its variant

[10] $[e = s(c)]$

take us one very large step forward, in answering this question, for if [8] or [10] is true, as I have assumed it is, then, for some relation R, $[p^e = (p^s R \, p^c)]$, whatever p^s and p^c come to and however exactly they are related. The remaining and difficult question is how *s* and *c* are related (the dummy relation term '*R*' in the curved brackets doesn't rule out identity).

The polarity and non-identity of *s* and *c* is fundamental to our thought, but I proposed on p. 169 that *c* is in some way constitutive of the very existence of *s*, and the converse proposal also seems apt. For what is *c*? *c* is *living content*. It is an actual occurrence of content that is (necessarily) an actual *entertaining* of content, an episode that necessarily involves there being 'what-it's-likeness' in the world, and its very life and reality—its being something concrete and particular, rather than being an uninstantiated what-it's-likeness *type*—just is its being lived, had, animated, *by a subject*. It is impossible for *c*—this very occurrence of experiential content—to exist without *s*—this very (thin) subject existing and being its 'animating principle'.

As for *s*—*s* does not exist at all when *e* does not exist, the experience of which it is the subject, and *e* does not exist at all without *c*, its content, which is its very matter. If one reflects it can begin to seem that there is after all no obvious asymmetry between *s* and *c* as regards their mutual dependence. The egalitarian implication of the colon symbol in '*s:c*'—the suggestion of (ontological) parity, commutativity, relational symmetry—may begin to seem less problematic than before.

Suppose this is so. What then remains to favour ':' over '='? Well, the colon, unlike the identity sign, continues to stand up for the apparently adamantine fact that *s* and

---

[74] I am assuming that materialism builds in the traditional (if ultimately questionable) idea that concrete reality consist of very small ultimate parts in various combinations.

c must be *somehow* distinct however intimate their relation of mutual dependence. The idea that they are at least *conceptually* distinct, even if they are not *really* distinct, is surely non-negotiable.

—But what does this mean, applied to particulars? Surely the notion of a merely conceptual distinction applies only to properties? Two *properties* like trilaterality and triangularity can be merely conceptually distinct, because unable to exist apart, while remaining clearly different properties, but how could two (concrete) *particulars* possibly be absolutely unable to exist apart without being the same single thing . . .

Hang on a moment—

. . . but it hardly matters, because you've simply *defined* these entities into this intense degree of metaphysical intimacy, and although you may not have meddled much with the notion of an *experience*, or the (somewhat peculiar) notion of *occurrent content* in doing so, you've had to bend the notion of a *subject of experience* right out of shape to get anywhere near where you think you are now.

Out of shape? I think that's terminological prejudice, for reasons given earlier. Why should 'subject of experience' have a dispositional reading, i.e. a reading that allows there to be a subject of experience when there is no experience? What's the *evidence* that a subject of experience continues to exist when there is no experience?

This is a silly question, because the matter under discussion is not a matter of fact, but that's the point of the question. It makes it vivid that it is a terminological decision to say that subjects of experience are things that can continue to exist when there is no experience. Human beings do so continue, of course, and brains, and parts of brains that are capable of being recruited into experience-constituting and subject-constituting synergies; but I don't think subjects of experience do. You don't disagree with me, on my terms. You simply choose to put things differently.

—But [9], the proposal that [*e* = *s* = *c*], is perfectly absurd. The experience *is* the subject? The subject *is* the content? Contents have *experience*? *Experiences* have experience? Experiences experience *themselves*? [8], the claim that [*e* = *s:c*], may come to seem relatively tolerable once one has acclimatized to the thin use of 'subject'. It simply states that a particular experience-occurrence is a particular subject-entertaining-a-content-occurrence, and that is certainly true, on the present terms. But why go on to the triple identity?

I suspect that [*e* = *s* = *c*] is a deep truth.[75] On the one hand it seems to me that the claim made earlier—that *s* and *c* stand in an intensely intimate relation given which they cannot possibly exist apart, so that there is (in Cartesian terms) at most a conceptual distinction and no real distinction between them—has considerable force. On the other hand the putative objection made earlier—that if two concrete particulars can't exist apart, and are therefore at most *conceptually* distinct rather than *really* distinct, then they must be numerically identical—seems pretty irresistible.[76]

---

[75] It is on the face of it much stronger than the proposal in the epigraph from Rosch (p. 151 above); but this may be just a matter of terminology.
[76] See further Strawson 2008.

And if this is right then unless one can show a real distinction—a more than merely conceptual distinction—between *s* and *c* one will I think be driven to

[10] $[s = c]$

even if [10], like [9], seems as crazy as ever.

Be that as it may, let me now formally endorse the principle that if there is at most a conceptual distinction between two apparently distinct (concrete) particulars, if they cannot possibly exist apart, then they are not really two but only one: they are identical (that is, *it* is—of course—identical with itself).[77] The question is then this: is

[11] $[s \Leftrightarrow c]$

true, or can *s* and *c* possibly exist apart after all?

The answer No is contained in what has gone before. Certainly *c* cannot possibly exist without *s*; no actual, concrete, occurrent content occurring at some particular place at some particular time can possibly have any subject other than the subject it does have, whatever the subject's girth (thick, traditional inner, thin inner). This is

[4] $[c \Rightarrow s]$

a point covered, as noted, by the old slogan that ideas (experiences) are 'logically private'. You reject the converse

[6] $[s \Rightarrow c]$

arguing that *s* and *c* can begin to exist together at time t_1, *c* being cut short after 10 milliseconds, at $t_{1.1}$ and seamlessly replaced by c^* *c*, which which lasts until t_2, while *s* continues to exist. I reply that this is not so on my view. *c* is the very body of *s* without which *s* cannot exist. In this story, *s* ceases to exist at $t_{1.1}$ and a completely new subject comes into existence. One experience/subject-upsurging is cut short, another crosses the line into existence at the same moment (see Figure 6.2).

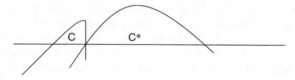

Figure 6.2.

Here as before the fact that certain sorts of counterfactual speculation run smoothly in everyday thought has no force against [6]. To appeal to this fact is simply to presuppose that *s* is substantially distinct from *c* in some way. It is to beg the question.

---

[77] I am concerned only with concrete particulars, so apparent counterexamples that cite abstract objects—e.g. the case of Louis and the singleton set (considered as an abstract object) whose only member is Louis—are not to the point. And I am concerned only with concrete particulars considered independently of human intentions and conventions (this clause is designed to deflect the kinds of cases adduced in Johnston 2003). 'What about a ball and its surface?' Well, either its surface is not a concrete object or it is a concrete object and is therefore a collection of ultimates that can possibly exist independently of the ball . . . and so on.

One needs some independent reason to think that *s* is substantially distinct from *c*. But what gives one an independent fix on the identity of *s* that allows one to say such a thing?

—Fine; just give me a reason for saying that *s* can't possibly exist without *c* that doesn't equally beg the question. It isn't enough for you to appeal to your definition of 'subject' according to which a subject exists in the L-reality only if experience exists in the L-reality. My proposal blocks that move with the phrase 'seamlessly replaced': there is no time between t_1 and t_2 at which there is no experience in the L-reality.

I'll take back 'begs the question', but this reply fails, for it does not follow, from the fact that there is temporally seamless experience in the L-reality between t_1 and t_2, that there is a single thin subject. This issue arose in §3, where I proposed that new experiences, and so new subjects, arise constantly as old ones die away, in the human case, each such experience-and-subject being a primitive unity, a matter of a certain sort of upsurging of activity in and across neurons, each such upsurging essentially numerically distinct from the next. I believe that this is what the phenomenon of there being a subject of experience actually consists in, in the human case. This is the reality that underlies all the subjective phenomena of continuity and flow in experience, and the whole natural picture of the persisting inner self or subject.

What more can be said? I argued in §3 that it is helpful to have a realistically processual understanding of the nature of physical objects. This point combines with §7's account of the relation between an object and its properties to take (or so I hope) any remaining felt strangeness out of the claim that subjects—even thin subjects—are best (or well) thought of as objects in fundamental metaphysics. Having said that, I am happy to agree that this may be one of those points at which it is helpful to put 'subjectivity' in place of 'subject', taking it as a constituent of a count-noun ('an event or episode of subjectivity'). [11] is then the claim that the existence of *s* (this particular episode of subjectivity) is really nothing over and above the existence of *c* (this particular occurrent living content). The existence of this subjectivity entails—indeed is—the existence of this occurrent content, the existence of this occurrent content entails—indeed is—the existence of this subjectivity; neither is in any way ontologically distinct from the other.

It is I think the tremendous inertial force of the (ordinarily unexceptionable but occasionally theoretically disastrous) ordinary notion of what an object is, and so of what a subject-considered-as-an-object is, that makes many meditators want to deny the existence of any such thing as the subject (even when the subject is supposed to be something fleeting, as here), and throw up their hands at the further idea that the subject might have as much claim to be called an object as anything else in reality. In certain theoretical frames, the idea that the correct thing to say is that there is no subject, only occurrent subjectivity or occurrent consciousness, seems an early, easy lesson of meditation. An experience many find it natural to characterize as experience of the non-existence of the self or subject can seem inescapable in the present moment of meditation if it is practised with any success.[78] In the present frame, however, this does not give any reason to think that the notion of the subject is in any way inappropriate in the description of reality, either in general or in the description of certain meditative states. In the present frame it is a trivial (definitional) point that it is appropriate to speak of a subject whenever it is appropriate to speak of subjectivity: whenever there is experience, with its necessary *for*-ness. It is, more bluntly, a necessary truth that there is a subject whenever there is subjectivity.[79]

It is equally trivial, on the present terms, that there is a *object* that is a subject of experience whenever there is subjectivity. To think that the idea that subjects of experience are objects can be put in question by what meditation reveals is simply to have an excessively *lumpen* picture of what physical objects are.

10   THE PURPLE PULSE

I suppose I'm offering the triple identity as some sort of necessary truth—but let me try for a moment to present it as if it were a merely empirical claim about the material world. e is (by materialist hypothesis) identical with a two-second synergy of process-stuff p^e ($[e = p^e]$), s is identical with a two-second synergy of process-stuff p^s ($[s = p^s]$), and c is identical with a two-second synergy of process-stuff p^c ($[c = p^c]$), and the proposal is that as a matter of fact

$[9^p]$ $[p^e = p^s = p^c]$

—that in any and all cases of experience the process-stuff that is the experience just is the process-stuff that is the subject, which in turn just is the process-stuff that is the content. We cannot section p^e into regions, a p^s region and a p^c region. In which case $[e = s = c]$.

Suppose that the art of mapping the neural constituters of consciousness has been perfected, and that we have picked out the synergy of process-stuff p^e that is directly constitutive[80] of experience e. And suppose we find that we can somehow independently identify the subject synergy p^s that must exist given that e exists and the content synergy p^c that must exist given that c exists. The present claim is that in this case we will find that p^s and p^c are the same, and that both are the same as p^e.

If we suppose instead that we can corral out a subject subsynergy p^s of p^e or a content subsynergy p^c of p^e, neither p^c nor p^s being identical with p^e, then the claim is that p^s and p^c will still always be the same.

This last supposition about a subject/content subsynergy is directly contrary to $[9^p]$, and so to [9], but I think it is worth pursuing a little way. And in order to do so I will depart slightly from my present expository scheme. I proposed earlier that

---

[78] The occurrence of this experience is entirely banal and reliable, entirely 'robust' in the sense of experimental psychology (it can occur without delivering any particular spiritual benefits).
[79] This would be my—I take it conciliatory—reply to the doubts raised in Jim Stone (2005).
[80] See p. 164.

the 'process-stuff' idiom allows one to refer to e $(= p^e)$ in a very fine-grained way that excludes any and all matter (process-stuff) that is not *directly constitutive* of e, and thereby excludes things like cell-wall-constituting ultimates, delivering e_e as object of thought (and indeed as candidate physical object). Here, however, I want to think of e, i.e. p^e, as something that can have parts like cell-wall-constituting ultimates that are *not* themselves directly experience-constituting parts.[81]

With this in place, consider the following 'empirical' challenge to the claim that if we could identify a subject subsynergy p^s or a content subsynergy p^c within an experience-synergy p^e existing from t_1 to t_2, p^s and p^c would have to turn out identical. Suppose there seem at first to be good intuitive reasons—simple spatial reasons, say—for distinguishing p^s from p^c. At t_0, say, one is considering the collection of ultimates, K, that will participate in the constituting of p^e from t_1 to t_2. K, modelled in colour in two dimensions, has the shape of a blue crescent moon curled tightly to the side of an orange ball. There are little nodes on the crescent/ball boundary, and pathways for sensory inputs lead to the ball and only to the ball. At t_0 sensory inputs flow into the ball. A flush of red suffuses rapidly across the ball and through the nodes into the crescent. Pulses of blue shoot out from the crescent through the nodes, and at t_1 the whole crescent-ball complex pulses purple for two seconds—this is the existence of p^e—until t_2, when K precipitately loses its purple colour as neurons (or ultimates) constitutive of p^e become inactive with respect to s's experience, or are rapidly recruited into other transient experience-synergies.

The idea is that one might think it right to say that the purple-pulsing crescent is p^s while the purple-pulsing ball is p^c. But nothing in this story gives one good reason to suppose that an actually existing (hence actually experiencing) thin/live subject s $(= p^s)$ is ontologically distinct from an actually existing occurrent 'living' content c $(= p^c)$. For e, in this story, is purple-pulsing p^e. No (thin) subject exists in the K-reality before t_1, although there is a crescent formation; nor is there any occurrent (conscious) content in the K-reality before t_1, although there is an orange ball formation that has been suffused with red. Neither s nor c exists at all before the onset of purple at t_1. They begin together. The occurrent content c is the body of s without which s cannot exist at all and the subject s is the animation of c without which c cannot exist at all. The crescent-ball story supplies no reason to think that the crescent formation between t_1 and t_2 is s while the ball formation is c.

How might we express the suggestion (rejected on p. 178) that s could continue to exist even if c were replaced by $c^* \neq c$? It won't do to imagine that the red flush in the ball (material for an F-type experience, say) is annihilated and seamlessly replaced at $t_{0.9}$ by a differently caused darker red flush (material for a G-type experience) before any empurplement occurs, for s does not yet exist at all in this story, and nor does c; experience has not yet begun. We have to suppose instead that empurplement has taken place at t_1 (experience has begun, s exists) and that the ball part

---

[81] The neural (direct) *constituters* of e are (I take it) a very small subset of the neural *correlates* of e, given that 'n is a neural correlate of e' entails only that if e occurs/exists then n must occur/exist. (Note that talk of correlates invites a type reading, but can be given a token reading, as here.)

of the purple process-stuff is then annihilated and seamlessly replaced by different (darker) process-stuff at $t_{1.1}$ while the crescent part of the process-stuff remains the same.[82]

Suppose we admit this possibility. Is it a case in which s continues while c does not? No. For the *subjectivity* of e is no more located in the crescent than in the ball—the subjectivity of the experience is undisentanglably distributed across p^e. So s does not continue to exist with this replacement. I like to think that something like this (considered in an appropriately general manner) is the present consensus among the neurophysiologically informed about how experiences exist in the brain; both among those who are genuine (real) realists about consciousness, and those, like Dennett (in so far as I understand him), who are not.[83] On this view, there is simply no locus in the brain, however scattered, that is [a] the locus of the subject of experience and [b] distinct from the place where the neuronal activity in virtue of which the experience has the content it does is located.

11 CONCLUSION

What next? I think this is enough for now. When we try to approach this part of reality our categories of thought seem close to breaking point. The standard conception of the relation between a thing and its properties is locked into the terms 'experience', 'subject of experience' and 'content' in a way that makes it almost impossibly hard for us to grasp, let alone endorse, the proposed identity—even if the best current neurophysiology seems to support something like it. We can, it seems, pull c into line with e to get

[12] $[e = c]$

—as in the traditional misunderstanding of Hume. And, jumping off from the $[e = s{:}c]$ picture, or the $[e = s(c)]$ picture, we can perhaps pull s into line with e to get

[13] $[e = s]$.

But as soon as we have done this with one of s or c—as soon as we have achieved some sort of grip on the proposal that one of s or c is identical with e—the other pops out of line, deliquescing and recrystallizing as propertyish or aspectish.

Thus suppose we've managed to set things out in such a way as to give some plausibility to the claim that the existence of the experience *just is*—is just—the existence of the subject (the thin subject that does not and cannot exist unless experience exists). In this case the content of the experience seems left out, and it seems we can get it back

---

[82] The same ultimates may be involved: to constitute a numerically distinct portion of synergetic process-stuff they need only be in a different state of activation.

[83] If some form of panpsychism is as I think the most parsimonious and 'hard-nosed' option for materialists (see Essay 2), the way now lies open for a spectacular *Aufhebung* (makeover, takeover) of Dennett's (2001) apparently reductionist, consciousness-denying account of consciousness as 'just' 'cerebral celebrity' or 'fame in the brain' into a fully realist, genuinely consciousness-affirming account of consciousness. This, however, is a story for another time.

in only by thinking of it as an aspect or property or 'modification' of the subject (back to $[e = s{:}c]$ or $[e = s(c)]$).

Suppose, alternatively, that we have coaxed our intuitions closer to the thought that the experience *just is*—is just—the occurrent content. In this case the subject seems left out, and it seems we can get it back in only by thinking of it as the (essential) subject*ivity* of occurrent content: $[e = c_s]$, as it were.

But the subjectivity (so I have proposed) just is the subject . . . and in spite of all these troubles I suspect that $[e = s = c]$ is true, and that similar wonders of identity apply in the case of all other physical objects—masked by the bad picture of objects and their properties to which our minds keep defaulting.[84]

I think, in fact, that the case of the relation between an experience, the subject of the experience, and the content of the experience—the sheer difficulty of the triple identity—may be exemplary. We can perhaps get closer to apprehending the identity of a thing and its properties (the identity of its being and its being, I am inclined to say, the identity of its existence and its qualitative nature) in this case than in any other. Perhaps $[e = s = c]$ gives us a glimmering of an extremely general metaphysical truth, opening a small frosted window onto the nature of things in a way that nothing else can. (The frosting is in the mind, not the glass, given that intellectual insight can bring us, however transiently, to transparency.)

12 CODA

—All this time you've been avoiding an obvious, fatal objection. It's true on your terms that s can't exist without c and that c can't exist without s, but this fact is no more difficult than the fact that no object that has an essential property can exist without having that property. c is really just a *property* of s, and is on your terms (your thin conception of the subject) an essential property of s. That's why s and c are unbreakably locked. And this doesn't force us into any strange identity claim. You should stick to [8] $[e = s{:}c]$.

I used to think that [8] was the most that could be said. Now, though, I think that this objection draws any force it has from the reality-fogging inadequacy of the standard account of the relation between an object and its properties.

—I'll grant this for argument's sake. I'll even grant that in fundamental metaphysics 's' and 'c' name things that have as good a claim to be physical objects as anything else, so that the question of their identity can be posed. But an identity claim entails that the 'two' things that are said to be identical have all their properties in common (because they are after all only one thing). And s and c do not have all their properties in common. If one thing is certain, subjects experience things, and contents don't.

The triple identity claim is in flagrant conflict with ordinary thought and talk. If you're content to rely on them they will secure your case. My hope is that we're beyond this sort of objection by now. s is not a subject as conceived in your objection,

---

[84] I feel that Leibniz should be on my side, and Descartes. See e.g. Strawson 1994: 124–7, and *Selves* §7.4.

c is not a content as you conceive it. What we have is an experience e; a living content; a content-bodied subject s/c; a subject-animated content c/s: $[e = s = c]$.[85]

[85] This paper was abandoned rather than finished, in true Paul-Valéry style. I thank Jesus Aguilar, Torin Alter, Barry Dainton, Brie Gertler, Mark Greenberg, Mark Johnston, Adrian Moore, Martine Nida-Rümelin, Ben Olsen, Jim Stone, P. F. Strawson, and Dean Zimmerman. Thanks also to the members of the 2002 Pew Charitable Trusts Workshop on 'The Metaphysics of the Human Person' and the 2002 NEH Summer Institute on 'Intentionality and Consciousness'.

7

Against Narrativity

1

Talk of narrative is intensely fashionable in a wide variety of disciplines including philosophy, psychology, theology, anthropology, sociology, political theory, literary studies, religious studies, psychotherapy, medicine, and law. There is widespread agreement that human beings typically experience their lives as a narrative or story, or at least as some sort of collection of stories. I am going to call this the *psychological Narrativity thesis*, using the word 'Narrative' with a capital letter to denote a specifically psychological property or outlook: if one is Narrative then (as a first approximation)

[N] one sees or lives or experiences one's life as a narrative or story of some sort, or at least as a collection of stories.

As it stands the psychological Narrativity thesis is a straightforwardly descriptive, empirical psychological thesis about the way ordinary, normal human beings experience their lives. This is how we are, it says, this is our nature. But it is often coupled with a normative thesis, which I will call the *ethical Narrativity thesis*, according to which a richly Narrative outlook on one's life is essential to living well, to true or full personhood.

The descriptive thesis and the normative thesis have four main combinations. One may, to begin, think the descriptive thesis true and the normative one false. One may think that we are indeed deeply Narrative in our thinking and that it's not a good thing. The protagonist of Sartre's novel *La nausée* holds something like this view.[1] It is also attributed to the Stoics, especially Marcus Aurelius.

Second, and contrariwise, one may think the descriptive thesis false and the normative one true. One may grant that we are not all naturally Narrative in our thinking but insist that we should be, and need to be, in order to live a good life. There are versions of this view in Plutarch[2] and a host of present-day writings.

Third, one may think both theses are true: one may think that all normal non-pathological human beings are naturally Narrative and also that Narrativity is crucial to a good life. This is the dominant view in the academy today, followed by the second view. It does not entail that everything is as it should be; it leaves plenty of room for the idea that many of us would profit from being more Narrative than we are, and the idea that we can get our self-narratives wrong in one way or another.

---

[1] Sartre 1938.   [2] See e.g. 100 CE: 214–17 (473B–474B).

Finally, one may think that both theses are false. This is my view. I think the current widespread acceptance of the third view is regrettable. It's just not true that there is only one good way for human beings to experience their being in time. There are deeply non-Narrative people and there are good ways to live that are deeply non-Narrative. I think the second and third views hinder human self-understanding, close down important avenues of thought, impoverish our grasp of ethical possibilities, needlessly and wrongly distress those who do not fit their model, and are potentially destructive in psychotherapeutic contexts.

2

The first thing I want to put in place is a distinction between one's experience of oneself when one is considering oneself principally as a human being taken as a whole, and one's experience of oneself when one is considering oneself principally as an inner mental entity or 'self' of some sort—I'll call this one's self-experience. When Henry James says, of one of his early books, 'I think of . . . the masterpiece in question . . . as the work of quite another person than myself . . . a rich . . . relation, say, who . . . suffers me still to claim a shy fourth cousinship',[3] he has no doubt that he is the same human being as the author of that book, but he does not feel he is the same self or person as the author of that book. It is this phenomenon of experiencing oneself as a self that concerns me here. One of the most important ways in which people tend to think of themselves (quite independently of religious belief) is as things whose persistence conditions are not obviously or automatically the same as the persistence conditions of a human being considered as a whole. Petrarch, Proust, Parfit, and thousands of others have given this idea vivid expression. I'm going to take its viability for granted and set up another distinction—between 'Episodic' and 'Diachronic' self-experience—in terms of it.

3

The basic form of Diachronic self-experience is that

[**D**] one naturally figures oneself, considered as a self, as something that was there in the (further) past and will be there in the (further) future

something that has relatively long-term diachronic continuity, something that persists over a long stretch of time, perhaps for life. I take it that many people are naturally Diachronic, and that many who are Diachronic are also Narrative in their outlook on life.

If one is Episodic, by contrast,

[**E**] one does not figure oneself, considered as a self, as something that was there in the (further) past and will be there in the (further) future.

[3] 1915: 562–3.

One has little or no sense that the self that one is was there in the (further) past and will be there in the future, although one is perfectly well aware that one has long-term continuity considered as a whole human being. Episodics are likely to have no particular tendency to see their life in Narrative terms.[4]

The Episodic and Diachronic styles of temporal being are radically opposed, but they are not absolute or exceptionless. Predominantly Episodic individuals may sometimes connect to charged events in their pasts in such a way that they feel that those events happened to them—embarrassing memories are a good example—and anticipate events in their futures in such a way that they think that those events are going to happen to them—thoughts of future death can be a good example. So too predominantly Diachronic individuals may sometimes experience an Episodic lack of linkage with well-remembered parts of their past. It may be that the basic Episodic disposition is less common in human beings than the basic Diachronic disposition. I suspect that the fundamentals of temporal temperament are genetically determined, and that we have here to do with a deep 'individual difference variable'—to put it in the language of experimental psychology. If this is right individual variation in time-style, Episodic or Diachronic, Narrative or non-Narrative, will be found across all cultures, so that the same general spread will be found in a so-called 'revenge culture', with its essentially Diachronic emphasis, as in a more happy-go-lucky culture.[5] Compatibly with that, one's exact position in the Episodic/Diachronic/Narrative/non-Narrative state-space may vary significantly over time according to what one is doing or thinking about, one's state of health, and so on; and it may change markedly with increasing age.

Certainly poor memory has nothing to do with Episodicity. In his autobiography John Updike—a man with a powerful memory and a highly consistent character—says of himself 'I have the persistent sensation, in my life and art, that I am just beginning.'[6] I have the same sensation, and I think Updike accurately describes how things are for many people when it comes to their experience of being in time and, in particular, their sense of themselves as selves. But he shows by his own memorious case that this experience of always beginning has nothing essentially to do with having a poor autobiographical memory, let alone one that almost never impinges spontaneously on one's current life.[7]

[4] The Episodic/Diachronic distinction is not the same thing as the Narrative/non-Narrative distinction, as will emerge; but there are marked correlations between them.

[5] Although a culture could in theory exert significant selective pressure on a psychological trait. For descriptions of revenge cultures see Blumenfeld 2003.

[6] 1989: 239. See also the remarkable Portuguese poet Fernando Pessoa (1888–1935) an extreme Episodic: 'I always feel as if I've just been born/Into an endlessly new world' (1914: 48).

[7] The sense of perpetual beginning is not at all a sense of perpetual inchoateness. That which is always launching out may be well or strongly formed and may be felt to be. Updike also talks in a Narrative fashion of our 'religious . . . persistence, against all the powerful post-Copernican, post-Darwinian evidence that we are insignificant accidents within a vast uncaused churning, in feeling that our life is a story, with a pattern and a moral and an inevitability' (1989: 216); and although this has no resonance for some, it fulfils a powerful psychological need in many and is common.

In one respect, I think that the sense of being always just beginning is nothing more than an accurate reflection or surfacing in consciousness of the actual nature of all conscious being in time, at least in the human case. I think it may also be an ever-present feature of ordinary everyday experience that is accessible to everyone but rarely attended to.[8] But this view may simply reflect my own experience. And if there is any respect in which the experience of being always just beginning is universal, then this, at least, cannot be part of what distinguishes Episodics from Diachronics.

It may be said that the sense of perpetual beginning is simply more salient or vivid for Episodics; but it need not be. An Episodic considering the character of her present experience may feel that consciousness is a flowing stream, and have no particular positive experience of perpetual rebeginning, while lacking any significant sense that she was there in the (further) past and will be there in the future. A Diachronic may experience consciousness as something that is always re-engaging or always setting out without feeling that this undercuts his sense that he was there in the past and will be there in the (further) future. Episodics may well have a general tendency to experience things more in one way than the other, and so too Diachronics, but there are perhaps no necessary linkages between the Diachronic and Episodic dispositions and these sorts of phenomenological particularities. The key—defining—difference is simply as stated: it is the difference between those who do and those who do not naturally figure or experience themselves, considered as selves or subjects, as things that were there in the (further) past and will be there in the (further) future.[9]

Diachronics and Episodics are likely to misunderstand one another badly. Diachronics may feel that there is something chilling, empty, and deficient about the Episodic life. They may fear it, although it is no less full or emotionally articulated than the Diachronic life, no less thoughtful or sensitive, no less open to friendship, love, and loyalty. Certainly the two forms of life differ significantly in their ethical and emotional form. But it would be a great mistake to think that the Episodic life is bound to be less vital or in some way less engaged, or less humane, or less humanly fulfilled. If Heideggerians think that Episodics are necessarily 'inauthentic' in their experience of being in time, so much the worse for their notion of authenticity.[10] If Episodics are moved to respond by casting aspersions on the Diachronic life—finding it somehow macerated or clogged, say, or excessively self-concerned, inauthentically second-order—they too will be mistaken if they think it an essentially inferior form of human life.

There is one sense in which Episodics are by definition more located in the present than Diachronics, so far as their self-experience is concerned. But it does not follow, and is not true, that Diachronics are less present in the present moment than Episodics, any more than it follows, or is true, that the present is somehow less informed by or responsible to the past in the Episodic life than it is in the Diachronic life. What is true is that the informing and the responsiveness have different

8 I hope to discuss this in *Life in Time*. For a sketch, see Strawson 1997: §9.
9 As noted, this difference tends to run alongside the difference between Narratives and non-Narratives, but is certainly not coextensive with it.
10 Cf. e.g. Heidegger 1927.

characteristics and different experiential consequences in the two cases. Faced with sceptical Diachronics, who insist that Episodics are (essentially) dysfunctional in the way they relate to their own past, Episodics will reply that the past can be present or alive in the present without being present or alive *as* the past. The past can be alive—arguably more genuinely alive—in the present simply in so far as it has helped to shape the way one is in the present, just as musicians' playing can incorporate and body forth their past practice without being mediated by any explicit memory of it. What goes for musical development goes equally for ethical development, and Rilke's remarks on poetry and memory, which have a natural application to the ethical case, suggest one way in which the Episodic attitude to the past may have an advantage over the Diachronic: 'For the sake of a single poem', he writes, 'you must have . . . many . . . memories . . . . And yet it is not enough to have memories . . . . For the memories themselves are not important.' They give rise to a good poem 'only when they have changed into our very blood, into glance and gesture, and are nameless, no longer to be distinguished from ourselves'.[11]

Among those whose writings show them to be markedly Episodic I propose Michel de Montaigne, the Earl of Shaftesbury, Laurence Sterne, Coleridge, Stendhal, Hazlitt, Ford Madox Ford, Virginia Woolf, Jorge-Luis Borges, Fernando Pessoa, Iris Murdoch (a strongly Episodic person who is a natural story teller), Freddie Ayer, Bob Dylan. Proust is another candidate, for all his remembrance (which may be inspired by his Episodicity); also Emily Dickinson. Diachronicity stands out less clearly, because it is I take it the norm (the 'unmarked position'), but one may begin with Plato, St Augustine, Heidegger, Wordsworth, Dostoievski, Graham Greene, Evelyn Waugh, and all the champions of Narrativity in the current ethico-psychological debate. I find it easy to classify my friends, many of whom are intensely Diachronic, unlike my parents, who are on the Episodic side.[12]

4

How do Episodicity and Diachronicity relate to Narrativity? Suppose that being Diachronic is at least necessary for being Narrative. Since it's true by definition that if you're Diachronic you're not Episodic and conversely, it follows that if you're Episodic you're not Narrative. But I think that the strongly Episodic life is one normal,

[11] 1910: 91.

[12] In an earlier published version of this paper I classified Joseph Conrad as Narrative, and this was cogently questioned by John Attridge in the Letters column of the *Times Literary Supplement* (10 December 2004). In his 'personal remembrance' of Conrad, Ford Madox Ford observes that 'Conrad had very strongly the idea of the Career. A career was for him something a little sacred: any career . . . . A frame of mind, a conception of life, according to which a man did not take stock of the results of his actions upon himself, as it were at long range, was something that he had never contemplated' (1924: 130–5). It seems, though, that this was an effort that Conrad made, something that did not flow from any natural Narrativity, something learnt, like the neatness of sailors, to which Ford compares it. Attridge notes Conrad's 'youthful indifference to the overall plot of his existence', and quotes Conrad's judgement of his youthful self as 'not having any notion of life as an enterprise that could be mismanaged'.

non-pathological form of life for human beings, and indeed one good form of life for human beings, one way to flourish. So if Diachronicity is necessary for Narrativity (see §9 below) then I reject both the psychological Narrativity thesis and the normative, ethical Narrativity thesis.

I need to say more about the Episodic life, and since I find myself to be relatively Episodic, I'll use myself as an example. I have a past, like any human being, and I know perfectly well that I have a past. I have a respectable amount of factual knowledge about it, and I also remember some of my past experiences 'from the inside', as philosophers say. And yet I have absolutely no sense of my life as a narrative with form, or indeed as a narrative without form. Absolutely none. Nor do I have any great or special interest in my past. Nor do I have a great deal of concern for my future.

That's one way to put it—to speak in terms of limited interest. Another way is to say that it seems clear to me, when I am experiencing or apprehending myself as a self, that the remoter past or future in question is not my past or future, although it is certainly the past or future of GS the human being. This is more dramatic, but I think it is equally correct, when I am figuring myself as a self. I have no significant sense that *I*—the I now considering this question—was there in the further past. And it seems clear to me that this is not a failure of feeling. It is, rather, a registration of a fact about what I am—about what the thing that is currently considering this problem is.

I will use 'I*' to represent that which I now experience myself to be when I'm apprehending myself specifically as an inner mental presence or self. 'I*' comes with a large family of cognate forms—'me*', 'my*', 'you*' 'oneself*', 'themselves*', and so on. The metaphysical presumption built into these terms is that they succeed in making genuine reference to an inner mental something that is reasonably called a 'self'. But it doesn't matter whether or not the presumption is correct.[13]

So, it's clear to me that events in my remoter past didn't happen to me*. But what does this amount to? It certainly doesn't mean that I don't have any autobiographical memories of these past experiences. I do. Nor does it mean that my autobiographical memories don't have what philosophers call a 'from-the-inside' character. Some of them do. And they are certainly the experiences of the human being that I am. It does not, however, follow from this that I experience them as having happened to me*, or indeed that they did happen to me*. They certainly do not present as things that happened to me*, and I think I'm strictly, literally correct in thinking that they did not happen to me*.

—That can't be right. If one of my remembered experiences has a from-the-inside character it must—by definition—be experienced as something that happened to me*.

This may seem plausible at first, but it's a mistake: the from-the-inside character of a memory can detach completely from any sense that one is the subject of the remembered experience. My memory of falling out of a boat has an essentially from-the-inside character, visually (the water rushing up to meet me),

---

[13] The term 'I*' and its cognates can function in phenomenological contexts to convey the content of a form of experience that incorporates the presumption whether or not the presumption is actually correct. I'll omit the '*' when it's not necessary.

kinaesthetically, proprioceptively, and so on.[14] It certainly does not follow that it carries any feeling or belief that what is remembered happened to me*, to that which I now apprehend myself to be when I am apprehending myself specifically as a self.

This doesn't follow even when emotion figures in the from-the-inside character of the autobiographical memory. The inference from [1] The memory has a from-the-inside character in emotional respects to [2] The memory is experienced as something that happened to me* is simply not valid, although for many people [1] and [2] are often or usually true together.

For me this is a plain fact of experience. I'm well aware that my past is mine in so far as I am a human being, and I fully accept that there's a sense in which it has special relevance to me* now, including special emotional and moral relevance. At the same time I have no sense that I* was there in the past, and think it obvious that I* was not there, as a matter of metaphysical fact. As for my practical concern for my future, which I believe to be within the normal human range (low end), it is biologically—viscerally—grounded and autonomous in such a way that I can experience it as something immediately felt even though I have no significant sense that I* will be there in the future.

5

So much, briefly, for the Episodic life. What about the Narrative life? And what might it mean to say that human life is 'narrative' in nature? And must you be Diachronic to be Narrative? There are many questions.

One clear statement of the psychological Narrativity thesis is given by Roquentin in Sartre's novel *La nausée*:

a man is always a teller of stories, he lives surrounded by his own stories and those of other people, he sees everything that happens to him *in terms of* these stories and he tries to live his life as if he were recounting it.[15]

Sartre sees the narrative, story-telling impulse as a defect, regrettable. He accepts the psychological Narrativity thesis while rejecting the ethical Narrativity thesis. He thinks human Narrativity is essentially a matter of bad faith, of radical (and typically irremediable) inauthenticity, rather than as something essential for authenticity.

The pro-Narrative majority may concede to Sartre that Narrativity can go wrong while insisting that it's not all bad and that it is necessary for a good life. I'm with Sartre on the ethical issue, but I want now to consider some statements of the psychological Narrativity thesis.

[14] It does not have any sort of 'from-the-outside' character (that would be a bit like my seeing a film of myself falling taken by a third party).
[15] 1938: 64. Sartre is as much concerned with relatively short-term passages of life as with life as a whole.

It is as I've said widely believed. Oliver Sacks, for example, holds that 'each of us constructs and lives a "narrative" '. He says that 'this narrative *is* us, our identities'. The distinguished psychologist Jerry Bruner writes similarly of 'the stories we tell about our lives'. He claims that 'self is a perpetually rewritten story', and that 'in the end, we *become* the autobiographical narratives by which we "tell about" our lives'.[16] Dan Dennett claims that

we are all virtuoso novelists, who find ourselves engaged in all sorts of behaviour, and we always try to put the best 'faces' on it we can. We try to make all of our material cohere into a single good story. And that story is our autobiography. The chief fictional character at the centre of that autobiography is one's self.[17]

Marya Schechtman goes further, twisting the ethical and the psychological Narrativity theses tightly together in a valuably forthright manner. A person, she says, 'creates his identity [only] by forming an autobiographical narrative—a story of his life'. One must be in possession of a full and 'explicit narrative [of one's life] to develop fully as a person'.[18]

Charles Taylor presents it this way: a 'basic condition of making sense of ourselves', he says, 'is that we grasp our lives in a *narrative*' and have an understanding of our lives 'as an unfolding story'. This is not, he thinks, 'an optional extra'; our lives exist 'in a space of questions, which only a coherent narrative can answer'.[19] He is backed up by Claire in Doug Copeland's novel *Generation X*: 'Claire . . . breaks the silence by saying that it's not healthy to live life as a succession of isolated little cool moments. "Either our lives become stories, or there's no way to get through them" '; but Taylor builds a lot more ethical weight into what's involved in getting through life. It is

because we cannot but orient ourselves to the good, and hence determine our place relative to it and hence determine the direction of our lives, [that] we must inescapably understand our lives in narrative form, as a 'quest' [and] must see our lives in story.[20]

This, he says, is an 'inescapable structural requirement of human agency',[21] and Paul Ricoeur appears to concur:

How, indeed, could a subject of action give an ethical character to his or her own life taken as a whole if this life were not gathered together in some way, and how could this occur if not, precisely, in the form of a narrative?[22]

Here my main puzzlement is about what it might be to 'give an ethical character to [one's] own life taken as a whole' in some explicit way, and about why on earth, in the middle of the beauty of being, it should be thought to be important to do this. I think that those who think in this way are motivated by a sense of their own importance or significance that is absent in other human beings. Many of

---

[16] Sacks 1985: 110; Bruner 1987: 11, 15, 12; 1994: 53.
[17] Dennett, D. (1988), *Times Literary Supplement*, 16–22 September.
[18] Schechtman 1997: 93, 119.   [19] 1989: 47, 52.
[20] 1989: 51–2. I reject the 'because' and the second 'hence'.
[21] 1989: 52.   [22] 1990: 158.

them, connectedly, have religious commitments. They are wrapped up in forms of religious belief that are—like almost all religious belief—really all about self.[23]

Alasdair MacIntyre is perhaps the founding figure in the modern Narrativity camp, and his view is similar to Taylor's. 'The unity of an individual life', he says, 'is the unity of a narrative embodied in a single life. To ask "What is the good for me?" is to ask how best I might live out that unity and bring it to completion. . .' The unity of a human life, he continues,

is the unity of a narrative quest . . . [and] the only criteria for success or failure in a human life as a whole are the criteria for success or failure in a narrated or to-be-narrated quest . . . . A quest for what? . . . a quest for the good . . . the good life for man is the life spent in seeking for the good life for man.[24]

MacIntyre's claim seems at first non-psychological: a good life is one that has narrative unity. But a good life is one spent seeking the good life, and there is a strong suggestion that seeking the good life requires taking up a Narrative perspective; in which case narrative unity requires Narrativity.

Is any of this true? I don't think so. It seems to me that MacIntyre, Taylor and all other supporters of the ethical Narrativity thesis are really just talking about themselves. It may be that what they are saying is true for them, both psychologically and ethically. This may be the best ethical project that people like themselves can hope to engage in.[25] But even if it is true for them it is not true for other types of ethical personality, and many are likely to be thrown right off their own truth by being led to believe that Narrativity is necessary for a good life. My own conviction is that the best lives almost never involve this kind of self-telling, and that we have here yet another deep divider of the human race.

When a Narrative like John Campbell claims that 'identity [through time] is central to what we care about in our lives: one thing I care about is what I have made of my life'[26] I'm as bewildered as Goronwy Rees when he writes

For as long as I can remember it has always surprised and slightly bewildered me that other people should take it so much for granted that they each possess what is usually called 'a character'; that is to say, a personality [or personality-possessing self] with its own continuous history . . . . I have never been able to find anything of that sort in myself . . . . How much I admire those writers who are actually able to record the growth of what they call their personality, describe the conditions which determined its birth, lovingly trace the curve of its

---

[23] Excessive self-concern is much more likely to be the cause of religious belief in someone who has come to religion than in someone who has been born into it. That does not change the fact that religious belief in general, ostensibly self-denying, is one of the fundamental vehicles of human narcissism.

[24] 1981: 203–4.

[25] One problem with it, and it is a deep problem, is that one is almost certain to get one's 'story' wrong, in some more or less sentimental way—unless, perhaps, one has the help of a truly gifted therapist.

[26] 1994: 190.

development.... For myself it would be quite impossible to tell such a story, because at no time in my life have I had that enviable sensation of constituting a continuous personality.... As a child this did not worry me, and if indeed I had known at that time of *Der Mann ohne Eigenschaften* [*The Man without Qualities*, a novel by Robert Musil], the man without qualities, I would have greeted him as my blood brother and rejoiced because I was not alone in the world; as it was, I was content with a private fantasy of my own in which I figured as Mr. Nobody.[27]

Unlike Rees, I have a perfectly good grasp of myself as having a certain personality, but I'm completely uninterested in the answer to the question 'What has GS made of his life?', or 'What have I made of my life?'. I'm living it, and this sort of thinking about it is no part of it. This does not mean that I am in any way irresponsible. It is just that what I care about, in so far as I care about myself and my life, is how I am now. The way I am now is profoundly shaped by my past, but it is only the present shaping consequences of the past that matter, not the past as such. I agree with the Earl of Shaftesbury:

The metaphysicians ... affirm that if memory be taken away, the self is lost. [But] what matter for memory? What have I to do with that part? If, *whilst I am*, I am as I should be, what do I care more? And thus let me lose *self* every hour, and be twenty successive selfs, or new selfs, 'tis all one to me: so [long as] I lose not my opinion [i.e. my overall outlook, my character, my moral identity]. If I carry that with me 'tis I; all is well.... —The *now*; the *now*. Mind this: in this is all.[28]

I think, then, that the ethical Narrativity thesis is false, and that the psychological Narrativity thesis is also false in any non-trivial version. What do I mean by non-trivial? Well, if someone says, as some do, that making coffee is a narrative that involves Narrativity, because you have to think ahead, do things in the right order, and so on, and that everyday life involves many such narratives, then I take it the claim is trivial.[29]

Is there some burden on me to explain the popularity of the two theses, given that I think that they're false? Hardly. Theorizing human beings tend to favour false views in matters of this kind. I do, though, think that intellectual fashion is part of the explanation. I also suspect that those who are drawn to write on the subject of 'narrativity' tend to have strongly Diachronic and Narrative outlooks or personalities, and generalize from their own case with that special, fabulously misplaced confidence that people feel when, considering elements of their own experience that are existentially fundamental for them, they take it that they must also be fundamental for everyone else.[30]

---

[27] 1960: 9–10. Pessoa also experiences himself as not really having or being a specific self at all, and this feature, valued in many religious traditions, may well be positively correlated with Episodicity when it occurs naturally. Pessoa, however, experiences himself as multiply personalitied, and this is quite another matter.

[28] Shaftesbury 1698–1712: 136–7; Epictetus is an important influence.

[29] Taylor is explicit that it is when I am not 'dealing with such trivial questions as where I shall go in the next five minutes but with the issue of my place relative to the good', that 'making sense of my present action ... requires a narrative understanding of my life' (1989: 48).

[30] I think this may be the greatest single source of unhappiness in human intercourse.

6

—All very interesting, but what exactly is (upper-case) Narrativity? You still haven't addressed the question directly, and you're running out of space.

Perhaps the first thing to say is that being Diachronic doesn't already entail being Narrative. There must be something more to experiencing one's life as a narrative than simply being Diachronic. For one can be Diachronic, naturally experiencing oneself(*) as something existing in the past and future, without any particular sense of one's life as constituting a narrative.

—Fine, but you haven't told me what a (lower-case) narrative is either.

Well, the paradigm of a narrative is a conventional story told in words. I take the term to attribute—at the very least—a certain sort of *developmental* and hence temporal *unity* or *coherence* to the things to which it is standardly applied—lives, parts of lives, pieces of writing. So it doesn't apply to random or radically unconnected sequences of events even when they are sequentially and indeed contiguously temporally ordered, or to purely picaresque or randomly 'cut-up' pieces of writing.[31]

—'This doesn't take us very far, because we still need to know what makes developmental unity or coherence in a life specifically *narrative* in nature. After all, there's a clear sense in which every human life is a developmental unity—a historical-characteral developmental unity as well as a biological one—just in being the life of a single human being. Putting aside cases of extreme insanity, any human life, even a highly disordered one, can be the subject of an outstanding biography that possesses all the narrative-unity-related virtues of that literary form. But if this sort of developmental unity is sufficient for narrative structure then it's trivially true that all human lives have narrative structure. Actually, even dogs and horses can be the subject of excellent biographies.'

True. And this, I think, is why the distinctive claim of the defenders of the psychological Narrativity thesis is that for a life to be a narrative in the required sense it must be lived Narratively. The person whose life it is must see or feel it as a narrative, construe it as a narrative, live it as a narrative. One could put this roughly by saying that lower-case or 'objective' narrativity requires upper-case or 'subjective' Narrativity.[32]

—Now you're using the notion of upper-case psychological Narrativity to characterize the notion of lower-case 'objective' narrativity, and I still don't have a clear sense of what upper-case Narrativity is.

[31] There are, however, many interesting complications. See *Life in Time*.
[32] MacIntyre does not in the passages I have quoted explicitly say that the narrativity of a life requires Narrativity. In *After Virtue* he is particularly concerned with the idea that 'to think of a human life as a narrative unity is to think in a way alien to the dominant individualist and bureaucratic modes of modern culture' (1981: 211), and this remark was principally a criticism—an excellent one—of the social sciences of the time.

Well, it's not easy, but perhaps one can start from the idea of a *construction* in the sense of a construal. The Narrative outlook clearly involves putting some sort of construction—a unifying or form-finding construction—on the events of one's life, or parts of one's life. I don't think this construction need involve any clearly intentional activity, nor any departure from or addition to the facts. But the Narrative attitude must (as we have already agreed) amount to something more than a disposition to grasp one's life as a unity simply in so far as it is the life of a biologically single human being. Nor can it consist just in the ability to give a sequential record of the actual course of one's life—the actual history of one's life—even if one's life does in fact exemplify a classical pattern of narrative development independently of any construction or interpretation. One must in addition engage—to repeat—in some sort of construal of one's life. One must have some sort of relatively large-scale coherence-seeking, unity-seeking, pattern-seeking, or most generally

[F] *form-finding* tendency

when it comes to one's apprehension of one's life, or relatively large-scale parts of one's life.[33]

—But this doesn't even distinguish Narrativity from Diachronicity, for to be Diachronic is already to put a certain construction on one's life—on the life of the human being that one is: it is to apprehend that life through the life-unifying sense that one (*) was there in the past and will be there in the future. And yet you say being Diachronic is not enough for being Narrative.

I'm prepared to allow that to be Diachronic is already to put a certain construction on one's life in the sense you specify. Nevertheless one can be Diachronic without actively conceiving of one's life, consciously or unconsciously, as some sort of ethical-historical-characterological developmental unity, or in terms of a story, a *Bildung* or 'quest'. One can be Diachronic without one's sense of who or what one is having any significant sort of *narrative* structure. And one can be Diachronic without one's apprehension of oneself as something that persists in time having any great importance for one.[34]

—You've already said that, and the question remains unanswered: what sort of construal is required for Narrativity? When does one cross the line from mere Diachronicity to Narrativity? This is still luminously unclear.

I agree that the proposal that form-finding is a necessary condition of Narrativity is very unspecific, but its lack of specificity may be part of its value, and it seems clear that Diachronicity (D) and form-finding (F) are independent of each other. In practice, no doubt, they often come together, but one can imagine [−D +F] an Episodic person in whom a form-finding tendency is stimulated precisely by lack of a Diachronic outlook, and, conversely, [+D −F] a Diachronic person who lives, by force of circumstance, an intensely picaresque and disjointed life, while having absolutely

---

[33] From now on I will omit the qualification about 'parts of one's life' and take it as read.
[34] 'Discern', 'apprehend', 'find', 'detect' all have non-factive readings.

no tendency to seek unity or narrative-developmental pattern in it. Other Diachronics in similar circumstances may move from [+D −F] to [+D +F], acquiring a form-finding tendency precisely because they become distressed by the 'one damned thing after another'[35] character of their lives. The great and radically non-Narrative Stendhal might be judged to be an example of this, in the light of all his chaotic autobiographical projects, although I would be more inclined to classify him as [−D +F].[36] Either way, the fact remains that one can be Diachronic while being very unreflective about oneself. One can be inclined to think, of any event in one's past of which one is reminded, that it happened to oneself*, without positively grasping one's life as a unity in any further—say specifically narrative—sense.

I think that the notion of form-finding captures something that is essential to being Narrative and that goes essentially beyond being Diachronic, and one view might be that form-finding is not only necessary for Narrativity, but also minimally sufficient. Against that, it may be said that if one is genuinely Narrative one must also (and of course) have some sort of distinctive

[S] *story-telling* tendency

when it comes to one's apprehension of one's life—where story-telling is understood in such a way that it does not imply any tendency to fabrication, conscious or otherwise, although it does not exclude it either. On this view, one must be disposed to apprehend or think of oneself and one's life as fitting the form of some recognized narrative genre.

Story-telling is a species of form-finding, and the basic model for it, perhaps, is the way in which gifted and impartial journalists or historians report a sequence of events. Obviously they select among the facts, but they do not, we suppose, distort or falsify them, and they do more than merely list them in the correct temporal order, for they also place them in a connected account. In its non-falsifying mode story-telling involves the ability to detect—not invent—developmental coherencies in the manifold of one's life. It is one way in which one may be able to apprehend the deep personal constancies that do in fact exist in the life of every human being—although I believe this can also be done by form-finding without story-telling.

So story-telling entails form-finding, and story-telling in addition to form-finding is surely—trivially—sufficient for Narrativity.

7

A third and more troubling suggestion is that if one is Narrative one will also have a tendency to engage unconsciously in invention, fiction of some sort—falsification,

[35] Hubbard 1909: 32.
[36] I judge Stendhal to be strongly Episodic but subject to Diachronic flashes. Jack Kerouac is I think a clear case of an Episodic looking for larger form. There are also clear elements of this in Malcolm Lowry. Laurence Sterne makes comedy out of Episodicity. Jerry Fodor cites Anthony Powell, whom I have not read, as a fine example of an Episodic aspiring to Narrativity.

confabulation, revisionism—when it comes to one's apprehension of one's own life. I will call this

[R] revision.

According to *the revision thesis* Narrativity always carries with it some sort of tendency to revision, where revision essentially involves more merely than changing one's view of the facts of one's life. (One can change one's view of the facts of one's life without any falsification, simply by coming to see things more clearly.)

Revision in the present sense is by definition non-conscious. It may sometimes begin consciously, with deliberate lies told to others, for example, and it may have semi-conscious instars, but it is not genuine revision in the present sense unless or until its products are felt to be true in a way that excludes awareness of falsification.[37] The conscious/non-conscious border is both murky and porous, but I think the notion of revision is robust for all that. The paradigm cases are clear, and extremely common.

If the revision thesis were true, it would be bad news for the ethical Narrativity thesis, whose supporters cannot want ethical success to depend essentially on some sort of falsification. I have no doubt that almost all human Narrativity is compromised by revision, but I don't think it must be. It is in any case a vast and complex phenomenon, and I will make just a very few remarks.

It is often said that autobiographical memory is an essentially *constructive* and *reconstructive* phenomenon (in the terms of experimental psychology) rather than a merely *reproductive* one, and there is a clear sense in which this is true.[38] Memory deletes, abridges, edits, reorders, italicizes. But even if construction and reconstruction are universal in autobiographical memory, they needn't involve revision as currently defined, for they may be fabrication-free story-telling or form-finding. Many have proposed that we are all without exception incorrigible self-fabulists, 'unreliable narrators' of our own lives,[39] and some who hold this view claim greater honesty of outlook for themselves, and see pride, self-blindness, and so on in those who deny it. But other research makes it pretty clear that this is not true. It's not true of everyone. We have here another deep dimension of human psychological difference. Some people are fabulists all the way down. In others, autobiographical memory is fundamentally non-distorting, whatever automatic processes of remoulding and recasting it may invariably involve.[40]

Some think that revision is always *charged*, as I will say—always motivated by an interconnected core group of moral emotions including pride, self-love, conceit,

---

[37] It's well known that fully conscious lies can forget their origins and come to be fully believed by their perpetrators.

[38] For good discussions, see e.g. Brewer 1988; McCauley 1988.

[39] Cf. e.g. Bruner 1987, 1990, 1994. The notion of an 'unreliable narrator' derives from literary criticism. In *The Mind's Past* (1998a) Gazzaniga seems to support a strongly reconstructive view of human memory, but he later says only that personal memory tends to be 'a bit fictional' (1998b: 713).

[40] Brewer (1988) argues that the evidence that supports 'the reconstructive view of personal memory . . . does not seem very compelling'. See also Wagenaar 1994; Baddeley 1994: 239; Swann 1990. Ross (1989) argues that revision that seems to serve self-esteem may be motivated by nothing more than a concern for consistency.

shame, regret, remorse, and guilt. Some go further, claiming with Nietzsche that we always revise in our own favour: ' "I have done that", says my memory. "I cannot have done that", says my pride, and remains inexorable. Eventually—memory yields.'[41]

It seems, however, that neither of these claims is true. The first, that all revision is charged, is significantly improved by the inclusion of things like modesty or low self-esteem, gratitude or forgiveness, in the core group of motivating moods and emotions; some people are just as likely to revise to their own detriment and to others' advantage as the other way round. But the claim that revision is always charged remains false even so. Revision may occur simply because one is a natural form-finder but a very forgetful one and instinctively seeks to make a coherent story out of limited materials.[42] Frustrated story-tellers may fall into revision simply because they can't find satisfying form in their lives and without being in any way motivated by a wish to preserve or restore self-respect. John Dean's recall of his conversations with Nixon at the Watergate hearings is another much discussed case of uncharged revision. When the missing tapes were found, his testimony was revealed to be impressively 'accurate about the individuals' basic positions' although it was 'inaccurate with respect to exactly what was said during a given conversation'. His recall of events involved revision in addition to routine forgetting and morally neutral reconstruction, in so far as it contained positive mistakes, but there is no reason to think that it was significantly charged.[43] 'Flashbulb' memories (such as the memory of what was one doing when one heard about the shooting of President Kennedy, or about 9/11) can be surprisingly inaccurate—astonishingly so given our certainty that we remember accurately—but once again there seems no reason to think that the revision that they involve must be charged.[44]

Even when revision is charged, the common view that we always revise in our own favour must yield to a mass of everyday evidence that some people are as likely to revise to their own detriment—or simply forget the good things they have done.[45] When La Rochefoucauld says that self-love is subtler than the subtlest man in the world, there is truth in what he says. And revising to one's own detriment may be no more attractive than revising to one's advantage. But La Rochefoucauld is sometimes too clever, or rather ignorant, in his cynicism.[46]

Is a tendency to revise a necessary part of being Narrative? No. In our own frail case, substantial Narrativity may rarely if ever occur without revision, but story-telling is sufficient for Narrativity, and one can be story-telling without being revisionary. So the ethical Narrativity thesis survives the threat posed by the revision thesis. When Bernard Malamud claims that 'all biography is ultimately fiction',

---

[41] 1886: §69.
[42] Perhaps 'confabulation' in patients with Korsakov's syndrome is an extreme and pathological example of revision. See e.g. Sacks 1985; Gazzaniga 1998.
[43] Brewer 1988: 27. Cf. Neisser 1981.   [44] See e.g. Pillemer 1998: ch. 2.
[45] For more formal evidence, cf. e.g. Wagenaar 1994, 'Is memory self-serving?'.
[46] Even if we did all tend to see our lives in a favourable light, it would not follow that we were all revisers: some will have self-favouring, self-respect-preserving justifications of their actions already in place at the time of action, and so have no need for subsequent revision.

simply on the grounds that 'there is no life that can be captured wholly, as it was', there is no implication that it must also be ultimately untrue.[47]

8

I've made a number of distinctions, but none of them cut very sharply, and if one asks how Diachronics [D], form-finders [F], story-tellers [S], and revisers [R] relate to each other, the answer, as far as I can see, is that almost anything goes. Story-telling entails form-finding because it is simply one kind of form-finding, but I see no other necessary connections between the four properties. Some think that all normal human beings have all four of these properties. I think that some normal human beings have none of them. Some think that Narrativity necessarily involves all four. I think (as just remarked) that the limiting case of Narrativity involves nothing more than form-finding story-telling (it does not even require one to be Diachronic). If, finally, 'Narrativity' is taken simply as a name for *whatever kind of reflective attitude to oneself and one's life is rightly considered valuable* then I think the limiting case of 'Narrativity' involves nothing more than form-finding, and does not involve anything distinctively Narrative at all.

How do the authors I've quoted classify under this scheme? Well, Dennett is someone who endorses a full blown [+D +F +S +R] view of what it is to be Narrative, and he seems to place considerable emphasis on revision:

our fundamental tactic of self-protection, self-control, and self-definition is not spinning webs or building dams [like spiders and beavers], but telling stories, and more particularly *concocting* and controlling the story we tell others—and ourselves—about who we are.[48]

Bruner, I think, concurs with this emphasis. I take it that Sartre endorses [+F +S +R], and is not particularly concerned with [D] in so far as he is mainly interested in short-term, in-the-present story-telling. Schechtman's account of Narrativity is [+D +F +S ±R]. It assumes that we are all Diachronic and requires that we be form-finding and story-telling and explicitly so

constituting an identity requires that an individual conceive of his life as having the form and the logic of a story—more specifically, the story of a person's life—where 'story' is understood as a conventional, linear narrative[49]

but it is important, on her view, that there be no significant revision, that one's self-narrative be essentially accurate.

I take myself to be [−D −F −S −R]. The claim that I don't revise much is the most vulnerable one, because it is in the nature of the case that one has no sense that one revises when one does. So I may be wrong, but (of course) I don't think so.

[47] Malamud 1979.

[48] 1991a: 418; my emphasis. Dennett takes the story to be primarily about *who* we are, and to that extent it seems that the word 'account' would do as well as 'story', even though it will refer to particular events in one's life.

[49] Schechtman 1997: 96. This is a strong expression of her view, which has usefully weaker forms (cf. e.g. pp. 117, 159).

On the strong form of Schechtman's view, I am not really a person. Some sentient creatures, she says, 'weave stories of their lives, and it is their doing so which *makes* them persons'; to have an 'identity' as a person is 'to have a narrative self-conception . . . to experience the events in one's life as interpreted through one's sense of one's own life story'. This is in fact a common type of claim, and Schechtman goes further, claiming at one point that 'elements of a person's narrative' that figure only in his 'implicit self-narrative', and that 'he cannot articulate . . . are only partially his—attributable to him to a lesser degree than those aspects of the narrative he can articulate'.[50]

This seems to me to express an ideal of control and self-awareness in human life that is mistaken and potentially pernicious. The aspiration to explicit Narrative self-articulation is natural for some—for some, perhaps, it may even be helpful—but in others it is highly unnatural and ruinous. My guess is that it almost always does more harm than good—that the Narrative tendency to look for story or narrative coherence in one's life is, in general, a gross hindrance to self-understanding: to a just, general, practically real sense, implicit or explicit, of one's nature. It's well known that telling and retelling one's past leads to changes, smoothings, enhancements, shifts away from the facts, and recent research has shown that this is not just a human psychological foible. It turns out to be an inevitable consequence of the mechanics of the neurophysiological process of laying down memories that every studied conscious recall of past events brings an alteration.[51] The implication is plain: the more you recall, retell, narrate yourself, the further you are likely to move away from accurate self-understanding, from the truth of your being. Some are constantly telling their daily experiences to others in a storying way and with great gusto. They are drifting ever further off the truth. Others never do this, and when they are obliged to convey facts about their lives they do it clumsily, stumblingly, and uncomfortably, and in a way that is somehow essentially and powerfully narrative-resistant. There are, among the non-Narratives, anti-Narratives, those for whom any storying of their life—suppose someone is recounting an incident in your life to a group of friends in your presence—seems to be missing the point, missing the truth, even if all the facts are right.

Certainly Narrativity is not a necessary part of the 'examined life' (nor is Diachronicity), and it is in any case most unclear that the examined life, thought by Socrates to be essential to human existence, is always a good thing. People can develop and deepen in valuable ways without any sort of explicit, specifically Narrative reflection, just as musicians can improve by practice sessions without recalling those sessions. The business of living well is, for many, a completely non-Narrative project. Granted that certain sorts of self-understanding are necessary for a good human life, they need involve nothing more than form-finding, which can exist in the absence of Narrativity; and they may be osmotic, systemic, not staged in consciousness. It may be said that the acquisition of self-understanding in psychotherapy, at least, is an essentially Narrative project, and it's true that therapy standardly involves identifying key causal connections between features of one's early

[50] 1997: 117.   [51] See McCrone 2003; Debiec, LeDoux and Nader 2002.

life and the way one is at present. But even though the thing one learns is of the form 'It is because X and Y happened to this child that I am now Z', there need not be anything distinctively or even remotely Narrative in one's psychological attitude to the acknowledged causal connections, any more than there need be when one discovers as an adult that a (physical) scar was caused by one's falling out of a pram. This is not a condition of effective therapy—and one certainly doesn't have to have any Diachronic sense that the child encountered in therapy was oneself*. Even more certainly, one does not have to have a satisfying narrative 'forged' for one by the therapist, or in the process of therapy, in order to live well. Heaven forbid.

9

—I'm sorry, but you really have no idea of the force and reach of the psychological Narrativity thesis. You're as Narrative as anyone else, and your narratives about yourself determine how you think of yourself even though they are not conscious.

Well, here we have a stand off. I think it's just not so, and I take it that the disagreement is not just terminological. Self-understanding does not have to take a narrative form, even implicitly. I'm a product of my past, including my very early past, in many profoundly important respects, but it simply does not follow that self-understanding, or the best kind of self-understanding, must take a narrative form, or indeed a historical form. If I am charged to make my self-understanding explicit, I may illustrate my view of myself by reference to things I (GS) have done, but it certainly will not follow that I have a Diachronic outlook, still less a Narrative one.

At this point Heidegger informs us, in a variation on Socrates, that a human being's existence—'Dasein's' existence—is constituted by the fact that its being is an issue for it. Fine, but it's not at all clear that being a thing whose being is an issue for it need involve any sort of Narrative outlook. Heidegger takes it that one's 'self-understanding is constitutive of [one's] . . . being what or who [one] is', and that this self-understanding consists largely in one's 'determining oneself as someone by pressing ahead into a possible way to be'.[52] And here he seems (but I do not understand his notion of temporality) to be insisting on the importance of being Diachronic and indeed Narrative. But if this is his claim then—once again—it seems to me false: false as a universal claim about human life, false as a claim about what it is for human beings to be what or who they are, false as a normative claim about what good or authentic human life must be like, false about what any self-understanding must involve, and false about what self-understanding is at its best. Perhaps Heideggerian authenticity is compatible with the seemingly rival ideal of living in the moment—'Take therefore no thought for the morrow: for the morrow shall take

[52] Blattner 1999: 32, 41; I substitute 'one' for 'Dasein'. Cf. Heidegger (1927: 344): 'In the light of the "for-the-sake-of-which" of one's self-chosen ability-to-be, resolute Dasein frees itself for its world.'

thought for the things of itself. Sufficient unto the day is the evil thereof'[53]—but this will not win me over.

10

There is much more to say. Some may still think that the Episodic life must be deprived in some way. But truly happy-go-lucky, see-what-comes-along lives are among the best there are, vivid, blessed, profound.[54] Some think that an Episodic cannot really know true friendship, or even be loyal. They are refuted by Michel de Montaigne, a great Episodic, famous for his friendship with Etienne de la Boétie, who judged that he was 'better at friendship than at anything else' although

there is nobody less suited than I am to start talking about memory. I can find hardly a trace of it in myself; I doubt if there is any other memory in the world as grotesquely faulty as mine is![55]

Montaigne finds that he is often misjudged and misunderstood, for when he admits he has a very poor memory people assume that he must suffer from ingratitude: 'they judge my affection by my memory', he comments, and are of course quite wrong to do so.[56] A gift for friendship doesn't require any ability to recall past shared experiences in detail, nor any tendency to value them. It is shown in how one is in the present.

But can Episodics be properly moral beings? The question troubles many. Kathy Wilkes thinks not.[57] So also, perhaps, do Plutarch and many others. But Diachronicity is not a necessary condition of a properly moral existence, nor of a proper sense of responsibility.[58] As for Narrativity, it is in the sphere of ethics more of an affliction or a bad habit than a prerequisite of a good life. It risks a strange commodification of life and time—of soul, understood in a strictly secular sense. It misses the point. 'We live', as the great short story writer V. S. Pritchett observes, 'beyond any tale that we happen to enact.'[59]

---

[53] *Matthew* vi. 34. This way of being in the present has nothing to do with the 'aesthetic' way of being in the present described and condemned by Kierkegaard.

[54] Note, though, how Tom Bombadil in *The Lord of the Rings* can produce a certain anxiety.

[55] 1563–92: 32.

[56] Op. cit. p. 33. 'A second avantage' of poor memory, he goes on to note, 'is that . . . I remember less any insults received'.

[57] Wilkes 1999.   [58] I discuss Episodic ethics in Essay 8.

[59] Pritchett 1979: 47. I am grateful to audiences in Oxford (1999), Rutgers (2000), and Reading (2003) for their comments and to Alan Jenkins at the *Times Literary Supplement*.

8

Episodic Ethics

I guess I wont send that note now, for the mind is such a new place, last night feels obsolete.

Emily Dickinson (1870: 211)[1]

She said: 'Rejoice, for God has brought you to your fiftieth year in the world!' But she had no inkling that, for my part, there is no difference at all between my own days which have gone by and the distant days of Noah about which I have heard. I have nothing in the world but the hour in which I am: it pauses for a moment, and then, like a cloud, moves on.

Samuel Hanagid (c.1046)

1 FOUR TEMPORAL TEMPERAMENTS

The first thing I want to put in place is a distinction between one's experience of one-self when one is apprehending oneself principally as a human being taken as a whole, and one's experience of oneself when one is apprehending oneself principally as an inner mental entity or 'self' of some sort—I'll call this one's self-experience. When Henry James says, of one of his early books

I think of . . . the masterpiece in question . . . as the work of quite another person than myself . . . a rich . . . relation, say, who . . . suffers me still to claim a shy fourth cousinship'[2]

he has no doubt that he is the same human being as the author of that book, but he doesn't feel he is the same self or person as the author of that book. It's this phenomenon of experiencing oneself as a self that concerns me here. One of the most important ways in which people tend to think of themselves (quite independently of religious belief) is as things whose persistence conditions are not obviously or automatically the same as the persistence conditions of a human being considered as a whole.

---

[1] When I cite a work I give the first publication date or estimated date of composition, while the page reference is to the text listed in the bibliography.
[2] 1915: 562–3.

I'm going to use the terms 'Diachronic', 'Episodic', 'Narrative' and 'non-Narrative' with capital letters to denote four psychological tendencies, four natural ways of experiencing life in time. To be *Narrative* is

[N] to see or live or experience one's life as a narrative or story of some sort, or at least as a collection of stories.

To be *non-Narrative* is not to live one's life in this way; one may simply lack any Narrative tendency, or one may have a positively anti-Narrative tendency.

Everyone, I think, agrees that there is such a thing as Narrativity, although there's a large debate about what it is, exactly, and about whether or not it's a good thing. I'm not going to say much about it here, though, because I'm more concerned with the less familiar distinction between Episodics and Diachronics.[3]

If one is *Diachronic*

[D] one naturally figures oneself, the self or person one now experiences oneself to be, as something that was there in the (further) past and will be there in the (further) future.

Diachronics needn't be Narratives, even if (as may be doubted) Narratives are bound to be Diachronics, for the basic Diachronic experience of self and life can exist as just defined in the absence of any specifically Narrative—story-discerning, unity-seeking—attitude to one's own life.

Many human beings, it seems, are Diachronic. Others are Episodic, where the defining feature of being *Episodic* is that

[E] one doesn't figure oneself, the self or person one now experiences oneself to be, as something that was there in the (further) past and will be there in the (further) future

although one is of course fully aware that one has long-term—lifelong—continuity considered as a human being. Episodic experience is the direct opposite of Diachronic experience.

Many think that a good human life must be both Narrative and Diachronic. They think that an Episodic person cannot live a fully moral life. An Episodic, they say, cannot properly inhabit the realms of responsibility, duty and obligation—not to mention those of friendship, loyalty, and so on.[4]

Is this true? In discussing the question I'll sometimes use 'I*' ('me*', 'mine*', etc.) as I've done before to represent that which I experience myself to be when I'm apprehending myself specifically as a self or inner subject considered as something different from GS, that is, the human being that I am considered as a whole. (The asterisk attaches equally well to other personal pronouns and adjectives—'you*', 'their*', etc.—to denote others' sense of themselves as selves or inner subjects as opposed to their sense of themselves as human beings considered as a whole. 'I' does not exclude 'I*', and one's thought about oneself can flicker between thought of oneself as a whole

---

³ I discuss Narrativity in Essay 7.

⁴ The notion of Diachronicity is close to the special notion of 'consciousness' of past events that Locke employs in his discussion of personal identity. Consciousness in his sense is essentially accompanied by 'concernment', a sense of ownership and involvement. See Schechtman 1996: 105–9; Strawson in preparation b.

human being and thought of oneself specifically as a self, or remain unspecific in that respect.)

According to Kathy Wilkes,

morality is a matter of planning future actions, calculating consequences, experiencing remorse and contrition, accepting responsibility, accepting praise and blame; such mental phenomena are both forward—and backward—looking. Essentially.... Emotions such as love or hate, envy or resentment, would not deserve the name—except in some occasional rare cases—if they lasted for but three seconds, and were thereafter claimed, not by any me*, but by some former self. ...; we must have a life, or self, with duration. We are, and must consider ourselves as, relatively stable intentional systems. Essentially.[5]

This is forcefully put, and I agree with quite a lot of it. It does, however, misrepresent what it is to be Episodic, and I think its central claim is false. The Episodic life is certainly not the same as the Diachronic life, any more than the non-Narrative life is the same as the Narrative life, but it's certainly not less moral, or less feeling. Nor is it less human or humane, less vivid, less understanding, or less responsible. A happy-go-lucky person can be the best among us.

To some this is obvious, others find it hard to see. Human beings have radically different moral styles or personalities, and some types have a rather dim view of others.[6] Diachronics may think that an Episodic's attitude to others must be thin or cold or incomplete in some way. There is, however, no systematic quantative difference in the warmth, completeness and depth of Episodics' and Diachronics' relations with others. Human beings can flourish in very different ways, and Plutarch shows great ignorance when he writes in *On Tranquillity* as follows:

the present good, which permits us to touch it only for the briefest period of time and then eludes perception, seems to fools to have no further reference to us nor to belong to us at all. As in that painting of a man twisting rope in Hades, who allows a donkey grazing near by to eat it up as he plaits it, insensible and thankless forgetfulness steals upon most people and takes possession of them, consuming every past action and success, every pleasant moment of leisure, companionship and enjoyment. Forgetfulness does not allow life to become unified, as when past is interwoven with present. Instead, separating yesterday from today as though it were different, and also tomorrow, it immediately makes every event to have never happened because it is never recalled.

Those in the Schools who deny growth and increase, on the ground that Being is in continual flux, turn one into ... a series of persons different from oneself. So too, those who do not preserve or recall former events in memory, but allow them to flow away, make themselves deficient and empty each day and dependent on tomorrow—as though what had happened last year and yesterday and the day before had no relation to them, and had never happened at all.[7]

---

[5] Wilkes 1998: 15, criticizing Strawson 1997 (my emphasis).

[6] Cf. e.g. Flanagan 1991. One of the most profound differences is between those for whom the moral–emotional categories of resentment and humiliation are central, and those for whom they hardly figure.

[7] *c*.100: 214–17 (473B–474B); my thanks to Richard Sorabji for showing this to me. Forgetfulness is not in fact a necessary part of Episodicity, but Plutarch's overall opposition to the Episodic life is clear.

Diachronics may see a lack of interest in what one has made of one's life as chilling or alien—even slightly frightening—when set down on paper. They shouldn't, however, conclude that they'll find people who experience things in this way chilling or frightening; some of their best friends may be like this. It's not hard to develop a sense of where people fall on the Diachronic–Episodic spectrum, although one needs to bear in mind that things like increasing age may bring about significant change, and that the strength and emotional loading of one's awareness of oneself* as something that has a past or a future can vary considerably according to what one is thinking about.

Adequate studies of the ethical differences between Diachronics and Episodics would fill a bookshelf—they already fill many, if one looks to literature—and I'm not going to attempt a systematic exposition. After forestalling one possible misapprehension I'm simply going to offer, in no particular order, a number of points in defence of the flourishing Episodic life. (It is a further question whether the non-Narrative life can be a fully moral or human life; the answer is 'Of course'.)

The misapprehension is this. In the passage quoted above Wilkes is replying to a paper in which I propose that the best thing to say about human selves, given the assumption that such metaphysical entities exist at all, is that they exist for at most two or three seconds. Now this, however foolish, is a strictly metaphysical proposal, motivated partly by considerations from experimental psychology, and it's meant to apply equally to all of us, Diachronics and Episodics alike, however we experience ourselves in time. It doesn't carry any sort of suggestion that anyone's subjective experience of their* duration will tend to be of the order of two or three seconds, and the grounds for making it would remain the same even if we were all profoundly Diachronic. As things are, it seems that some Episodics experience their* duration as the same as that of the specious present, around a half a second; for others, perhaps, it's experienced as considerably longer, extending, perhaps, for a few minutes, or half an hour, or a day, or for some longer indeterminate period of time, in the Proustian or (Henry) Jamesian manner.

Many will look no further than their friends and acquaintances, real and fictional, in realizing that Episodics are not as a group somehow morally worse off than Diachronics—although strong Diachronics may have to make more effort than others, in as much as they assume that the Diachronic form of moral experience is required.[8] The fact that Episodics are not morally inferior as a type should also be immediately clear to many moral philosophers—all those, for example, who hold that moral principles are either consequentialist, or deontological, or rights-based, or some mixture of these. For respect for these principles need not depend in any way on whether one is Episodic or Diachronic.[9] The same is true in the case of 'virtue

---

[8] Almost all of us assume that others are more like ourselves, psychologically, than they are. In this domain we automatically employ something like the 'argument from analogy' and are seriously restricted in our capacity to imagine radical difference. We fail, as Murdoch (following Simone Weil) says, to think of others with sufficient realism, imagination, and attention—where these three virtues are indissolubly connected (Murdoch 1970).

[9] Still less should it. Consider a group of people who subscribe to a morality of divine command and who have an equal degree of religious belief. Suppose we find out that the Diachronics among

ethics', but some virtue ethicists, by which I mean those who take the concepts of virtue and moral character to be central to ethics, may think it obvious that Episodics must fall short of Diachronics.

To make their case, these virtue ethicists will have to show that there are some dispositions of character that are not only essential to a fully moral life (whether or not they are rightly called 'virtues') but are also unavailable, or significantly less available, to Episodics. I don't think this can be shown. I am, however, going to accept Wilkes's terms of debate, and take it that we're concerned with the conditions of a 'richly moral and emotional' life in her sense, not just with moral life more narrowly construed. Moral goodness is fundamentally a matter of feeling and desire, of right feeling and right desire, and there's a clear sense in which machine-like consequentialists or crabby 'Kantians' fail to live a richly moral and emotional life even if they're morally impeccable by their own standards.[10]

2   REMORSE, CONTRITION, REGRET, GUILT

It's important, to begin, that the Episodic sense of self isn't absolute in the way Wilkes imagines. Episodics vary greatly among themselves, from extreme to moderate, and one's general sense of one's temporal being may also vary considerably depending on what one is doing or thinking about, or one's chemistry or mood.[11] There are things in what is for most people the remoter future—e.g. their death—and the remoter past—e.g. moments of great embarrassment—that even strong Episodics may tend to figure as involving themselves*. They may apprehend a past triumph as involving themselves* and feel satisfaction. They may apprehend dubious actions in the remoter past as involving themselves* and duly feel remorse or contrition.

Remorse and contrition seem particularly important, when one asks whether an Episodic can be a fully moral being. They seem to be emotions to which one ought to be susceptible in certain circumstances. Neither of them, however, depends on any sort of Diachronic connection with one's remoter past, for both are often felt intensely immediately after action, and are for that reason alone as available to a strong Episodic as anyone else. Nor is either of them essential to the moral life. One can rightly regret things one has done without any special experience of remorse or contrition (in many cases neither is appropriate), and a morally good agent may never have occasion to feel either.

—Isn't the *capacity* to feel remorse or contrition, at least, essential to the moral life?

The first reply is that an Episodic may have this capacity as robustly as anyone else, as just remarked. The second reply is No. There is, for one thing, a distinctively

them are somewhat more likely than the Episodics to observe the dictates of that morality. That will hardly show that they are, intrinsically, morally better people. It may be that they are more self-concerned, or simply that the practical effects of self-concern are different in Episodics and Diachronics.

[10] For a striking discussion of how adherence to Kantian principles can go wrong, see Annas 1984.
[11] See e.g. Strawson 1997: 419–21.

moral species of sinking feeling that lacks the special phenomenology of remorse and contrition although it possesses in equal measure anything that is good about them. There is a certain distinctive negative thud of realization of what one has done that has the same ethical value, whatever exactly that value is. There is a kind of dismay of which the same is true, and one's own actions can occasion sorrow or sadness in one in an ethically influential way, and in a way in which others' actions (or indeed news of disaster) would not, without being self-concerned in the manner of remorse or contrition or mortification. There is, again, a kind of matter-of-fact moral self-criticism that isn't a morally inferior way of experiencing one's own wrongdoing even though it may have very little of moral emotion in it (in so far as it is accompanied by emotion this isn't a matter of remorse and contrition, but rather a kind of condemnatory exasperation or crossness with oneself, a feeling of severity).[12]

When this sort of moral self-criticism occurs in an Episodic like myself it's directed at me* experienced as something existing in the present, even if it is thought about the past that brings it on. But it doesn't follow from the fact that it is thought about the past that brings it on that I do really, and in spite of my assertion of my Episodicity, think of myself* as there in the past. For one thing, thought about the past can bring it on because I am as I know a person of a certain kind and my GS-past can be a very good indicator of what kind of person $I^{(*)}$ am (it is an understatement to say that my GS-past has special relevance to me as I am now). The content of the experience is plain: the object of my attention is simply me* now, and I have no sense that I* was there in the past. My concern in this moral self-criticism is with my* moral nature or being, and this no more includes my past than my present physical being includes all the particles of matter that have previously made me up. I* was not there in the past. But this is not to say that $I^{(*)}$ cannot feel bad about past harm I have done to others; $I^{(*)}$ can.

—Shouldn't this feeling become indistinguishable, in an Episodic, from feeling bad about past harm that others (strangers) have done?

It might in some Episodics, but it need not—to any extent that it should not. Feelings are not bound by consistency or rationality considerations, although they can certainly respond to such considerations, and it is, as just remarked, an understatement to say that my GS-past has special relevance to me as I am now. If, then, some difference remains between my feelings about my own past wrongdoing and my feelings about others' past wrongdoing, we need not be surprised.

We should also bear in mind that contrition, appropriate and attractive as it can be, is the more attractive the more fully it involves grasp of and sorrow about the harm done, and the less it involves focus on the fact that it was oneself who did it. This last element cannot disappear altogether if the feeling is to count as contrition, but the focus on self grows suspect if the emotion persists too long, and even contrition can easily become entangled with elements of self-indulgence. The same is (all too) true of remorse and feeling mortified, which are emotionally thicker than contrition

---

[12] It may also be accompanied, dangerously for some, by self-disdain, self-contempt.

along a certain dimension, but are a good thing for the same reasons.[13] These moral emotions may be instrumentally useful both personally and socially, in as much they dispose people to future good behaviour; they are, so far, good things in their place. And we feel warmly about contrition and remorse even when we consider them non-instrumentally, especially in so far as they are fuelled more by an awareness of harm to others than by an essentially negative attitude to oneself. Susceptibility to such feelings is not, however, a necessary ground of future good behaviour, nor a very good one, even when it is practically effective.

Certainly *guilt* adds nothing—nothing good—to moral being. It is a common feeling, but it is rightly not mentioned by Wilkes. Cyril Connolly has guilt-trouble—

When I contemplate the accumulation of guilt and remorse which, like a garbage-can, I carry through life, and which is fed not only by the lightest action but by the most harmless pleasure, I feel Man to be of all living things the most biologically incompetent and ill-organized. Why has he acquired a seventy years life-span only to poison it incurably by the mere being of himself? Why has he thrown Conscience, like a dead rat, to putrefy in the well?[14]

—but the fact that experiencing guilt is disagreeable does not alter the fact that there is in the end nothing in it that is not essentially superficial, essentially self-indulgent (especially when associated with religious belief) and above all petty, as Connolly would be quick to grant. It is, to be sure, a chimpanzee thing, and wholly so, an ancient adaptive emotional reflex in social animals, encrusted, now, with all the fabulous complications and dreadful superstitions of human consciousness, but otherwise unchanged, an internal prod that evolved among our remote but already highly social ancestors.[15]

Some think that it's impossible for anyone who takes such a negative view of guilt to be fully moral. They think that such a view shows a basic failure of moral understanding. This, though, is an unfortunate charge, because it proves in its proponents what it charges in others. The negative view of guilt isn't a strategy of self-exculpation. It isn't a view held by moral flippertygibbets or strident self-styled 'Nietzscheans', or by those who don't themselves feel guilt. It's at least as likely—perhaps more likely—to be held by those who are susceptible to guilt. It isn't a comfortable self-protective truth. It's an uncomfortable self-exposing truth (at least at first). It is much less comfortable than guilt for the millions who make their comfortably uncomfortable home in guilt, and grasping it is, perhaps, the beginning of genuine personal morality.

—I agree that there's a great ocean of unwarranted guilt, bad guilt, narcissistic, masochistic guilt. But what about feelings of guilt that occur in people because of

---

[13] Nietzsche attacks remorse, predictably, but fails to distinguish it sufficiently from guilt ('Against remorse', 1887: 192).

[14] 1944–5: 4–5.

[15] My father and eldest son once startled me by maintaining that there is nothing more to feeling guilty than fear of being found out. Reflecting on this view is a good exercise for those given to guilt, but it cannot be wholly right because one can feel guilty about actions performed in full view of others, and feelings of guilt can persist even when one's misdemeanour is discovered. We need to add fear of being ill thought of and punished, at least, to the fear of being found out.

genuine wrongdoing on their part? Aren't these feelings of guilt, at least, intrinsically morally good, rather than (at most) instrumentally valuable?

Surely not. There can be sorrow and remorse without guilt, as already remarked. There can be regret and contrition and just self-reproach. None of these things is self-indulgent or self-important in the way that guilt is, and the same is true of shame, although shame is delicately balanced. It has forms that are not in any way self-indulgent (their availability is as likely to be a matter of cultural differences as of individual psychological differences), but it can, like self-hatred (fatally easy for some, unimaginable for others), degenerate fast into a particularly insidious form of self-indulgence.[16]

It is a striking fact that a capacity for negative self-concerned moral emotions (remorse, guilt, and so on) is widely thought to be essential to fully-fledged moral being—especially, I have found, when the issue of Episodic ethics is raised—while there is much less tendency to hold similar views about the indispensability (or even importance or desirability) of positive self-concerned moral emotions.[17] We don't really seem to have words for attractive, positive, distinctively moral self-concerned emotions, although we have a rich way of talking about unattractive ones—as when we say that people are self-satisfied, smug, self-righteous, complacent, and holier-than-thou.[18] We tend to be overcome by the idea that if positive self-concerned moral emotions were in any way agreeable to those who felt them then they would diminish or destroy the value of the very thing that would otherwise justify them, as when a child's charm is spoilt by the fact that she is aware of it. We are too aware of how such emotions might constitute a suspect motive for being moral, or become infected with self-deception. Our model of morally good people seems to require that they be somehow ignorant of the fact that they are morally good, on pain of corruption; or at least that they be utterly unmoved by it. If positive moral emotions are to be a matter of occurrent feeling at all, then they must somehow be ghostly to the point of invisibility. If we posit as attractive an emotion of quiet happiness in doing justice, say, it must not know or examine itself, it must somehow ignore itself.

It is not as if there is no room at all, in our ordinary moral scheme, for positive feeling to flow from, and in that sense be concerned with, one's moral behaviour. Everyone—even Kant—can agree that good deeds may give one a sense of being in harmony with things, and with oneself, and that this is a good and desirable thing, that virtue in this sense can be its own reward.[19] Few would find anything wrong in a person's being filled with happiness by being kind and thoughtful. Once again,

---

[16] Guilt in the Christian manner seems irredeemably obnoxious, but there is a Jewish cultural tradition that treats it as an object of rueful humour in a way that makes it seem positively charming.

[17] It is an ancient idea that you have to like yourself—well enough—to live a good life, and similar ideas are common in present-day psychotherapy; but they do not usually extend to positive self-concerned emotions that are specifically moral in character.

[18] 'Pride' names something good as well as something bad, but it is hard for us to think that 'moral pride' might be a good thing.

[19] I'm interpreting the dictum narrowly and psychologically as a statement about the positive effects of virtuous action on one's subjective state. A wider reading finds rewards beyond any subjective effects.

though, it seems that these feelings cannot themselves be moral feelings in the sense that they involve a moral opinion about oneself. It is all right to feel oneself to be morally bad, but it is simply too dangerous, according to our ordinary scheme, to feel oneself to be morally good.[20] Even when theorists allow that a sense of harmony deriving from good conduct may have considerable intrinsic and instrumental value—against the standard background of the view that negative self-concerned moral emotions are important or essential to fully moral being—one hears little or nothing of the correlative idea that susceptibility to such positive emotions might be important or even essential to being a genuinely moral agent.

Well, I'm not at all sure it is essential, but why is there this sour bias? Why isn't the disposition to feel the negative emotions also judged to have instrumental value at most, and to be otherwise regrettable and in any case inessential to full-fledged moral flourishing? The detailed answer lies in the difficult domain of evolutionary psychology. Here it is enough to note that the question bears immediately on the question of Episodic ethics, for if I am right that ethical wellbeing and responsibility don't require susceptibility to the negative emotions then it does not follow, from the claim that these emotions require a Diachronic outlook, which is in any case dubious, that only Diachronics can be fully moral.

Suppose we think that susceptibility to the positive emotions is a good thing, but not a morally good thing. Should we continue to maintain that susceptibility to the negative feelings is specifically a morally good thing, even after having abandoned the idea that it is essential to fully moral being—continuing to insist that an individual's possession of a disposition to have the negative feelings is not merely instrumentally valuable but also makes that individual an intrinsically better person, morally speaking? This seems utterly dubious. It may at first be thought to connect with and derive support from the venerable idea that morality is at bottom to be negatively defined,[21] as a device to counteract egoism, say, but that doctrine typically incorporates a strongly instrumental attitude to morality, and is vulnerable to Nietzschean polemic and Aristotelian puzzlement.

It may be added that an instrumentally valuable negative attitude to one's own wrongdoing need not involve any particular moral emotion. As for the supposed instrumental value of guilt—the belief that one has done something wrong can motivate one to act without any trace of the feeling of guilt, and I would back clear belief over guilt any day, if there is any hope of the wrongdoer making things better. And consider dear Lucy, who has, regrettably, performed some action A. Suppose that she is thinking that A-ing is wrong, and suppose she has acquired a particularly vivid sense that A-ing is wrong specifically because she herself has A-d in the past. This can be so without her being in any way disposed to fix on or give special weight or attention to the fact that *she herself* has A-d.[22] Even if it is the experience of actually performing

[20] Perhaps there are cultural differences at work here—American/European differences, for example.

[21] See e.g. Hobbes 1651; Warnock 1971.

[22] She may be equally likely to acquire a vivid sense that A-ing is wrong from being the victim of someone else's A-ing.

the action that has provoked her sense of its wrongness she needn't be specially fixed on the fact that it was she herself who A-d, and it is better if she isn't.

She may be Diachronic or Episodic, Narrative or non-Narrative; it makes no difference. Newly acquired moral understanding, like many other kinds of understanding, can be integrated into how one is without being explicitly tagged as deriving from something one did in the past, even if it is the fact that one did it in the past that has made its wrongness especially plain to one. There is a powerful, phylogenetically ancient psychological mechanism by which many of us learn vividly about morality from our own actions, and the attendant sanctions of others, but the learning of the lesson does not depend on any marked or sustained self-concern, or any persisting sense of oneself* as having been the agent of those actions. The operation of the mechanism may be accompanied by such forms of self-concern in Diachronics and may seem to depend on them, but it does not.

3   THE EMOTIONAL PRIORITY THESIS

When we consider the complexities of conscience and moral emotion specifically as they relate to a person's past, I think we are in danger, as theorists, of getting things the wrong way round. It may seem to us that these feelings depend essentially on possession of a Diachronic sense of self (although not necessarily on Narrativity). But the true dependence, I suggest, runs the other way. The grounds of the mechanisms—the feeling-mechanisms—of conscience and responsibility are ancient. They predate the Diachronic sense of self, both phylogenetically and ontogenetically, and they are in that straightforward sense independent of it and can operate without it. Rather than being essentially dependent on the Diachronic sense of self, which is after all something that can exist only in creatures like ourselves that have evolved into fully-fledged concept-exercising self-consciousness, they are among its deep foundations.

One might call this the 'Emotional Priority Thesis'. It states that the past-concerned moral emotions, and in particular the feeling of responsibility, do not in their basic forms presuppose a Diachronic outlook, although we tend to conceptualize them in ways that make it seem analytic that they do. It is because the independently and phylogenetically grounded feeling of responsibility is so salient and vivid among the many things that nourish and structure the Diachronic outlook, in those who have it, that the former comes to seem to depend on and presuppose the latter.

There is a clear parallel between the Emotional Priority Thesis and P. F. Strawson's argument in his famous paper 'Freedom and Resentment'.[23] We all ordinarily believe that people are free agents in some strong, straightforward and unequivocal sense given which they are truly and wholly and ultimately responsible for what they do in some equally strong, straightforward and unequivocal sense, and this belief is vividly manifested in what Strawson calls our 'moral-reactive' and 'personal-reactive' attitudes to other people—our feelings and attitudes of gratitude, resentment, and so

---

[23] Strawson 1962.

on. It seems plain that such reactive attitudes are unwarranted, inappropriate, out of place, fundamentally mistaken, if people do not really have 'strong' free will of the sort just outlined: it seems plain that the reactive attitudes depend logically on the belief in strong free will for their full appropriateness.

There is, however, an extremely powerful argument, which I will not give here, that shows that strong free will of this sort is incoherent, logically impossible.[24] Does this mean that we should give up the reactive attitudes? The question does not really arise for us, as Strawson points out, for it raises the question whether we can give them up, and the answer to that question is, for all practical purposes, No. And although the reactive attitudes do clearly depend logically on the belief in strong free will for their full appropriateness, in spite of the fact that feelings are not bound by logic, it does not follow that they depend *causally* on this belief in such a way that it must in some sense precede them and give rise to them and sustain them. It seems, on the contrary, and as Strawson says, that it is the other way round. The reactive attitudes are the primary and prior phenomenon. They are the true foundation of the typically wholly unexamined and utterly-taken-for-granted belief in strong free will, rather than being founded on it. Logically, the reactive attitudes depend on belief in strong free will for their full appropriateness. Causally, the dependency is the other way round.[25]

It is not just that the reactive attitudes clearly precede any clear and explicit form-ation of a belief in strong free will, both phylogenetically and ontogenetically, and standardly persist untouched in the face of extremely powerful theoretical arguments directed against the possibility of strong free will (arguments that lead many to say, quite sincerely, that they do not believe in free will). The further claim is that the belief in strong free will actually arises from the reactive attitudes (it is perhaps best seen as a kind of conceptualized *post hoc* expression of the reactive attitudes, rather than as an independent element in a person's mental economy). The corres-ponding claim about Diachronicity is that feelings that apparently presuppose Dia-chronicity—embarrassment, guilt, resentment, remorse and so on—actually precede it. They are not essentially posterior to Diachronicity and dependent on it. They are part of what drive and vivify Diachronicity in those who are Diachronically inclined.[26] Most strongly put, the claim is that the Diachronic outlook is not the necessary ground of the feelings it seems to be the ground of. It is, rather, grounded in them—in those who have it at all.

The parallel between the Emotional Priority Thesis and Strawson's argument is partial, for in the free will case it is not only the reactive attitudes but also the belief in strong free will itself that seem to survive acceptance of the force of the argument that strong free will is impossible; the reactive attitudes and the belief in strong free will are very tightly locked together. In the present case, by contrast, the starting assumption is that the person is Episodic and simply does not have the belief that constitutes the

[24] See e.g. Strawson (1994a), where I offer a further characterization of strong free will.
[25] I differ from my father in suspecting that the most fundamental source of the continuing conviction of strong free will is one's experience of one's own agency rather than from one's experience of one's reactive attitudes to others (see G. Strawson 1986: ch. 5).
[26] By the same token, people who are naturally low in the feelings that most powerfully underwrite the Diachronic outlook may be less Diachronic for that reason alone.

Diachronic outlook, and the question is to what extent moral feelings and attitudes that seem to presuppose the Diachronicity belief can survive or even exist in such a person.

4   RESPONSIBILITY AND CONSCIENCE

I do not need to show that this is possible in the case of feelings that are not essential to fully moral being, for my aim is only to show that Episodics can be fully moral. But even when we have put aside guilt, and even remorse and contrition, there are some feelings—feelings of responsibility, feelings of obligation, feelings involved in having a conscience—that may seem to be essential to fully moral being and, equally, to depend essentially on the Diachronicity belief.

I will begin with responsibility, where the central point is quickly made, because the heart of moral responsibility, considered as a psychological phenomenon, is just a sort of instinctive *responsiveness* to things, a responsiveness in the present whose strength or weakness in particular individuals has nothing to do with how Episodic or Diachronic or Narrative or non-Narrative they are. Moral responsibility in this fundamental sense is non-historical. Fully moral being, fully felt awareness of moral right and wrong, no more depends on a sense of one's past, or on a sense that one* was there in the past, than mathematical knowledge.

—'I disagree. Episodics will inevitably lack a proper sense of responsibility if they don't feel that it was they themselves* who performed their past actions.'

Not true. Full moral responsibility is in no sort of conflict with an Episodic outlook. If my past acts have given me obligations, including obligations of reparation, these are obligations I* now fully feel myself to have without any sense that I* performed those actions. This is an experiential fact for many Episodics, make of it what you will.[27] A proper sense of responsibility for my (GS's) past actions is lodged in me* as I am in the present, even though I do not feel that it was I* who performed those actions, just as memories of my (GS's) past experiences are lodged in me* as I am in the present, although I have no sense that it was I* who had those experiences. This is hardly surprising, if only because I know as well as any Diachronic that other people have legitimate GS-related expectations in the present—and what more could one need for a proper sense of responsibility? *Nothing* depends on my sense of myself in the past. I am and now experience myself as myself*, who was not there in the past, but I am also GS, and I know this, and I know that others know this, and I know that I am for others fundamentally GS, the continuing person and human being, and there is for this reason alone a straightforward respect in which that is how I primarily figure myself when I am engaged with others. Although there is a sense in which my primordial referential intention always cleaves first and foremost to I*, my overall referential

---

[27] Fulfilling legitimate expectations is for many people a great pleasure. It is not experienced as a burden.

intention can equally well embrace both I* and GS, and when I am thinking about and mentioning myself in public I certainly and solidly mean GS, whatever else I mean. One might say that the GS reference is automatically secured for me by the pragmatics of the context, independently of the way I figure myself in my referential intention; but there is more to it than this, because I am of course aware of the context and this awareness is active in my referential intention.[28]

Consider the sense one has that one ought to do what one has said one will do because one has said one will do it. If Lucy tells Louis she will do A, and dear Louis is expecting or relying on this, then, other things being equal (A is not, for example, something bad), she ought to do A. Anyone who agrees with this should agree that the fact that she ought to do A does not depend on her having a Diachronic sense of herself. But nor does Lucy's sense or feeling that she ought to do A depend on her having a Diachronic sense of herself. All she needs is an awareness of the fact of obligation, given the fact of expectation. If it is true that she has an obligation, it is a truth that is independent of the particularities of the way she experiences herself* in time. And just as there's no difference between Diachronics and Episodics, in such cases, in respect of the fact that they have an obligation to do what they have said they will do, so too there's no systematic or significant difference between Diachronics and Episodics in respect of the strength of their feeling that they ought to do what they have said they will do.

If the brakes fail in my car through no fault of mine, and it damages another car, I feel full responsibility for the damage, even if I also think I have had bad luck. This is worth noting because it shows the facility of the feeling of responsibility, but it shouldn't be misinterpreted. In having a normal—strong—sense of responsibility for one of GS's past failures I do not as an Episodic have any sense in the present that it is my* bad luck that GS did whatever regrettable thing he did in the past; nor do I lack awareness of the fact that I have some sort of special connection with the action that I do not have with my car or its brakes.

There are other relevant facts of this sort, such as the way in which people feel responsible for (ashamed of, proud of) the actions of members of their family or community, country or species, even though they did not perform the actions themselves. We can, though, put all such things aside, for the basic fact is simply that there is a phenomenon of natural transmission of a sense of responsibility that does not depend in any way on Diachronic self-experience. In the same way, I can take on the debts of a member of my family.

Turning to the notion of conscience, one might put the point by saying that conscience is not essentially retrospective. The thing for which it is best known—the stab from the past, the essentially retrospective 'agenbite of inwit'[29]—is not its essence, or

---

[28] The intended reference of 'I' in everyday thought and talk is sometimes oneself*, sometimes the whole human being that one is, sometimes both these things, and sometimes indeterminate. It is a common mistake in analytic philosophy to think that it can only be to the whole human being (see e.g. Strawson 2002b).

[29] The re-bite of conscience, 're-bite' deriving from Latin *remordere*, from which we get 'remorse', a word which has since (like 'poignant') acquired a softer meaning. James Joyce famously uses this phrase eight times in *Ulysses*.

what constitutes it. It is simply one of its consequences. Conscience casts its lines into the future as readily as the past and is in its most general, original sense simply a matter of inner mental self-awareness in the present.[30] Taken in a slightly narrower sense it is a faculty of self-awareness specifically concerned with thought or action, by means of which one is aware of what one is up to when one is up to it, and a small further narrowing brings us to the standard meaning: conscience is a matter of being aware of what one is up to *within a specifically moral frame of thought*, a matter of moral self-awareness. But here too it is in the basic case wholly directed on the present moment. It is nothing other than the self-aware play of moral sense or understanding on the situation in which one finds oneself. It need not involve any memory of one's past actions at all (you are not deprived of your conscience in suffering amnesia), let alone any Diachronic or Narrative sense of involvement with them. It is neither an essentially backward looking faculty nor an intrinsically recriminatory one.

This isn't a hopeful piety or a revision of ordinary understanding. It records a fundamental part of our most ordinary understanding of what conscience is. The affective snap of the agenbite of inwit is, as remarked, merely one of the consequences that having a conscience has in certain circumstances. One's past can be preserved, active, in conscience, just in so far as one has a negative (or positive) attitude to certain sorts of actions partly because one has oneself performed them in the past. One need not have any sense that one* performed such an action, nor, of course, any sense of guilt (pride). Human beings can grow and deepen in ethical efficacy by a kind of unstudied osmosis that draws particularly on their own past performances without any explicit book-keeping or any Narrative or Diachronic sense of themselves and their deeds. Certainly Episodicity and non-Narrativity are compatible with profound constancy of character, personality and general outlook, and with a deep, steady and unwavering sense of who one is (which need not, of course, be something that one reflects upon, or could easily express in words). This is my own experience, although I am not I think an extreme Episodic. There may even be a connection between the two things, in as much as felt steadiness of personal identity removes any need for one of the things that Diachronicity and Narrativity may exist to provide.

—You claim that one can have a proper sense of responsibility for one's past actions although one does not feel or believe that one* performed them. But it seems to me that to have a proper sense of responsibility with regard to one's past actions just is—*eo ipso*—to have a Diachronic outlook. Diachronicity is not a merely theoretical attitude to oneself, it is expressed in action; essentially. If this is not so given your definition of 'Diachronic', then your definition is wrong. I agree with your criticism of views that tie a proper sense of responsibility to a capacity to feel guilty, chronically remorseful, and so on. The fact remains that any viable definition of Diachronicity must register the fact that it is a necessary precondition of a proper sense of responsibility, that if you have a proper sense of responsibility you must have a Diachronic outlook. What is your definition? You say that to be Diachronic is simply to 'have a sense that one* was there in

---

[30] In French 'conscience' still means 'consciousness' as well as 'conscience' in the English sense. The 'con' prefix introduces the reflexive element. See e.g. Locke 1689–1700: 2.27.9.

the past and will be there in the future'. So be it. I say that having a proper sense of responsibility just shows that one does have a sense that one* was there in the past and will be there in the future—*even if it can somehow seem to one that one does not* (I'm not doubting the sincerity of your claim to be Episodic, or to have a proper sense of responsibility so far as your past actions are concerned).

Our disagreement is clear.

—But you can't just leave it at that! There's a great deal at stake. One loses a vital moral constraint on action if one cares little about one's past.

Many have made this objection, but it is a mistake. One doesn't have to care about one's past in any essentially self-concerned way, still less feel or conceive it as one*'s own, in order to act well or be disposed to act well. What matters morally in any situation one is in is the moral structure of that situation. In some cases facts about one's past actions are part of the moral structure of the present situation, in which case one's own past is part of what matters, but, again, one will not need to care about it in an essentially self-concerned way, or now conceive it as one*'s own. There is no more difficulty in this idea than there is in the idea that Louis can be and feel legally and morally related to Lucy in such a way that he can inherit her debts and obligations. The legal and moral relation can hardly be stronger than it is in the present case, for one is of course the same person in 2000 as one is in 2020, legally and morally and bodily speaking, just in so far as one is the same human being, and one is also (barring certain sorts of brain lesions and major changes in brain chemistry) fundamentally the same in respect of character and personality, however spectacular the phenomena of personal revolution; however Episodic one is.

One does not, then, lose any vital constraint on one's action if one does not care about one's past in any self-concerned way or feel or conceive it as one*'s own. Nor does one have to be governed by concern about one's *future past* (the past one will have, and have to live with, in the future) in order to be a fully moral being, or to act well. I encountered this objection the first time I defended Episodic ethics in a lecture in 1997, but it seems particularly unfortunate and is positively at odds with most moral outlooks (it has affinities with the idea that it is a good thing if people are worried about their fate in the 'afterlife' because it helps them to stay morally in line). Being a moral agent makes one responsible in the future for what one has done in the past, but it does not follow, and is not true, that one's sense of oneself as an agent confronted in the present with a moral issue need include any sense of oneself(*) as something having a future. Many people, I believe, find concern about their future past completely absent from the phenomenology of moral engagement. Many also find concern about their actual past as irrelevant as concern about their future past. Most, in so far as they are moved by moral considerations, find that their concern is simply to do what should be done because it is what should be done, or—omitting the Kantian layer—simply to do what should be done. Judgements about what to do obviously require one to take account of the consequences of one's actions and so to look to the future, but, equally obviously, Episodics can do this as well as Diachronics. One can take account of the future without having any clear sense that one* will be there in the future.

One can even adopt Nietzsche's doctrine of the eternal return considered specific-ally as a technique of moral seriousness (the idea is that when you are facing a choice about which action to perform you should have it vividly in mind that whatever action you choose to perform will be repeated by you for ever in the eternal return) without any trace of a Diachronic or Narrative outlook. One can care passionately about the moral quality of the action, and about the fact that performing it will not only make it part of the history of the universe for ever but will in addition cause sim-ilar such actions to occur over and over again, for ever, without thinking about oneself or one's moral standing at all.[31] To factor in the eternal return when trying to decide what to do is certainly to look to the future, and to give weight to the thought of the future, but, once again, one need not conceive it as one*'s own future in Diachronic fashion in order to be strongly motivated to avoid bad actions.

Episodics are less likely to suffer in Yeats's way:

> Things said or done long years ago,
> Or things I did not do or say
> But thought that I might say or do,
> Weigh me down, and not a day
> But something is recalled,
> My conscience or my vanity appalled[32]

but if Diachronics propose that the inability of Episodics to be weighed down in Yeats's way is a moral failing, Episodics may be provoked to reply that when it comes to the past, most of what is thought to be conscience, and so good, is merely egoism and vanity—not good at all. It does not make one a better person if one is, or capable of being, weighed down like Yeats. It certainly does not make one a better person in some internal spiritual sense, in respect of 'beauty of soul'. As for the idea that Narrat-ives or Diachronics may behave better overall, morally speaking, than non-Narratives or Episodics, that is an empirical claim and evidently false.

5 LOYALTY, VENGEFULNESS, RESENTMENT, HATRED, FRIENDSHIP, GRATITUDE

I have argued that a Diachronic outlook is neither necessary nor sufficient for a proper sense of responsibility. Diachronic personalities are certainly not more punctilious than Episodic personalities. Diachronics can fail to feel properly responsible for their past actions even though they feel that it was they* who performed them; Episodics can feel properly responsible for their past actions even though they do not feel that it was they* who performed them. Diachronics can fail to take responsibility for

---

[31] This use of the doctrine of the eternal return as a technique of moral guidance is of course strictly speaking incompatible with its status as a deterministic metaphysical doctrine to which the appropriate ethical response is *amor fati*, for one is already just repeating one's forever unalterable pattern. (There are obvious connections, here, with the psychology of strict Calvinism.)

[32] 1933: 284.

their past actions even if they do feel that it was they* who performed them; Episodics can behave highly responsibly, given their past actions, even though, once again, they do not feel that it was they* who performed them. There is no significant positive or negative correlation between either Diachronicity or Episodicity and responsible behaviour.

I am now going to downplay the real and important differences between 'Episodic' and 'non-Narrative', on the one hand, and 'Diachronic' and 'Narrative', on the other. I will use 'EN' to join the former pair and their lexical cognates and 'DN' to join up the latter pair and their lexical cognates. 'EN' and 'DN' may be read to mean 'Episodic or non-Narrative' and 'Diachronic or Narrative' where 'or', as in classical logic, does not exclude 'and'.[33] The question, then, is whether there are any essentially DN moral traits. Guilt is not an example, and nor is shame, if only because both can be rapid reactions as available to ENs as to DNs, as powerful in acute (short-lived) form as in any chronic form. The same goes for almost all moral-psychological traits: they can be rapidly manifested in their fullest form, and they are not less themselves for being immediate.

Isn't loyalty, at least, an essentially DN virtue? Not. Loyalty may be deep and intense in those who are Episodic and picaresque and it has a non-Narrative form as strong as any Narrative form. Loyalty is a matter of one's attitude and relation to a person in the present, and the EN/DN difference is no more than the difference between those whose loyalty happens to be psychologically linked in some way to an ability or tendency to think about the past they share with those to whom they are loyal and those whose loyalty is not so linked. The phenomenon of loyalty may be grounded in the past in the EN case as much as it is in the DN case, but it need not be bound up with any tendency to think of the past, still less with any tendency to think of one's own past specifically as one*'s own.[34]

It is worth adding that loyalty, like other virtues, has intensely powerful false forms. A great deal that passes for loyalty is a blend of self-love, narcissism, and fear. Those who genuinely possess the virtue are slow to attribute disloyalty to others and tend to react to evidence of disloyalty with doubt, and to proof of disloyalty with grief and regret. Those who possess the mixed vices masquerading as the virtue are quick to suspect disloyalty where there is none and have a strong tendency to react to disloyalty to themselves (real or imagined) with sulkiness, anger, accusation, and a desire for revenge.

What about resentment, vengefulness, susceptibility to humiliation or insult? Are these essentially DN emotions, in the sense that a DN outlook is a necessary condition of their instantiation? No. They all have EN versions in their acute form, although not their chronic form. If it is taken to be definitive of resentment that it requires a present sense that one* has been insulted, humiliated, cheated or

---

[33] One might say that the [A or B] form is best understood to abbreviate the following more complex form: [[A or at least B] or [B or at least A]].

[34] It is a striking fact (neutral for the purposes of the present case) that intensely powerful feelings akin to feelings of loyalty can spring up almost immediately in human beings who have been divided into different teams for a game.

otherwise done down, then ENs are not able to sustain it very well, and there is a way of brooding over past wrongs that is not available to them. To the extent that resentment is wrongly thought of as an essentially chronic condition, ENs are not very good at it.[35] ENs may mistrust, or dislike, or have a sinking feeling about, individuals who have wronged them in the past if they think of them, or come up against them in the present, but one can mistrust or dislike someone—this being a standing condition—, and dislike them specifically because of past wrongs, without any persisting feelings of resentment or vengefulness, insult or humiliation, just as one can be put off a food for life after it has made one ill (the mechanism is essentially the same).

So much the better, for every second spent on vengeful feelings—after the heat of the moment—is a further defeat by the person who inspires them in one. Some exult in chronic resentment and thoughts of revenge; it gives form to their lives. Others see perseveration in such feelings for what it is—a form of subjugation to the one resented. 'Pleasure in revenge is proof of a weak and narrow mind', as Juvenal says; 'revenge is sweeter than life itself—so think fools.'[36] Whole cultures can be weak, fools, narrow in this way. Retaliation may sometimes be necessary, as the Dalai Lama in his wisdom has observed about the school playground, but retaliation is not a feeling.[37]

Plainly all this could be true—ENs could have special immunity to chronic forms of these disagreeable emotions—while the individuals who were in fact least touched by them, on this earth, at this time, were predominantly Diachronic and Narrative.

—But if ENs are not much good at chronic resentment, because they do not feel that they* were there in the past, presumably they are not much good at lasting gratitude either, and for the same reason. Surely they must fall down badly here?

Gratitude is the greatest *prima facie* problem for Episodic ethics. I will approach it by way of fidelity, love, and forgiveness.

Fidelity, like loyalty, is equally available to both sides. ENs are far less likely to experience fidelity as a kind of answerability to or honouring of the past, but this offers no support to the idea that they experience the emotion of fidelity with any less strength than DNs. Fidelity of heart, including true sexual fidelity, is a matter of present commitment, wholly a matter of present feeling, and is found equally on both sides with equal strength.

The same is true of love. Enduring love of a person is, at any moment, a matter of present disposition. Its manners and customs may be shaped by the past, but

---

[35] For some people, resentment is balefully cumulative, but this is no part of its essence. In others resentments are intense but short lived, vanishing on the air as if they had never been.

[36] 'Semper et infirmi est animi exiguique voluptas Ultio', *Satires* XIII: 189–90; 'vindicta bonum vita jucundius ipsa nempe hoc indocti', *Satires* XIII: 180. See Blumenfeld 2003 for some remarkable stories of vengefulness.

[37] Alas for cultures that say 'revenge is a dish best eaten cold', or that a person who has waited thirty years to take revenge has been 'hasty'. (The fundamental ground of chronic vengefulness is boredom: as a specifically cultural phenomenon it dates back to a time when there was far less to entertain people outside their work. This is vividly observed by Gorky in his great *Autobiography*.)

it does not require any tendency to engage in explicit recollection of the past, nor any trace of any Diachronic sense that one*—or the one* one loves—was there in the past. (The deep reason why Jill matters to Narrative Jack, unfortunately, is that Jill is part of *Jack's* life and past; his feeling is fundamentally about himself. He feels safe—validated and at home—in his sense or story of his past and clings to things, including people, that it contains principally for reasons of self-love and self-support, or out of fear of the unknown.)

The same goes for friendship. Michel de Montaigne, a great Episodic, renowned for his friendship with Etienne de la Boétie, famously gave the best possible answer, when asked why their friendship had been what it was: 'because it was him, because it was I'. A gift for friendship doesn't require any ability to recall past shared experiences, nor any tendency to value them. It is shown in how one is in the present. Montaigne judges that he is 'better at friendship than at anything else' although

there is nobody less suited than I am to start talking about memory. I can find hardly a trace of it in myself; I doubt if there is any other memory in the world as grotesquely faulty as mine is![38]

He finds that he is often misjudged and misunderstood, for when he admits he has a very poor memory people assume that he must suffer from ingratitude: 'they judge my affection by my memory', he comments, and are of course quite wrong to do so. 'A second advantage' of poor memory, he goes on to note, 'is that . . . I remember less any insults received'.[39]

—Narrative or Diachronic lovers and friends can be present in the present in every way in which their Episodic counterparts are, but they also have something more—their sense of themselves(*) as together in the past. Their history can be alive in their thought as their their(*) history, and this is a great good unavailable to Episodics.

Episodics may reply that this may be so, but that the dangers of sentimental falsification and confabulation are awesome, and that they also and equally have something more—a way of being present in the present in which the past is present without being present as the past—that is unavailable if one's shared history is or tends to be alive in one's thought as one*'s shared history. Each side may concede that there is something they cannot know, and all will be well on all sides as long as no one proposes that Narrative or Diachronic love is somehow essentially deeper or more powerful than Episodic and non-Narrative love, or forgets that many couples are happily made up of a DN and an EN. (Explicit recognition of this fact can be helpful in a relationship.)

Forgiveness? Once again, neither side is intrinsically more disposed to be forgiving than the other. One can't, perhaps, forgive if one has forgotten, but one may have forgotten because one has already forgiven. It may be said that one must not only remember what was done to one, in order to be able to forgive, but must also feel that it was oneself* who was there in the past—so that ENs may lose opportunities for forgiveness even when they have excellent memories. But I can see no reason to believe this. There do not seem to be any deep differences, specifically so far as the phenomenon of forgiveness is concerned, between the case in which one forgives a wrong done to oneself(*) and the case in which one forgives a wrong done to another (unlike someone who says 'I cannot forgive him for what he did to her'). And if this is so, then even if one does not think that it was one* who was there in the past, one's capacity for forgiving a wrong is not touched; only the emotional accompaniments are different. And if there is after all some sense in which ENs do lose opportunities for forgiveness, in spite of having excellent memories, these will be opportunities of which they have no need. 'Mirabeau had no memory for insults and vile actions done him and was unable to forgive simply because he—forgot. . . . Such a man shakes off with a single shrug many vermin that eat deep into others.'[40]

What about the wrongdoers, in such cases? They may feel a need for forgiveness, and feel that it is denied them by ENs. But they already have it in sufficient measure, for the ENs no longer feel wronged, although they remember what happened, and that is forgiveness. If a DN wrongdoer wants something more, and feels that a wronged EN individual is not really giving it to her, her desire is merely selfish—and perverse.

Can one fail to forgive a past wrong done to one even though one genuinely doesn't feel that it was oneself* who suffered it in the past? One's present actions might make this seem the best thing to say. Others, though, may interpret these actions differently. What such a behaviourally manifested failure to forgive shows, they may say, is that really one does still have a sense that it was oneself* who was there in the past, and deludes oneself when one denies it.

This is an objection in a by now familiar pattern. It assumes that an adequate explanation of the unforgiving feelings that have been attributed to one (perhaps wrongly) on the basis of one's behaviour must cite a belief that it was oneself* who was there in the past; so that one can after all infer a fundamentally DN outlook from indirect behavioural evidence of the presence of unforgiving feelings. I think, on the contrary, and in line with the Emotional Priority thesis, that the existence and naturalness of such feelings may be a crucial part of what gives rise to or sustains the DN outlook, and that such feelings can persist, though perhaps only in a relatively attenuated form, even in the absence of the DN outlook. As P. F. Strawson observes, moral emotions like resentment and gratitude *effortlessly* survive acceptance of the force of the argument that the (strong) free will that they presuppose is impossible. So too, moral

---

[40] Nietzsche, quoted in Sommers 2007. Some are less able to forgive a wrong done to someone else—whether or not it is someone they know well—than a wrong done to themselves, but it is not as if something good lies behind this. It is rather something extremely dangerous, very ugly, and very human, the most dangerous force in all human public affairs: righteous indignation in the pejorative sense, righteous indignation felt on behalf of others or on behalf of the group of which one is part. Righteous indignation of this sort often incorporates a sense of absolute justification precisely because it is (ostensibly) not self-concerned—a sense of purity of justification that seems to those who feel it to license absolute violence. Its deep root, no doubt, is anger felt about one's own life or situation, anger that, once disguised in this way, is able to express itself without any inhibition.

emotions like gratitude and resentment may exist in an Episodic who genuinely does not feel that it was he* to whom good or ill was done in the past, even if such moral emotions seem logically to require that he does think that it was he* to whom good or ill was done in the past.

It is, however, far less clear that these emotions can remain untouched in the case of Episodicity, as compared with the case of belief in strong free will. In the latter case it seems that not only the moral emotions but also the very belief in strong free will survive acceptance of the force of the argument that strong free will is impossible. In the former case, by contrast, and as remarked, the starting assumption is that the person genuinely lacks a Diachronic outlook (this is the parallel to genuinely lacking the belief in free will) and the question is to what extent the moral emotions that seem to presuppose the Diachronic outlook can survive in such a person.

My own experience, self-deluded or not, is that the feeling of gratitude survives while the feeling of resentment does not.[41] Resentment of a person can quickly decay into negative affect that entirely lacks the peculiar phenomenology of resentment and on into neutrality (it may yet leave one specially tuned to resent that person for new reasons). Gratitude, by contrast, standardly survives in a form of liking whose special tone distinguishes it quite clearly from liking that has no foundation in gratitude.[42]

Montaigne, evidently, felt the same, and I have seen it in many others. But how is this asymmetry possible? Well, it can't be any more surprising than the asymmetry found in people in whom resentment persists even while gratitude decays, and this second asymmetry may be said to restore a basic symmetry between gratitude and resentment, in as much as either can decay while the other does not. I like to think that empirical tests would show that gratitude is more robust than resentment in the population as a whole, given reasonable conditions of life (including sufficient means of entertainment—see note 37), and other things being equal; but there are, certainly, those in whom resentments and grudges accumulate year on year, whether or not gratitude decays.[43] This last fact, though, has no special bearing on the Episodic predicament, where my sense, to repeat, is that gratitude is more likely to persist than resentment, in a form of liking that has a special tone.

It may be said that resentment must persist in a similar fashion, in a form of dislike whose special tint distinguishes it quite clearly from dislike that has no foundation in resentment. This doesn't seem accurate to me, but it is plain that this could happen to some Episodics, given other features of their personality and circumstances. The

---

[41] The word 'gratitude' is not only used to denote a feeling—one can say truly that one is grateful to someone without any feeling of gratitude—but I will put aside this other use. (It is a question whether one can really feel gratitude to someone one doesn't like. It seems so—at least at first.)

[42] It is perhaps diagnostic of the emotion of gratitude that it can persist, in the face of disagreeable behaviour on the part of its inspirer, in cases where mere liking does not persist.

[43] There are also those in whom reasons for gratitude become causes of resentment. Some fear that this process is inevitable and universal; see e.g. Joseph Conrad as described in Ford 1929: 131ff.

question whether it is the glow of gratitude or the stain of resentment that is more robust in Episodics is open to empirical test. Some people are immune to bitterness, others are largely made of it, but what happens in an individual case may be more a function of external circumstances than fundamental character.

Could it be that resentment decays because it is a psychological burden (and a waste of time), while genuine gratitude is not? It is plain that some people have this happy disposition, but it is no less plain that others lack it. So too, some retain memories of other people's kindness and lose memories of their ill-doing, while others are the other way around. There is nevertheless something in this idea. In the long run, I think, many people have a lot of good sense. They have, in particular, a fundamental capacity for *acceptance*, where this does not involve any sort of capitulation or admission of defeat or retreat from humanity, but is rather a matter of wider perspective, an increase of humanity, of realism, an understanding, however late, that some things are indeed a waste of time. Acceptance of this sort undermines resentment by its very nature, while having no adverse effect on gratitude. One reason why we may underestimate its presence and force in human life, I think, is that it receives far less attention in novels, films, and songs than most other important features of human psychology.

So I continue to believe that there is a positive asymmetry. And this belief finds further support, perhaps, in an apparent asymmetry between gratitude and resentment that has nothing to do with their rates of decay. We often feel grateful—the quality of the emotion is unmistakable—for a cool breeze or an outbreak of sun, but we are certainly not resentful, rather than disappointed, when the breeze drops or the day turns muggy.[44] Gratitude, it seems, has a greater natural reach than resentment. The case cannot be cordoned off by saying that there are two kinds of gratitude, personal and meteorological (impersonal), and that the first is independent of the second, and that the second impersonal kind cannot really ('logically') be the real thing. We use the same word for the cool breeze and the kind act because it is the same basic feeling, whatever other differences of feeling are found in the two cases.

I don't think we have to personify nature to have this feeling of gratitude, animistic and anthropomorphizing though we are as a species. (If meteorological gratitude depended on surreptitious personification, we would, *ceteris paribus*, expect meteorological resentment in equal measure.) To this extent it seems that gratitude has, in some way, an impersonal or at least larger field, while resentment remains essentially personal. This does not mean that one can't resent one's washing machine; only that one has to adopt a psychologically anthropomorphic attitude to it. But perhaps the weather is a special case; for I do not think one could feel gratitude towards one's washing machine without some sort of animistic attitude to it.[45]

[44] See Sommers 2005.

[45] Note added in 2008, after reading a paper about gratitude by my colleague Philip Stratton-Lake which revived the following memory. About ten years ago I walked to my car, which was parked in the street, and found that the right rear wheel had been stolen. The rear axle was resting on a couple of bricks. I was dismayed and annoyed. When I crouched down to investigate, I found that the four wheel nuts had been tucked carefully beside the bricks, just out of sight. I was immediately touched by this considerateness. It triggered a sense of fundamental human community

There are no strong generalizations to be made in this area. Our moral-emotional personalities are too complex and too varied. Obviously it seems very neat for an Episodic like myself to claim that he can't manage to sustain significant resentment for more than a few days (although it can be reanimated in conversation) but has no such trouble with gratitude. I am nevertheless going to leave you with that claim.

6   CONCLUSION

My larger claim is that Wilkes is wrong to think that the EN life could not be richly moral and emotional. There is I suggest no interesting correlation between moral worth and being Episodic or Diachronic, Narrative or non-Narrative, although ENs and DNs may experience morality in significantly different ways. There is no special connection, let alone a necessary connection, between [a] a lack of felt connection with one's past of the sort characteristic of Episodics and [b] a propensity to behave badly or, more particularly, [c] a propensity to behave worse than those who have a characteristically Diachronic sense of connection with their past. All moral traits have both EN and DN forms of expression, even if some achieve their fullest or most familiar expression only in ENs or DNs.[46]

---

and gratitude, although it had cost the thieves nothing and although the shock persisted. When I remembered this recently I encountered nothing but a feeling of gratitude and warm emotion. Since then it's come back to me several times, always with the same effect. I have to think about the theft for some time before I can recover any negative feeling, or appreciate that my initial reaction is open to ethical criticism.

[46] Some have suggested an association between Episodicity and depression and dissociation (Lampinen, Odegard, and Leding 2004). It may be, though, that while this is characteristic of depressed and dissociated Diachronics, the reverse is true in the case of Episodics—in whom greater Diachronicity could be a form of dissociation.

I would like to thank members of the audiences at Union College, Schenectady, NY, at the 2005 Royal Institute of Philosophy conference on 'Narrative and Understanding Persons', and at the 2006 Eunice Belgum Lectures at St. Olaf's College, Northfield MN, for their comments.

9

Mental Ballistics: the Involuntariness
of Spontaneity

'The mind only begins a train of thinking or keeps it in one particular track,
but the thoughts introduce one another successively. . . . Whoever will carefully observe what he does when he sets himself down to study, may perceive
that he produces none of the thoughts in his mind.'

Abraham Tucker (1765: 14–15)

1

It is sometimes said that reasoning, thought and judgement essentially involve
action.[1] It is sometimes said, in Kantian style, that they involve *spontaneity*, where
spontaneity is taken to be connected in some constitutive way with action: intentional, voluntary and indeed free action.[2] There is, however, a fundamental respect
in which reason, thought and judgement neither are nor can be a matter of intentional action; and the same goes (a fortiori) for belief and belief-formation.[3] I think
the point is obvious, and perhaps no one disagrees with it; but it may be worth an
airing.

2

Actually, I don't think that a reasoning, thinking, judging self-conscious creature
need be an agent at all. Nothing in what follows depends on this view—but
there is no *incoherence* in the idea of a Pure Observer, a motionless, cognitively
well-equipped, highly receptive, self-conscious, rational, subtle creature that is well
informed about its surroundings and has, perhaps, a full and vivid sense of itself as an

[1] For recent examples see Burge 1998 and Peacocke 1999. When I cite a work I give its original
publication date (or sometimes the date of its completion), while the page reference is to the edition
listed in the bibliography.
[2] McDowell 1994, 1998a, 1998b stresses the notion of spontaneity in judgement and links it to
the notion of freedom, but there is I think no incompatibility between the account of spontaneity
given here and the core of McDowell's view (see §10 below).
[3] So that the thesis of 'doxastic voluntarism' is false in any remotely robust formulation. For a
good recent discussion, see Audi 1999. See also Wiggins 1970.

observer although it has no capacity for any sort of intentional action, nor even any conception of the possibility of intentional action (from now on I use 'action' to mean intentional action). Things impinge on a Pure Observer. It forms beliefs, hypotheses, expectations, it is host to—it is the entertainer of—trains of reasoning that are as automatic as most of our own. But none of this is in any way a matter of action. It is excessively unlikely that any such creature could evolve naturally, but that is another matter.[4]

—The Pure Observers are impossible because *thought* of any sort already necessarily involves mental action, mental *agency*—mental activity that is a matter of action. This decides the case against the Pure Observers even before we ask whether it is intelligible to suppose that there could be mentally complex creatures that were constitutionally incapable of any large-scale intentional bodily movement.

I disagree. Obviously thought involves—is—mental *activity*, but activity, whether mental, chemical or volcanic, does not always involve action. And if we consider things plainly, we find, I think, that most of our thoughts—our thought-contents—*just happen*. In this sense they are spontaneous: 'instinctive', as the *Shorter Oxford English Dictionary* has it, 'involuntary, not due to conscious volition',[5] not actions at all. Contents occur, spring up—the process is largely automatic. Even when our thoughts are most appropriate to our situation and our needs as agents, action and intention need have little or nothing to do with their occurrence.

The case of thought in conversation is striking, for one does not act to generate material for one's reply, as the other is speaking. It just comes, often before the other has finished speaking, and one often knows—in a flash, for 'thought is quick'[6]—both that the essential content of the reply is ready to hand in the mind, and, in some ineffably compressed manner, what its content is, before one has run through all its detail in any way.[7]

This is how it is for me, at any rate. Some claim to experience things differently, and I am sure they are sincere. So I want to consider not only the extent to which human mental goings on are in fact a matter of action, but also the extent to which they are experienced as action.

---

[4] Compare the 'Weather Watchers' discussed in Strawson 1994: ch. 9. The Pure Observer's inability to act does not mean that it cannot experience movement through space of the sort sometimes said to be essential to a grasp of the three-dimensionality of space. Its sister, resident on a giant drifting lily pad, may have exactly the same mental and bodily equipment and experience movement through space. Its second cousin, one of the Weather Watchers, may have complicated preferences and desires, a marked personality, and still lack any capacity for, or conception of, action. See also the 'Spectator Subject' and the 'Natural Epictetans' in Strawson 1986: chs. 12 and 13; and Camus's Meursault (Camus 1942). I hope no one still thinks that 'Wittgensteinian' objections to the Pure Observer have any force.

[5] 1993: 2998; see further §10 below.

[6] Hobbes 1651: §1.3.

[7] This, I take it, is what Wegner calls the 'abstract cognitive plan that reflects the gist or intention' of what the speaker will say (2002: 87, citing Hoffman 1986). As one starts speaking one often elaborates on what had already come to mind, and adds new material, but that is a further matter.

3

When I consider my mental life I find that things constantly impinge on me. I remember that I have to do X—it strikes me that Y is true. I want some coffee—I wonder where the filter papers are. I know I have to go to Charing Cross—I find myself thinking about the best way to travel. Thought, it seems, is often a matter of things just happening, and the passive or non-agentive nature of the ordinary experience of thought is vividly expressed in many of our idioms: 'I realized that *p*', 'It struck me that *q*', 'I had an idea', 'I noticed that *r*', 'Then I understood', 'The scales fell from my eyes', 'The thought crossed my mind'; 'I saw the answer', 'It suddenly came to me', 'It occurred to me—it dawned on me', I remembered that *s*', 'It hit me that *t*', 'I found myself thinking that *u*', '*v*!—of course—how stupid of me!'

It's just started to rain, and I've just thought that Harry is going to get wet, and we naturally say that this is something I do. But we also say this about sneezing, yawning and tripping over, and my spontaneous and involuntary thought about Harry is certainly not a matter of action. And yet some seem to think—or feel—that having a thought or taking a step in thought is standardly a matter of action, something crucially located in the general domain of action.

The cases of judging and reasoning—directed thought in general—are central for those who hold this view, and there are a number of idioms that seem to support the idea that an agentive view of the matter is at least as natural as a non-agentive view: 'I've worked it out', 'I judged that *p*', 'My considered judgement is that *p*', 'After reflection I endorsed the view that *q*', 'I reasoned that *r*', 'I decided that *s*', 'I came to the conclusion that *t*', 'I assented to the proposition that *u*', 'I speculated, hypothesized, that *v*, and judged that if *v*, then *w*', 'I accept that *x*'.

All these more agentive idioms have an easy and natural passive reading, in fact, while the preceding passive idioms do not have any natural agentive reading, but the issue is not to be decided by appeal to idioms, let alone their relative weight of numbers, and when we put the idioms aside, what is left over, it seems, is simply a difference of attitude or temperament. Some people standardly figure having a thought or taking a step in thought as a matter of action; others figure it as something that just happens. Some seem pervasively committed to the idea that the occurrence of new content in thinking, judging, reasoning, is itself a matter of action; others like myself find this mystifying. This, I think, is another of those deep differences among human beings—another of the great dividers of the human race—that exist independently of philosophical training or any specific theoretical commitment.[8]

What might explain it? I don't think it stems from a dramatic difference between those who really do routinely operate as conscious intentional agents in major parts

[8] For recent examples of the 'thought is action' view see Burge 1998; Peacocke 1999. Peacocke is forthright. He claims that 'judgements are in fact *actions*, a species of mental action' (1999: 238; see also 19–20). Burge claims that 'events guided by reasons issuing from a thinker's uncoopted central rational powers are acts'; 'to understand reasoning . . . one must regard reasons as effective in

of their mental lives and those who don't. The deep difference, I think, is just the difference of opinion or rather feeling—between those who are inclined to experience themselves primarily as agents in their mental lives, and those who aren't. The strength and reach of 'the tendency to attribute control to self is a personality trait', as Wegner says, and in some the sense of control—or origination—extends further than in others.[9] Some of us are much more likely than others to experience what he calls an 'emotion of authorship' in reason, thought, and judgement.[10] I never experience anything of the sort.

There is of course such thing as mental action. There is mental action in every sense in which there is bodily action. And there may well be significant differences between people when it comes to the question of how much their mental lives are a matter of action. But those who take it, perhaps very unreflectively, that much or most of their thinking is a matter of action are I believe deluded.

4

The central point is this: the role of genuine action in thought is at best indirect. It is entirely *prefatory*, it is essentially—merely—*catalytic*. For what actually happens, when one wants to think about some issue or work something out? If the issue is a difficult one, then there may well be a distinct, and distinctive, phenomenon of setting one's mind at the problem, and this phenomenon, I think, may well be a matter of action. It may involve rapidly and silently imaging key words or sentences to oneself, rehearsing inferential transitions, refreshing images of a scene, and these acts of *priming*, which may be regularly repeated once things are under way, are likely to be fully fledged actions.

What else is there, in the way of action? Well, sometimes one has to shepherd or dragoon one's wandering mind back to the previous thought-content in order for the train of thought to be restarted or continued, and this too may be a matter of action. We talk of concerted thought, and this *concertion*, which is again a catalytic matter, may be (but need not be) a matter of action: it may involve tremendous effort and focused concentration of will. Sometimes thoughts about the answer to a question come so fast that they have to be as it were stopped and piled and then taken up and gone through one by one; and this, again, can be a matter of action.[11] Sometimes one has a clear sense that there is a relevant consideration that is not in play, although

---

one's judgements, inferences, and other activity. Doing so amounts to an acknowledgement of one's agency' (1998: 251). This last claim seems to be a non sequitur, and it is striking that Burge's paper shifts constantly between active and passive characterizations of thought and reasoning. It is as if he keeps trying to coax his subtle, correct, but essentially non-agentive descriptions of the process of judgement into being something more agentive in order to secure for the latter the plausibility of the former. In one active-passive fusion he speaks of 'the practice of being moved by reasons' (257).

[9] 2002: 330, citing Rotter 1966.   [10] Wegner 2002: 318, 325–6.

[11] I am thinking of the speed and wealth of sober focused thought when one is alert, not the mental torrent of illness or the drugged or drunken mind, where typically nothing can be done about the content.

one doesn't know what it is. One initiates a kind of actively receptive blanking of the mind in order to give any missing elements a chance to arise. This too can be a matter of action, a curious weighted intentional holding open of the field of thought. Attention, too, can be a matter of action, of maintaining attention; but 'attention *creates* no idea', as William James remarked.[12] In itself it delivers no new content, and it need not be a matter of action, any more than being keyed up and tensely expectant are: one may be gripped, fascinated, absorbed, swept away, one's attention may be held: all these descriptions correctly imply lack of action.

No doubt there are other such preparatory, ground-setting, tuning, retuning, shepherding, active moves or intentional initiations.[13] But action, in thinking, really goes no further than this. The rest is waiting, seeing if anything happens, waiting for content to come to mind, for the 'natural causality of reason' to operate in one.[14] This operation is indeed spontaneous, but in the sense of 'involuntary, not due to conscious volition'. There is I believe no action at all in reasoning and judging considered independently of the preparatory, catalytic phenomena just mentioned; considered in respect of their being a matter of specific content-production or of inferential moves between particular contents. Nor is catalysis crucial: in his short story 'Giving Blood' Updike introduces a sentential operator that perfectly fits one of the things that goes on when one is doing philosophy: 'The thesis developed upon him that [*p*].'[15]

To this extent Philo was radically understating things when he said that 'a man's thoughts are sometimes not due to himself but come without his will'.[16] It is not just that 'the faculty of voluntarily bringing back a wandering attention, over and over again, is the very root of judgment', as William James remarked; although that is also true.[17] It is that this catalytic bringing back is all there is in the way of action, in judgement. This, just this, is the true extent of what Descartes called '*directio ingenii*', the direction of the mind in thought—'the voluntary . . . decision to direct the mind in ways which will allow its natural rational powers to operate properly and productively'.[18] Call what goes on mental spontaneity if you like, allow the arising of contents to be a matter of spontaneity; but admit, then, that spontaneity has nothing particularly to do with action or will, and nothing at all to do with freedom of choice.

'The solution of problems is the most characteristic . . . sort of voluntary thinking.'[19] James seems to be right about this too (although there is also directed daydreaming to consider). He suggests that trying to solve a problem is in many ways like trying to remember a forgotten name or idea, and the comparison is telling. There is plenty of action—catalytic, priming (and strangely indirect) action—in trying to

---

[12] 1890: 1.450.

[13] Sophisticated automobile engines are said to retune themselves several thousand times a second. Perhaps something similar to this goes on, at comparatively leisurely speeds, in concentrated thought—something similar to the constant refreshal of a computer monitor.

[14] I use this expression in Strawson 1986, e.g. pp. 93–4, 105. See also Hume 1748: 165–8, 'Of the reason of animals', and Brewer 1995.

[15] 1962: 367. Here Updike sounds like Henry James, as he surely knows.

[16] 20–50 CE: V.266.   [17] 1890: 1.424. The root is not, I take it, the essence.

[18] Cottingham 2002: 352. This accurate description attributes no intentional agency to the operation of reason.

[19] 1890: 1.584.

remember a name, but there is nothing voluntary about what new content comes to mind. Pointers arise, as we press the mind, but they '*arise independently of the will*, by the spontaneous [*nb*] process we know so well. *All that the will does is to emphasize and linger over those which seem pertinent, and ignore the rest* . . . even though there be a mental spontaneity, it can certainly not create ideas.'[20]

So too, all the *cognitive work* that thought involves, all the *computation* in the largest and most human sense, all the essential *content-work* of reasoning and judgement, all the motion or progress of judgement and thought considered (so to say) *in its contentual essence*—the actual confrontations and engagements between contents, the collaborations and competitions between them, the transitions between them—, is not only not a matter of action at all but also non-conscious or sub-experiential.[21] It is not itself a phenomenon of consciousness, however much it is catalysed by conscious primings. Rather, the content outcomes are delivered into consciousness so as to be available in their turn for use by the catalytic machinery that is under intentional control. One knows that P is true and wonders whether $[P \rightarrow Q]$, holding this content in consciousness. Into consciousness comes 'No; possibly $[P \wedge \neg Q]$'; immediately followed, perhaps, by 'But R, and $[[P \wedge R] \rightarrow Q]$, so Q.'[22]

This non-consciousness is itself an important fact, I think, and invites reflection. Some may think that it amounts already to the point that the essence of thinking (as opposed to the supporting work of catalysis and priming) is not a matter of action. This may not be the right reaction, all things considered (see §8 below), but the main claim remains: no ordinary thinking of a particular thought-content, conscious or otherwise, is ever an action. No actual natural thinking of a thought, no actual having of a particular thought-content, is ever itself an action. Mental action in thinking is restricted to the fostering of conditions hospitable to contents' coming to mind. The coming to mind itself—the actual occurrence of thoughts, conscious or non-conscious—is not a matter of action.

5

—I'm now going to think that grass is green, and my thinking that grass is green is going to be a premeditated action: *grass is green*. There. And now I'm going to think something—I don't yet know what—and my thinking it is going to be a premeditated action: *swifts live their lives on the wing*. Both these actions disprove your last claim.

Well, they are hardly natural cases of thought, but let us consider them. In the first case, that of thinking *grass is green*, it may seem that there is an especially concentrated, fully-fledged action of comprehension-involving entertaining of a content. But

---

[20] 1890: 1.586, 594. See also James's brilliant discussion of trying to remember something on 1.251–2.

[21] 'Sub-personal', as some say; but the distinction holds in dogs as much as in human beings.

[22] Certainly associationism of Tucker's kind takes away nothing from our powers of reasoning.

is this really so? Is there really any such thing as an *action* of comprehension-involving entertaining of a content? What one finds, I think, if one reflects, does at one stage involve some sort of action, but this is just a matter of a silent mental imaging of words (as sounds or visual marks, say): the actual *comprehending thinking of the content* is something that just happens thereafter or perhaps concurrently.

In this case a comprehending entertaining of *grass is green* has already previously occurred—it has already been held in mind as an intended object of thought. Another event of (particularly emphatic) comprehending entertaining is then brought about by one's doing something of the priming or catalytic kind, such as generating a silent acoustic image of 'Grass is green' to oneself in some way—something that has already been allowed to be a genuine instance of mental action. But the event of entertaining itself is not an action, any more than falling is once one has jumped off a wall.

In the case of *swifts live their lives on the wing* there is again a certain sort of action: an action of setting oneself to produce some content or other. But what happens then is—a content just comes. Which particular content it is is not intentionally controlled; it is not a matter of action. It cannot be a matter of action unless the content is already there, available for consideration and adoption for intentional production. But if it is already there to be considered and adopted it must already have 'just come' at some previous time in order to be so available. And this takes us back to the first case, while throwing more light on the general respect in which the occurrence of a particular event of entertaining and consciously comprehending a particular thought content neither is nor can be an action, still less an action in which the intention is to comprehendingly entertain that very thought-content. One can make such an event occur, but only by doing something else.

—Actions have many true descriptions and it is a familiar point that they can be redescribed in terms of their consequences, intended or not. I cross the threshold, activate the lighting, illuminate the conservatory, alarm the parrot, wake the burglar. I move my leg, kick the ball, score the goal. So too I aim to think some thought or other, I make millions of neurons fire, I think *swifts live their lives on the wing*; or I aim to work out the truth about some specific matter, and finish up thinking P. Why aren't these cases of the same sort? Why can't all intentional mental actions of catalysis and focusing be truly described in terms of their consequences, so that when I focus my mind in order to try to work out what the truth is, and end up thinking P, my entertaining this content is correctly said to be an action?

If you think the cases are the same, fine. Certainly one is not thereby obliged to assimilate the case of coming up with the particular thought-content one does to the case of waking the parrot—although it is very important that the upshot targeted in intention can be specified only generally in the normal case, either as just: thinking some thought or other, or, in the case of trying to work something out, as: thinking whatever is the truth about the question under consideration. Given this way of describing things, perhaps the only error that some people make, in considering these matters, is to conceive of the issuing of a particular thought-content as a 'basic' action:

something one does, and does intentionally, and does not do by doing anything else. Here as elsewhere I think it is the psychological difference between those who feel thought as action and those who don't that is most interesting—each side finding the other remarkable.

—Suppose you initiate a line of thought that will lead you to the answer to the question 'Is *a F* or *G*?'. You already know the answer (*a* is *G*), but you can't remember the course of the argument that gets you to it. But you know the premises, and you know that going through the argument will lead you to the answer, so that you will finish up thinking vividly that *a* is *G*. Isn't this, at least, a case in which entertaining a particular thought is an action in which the intention is to produce that very thought-content?

Your thought that *a* is *G* is precipitated by the staging of an argument in thought. You cause the thought to come about by action. You actively initiate the line of argument by bringing the premises to mind, and maintain it in being as necessary (it may run by itself). Once again, though, the final occurrence—your explicit and convinced thinking that *a* is *G*—is not itself an action, still less an action in which the intention is to produce that particular thought-content. Your thinking that *a* is *G* can be allowed to be the product of an action or actions performed with the intention to produce that particular thought-content, but it is not itself an action, any more than an increase in one's physical fitness is when one goes in for regular exercise. In many respects thinking is like seeing. Opening one's eyes, turning one's head in the direction of X, concentrating on the scene in the attempt to pick out X—all these things can be a matter of action, but seeing X can't be.

—Just ask me to think about God, the number 1,000,000, or democracy (or the concepts of God, the number 1,000,000 or democracy), and I will. Just ask me to consider the proposition P, and I will.[23]

Certainly these are things we can do at will and on demand, things we can do and do and do intentionally. And these are cases in which we do not have a fully pre-given content, like *grass is green*, only a pre-given topic. But the component of action is the same as before. It is the setting of the mind at a given topic (triggered in one's mind by another's speech) and waiting for content to come.

What do I do when asked to think about democracy? Let me try. I find I bring the word 'democracy' before my mind in the familiar, superfast, insubstantial, quasi-acoustic way. What happens then? Nothing comes immediately, apart from a mood-flash of boredom at the idea of democracy, which arises in spite of the fact that I'm all for it, and a concurrent sense that a passable dictionary definition of democracy is 'access-conscious' in Block's sense—immediately available to thought—although I do not spell it out to myself (it is as it were 'compressed' in the sense of a computer file). I try to give things a push—again this is a matter of action of the catalytic sort discussed above—and I get a muddled bundle of things: some Greek etymology, the name Churchill, a primitive sketch of his remark about democracy, a thought

---

[23] Ward Jones's challenge, for which I am grateful.

about communism.[24] But none of these comings and entertainings of content are themselves a matter of action.

We can replace 'judgement' by 'thought' in the passage quoted earlier from William James: 'the faculty of voluntarily bringing back a wandering attention, over and over again, is the very root of thought', the very root of a person's concerted thinking about something. Is the root of a thing its essence or that from which it grows? The latter, no doubt; but if you think it is the former, then you can say that thought—concerted thought—is action through and through. The point remains: no actual passage to judgement, no actual accession to a new belief, is itself a matter of action. It is just what happens after the exercise of the faculty of bringing back one's wandering attention to the matter at hand.

'Every kind of reasoning is nothing, in its simplest form, but attention', as Shadworth Hodgson remarked.[25] It is a laying open of oneself to the 'natural causality of reason', an induction of oneself into a receptive, actively passive state, tuned this way or that. And everything that applies in the case of thought, reason, and judgement applies equally in the case of belief and belief-formation. So here I am in direct disagreement with the proponents of 'doxastic voluntarism'. I am directly opposed to Peacocke, for example, who advances from the claim that 'judgements are in fact *actions*' and the claim that 'to make a judgement is the fundamental way to form a belief' to the conclusion that coming to form a belief is also standardly a matter of action.[26] Peacocke allows that 'not every case of coming to believe something is an action', but the view defended in this paper is that no normal cases of coming to believe something are actions.[27]

6

—Even if reason, judgement, thought and belief-formation are not in their contentual essence—their intrinsic contentual evolution and outcome—a matter of action, imagination is, and so are choices and decisions. Reason, judgement, thought and belief-formation aim at truth—they all operate under the constraint of truth. For this reason alone they cannot plausibly be supposed to be exercises of spontaneity in any sense that connects spontaneity interestingly with freedom of choice; and this is a point that holds quite independently of most of the claims that you have made so far. But imagination and decision are not like this at all. It is clear—to begin with the former—that

[24] 'No one pretends that democracy is perfect or all-wise. Indeed, it has been said that democracy is the worst form of government except for all those other forms that have been tried from time to time' (speech in the House of Commons, 11 November 1947).

[25] 1870: 1.400, quoted in James 1890: 1.589.

[26] Peacocke 1999: 19–20, 238.

[27] 'Belief is more properly an act of the sensitive, than of the cogitative part of our natures', according to Hume (1739–40: 183/1.4.1.8), but belief-formation is not a matter of action in either case (no interesting objections arise from visits to the hypnotist to acquire the belief that P, or the phenomena of 'self-deception', or cases like the one in which one opens a box in order to acquire a belief about what is inside).

imagining really is, quite straightforwardly, a matter of action. The production and entertaining of new content in imagination is itself, and quite directly, a matter of action, in a way that has and can have no parallel in the case of truth-aimed cognition. Summon up an image of a giraffe now, and have it turn round and run away. This is a matter of action, something you can do and control and develop.

Imagination can have a remarkable effortlessness or fluency, and can seem like a paradigm case of action—something we do and do intentionally—and indeed like a matter of 'basic' action—something we do intentionally and do not do by doing anything else. And my principal present aim is merely to resist the idea that reasoning, thought, judgement, and belief-formation are in their contentual progression a matter of action (their contentual progression considered just as such, as when, believing that P, one has the thought that Q after realizing that [P → Q]). But let me try very briefly to extend the passivist proposal a little. Even in the case of imagination there seems to be a sense in which the entertaining of content is not itself any sort of action, but, rather, a kind of involuntary response that we are prone to experience as action, as something we do intentionally, when it occurs (as it normally does) without any sort of resistance.[28]

If I ask you to conjure up in imagination a tree, a bottle, a naked body, a pink elephant, a zebra-striped giraffe, you can probably do it effortlessly, in whatever way it is that you do imagine things—however sketchily or schematically, however non-pictorially, however impoverished your visual imagination.[29] But if I ask you instead *not* to conjure up a black-and-white-striped giraffe, you may find it hard to comply.[30] Obviously you have to grasp what 'black-and-white-striped giraffe' means, and so have the concept of a black-and-white-striped giraffe in mind, in order to know what I am asking you not to conjure up. The further claim is that you are very likely to be unable not to conjure up a black-and-white-striped giraffe, at least momentarily (for thought is quick), in whatever way you do conjure things.[31] Even if one has mastered a special thought-blocking technique (whose initiation may be a matter of action), one is likely to be able to close the door of imagination only after it has already intimated something black-and-white-striped-giraffish.

Now this imagining is evidently not a matter of action—it is involuntary, a reflex mental response—and one may ask whether anything similar might be true in the case in which one has set oneself to imagine something. Is what then occurs straightforwardly something one does and does intentionally? Isn't it rather an automatic occurrence of content which, welcome as it is, meeting no resistance, is (in many

---

[28] I take imagination to involve non-conceptual content (by which I mean representation in some not purely conceptual medium) essentially. I am concerned with whatever content imagining a silver horse adds to merely thinking *silver horse*.

[29] People vary enormously in the vividness and experiential modalities of their imagining. William James's discussion of this is probably still as good as any (1890: ch. 18).

[30] It is probably already too late. Experimental psychologists know this as the 'pink-elephant phenomenon'.

[31] One might as well try not to understand the sentence 'this giraffe is tall' when one hears it clearly enunciated (on the involuntariness of linguistic understanding, see Strawson 1994: 6–7).

people) invested with a glow of ease that makes it feel like some sort of intentional achievement? The dear self[32] may like to claim what then occurs as its own intentional performance, but it may be that the sense of intentional authorship arises merely from the resistlessness, together with the ambient sense of agency involved in any catalytic activity that may also be going on.

Might it also arise from an extremely fast, automatic, rubber-stamping *nihil-obstat*ing of what simply *happens* given the initial imaginative project and the fact that one has no objection to it? Perhaps—but if this has any mental reality I think it is not itself something conscious, even if it leaves a wake in consciousness; and sometimes the passage from project to delivery seems too fast for any lightning *fiat* or *nihil obstat*.

If the process as a whole is largely automatic, is the particular content of one's imagining, at least, an intentional production? When one has set oneself to imagine something one must obviously start from some conceptual or linguistic specification of the content (*spangled pink elephant*), and given that one's imagining duly fits the specification one may say that it is intentionally produced. But there isn't intentional control in any further sense: the rest is a matter of ballistics, mental ballistics.[33] One entertains the verbal specification and waits for the mechanism of imagination—the (involuntary) spontaneity of imagination—to deliver the image.

The pro-action camp may grant this, or some of it, while continuing to insist that the sustaining and developing of imaginings are another matter. And it seems clear that such sustainings and developings can involve action. But it should be noted, first, that imagining or fantasy has, notoriously, an internal (and again 'spontaneous') dynamic of its own that is not a matter of action; it can run riot, agreeably or disagreeably, without any input in the form of intentional direction, and indeed in spite of any such input.

Note, also, that the occurring of an idea about what to add to an imagined scene is not itself a matter of action, although it may well be triggered by intentional, directed, catalytic processes of attention and focusing; nor, I think, is what then actually happens in imagination by way of addition and development. Although the sustaining or facilitation of what happens may again involve catalytic action, the imaginative content itself is, again, up to one's Muse, given that it is something over and above any explicitly cognitively prefigured content—*spangled pink + elephant* for example.[34] When one sets oneself to imagine anything there comes a moment when what one does is precisely to relinquish control. To think that the actual content-issuing and content-entertaining that are the heart of imagining are themselves a matter of action seems like thinking, when one has thrown a dart, that the dart's entering the dartboard is itself an action.

---

[32] 'The dear self is always turning up' Kant *Grundlegung* 1785: ch. 1. Compare the way in which some, most strangely, behave—feel—as if they deserve to be given credit for their natural talent.

[33] In the technical (psychophysiological) sense in which the motion of one's leg, after one has done whatever one does neurally in initiating a kick, is merely ballistic—as ballistic as the motion of the ball after it has ceased to be in contact with one's foot.

[34] There are, evidently, different catalytic techniques, different gifts, different deficits.

In these directed cases, one has the intended content in mind under one fairly precise mental identifier: as likely as not, actual images of words (visual or acoustic) are somehow present to mind, along with understanding of their meaning. And one can indeed be said to be doing just what one intends to do in imagining what one imagines. And in this sense, at least, it may be said, imagining is as robust a case of action as any. So too when one aims at the bullseye and hits it, one's hitting it is an action on one's part. But all the previous points about the limits on mental action remain in place.

A final remark: although imagination does not operate under the constraint of truth in the way that reason, judgement, thought and belief-formation do, it is standardly employed in the search for truth, in trying to work out what is likely to happen, what will happen if X, what probably has happened given Y; in rehearsing possibilities of action, anticipating dangers, planning well. In this core use it is integral to effective truth-seeking thought, reasoning, judgement, and belief-formation.[35] But it is not always directly answerable to truth considerations in the way that these other things are, in their normal operation, and that, perhaps, is the main reason why its specific content-productions can seem to be a matter of action, even under theoretical scrutiny, in some way that has no parallel in the case of these other things.

7

—'What about choices and decisions? These are clearly mental actions.'

Some are, but the case is far from clear. And we need to consider the mental goings on that precede choices and decisions. Are these a matter of action, at least in part?

Well, it depends on the case. Very often there is no action at all: none of the activation of relevant considerations is something one does intentionally. It simply happens, driven by the practical need to make a decision. The play of pros and cons is automatic—and sometimes unstoppable. At other times there is a deliberate setting of the mind at the problem of what to do, a process of focusing on the problem, a concertion of thought, and this can be a matter of action. But what follows is, again, just a waiting for content to occur. As in the case of theoretical thought there may well be a process of refocusing and re-refocusing—that curious ballistic launching and relaunching of the mind after it has stalled or stumbled or been distracted, a recasting of it (in the fishing sense) after it has started to settle in one direction, so that it will be receptive to hitherto unengaged relevant considerations. But here again action is the underlabourer, preparatory, catalytic. There is no direct action in the actual issuing of new content, any more than there is in the growth of trees one has planted.

In many situations of practical uncertainty, pressing or not, one believes, often rightly, that there is a straightforwardly right or best answer to the question what to do. And in all cases of this sort reaching a decision need not—I am inclined to say

---

[35] There is also what one might call cognitive imagination, imagination at the service of theoretical rather than practical enquiry.

should not—involve any *agency in decision*, nor any sense of agency in decision. What happens is that one considers and reconsiders the pros and cons, perhaps involuntarily, perhaps calmly, perhaps frenetically, and what one wants is that it should become clear which is the right choice. One simply wants to come to see what is best (morally or otherwise), and there is *nothing* in the experience of wanting this, or of actually coming to see what is best, that necessarily or even properly involves any sense of intentional agency or free decision.[36] Some, no doubt, have such a sense, but the case seems similar to the case of imagination. Mere openness to, simple lack of resistance to, harmony with, one's own natural, internal, automatic, non-agentive operations of content-processing, is experienced by some as action, as something intentionally done, when really these operations are (catalytics aside) nothing of the sort. The movement of the natural causality of reason (practical reason in this case) to its conclusion in choice or decision is lived (by some) as action when it is really just reflex; distinctively rational reflex, to be sure, but not in any case a matter of action.[37] All in all, it seems to me that most of deciding what to do is best seen as something that just happens, even if there is also, and crucially, some sort of genuine action of positive commitment to the decision, either at the time it is reached, or at the moment of the 'passage à l'acte'.[38]

One could press the passivist line harder, and raise free-will issues, but I will move on.

8

I have argued that there is relatively little action in mental life, especially in the case that most concerns me: cognition in the widest sense. No coming to entertain a content, and no comprehending entertaining of a content, in reasoning, thinking, judging, or anything else, is itself an action. People may differ in the degree to which they are agents in their mental lives, as remarked. We can train ourselves to exercise more agency in our mentation. Some people engage in a great deal of concerted thought, others in almost none. But any action in cognition is of the catalytic sort. And, once again, the really intriguing difference between people is not the difference between those who are regularly agents (catalytic agents) in their cognition and those who are not, but between those who *feel* strongly that they are agents in their cognition, agents in what they think, and who set great store by this idea, and those who do not.

[36] Compare trying to decide which of a number of melons is ripest, or trying to read the words on a distant sign.

[37] This is not any sort of reductive remark so far as the rationality of the processes (or of the people in whom they take place) is concerned. On this I agree fully with Brewer 1995.

[38] Perhaps it was awareness of this point that drove the existentialists into the strenuous artifice of the 'acte gratuit'. It might be argued that choices and decisions are fully-fledged actions only in the limiting case in which it is rational to choose either A or B but one has no reason for favouring one over the other; the case in which there is precisely 'nothing to choose' between A and B, so that there has to be some sort of coin-tossing, non-rational plumping for one or the other.

In large-scale bodily action, Davidson remarks, 'we never do more than move our bodies; the rest is up to nature'.[39] In cognition we never do more than aim or tilt our minds; the rest is up to nature, trained or not. Much bodily movement is ballistic, relative to the initiating impulse; the same goes for thought.[40]

Benjamin Libet's experimental work deserves a mention here, for it has been cited in support of the view that we never really make choices or decisions in the present moment of consciousness in the way we think we do. Our natural sense of things, plainly, is that many of our actions depend on and flow causally from our consciously made choices and decisions and resolutions.[41] In these cases we experience ourselves as consciously deciding or resolving what to do, and as consciously deciding or judging that *now* is the time to act, and as then (subsequently) acting. Such experience is routine and often vivid, and in the normal case one has no sense that the time of these choices or resolvings, or the time of their triggering action, is other than the time at which they are consciously experienced as being made and as triggering action. Libet's experiments, however, suggest that the experience of conscious choice to perform an action occurs about 350 milliseconds after the time at which the brain activity leading to the performance of the intended action (the readiness potential) has got under way. To that extent, they suggest that there is a key sense in which the conscious experience of choice occurs some time after the choice has been made, non-consciously, in the mind or brain. Indeed it seems that the time of the experience of conscious choice or decision is simply the time at which the content of the choice or decision or resolution first becomes available to consciousness.[42]

Roughly put, then, Libet's claim is that the neurophysiological evidence shows that the experience of conscious choice is strictly speaking illusory. It occurs only when a choice that has already been made and has already begun to be acted on is (as it were) presented in consciousness. If this is right, it undermines an intensely natural picture of agency according to which it is, essentially, the *conscious I* that is the agent: we take it that in so far as we are deciders, choosers and initiators of action, true exercisers of

---

[39] 1971: 23.

[40] There are in fact powerful reasons for drawing the line between what we do and what happens further in than Davidson does: perhaps between the intentional-bodily-movement-initiating brain impulses in the cerebral cortex and all that then follows. In the case of motor action 'the final 50 ms. before the muscle is activated is the time [needed] for the primary motor cortex to activate the spinal motor nerve cells', and during this time things go ballistic: 'the act goes to completion with no possibility of stopping it by the rest of the cerebral cortex' (Libet 1999: 51). Clearly these neurological facts do not in themselves settle any philosophical questions about what things it is best or most natural to designate as actions.

[41] Although the vast majority—from typing to driving to shifting position to taking the next step down the road—do not.

[42] See e.g. Libet 1985, 1987, 1989; Gazzaniga 1998; Wegner & Wheatley 1999; Wegner 2002. There is a very helpful account of Libet's work in Norretranders 1991: ch. 9. See also Libet 2000. In his experimental work Libet concentrates on cases in which the decision is not simply a decision about what to do but a decision to do it now, for these cases are more susceptible of experimental test. But if his findings are valid we may take it that they may be valid for all events of decision and choice.

agency, it is (essentially) as conscious beings who are present in the present moment of consciousness. And yet the experimental results suggest that:

it is not a person's conscious *I* that really initiates an action . . . The *I* does not want to accept this. The thinking, conscious *I* insists on being the true player, the active operator, the one in charge. But it cannot be.[43]

Is this claim true? It looks as if it may be, although it should be said that it is not really an empirical question whether the onset of the readiness potential should count as a choice.[44] If it were true, would it undermine anything that matters? No. Even on their strongest interpretation Libet's results do not in any way threaten the view that we really do make decisions and choices, and are indeed the authors of our actions. For our decisions and choices and actions, mental or bodily, are not in any sense not our own, or in any way less our own, because their original occurrence is not conscious (the same goes for our thoughts, reasonings, judgements). Libet's results do not threaten any defensible sense in which we can be said to have free will or to be responsible for what we do. The experience one has of being the author or origin of one's decision or choice is mistaken only in so far as it may not be oneself considered very narrowly (conscious-egoistically) as the conscious *I* present in the moment of the conscious experience of making the choice or decision that actually makes the choice or decision. The choice or decision is, to repeat, no less one's own for occurring outside consciousness (it is certainly no one else's). It flows from oneself, from one's character and outlook, from what one is, mentally. The most that Libet's experiments show (if the conclusions drawn from them are indeed correct) is that one does not resolve on one's actions at quite the time one thinks one does, or make one's choices and decisions consciously in the way one thinks one does. But any such misdating is utterly unimportant.[45]

—Quite so; and this point has a natural extension. Just as it does not follow, from the claim that the 'conscious *I*' never makes choices or decisions, that there is any sense in which one's choices and decisions are not one's own, or in any way less one's own, so too it does not follow, from the fact that the processes that lead to the arrival of thought contents in consciousness are not themselves conscious, either (a) that they are in any sense not truly our own thoughts or (b) that they are in any sense not a matter of action.

I agree with (a) but not (b). I agree that our thoughts and judgements are not in any sense not our own, or less our own, for not being direct products of consciousness;

[43] Norretranders 1991: 257.
[44] It has been subjected to much criticism. For recent examples see e.g. Dennett 2003: 227–42; Mele 2005.
[45] See Norretranders 1991: 257, Strawson 1994: 172. Libet has also argued that at the time of the conscious experience of making the choice one still has a power to abort or 'veto' the action process that is already under way (see e.g. Libet 2000; 1985). This, presumably, would put the 'conscious I' back in control in some sense; but the respect in which choices may be non-conscious remains untouched, and I do not think that Libet succeeds in answering the objection that the veto, too, is presumably under way non-consciously before it becomes conscious (Libet also mislocates the threat to free will, as do many participants in the debate, for reasons just given).

the fear that Libet's findings constitute a threat to any remotely defensible account of autonomy, freedom, and responsibility is psychologically telling but superficial. I also agree that the occurrence of our thoughts and choices can be partly caused by genuinely intentional mental actions on our part—the catalytic business discussed earlier, the girding of the mind to engage the problem at hand.[46] But I see no reason to say that the operation of the mental system that is catalysed in this way, and that culminates in a thought or judgement, is itself a matter of action, rather than being automatic and standardly involuntary. We return to the fundamental point: human minds are powerfully governed by deep, natural, non-agentive principles of operation. This is the spontaneity of reason and understanding: the 'natural causality of reason'. But it is also, more broadly, the natural causality of the profound entanglement of human cognition and emotion. More broadly still, it is the natural causality of the whole huge engine of innate mental equipment as activated and tuned by experience.

9

We are incessantly engaged in actions of one sort or another, major and minor. Are we then bound to have some vivid sense of ourselves as agents in our mental lives (short of mental illness)? Is this a psychological necessity for us? By no means. Such a sense of agency is not a human universal. Human beings need have no significant sense of themselves as agents in their mental lives. In this respect, as in so many others, we are widely distributed on a long spectrum of temperamental difference, and have equal opportunities for flourishing and failure, however dubious we are about the claims of those unlike ourselves. One can live a good—amazing—human life without any significant experience of oneself as an agent in one's mentation.

Certainly a sense of responsibility, and responsibility itself (understood as a general trait that a person may have or lack), does not depend on any sense of mental agency. In moral matters as much as in non-moral, certain courses of action present as things one should do, or should not do; and one's sense that this is indeed what they are, one's living of the fact that this is what they are, certainly does not require any sort of positive, active endorsement of them, nor any sense of any such positive active endorsement. On the contrary; they are likely to seem like things one can do nothing about, like the wetness of water. Responsibility as a trait of being is not a matter of action at all, although cultivating it can be. It's a set or cast of mind that has consequences for action. Responsibility is something one finds in oneself. It's there, like one's hands. There is *no* correlation between a lack of a sense of action in mentation and irresponsibility or moral deficiency. But for some—caught up in the picture of pervasive inner agency—this may be hard to see.

---

[46] No doubt these catalytic mental actions, like bodily actions, are initiated and already under way before they are experienced as being initiated by the conscious *I*.

The effects of spiritual discipline on human mentality should not be underestimated. Descriptions of the experiential character of states of spiritual advancement appear to be extremely robust,[47] and Krishnamurti reports an experience that many, perhaps, have had when he claims that

you do not choose, you do not decide, when you see things very clearly: then you act which [*sic*] is not the action of will. ... Only the unintelligent mind exercises choice in life. ... A truly intelligent [spiritually developed] mind ... simply cannot have choice.[48]

To lose a sense of agency here may simply be to pass beyond experience of indecision and, equally, beyond any need to push or catalyse one's thinking. It most certainly does not involve any loss or diminution of responsibility.

It is worth adding that pathological human experience is as real as any other, and important in its own right. Experience of oneself as an agent in one's mental life can be lost in depersonalization, for example, while basic awareness of oneself as a locus of consciousness or mental presence remains undiminished. Something like this, pathological or not, afflicted Coleridge. He got up in the morning and put on his boots. He lived from day to day. He wrote letters and walked into town. But he felt that he entirely lacked the 'self-directing Principle', and was, 'as an *acting* man, a creature of mere Impact'.[49] Camus's Meursault also comes to mind.[50]

Experiences of creativity or composition also commonly have this form. You do not have to be a poet or a genius to agree with Rimbaud when he writes

It's false to say: I think. One ought to say 'it thinks [in] me ... for *I* is an other ... It's obvious to me that I am a spectator at the unfolding of my thought: I watch it, I listen to it.[51]

This is how it is for me when I think about what to say here. Any action lies in the catalytic prompting of mentation, in the choice of focus as several things strike me when, stuck, I re-read the previous sentence or two and wait to see what happens.[52] Apart from that, the usual ambient activity, a restless scanning that goes on automatically, an apparently empty-headed, purposefully aimless ranging (it has, somehow, a spatial character to it) which is not in fact aimless because it has become tuned to a specific subject-matter. Then Nietzsche's 'small terse fact that a thought comes when "it" wishes and not when "I" wish'.[53]

I will finish with a few further remarks about spontaneity.

[47] In the sense that there is a high measure of agreement as to their basic character across different traditions.
[48] Quoted in Lutyens 1983: 33, 204; see Strawson 1986: ch. 13. Compare Spinoza's view that 'God ... cannot be said ... to act from freedom of the will' (1675: 435 (*Ethics* Pt. 1, Prop. 32, Coroll. 2)).
[49] Holmes 1989: 315.
[50] Camus 1942. See also Roquentin's bad moments in *La nausée* (Sartre 1938), and n4 above.
[51] 1871: 249, 250.
[52] I often lose an idea and trust that it will find its way back if it is any good. Dennett (1991a, 2001) gives some striking descriptions of how contents compete for entry into consciousness.
[53] 1886: §17. Compare Federico in Ernest Hemingway's (1929) *A Farewell to Arms:* 'I never think, and yet when I begin to talk I say the things I have found out in my mind without thinking.' And remember the little girl in Graham Wallas's *The Art of Thought* (1926) 'who, being told to be

10

One cannot be spontaneous, in the everyday sense of the word, if one is trying or intending to be. The project is self-defeating. This is a familiar point outside philosophy, and it seems that a version of it applies equally to the idea that there is spontaneity in cognition: if the notion of spontaneity is brought into close connection with the notion of (intentional) action, or with any notion of freedom other than the Spinozan–Kantian notion according to which to be free is simply to be governed by reason,[54] then there is I think nothing in reasoning, thought, judgement, and belief-formation ('cognition' for short) that can constitute being spontaneous. Spontaneity conceived of in this way is not, should not be, and cannot be what determines one's thoughts' having the particular content they do as they arise in cognition.[55]

The dictionary definition of 'spontaneous' contains interesting stresses. The first and most straightforward meaning is 'occurring without external cause or stimulus', and this is what Kant means by the term, but it continues as follows:

coming naturally or freely, unpremeditated; voluntary, done of one's own accord ... acting voluntarily or without premeditation ... (of movement) instinctive, prompted by no motive ... involuntary, not due to conscious volition.[56]

I have argued that it is only in so far as spontaneous means 'involuntary' that there is any spontaneity in reason, thought, and judgement.

I don't think that this puts me in conflict with McDowell's basic Kantian characterization of the link between spontaneity and freedom. He, after all, is concerned with the 'freedom, exemplified in responsible acts of judging, [that] is essentially a matter of being answerable to criticism in the light of rationally relevant considerations', the freedom that is a matter of 'rational necessitation', namely, determination by reason;[57] and if freedom resides in the autonomy that consists in rational necessitation, then to the extent that spontaneity is to be identified with freedom, there seems to be a clear sense in which freedom increases in proportion as spontaneity becomes irresistible, natural, automatic, involuntary, instinctive, reflex, second nature. True freedom, on this Spinozan–Kantian±Krishnamurtian view, is—once

---

sure of her meaning before she spoke, said "How can I know what I think till I see what I say?" ' She speaks for many, although not for all at all times.

   Nietzsche continues 'so that it is a falsification of the facts of the case to say that the subject "I" is the condition of the predicate "think" '. I think there's a clear sense in which this is wrong, for reasons given in discussion of Libet, but it is right about what many people think that the 'I' of consciousness is.

   54 'I call him free who is led by reason alone' (Spinoza 1675: 584).
   55 I take this to include moral cognition.
   56 *SOED* 1993: 2998. Compare Philip Roth 2001: 141: 'With Consuela, there's a semiconscious spontaneity in whatever she does, a rightness, though she may not know quite what she's doing or exactly why. [.... What she does] is very close to nature, to an original drifting thought, to intuition, and there is no deliberate reasoning behind it.'
   57 McDowell 1998: 434, 1994: 5.

again—*necessitation* by reason—that is, something that does not itself involve any sort of action,[58] although it affects—governs—the nature of the actions that one does perform. This is a notion of freedom that is remote from the ordinary notion of freedom of choice, but it is venerable, important, and perfectly clear.[59]

McDowell writes that

judging, making up our minds what to think, is something for which we are, in principle, responsible—something we freely do, as opposed to something that merely happens in our lives[60]

and here his may view seem directly at odds with my claim that there is a crucial sense in which judging 'just happens'. There are, however, different ways in which things just happen, and as far as I can see the sense in which judgements and makings up of minds just happen subtracts nothing from the autonomy or freedom or responsibility that human beings have on McDowell's view (or indeed from any autonomy or freedom or responsibility that human beings can be coherently supposed to have). Certainly in 'just happening' they can be wholly spontaneous in the Kantian sense; they do not impinge on us from outside us in any freedom-diminishing way. They

---

[58] It's not up to you that, believing [P → Q], you come to believe Q on coming to believe P.

[59] By my count 'spontaneity' and its cognates appears twenty-seven times in Kemp Smith's translation of *Critique of Pure Reason* (I count occurrences in a single paragraph as a single occurrence), usually translating 'Spontaneität', but sometimes 'Selbsttätigkeit' (self-activity), or a phrase like 'von Selbst'. The first use is non-technical, twenty of the others are concerned with the spontaneity of the understanding, six with the 'absolute' spontaneity supposedly required for free will. The basic meaning is the same in all cases, and is fully conveyed by the first definition given in the *SOED*: 'occurring without external cause or stimulus'. If we allow ourselves to talk temporally within the Kantian frame, and say that the operation of the spontaneity of the understanding can be triggered by input from sensibility, Kant's claim is that it is what the understanding does *after* that that is spontaneous: that is, the understanding is not in its own principles of operation subject to or affected by any external cause or stimulus or determinant.

The *SOED* definition applies equally to the spontaneity associated with freedom of action. Spontaneity is 'a power of absolutely beginning a state' [A445/B473], a power whereby something 'begins *of itself*' [A447/B475] without any (prior) external cause, and is therefore absolutely self-determining. 'By freedom . . . I understand the power of beginning a state *spontaneously*' [von Selbst], i.e. undetermined by anything external. [A533/B561]. Kant sticks strictly to the use McDowell adopts from him, and says nothing to suggest that he thinks that the practical employment of thought or reason is a matter of freedom in the sense of freedom of choice.

The same goes for the only occurrence in the *Grundlegung* (1785: 120, Ak. 4. 452; Kant is explaining the sense in which the spontaneity of reason is more 'pure' than that of the understanding), and for at least four of the seven occurrences in the Beck translation of the *Critique of Practical Reason*. Of the remaining three, two are used to characterize something Kant disparages in so far as it preempts or interferes with a proper sense of duty and obligation—'spontaneous inclination' and 'spontaneous goodness of heart', and the last is unclear but no basis for an objection to the present position is 'whether it is a perfect duty to devote one's self to . . . the magnanimous sacrifice of life for the safety of one's country . . . spontaneously and unbidden'). In the Greene and Hudson translation of *Religion Within The Bounds of Reason Alone* (five occurrences), Kant continues to use the term to mean 'occurring without external cause or stimulus' and has no other or more exciting brief. All in all, I think, the term has no special load or importance for Kant (there are only forty occurrences of the root '*spontan*' in the whole Kantian Corpus including the pre-Critical writings, of which twenty are in the *Critique of Pure Reason*).

[60] 1998: 434.

are part of us, part of our natural inner working. Suddenly seeing the answer is not the same as tripping over a stone.

'A belief', McDowell continues,

is not always, or even typically, a result of our exercising this freedom to decide what to think. But even when a belief is not freely adopted, it is an actualization of capacities of a kind, the conceptual, whose paradigmatic mode of actualization is in the exercise of freedom that judging is. This freedom, exemplified in responsible acts of judging, is essentially a matter of being answerable to criticism in the light of rationally relevant considerations. So the realm of freedom, at least the realm of freedom of judging, can be identified with the space of reasons.[61]

And in another place, after asking 'why it seems appropriate to describe the understanding, whose contribution to this co-operation is in terms of its command of concepts, in terms of spontaneity' he responds as follows:

a schematic but suggestive answer is that the topography of the conceptual sphere is constituted by rational relations. The space of concepts is at least part of what Wilfrid Sellars calls the 'space of reasons'. When Kant describes the understanding as a faculty of spontaneity, that reflects his view of the relation between reason and freedom: rational necessitation is not just compatible with freedom but constitutive of it.[62]

Both these passages seem to confirm that there is no deep conflict between McDowell's view of spontaneity and mine, for this freedom of rational necessitation is fully available given the present account of the involuntariness of spontaneity.[63]

—But McDowell also writes that

conceptual capacities, which are actualised in our possession of beliefs or a world-view, . . . are appropriately described as belonging to a faculty of spontaneity. It is essential to them that they can be exercised in an activity of thinking responsibly undertaken by a subject who is in control of the course of the activity;[64]

Isn't his use of the notion of control in this passage plainly irreconcilable with your view?

Again I don't think so (McDowell may correct me). For, first, much of the catalytic business is precisely a form of control, and is responsibly undertaken by a responsible person. Second, and more interestingly, control in thought may well be spontaneous in the sense of being involuntary, unpremeditated, coming naturally. It can be—and ideally is—as involuntary as the spontaneous, effortless control with which we normally maintain balance and mastery of our limbs in walking or running. Control does not require explicit awareness of control. Ask any seagull on the wind. In our own case both sorts of control, mental and physical, are acquired in accordance with a

---

[61] 1998: 434.   [62] 1994: 5.

[63] There is also a link to McDowell's correct observation (McDowell 1979) that the sound moral judgement of moral virtue is a matter of being tuned to how things are in such a way that one 'just sees' what needs to be done (it is in that sense a sensitivity, a kind of tuned receptivity). It is an old idea that in the highest state of virtue right action is effortless and automatic. *Dilige et quod vis fac*, love and do what you will, in St Augustine's words.

[64] 1998b: 365, 367.

genetic predisposition to acquire them, both become second nature, all being well, and both can be worked on and refined way beyond their ordinary levels, whether in the circus or the seminar room. So once again I find no important conflict here, and no reason not to welcome the idea that the freedom—and control—constitutive of the spontaneity involved in cognition increases in proportion as the spontaneity—or control—'comes naturally . . . , [is] unpremeditated, . . . instinctive'.[65]

[65] *SOED* 1993: 2998. This paper develops material in Strawson 1986, 1994. I am very grateful to John Cottingham, Dylan Futter, Ward Jones, Eusebius McKaiser, Julia Simon, and Tamler Sommers for their comments.

10

Intentionality and Experience: Terminological Preliminaries

1 INTRODUCTION

The current discussion of intentionality in analytic philosophy presents as an important substantive debate. I think it is little more than a terminological squabble. I can't offer a full case for this here, but I want to make some terminological proposals—some unfashionable—that may help us to see more clearly what is going on.

The claim that the current disagreements are largely terminological is a substantive claim that would be rejected by nearly all participants in the debate. To underwrite it, I think, would be to see what it is to naturalize intentionality and to see that there is no particular philosophical difficulty in it. So it should be worth trying to make a start. If I seem to wander, I hope you will be patient.

Most of the key terms in analytic philosophy of mind have been put through the mangle and no longer have any clear agreed use. I will try to say what I mean by certain words by using other words that don't require me to say what I mean by them. Sometimes, though, it will be impossible for me to avoid using a mangled word in trying to say what I mean by another mangled word before I have had a chance to say what I mean by the first one. It will be like Otto Neurath's boat. Sometimes you have to stand on one part to rebuild another part before standing on the other part to rebuild the first, or even jump between them as you go along.

2 'NATURALISM', 'PHYSICALISM', 'EXPERIENCE'

Most present-day philosophers of mind favour *naturalism* and *physicalism*. They want a naturalistic account of mind and take it that it must be a materialist or physicalist account. In this paper I'm going to assume that they are right, and that 'naturalist(ic)' can always be replaced by 'physicalist' when the mind is in question, and vice versa. I will use one or the other term *au choix*.[1]

So naturalism is physicalism, and physicalism is a view about the actual universe, the view that every real, concrete phenomenon in the universe is . . . physical! What is it for something to be physical? An interesting question, if only because the only

[1] I take 'materialist' and 'physicalist' to be equivalent and use 'physicalist'.

thing we know for certain to be physical, given that physicalism is true, is conscious experience, for conscious experience is the only thing we know for certain to exist.

Many think that a naturalistic account of mind faces two central problems: conscious experience and intentionality. The alleged problem of conscious experience is that it exists. I will use the noun 'experience' (in its non-count-noun form) to refer to it, together with the adjective 'experiential', taking it that experience is by definition conscious.[2] More precisely, I will use 'experience' and 'experiential' to refer specifically and only to the *experiential qualitative character* of conscious mental phenomena, to the phenomenon of experiential 'what-it's-likeness'; and I will use 'EQ' as short for 'experiential qualitative'.[3]

Experience is not in fact a problem for naturalism, for one thing is certain. You're not a serious physicalist, you're not a real or realistic physicalist, if you deny the existence of the natural phenomenon whose existence is more certain than the existence of anything else: experience, experiential 'what-it's-likeness', feeling, sensation, explicit conscious thought as we have it at almost every waking moment. This is where we start from. There is nothing more certain in philosophy and life. Real physicalism can have nothing to do with *physicsalism*, the view that the nature or essence of all concrete reality can in principle be fully captured in the terms of (human) physics.[4] If you think that physicalism can be physicsalism you must suppose that the terms of physics can fully capture the nature or essence of experience. But this is obviously—provably—false.[5] The only alternative is to deny the existence of experience altogether. But this is the Great Silliness: the silliest claim ever made in the whole history of philosophy.[6]

A major terminological obstacle here is that there is a venerable tradition of using 'mental' (where the mental either is or includes the experiential) and 'physical' as mutually exclusive terms. This traditional opposition is fine if you are, say, Descartes, but it is not available to serious physicalists. Why not? Because they hold that everything concrete is physical and must acknowledge the existence of experience, the most certain concretely existing thing there is. It follows that they must hold that the mental/experiential is physical. They cannot therefore oppose the terms 'mental' and 'physical' and must instead use 'mental' and 'non-mental', or 'experiential and non-experiential'.[7]

I choose to use 'experience' instead of 'consciousness' because although 'consciousness' is perfectly adequate for philosophical purposes it has been very heavily

---

[2] The count-noun form of 'experience' remains available for talking of experiences [plural] as things that have non-experiential being as well as experiential being.

[3] I qualify 'qualitative' by 'experiential' because every intrinsic or non-relational property of a thing contributes to its qualitative character, and experiences also have non-experiential being—hence non-experiential qualitative character—according to standard physicalism.

[4] See e.g. Dennett 1991a: 40.   [5] See e.g. Strawson 1994 (henceforth *MR*): §3.6.

[6] See e.g. Essays 1 and 2.

[7] Hume is clear about this in his *Dialogues Concerning Natural Religion*, and Russell gives a dramatic statement of the serious physicalist's position: 'We know nothing about the intrinsic quality of physical events except when these are mental events that we directly experience'; 'as regards the world in general, both physical and mental, everything that we know of its intrinsic character is derived from the mental side' (1956: 153, 1927a: 402; Russell's use of 'intrinsic' is misleading and too strong as it stands—see Essay 1: 27–8).

mangled. It has been forced through the terminological looking glass by philosophers like Dennett who use it to mean precisely something that involves no consciousness.[8] I will mark this by saying that Dennett uses the word 'consciousness' to mean consciousness^{LG}, where the 'LG' stands for 'looking-glass'. Dennett looking-glasses the term 'consciousness', where to looking-glass a term is to use it in such a way that whatever one means by it, it excludes what the term means.

To looking-glass a term is not the same as using a term to mean both what it means and also something that it does not mean. I will call this *starring*: to use the term 'mental' so that it covers essentially non-mental phenomena as well as mental phenomena is really to use the term 'mental*'. The difference between looking-glassing and starring is the difference between using 'gold' to mean pizza ('gold^{LG}') and using it to mean gold and pizza ('gold*'). The cases that concern us in philosophy are less frivolous, although not always less bizarre. (There are many other possibilities such as using 'animal'—'animal*'—to mean animals and statues of animals; or just mammals; or mammals and statues of mammals; and so on.)

I'm not saying that attaching asterisks to terms is a bad thing in philosophy; it's often very helpful. I'm just using the verb 'star' in this paper to mark a bad thing. I'm not any sort of linguistic prescriptivist, and I'm not against terminological innovation. Words in human language soak similarities and metaphorical extensions into themselves with extraordinary ease, and although the facility with which we accept such extensions can cause havoc in philosophy it is one of our greatest cognitive gifts.

3 'INTENTIONALITY', 'ABOUTNESS'

The second supposed problem for naturalism, the problem of *intentionality*, is posed by the fact that natural entities like human beings and dogs can have something in mind, can be aware of something, mentally in touch with something, cognizant of something in thought or feeling or perception. We can think about things. We can target, hit, refer to, mean, intend an object, present or absent, concrete or not, in thought.

I will call this 'concrete intentionality', for it is intentionality considered as a concretely existing phenomenon, that is, as something correctly attributed to concrete (states of or occurrences in) entities like ourselves and dogs, rather than intentionality considered as a property of entities like propositions that are not concrete entities ('abstract intentionality'). Since I am only concerned with concrete intentionality in this paper, I will simply call it 'intentionality'.

Many present-day philosophers quickly start talking about experienceless entities like robots and pictures, computers and books, when they talk about intentionality, claiming that such things can be in intentional states or 'have' intentionality even if they are not mental beings.[9] This is extremely startling to those unfamiliar with the

---

[8] See e.g. Dennett 2001.
[9] I am going to assume that all robots and computers are experienceless for the purposes of discussion.

current debate, but the link is made as follows. First, we naturally say that such experienceless or non-mental entities are about or of things, or are in states that are about or of things. Second, it has come to seem natural to say that the problem of intentionality is nothing other than the problem of how natural phenomena can be about things or of things.[10] Intentionality is thus equated with aboutness-or-ofness, which I will call *aboutness* for short, and the conclusion that non-mental entities can have intentionality follows immediately.[11]

I think, though, that this terminological equation leads to many unnecessary difficulties. Everyone can agree that intentionality entails aboutness (I → A) but the converse (A → I) requires reflection. It seems to me that one can either accept (A → I) and be tight with aboutness, or reject it and be generous with aboutness. My choice in this paper is to reject (A → I) and be generous with aboutness, in line with everyday talk (elsewhere I consider accepting it and being tight with aboutness). What I think one cannot wisely do—it is a terminological matter—is accept that aboutness entails intentionality and be generous with aboutness, and hence also with intentionality. But this is today a very popular choice.

Here, then, we reach a terminological parting of the ways. Some think it obvious that only mental entities or states or events in mental entities can be intentional or have intentionality; others are prepared to ascribe intentionality—*intentionality*, no less—to things that no ordinary person wishes to call mental.[12] I take intentionality to be an essentially mental and indeed essentially experiential (conscious) phenomenon. This is terminologically unorthodox in present-day analytic philosophy, and I adopt it not so much because it's simply correct in the English that I speak but because I think it offers the best way to put things when trying to get a clear general view of the phenomenon of intentionality and, more broadly, the phenomenon of one thing's being about another.

I accept that it will be seen as a terminological *choice* in the current terminological pandemonium. Fine, so long as it is clearly understood that I'm not denying the reality of any of the phenomena that have led philosophers to say that non-experiential and even non-mental (ordinary understanding of the word—see §5) entities can be intentional entities or have intentionality. I'm quite sure I don't disagree with these philosophers on any relevant matter of fact.

4 NO DISPOSITIONS ARE INTENTIONAL

One obvious consequence of the decision to define intentionality as essentially experiential is that dispositional phenomena like belief dispositions are not properly counted as intentional phenomena. Since all experiential phenomena are occurrent

---

[10] 'About', unlike 'of', tends to imply an essentially discursive form of representation, but I won't make anything of this.

[11] Harman, 1998: 602, holds that grass needing water is an intentional phenomenon.

[12] My use of 'mental' here is meant to be that of ordinary thought, but it is also Neurathian because 'mental' has been looking-glassed and starred in all sorts of ways; see §5.

phenomena, only occurrent phenomena can be intentional phenomena, properly speaking.[13]

Some analytic philosophers may feel that it isn't worth reading any further. Terminological habits are as powerful as any in human life and there is no way of talking more deeply engrained in the analytic-philosophy community than the one that allows that dispositional states can be contentful intentional states.

This is a very striking fact, for it takes only a very little reflection to see that a *disposition* (e.g. the disposition to answer Yes if intending to speak truly when asked if grass is green) is just not the kind of thing that can possibly be contentful in the way that it needs to be if it is to be an intentional thing. This is plainly so even if it can be identified as the disposition it is only by reference to the content *grass is green*. To think that a disposition is, metaphysically, the kind of entity that can be contentful in itself, and so intentional, is a bit like thinking that an object's disposition to cause red-experience or square-experience in human beings (in certain circumstances) is itself something red or square; or like thinking that if an object has a fragile disposition then it already in some sense contains or involves actual breaking.[14]

Obviously many ways of talking that are unacceptable taken strictly are fine as *façons de parler*; the long-known danger is that *façons de parler* turn into metaphysical systems.[15] Much of the recent history of analytic philosophy of mind could be written as the story of what happened when intentionality was allowed to exist without experience (consciousness)—the story of how far philosophers were prepared to go in their uses of words like 'mental', 'mind', 'think', 'understand', and so on, in order to accommodate the chain reaction set off by this particular terminological decision. Another connected part of the story is about what happened when it became common to talk in a strongly reificatory way about mental states as if they were things in us, rather than things—states—we are in. The combination was lethal.

[13] I will take beliefs to be essentially dispositional phenomena although I think one can talk of conscious beliefs, meaning conscious assenting entertainings of believed propositions.

[14] An object may cause red-experience or square-experience in human beings because it is red or square, and it may be disposed to cause red-experience or square-experience in human beings because it is red or square, but a disposition—as ordinarily understood—is not the kind of thing that can itself be red (for the qualification 'as ordinarily understood' see Strawson 2006: 262 n). Even if one thinks that the *categorical ground* of the disposition is itself red or square, one can't coherently think this of the *disposition* to cause red-experience or square-experience; and no one, I think, will want to turn to the (non-experiential, neural) categorical ground of the belief disposition to provide a truly, intrinsically mentally contentful *grass-is-green* item.

There are of course important differences (e.g. causal differences) between belief dispositions and colour and fragility dispositions. Setting them out takes one straight to the heart of a great instability in the standard analytic-philosophical account of mental dispositions like beliefs: briefly, Dennettian anti-realism about belief dispositions as items with content turns out to be the only reasonable view, given the standard account. This is all to the good, on my view, for Dennettian anti-realism amounts to a rejection of the idea of mental dispositions as entities with content (I hope to discuss this further in *Intentionality!*).

[15] 'It is astonishing what havoc is wrought in [philosophy of mind] by admitting at the outset apparently innocent suppositions, that nevertheless contain a flaw. The bad consequences develop themselves later on, and are irremediable, being woven through the whole texture of the work' (James 1890: 1.224; I have substituted 'philosophy of mind' for 'psychology').

5 'MENTAL'/'NON-MENTAL'

I will return to states in §9. Here it must be said that it's not much use invoking the mental/non-mental distinction, because the word 'mental'—along with every other key word—has been chewed up beyond all recognition in the last fifty years.[16] It would be nice to be able to say that we have at least one firm grip on it, in the current definitional pandemonium, simply because experience is an intrinsically and essentially mental phenomenon whose essential nature (or, at the very least, part of whose essential nature) we apprehend just in having it.[17] And of course we do. But even this has been flatly denied—it has even been *held to be false as a matter of meaning*—in the theoretico-terminological bedlam induced by behaviourism and its various offspring. 'Mental' has been starred, if not looking-glassed, in every imaginable way.

Sometimes I think the only thing to do is to abandon the mental/non-mental distinction and fall back on the very clear and indisputably real experiential/non-experiential distinction; or else collapse the two distinctions together, and say with Descartes that experiential phenomena are the only truly mental phenomena, the only irreducibly mental phenomena; or rather, and more specifically, that experiential phenomena are the only truly *mentally contentful* phenomena.

I think this last suggestion is rather a good one, and I will take it further in §§8 and 10. For now, consider a thesis about 'mental' that seems hugely natural to many although we have got to the (terminological) point where others think it absurd. According to this thesis a mental episode, and a fortiori an intentional episode, can occur only in a being that is capable of experience. One could call this the *Only In An Experiential Being* thesis.

A question arises about what could justify it—it is a remarkable fact that it is open to the charge of complete arbitrariness in the current terminological environment—but I shall not try to answer it here.

It doesn't really need a justification, of course. It's just a fact about what the word 'mental' means. Some, though, think that the Only In An Experiential Being thesis is an obsolete intuition, frozen into the conventional meaning of the word 'mental', from which we must liberate ourselves.

Hmm. Sometimes our terms do change their meaning, and in a valuable way, but there's no profound paradigm shift occurring here, no new discovery or insight calling out for certification in a radically new way of talking. I've felt the pull of this use of 'mental', as have many, but reflection in a cool hour finds nothing more than a war of words that has deluded itself into thinking that it is a substantive debate.

Many think that developments in Artificial Intelligence oblige us to admit that the realm of the mental, and of mental beings, is larger than we used to think, but the

---

[16] Obviously this is normal and perhaps inevitable in philosophy, and probably it is not always a bad thing.

[17] This apprehension is a matter of direct acquaintance, it is 'non-thetic' in the phenomenologists' terms, i.e. it does not involve any explicit taking of one's experience as the object of one's thought, although we can also do this.

opposite view is at least as plausible: what developments in AI show is that the realm of the distinctively mental is actually smaller than we used to think, since so many of the abilities or properties that we used to take to be distinctively mental can now be seen to be possessed by things that are experienceless, and are not mental beings at all. On this view, developments in AI do not lead to the realization that mentality has nothing essentially to do with experience. Instead they confirm the Cartesian-naturalist view that the only thing that is distinctively and essentially mental—or at least (more narrowly) mentally *contentful*—is, precisely, experience.[18]

I need to put the case for this view—this terminological proposal. I will do so in §§8 and 10. First I need to say something about cognitive phenomenology, cognitive experience.

6 COGNITIVE EXPERIENCE

Recent philosophy has insisted on separating the notion of cognitive or conceptual mental content sharply from the notion of experience (there are, in the long wake of the British empiricists, real and fictional, some very good reasons for doing so). But this has had one very unfortunate consequence. It has become hard for many philosophers to hold onto the evident fact that there is such a thing as *cognitive experience* as well as sensation-mood-emotion-image-feeling experience, which I'll simply call *sensory experience* for short.[19] The existence of cognitive experience has been well argued for in recent years[20] and it is increasingly regaining acceptance, but it is still doubted by many and it is worth proving its existence because it is central to the problem of intentionality.

Proof 1. Life would be fabulously boring if this were not so. Life is not fabulously boring.

Proof 2. Many things which are not utterly mysterious would be utterly mysterious.

We would, for example, have no explanation of why you are gripped by a talk, say, other than that you are fascinated by the sounds the speaker makes considered as merely auditory phenomena. It is no reply to say that the talk is objectively fascinating and that the qualitative character of your experience has nothing to do with it, for your distinguished neighbour in the audience—who has three heads and makes Mr Spock seem as impassive as Maria Callas—understands the talk as well as you and does not know what you are talking about when you say you are fascinated.

The same goes for books, *mutatis mutandis*. It goes for anything whatever that goes beyond sensory experience, interoceptive or exteroceptive—cricket, antwatching,

---

[18] This is to express things in overtly substantive, metaphysical terms, but the standoff is really terminological. The two sides can agree on all the facts however much they fuss about the words. See *MR* ch. 11.

[19] I am not concerned in any way with the current debate about 'non-conceptual content', and I'm taking the notion of sensory or non-cognitive experience for granted.

[20] See e.g. Ayers 1991: 1.277–88; Siewert 1998; Loar 2003; Pitt 2004.

dominoes, and so on. Here, however, I am particularly interested in the cognitive experience involved in comprehendingly entertaining propositions in reading, listening, or thinking, and I am going to limit my attention to this.

These two proofs are indirect in as much as they draw attention to a reaction that presupposes the existence of cognitive experience. I will leave them without further comment, although many may not be convinced. It can take time to appreciate the point, given the current philosophical climate and the robust externalism of ordinary talk. (If you say 'It's the content that arouses my interest, not my cognitive experience!' I reply 'Of course it is'.)

Proof 3 is more direct. You are understanding this very sentence as you hear it. Clearly this understanding—it is going on right now—is part of the character of the current course of your experience. It is part of the experiential character, the EQ character, of your experience at this moment.[21] Your experience would have been very different if the words had been 'The objection to the Realist Regularity theory of causation is accordingly very simple. It is that the theory is utterly implausible in asserting categorically that there is no reason in the nature of things for the regularity of the world.' And the difference wouldn't have been merely visual—a matter of the difference in the shapes and order of the letters on the page, the overall Gestalt of the sentences' appearance, and so on.[22] It is the meaning of the sentences—and now of this very sentence—that is playing the dominant part in determining the overall EQ character of this particular stretch of the course of your experience, although you may also be aware of page, print, sunshine, birdsong, and so on, and although the meaning would be more effortlessly to the fore, experientially, if you were not currently engaged in this particular exercise of self-inspection.

A little less introspectively: consider (experience) the difference, for you, between my saying 'I'm reading *War and Peace*' and my saying 'barath abalori trafalon'. In both cases you experience sounds, but in the first case you experience something more: you have an understanding-experience, a cognitive experience.[23]

Why isn't this point universally acknowledged? *Have you had only sensory experience for the last two minutes?* One problem is that there has been a terminological lock-in. When analytic philosophers talk generally about what I call 'EQ content'—when they talk generally of the 'subjective character' of experience, or 'what-it's-likeness', or 'qualitative character', or 'phenomenology' in the current deviant use of the term[24]—they standardly have only *sensory* EQ content in mind, and

---

[21] Strictly speaking it is the experience of *or as of* understanding these particular sentences, not the understanding itself, that has cognitive EQ content, for *mis*understanding the sentences would equally involve cognitive experience, experience as of understanding (see Strawson 1994: 6–7; the same goes for 'comprehend' below).

[22] Visual and quasi-auditory if we include the rapid silent imaging of the sound of the words that most experience when reading; audio-somatosensori-visual if we include visceral reactions to words; and so on.

[23] This is a large part of the subject matter of 'cognitive phenomenology' (Strawson 1986: 30, 55, 70, 96, 107–9). I call it 'understanding-experience' and 'meaning-experience' in *MR*: 5–13.

[24] It is incorrect first because 'phenomenology' is the study of experience, not experience itself, second because when it used to mean experience itself it is used too narrowly to mean only sensory content.

the mistake has already been made. For this terminological habit simply forbids expression of the idea that there may be non-sensory or *cognitive* EQ content.

One doesn't have to be Husserl to be astounded by this terminological folly, and the metaphysical folly that it entrains (the denial of the existence of cognitive experience), as one negotiates the unceasing richness of everyday experience. It beggars belief. It amounts to an outright denial of the existence of almost all our actual experience, or rather of fundamental features of almost all (perhaps all) our experience. And yet it is terminological orthodoxy in present-day analytic philosophy of mind.

How did this happen? It was, perhaps, an unfortunate byblow of the correct but excessively violent rejection, in the twentieth century, of the 'image theory of thinking' or 'picture theory of thinking' seemingly favoured, in various degrees, by the British empiricists and others. But rejecting the picture theory of thinking didn't require denying the existence of cognitive experience. On the contrary. Liberation from the picture-theory idea that cognitive experience centrally and constitutively involves sensory experience, and is indeed (somehow or other) a kind of internal sensory experience, is a necessary first step towards a decent account of what cognitive experience is. Schopenhauer certainly didn't reject the existence of cognitive experience when he refuted the picture theory of thinking in 1819 in terms that no one has improved on:

> While another person is speaking, do we at once translate his speech into pictures of the imagination that instantaneously flash upon us and are arranged, linked, formed, and coloured according to the words that stream forth, and to their grammatical inflexions? What a tumult there would be in our heads while we listened to a speech or read a book! This is not what happens at all. The meaning of the speech is immediately grasped, accurately and clearly apprehended, without as a rule any conceptions of fancy being mixed up with it.[25]

When it comes to EQ content, then, when it comes to *the strictly qualitative character of experience*, which is wholly what it is considered entirely independently of its causes, there is *cognitive* EQ content as well as sensory or non-cognitive EQ content. There is cognitive experience. Its existence is obvious to unprejudiced reflection, but some philosophers have denied it fiercely and, it must be said, rather scornfully.

It can seem difficult to get a decent theoretical grip on it. It is, for one thing, hard to pin down the contribution to the character of your current experience that is being made now by the content of this very sentence in such a way as to be able to take it as the object of reflective thought. (It is far easier to do this in the case of the phenomenological character of an experience of yellow, let the 'transparentists' say what they will.) In fact, when it comes to the attempt to figure to oneself the phenomenological character of understanding a sentence like 'Consider your hearing and understanding of this very sentence and the next' it seems that all one can really do is rethink the sentence as a whole, comprehendingly; and the trouble with doing this is that it seems to leave one with no mental room to stand back in such a way as to be able to take the phenomenological character of one's understanding of the sentence, redelivered to one by this rethinking, as the principal object of one's attention: one's mind

[25] 1819: 39.

is taken up with the sense of the thought in such a way that it is very hard to think about the experience of having the thought.[26]

This is, as it were, a merely practical difficulty. It is I think a further point that there is in any case something fundamentally insubstantial, intangible, unpindown-able, about the character of much cognitive experience, and that this is so even though cognitive experience can also and simultaneously have a character of great determ-inacy. Consider, for example, your experience of understanding this very sentence, uneventful as it is. Or the sentence 'This sentence has five words.' Determinate but insubstantial.[27]

I use quiet sentences to make the point, rather than sentences like 'A thousand bonobos hurtled past on bright green bicycles', simply because it helps to still the ima-gistic or emotional accompaniments of thought or understanding as far as possible. It is then easier to see that what is left is something completely different, something that is equally real and definite and rich although it can seem troublesomely intan-gible when one tries to reflect on it: the experience that is standardly involved in the mere comprehending of words, read, thought, or heard—right now—, where this comprehending is (once again) considered quite independently of any ima-gistic or emotional accompaniments. Cognitive experience, we may say, is a mat-ter of whatever EQ content is involved in such episodes after one has subtracted any non-cognitive EQ content trappings or accompaniments that such episodes may have.

I think we have no choice but to grant that our capacity for cognitive experience is a distinct naturally evolved *experiential modality* that is, whatever its origins, funda-mentally different from all the sensory experiential modalities (at least as we currently understand them). This is a radical claim in the current context of discussion of exper-ience or consciousness, especially given all the input from psychology and neuropsy-chology, which very strongly constrains people to think that all experience *must* be somehow sensory.[28]

We also have to think through very clearly the initially difficult fact that cognitive EQ content is, in itself, purely a matter of experiential qualitative character, wholly what it is considered entirely independently of its causes. We may have to dwell on the point, work on it, especially if we have been trained up as analytic philosophers at any time in the last fifty years. Try now to imagine life without cognitive experience being part of the (experiential) qualitative character of experience. Consider yourself reading this now and try to convince yourself that all that is going on is sensory exper-ience (accompanied by non-experiential changes in your dispositional set).

One of the difficulties that philosophers have with the idea of cognitive EQ con-tent may derive from the fact that they fail to distinguish it sharply from cognitive

[26] Compare the 'transparency' or 'diaphanousness' of ordinary visual experience stressed, exag-gerated, and regularly theoretically abused by 'representationalists'.
[27] When I talked inaccurately of the 'diaphaneity' of cognitive experience in *MR* (see e.g. 182–3), I meant only this gauziness, insubstantiality, intangibility.
[28] Even the best philosophizing psychologists, like Antonio Damasio and Jeffrey Gray, seem to accept this view. I think they underestimate evolution (it may well be that cognitive experience is at least partly located in early sensory areas of the brain).

content as currently understood. So let it be said: *cognitive EQ content is not the same thing as cognitive content*. Cognitive content as we now understand it is not an EQ matter at all. The cognitive content of a thought-episode is (necessarily) *semantically evaluable*—assessable as true or false, accurate or inaccurate; the cognitive EQ content of the thought-episode is *in itself* no more semantically evaluable than sensory EQ content considered entirely independently of its causes. The cognitive EQ content of one's 'Twin-Earth' Twin's thoughts and experiences is by hypothesis identical to one's own in every respect although the cognitive content of one's Twin's thoughts and experiences is quite different. The same goes for one's 'Brain-in-a-Vat' Twin, and, for good measure, one's 'Instant' Twin who has just now popped flukishly into being. (Note that identity of cognitive EQ content across Twins must be conceded even by philosophers who claim that Instant-Twins don't really have thoughts—cognitive content—at all.)

Recognition of the existence of cognitive EQ content brings immediate relief to those who find it impossible to accept the popular idea that one fails to think a thought *at all* when one takes oneself to think that *a* is *F* in the case in which there is in fact no such thing as *a*. For in this case one can and must allow that there is a fully fledged thought-*experience*, with full cognitive *EQ* content, even if one wishes to say that there is no propositional content properly speaking, no 'Russellian' thought.[29]

Let me say it again: the cognitive EQ content of a thought is not the propositional content of the thought, which many nowadays simply call 'the content'.[30] It is that without which it cannot be true to say that the propositional content is being consciously entertained by someone (the comprehending entertaining of the content of a thought tends to be orders of magnitude faster than it is when it is no faster than the verbal spreading out of the thought in silent inner speech). We need to recognize it fully, now, in analytic philosophy of mind, because we have got into a sorry state without it.

—Philosophers' Twins are one thing—their experience is identical by hypothesis—but I'm still confused, and one crucial question, it seems to me, is this: Do two ordinary people thinking the same thought (entertaining the same cognitive content) necessarily have the same cognitive experience, the same cognitive EQ content? Suppose you and I both think 'The river is deep and wide'. Do we then have the same cognitive EQ content, according to you? Do we necessarily have the same cognitive EQ content?

This is a natural question and the answer is No, it would be hugely surprising if we had exactly the same cognitive EQ content, given that we're not Twins.

One way to put the point, perhaps, is to allow, strictly for purposes of discussion, that there is a sense in which we almost certainly don't have exactly the same river concept. This is like a key idea in 'conceptual role semantics', according to which

[29] Perhaps cognitive EQ content is what you get when you give Kaplan's notion of character an explicitly experiential reading. I'm not sure. What I do know is that full and unqualified acknowledgement of the existence of cognitive EQ content, cognitive experience, is compatible with robust externalism.

[30] This is why most of my uses of 'content' are Neurathian—at least until the next section.

we all have somewhat different river concepts because the concept RIVER[31] has different semantic or conceptual associations for us, sitting as it does in a different web of cognitive connections in each of us. One does not have to accept conceptual role semantics—I don't—in order to accept this as a helpful way of expressing how your and my *cognitive EQ content* can be different when we both think that the river is deep and wide. One can just as well be an outright Fodorian, a strong-as-you-like externalist about the (actual semantic) content of concepts.

The point can be put differently and perhaps better by saying that when we try to characterize the nature of cognitive EQ content we have to take account of what William James, talking of words, calls 'the halo, fringe or scheme in which we feel the words to lie'.[32] Or one might distinguish between the external and internal aspects of a concept considered as a mental particular—between $RIVER_I$ and $RIVER_E$ ($GOLD_I$ and $GOLD_E$), as it were. A huge and unnecessary debate in philosophy of mind has arisen from the fact that polarizing, adversarial philosophers have either stressed $RIVER_E$ at the expense of (or to the exclusion of) $RIVER_I$ or vice versa. And here the slippage between thinking of concepts as concrete mental particulars and thinking of them as abstract objects has much to answer for.

—But suppose you and I both focus furiously just on the cognitive content *The river is deep and wide,* or *All squares have four sides.* Won't we then have the same cognitive experience, perfectly focused as we are—won't we *necessarily* have exactly the same cognitive EQ content? And isn't that a very implausible thing to have to say?

Yes to your second question, No to your first—for the reasons already given. Necessary sameness of cognitive EQ content does not follow from perfect focusing, although the differences between us may indeed be small. The conceptual role semantics analogy is perhaps particularly helpful in as much as it introduces the possibility of difference right into the middle of the cognitive EQ content involved in thinking 'The river is deep and wide' by lodging it within the concepts deployed. On the face of it, the Jamesian fringe doesn't do this, but really the two analogies do the same thing, and it isn't hard to come up with others.

There is more to say about this issue, but this is enough for now. In conclusion, note that recognition of the existence of cognitive EQ content promises a complete and benign resolution of the conceptual role semantics debate, while at the same time explaining (socio-psychologically) the fact that it occurred. On the one hand, the existence of cognitive EQ content accounts naturally for the internalist (inscape) intuitions of those who favour conceptual role semantics. On the other hand, it allows all the externalist (outreach) Wittgensteinian and Fodorian intuitions to remain intact.

The debate between externalist and internalist construals of the notion of a concept has, in numerous forms, been one of the central topics of analytic philosophy at

[31] 'The concept RIVER' is shorthand, in so far as it is being questioned whether there is a single concept RIVER that we all possess. It stands for something like 'the concept that is, in any given one of us, the best candidate for being the concept RIVER on the assumption that there is only one river concept'.

[32] James 1980: I. 260. I am focusing for theoretical purposes on the conceptual aspect of the halo to the exclusion of the sensori-emotional aspect, although they are not disentanglable in everyday life.

least since the 'incommunicability of content' debate of the 1920s and 1930s against which Wittgenstein reacted, and there have been correct—hence wholly reconcilable—intuitions on both sides. The debate is an almost constant presence in philosophy, in fact (it's only one step back to Frege . . .). But all we need to resolve it is a well-developed recognition of the existence of cognitive EQ content and of the difference between it and cognitive content as currently understood. With this in hand we don't have to have a psychologism vs anti-psychologism shoot out every time we consider the relations between thought, language and reality. The intuitions of both sides can be fully preserved in the simple framework obtained by adding the notion of cognitive EQ content to the existing scheme of things.

By now it will be clear to many that the notion of cognitive EQ content is nothing new (it took me a while to see). It has been around in some form or other for as long as philosophers have grasped the tension between acknowledging thought to be the psychological phenomenon it is and taking full account of the fact that it allows us to think—and talk to each other—about reality. It is in Locke in all essentials; I am sure the scholastics had it clear; and so on into all the great past realms of philosophy.

7 'CONTENT', 'REPRESENTATIONAL CONTENT', 'MENTAL CONTENT'

I'm continuing to ignore those—behaviourists, neo-behaviourists, functionalists, neo-functionalists, 'strong representationalists', and so on—who don't really believe in EQ content at all. These people do not need to be met with argument. They do however pose a practical problem, for many of them *pretend* that they believe in EQ content (sensory EQ content, that is). They star or looking-glass the standard terms for it—'phenomenology', 'qualia', 'consciousness', 'what-it's-likeness'—raising a great dust and then complaining that no one else can see. Many present-day 'representationalists', for example, say that experiences—such as perceptions—do have EQ content. ('Of course they do!', they say, 'Of course we don't deny this!') But then they go on to say that the EQ content of a perception P is really just its 'representational content'. And then it turns out that what they mean by the 'representational content' of P is typically something *wholly non-experiential*—a stickshift, a mountain, a hagfish, a moon; together with the functional role of P, its systemic causal role in the experiencer's mental economy, or some such.[33]

There is no clear defence against this terminological trick, because one can't move in the philosophy of mind without using terms that these philosophers immediately co-opt and turn inside out. My only resource is pleonasm: sometimes I will call EQ content 'real EQ content', because when the 'strong' representationalists (for

---

[33] See e.g. Dennett 2001; Dretske 1995; Lycan 1996. If P is an apprehension of someone else's feelings, Niobe's sorrow or Ivo's elation, then it will on the representationalists' terms have EQ content as (part of) its representational content. But in this case although P's content will be at least partly EQ content it will be nothing to do with P's own EQ content! (And the EQ content will be EQ content[LG].)

example) say that a perception of some non-experiential phenomenon does of course have EQ content they don't mean what they say; they mean that it has EQ content[LG], i.e. something wholly non-experiential: they looking-glass 'EQ content', even as their milder companions star it.

One finds the same terminological inversion with the expression 'representational content'. This expression has traditionally referred to properties that an entity like a mental occurrence has *considered completely independently of whatever it actually represents*. In the ordinary sense of 'representational content' a veridical perception and a qualitatively identical hallucination have exactly the same representational content, as do a portrait of X and a painting of an imaginary person that is qualitatively identical to the portrait of X. Their shared representational content is a matter of their indistinguishability as representational *vehicles*, their sameness of intrinsic EQ content as potential representations.[34] According to current terminological orthodoxy, by contrast, the representational content of an experience has *nothing* to do with its EQ content, nothing to do with its nature considered as a vehicle of representation in the above sense. The representational content of my experience of the moon is just the moon itself, the non-experiential, non-representational, non-mental entity the moon.[35] It is not, then, representational content; it is representational content[LG].

Confusing; though not, now, for those soaked in the new terminology, who have passed through the looking glass and may feel queasy at the idea that 'representational content' could mean anything other than what they have been conditioned to understand it to mean.

The confusion grows when philosophers go on to say that *all* mental content is representational content—by which they mean representational content[LG]. For now the same terminological trick is turned: 'mental content', standardly shortened to 'content', is understood in such a way that the EQ content of a conscious mental episode M is no part of M's content—no part of M's mental content! All conscious mental episodes have EQ content by definition, but the present terminology has it that M's content is only what M is *of* or *about*, so that M has EQ content as part of its content only if M is of or about some EQ content or other that exists quite independently of M—Iphigenia's apprehension or Harry's feeling of peace. As for M's own EQ content, that can now be part of M's own content only in the vanishingly rare case in which M is about itself![36]

This looking-glassed—or at least heavily starred—use of the general phrase 'mental content' is now deeply entrenched. Many have grown so accustomed to it that they can no longer hear that there is anything wrong with it: it sounds to them obvious,

---

[34] Bear in mind that this intrinsic EQ content includes cognitive EQ content, e.g. the *taking what one is seeing to be an F* that is standardly built into seeing an F or hallucinating an F.

[35] Plus the experience's systemic functional role or some such: I will omit this qualification from now on.

[36] Is this possible? If M is about itself (*This very thought is puzzling*) then it is automatically about its own content in the representationalists' terms because it is itself its own content. But it is not at all clear that it can be about its own (real, non-looking-glassed) EQ content. It depends on the extent to which thought on the wing can be immediately self-aware (see Strawson 1999: §10 on the self-awareness of the thinking subject).

accurate, and unambiguous, just as 'gold' becomes an obvious, accurate, unambiguous word for pizza for those who use it for long enough to mean pizza. It is for all that hopelessly counterintuitive in what it excludes. For EQ content (real EQ content) is, evidently, mental content, given any remotely sensible use of the term 'mental content'.[37]

I can imagine terminological contexts in which I might allow that what is now often called 'mental content' (stickshifts, hagfish, etc.) can indeed be called mental content; but the people who like to talk in this way would at least have to allow in return that EQ content is *also* mental content (in this case the term 'mental content' would be starred, not looking-glassed). And they won't, or many of them won't. So let me for the sake of clarity match them in terminological intransigence. The question is this. Given that (real) EQ content is obviously mental content, should 'mental content' also be taken to cover propositional/cognitive content, 'content' in the straitened externalist sense just described? And now, intransigently, I say No. When 'content' is understood in this way, *the content of a mental state or occurrence is not mental content*. Obviously. The opposition really have looking-glassed 'mental content', rather than just starring it.

Does this sound strange? It shouldn't, for it is a straight consequence of standard externalism, and of all the overexcited statements of externalism that have led to this strange new way of talking.[38] For when the planet Mars, the very thing itself, is said to be (part of) the content of a mental state or occurrence M, in the externalist manner, it certainly does not follow, and is certainly not true, unless you are Berkeley (on one reading of him), that Mars, the thing itself, 150 million miles away from M, is itself a matter of mental content.[39] So too for everything else we can perceive or think about that is not itself a mental phenomenon in the traditional sense. To think that the externalistically understood content of a mental state or occurrence is itself mental content, i.e. something that is itself in some way mental in nature, is the very antithesis of externalism.[40] It's like thinking that the content of my bucket, these potatoes, is not just in the bucket, but partakes of buckethood in its intrinsic being by virtue of being in the bucket. Clearly one should not infer from 'A is the content of a B-ish container' to 'A is B-ish'.

Chorus of voices saying of course they never meant anything like this. Of course—but concede the unclarity of the usage (read Arnauld). So too for 'representation'.

---

[37] How did this happen? It got a boost when 'externalism', a doctrine which, correctly understood, is accepted by all sensible people, including of course Descartes, went mad and metaphysical. Pyle 2003: ch. 5, gives a nice account of Arnauld's defence of the externalist and direct realist Cartesian position against the terminologically slippery Malebranche.

[38] Overexcited: externalism is as old as thought and—as just remarked—fully Cartesian. Note that Descartes is also a representationalist on a sensible (EQ-content-acknowledging) understanding of the term, holding that all sensations (including e.g. pains) have representational content and are therefore intentional. Their defect, as representations, is that they are confused, not clear and distinct.

[39] See, though, n36.

[40] Of course they reject the 'i.e.', but to do that one has to Humpty-Dumpty around for a long time until it sounds OK. Arnauld set all this out beautifully in *On True and False Ideas* (1683: esp. pp. 54–73, paras. 76–7).

In the current idiom the content of a particular representation R of Mars—namely Mars itself—is its representational content (it is representational content^{LG}). What's more, many want to say that Mars is, in being the representational content of R, part of R itself. In the village I come from, however, a representation of something is wholly ontologically distinct from the thing it is a representation of (except in very rare cases). In the village I come from we always find that there is, on the one hand, the representation, a concrete particular thing, and, on the other hand, the thing represented, another particular concrete thing (putting aside 'abstract objects'). There is, certainly, a causal connection between representation and represented, in the case of a representation of a concrete entity; but this merely confirms the point, inasmuch as things that stand in causal relations are 'distinct existences'.

8   ALL MENTALLY CONTENTFUL PHENOMENA ARE EXPERIENTIAL PHENOMENA

Now for the sense in which all truly, genuinely, intrinsically, categorically[41] mentally contentful phenomena are experiential phenomena. I say 'the sense in which' because all I am going to do is to offer a way of putting things that certainly says something true when its terms are accepted even if many find its terms unacceptable.

In *The Mind Doesn't Work That Way* Jerry Fodor writes that:

our pretheoretical, 'folk' taxonomy of mental states conflates two quite different natural kinds: the intrinsically intentional ones, of which beliefs, desires, and the like are paradigms; and the intrinsically *conscious* ones, of which sensations, feelings, and the like are paradigms.

Fodor makes, here, a popular terminological choice about the word 'intentional'. Then, observing that some intentional states are conscious, he adds a footnote:

It is rather an embarrassment for cognitive science that any intentional mental states are conscious. 'Why aren't they all unconscious if so many of them are?' is a question that cognitive science seems to raise but not to answer. Since, however, I haven't got the slightest idea what the right answer is, I propose to ignore it.[42]

But if cognitive science raises Fodor's question then perhaps it also raises the complementary question: Why aren't they all conscious if so many of them are—all the tens of thousands of perceptions and conscious thoughts that fill every waking day? And perhaps the best answer to this question, all things considered, is that they are all conscious: that, strictly speaking, every genuinely intentional state is a conscious state.

This is my view—my terminological choice. It's hardly iconoclastic, for it is the view (terminology) of the vast majority of philosophers, from Aristotle to Avicenna to Brentano and Husserl and right up to the present-day community of philosophers

---

[41] Such words may be thought vague or vacuous or question-begging, but they have some useful force in contexts like the present one.

[42] Fodor 2000: 4–5, 106.

excluding its analytic division. I really do think it is the best way to put things, once one has become clear about the existence and utter centrality to our lives of cognitive experience. (Why is cognitive experience relevant? See Essay 11.) It is true to say of you now that you have thousands of beliefs about things of which you are at present in no way conscious, but it doesn't follow that you are now in any truly or genuinely or intrinsically (etc.) contentful mental states that are about these things. And—outside today's terminological prison—it's obvious that you aren't.

Why have we gone wrong? It is here, I think, that uncritical use of the expression 'mental state' has done most damage in the philosophy of mind, and this deserves a brief separate comment.

9 'MENTAL STATES'

Many philosophers talk in a strongly reificatory way about mental states as if they were things in us, rather than things—states—we are in, and this (mixed in with the whole long behaviourist folly) has led many to find it natural to conceive of belief dispositions, preference dispositions, and so on as mentally contentful somethings that are 'in us' and are rightly thought of as intrinsically mentally contentful entities ('belief states', 'desire states') quite independently of the content of our present experience.[43] The use of plain count-noun forms like 'belief' and 'desire' for dispositional mental phenomena already leads us into metaphysical temptation (for we are weak, and these nouns do not have explicitly dispositional 'ility' endings). It dangerously smooths the way to the sense that a belief (for example) is somehow a categorical item rather than (or as well as) a disposition. The common use of 'belief' as a near synonym of 'proposition' makes things worse. It adds to the aura of categoricality and substantivality, for propositions are undoubtedly intrinsically contentful and non-dispositional entities, albeit abstract ones.

A proposition, however, is not a disposition. And a disposition is not a proposition. We know this, but there is leakage.

The point can be put concisely by saying that *to have a belief is not to be in any contentful mental state*. This sounds bizarre, given current terminological orthodoxy, although it sounded self-evident a hundred years ago, but to say that a person has a certain belief is simply to say that he is disposed in a certain way. It is, certainly, wholly natural—correct—to call this disposition a *mental* disposition, because it is a disposition to be in certain sorts of mental states in certain circumstances. But to say that someone has a certain mental disposition, a belief disposition, for example, is not to say that she is actually in any contentful mental state. To be in a state of dreamless sleep is not to be in any contentful mental state at all, although one has, asleep, tens of thousands of beliefs, preferences, and so on. And one must not (to repeat) think of one's mental dispositions as quasi-substantival intrinsically contentful somethings

---

[43] This is very well analysed by Helen Steward 1997: ch. 4. Recall from your pre-philosophical life how extraordinarily unnatural it is to use the phrase 'mental state' of beliefs and their like at all, rather than of states of anxiety, overexcitement, and relaxation.

that are 'in' one. This is a case in which terminological choice kicks off metaphysical error.[44]

Some will think this obviously wrong. The phenomenon of linguistic conditioning is remarkable. It can make someone unable to see the duck-rabbit figure as anything other than a rabbit even in a context that makes it almost impossible to see it as anything other than a duck. I think it's not uncommon to have direct experience of this in a philosophical career, coming to see a possibility that one simply couldn't see—couldn't really see—before. It has happened to me.

Some will be as impatient as I used to be when others drew attention to the dangers of terminology. They will be confident that they can philosophize in their familiar idiom without being in any way misled; and it is true that a piece of terminology can work very well and introduce no distortion in many contexts even though there are other contexts in which it is disastrous. This is, in fact, a large part of the problem, because the contexts in which the use does no harm confer a false air of unrestricted legitimacy.

10   ALL MENTALLY CONTENTFUL PHENOMENA ARE EXPERIENTIAL PHENOMENA (CONT)

So much for mental states. Here now is Louis, a representative human being, lying for our theoretical convenience in dreamless sleep during a thirty-second period of time t.[45] Consider the portion of reality that consists of Louis, which I call the *Louis-reality*—the *L-reality* for short (it is a rough notion, for as a physical being Louis is enmeshed in wide-reaching physical interactions, but it is serviceable and useful none the less). We truly ascribe beliefs, preferences, and many other so-called 'propositional attitudes' to Louis as he lies there at t, and he undoubtedly has tens, hundreds of thousands of *dispositions* to behave in all sorts of ways, verbal and non-verbal, and to go into all sorts of states, mental and non-mental. Many, many disposition-ascribing *mental predicates* are true of Louis, true without qualification. Many propositional-content-citing predicates (e.g. 'believes that p', 'wants X to embrace Y', etc.) are true of him. Certainly. And yet there aren't really any truly mentally contentful entities in the L-reality during t, on the present view. Nor, therefore, are there any intentional phenomena.[46]

So what it is about Louis, lying there so dreamlessly at t, that makes it true to say that he believes that the sixth-century church of San Vitale is in Australia or that every even number greater than 2, except one, is the sum of two different prime

[44] Note that any supposed problems arising from the need to make a distinction between explicit and implicit beliefs vanish when the dispositional approach is taken seriously.

[45] Here I draw on *MR* §6.6.

[46] I'm assuming for the purposes of argument that there aren't any other subjects of experience other than Louis in the L-reality. My 'micropsychism' (the view that some if not all of the ultimate constituents of reality have experiential being) commits me to saying that there are in fact other subjects of experience in the L-reality, but it is not relevant here.

numbers? What is it in the current L-reality that makes this true?[47] The standard naturalist physicalist answer is: a certain arrangement of neurons, call it N. By hypothesis N is not—does not constitute—a conscious, experiential state of Louis, nor is it any part of such a state. It is simply the neural categorical ground of one of Louis's mental dispositions. Is it nonetheless a genuinely mentally contentful, intentional entity, considered in its total intrinsic being, which is wholly non-experiential being? Surely not—whatever has caused it to exist as it does (for a concession on this point see Essay 11: §6). Louis's brain has—by hypothesis—only non-experiential being at t, and we may therefore, in line with standard physicalism, take its nature at t to be wholly capturable, at least in principle, in the terms of neurophysiology and physics. Will these record any mental content, or intentionality at t, in their account of the being of N? Evidently not. They may tell us the bottom truth about why Louis is disposed to deny that San Vitale is in Italy, just as physics will tell us the bottom truth about why this calculator is disposed to display the numeral 49 when its keys are struck in a certain way, but they will not reveal anything intrinsically mentally contentful in Louis's brain at t, even while they reveal everything there is to Louis's brain at t. Certainly you won't get a difference between Louis and the calculator without the Only In An Experiential Being thesis, and that alone won't be enough.

Take up your superpsychocerebroscope and aim it at Louis's brain during t. It has one switch with two positions. Switching to A reveals all experiential goings on, switching to B reveals all non-experiential goings on. You switch to A: nothing. You switch to B: all the unbelievably complex goings on accounted for in a perfected (non-experiential) physics. Question: when the psychoscope is switched to B, does it reveal any truly mentally contentful goings on (or entities) whose contents are what make the thousands of dispositional mental predicates that are true of Louis true of him? No, say I.

Imagine, in the spirit of the 'extended mind' hypothesis,[48] a prosthesis that gives you immediate mental access to a database on a memory storage device stitched in under your ribs. Thanks to this prosthesis, if someone asks you what the atomic numbers of platinum and mercury are, it comes immediately to your mind that they are 78 and 80 respectively, although you didn't know this before. The vast quantity of information on the device isn't intrinsically mentally contentful before you plug in. Does all of it become so immediately you plug in? It's hard to see how one could say No, on the view according to which dispositional phenomena can be intrinsically mentally contentful entities.

I think this is a serious problem for the whole idea that dispositional phenomena are intrinsically mentally contentful phenomena even after one has put aside the (already decisive) point that dispositions just aren't the right kind of thing, metaphysically, to be intrinsically mentally contentful. Dreamless Louis was plugged in during t without him feeling a thing. Did a whole new realm of real, actually existing, concrete mental content come into existence at that moment? Surely not.

---

[47] In the case of San Vitale a causal connection is also necessary, but it is not part of what is in the L-reality.

[48] See Clark and Chalmers 1998; Clark 2001: ch. 8.

I don't say this because I doubt that the 'extended mind' hypothesis is any real help with seeing how things are in (mental) reality, although I do doubt this. What's relevant here is that the proponents of the extended mind thesis have anticipated this objection. They have seen that claiming that there is such a thing as *experienceless intentionality* will require one to agree that a whole new realm of concrete mental content leaps into being the moment we plug in the device, and they have accordingly—fatally—bitten the bullet.

In some ways my view is close to Searle's. When there is no experience, he says, 'what is going on in the brain is neurophysiological processes [here he means non-experiential goings on] . . . and nothing more'.[49] There are no truly mentally contentful phenomena to be found when there is no experience. Nor, therefore, are there any truly intentional phenomena.

At certain points, however, Searle says that although belief dispositions are non-experiential they are none the less intrinsically intentional.[50] I deny this outright, but in the end we may differ only in emphasis, for he goes on to say that 'the ontology of mental states, at the time they are unconscious, consists entirely in the existence of purely neurophysiological phenomena,'[51] and here again by 'purely neurophysiological phenomena' he means non-experiential phenomena, the point being that they are phenomena that cannot *really* be said to be intrinsically mentally contentful or genuinely intentional, considered in themselves, in their total physical being, any more than a CD of Shostakovich's Fifteenth String Quartet can be said to be intrinsically musically contentful, considered in itself, in its total current physical being.

One's mental dispositions are no less than they are; but neural phenomena in the absence of experiential phenomena aren't intrinsically mentally contentful intentional phenomena any more than pits in a CD are intrinsically musically contentful. A perfect physical duplicate of a CD could come into existence by chance, or as a result of the impacts of random radio signals on a CD burner. So too, *mutatis mutandis*, for the non-experiential neural phenomena that ground a mental disposition.[52]

So the claim remains: all true, actual, mental content is, necessarily, (occurrent) experiential content, and there just isn't any in the L-reality during *t*. The intensely natural picture according to which it is just obvious that there is no mental content in the L-reality at *t* (I have put micropsychism aside) has become invisible to many present-day analytic philosophers, but from the perspective of this paper the view that there is mental content in the L-reality during *t* given Louis's mental dispositions is a bit like the view that there are intrinsically breakage-involving states or goings on actually present in a fragile but undisturbed object.

---

[49] 1992: back cover.   [50] 1992: 158.

[51] 1992: 159. Note that the present proposal obviates Searle's need for what he calls the 'Connection Principle', which has trouble with Freud and raises puzzles about 'implicit' (never consciously entertained) beliefs.

[52] I discuss the CD analogy in *MR* ch. 6, imagining a normal human brain permanently and irreversibly deprived of its capacity for consciousness but otherwise running normally. This brain has long been harnessed to a light-show-producing machine and produces spectacular displays. Does it contain beliefs, preferences and so on? Certainly there are plenty of true counterfactuals about what would happen if you placed it back in a normal human body. . . .

—The view that there are intrinsically mentally contentful states inside the head of dreamless Louis isn't a philosophical concoction. Ordinary thought says the same, and philosophy should always treat ordinary thought with respect.

Yes. But, first, ordinary thought is not a good general guide to philosophical or scientific truth. Second, it won't help to appeal to it here. For even if it does endorse the view that there are intrinsically mentally contentful states in dreamless Louis, I am quite sure that it does not endorse the standard philosophical view that *dispositions* are intrinsically mentally contentful phenomena. This point is hidden by the current terminology of analytic philosophy, because it takes over ordinary words like 'belief' and uses them for things it classifies as strictly dispositional phenomena (even as the word 'belief' creates a vague sense that beliefs are somehow categorical items). But in doing this it completely loses touch with ordinary thought, which takes it (it seems to me) that there are intrinsically mentally contentful phenomena in dreamless Louis only in so far as it pictures them non-dispositionally as little packets of intrinsic content laid up in the head and available for activation by consciousness. Ordinary thought pictures them as non-dispositional, categorically mentally contentful intentional entities (a bit like sentences in a book where a book is naively and wrongly conceived as intrinsically intentional). And when ordinary thought does consider mental dispositions, it does not think of them as mentally contentful at all. We say, for example, that Cordelia has a gentle disposition. But here we do not think that there is an actual gentleness *content*, a *contentful state of gentleness*, sitting there all the time in virtue of which it is true to say that Cordelia is a gentle person (or intelligent, or proud). And it seems to me that in so far as we talk of beliefs as dispositions, we should not treat them differently.

—Look, sometimes we move straight to action on the basis of our beliefs and preferences without any conscious contentful experiential episodes at all. We do A because we believe B and like C. This can be a straightforwardly true explanation of our action, as true as 'squares have four sides'. How can you possibly say that the B and C dispositions are not themselves intrinsically mentally contentful states, given that they have this causal and explanatory role?

No problem. I have no more reason to say this than I have to say that this glass's being fragile right now involves intrinsically breakage-involving goings on right now (even given the important differences between fragility dispositions and belief dispositions—see note 14). In fact I not only think that the B-disposition and the C-disposition are definitely not intrinsically mentally contentful states. I also think that any *occurrent* but non-experiential episodes to which they give rise in leading to A, episodes that comfortable, familiar theory may seem to require us to think of as intrinsically mental-content-carrying, are not intrinsically mentally contentful, even though they, unlike dispositions, are not immediately ruled out for fundamental metaphysical reasons (see, though, Essay 11: §6).

Here, perhaps, I am genuinely in conflict with ordinary thought. Perhaps I should allow that these occurrent non-experiential episodes can have aboutness, at least, given their causes, even though they can't be said to be intentional (because intentionality requires experience). Certainly I don't mind saying that they 'carry information'.

In the long run, though, I think that if one allows true mental contentfulness to any non-experiential occurrences in the brain one will in the end have to allow that robots and pocket calculators can be in truly mentally contentful states in every sense in which we can. Nor will one be able to stop at pocket calculators. And that is a *reductio*.

You may retain some respect for the word 'mental' (many don't, and think it's deep not to) and try to exclude the robots and calculators by endorsing the Only In An Experiential Being thesis; but this thesis does nothing to help the metaphysically incoherent idea that *dispositions* are entities that can be intrinsically mentally contentful entities. The fact is that dispositional mental predicates can be wholly and straightforwardly true of Louis at *t* without there being any truly mentally contentful phenomena in the L-reality; just as 'fragile' can be true of an object without there being any actual breaking going on in that object.

Can we meet in the middle? You concede to me that dispositions cannot be truly mentally contentful, that only occurrent phenomena can. Then you return to the point that there are plenty of occurrent phenomena to be found connecting the B and C dispositions and the occurrence of A in such a way that A is appropriate given the nature of the B and C dispositions, and ask me to concede in return that non-experiential (sub-experiential) occurrent states as well as experiential states can be mentally contentful.[53] 'The null hypothesis', you say,

is that there isn't (that is, needn't be) any difference between a robot thinking 'it's raining' and me thinking 'it's raining'. I think that must be right because I don't think my thoughts are usually conscious (or, anyhow, consciously noticed); and, surely, my thought that it's raining is the thought that it's raining, whether or not I'm aware of having it.[54]

For myself I'm eirenic, but my terminology is adamant. It says that if occurrent non-experiential states can be truly mentally contentful, then truly mentally contentful states can be found in zombies, robots, calculators, and so on.[55] But they can't, so they aren't. Fodor contraposes: they are, so they can. But it's only terminology, as Cole Porter said. We don't disagree on the facts. We're sticking over a word. I'm happy to allow that any content or 'content' or 'aboutness' that can be ascribed to goings on in experienceless entities can be equally well ascribed to certain of our non-experiential neural states goings on, and vice versa. In fact I think one has to allow this to get a remotely plausible picture of how the world works. But there is nothing truly mentally contentful going on in this case (so too there is nothing truly musically contentful going on in a CD, and nothing truly breaking or broken in the panes of glass in the window in front of me), and there is no intentionality.

[53] That, you say, is how the problem you had when you set out for Scotland was solved when you got there even though you hadn't given it any thought.

[54] Fodor, private correspondence, 2002.

[55] In Essay 11 I argue that one can't stop there—one has to let in footballs, electrons, everything. The aim of the argument is a *reductio ad absurdum* of the view that there can be non-experiential intentionality.

The alternative is to say that calculators and so on have intentionality in every sense in which we do. But I say to you again, no intentionality without mind, and no mind without, in a word, *mind*.

—What about a Freudian unconscious belief? However much you obfuscate in other cases, in this case it's absolutely clear that you are in a state that is about Great Aunt Lulu. This is fact, objective fact about the concrete world. It is a fact about you as a physical system considered now in your intrinsic physical nature. That means it's a fact about you now considered wholly independently of everything else including your past and shaping causes. There is Lulu-intentional content lodged in you, period.

So far as dispositions are concerned, the case of Freud-unconscious beliefs is no different from that of any other beliefs: dispositions aren't and can't be mentally contentful entities. Nor can the categorical neural grounds of mental dispositions, fully describable by physics and neurophysiology, be mentally contentful entities. But the Freudian unconscious pulls hard on people's intuitions. Surely, we think, there is a little packet of intrinsic Lulu content somewhere in the folds of my brain right now? If Wilder Penfield poked his neurosurgical probe in the right place, I would light up with a dread memory of Lulu in her satin combinations. So surely Lulu stamped Lulu-content into me in such a way that it is in me, now, intrinsically, considered simply as the physical system I now am, and so considered wholly independently of my undeniably Luluish past?

I think nearly all philosophers reject the idea of little packets of intrinsic content thus conceived. And yet the idea that there is absolutely nothing intrinsically mentally contentful and in particular Lulu-contentful inside Louis, when one of these Freud-unconscious states is actively moving him, may seem hard to defend; even though whatever is going on in him is by hypothesis non-experiential.

This is the issue just raised: can occurrent non-experiential goings on, at least, be said to be mentally contentful? How do I respond? First, I repeat that there is nothing special about the case of Freud-unconscious occurrent goings on, for the sub-experiential processes that go in in me when I find myself ready with a reply to your last remark cannot be less worthy, as candidates for mental contentfulness. Anything else? Not really. I grant that the intrinsic-content intuition is intensely natural for us given our actual unquestioned causal-environmental embeddedness, but my position remains the same. The sense in which there is something intrinsically mentally contentful here is exactly the same as the sense in which occurrent, processual radio waves travelling out into space from the studios of BBC Radio Three are, considered in their intrinsic physical nature as it is now and so wholly independently of everything else including its past and shaping causes, intrinsically Shostakovich's-Fifteenth-Quartet-contentful. There is no more intrinsically resident musical content in the occurrent radio-wave process than there is in the CD.[56]

[56] It's worth noting that the idea that the radio waves are intrinsically processual in some way in which the CD is not is metaphysically superficial.

Some may find my terminological preferences counterintuitive to the point of offence or error, but I am sure, as already remarked, that I do not disagree with them on any matter of fact.[57]

There is much more to say, but the general terminologico-substantive position is clear.[58] Intentionality is essentially categorical, never dispositional. More than that, it is essentially 'live', occurrent, mental, and indeed experiential. This, I propose, is the best way to talk. Fodor once disagreed when he said that a 'good theory of content might license the literal ascription of (underived) intentionality to thermometers',[59] and the proposal is obviously revisionary relative to current terminological fashion. But the claim remains: everything true that can be said in the current standard terms can be said equally clearly, and I think better, in these terms. The claim that mental dispositions are themselves intentional phenomena is not only metaphysically incoherent; it also puts one on a slippery slope that slides all the way down to intentional thermometers and beyond. The same slippery slope awaits the (admittedly far less bizarre) claim that occurrent non-experiential mental phenomena can be truly intentional phenomena. These points are something about which Fodor, for one, has always been very clear. But it's just a way of talking, and I want to try another way. I would be astonished if Fodor and I disagree about any relevant matter of fact.

You have to choose your implausibility. If you allow that states of a person in dreamless sleep can be genuinely intentional phenomena, your problem is to stop the slide down to intentional thermometers and beyond without invoking the seemingly arbitrary Only In An Experiential Being thesis.[60] That's Fodor's problem, but of course he doesn't think it's really a problem. If on the other hand you deny that occurrences in and states of a person in dreamless sleep can be genuinely intentional phenomena, your problem is to stop the intentional realm shrinking into the experiential realm. That's my problem, but then I don't think it's really a problem.

Many who dismiss the Only In An Experiential Being thesis may want to deny that puddles and mirrors (and perhaps thermometers) have intentionality while insisting that robots, cruise missiles, and so on do. They are drawn to what one might call the *Only In A Behaviourally Purposive Being* thesis, which is, I take it, extensionally equivalent to Dennett's notion of the 'intentional stance' according to which intentional phenomena are to be found only (and also *ipso facto*) in a being to which we naturally or usefully attribute beliefs and goals when we attempt to explain or predict its behaviour.[61]

It seems to me, though, that the Only In A Behaviourally Purposive Being thesis is no less arbitrary than the Only In An Experiential Being thesis. It is, furthermore,

---

[57] See further *MR* 160–2, 168–72. Obviously many intuitions are highly context-sensitive. I can pull my own in different direction by altering the surround.

[58] Understandably enough, participants in the 2002 NEH Summer Institute on 'Consciousness and Intentionality' did not take to the term 'terminologico-substantive'.

[59] 1990: 130.

[60] Note that it imposes a looser requirement than Searle's 'Connection principle' (Searle 1992).

[61] See Dennett 1971, 1981, 1991b. I say 'extensionally equivalent' because I think that some who endorse the Only In A Behaviourally Purposive Being thesis reject Dennett's profoundly anti-realist attitude to intentionality, consciously or not.

quite unclear what should count as behavioural purposiveness. Most of those who are drawn to the Only In A Behaviourally Purposive Being thesis would not attribute intentionality to a plant that responds variously to environmental conditions (say), or to a developing embryo operating according to a fixed program, or to a host of other such things. But it is entirely unclear what, other than a certain zoomorphic prejudice, can justify including robots that operate according to a fixed program while excluding plants and so on.[62]

The arbitrariness of the Only In A Behaviourally Purposive Being thesis is not a problem for Dennett, of course. It is something that he is quite clear about, given his wholly behaviourist, anti-realist, functionalist, instrumentalist, interpretationist approach to questions of mind. It is, indeed, something he rather welcomes. There isn't, for him, any genuine metaphysical issue about the nature of intentionality. Like many, I utterly disagree, and am dismayed that the real metaphysical issue has been lost. This paper is an attempt to recover it, but it is only the beginning.[63]

---

[62] The Only In A Behaviourally Purposive Being thesis has interesting variants, e.g. the Only In A Behaviourally Purposive Being Capable of Misrepresentation thesis, and the Only In A Behaviourally Purposive Being Capable of Learning thesis. Some think they can stop the slide down to intentional thermometers in such highly specific ways (see e.g. Dretske 1988, 1995). I'm sceptical, though, as is Fodor. For other functionalist strategies to stop the slide see e.g. Tye 1995; Lycan 1996. I reject these briefly in Essay 11: §3, and also in *Intentionality!*

[63] This paper began as an unfinished presentation to the 2002 NEH Summer Institute on 'Consciousness and Intentionality' held at Santa Cruz in 2002. I would like to thank the participants —especially David Chalmers and John Hawthorne—for their sceptical comments.

1 1

Real Intentionality 3: Why Intentionality Entails Consciousness

1 'INTENTIONALITY', 'EXPERIENCE', 'PHYSICALISM', 'NATURALISM'

My subject is intentionality, the phenomenon of a thing's being about something or having something as its topic, or subject, or object. More particularly, my subject is concrete intentionality, that is, intentionality considered as a real, concrete phenomenon, something that can be correctly attributed to concrete entities like ourselves and dogs—to concrete states we are in or concrete occurrences in us. I'm not at all concerned with intentionality considered as a property of entities like propositions.[1]

Since I'm only concerned with concrete intentionality I'll simply call it 'intentionality'. My question is: What is intentionality? What is it for intentionality to exist? I take this to be a straightforwardly metaphysical question.

I'm going to assume that intentionality exists, and that conscious states or events can and standardly do have intentionality. I'm going to focus on intentionality with respect to concrete objects like trees rather than abstract objects like the number 2, and argue for the old but now widely rejected view that the best thing to say about intentionality is that only conscious states or events can have it. On this view, all real or true intentionality essentially involves consciousness, conscious experience.

My preferred term for talking about consciousness is 'experience', because the words 'conscious' and 'consciousness' have been looking-glassed in recent philosophical discussion.[2] I use 'experience' (taken as a mass term) and the adjective 'experiential' to refer specifically and only to the *experiential qualitative* character of conscious mental goings on, to the phenomenon of experiential 'what-it's-likeness' whose general nature is clearly and accurately understood by everyone except an extremely small number of philosophers.[3]

---

[1] Propositions are 'abstract' entities, and in this paper 'concrete' means 'not abstract': for the purposes of this paper one can take it to be equivalent to 'spatiotemporally located' (a body of gas is as concrete as a lump of reinforced concrete).

[2] To looking-glass a term is to use the term in such a way that whatever one means by it, it excludes what the term means; see Essay 10: 257.

[3] I qualify 'qualitative' by 'experiential' because the word 'qualitative' has nothing especially to do with experience; a stone has many qualities.

The claim, then, is that only experience-involving phenomena can have intentionality. It follows that no dispositional states can be intentional phenomena. This is likely to be thought counterintuitive, because dispositional states are almost universally treated as if they are paradigm cases of intentionality in current philosophical discussion. It is, however, an elementary point in metaphysics that dispositional states can't themselves be intentional entities. They can't be intentionally contentful any more than they can be coloured, even if they are individuated as the dispositions they are by reference to intentional contents—a point to which I will return to at the end of the paper.[4]

I'm also going to assume that 'physicalism' and 'naturalism' are true, so far as concrete reality is concerned, and that they amount to the same thing. I don't, however, mean what many people today mean by these two terms, because my naturalism starts from real realism—outright realism, ordinary-person, Clapham-omnibus realism—about experience (or consciousness). This is because *experience is itself the fundamental given natural fact*. Its existence is evident and provably non-illusory. It is provably non-illusory because its seeming to exist (which very few deny) is a sufficient condition of its actually existing.[5]

Experience is in fact the only concrete natural phenomenon that we know for certain to exist (unless it can be shown—which I doubt—that a subject of experience ontologically distinct from experience must exist if experience exists). It follows that to be a physicalist or naturalist, a real physicalist or naturalist, a realistic, thoroughgoing physicalist or naturalist, is necessarily to believe that experience exists. It is therefore to believe that experience is wholly physical.

There is nothing so misleading as to use the word 'naturalism' to mean, not physicalism, which I am taking to be the view that everything concrete, including experience, is physical, but *physicsalism*, the view that the fundamental nature of everything concrete can be accounted for in the terms of physics. The word 'physical' is a natural-kind term and refers to the physical as such, whatever its fundamental nature. It does not just refer to the physical as described by physics, and one thing that is certain if physicalism is true is that there is more to the physical than what is (or can be) described or accounted for by physics—by present-day physics or any non-revolutionary extension of it that we can imagine.

2   'INTENTIONALITY', 'ABOUTNESS'

Many people equate intentionality with aboutness, but I am now going to distinguish them for the purposes of this discussion.[6] This is a terminological decision that will seem unnatural to some, given the recent use of 'intentionality' in analytic philosophy, but it will I hope be helpful.

---

[4] p. 297 below. For further discussion see Essay 10: 258–9, 271–5.

[5] This is an old point. See e.g. Essay 2, n7.

[6] I will use 'aboutness' widely to cover all cases in which it is more natural to use 'of' than 'about' ('picture of', 'representation of').

I allow of course that having intentionality (I) entails having aboutness (A)

$$[I \rightarrow A]$$

for if something has intentionality it is necessarily about something, but I deny that having aboutness entails having intentionality

$$\neg[A \rightarrow I].$$

Books and photographs, for example, are certainly *about* things, on my terms, but they certainly do not involve *intentionality*, on my terms. There is a lot more aboutness in the world, on these terms, than there is intentionality, for although all intentionality involves aboutness, not all aboutness involves intentionality.

How does this distinction interact with the familiar distinction between 'underived' (or 'original' or 'intrinsic') intentionality, on the one hand, and derived intentionality, on the other? Well, the paradigm cases of underived intentionality are conscious or experiential states, while the paradigm cases of derived intentionality are non-experiential things like inscriptions, books, road signs (so far as entities that are not capable of behaviour are concerned), and computers, programmed robots and so on (so far as entities that are deemed capable of behaviour are concerned). Dennett and others reject the distinction, because it marks no real line on their view, when applied to the things that concern them, i.e. entities that are capable of behaviour,[7] and I also reject it, because I hold that the best thing to say about intentionality is that all genuine intentionality is experience-involving and cannot be possessed in any 'derived' form by things like books. I can nevertheless allow that there is a genuine distinction between derived and underived *aboutness*, even while I deny any genuine distinction between derived and underived *intentionality* (on the ground that there is no derived intentionality). Experiential states can have underived aboutness and books can have derived aboutness.

Aboutness, then, is necessary but not sufficient for intentionality. The question, on these terms, is: What does aboutness have to be like to be or involve intentionality?

I am going to assume that derived aboutness can never be sufficient for intentionality, and put it aside completely for the purposes of this paper: if aboutness is to qualify as intentionality it must at least be underived aboutness. Justification for this assumption will emerge in what follows.

This next question is whether underived aboutness is not only necessary but also sufficient for genuine intentionality, and this raises the question: What sorts of underived aboutness are there?

We know that there is *experiential* underived aboutness, for the paradigm of genuine intentionality is experiential underived intentionality, which entails experiential underived aboutness. The key question, then, is whether there is also *non-experiential*

---

[7] They hold that all attributions of intentionality are simply a pragmatic matter of taking up a certain interpretative stance to something when trying to explain and predict its behaviour.

underived aboutness, underived non-experiential aboutness, *UNA* for short. Or, to put it slightly differently

Can there be *underived aboutness in a non-experiential entity— UNA^{NE}* for short?[8]

If the answer is Yes, and if underived aboutness is not only necessary but also sufficient for intentionality, then experience is not necessary for intentionality after all.

Many take it that the answer to the key question is plainly Yes: UNA can and does exist. A puddle, for example, may reflect San Vitale, and in that sense genuinely contain or constitute a representation of San Vitale, and representation entails aboutness, which is in this case wholly underived (there is no other aboutness around for it to be derived from). In the same way a mirror may reflect an image of you, so that it is natural to say that there is a representation of you right in front of you independently of any views you may have on the matter. Some theorists are happy to say that certain of the states of phototropic beetles represent light, or at least represent certain opportunities for behaviour,[9] even if the beetles are experienceless, and perhaps we can also say that the fingerprint on this guitar has aboutness. Certainly it carries information that uniquely identifies you. Many are inclined to say the same about tree rings that carry information about climate and the tree's age, and it is arguable that everything is about everything else, for according to Mach's Principle 'the slopping of your drink in [a] lurching aeroplane is attributable to the influence of all the matter in the universe'.[10]

This may be going too far (we shall see), but some of these UNA claims seem both uncontroversial and very natural, and their naturalness, combined with the standard identification of intentionality with aboutness, can seem to sweep us smoothly into a perspective from which the phenomenon of intentionality-involving aboutness, which I am taking to be essentially mental, and indeed essentially experiential, appears fundamentally similar to, deeply continuous with, forms of aboutness that are non-experiential and underived and occur in wholly non-experiential entities,[11] in such a way that both are correctly classified as cases of genuine intentionality.

I agree that there are important similarities and continuities between ourselves and experienceless phototropic beetles, TV cameras, heat-seeking missiles, thermometers, and so on. More generally, I'm quite certain that I don't disagree on any actual matter of fact with those who like to say that states of robots, microbes, grass, thermometers, and so on can have intentionality. I don't, however, think that saying this is a good way to characterize the similarities between ourselves and these things. I think, in fact, that the best thing to say may be that there is no UNA^{NE} at all: that, once we put the case of derived aboutness aside, as here, *no states of non-experiential entities are ever really about anything at all.*

---

[8] The suffix leaves open the possibility of saying that there can be UNA in an experiential being (see e.g. n57 below) but I will standardly omit the suffix, taking it as read.

[9] 'The frog doesn't represent either flies or pebbles, but, instead, represents the opportunity for tongue flicking and eating' (Bickhard 2003: 143). In this way Bickhard offers a solution to the 'disjunction problem'.

[10] Davies 2001.

[11] There is no reason to deny that UNA can also occur in experiential entities like ourselves.

—How can this possibly be right? Consider a crack in the curtains that functions fortuitously to create a *camera obscura*, casting a perfect upside-down image (representation) of the view from a window onto the opposite wall. Surely this is a case of UNA^{NE}? Consider a camera functioning on its own, taking photographs and films that are indisputably about or of things. You don't need to have someone who intends to take a photograph of X, or indeed of anything, to get a photograph of X. It's true that cameras are designed to do what they do, and this can seem to be a reason for saying that films and photographs have derived aboutness, but a thing physically identical to a functioning camera could conceivably come into existence by cosmic accident and produce admirable films and photographs of things. These would be about things and they would no more have derived aboutness than all the naturally occurring *camerae obscurae* in the world.

Consider also R1, an experienceless robot that travels round a room littered with multicoloured geometrical shapes picking up all and only the purple pyramids and dropping them in a box, thereby replenishing its energy supply. R1, also known as Luke, is built and programmed by us to perform the pyramid task straight out of the box, and may accordingly be said to have derived aboutness. But there is also R2, hardware-identical to R1 but 'programmed' entirely by a freak burst of radiation that makes it software-identical and hence behaviourally identical to R1. And then there is R3, hardware-identical to R1 and programmed by us, not in such a way that it can perform the pyramid task straight off, but rather in such a way that it learns to perform the pyramid task. Then, importantly, there is R4, also known as Fluke, physically (hardware and software) identical to R1 although it came into existence by cosmic fluke. Finally, there is R5, another product of cosmic accident that is physically (hardware and software) identical to R3. I assume you'll allow derived aboutness to R1 and perhaps R3, but how, as they continue to function perfectly over the years, are you going to deny underived aboutness, UNA, to the rest of them? Surely they are all indisputably in states that *represent* purple pyramids and all sorts of other things and are *about* these things?

I know it can seem natural to say this. But if you insist on talking in this way, as is of course your terminological right, then I think you will find there is just too much UNA, more than you can handle.

3   THE UBIQUITY OF UNA

As far as I can see, this follows almost immediately from some very general considerations about causation and information.[12] I take it, to begin, that

[1] there are objectively legitimate ways of cutting the world, the worldflow, into causes and effects[13]

and that this can be done in such a way that

[2] the things picked out as effects are reliable signs of the things picked out as their causes

[12] Compare Searle 1992: 81.
[13] Here I put aside my Nagarjunan metaphysical preferences. There are everyday ways of cutting the worldflow into causes and effects, scientifically useful ways of doing so, ways that are useful for pursuing certain sorts of conceptual or philosophical enquiries, and so on.

and that in this sense

[3] every effect may be said to 'carry information' about its cause.[14]

It may be, in fact, that there is a way of cutting the world into causes and effects in such a way that

[4] every effect carries uniquely identifying information about its cause.[15]

But whether or not this is so—it doesn't matter if it isn't—it seems plausible, to expand [3], that

[5] every effect can be said to carry information about its cause, and in that sense to be about its cause, and in that sense to represent its cause,

and therefore that

[6] UNA is utterly ubiquitous.

The first objection is likely to be that if one is going to talk in this way then one has to acknowledge that there is aboutness and aboutness, and that not all aboutness is aboutness of the kind we care about when we are interested in content, intentionality, and so on, and that this is so even when we are concerned only with UNA. On this view, the alleged UNA of the flight of a kicked ball that, on the present view, carries information about its cause and can in that sense be said to be about—to carry or constitute a representation of—its cause is of a completely different order from the UNA of a reflection of the moon in a puddle, or an image of the moon produced by a (fluke) camera. The puddle and camera cases are somehow special, and involve real representation, while the football case doesn't.

This seems at first an intuitive distinction; the question is whether it can be defended in such a way as to stop the supposedly more special cases of UNA from being swallowed up in the ubiquitous UNA of the whole heaving universe. I don't think it can. If we find the UNA of the puddle or the fluke camera image special it is because we are overcome, as so often, by the vividness of light-involving cases which we assimilate to our experience of vision. In order to find a candidate for moon-aboutness in the puddle we have to imagine an observer, and an observer in a particular position (there are infinitely many ways of looking at the puddle that do not render an image of the moon). This is because all that we have, in fact, in the case of the puddle, is a body of water and the incidence upon and reflection by its surface of certain wavelengths of

---

[14] If determinism is true, as it may well be, we can replace 'every effect' by 'every event'.

[15] The idea is that the microdetail of the effect or effect-type will be such that only one kind of event could have caused just that. Suppose, briefly, that we start with the point that the things we pick out as causes in everyday thought are generally neither necessary nor sufficient for their effects, but are rather Mackiean 'inus' conditions of their effects: insufficient but non-redundant parts of unnecessary but sufficient conditions (Mackie 1974: ch. 2). If we then describe the thing picked out as the effect in greater and greater detail, producing an increasingly exclusive type-description, the number of types of things that could be its cause dwindles away, arguably down to one, and vice versa; while information about spatiotemporal location brings us down to the actual cause and effect (causal overdetermination phenomena raise no relevant problem here).

light, and when we consider it this way, taking, as it were, the 'view from nowhere',[16] it seems that we face a choice. Either there is no good reason to say that there is anything here that is about anything or intrinsically a representation of anything, or, if we allow that there is good reason to say this, then there is certainly no more reason to say it when considering the incidence and reflection of light waves than when considering the incidence and reflection of sound waves, or indeed the causal impacts of anything on the puddle. In fact, as far as I can see, there is in the case of any entity X and any possible physical effect of X on the puddle a possible observer who, on detecting this effect, naturally experiences it as being or giving rise to a representation of something, and indeed as a representation of X or an X-type thing. What distinguishes us is simply that we feel particularly happy and familiar with visual cases or cases analogous to visual cases.

The case of the photograph may seem more compelling than that of the puddle, but here again we are overimpressed by a light-involving case assimilable to vision, and here too we have to introduce a possible sighted observer to give body to the idea that we have some special sort of aboutness and not just a certain sort of effect, one among trillions, that is no more (and if you like no less) intrinsically *about* anything or a representation *of* something than the flight of the ball or the sonic effects of the traffic on the puddle or the precise nature and pattern of the digestive processes now occurring in someone's alimentary canal. The universe is alive with information transfer; some say that it consists of (concrete) information and information transfer. And if information transfer entails representation, then representation is everywhere, and so is aboutness, and there is no way of holding on to cases like the photo while ruling out almost everything else. Conclusion: if UNA exists at all, then, it is ubiquitous. If any photo has it, so does any photon.

Some philosophers (e.g. defenders of 'teleological' theories of content) may now say that there is something very special about the representational states of biological entities (at present we are considering only experienceless ones) because their capacities to enter into such states were 'designed' by evolution for specific tasks. But there is no deep difference here, in the great story of the universe. Nor will any such biological criterion distinguish light-detecting states of experienceless phototropic beetles from states of developing foetuses that appear to engage in fiendishly cunning behaviour in the womb (pursuing, roughly, the be-as-selfish-as-possible-short-of-killing-your-host strategy). Defenders of teleological theories of content will also have to accept that experienceless beings can have aboutness if naturally evolved while their cosmic-accident perfect duplicates can't—ever. They will have to accept that naturally evolved experiencing beings like Freddy the frog, Fido and myself can have aboutness and intentionality, while our cosmic-accident Twins can't—ever. And this seems very unfair (fabulously counterintuitive).[17] Other philosophers try to narrow things down in another way: by according special status to representational states in individuals that depend on some kind of ontogenetic learning process (I'm allowing

[16] In Nagel's phrase (1986).
[17] Papineau 1987: 72–5 faces the issue squarely and is prepared to bite the BB.

that experienceless entities can learn), and not on something entirely hard-wired.[18] But the case is at bottom the same.

Others again seek to restrict the class of experienceless entities that can be said to have intentionality or (underived) aboutness in a 'functionalist' way. On this view a state of or episode in an entity X has aboutness only if it has some functional role in X: only if it is disposed to interact with other features of X and thereby affect X's behaviour. But this imposes no significant restriction at all if we take the notion of function generally, that is, in a non-normative way that does not tie the very general notion of function to the very specific notion of being something that contributes to X's survival or flourishing; it lets in atoms as automatically as animals. If instead we take the notion of function normatively, by connecting it to the desiderata of survival and flourishing, it appears to render the idea of God's intentionality (aboutness) incoherent. God aside, a conscious, cognitively sophisticated 'Pure Observer' or 'Weather Watcher', a being constitutionally incapable of any sort of adaptive behaviour, could conceivably come into existence and enter into many intentional/aboutness states although none of them ever had or could have anything to do with its survival or well-being.[19]

Another popular suggestion is that aboutness comes on the scene only when we can make sense of the idea that X (or states of or episodes in X) can be said to *misrepresent* something. There has been a great quantity of sophisticated argument about what is required for the notion of misrepresentation to be properly applicable, and it seems clear enough that it does impose a significant restriction on candidates for aboutness. It seems clear that the puddle's representation of the moon doesn't pass the test, for example, along with almost all the rest of the causation in the universe.

One problem with this idea, however, and very briefly, is that the discussion has tended to take it for granted that we need a survival-and-well-being-based normative notion of function in order to make sense of the notion of misrepresentation (it has focused on finding the minimal case of aboutness, canvassing frogs, robots, bacteria and such like). This cannot be right, for there is again no *incoherence* in the idea of a Pure Observer who can represent and misrepresent, and know it, in a way completely unconnected with any such notion of function. The Pure Observers show with great clarity that intentionality and aboutness can exist in cases where there is no question of survival-and-well-being-based function. They are, however, fatal to a whole realm of theories, and are therefore fogged over for many philosophers.

—I don't have to consider such a case in trying to give a 'naturalistic' account of intentionality because it's not a case that involves a natural being.

This response misunderstands the nature and scope of the philosophical problem of giving a naturalistic or physicalist account of intentionality. To allow it is to let

---

[18] See e.g. Dretske 1988, 1995.

[19] See e.g. Strawson 1994: ch. 9. This is not to deny that the notions of intentionality and aboutness can be conceptually linked to notions of behaviour by sufficiently complicated counterfactuals.

naturalism come apart from physicalism in such a way that the naturalist problem of intentionality can be treated as having been solved by this manoeuvre (solving by shelving) while the physicalist (real physicalist) account of intentionality remains untouched, given that Pure Observers are physically possible entities.

It seems, further, that even if we accept the tie between aboutness and misrepresentation (± normative function) it won't stop UNA spreading everywhere. For we can make sense of the idea that an X-type particle may go anomalously into state S1, a state that it normally goes into only when interacting with a Y-type particle, even though it has not interacted with a Y-type particle, and on one view this is already enough for misrepresentation. We can further suppose that the X particle normally goes into S2 when and only when it has gone into S1, and that going into S2 in the absence of a Y particle shortens its 'life', and is in that sense dysfunctional for it, although its tendency to go into S2 on going into S1 is not the product of any process of evolution by natural selection.[20] Similarly, we can make sense of the idea that a non-self-moving organism like a tree may go into the state it would have gone into if it had been exposed to certain environmental conditions (its propensity to go into that state in those conditions being an evolved response) although those conditions do not obtain, this 'misrepresentation' being fatal for it.

It may be said that these kinds of cases are irrelevant, because we are interested in 'purposive' behaviour, pursuit of goals, and so on. But this fact about human interests can't ground any kind of metaphysically solid distinction. Any line that we try to draw between purposive behaviour and non-purposive behaviour in the domain of the experienceless (for we are still in pursuit of UNA^{NE}) will, once again, be wholly a matter of anthropomorphic/zoomorphic human prejudice. There is no metaphysically fundamental line to be drawn between the complex reactive behaviour of a developing embryo, which can look intensely and sophisticatedly goal-directed, or indeed of any self-maintaining system like an individual cell (or any of its biologically distinguishable subparts) and the 'purposiveness' of an undesigned robot like Fluke or—supposing for the sake of argument that birds are experienceless—a nesting bird. It is just that we find it more intuitive to call the last two sorts of behaviour 'purposive', given the biases built into our zoomorphic interests and ways of understanding things.[21] We naturally and heavily favour things that move around on their own in pursuit of things in their environment, for example, over embryos and cells with locally fixed positions.

One proposal, then, is that misrepresentation goes all the way down, in which case the misrepresentation requirement places no significant restriction on UNA. One may counter this by stipulating that misrepresentation (and so aboutness) can only occur in entities to whom the very specific survival-and-well-being-related notion of normative function applies, and this is a pretty good first shot at a significant restriction on genuine aboutness. It looks as if it excludes about 99.9 recurring per cent of

---

[20] It may be, though, that it is a product of the evolution of stable universes by natural selection in the sense of Smolin 1997.

[21] As remarked, Dennett has been quite clear about this through the decades; see e.g. Dennett 1971, 1981, 1991b, 2001.

all the candidate cases of UNA in the universe. It isn't enough, though, for it still lets through a vast array of the states of the embryo that govern its complex reactive behaviour, not to mention states of individual cells and their biologically distinguishable subparts. It seems that yet another restriction is needed to get us anywhere near a satisfactorily limited notion of UNA: restriction to a certain subclass of phenomena that we happen to find particularly interesting and intuitively classify as instances of 'purposive behaviour'. But this restriction simply begs the question, in the present context, and is completely arbitrary from a metaphysical point of view, which can take no special account of human interests.

No doubt other reasons can be given for discerning UNA only at certain special points in the great nexus of cause and effect. I think, though, that they are bound to be metaphysically superficial, for reasons just given. The idea needs development, but it is I think plain. It's not as if it can be undermined by special theories of causation. Nor does it depend on determinism. Even if determinism is false, and there are events that carry no information about the past, there are innumerable events that do, and the claim remains the same: if there is any underived aboutness to be found in non-experiential entities then it is all pervasive. And that's only the half of it. The problem is not only that almost everything (if not everything) has aboutness, it's also that everything that has it has far too much of it—perhaps an infinite amount. Suppose E carries information about D (with sufficiently detailed information about E we can know that D happened because only a D could have brought about E) and that the same goes for D and C, C and B, B and A. In that case the same also goes for E and A—E is as much about A as it is about D—and all stations in between and beyond.[22]

I will return to this second problem of excess shortly. So far we have the idea that if UNA$^{(NE)}$ exists at all it is all pervasive.

How should we treat this conclusion? We could contrapose. We could declare that it's all too much, and that the best thing to say (the only sensible thing to say, given our starting theoretical interest in intentionality) is that there isn't really any such thing as UNA^{NE}, there isn't ever any real or true underived aboutness in a non-experiential entity. I think this is a natural terminological reaction, and the most intuitive in certain contexts, if only because it allows one to withdraw the rejection of [A → I] that must have seemed so unnatural to many in §2.[23] For the moment, though, I am going to take the second option of continuing to allow that there is UNA$^{(NE)}$ while insisting [a] that UNA falls *infinitely* short of any kind of genuine intentionality and [b] that UNA is utterly ubiquitous, if it exists at all, in such a way that none of the usually favoured candidates—from states of naturally evolved experienceless organisms to states of cosmic-accident robots—are special in any way at all, as compared with kicked footballs, ripples in ponds, gravitational effects, and so on. There is, I suggest, no significant or substantive metaphysical line, of the sort that one would expect when dealing with a fundamental, real-world, concrete

---

[22] If indeterminism is true, there will be a progressive widening in the description of the cause-type.

[23] The philosophically uninteresting phenomenon of derived aboutness has been put aside.

phenomenon like intentionality, to be drawn between the sense in which states of a purposively efficient naturally evolved experienceless organism or cosmic-accident-programmed robot can be said to be about purple pyramids and the sense in which any effect is about its cause(s). There are plenty of compelling, intuitive, anthropomorphizing, human-interest, purposive-behaviour-focused lines to be drawn between the two cases, but that is quite another matter.

Dan Dennett nods his head, I think, and the choice seems stark. Either Dennett is right across the board—there's really no such thing as intentionality, it's just natural and useful to *talk* in such terms when explaining and predicting the behaviour of certain things—or I am right that there really is intentionality, but that all intentionality is experiential.[24] There is no middle ground—and this is something about which Dennett, unlike so many others, has always been admirably clear. Those who are tempted to burst out that they *know* that their conscious thoughts really are about particular things as a matter of metaphysical fact, quite independently of any explanation and prediction of their behaviour, have my sympathy, and are in fact, as I have yet to argue, quite right.[25]

—But if experience is necessary for this thing you're calling 'intentionality', what exactly do you have in mind? And what is the nature of the relation between experience and this thing you're calling 'intentionality' that makes the former necessary for the latter—whether we're thinking about a purple pyramid we can see right in front of us, the church of San Vitale a thousand miles away, the tallest tree in the Amazonian jungle, π, W. V. Quine's second-best sloop, marshmallow camshafts, or round squares? What *exactly* does your and my conscious thinking about the pyramid add to whatever it is in robots like Luke and Fluke that is involved in their efficient and successful search for the pyramid and their depositing of it in a designated box? What exactly does my conscious experience add to my thinking about π, given that Luke and Fluke (equipped with a maths module) are now smoothly engaged in calculating π's decimal expansion?

To answer this question I must first say something about cognitive experience.

4   COGNITIVE EXPERIENCE

When people today talk of experience,[26] of experiential qualitative content, *EQ* content for short, they standardly have in mind only things like sensations and sensory images, emotional feelings and moods considered (so far as they can be) just in respect of their non-cognitive felt character—all of which things I will for the

[24] In §6 I consider the proposal that derived non-experiential intentionality may occur in experiential beings. For some discussion of the 'Only In An Experiential Being thesis' see Essay 10: 260, 278–9.

[25] They are right even if they are 'brains in vats', although they are then more wrong about the nature of the things their thoughts are about than they know.

[26] Although the words 'experience' and 'experiential' have been defined in §1 as referring only to the phenomenon of the experiential qualitative character of conscious mental phenomena I will for purposes of emphasis sometimes speak pleonastically of the 'qualitative character of experience' or 'experiential qualitative character of experience'.

purposes of the present discussion bring under the inelegant heading *sensory-affective EQ content* or *sensory-affective experience*. This is unfortunate, because there is also EQ content that is not sensory-affective content. There is *cognitive EQ content*, or *cognitive experience*, as I will call it, and philosophical analysis allows us to distinguish cognitive EQ content or experience sharply from sensory-affective EQ content or experience although the two things are utterly undisentanglable in daily life.[27] The existence of such cognitive experience, of non-sensory-affective EQ content, is hopelessly obvious to unprejudiced reflection, for it fills almost every moment of our lives. In analytic philosophy, however, its existence has very often been denied or at least ignored. Most strikingly, it has been denied or ignored even by those who fully acknowledge the existence of sensory-affective experience, sensory-affective EQ content.[28]

What do I have in mind? I use the term 'cognitive experience' to cover every aspect of experience that goes beyond sensory-affective experience considered just as such. It sweeps up whatever is left over after one has isolated in thought the merely sensory-affective content of experience. If one could somehow quantify the respective contributions of cognition and sensory affection to experience, I think that the vast bulk of experience would classify as cognitive. It saturates everything—swimming and digging as much as philosophizing. Here, however, I am going to limit my attention to the cognitive experience involved in comprehendingly entertaining propositions in reading, writing, listening, or thinking.

I have argued the point elsewhere[29] and will be brief. You are now understanding this very sentence. This understanding is contributing to *the character of the current course of your experience*. It is contributing to the overall experiential character, the EQ character, of your current experience.[30] Your experience in the last few seconds would have been very different if the last two sentences had been 'The objection to the Realist Regularity theory of causation is very simple. It is that the theory is utterly implausible in asserting categorically that there is no reason in the nature of things for the regularity of the world.' And the difference wouldn't have been merely visual. It's the conceptual content of the sentences—and now of this very sentence— that plays the dominant part in determining the overall character of this particular stretch of the course of your experience, although you may also be aware of many

---

[27] Some may say that it is not just impracticable but also illegitimate to distinguish these two things—even for purposes of philosophical analysis—because they are so entangled in our experience. I prefer Kant's view that 'the understanding can intuit nothing, the senses can think nothing. Only through their union can knowledge arise. But that is no reason for confounding the contribution of either with that of the other; rather is it a strong reason for carefully separating and distinguishing the one from the other' (Kant 1781–7: A51-2/B75-6). I take it that one can appreciate Sellars's 1956–63 and McDowell's 1994 stress on the essentially conceptual nature of the content of experience without in any way questioning the analytical legitimacy of the distinction between the sensory and the cognitive.

[28] 'Eliminativists' deny the existence of sensory-affective EQ content as well.

[29] 1994: 5–13 and Essay 10: §6. See also (e.g.) James 1890: ch. 9; Siewert 1998; Pitt 2004.

[30] Strictly speaking it is the experience of *or as of* understanding these particular sentences that has cognitive EQ content, for *mis*understanding the sentences would equally involve cognitive experience, experience as of understanding (see Strawson 1994: 6–7; the same goes for 'comprehend' below).

other things.[31] Consider (experience) the difference, for you, between my saying 'I'm reading *War and Peace*' and 'barath abalori trafalon'. In both cases you experience sounds, but in the first case you experience something more: you have understanding-experience, cognitive experience.[32] Cognitive experience of the sort I am focusing on at present is a matter of whatever EQ content is involved in episodes of consciously entertaining and understanding specific cognitive or conceptual contents after one has subtracted any sensory-affective EQ-content trappings or shadings or accompaniments that such episodes may have.

Here is another proof of its existence. *Have you really been having merely sensory-affective experience for the last two minutes?* That's a rhetorical question—Of course not. But if there's no such thing as cognitive experience the answer is certainly Yes. One can imagine the rhetorical question being interrupted. . . . Have you really RELIGIOUS DISSENT had nothing WILLIAM JAMES'S PLUMBER'S BILL but sensory-affective experience SHOW ME SOME DARK MATTER for the last thirty seconds? If there's no such thing as cognitive experience, cognitive EQ content, the answer is certainly Yes.

I think that the main difficulty that philosophers have with the idea of cognitive EQ content derives from the fact that they fail to distinguish it sharply from cognitive content, as this is now ordinarily understood. So let it be said: *cognitive EQ content is not the same as cognitive content.* Suppose you think consciously *The average distance from the moon to the earth is 238,888 miles.* What is the cognitive EQ content of this thought-episode? Well, consider your 'Twin-Earth' Twin, and your 'Brain-in-a-Vat' Twin, and your 'Instant' Twin who has just now popped flukishly into being. By hypothesis, all three of them have exactly the same cognitive EQ content, the same thought-*experience*, as you do. The cognitive EQ content of your thought-episode is precisely what you have in common with them, experientially speaking.[33]

So much for your thought-episode's cognitive EQ content. What, now, of its cognitive content? Accounts differ. According to one central account, cognitive content, whatever the details of its nature, is something that is essentially semantically evaluable, evaluable as true or false, accurate or inaccurate. This is the account that will concern me.

There is a different and currently fashionable account I mention to put aside: the externalist, direct-reference, 'representationalist', 'Russellian' (etc.) account, according to which the cognitive content of the thought-episode consists of the moon itself, the earth itself, and the distance between them itself, or the state of affairs that consists of the moon's being this far from the earth. Since the moon and the earth are not

---

[31] Imagine a language in which the first of these pairs of sentences has the same meaning that the second pair has in English.

[32] I called the study of this phenomenon 'cognitive phenomenology' in Strawson 1986: 30, 55, 70, 96, 107–9, and used the terms 'understanding-experience' and 'meaning-experience' in Strawson 1994: 5–13.

[33] Your Twin's course of experience when reading this paper is exactly the same as yours. The point that there is no natural language in which we can specify this common content in detail (see e.g. Pettit and McDowell 1986) is no grounds for an objection.

semantically evaluable entities, or representational entities, or mental entities, being things that could exist without there being any minds or representations at all, they are in no danger (one lives in hope) of being confused with the EQ content of a thought-episode, which is an essentially mental phenomenon that could not exist if there were no minds at all. I take it, accordingly, that the danger of failing to distinguish cognitive EQ content sharply from cognitive content arises only when cognitive content is at least taken to be something semantically evaluable and hence something that represents something,[34] and hence something that is as a representation ontologically distinct from what it represents.[35] The possibility of confusion is then provided for, because we also often take mental phenomena to represent something—and to be of course ontologically distinct from what they represent.

Both sorts of cognitive content can happily coexist, so long as they do not insist on being called the same thing, and they can equally well coexist with cognitive EQ content. In the case of my thinking *The average distance from the moon to the earth is 238,888 miles*, there is [1] the Russellian cognitive content of my thought-episode, i.e. the moon, the earth, and so on plus [2] the cognitive EQ content of my thought-episode, that is, that which I share fully with my Twins, plus [3] the semantically evaluable cognitive content of my thought-episode, that is, that feature of the representation that is my thought-episode, whatever your preferred theory of its nature, in virtue of which it has the property—which it certainly has, given its causal embedding—of being able to be true or false. ([3] is an essentially 'externalist' notion, at least in part.)

It remains only to say that the cognitive EQ content of my thought-episode, which is by hypothesis identical to the cognitive EQ content of my Twins' real or apparent thought-episodes, is in itself no more semantically evaluable than sensory-affective EQ content—by which I mean sensory-affective EQ content considered just as such, that is, entirely independently of its causes.[36] Cognitive EQ content is just a matter of the qualitative character of experience and the fundamental block to understanding it clearly and distinguishing it cleanly from cognitive content is simply a profoundly inadequate (because merely sensory-affective) conception of the (experiential) qualitative character of experience.

I don't see how there can be any real progress with the problem of intentionality until we recover a good grasp of the reality of cognitive EQ content and its all-importance in human life. The key to the problem of intentionality (including the supposed problem of intentionality with respect to so-called 'non-existent objects')

---

[34] It's a necessary truth that to be semantically evaluable is to be representational, so if you think that propositions are true or false you must think they're representations, and if you think that propositions aren't representations then you can't think they're true or false (you may be thinking of them as states of affairs). God preserve us from any terminology that doesn't recognize this point—the word 'proposition' has proved to be distressingly slippery under philosophical distortion.

[35] God preserve us, also, from those who have recently twisted the word 'representation' in such a way as to muddy this distinction (see Strawson 2005).

[36] It is helpful to note that identity of cognitive EQ content across Twins must be conceded even by philosophers who claim that Instant-Twins don't really have thoughts—cognitive content—at all.

lies here, and yet many analytic philosophers deny the existence of cognitive EQ content, making a mistake comparable to the mistake made by those by no means entirely legendary philosophers who thought that thinking was wholly a matter of having images in the head.[37]

5 WHAT IS THE RELATION BETWEEN EXPERIENCE AND INTENTIONALITY?

With the notion of cognitive EQ content in hand, we can return to the question raised at the end of §3: What is the relation between experience and intentionality? Consider Lucy and Louis, who live in the real world, as we do, and who are having qualitatively identical experience — call it 'M-experience'. It is experience just like experience of thinking about, or perhaps visualizing, or seeing, a moose. In fact it is just like the experience someone might have if thinking about, or visualizing, a certain real moose, Mandy, '*M*' for short. And in fact Lucy's M-experience has normal causal links to seeing M or pictures of M, or reading about M. Louis's M-experience, by contrast, and his whole accompanying M-experience-related dispositional set, which I assume to be identical to Lucy's in all relevant respects,[38] are caused by a freakish brainstorm. He has had no contact with moose, still less with M.

Lucy's M-experience is about M; it has classic intentionality with respect to M. Louis's M-experience isn't; it has no intentionality with respect to M. It is not about any concrete object, although Louis thinks it is. So the two experiences differ dramatically in their intentionality. But the only relevant difference between them lies in their causes. It does not (by hypothesis) lie in their intrinsic EQ character as experiences. Nor is there any difference between Lucy and Louis so far as their relevant behavioural dispositions (including their mental-activity dispositions) are concerned, for I have supposed that they are identical in this respect. It is simply the difference in the causes of their experiences that makes the difference in respect of M-intentionality. And this causal difference is not itself philosophically mysterious. It is not significantly different from the causal difference that explains why this picture is a picture of Isaiah Berlin (it is a photograph or portrait of Isaiah Berlin), whereas this qualitatively identical picture is not, since it is a work of pure imagination or a complex accident of paint.

We have, then, a very plain causal factor, and it raises a problem that is familiar from other causal theories like the causal theory of perception. For the fact is that Lucy's thought is about M — *Mandy*. It is not about the neuronal happenings that directly causally precede and precipitate the (neural happenings that are the) thought,

[37] It is arguable that the second mistake arose out of a violent overcorrection of the first. This is a story for another time.

[38] Louis's M-experience-related dispositional set is identical to Lucy's in the sense that if Louis and Lucy swapped all their other properties then Louis would do just what Lucy would do given his M-experience-related dispositional set (one could run the case more simply with Lucy and a duplicate of Lucy). I understand dispositions in the natural 'internalist' way according to which one shares all one's behavioural dispositions with one's 'Twins' (Instant, Vat, etc).

for example. Nor is it about the light waves and optic-nerve electrical activity that are causally involved in Lucy's coming to know about M by seeing or reading about her. Her thought is *quite unequivocally* about M rather than any of these other things. This is not merely some kind of natural *interpretation* of the situation. It is not just some kind of 'intentional-stance' hypothesis. It is an immoveable objective fact (you can test it by thinking of an absent friend).

But what makes Lucy's thought unequivocally about M and M alone? How do we—how does intentionality—know where to stop? We may compare the question of what justifies taking photographs and sound recordings to be only of things that are located at a certain stage in their causation. Is it an immoveable objective fact that these things, rather than light waves or sound waves, are what the photographs and recordings are of or about, quite independently of what we human beings take them to be about, or do we find such objective facts only in cases like Lucy's?

The problem of where to stop (how to stop) is, as remarked, a routine problem in theories that have a causal component. It certainly doesn't constitute a difficulty that is peculiar to the present account of intentionality. On the contrary: it is precisely the stopping problem that justifies the present account's insistence on the necessity of experience. For what we need is an account of how, given all its causes, Lucy's thought manages to be only and precisely about M.[39] And here we reach the crux: it is precisely the EQ[40] character of her experience, and in particular her cognitive experience, that allows us to stop at a certain specific point as we proceed down the chain of causes—in a way that nothing else can. How can it do this? Because the EQ character of her experience includes her sense, her conception, of what particular thing—M—her experience is about; it includes her taking her experience to be experience of a certain particular thing. It is this taking, which is part of the EQ character or content of her experience, and in particular the cognitive-experiential character or content of her experience, that settles the question, given her causal context, of which of her thought's causal antecedents her thought is about—*in a way that nothing else can*. Her experience is a real, concrete, natural, empirical phenomenon, albeit not one that is open to public inspection, and its EQ character, cognitive or otherwise, is equally a concrete empirical phenomenon, albeit one that is not open to public inspection.[41]

Consider a simple perceptual case. There is a wineglass in front of you. You are thinking about it and it alone. How can you do this? What makes it the case that you are thinking about the glass, rather than about the neural activity immediately preceding your thought, or the stimulus pattern on your retina, or the glass-reflected light waves a metre away from your eye? There are really only two candidates in play. Either it is [1] the EQ character, and in particular the cognitive EQ character, of your current experience—the fact that your experience includes your taking it to be experience of a

---

[39] There is plenty of room for philosophical cleverness about ways in which Lucy's thought is indeterminate (see e.g. the discussion of 'vague objects'); they do not change the fact that her thought is about M.

[40] 'EQ' is strictly speaking redundant whenever it qualifies 'character'.

[41] Many have come to think, quite wrongly, that 'empirical' implies 'open to public inspection'.

certain thing (note that one does not have to posit any kind of higher-order experience to account for this 'taking'; the taking in question is simply built in to the character of the experience). Or it is [2] your current overall behavioural disposition, plus anything else about you that anyone wants to cite so long as it excludes [1], the very existence of which is denied by many participants in the debate.

It is, however, silly to think that behaviour can settle this question. It is not really a candidate at all. It has seemed to be a candidate (when the question has been faced) only because many have either denied the existence of EQ character outright, or have allowed it but denied that it is in any way relevant to the question of intentionality, and have been left with nothing else. Consider the experienceless, pyramid-fixated robot. It may be overwhelmingly natural for us to say that certain of the states that it is in when it is interacting with purple pyramids—I'll call them P-states, where P-states are understood to be identified by their intrinsic or non-relational character—are about the pyramids, given how it behaves (it picks up the pyramid and drops it in the box). But this behaviour doesn't really show that its P-states are about the pyramid in any sense in which they are not equally about the proximal inputs to its central control system, or about what causally precedes those inputs by 50 ms, and so on. One can train the robot in a virtual environment on an electronic simulator until it is rich in P-states and many other such states (R-states for red spheres, to be sedulously avoided, B-states for blue cubes, to be ignored), and then transfer it into an exactly matching physically real environment in which there are purple pyramids, red spheres, blue cubes. (An alternative is that its software configuration is a product of cosmic fluke.) Its P-states are not about the real pyramids before it is transferred, and the transfer, the embedding in the real world, cannot make it true that its P-states are now determinately about the pyramid in any sense in which they are not equally about the proximal inputs to its control system, or whatever immediately causally precedes the proximal inputs; and so on. Nor can there be any sense in which it is wrong about what its states are about.

I think you have to choose. Either experience is essential to intentionality, or Dennett is right, across the board, and there is really no such thing as intentionality, there are no matters of fact about intentionality, all attributions of intentionality are just a matter of theoretical convenience. There is, to repeat, no tenable middle ground. (It will not help to include linguistic behaviour, or appeal to facts about the public nature of language.)

This returns us to the second problem of excess, the problem that if there is any UNA then anything that has it has far too much of it (the first problem is that if any experienceless entity has UNA then everything or almost everything does). Compare what happens when we, brought up in the real world, are switched unknowingly onto a perfect simulator. We are then wrong, completely wrong, about what our thoughts and experiences are about. We can get things completely wrong because there are hard, wholly non-behavioural, real-world, concrete facts—cognitive-experiential mental facts—about what we take our experiences to be about. These takings are themselves real-world, concrete phenomena—EQ phenomena. They are features of the cognitive EQ character of our experience, and they, and they alone, make it possible for us to get things wrong. They alone can confer sufficient determinateness on intentionality, determinateness sufficient for making sense of error. The experienceless do not and cannot get things wrong, so if their states are about anything they are indiscriminately about all those of their causes of which they are reliable indicators. When it comes to aboutness and intentionality, consciousness kicks.[42]

There are standard complications. If Lucy is contemplating a rock in the mist which she takes to be a moose, and indeed to be M, then that taking-something-to-be-a moose, which is also a taking-something-to-be-M, and is, considered as a taking in the present sense, entirely a matter of cognitive EQ content, is obviously not going to settle the question of which of her experience's local causal antecedents it is about (i.e. the rock).[43] Fortunately, however, she also takes it that *that thing* (the thing she takes to be a moose, and to be M) is a physical object over there in the mist, and that taking, too, is part of the content of her experience, and it does allow us to stop at a particular place as we go back up the chain or cone of causes. The same goes if the thing in question is just a dark curl in the mist. If the cause of her thought is a brainstorm, on the other hand, then it is not about that brainstorm, but it is still about moose, and indeed about M. And so on.[44]

Perception provides the most vivid cases, but the point is general, and exclusive concentration on perceptual cases is likely to mislead. For it's not just that the EQ content of my experience allows me to stop (makes it the case that I stop) at the right

---

[42] 'Some may still be worried by the elusiveness of understanding-experience [*sc* cognitive experience, cognitive EQ content]. They may be prepared to concede that there is something that may reasonably be called "understanding-experience" but be struck by the fact that one can't really do anything much with the idea, theoretically. And they may feel that being able to do something with the idea theoretically is a necessary part of genuinely understanding it, philosophically. They may even think that being able to do something with it theoretically is a necessary condition of accepting it as real. And there is another pragmatic difficulty with achieving a satisfactory grip on the notion of understanding-experience. Suppose that one hears it put forward and discussed, and concludes that there is indeed something that may reasonably be called "understanding-experience". One may still remain uncertain as to whether one really knows what it is. This may now be because one is too close to what one is trying to think about, so that it is like looking at an elephant from three inches away. I don't, however, think either of these problems is serious. One doesn't have to do anything much theoretically with the notion of understanding-experience. Nor does one have to try to get an impossibly detached perspective on it. What philosophy requires of one is simply that one should acknowledge its reality and bear it in mind when trying to form an adequate general conception of the nature of experience. One needs to have such a conception in order to stay balanced in the philosophy of mind. (Strawson 1994: 11–12).

[43] Note that cognitive-EQ-content-denoting expressions like 'taking-something-to-be-Mandy (a moose)' are rough, because specification of their content doesn't involve any reference to actual Mandy (moose). Their EQ content is 'purely qualitative' or general, as is evident from the fact that Milly's experiential Twins have identical EQ content.

[44] More benign complications. It is possible to construct a case in which Lucy has a thought that is [i] caused by a previously unencountered thing X and [ii] just like how a thought about X would be for her, experientially speaking, but [iii] not about X at all. Equally she can have a thought that is [i] caused by a previously encountered thing Y and [ii] about Y although she is very wrong about what has been going on causally. And she can in this case be right about what Y is or, again, be very wrong about what Y is. And so on. There are many further issues about how wrong Lucy can be about things she stands in an intentional relation to. See e.g. Evans 1982 and Montague forthcoming.

thing when I am having a perceptual experience of an object. The same holds equally in the case of my thoughts about absent objects, and in the case of the concepts I deploy in thought, given always that I am in a certain causal context—given that I am in fact in a real world more or less as I suppose myself to be. Suppose I am thinking about moose, or about some particular moose. The EQ character of my thought when I deploy the concept or thought-element MOOSE makes the object of my thought determinate, given my overall causal context, in a way that no represent-ation in any non-experiential entity can ever be (obviously the EQ character of my thought can't do it all on its own; causal context is essential). This is not to say that it makes it determinate in some magically absolute way.[45] The claim is just this: given that we are in a real world more or less as we suppose ourselves to be, the intentional-ity of Lucy's overall experiential state is sufficiently fixed (sufficiently 'disambiguated', one might say) by the fact that she takes it to be experience of a particular moose, and is suitably causally connected to M.[46]

The next stage in a general account of intentionality is to extend the point from thought about concrete objects to thought about 'abstract' objects like the number 2, where there is no stopping problem of the kind one encounters when one is dealing with a causal process. It looks as if it is not just concentration on perceptual cases that is likely to mislead, but also, and more generally, concentration on cases of intention-ality with respect to concrete entities. In this paper, however, I'll continue to focus on the case of intentionality with respect to concrete entities.

—I don't see how you're going to deal with the number 2, but my question is in any case general. What exactly is this 'taking', that is, you say, part of the content of her experience?

It is an all-pervasive feature of our experience; your current experience is flooded with it. It is as plain as day, but obscure to philosophers who have so embrangled the notion of mental content. It is simply a matter of cognitive EQ content, something that Lucy and Louis have wholly in common, so far as their M-experience is concerned, although Lucy is thinking about M and Louis is not.[47] All one has to do, to know what it is, is to think about what Lucy and Louis have in common, in the case in question (or Lucy and her experiential duplicate, whom we may now suppose to have no causal connection to moose at all).

One might say that it is *cognitive intent, intentional intent*, which is part of the cognitive-experiential content of a thought, that fixes intentionality in con-junction with the causal factor. It fixes what the thought is about in its causal context. It is essential. Nothing else will do. Every other attribution of intentional-ity is convenient fiction, 'intentional-stance', down-with-metaphysics, behaviourist-or-neobehaviourist, don't-care anti-realism about mental states. When the robot or

---

[45] The determinateness claim is compatible with irreducible fuzziness in some dimensions; see e.g. Schiffer 1987: ch. 3.

[46] There are interesting things to say about the nature of one's intentionality if one is a brain engendered and permanently resident in a vat.

[47] Perhaps cognitive EQ content is what you get when you give Kaplan's notion of character an explicitly experiential reading. I'm not sure, but I think we are close.

zombie comes off the simulator and enters the real world, it doesn't, to repeat, get anything wrong. Nor does any UNA that we allow it to have suddenly start to be about real, concrete, spatiotemporal, distal things in any sense in which it is not equally about its proximal inputs. The same goes when we put it back on the simulator. When you and I transfer between real world and simulator, by contrast, all sorts of things change. We are wrong about our situation, for example, because our intentionality is effectively determinate.

—But how can experience ever deliver determinateness?

It just can. Cognitive experience in causal context can do just this. Such is its power. (When it comes to the number 2, it doesn't even require causal context.) Cognitive experience is a remarkable thing. The whole philosophical difficulty, for some, is simply to accept this fact; to see that there is absolutely nothing suspect or question-begging or anti-naturalistic about it. It takes some getting used to if one has been brought up philosophically in a certain way.

—But 'cognitive intent', if there is such a thing (I don't really know what you mean) must be supposed to be non-experiential in many cases, if not in most cases, something implicit, part of the background out of which thought arises, not something that is normally present in any way in the (EQ) content of conscious experience.

In my use the term stands for something experiential—I'll call it 'conscious cognitive intent' if you prefer. One can use the phrase 'cognitive intent' in a way that allows it to be non-experiential, to be something that can be wholly latent, when one is thinking or perceiving, in such a way that there is no sense in which it is part of the EQ content of one's thought or perception. One will first, however, need to acquire a realistic view about how much can be genuinely part of the EQ content of experience without being in the focus of attention, for this is vastly underestimated in the analytic tradition.[48] And even when one has done this I will continue to insist that genuine intentionality comes on the scene only when cognitive intent is part of the EQ content of thought (stressing, again, how much can be part of the EQ content of experience without being in the focus of attention); so that whatever non-experiential cognitive intent may be supposed to be, in experiencing beings like ourselves, it doesn't deliver intentionality. Nor does it deliver determinate aboutness, for it is subject to all the uncontrollability of UNA. When there is experiential cognitive intent, by contrast, everything is transformed.

—'When there is experiential cognitive intent everything is transformed.' This is magic. You're simply asserting that experiential cognitive intent + causal context can constitute intentionality while no non-experiential cognitive intent, conceptual capacity, or whatever can ever constitute intentionality. Your thesis is that when there's experience, *pff!*, there's intentionality.

---

[48] Some will think I am subject to a colossal illusion in this matter; I recommend a reading of selected passages of Husserl. Nor should anyone who is in any doubt venture a firm opinion before reading ch. 9 of William James's *The Principles of Psychology*.

I'm saying that there's intentionality only when there's experience, but I think I see what you mean. I think you're imagining a case in which everything that can possibly contribute to the existence of intentionality is present, including everything that is possible in the way of experiential conditions given that conscious cognitive intent (intentional intent) is absent. And I think you're saying that simply adding conscious cognitive intent—that is, a mere piece of experiential what-it's-likeness, albeit cognitive what-it's-likeness—could not make the difference.

If so, I disagree. I do hold the *pff!* thesis. It's a bit like looking at one of those pictures where you can't see what it is a picture of, and then suddenly you see. Suppose Louis is confronting a real scene in the world, and is seeing it, on account of some temporary mental fugue, just as an array of colours, without even any automatic taking of it as of the real world, without even any grasp of it as experience of anything at all. No intentionality here, I say, none at all. Then he comes to, he sees buildings, leaves, whatever it is. Such 'brown-study' fugues, in which intentionality fades to nothing, are not that uncommon in ordinary life, and one can precipitate them quite easily, fixing one's stare and letting go. Total intentional decoupling—because of the lapse in conscious cognitive EQ content or cognitive intent.[49]

—But what *is* this cognitive intent? You can't propose to analyse intentionality in terms of intent, intentional intent, announce that this intent is essentially experiential, and that's it.

Given the way the notion of intentionality has been detached from mind and experience in current debate, to move from the notion of intentionality to a notion of intent isn't to move in anything like a circle of terms; for there is no intent in the experienceless. And if and in so far as it is to move in a circle it brings insight, given the current debate in analytic philosophy, to see that this is so. It brings the notion of intentionality home, and it's a big step forward to see this—to see that this is home.

—It's still magic. How can the quality of experience pin things down determinately, or at least as determinately as you say it can? How can it be any more determinate than behaviour, in the end, in determining intentionality? You are, at bottom, dreaming.

'Determinate' and its cognates are tricky words because they have metaphysical/epistemological slippage built in to them. I can't answer until I'm sure that you're not using 'determinate' in any (to me uninteresting) epistemological sense, but only in a metaphysical sense; and that you don't think, as so many did in the last century (and perhaps some still do), that a thing cannot be metaphysically determinate unless it can in principle be epistemologically determinate for us human beings.

—I'm not sure you can cut metaphysics off from epistemology like this, but I'll let it go.

Good, then my answer to your question 'How can the quality of experience pin things down determinately' is: It just can. That's how it is. This is what we do. This is the

---

[49] A less successful coming-to might leave Louis experiencing his experience as experience of the real world but nothing more. Its intentional object would then be fixed as *the world*, and the proximal sensory inputs (e.g.) would no longer be equally good candidates.

power of the entirely natural phenomenon of conscious thought. My intent (taking) fixes it that I'm thinking about the tree, not the proximal inputs. If God could look into my mind[50] and apprehend the cognitive EQ content of my experience he would certainly know what I was thinking about, given that he also knew—and how could he not—about my causal circumstances. He would know, given the (cognitive) EQ character of my experience, that I was thinking about the tree, that tree, not any intervening causal goings on, light waves, optic nerve electrical activity, and so on. It is the same power that makes it the case that I can think determinately about the number 2 although there is no relevant causal context. *Pff!*—I just can—such is the power of thought. This is the correct account of how it is that content can be determinate in spite of all the problems raised for this idea by Kripke in his book *Wittgenstein on Rules and Private Language.*[51] The difficulty, in the current frame of discussion, is to see that it is adequate.

It may be hard to grasp—the reality, the power of conscious thought—after nearly a century of behaviourist and post-behaviourist (functionalist, interpretationist, 'representationalist') folly.[52] It may seem like mere assertion, or trying to have something (something impossible) for free. It may seem like sheer irresponsibility, or a naïve relapse into hopeless old ways of thinking. It is a return to old ways of thinking, but it is not a relapse and it is not I think naïve. I suspect, however, that it will leave a feeling of dissatisfaction, partly because it terminates in something primitive, not further analysable: the mere existence of the experiential modality of cognitive experience, the mere existence of the phenomenon of cognitive EQ content.

The only way to make progress here, I think, is to let go: to see that there is nothing to press for here, no legitimate philosophical demand that is not being met. The fact that cognitive experience exists, just as visual and auditory experience exist, is a fact we encounter—right on our doorstep—in naturalistic investigation. The key is to see that it raises no greater problem for (evolutionary) naturalism than the existence of any other kind of developed experiential modality, like vision or hearing. There is no new problem of principle. There is in the world cognitive EQ content, intentional intent, cognitive-experiential intentional intent, just as there is pain.[53]

---

[50] Cf. Wittgenstein 1953: 217.

[51] Kripke 1982. My understanding is that Kripke himself believes that content can be determinate in spite of all the problems he catalogues.

[52] C. D. Broad annihilated behaviourism in four pages in 1925: 612–16. He then offered nine pages of further criticism, fearing that he might 'be accused of breaking a butterfly on a wheel' because the theory is 'so preposterously silly that only very learned men could have thought of' it. 'By a "silly" theory', he continues, 'I mean one which may be held at the time when one is talking or writing professionally, but which only an inmate of a lunatic asylum would think of carrying into daily life' (1925: 5).

[53] We are familiar with sensory modalities, but it looks as if these need to be subsumed under a more general category of experiential modalities. Each sensory modality is an experiential modality, and thought experience (cognitive experience) is an experiential modality to be reckoned alongside other experiential modalities. We have, so far, no explanation of how the systems of the eye and brain give rise to the phenomenology of colour-experience in the particular way that they do. In the same way, we have no explanation of how the systems of the brain that underlie or realize thought give rise to, or involve, conscious thought experience in the way in which they do. The fact remains that our cognitive lives are, as such, experientially rich. This is perhaps never more apparent

6 SAVING INTENTIONAL REALISM

It's plain that dispositional states (e.g. belief dispositions) cannot be intentional states, on the view I have expounded here, and this will worry many, as noted in §1. Terminological habits are as powerful as any in human life, and the way of talking that allows that dispositional states can be contentful intentional states is deeply engrained in analytic philosophy. Dispositional states have, indeed, been taken to be the paradigm cases of intentional phenomena.

This is odd, for it is an elementary point that a *disposition*, such as the disposition to answer Yes if intending to speak truly when asked if grass is green, is just not the kind of thing that can possibly be contentful in the way that it needs to be if it is to be an intentional thing—even if it can be identified as the particular disposition it is only by reference to the proposition (the content) *grass is green*, which is itself an (abstract) intentional entity. To think that a disposition is, metaphysically, the kind of entity that can be contentful in itself, and so intentional, is a bit like thinking that an object's disposition to cause red-experience or square-experience in human beings is itself something red or square; or perhaps it is like thinking that if an object has a fragile disposition then it already in some sense contains or involves actual breaking.[54]

There is in fact only one serious and metaphysically coherent candidate for a physicalist, when it comes to trying to find some intrinsically mentally contentful, non-experiential *grass-is-green* item in Louis (who is, we may suppose, now dreamlessly asleep), and that is the non-experiential, non-dispositional, concrete neural state in virtue of which it is true to say that Louis now believes that grass is green. But very few, I think, will want to say that such an item can be intrinsically *grass-is-green* contentful.

But perhaps there can be *occurrent* non-experiential intentionality (granted that there cannot be dispositional non-experiential intentionality)? This can seem a very attractive idea—especially when the non-experiential intentionality is supposed to occur in experiential beings like Louis and Lucy[55]—and I'd like to be able to allow it. But it gets you into all sorts of trouble. It's open to the same sorts of indeterminacy objections that confront all claims to non-experiential intentionality, and in the end Dennett claims your soul.

—You can't leave it at that. The principal difficulty remains. You're forgetting that *intentional realism* is true. You're forgetting that explanations of actions by reference

---

than when one is lying in the dark thinking of one thing after another, unable to sleep. My bet would be that cognitive experience is at least partly or principally located in what are known as the sensory areas of the brain.

[54] An object may cause red-experience or square-experience in human beings because it is red or square, and it may be disposed to cause red-experience or square-experience in human beings because it is red or square, but a disposition—as ordinarily understood—is not the kind of thing that can itself be red or square. (For the qualification 'as ordinarily understood' see Strawson 2008, where I argue that there is at most a conceptual distinction between categorical properties and dispositional properties, and no real distinction between them.)

[55] I consider the point in Strawson 1994: 168–72, and Essay 10: 275–6.

to the intentional content of dispositional mental states like beliefs and pro-attitudes can be straightforwardly and without qualification correct: see, for example, Fodor 1989. It's true that it's not the dispositions that are causally active, strictly speaking, but rather certain corresponding occurrent goings on but these occurrent goings on may well be non-experiential at the point of causal efficacy and they will therefore be wholly lacking in intentionality, on your view. Your view is therefore incompatible with intentional realism. You may say that thought is very quick and very rich,[56] and that there is in fact always some sort of rapid but real occurrent experiential episode when such occurrent states contribute to the production of action, at least in the normal case, but I can allow that too—if only for the sake of argument—because the 'normal case' qualification is fatal. What about Freud? What about the fact that unconscious mental occurrences that are concerned with—about—Great Aunt Tallulah can feature in straightforwardly true explanations of actions in beings like ourselves in whom they neither do nor can achieve experiential expression?[57]

My answer remains the same. Only experience, only cognitive-experiential taking, can confer genuine (sufficiently determinate) intentionality. We can allow that these unconscious mental occurrences have Aunt-Tallulah-determinate intentionality only if we can allow that they possess it in virtue of the causal-historical fact that Aunt-Tallulah-determinate cognitive-experiential taking was involved in the original processes of interaction that led to the presence of the dispositions that are now being manifested in the causing of an action by these unconscious mental occurrences.[58]

Can we allow this? Well, why not? Here I think we can find a robust use for the notion of derived intentionality, although it is strictly confined to states of experiential beings like Louis and is therefore quite unlike the standard use that ascribes derived intentionality to things like books.

Allowing such a notion of derived intentionality seems a small price to pay for preserving intentional realism, and suddenly I feel eirenic, ecumenical. I can hardly now protest if somebody wants to extend this notion of derived intentionality from certain of Louis's occurrent non-experiential states to those categorical (non-dispositional) neural states of Louis in virtue of which it is true to say that he has belief dispositions concerning grass, pro-attitude dispositions concerning *mozzarella di bufala*, and so on. And from there we may even go on to books. Fodor has spoken darkly of intellectual suicide, when considering positions that, like the present one, tie intentionality essentially to experience, but perhaps we can still reach some accommodation, somewhere between Dennett and Searle.[59]

[56] 'How very quick the actions of the mind are performed . . . many of them . . . seem to require no time . . . seem to be crowded into an instant' (Locke 1689–1700: 2.9.10).

[57] Fodor and Lepore press this case against Searle's attempt to confer intentionality on dispositional non-experiential states by appeal to the 'Connection Principle' (Searle 1992: 84, 155; Fodor and Lepore 1994).

[58] The taking must have picked out Great Aunt Tallulah, but it need not have picked her out as such.

[59] The present proposal about non-experiential (and essentially derived) intentionality is quite different from Searle's Connection Principle. (I would call Dennett 'Scylla', but Searle isn't anything like as bad as Charybdis.)

There are many more questions to address. There are questions about the minimal case of intentionality. If we suppose that new born babies don't have intentionality we will need to make sense of how intentionality dawns. If we take it (as I do) that cats have intentionality we need to say something about this; and just as we cannot hope to sort all conscious creatures scientifically into those that definitely have concepts (whatever exactly concepts are) and those that definitely don't, so too attributions of intentionality will sometimes be irredeemably uncertain. Questions about the innateness of the object concept, of the sort famously worked on by Spelke, Leslie and others, will be relevant; and they, no doubt, will link to questions about the innateness of intentional intent itself. There will be questions about the intentionality of dim or 'peripheral' awareness, and so on. For now this is enough.[60]

[60] This paper is a substantive reworking of Strawson 2004, which I was obliged to submit for publication before it was finished, and which appeared in an intermediate revised version as 'Stvarna intencionalnost 2' in *Filozofska Istrazivanja* vol. 102 (2006). I am grateful as before to Fiona Macpherson, Michelle Montague, and Dan Zahavi, and to participants in the 2002 NEH Summer Institute on 'Consciousness and Intentionality', where this paper began. I would also like to thank members of the 2004 CUNY Cognitive Science Symposium for their comments on an intermediate version, Christopher Pulman for pointing out a slip, and David Pitt for his very helpful comments on the original version.

12

On the Inevitability of Freedom
from the Compatibilist Point of View

According to standard compatibilist accounts of freedom, human beings act freely just in case they are, when they act, free from *constraints* of certain specified kinds. Such accounts of freedom are examples of what one may call *Constraint Compatibilism* (*CC*). I will argue that, properly understood, *CC* entails not only that we are virtually always able to act freely, but also that virtually all if not all our actual actions are free. The suggestion is not so much that this is a hitherto unnoticed consequence of *CC*, but, rather, that there is a certain way of conceiving of freedom implicit in *CC* that has not been taken sufficiently seriously.

1

One can distinguish act-theories and agent-theories of freedom. They aim to define 'free action' and 'free agent' respectively. The task of an *agent*-theory of freedom is to consider the various types of purposive agents, actual or possible,[1] and to say what a *purposive* agent must be like if it is to be, specifically, a *free* agent.

An *act*-theory of freedom presupposes the existence of an agent-theory. The main task of an act-theory is (1) to distinguish those sorts of circumstances in which a free agent (as defined by an agent-theory) is able to act freely from those sorts of circumstances in which it is not able to act freely (either in general, or in some particular way). An act-theory may also propose (2) to distinguish free actions from unfree or less than wholly free actions, among the actions of free agents. But this task is quite distinct from its main task. An act theory could in principle fulfil its main task without admitting the possibility of making this other distinction.

For present purposes I will assume that we have an agent-theory of freedom: I will assume that we have an acceptable compatibilist account of what an agent must be

As remarked in the Introduction, I think that this paper offers a general solution to the problem posed by Frankfurt's 1969 paper 'Alternate Possibilities and Moral Responsibility' (which I did not know at the time).

[1] Dogs, dolphins, human beings, Martians, etc.

like if it is to be a free agent, and that we ourselves are free agents according to this account. (All actual Constraint Compatibilists take this to be true; most of them simply assume it, without offering any detailed agent-theory of freedom at all.) Given such an agent-theory, we need an act-theory: given that we are free agents, we need to know in what circumstances we can and cannot, and in what circumstances we do, actually act freely.

CC is an act-theory; and, as remarked, it holds that a free agent acts freely just in case it acts, and is, with respect to the performance of that act, unconstrained. But the word 'unconstrained' is vague; and so, when it gets down to details, *CC* is usually much concerned with the specification of the particular kinds of constraints that are held to limit or eliminate freedom of action.[2] These details are of no importance to the present claim, however, which is entirely general in character, and is as follows: given the way in which *CC* supposes the presence of constraint to lead to the absence of freedom, it is committed to the view that if one is a free agent, then if one is able to act *at all* (in any given particular circumstances) one is *ipso facto* able to act *freely* (in those circumstances); and, similarly, that if one does act at all then one does act freely.

The point can initially be put as follows.

(1) Suppose that an action of some kind X is performed by an agent at some time t.[3] And call the occurrence of that which is held to constitute the action O.

Then

(2) it is integral to the notion of the agent's being genuinely able to perform an action of kind X at t that, in some ineliminable sense, the occurrence or non-occurrence of O, at t, must have been 'up to the agent'.

(3) Clearly, given the present compatibilism, the expression 'up to the agent' must be understood in such a way that it can be true that what happens is up to the agent even if determinism is true: it is true unless *constraints* are such that it is not up to the agent. (If constraints are such that it really is not up to the agent at all whether O occurs at t, then the agent cannot properly be held to have acted at all.)

But

(4) if the occurrence of O was indeed 'up to the agent', in the present sense, then the agent must (again relative to constraint, not determinism) have been both able to perform an action of kind X, at t, and able not to perform an action of kind X, at t.

For

(5) in some straightforward sense of 'initiated' that is entirely compatible with determinism (and materialism), the agent must itself have initiated the change that was the action, if it was indeed an action.

And

---

[2] Cf. Glover 1970.

[3] Here consideration is restricted to actions that are not intentional inactions, and that (roughly) involve some positive self-change or happening. See n5 below.

(6) it can truly be said to have done this, *as agent*, and in the required sense, at *t*, only if it can truly be said to have been able not to have done it, at *t*.[4]

It appears to follow immediately that a free agent is always able to act freely just so long as it is able to act at all; both in general, and with respect to any particular kind of action *X* which it is able to perform at any particular time *t*.[5] For, taking 'to *X*' to abbreviate 'to perform an action of kind *X*', the claim is that an agent must be both able to *X* and able not to *X* (or, to not-*X*), at time *t*, if it is truly able to *X* at all, at *t*.[6] It follows that the agent must be *unconstrained* at least in such a way that it is both able to *X* and able not to *X* (to not-*X*), at *t*. But if it is thus unconstrained with respect to *X*-ing, then (so the argument goes) it is *ipso facto* able to act *freely* in *X*-ing or not *X*-ing. That is, there is a fundamental sense of the phrase 'free action' in which this amount of unconstraint is already sufficient for free action, given *CC*'s account of free action. If the agent *X*-es (acts in any way) then it *ipso facto X*-es (acts) freely.

It is true that a threat or a natural accident may put a lot of pressure on one to do something—to *X*—that one would otherwise be very unwilling to do. But it is wrong to say that one is for that reason not able to act freely, in such a case: so long as one is indeed still both able to *X* and *able* not to, one is, in a natural and fundamental sense, free, absolutely free, either to *X* or not to *X* (to not-*X*). (This is discussed further in §3 below.)

Given *CC*, then, it seems that a free agent is actually able to act freely (given its capacities and circumstances) just so long as it is able (given its capacities and circumstances) to act at all. Since we are (when awake) virtually always if not always able to act in some way, it follows that we are virtually always if not always able to act freely. And for any particular kind of action *X*, if we can perform an action of kind *X* at all, at *t*, then, necessarily, we can also not perform an action of kind *X*.[7] That is, we must be *unconstrained* with respect to the performing or not performing of such an action, at the time we actually perform it, in such a way that if we *do* perform an action of that kind at that time then that action is, necessarily, a free action. So all our actions are free actions.

This is a very strong claim, and can hardly be maintained unqualified. A number of objections will be considered. One is worth discussing straight away, because it forces some changes in the phrasing of the argument.

---

[4] An agent can of course be in such a situation that if it does not act in a certain way at *t*, then its body will move at *t* in exactly the way in which it would have moved if the agent had acted in the way in question. But this is of no relevance to the present point. Its body may so move although it does not *act* at all. The problems that can be raised by reference to drug-addicts, or people who are subject to post-hypnotic commands, and so on, and of whom it may be claimed that they can truly be said to act in certain ways although they cannot not so act, will be considered below.

[5] In the case of actions (or 'actions') that are intentional inactions, where it is not so much a question of a change as of the absence of any change—a question of a 'non-change'—an agent can comprehensibly if inelegantly be said to cause a non-change to come to be or 'occur' simply in so far as an intentional inaction is the intentional not-doing of something *at a particular time* (or during a particular period of time). Here again, if the agent is truly able (relative to constraint, not determinism) to perform an action that is an intentional inaction, it must also be able not to do so.

[6] In fact this is not quite right; but it will do for the moment.

[7] This is still not quite right. See §2 below.

2

It may be objected that there are actions one can perform and yet cannot not perform. Suppose you are hanging on to two boats that are moving apart. You have to let go of one of them. It may be said that while you are able to perform the action of letting go with (at least) one hand, you are not able not to perform such an action; but although you are not able not to perform such an action, it is still an action you can perform. This raises no real problem. For here there are really at least two kinds of actions you can perform, and can also, therefore, not perform: you can let go, or not let go, with your right hand, and you can let go, or not let go, with your left hand. (You can also let go with both, of course.) For so long as this is true, whichever action you do perform you act freely in performing it, unattractive though your situation may be.[8] What this does show is that not just any action-kind description can be substituted for 'X', as it occurs in the argument in §1. But this does not amount to an objection to the strong claim, because the following remains true: whenever one is able to act at all, and does so, there will always be a true description of the action one performs given which it can be seen to be true that one could (relative to constraint) either have performed it or not have performed it, at the time of action. This description will reveal the vital sense in which it is true that if one acts at all then one is unconstrained in one's action in such a way that one's action is a free action—a fact that may be concealed by certain descriptions of what one does. All cases resembling the case just described are resoluble in the same kind of way.[9]

It may help to put the fundamental point in terms of doing rather than in terms of action. When a man a acts in some way, there are many different descriptions of what he does, in so acting (*or*: there are many different things he does).[10] There may even be several descriptions of what he does intentionally (*or*: there may be several things he does intentionally). But if he has acted at all, then it must be the case that there is something he did intentionally in so acting—call this thing ϕ—which is such that he could (relative to constraint) not have done ϕ. And for so long as this is true, he was not only able to act but also able to act freely.

Consider the example of the boats restated in the present terms. You know you cannot but let go with (at least) one hand, and you wonder which one it should be. Should you stay with your husband, who has two of your children, and food (left-hand boat), or with your other, third and youngest child (right-hand boat)? You are

---

[8] It is easy to tell a story in which your decision as to which action to perform has morally significant consequences. Telling such a story may make it clearer that such constricted choices can be fully free, as can the actions subsequently performed.

[9] Some intricate questions arise here, but they do not affect the main argument. Interesting problems in the philosophy of action arise from the fact (pointed out to me by Jennifer Hornsby) that there are apparently things one can do intentionally (in such a way that one's doing them is one's performing an action) which are also such that one cannot not do them. Thus human beings can move air (and/or oxygen) molecules intentionally; but it seems plausible to say that they cannot not move air (oxygen) molecules, so long as they are agents (and alive) at all. Such facts raise no problem for the present argument, however.

[10] I am not concerned with the relative merits of these two different ways of putting the matter.

shipwrecked, and the boats are ungovernable. You act. You let go with your left hand. You have acted, and in so acting you have done many things. There is something you have done intentionally which you couldn't not do: that is, let go with (at least) one hand. But there is also something you have done (that is, let go with your left hand), and have done intentionally, which you were (relative to constraint) able not to do. And so long as this is so, when you act, you act freely.

Whenever an agent acts, then, there is something that it does—ϕ—which is such that

(1) its acting is its ϕ-ing intentionally,

and

(2) it is true to say that it is when it acts both able to ϕ and able not to (though it cannot of course both ϕ and not-ϕ).

The objection currently being considered amounts to nothing more than the observation that not everything an agent does that fulfils (1) also fulfils (2).[11] But this is no objection to the claim that, given (1) and (2), there is a crucial sense in which all action is, just as such, necessarily unconstrained in such a way that *CC* is obliged to acknowledge that it is free action, or to the claim that there will in any particular case of action always be a way of describing what has happened that reveals how and why this is so.[12] (This said, it may also be observed that putatively problematic cases like the boat case are extremely rare.)

It might be thought that the essential point could be expressed in terms of the word 'power', simply as follows: if *a* is truly *able* (relative to constraint) to initiate and perform an action of kind *X*, at *t*, then it must be *in his power* (relative to constraint) to do so, at *t*. Obviously. But then it must also be in his power *not* to do so—for that is part of what it means to say that it is in his power to do so; the point is as simple as that.[13]

This way of putting it does again capture the essential point, but it is still open to the 'letting go with one hand' kind of objection just considered. A more careful statement is still needed, therefore. The conclusion remains the same. If a free agent acts at all, then it must be unconstrained in such a way that it acts freely in so acting. For the degree of unconstraint which is a necessary condition of all action whatever is sufficient condition of *free* action, according to a properly worked out *CC*.

It is—to recapitulate the argument in a rather more exotic form—a condition of something's counting as *a*'s action, as an actual intentional initiation of something by *a*, that it could (relative to constraint) possibly not have been thus initiated by *a*. A

---

[11] If, for example, ϕ = *letting go with (at least) one hand*, (1) is true but (2) is not.

[12] It would be wrong to think that what the more careful statement says is that the actions of free agents 'have descriptions under which' they are free actions, or some such thing. The claim is rather that all the actions of free agents are free actions, without any relativization to descriptions, and that a valid description of an action will always be available to show how this is so, in any particular case.

[13] Perhaps your hand will be forced down onto the button, if you do not press it. But you will in that case perform no action of pressing the button. (You will probably perform the action of resisting the downward pressure on your hand.)

fully intentional doing on the part of *a* must in some clear sense be a positive change made by *a*, who must be (so to say) properly situated in the field of the possibility of both making and not making the change. It is constitutive of the change's being an intentional doing, an action, that it occur in a field of possibility constituted by the agent's control of himself which is such that, up to the moment at which the change is brought about, it could (relative to constraint, not determinism) both have happened and not have happened.

I turn now to consider some other objections.

3

If all the actions of free agents are free actions, then the natural act-theory distinction between free actions and unfree or less than wholly free actions has no application, in the case of free agents. But most compatibilists would wish to reject this conclusion. So how might it be defended?[14]

One can dismiss one huge range of supposed cases of unfree action straight away. Consider a bank clerk at gunpoint, who calmly submits to a gangster's demands and hands over the money in her possession. She does not panic. She acts deliberately and after due consideration. And so she acts both freely and responsibly. For she chooses so to act, fully aware that she could do otherwise, simply refuse, try to dive under the counter, try to raise the alarm, and so on. This being so, she will find it extremely odd if someone says 'You were not responsible for what you did', rather than 'You were not responsible for what happened'. She may object strongly to such a comment. Someone better informed about her state of mind may say 'You acted very responsibly, in the circumstances', or 'You made the right decision'—implying freedom of decision.

She acts completely freely, on the present account, and is fully responsible for what she does. The point is simply that she is not blameworthy. It is not freedom or responsibility that is diminished by such constraint as this, but only blameworthiness. Something that is considered blameworthy in normal circumstances is not considered blameworthy in circumstances such as these. Symmetrical considerations apply to potentially praiseworthy actions.[15]

The same goes for the clerk's freedom of choice: so long as she is fully or genuinely aware that she is now both able to hand over the money and able not to hand over the money, she is *ipso facto* able to choose freely whether to do so or not. The gangster's gun does not diminish this freedom in any way—unless it causes panic, and blots out this awareness. But in the case of panic, her freedom of choice is not merely diminished. It seems, rather, that it is, with respect to the particular choice in question, annihilated: there seems to be an important sense in which ability to choose,

---

[14] The actions of purposive agents that are not free agents at all may be said to be unfree, of course. But their case is of little interest. What many compatibilists want to say is that free agents—ourselves, say—can act unfreely.

[15] Cf. Frankfurt 1975.

and, hence, freedom of choice, is all-or-nothing.[16] In which case there are no cases of unfree or less than wholly free choices: to be genuinely able to choose just is to be able to choose freely, from the compatibilist point of view, just as to be genuinely able to act just is to be able to act freely.

Sartre's claim that we are 'condemned to freedom' seems pertinent here. We are not free to choose whether or not to be free to choose (though the case can be imagined—we might now be free to choose whether or not to continue to be free to choose, or whether to submit to an operation that would deprive us of this freedom). If we are free at all, we are bound by our natures to be free. It is our inalienable gift (or burden), so long as we continue to be conscious and *compos mentis*. It is undiminished by imprisonment—and not because one may when imprisoned take an Epictetan view of one's circumstances. Imprisonment may restrict one's choices, but one remains fully free in the basic compatibilist sense. There remain many things that one can do or not do and can choose to do or not to do, and the ability to act freely disappears only when there is not even one kind of action one can perform or not perform. Given the present compatibilist account according to which we are free agents, it is probably true to say that very few if any of those who read this will, in their adult lives, ever have been in a situation in which they were not absolutely free agents, fully and inescapably able to act and choose completely freely. Just as one can act freely so long as one can act at all, so too there is a fundamental sense in which one has total freedom of choice so long as one has choice at all, however unpleasant the options are. After all, freedom of choice cannot be supposed to involve a completely unrestricted range of options; it is always somehow restricted. And, obviously, two options, however unattractive, are always minimally sufficient for genuine choice, so long as they are indeed what they are called—options.

Consider the question from another angle. Belief in freedom is often expressed as belief that one could do otherwise than one does do, in a given situation. This belief is very resilient under coercion; and, on the present compatibilist view (according to which the belief is false only if some constraint makes it so), it is very rarely false. For it is very rare that our actions or choices are determined by a post-hypnotic command or anything else that could count as a constraint of the sort that genuinely removes freedom of action or choice. Faced with the threat that a helpless child will be tortured for so long as one refuses to comply with some outrageous demand, one complies, if one does, not because one believes one could not possibly do otherwise, but because one is not prepared to do otherwise. In such a situation one acts freely and responsibly, but, quite possibly, not blameworthily.[17]

---

[16] Of course the mind can be slippery with self-deception, and fear. But so far as the presence or absence of awareness of options is concerned, one's situation is, in the borderline cases, much more like that of a light with a faulty connection which may flicker on and off, but which is either fully on or fully off, than it is like that of a light that can brighten and dim steadily along a continuous range.

[17] People may, like Luther, express their commitments by saying that they could not possibly have done other than they did do, but they will—unless they are idiotically fanatical—be prepared to admit the crucial, straightforward, common-sense sense in which they could have done other than they did.

True, to say that one does not act freely in such a case accords with one important way in which we use the word 'free'. But, given a properly developed *CC*, the sense according to which we can and do (and cannot but) act completely freely and responsibly in such a situation, if we are free agents at all, remains philosophically paramount.

4

Suppose that one agrees with this approach: one takes the whole vast class of cases of action in which (a) freedom and responsibility have traditionally and mistakenly held to be diminished or eliminated on account of the presence of various sorts of constraints, although (b) the constraints are not in fact really such that the agent really can do nothing but the thing it does do, and one denies that such cases are really cases of unfree or less than wholly free action. The only cases that then remain to be considered, so far as the question of whether there can be unfree (or less than wholly free) actions is concerned, are those cases that involve such rare things as kleptomania, obsessional neurosis and post-hypnotic command; cases where there is allegedly an action although it really is true that the agent couldn't not perform (or rather 'perform') it.

These cases are more difficult to deal with. I will first try to suggest how one might treat them if one wished to maintain unqualified the view that all the actions of free agents are free actions. Then I will briefly consider the concession that there can after all be said to be unfree actions.

Those who seek to defend the view that there is an act-theory distinction to be drawn between free and unfree (or less than wholly free) actions may first of all claim that most kleptomaniac thefts or obsessionally neurotic performances must be supposed to be intentionally carried out in *some* sense, for most of them clearly involve controlled and perhaps very complex bodily movement. They may then argue that this gives us very good reason to call these things *actions*, while the fact that kleptomania and obsessional neurosis are psychical constraints which can be such that the agent subject to them cannot but do what it does gives us good reason to say that they are not *free* actions. Therefore they are unfree actions.

Other apparently clear cases of unfree action involve post-hypnotic commands. *a* thinks he is choosing between pushing button *X* and pushing button *Y*—between *X*-ing and *Y*-ing, for short. But he is in fact being compelled to choose (or rather 'choose') to *X*, by a post-hypnotic command to *X*. He makes his apparent choice, and *X*-es. *X*-ing, he acts intentionally, and in a controlled and perhaps complicated fashion. As far as anyone including himself is aware, he acts completely normally. Surely this is a case of action? But since he was compelled by hypnotic command, it is an unfree action.

Replying first to this second case, and seeking to uphold the absolute view according to which all actions performed by free agents are free actions, one may grant that *a*'s *X*-ing is indeed unfree. But one must then claim that it is not an action, although it seems just like one.

A defence of this view might go as follows. It is not an action, for it is not *a*'s action if *a* truly cannot not do it (and it is certainly not anyone else's, such as the hypnotist's). It seems just like an action simply because the constraint is as it were routed through, and exploits, *a*'s normal action-producing and action-controlling system. But *a* is in effect taken over; he himself—he as we normally conceive him, the agent, the subject—does not act.

This may be found implausible. But is it? If *a* really cannot not *X* (relative to constraint), and yet produces an apparently intentional controlled movement of precisely the kind that is produced when he is both able to *X* and able not to *X*, and then *X*-es intentionally, there must be something quite extraordinary going on inside him. And it seems plausible to say that what is going on is, precisely, an exploitation of his normal action-producing and action-controlling system; an exploitation which is of such a kind that he himself does not act. We are deluded into thinking that there is an action precisely because something that must be counted as external to *a* so far as he is considered as an agent is routed through this system, and so causes something that looks just like an action to occur. But it is not really an action; for *a* is in a clear sense essentially constituted as an agent at *t*, with respect to any kind of action, by the property of being-able-to-do-or-not-do an action of that kind at *t*, and it is precisely this property that he does not now have, with respect to *X*-ing. So his *X*-ing now cannot be an action on his part. As remarked in §1, able-to-do-or-not-do-ness is a fundamental feature and necessary condition of all genuine intentional agency, and it is *ex hypothesi* true that *a* does not possess it, with respect to *X*-ing, in the present case.

One can also make the point by reference to the notion of responsibility, as follows. (1) Those who hold that there are unfree actions hold that those who perform such actions are not responsible for them, because they are unfree actions. (2) All action—all action properly speaking—is intentional action (the phrase 'intentional action' is, properly speaking, a pleonasm). (3) But if one is inclined to say that *a* is not *responsible* at all for what he did, surely one should be equally inclined to say that *a* did not really *act* (act intentionally) at all. For (4) it is really very odd indeed to say that *a* has acted intentionally and yet is in no way responsible for his action. How *can* one act intentionally and yet not be in any way responsible for one's action (within the compatibilist framework). It seems much more plausible to say that *a*—the person, the agent—did not really act at all, given that he is *in no way* responsible for what happened, than to say that he did act, but unfreely, and in such a way that he is in no way whatsoever responsible for what happened.[18]

Some may still wish to say that there is action in this case. And one reason for this may be that they shy away from the fact that we are simply complex psychophysical mechanisms, whatever else we also are. They do not like to think that we can, as mechanisms, be *used* in such a way that it looks exactly as if we are acting although we are not acting at all. But we can be so used: we do possess or contain complex

---

[18] Remember the level-headed bank clerk. She is not blameworthy when she hands over the money, but she is certainly *responsible* for her action. If she were not even *responsible* for her action—well, how could this be? How could it be true to say that it was really her action at all, an intentional action that she had performed, if she was not responsible for it?

intention-forming bodily-movement-controlling systems; and elements that are not the agent's intentions at all, and yet have exactly the same functional consequences as his intentions, can arise in or be introduced into this system in such a way that complex bodily movements ensue without the agent acting at all.

The same sorts of considerations apply to the first sort of cases mentioned above, cases of kleptomania and obsessional neurosis. These are less clear than cases of post-hypnotic command, however. For they are cases in which it is almost invariably much less clear whether the constraints on the agent which lead it to do what it does do are of such a kind that it really cannot but do what it does do.

It can, certainly, be maintained that the unclear cases are never cases of unfree or less than wholly free action, and that what is unclear is simply whether they are cases of action at all (and therefore *ipso facto* cases of free action), or whether they are cases of the compulsion (and therefore *ipso facto* not cases of action at all). But there are many complications here, and there would perhaps be little point in insisting on the all-or-nothing view.[19]

The all-or-nothing view is not in any case presupposed by the main conclusion of this paper: the conclusion (a) that if we are free agents at all, in the way that most compatibilist theories of freedom suppose we are, then virtually all if not all our actual actions are free actions; and (b) that we are virtually always if not always able to act freely. The fact that there are very murky cases, cases that may look like cases of unfree action, does not show that not all our actions are free; it may just be that in some situations no one can really tell whether someone who has done something has performed an action or responded to compulsion.[20]

But the point need not be pressed. Such cases are in any event extremely rare. And what remains true is that there is a fundamental sense in which, if one is a free agent, and if, as compatibilists suppose, free action is a matter of being able to do otherwise than one does (relative to constraint, not determinism), then all one's actions, all one's intentional self-change, must be free; simply because such 'being able to do otherwise' (relative to constraint) is not just a sufficient condition of free action, but also a necessary condition of all action.[21] Even if we do allow that actions and choices may be unfree, given the presence of certain constraints, I suspect that I have never

---

[19] This is very programmatic indeed. Defence of the all-or-nothing view requires, among other things, very careful consideration of what can be supposed to count as total constraint. I will mention just one problem case. A hypnotist induces in *a* a wish to *X* which is very likely to lead to an intention to *X*, but which is designed not to be compulsively overriding: it has to compete for a chance of fulfilment with *a*'s other wishes If *a* does *X*, then, he presumably retains the property of 'able-to-do-or-not-to-do-ness' with respect to *X*-ing, and can therefore reasonably be said to act. And yet it is arguable that his action is unfree simply on account of the provenance of the wish.

[20] Clearly the agent's own opinion is of no special significance. In the case of the post-hypnotic command *a* may be convinced that he has performed a fully intentional action.

[21] No objection can be raised by reference to cases in which one wants to do what one is compelled to do, cannot not do, and would have done anyway if one had had a choice in the matter. It remains true that if one's doing what one does is caused by the compulsion, then one does not act freely, or indeed act at all; nor is one morally accountable, praiseworthy or blameworthy, on account of what one does, although one's intentions or character may be found admirable or reprehensible in such a case.

really acted unfreely, and that the same is true of you. On the present view, human beings are born free, and everywhere remain so, whether they like it or not.[22]

---

[22] In fact, of course, libertarians can have as much reason to accept this general view as compatibilists. One challenge to it starts out from the claim that unconscious motives may not only give rise to such obviously pathological phenomena as the repetitious performances of obsessional neurosis (for example), but may also influence (or constrain) many of our most ordinary seeming actions in such a way that they are not really free actions. Discussion of this view is outside the scope of this paper, but one problem with it is that it risks treating too many of our ordinary actions as unfree actions. Indeed it may end up treating the conscious agent as some sort of plaything of the unconscious.

13

The Impossibility of Ultimate Moral Responsibility

1

There is an argument, which I will call the Basic Argument, which appears to prove that we cannot be truly or ultimately morally responsible for our actions. According to the Basic Argument, it makes no difference whether determinism is true or false. We cannot be truly or ultimately morally responsible for our actions in either case.

The Basic Argument has various expressions in the literature of free will, and its central idea can be quickly conveyed. (1) Nothing can be *causa sui*—nothing can be the cause of itself. (2) In order to be truly morally responsible for one's actions one would have to be *causa sui*, at least in certain crucial mental respects. (3) Therefore nothing can be truly morally responsible.

In this paper I want to reconsider the Basic Argument, in the hope that anyone who thinks that we can be truly or ultimately morally responsible for our actions will be prepared to say exactly what is wrong with it. I think that the point that it has to make is obvious, and that it has been underrated in recent discussion of free will—perhaps because it admits of no answer. I suspect that it is obvious in such a way that insisting on it too much is likely to make it seem less obvious than it is, given the innate contra-suggestibility of human beings in general and philosophers in particular. But I am not worried about making it seem less obvious than it is so long as it gets adequate attention. As far as its validity is concerned, it can look after itself.

A more cumbersome statement of the Basic Argument goes as follows.[1]

(1) Interested in free action, we are particularly interested in actions that are performed for a reason (as opposed to 'reflex' actions or mindlessly habitual actions).

(2) When one acts for a reason, what one does is a function of how one is, mentally speaking. (It is also a function of one's height, one's strength, one's place and time, and so on. But the mental factors are crucial when moral responsibility is in question.)

(3) So if one is to be truly responsible for how one acts, one must be truly responsible for how one is, mentally speaking—at least in certain respects.

(4) But to be truly responsible for how one is, mentally speaking, in certain respects, one must have brought it about that one is the way one is, mentally speaking, in certain respects. And it

---

[1] Adapted from G. Strawson, 1986: 28–30.

is not merely that one must have caused oneself to be the way one is, mentally speaking. One must have consciously and explicitly chosen to be the way one is, mentally speaking, in certain respects, and one must have succeeded in bringing it about that one is that way.

(5) But one cannot really be said to choose, in a conscious, reasoned, fashion, to be the way one is mentally speaking, in any respect at all, unless one already exists, mentally speaking, already equipped with some principles of choice, 'P1'—preferences, values, pro-attitudes, ideals—in the light of which one chooses how to be.

(6) But then to be truly responsible, on account of having chosen to be the way one is, mentally speaking, in certain respects, one must be truly responsible for one's having the principles of choice P1 in the light of which one chose how to be.

(7) But for this to be so one must have chosen P1, in a reasoned, conscious, intentional fashion.

(8) But for this, that is, (7), to be so one must already have had some principles of choice P2, in the light of which one chose P1.

(9) And so on. Here we are setting out on a regress that we cannot stop. True self-determination is impossible because it requires the actual completion of an infinite series of choices of principles of choice.[2]

(10) So true moral responsibility is impossible, because it requires true self-determination, as noted in (3).

This may seem contrived, but essentially the same argument can be given in a more natural form. (1) It is undeniable that one is the way one is, initially, as a result of heredity and early experience, and it is undeniable that these are things for which one cannot be held to be in any way responsible (morally or otherwise). (2) One cannot at any later stage of life hope to accede to true moral responsibility for the way one is by trying to change the way one already is as a result of heredity and previous experience. For (3) both the particular way in which one is moved to try to change oneself, and the degree of one's success in one's attempt at change, will be determined by how one already is as a result of heredity and previous experience. And (4) any further changes that one can bring about only after one has brought about certain initial changes will in turn be determined, via the initial changes, by heredity and previous experience. (5) This may not be the whole story, for it may be that some changes in the way one is are traceable not to heredity and experience but to the influence of indeterministic or random factors. But it is absurd to suppose that indeterministic or random factors, for which one is *ex hypothesi* in no way responsible, can in themselves contribute in any way to one's being truly morally responsible for how one is.

The claim, then, is not that people cannot change the way they are. They can, in certain respects (which tend to be exaggerated by North Americans and underestimated, perhaps, by Europeans). The claim is only that people cannot be supposed to change themselves in such a way as to be or become truly or ultimately morally responsible for the way they are, and hence for their actions.

---

[2] That is, the infinite series must have a beginning and an end, which is impossible.

2

I have encountered two main reactions to the Basic Argument. On the one hand it convinces almost all the students with whom I have discussed the topic of free will and moral responsibility.[3] On the other hand it often tends to be dismissed, in contemporary discussion of free will and moral responsibility, as wrong, or irrelevant, or fatuous, or too rapid, or an expression of metaphysical megalomania. I think that the Basic Argument is certainly valid in showing that we cannot be morally responsible in the way that many suppose. And I think that it is the natural light, not fear, that has convinced the students I have taught that this is so. That is why it seems worthwhile to restate the argument in a slightly different—simpler and looser—version, and to ask again what is wrong with it.

Some may say that there is nothing wrong with it, but that it is not very interesting, and not very central to the free will debate. I doubt whether any non-philosopher or beginner in philosophy would agree with this view. If one wants to think about free will and moral responsibility, consideration of some version of the Basic Argument is an overwhelmingly natural place to start. It certainly has to be considered at some point in a full discussion of free will and moral responsibility, even if the point it has to make is obvious. Belief in the kind of absolute moral responsibility that it shows to be impossible has for a long time been central to the Western religious, moral, and cultural tradition, even if it is now slightly on the wane (a disputable view). It is a matter of historical fact that concern about moral responsibility has been the main motor—indeed the *ratio essendi*—of discussion of the issue of free will. The only way in which one might hope to show (1) that the Basic Argument is not central to the free will debate would be to show (2) that the issue of moral responsibility is not central to the free will debate. There are, obviously, ways of taking the word 'free' in which (2) can be maintained. But (2) is clearly false nonetheless.[4]

In saying that the notion of moral responsibility criticized by the Basic Argument is central to the Western tradition, I am not suggesting that it is some artificial and local Judaeo–Christian–Kantian construct that is found nowhere else in the history of the peoples of the world, although even if it were that would hardly diminish its interest and importance for us. It is natural to suppose that Aristotle also subscribed to it,[5] and it is significant that anthropologists have suggested that most human societies can be classified either as 'guilt cultures' or as 'shame cultures'. It is true that neither of these two fundamental moral emotions necessarily presupposes a conception of oneself as truly morally responsible for what one has done. But the fact that both are widespread

---

[3] Two have rejected it in fifteen years. Both had religious commitments, and argued, on general and radical sceptical grounds, that we can know almost nothing, and cannot therefore know that true moral responsibility is not possible in some way that we do not understand.

[4] It is notable that both Robert Kane (1989) and Alfred Mele (1995), in two of the best recent incompatibilist discussions of free will and autonomy, have relatively little to say about moral responsibility.

[5] Cf. *Nichomachean Ethics* III. 5.

does at least suggest that a conception of moral responsibility similar to our own is a natural part of the human moral-conceptual repertoire.

In fact the notion of moral responsibility connects more tightly with the notion of guilt than with the notion of shame. In many cultures shame can attach to one because of what some member of one's family—or government—has done, and not because of anything one has done oneself; and in such cases the feeling of shame need not (although it may) involve some obscure, irrational feeling that one is somehow responsible for the behaviour of one's family or government. The case of guilt is less clear. There is no doubt that people can feel guilty (or can believe that they feel guilty) about things for which they are not responsible, let alone morally responsible. But it is much less obvious that they can do this without any sense or belief that they are in fact responsible.

3

Such complications are typical of moral psychology, and they show that it is important to try to be precise about what sort of responsibility is under discussion. What sort of 'true' moral responsibility is being said to be both impossible and widely believed in?

An old story is very helpful in clarifying this question. This is the story of heaven and hell. As I understand it, true moral responsibility is responsibility of such a kind that, if we have it, then it *makes sense*, at least, to suppose that it could be just to punish some of us with (eternal) torment in hell and reward others with (eternal) bliss in heaven. The stress on the words 'makes sense' is important, for one certainly does not have to believe in any version of the story of heaven and hell in order to understand the notion of true moral responsibility that it is being used to illustrate. Nor does one have to believe in any version of the story of heaven and hell in order to believe in the existence of true moral responsibility. On the contrary: many atheists have believed in the existence of true moral responsibility. The story of heaven and hell is useful simply because it illustrates, in a peculiarly vivid way, the *kind* of absolute or ultimate accountability or responsibility that many have supposed themselves to have, and that many do still suppose themselves to have. It very clearly expresses its scope and force.

But one does not have to refer to religious faith in order to describe the sorts of everyday situation that are perhaps primarily influential in giving rise to our belief in true responsibility. Suppose you set off for a shop on the evening of a national holiday, intending to buy a cake with your last ten pound note. On the steps of the shop someone is shaking an Oxfam tin. You stop, and it seems completely clear to you that it is entirely up to you what you do next. That is, it seems to you that you are truly, radically free to choose, in such a way that you will be ultimately morally responsible for whatever you do choose. Even if you believe that determinism is true, and that you will in five minutes time be able to look back and say that what you did was determined, this does not seem to undermine your sense of the absoluteness and inescapability of your freedom, and of your moral responsibility for your choice. The same seems to be true even if you accept the validity of the Basic Argument stated in §1, which concludes that one cannot be in any way ultimately responsible for the way one is and decides. In both cases, it remains true that as one stands there, one's freedom and true moral responsibility seem obvious and absolute to one.

Large and small, morally significant or morally neutral, such situations of choice occur regularly in human life. I think they lie at the heart of the experience of freedom and moral responsibility. They are the fundamental source of our inability to give up belief in true or ultimate moral responsibility. There are further questions to be asked about why human beings experience these situations of choice as they do. It is an interesting question whether any cognitively sophisticated, rational, self-conscious agent must experience situations of choice in this way.[6] But they are the experiential rock on which the belief in true moral responsibility is founded.

4

I will restate the Basic Argument. First, though, I will give some examples of people who have accepted that some sort of true or ultimate responsibility for the way one is is a necessary condition of true or ultimate moral responsibility for the way one acts, and who, certain that they are ultimately morally responsible for the way they act, have believed the condition to be fulfilled.[7]

E. H. Carr held that 'normal adult human beings are morally responsible for their own personality'. Jean-Paul Sartre talked of 'the choice that each man makes of his personality', and held that 'man is responsible for what he is'. In a later interview he judged that his earlier assertions about freedom were incautious; but he still held that 'in the end one is always responsible for what is made of one' in some absolute sense. Kant described the position very clearly when he claimed that 'man *himself* must make or have made himself into whatever, in a moral sense, whether good or evil, he is to become. Either condition must be an effect of his free choice; for otherwise he could not be held responsible for it and could therefore be *morally* neither good nor evil.' Since he was committed to belief in radical moral responsibility, Kant held that such self-creation does indeed take place, and wrote accordingly of 'man's character, which he himself creates', and of 'knowledge of oneself as a person who . . . is his own originator'. John Patten, a former British Minister for Education and a Catholic apparently preoccupied by the idea of sin, claimed that 'it is . . . self-evident that as we grow up each individual chooses whether to be good or bad'. It seems clear enough that he saw such choice as sufficient to give us true moral responsibility of the heaven-and-hell variety.[8]

---

[6] Cf. MacKay (1960), and the discussion of the 'Genuine Incompatibilist Determinist' in Strawson 1986: 281–6.

[7] I suspect that they have started out from their subjective certainty that they have ultimate moral responsibility. They have then been led by reflection to the realization that they cannot really have such moral responsibility if they are not in some crucial way responsible for being the way they are. They have accordingly concluded that they are indeed responsible for being the way they are.

[8] Carr in *What Is History?*, p. 89; Sartre in *Being and Nothingness, Existentialism and Humanism*, p. 29, and in the *New Left Review* 1969 (quoted in Wiggins 1975); Kant in *Religion within the*

The rest of us are not usually so reflective, but it seems that we do tend, in some vague and unexamined fashion, to think of ourselves as responsible for—answerable for—how we are. The point is quite a delicate one, for we do not ordinarily suppose that we have gone through some sort of active process of self-determination at some particular past time. Nevertheless it seems accurate to say that we do unreflectively experience ourselves, in many respects, rather as we might experience ourselves if we did believe that we had engaged in some such activity of self-determination.

Sometimes a part of one's character—a desire or tendency—may strike one as foreign or alien. But it can do this only against a background of character traits that are not experienced as foreign, but are rather 'identified' with (it is a necessary truth that it is only relative to such a background that a character trait can stand out as alien). Some feel tormented by impulses that they experience as alien, but in many a sense of general identification with their character predominates, and this identification seems to carry within itself an implicit sense that one is, generally, somehow in control of and answerable for how one is (even, perhaps, for aspects of one's character that one does not like). Here, then, I suggest that we find, semi-dormant in common thought, an implicit recognition of the idea that true or ultimate moral responsibility for what one does somehow involves responsibility for how one is. Ordinary thought is ready to move this way under pressure.

There is, however, another powerful tendency in ordinary thought to think that one can be ultimately morally responsible even if one's character is ultimately wholly non-self-determined—simply because one is fully self-consciously aware of oneself as an agent facing choices. I will return to this point later on.

5

Let me now restate the Basic Argument in very loose—as it were conversational—terms. New forms of words allow for new forms of objection, but they may be helpful nonetheless.

(1) You do what you do, in any situation in which you find yourself, because of the way you are.

So

(2) To be truly morally responsible for what you do you must be truly responsible for the way you are—at least in certain crucial mental respects.

Limits of Reason Alone, p. 40, *The Critique of Practical Reason*, p. 101 (Ak. V. 98), and in *Opus Postumum*, p. 213; Patten in *The Spectator*, January 1992.

These quotations raise many questions which I will not consider. It is often hard, for example, to be sure what Sartre is saying. But the occurrence of the quoted phrases is significant on any plausible interpretation of his views. As for Kant, it may be thought to be odd that he says what he does, in so far as he grounds the possibility of our freedom in our possession of an unknowable, non-temporal noumenal nature. It is, however, plausible to suppose that he thinks that radical or ultimate self-determination must take place even in the noumenal realm, in some unintelligibly non-temporal manner, if there is to be true moral responsibility.

Or:

(1) What you intentionally do, given the circumstances in which you (believe you) find yourself, flows necessarily from how you are.

Hence

(2) You have to get to have some responsibility for how you are in order to get to have some responsibility for what you intentionally do, given the circumstances in which you (believe you) find yourself.

Comment: once again the qualification about 'certain mental respects' is one I will take for granted. Obviously one is not responsible for one's sex, one's basic body pattern, one's height, and so on. But if one were not responsible for anything about oneself, how could one be responsible for what one did, given the truth of (1)? This is the fundamental question, and it seems clear that if one is going to be responsible for any aspect of oneself, it had better be some aspect of one's mental nature.

I take it that (1) is incontrovertible, and that it is (2) that must be resisted. For if (1) and (2) are conceded the case seems lost, because the full argument runs as follows.

(1) You do what you do because of the way you are.

So

(2) To be truly morally responsible for what you do you must be truly responsible for the way are—at least in certain crucial mental respects.

But

(3) You cannot be truly responsible for the way you are, so you cannot be truly responsible for what you do.

Why can't you be truly responsible for the way you are? Because

(4) To be truly responsible for the way you are, you must have intentionally brought it about that you are the way you are, and this is impossible.

Why is it impossible? Well, suppose it is not. Suppose that

(5) You have somehow intentionally brought it about that you are the way you now are, and that you have brought this about in such a way that you can now be said to be truly responsible for being the way you are now.

For this to be true

(6) You must already have had a certain nature N in the light of which you intentionally brought it about that you are as you now are.

But then

(7) For it to be true you and you alone are truly responsible for how you now are, you must be truly responsible for having had the nature N in the light of which you intentionally brought it about that you are the way you now are.

So

> You must have intentionally brought it about that you had that nature N, in which case you must have existed already with a prior nature in the light of which you intentionally brought it about that you had the nature N in the light of which you intentionally brought it about that you are the way you now are . . .

Here one is setting off on the regress. Nothing can be *causa sui* in the required way. Even if such causal 'aseity' is allowed to belong unintelligibly to God, it cannot be plausibly be supposed to be possessed by ordinary finite human beings. 'The *causa sui* is the best self-contradiction that has been conceived so far', as Nietzsche remarked in 1886:

> it is a sort of rape and perversion of logic. But the extravagant pride of man has managed to entangle itself profoundly and frightfully with just this nonsense. The desire for 'freedom of the will' in the superlative metaphysical sense, which still holds sway, unfortunately, in the minds of the half-educated; the desire to bear the entire and ultimate responsibility for one's actions oneself, and to absolve God, the world, ancestors, chance, and society involves nothing less than to be precisely this *causa sui* and, with more than Baron Münchhausen's audacity, to pull oneself up into existence by the hair, out of the swamps of nothingness . . . (*Beyond Good and Evil*, §21).

The rephrased argument is essentially exactly the same as before, although the first two steps are now more simply stated. It may seem pointless to repeat it, but the questions remain. Can the Basic Argument simply be dismissed? Is it really of no importance in the discussion of free will and moral responsibility? (No and No) Shouldn't any serious defence of free will and moral responsibility thoroughly acknowledge the respect in which the Basic Argument is valid before going on to try to give its own positive account of the nature of free will and moral responsibility? Doesn't the argument go to the heart of things if the heart of the free will debate is a concern about whether we can be truly or ultimately morally responsible in the absolute way that we ordinarily suppose? (Yes and Yes)

We are what we are, and we cannot be thought to have made ourselves *in such a way* that we can be held to be free in our actions *in such a way* that we can be held to be morally responsible for our actions *in such a way* that any punishment or reward for our actions is ultimately just or fair. Punishments and rewards may seem deeply appropriate or intrinsically 'fitting' to us in spite of this argument, and many of the various institutions of punishment and reward in human society appear to be practically indispensable in both their legal and non-legal forms. But if one takes the notion of justice that is central to our intellectual and cultural tradition seriously, then the evident consequence of the Basic Argument is that there is a fundamental sense in which no punishment or reward is ever ultimately just. It is exactly as just to punish or reward people for their actions as it is to punish or reward them for the (natural) colour of their hair or the (natural) shape of their faces. The point seems obvious, and yet it contradicts a fundamental part of our natural self-conception, and there are elements in human thought that move very deeply against it. When it comes to questions of responsibility, we tend to feel that we are somehow responsible for the way we are. Even more importantly, perhaps, we tend to feel that our explicit self-conscious awareness of ourselves as agents who are able to deliberate about what to do, in situations of choice, suffices to constitute us as morally responsible free agents in the strongest sense, whatever the conclusion of the Basic Argument.

6

I have suggested that it is step (2) of the restated Basic Argument that must be rejected, and of course it can be rejected, because the phrases 'truly responsible' and 'truly morally responsible' can be defined in many ways. I will briefly consider three sorts of response to the Basic Argument, and I will concentrate on their more simple expressions, in the belief that truth in philosophy, especially in areas of philosophy like the present one, is almost never very complicated.

(i) The first response is *compatibilist*. Compatibilists believe that one can be a free and morally responsible agent even if determinism is true. Roughly, they claim, with many variations of detail, that one may correctly be said to be truly responsible for what one does, when one acts, just so long as one is not caused to act by any of a certain set of constraints (kleptomaniac impulses, obsessional neuroses, desires that are experienced as alien, post-hypnotic commands, threats, instances of *force majeure*, and so on). Clearly, this sort of compatibilist responsibility does not require that one should be truly responsible for how one is in any way at all, and so step (2) of the Basic Argument comes out as false. One can have compatibilist responsibility even if the way one is is totally determined by factors entirely outside one's control.

It is for this reason, however, that compatibilist responsibility famously fails to amount to any sort of true *moral* responsibility, given the natural, strong understanding of the notion of true moral responsibility (characterized above by reference to the story of heaven and hell). One does what one does entirely because of the way one is, and one is in no way ultimately responsible for the way one is. So how can one be justly punished for anything one does? Compatibilists have given increasingly refined accounts of the circumstances in which punishment may be said to be appropriate or intrinsically fitting. But they can do nothing against this basic objection.

Many compatibilists have never supposed otherwise. They are happy to admit the point. They observe that the notions of true moral responsibility and justice that are employed in the objection cannot possibly have application to anything real, and suggest that the objection is therefore not worth considering. In response, proponents of the Basic Argument agree that the notions of true moral responsibility and justice in question cannot have application to anything real; but they make no apologies for considering them. They consider them because they are central to ordinary thought about moral responsibility and justice. So far as most people are concerned, they are the subject, if the subject is moral responsibility and justice.

(ii) The second response is *libertarian*. Incompatibilists believe that freedom and moral responsibility are incompatible with determinism, and some of them are libertarians, who believe that that we are free and morally responsible agents, and that determinism is therefore false. In an ingenious statement of the incompatibilist-libertarian case, Robert Kane argues that agents in an undetermined world can have free will, for they can 'have the power to make choices for which they have ultimate responsibility'. That is, they can 'have the power to make choices which can only and finally be explained in terms of their own wills (i.e. character, motives, and efforts of will)'.[9] Roughly, Kane sees this power as grounded in the possible occurrence, in agents, of efforts of will that have two main features: first, they are partly indeterministic in their nature, and hence indeterminate in their outcome; second, they occur in cases in which agents are trying to make a difficult choice between the options that their characters dispose them to consider. (The paradigm cases will be cases in which they face a conflict between moral duty and non-moral desire.)

But the old objection to libertarianism recurs. How can this indeterminism help with moral responsibility? Granted that the truth of determinism rules out true moral responsibility, how can the falsity of determinism help? How can the occurrence of partly random or indeterministic events contribute in any way to one's being truly morally responsible either for one's actions or for one's character? If my efforts of will shape my character in an admirable way, and in so doing are partly indeterministic in nature, while also being shaped (as Kane grants) by my already existing character, why am I not merely lucky?

The general objection applies equally whether determinism is true or false, and can be restated as follows. We are born with a great many genetically determined predispositions for which we are not responsible. We are subject to many early influences for which we are not responsible. These decisively shape our characters, our motives, the general bent and strength of our capacity to make efforts of will. We may later engage in conscious and intentional shaping procedures—call them S-procedures—designed to affect and change our characters, motivational structure, and wills. Suppose we do. The question is then why we engage in the particular S-procedures that we do engage in, and why we engage in them in the particular way that we do. The general answer is that we engage in the particular S-procedures that we do engage in, given the circumstances in which we find ourselves, because of certain features of the way we already are. (Indeterministic factors may also play a part in what happens, but these will not help to make us responsible for what we do.) And these features of the way we already are—call them character features, or C-features—are either wholly the products of genetic or environmental influences, deterministic or random, for which we are not responsible, or are at least partly the result of earlier S-procedures, which are in turn either wholly the product of C-features for which we are not responsible, or are at least partly the product of still earlier S-procedures, which are turn either the products of C-features for which we are not responsible, or the product of such C-features together with still earlier S-procedures—and so on. In the end, we reach the first S-procedure, and this will have been engaged in, and engaged in the particular way in which it was engaged in, as a result of genetic or environmental factors, deterministic or random, for which we were not responsible.

[9] Kane 1989: 254. I have omitted some italics.

Moving away from the possible role of indeterministic factors in character or personality formation, we can consider their possible role in particular instances of deliberation and decision. Here too it seems clear that indeterministic factors cannot, in influencing what happens, contribute to true moral responsibility in any way. In the end, whatever we do, we do it either as a result of random influences for which we are not responsible, or as a result of non-random influences for which we are not responsible, or as a result of influences for which we are proximally responsible but not ultimately responsible. The point seems obvious. Nothing can be ultimately *causa sui* in any respect at all. Even if God can be, we can't be.

Kane says little about moral responsibility in his paper, but his position seems to be that true moral responsibility is possible if indeterminism is true. It is possible because in cases of 'moral, prudential and practical struggle we . . . are truly "making ourselves" in such a way that we are ultimately responsible for the outcome'. This 'making of ourselves' means that 'we can be ultimately responsible for our present motives and character by virtue of past choices which helped to form them and for which we were ultimately responsible' (op. cit: 252). It is for this reason that we can be ultimately responsible and morally responsible not only in cases of struggle in which we are 'making ourselves', but also for choices and actions which do not involve struggle, flowing unopposed from our character and motives.

In claiming that we can be ultimately responsible for our present motives and character, Kane appears to *accept* step (2) of the Basic Argument. He appears to accept that we have to 'make ourselves', and so be ultimately responsible for ourselves, in order to be morally responsible for what we do.[10] The problem with this suggestion is the old one. In Kane's view, a person's 'ultimate responsibility' for the outcome of an effort of will depends essentially on the partly indeterministic nature of the outcome. This is because it is only the element of indeterminism that prevents prior character and motives from fully explaining the outcome of the effort of will (op. cit.: 236). But how can this indeterminism help with moral responsibility? How can the fact that my effort of will is indeterministic in such a way that its outcome is indeterminate make me truly responsible for it, or even help to make me truly responsible for it? How can it help in any way at all with moral responsibility? How can it make punishment—or reward—ultimately just?

There is a further, familiar problem with the view that moral responsibility depends on indeterminism. If one accepts the view, one will have to grant that it is impossible to know whether any human being is ever morally responsible. For moral responsibility now depends on the falsity of determinism, and determinism is unfalsifiable. There is no more reason to think that determinism is false than that it is true, in spite of the impression sometimes given by scientists and popularizers of science.

(iii) The third response begins by accepting that one cannot be held to be ultimately responsible for one's character or personality or motivational structure. It accepts that this is so whether determinism is true or false. It then directly challenges step (2) of the Basic Argument. It appeals to a certain picture of the self in order to argue that one can be truly free and morally responsible in spite of the fact that one

[10] He cites van Inwagen 1989 in support of this view.

cannot be held to be ultimately responsible for one's character or personality or motivational structure. This picture has some support in the 'phenomenology' of human choice—we sometimes experience our choices and decisions as if the picture were an accurate one. But it is easy to show that it cannot be accurate in such a way that we can be said to be truly or ultimately morally responsible for our choices or actions.

It can be set out as follows. One is free and truly morally responsible because one's self is, in a crucial sense, independent of one's character or personality or motivational structure—one's CPM, for short. Suppose one is in a situation which one experiences as a difficult choice between A, doing one's duty, and B, following one's non-moral desires. Given one's CPM, one responds in a certain way. One's desires and beliefs develop and interact and constitute reasons for both A and B. One's CPM makes one tend towards A or B. So far the problem is the same as ever: whatever one does, one will do what one does because of the way one's CPM is, and since one neither is nor can be ultimately responsible for the way one's CPM is, one cannot be ultimately responsible for what one does.

Enter one's self, S. S is imagined to be in some way independent of one's CPM. S (i.e. one) considers the deliverances of one's CPM and decides in the light of them, but it—S—incorporates a power of decision that is independent of one's CPM in such a way that one can after all count as truly and ultimately morally responsible in one's decisions and actions, even though one is not ultimately responsible for one's CPM. Step (2) of the Basic Argument is false because of the existence of S.[11]

The trouble with the picture is obvious. S (i.e. one) decides on the basis of the deliverances of one's CPM. But whatever S decides, it decides as it does because of the way it is (or else because partly or wholly because of the occurrence in the decision process of indeterministic factors for which it—i.e. one—cannot be responsible, and which cannot plausibly be thought to contribute to one's true moral responsibility). And this returns us to where we started. To be a source of true or ultimate responsibility, S must be responsible for being the way it is. But this is impossible, for the reasons given in the Basic Argument.

The story of S and CPM adds another layer to the description of the human decision process, but it cannot change the fact that human beings cannot be ultimately self-determining in such a way as to be ultimately morally responsible for how they are, and thus for how they decide and act. The story is crudely presented, but it should suffice to make clear that no move of this sort can solve the problem.

'Character is destiny', as Novalis is often reported as saying.[12] The remark is inaccurate, because external circumstances are part of destiny, but the point is well taken when it comes to the question of moral responsibility. Nothing can be *causa sui*, and in order to be truly morally responsible for one's actions one would have to be *causa sui*, at least in certain crucial mental respects. One cannot institute oneself in such

---

[11] Cf. C. A. Campbell 1957.

[12] e.g. by George Eliot in *The Mill on the Floss*, bk 6, ch. 6. Novalis wrote 'Oft fühl ich jetzt . . . [und] je tiefer einsehe, dass Schicksal und Gemüt Namen eines Begriffes sind'—'I often feel, and ever more deeply realize, that fate and character are the same concept.' He was echoing Heracleitus, Fragment 119 DK.

a way that one can take over true or assume moral responsibility for how one is in such a way that one can indeed be truly morally responsible for what one does. This fact is not changed by the fact that we may be unable not to think of ourselves as truly morally responsible in ordinary circumstances. Nor is it changed by the fact that it may be a very good thing that we have this inability—so that we might wish to take steps to preserve it, if it looked to be in danger of fading. As already remarked, many human beings are unable to resist the idea that it is their capacity for fully explicit self-conscious deliberation, in a situation of choice, that suffices to constitute them as truly morally responsible agents in the strongest possible sense. The Basic Argument shows that this is a mistake. However self-consciously aware we are, as we deliberate and reason, every act and operation of our mind happens as it does as a result of features for which we are ultimately in no way responsible. But the conviction that self-conscious awareness of one's situation can be a sufficient foundation of strong free will is very powerful. It runs deeper than rational argument, and it survives untouched, in the everyday conduct of life, even after the validity of the Basic Argument has been admitted.

7

There is nothing new in the somewhat incantatory argument of this paper. It restates certain points that may be in need of restatement. 'Everything has been said before', said André Gide, echoing La Bruyère, 'but since nobody listens we have to keep going back and beginning all over again.' This is an exaggeration, but it may not be a gross exaggeration, so far as general observations about the human condition are concerned.

The present claim, in any case, is simply this: time would be saved, and a great deal of readily available clarity would be introduced into the discussion of the nature of moral responsibility, if the simple point that is established by the Basic Argument were more generally acknowledged and clearly stated. Nietzsche thought that thoroughgoing acknowledgement of the point was long overdue, and his belief that there might be moral advantages in such an acknowledgement may deserve further consideration.[13]

---

[13] Cf. R. Schacht 1983: 304–9. The idea that there might be moral advantages in the clear headed admission that true or ultimate moral responsibility is impossible has been developed in another way by Saul Smilansky (1994).

APPENDIX

Review of *Freedom Evolves*, by Daniel C. Dennett*

In the last several years the philosopher Daniel C. Dennett has published two very large, interesting and influential books. The first, *Consciousness Explained* (1991), aimed to account for all the phenomena of consciousness within the general theoretical framework set by current physics. It failed, of course, and came to be affectionately known as *Consciousness Ignored*. But it was a very fertile and valuable piece of work. The second, *Darwin's Dangerous Idea* (1995), set out to make the case for the theory of evolution even more irresistible than it already is, and it was right on target: vivid, ingenious and illuminating, if sometimes huffy and overpolemical.

Now Dennett is advancing on free will. In *Freedom Evolves*, he wants to show how evolution can get us 'all the way from senseless atoms to freely chosen actions'. And he succeeds in his aim, given what he means by freedom. But he doesn't establish the kind of absolute free will and moral responsibility that most people want to believe in and do believe in. That can't be done, and he knows it.

So what does Dennett mean by freedom? Well, he's a 'compatibilist': he thinks that freedom is wholly compatible with determinism, although determinism is the view that everything that happens in the universe is necessitated by what has already happened, so that nothing can ever occur otherwise than it actually does. He thinks, in other words, that you can be wholly free and morally responsible for your choices and actions even if every single one of them was determined by events that happened long before your birth. You think this a strange notion of freedom? Me too. But here Dennett is part of an old tradition that stretches from the ancient Greeks through Hobbes, Locke, Hume, Mill and many others, and was the orthodoxy among analytic philosophers for most of the twentieth century.

This compatibilist freedom—call it C-freedom—seems intensely unsatisfactory. It doesn't give us what we want and are sure we have: ultimate, buck-stopping responsibility for what we do, of a kind that can make blame and punishment and praise and reward truly just and fair. It allows, after all, that the whole course of our lives may be fixed down to the last detail before we've even been conceived. But one of Dennett's main aims is precisely to convince us that C-freedom is all that is really worth having in the way of freedom. His basic position has not changed since his book *Elbow Room: The Varieties of Free Will Worth Wanting* (1984). It is restated here with new story-bells and example-whistles, and responses to recent work by other writers.

Dennett is a compatibilist about freedom, but a compatibilist can be a creationist and believe that we have immaterial souls. Dennett will have none of that. He's

* This review appeared in the *New York Times Book Review* of 2 March 2003. I've chosen to reprint it here because my wording was changed in the printed version in a way that gave rise to substantive misinterpretation in a discussion that took place in The Garden of Forking Paths, an impressive website devoted to 'Agency Theory' (http://gfp.typepad.com/). My thanks to Tom Clark on this matter.

a supercompatibilist. He not only grants that determinism may be true, he is also an 'uncompromising' materialist, one who holds that every phenomenon in the universe is wholly physical or material. He is also committed to a completely 'naturalistic' approach to the problem: one that rules out the existence of anything that would be classified as supernatural from the perspective of the natural sciences. And he thinks that everything about us can be explained within the framework of the theory of evolution. His claim, then, is that the existence of human freedom, free choice, free action, free will is entirely compatible with materialism, naturalism, determinism and the theory of evolution.

Is this plausible? Yes. Given that Dennett is talking only about C-freedom, I'm sure he's right. I'm sure he's right that all the freedom of choice and action and will that we actually have is a product of evolution. But his rhetoric is all wrong. He stands forth as the lone ranger of hard truth, the indomitable beleaguered word-warrior, fighting a vast rampant dragon of misguided and aggressive orthodoxy. But most philosophers (and a host of others) fully agree with him that determinism may be true and that a materialist, naturalistic, evolutionary approach is best, and find it obvious that C-freedom is compatible with all these things. They also know that there is no way in which the falsity of determinism—the existence of truly random or indeterministic occurrences in the universe—could help to give us greater freedom of will or moral responsibility (many have been beguiled by this last idea, though it doesn't take much thought to see that it won't work).

As for the basic story of how evolution gives rise to C-freedom, Dennettian free will, it's just the story of how we evolved, period. It has no special extra features. So if you already accept the general idea that we are products of evolution, you don't really have to look any farther to accept that C-freedom evolved. How does the story go? Well, it's obvious (looking across living species rather than backward in time) that we have more freedom than a chemically switched bacterium, or a clam that clams up by reflex when something strikes its shell, or a clever rat. We have more freedom than a bird that is as free as a bird, or a dog (even a very smart dog standing at the point of bifurcation of a raging river watching his master and mistress being carried away equidistantly down the two channels, looking agitatedly from side to side before plunging in after one or the other), or a smart chimpanzee. And we have more freedom, we take it, than a small child.

How so? It's simply that we have evolved into self-conscious, self-monitoring agents, language users, with all that that entails. We are creatures who are able to reflect consciously and deliberately on alternative courses of action before choosing between them. We are also creatures who live in complex societies, creatures whom evolution has endowed with natural concern for others, a conscience, a moral sense (Dennett gives a useful summary of how genuine moral feelings can evolve in a world of 'selfish' genes, following Robert Trivers, Robert Frank and others).

What is most striking, perhaps, is that our evolution into self-conscious agents has had the consequence that we find it impossible not to believe that we are radically free and responsible in our choices and actions, even if we're not: even if determinism is true and we have only C-freedom. And there is a peculiar respect, noted by Kant and Sartre, among others, in which we can seem to be rendered truly free for all the everyday purposes of life simply by believing that we are. Dennett makes this point, citing Dumbo the elephant, who was able to fly (at least in the first instance) only because he believed he had a magic feather that conferred the power of flight.

This belief in radical freedom, in ultimate responsibility, cannot actually make radical freedom exist. To be absolutely responsible for what one does, one would have to be *causa sui*, the cause of oneself, and this is impossible (it certainly wouldn't be any more possible if we had immaterial souls rather than being wholly material). There is nonetheless a sense in which our conviction that we are radically free provides a robust foundation for the whole sociocultural edifice of treating people as responsible and in particular as morally responsible; it provides an effective basis for our ordinary practices of punishment, reward and so on, even though these things can never be ultimately fair or just.

This, then, is the sense in which freedom and moral responsibility have evolved: they have evolved by cultural evolution on top of biological evolution. This is Dennett's story, which he is trying to make palatable to those who fear materialism, naturalism, determinism and the implacable beauty of evolution.

It's a worthy enterprise. But where is the lovely, ingenious Dennett? Scarcely to be found here. *Freedom Evolves* is a festival of his favourite themes, from memes to game theory to the Grand Old Problem of consciousness (Dennett continues to deny the existence of consciousness, and continues to deny that he is denying it). But the book is cluttered, overlong and too concerned with theatricals. Dennett claims dramatically that determinism does not imply inevitability, and is 'perfectly compatible with the notion that some events have no cause at all', but the first claim is a linguistic quibble and the second, embedded in a seriously muddled account of causality, is false by definition. There is an important point here—the point that fatalism is false even if determinism is true—but it's best stated in a couple of paragraphs, not buried in forty pages of unnecessary complication.

14

Consciousness, Free Will, and the Unimportance of Determinism

This paper begins with some brief reflections on the definition of determinism (§2), on the notion of the subject of experience (§3), and on the relation between conscious experience and brain events (§4). The main discussion (§§5–13) focuses on the traditional view, endorsed by Honderich in his book *A Theory of Determinism*, that the truth of determinism poses some special threat to our ordinary conception of ourselves as morally responsible free agents (and also to our 'life-hopes'). It is argued that this is half right: the truth of determinism does indeed threaten certain vital parts of our ordinary conception of ourselves as morally responsible free agents. The trouble is that the falsity of determinism does not diminish the threat in any useful way. The old, natural, and recurrent mistake is to think that we would really be better off, so far as free will and moral responsibility (and our 'life-hopes') were concerned, if determinism were false. It is argued that there is no important sense in which this is true, and that the question of whether determinism is true or false is therefore of no real importance, so far as the free will debate is concerned.

1   INTRODUCTION

Ted Honderich's *A Theory of Determinism* is wide-ranging and engagingly down to earth. It addresses a connected series of fundamental, philosophical issues: causation, determinism, the mind-body relation, the nature of action, and the freedom of the will. Broadly speaking I am in sympathy with Honderich's position. I agree that there is more to causation than regularity; that determinism may be true; that the causal theory of action is clearly correct. I think that Honderich places the right sort of constraints on any satisfactory account of the mind-brain or 'psychoneural' relation. He takes proper account of the fact that conscious mental states are part of ultimate reality, and that reductive physicalism is moonshine, given current conceptions of the physical.[1] Finally, I agree that if determinism is true, then free will, in one common

---

This paper was a contribution to a symposium on Ted Honderich's book *A Theory of Determinism* (1988). Unprefixed page references are to this book.

[1] 'Eliminativists' are 'out of their minds'. For the point of the restriction to current conceptions of the physical, see §4 below.

and central understanding of the phrase, is impossible. (It is impossible in any case; but of that more later.)

This response to Honderich's book is necessarily very selective. I will begin with some very brief remarks about determinism, consciousness, and the mind-brain relation. Then I will try to raise some more substantial doubts about his discussion of the consequences of determinism. This occupies part III of *A Theory of Determinism*, which I found quite hard to follow, largely on account of the looseness and variability of formulation of its key claims.

2   DETERMINISM

Is determinism conceptually viable? Certainly, despite J. L. Austin's odd remark that 'determinism . . . is . . . a name of nothing clear'.[2] For determinism, as a thesis about the existing world, is nothing more complicated than (1) the thesis that everything—everything that happens in the world now that it is up and running (and whatever its beginning)—has a cause, and hence an explanation; even if the explanation is inaccessible to us. (1) is often thought to be inadequate as a formulation of determinism, so I will briefly try to show that it isn't.

A familiar way of stating determinism follows from (1): this is the claim (2) that the history of the universe could not possibly have been, or be, different. One objection to (2), and to the claim that (2) follows from (1), is that statements of the following form may both be true: (3) X was, in fact, the cause of Y (at time t); but (4) X could equally have been the cause of Z instead (at t). Clearly, if (3) and (4) can be true together, then (1) does not entail (2). For if (3) and (4) are both true, then when X occurred the universe reached what one might call an 'objective branching point': either Y or Z could have occurred, although Y occurred in fact. If so, the history of the universe could have been different from how it is. So (2) is false. And yet (according to the objection) (1) is still true: it is still true to say that everything has a cause.

To state the objection is to see that it fails. For if (2) is to be false while (1) is true, then it must be possible for statements of the form of (3) and (4) to be true together. But if (1) is true, no statements of the form of (3) and (4) can be true together. For if (3) and (4) are both true, there is *ex hypothesi* no cause or explanation of Y's-happening-rather-than-Z's-happening; contrary to (1). So (1) does entail (2); and, properly understood, (1) is a perfectly adequate definition of determinism. If so, the thesis of determinism can be very simply stated—more simply, perhaps, than Honderich allows. This said, it should be noted that the definition of it given here employs the word 'cause', and that Honderich's principal concern in his opening chapters is to give an account of causation. This I will not discuss.

Given that determinism is conceptually viable, is it true? This is Honderich's next question. He grants that it can't be proved, but believes we have good reason to think it is true. He himself firmly believes that it is true, and yet he ends his discussion of

² J. L. Austin 1956: 131.

this issue with the cautious claim that the theory of determinism is 'certainly *as well supported as* a general theory of indeterminism' (p. 374, my emphasis).[3]

The two theories are obviously equal in respect of unprovability, and I think that Honderich is unnecessarily hesitant on the point that determinism cannot be proved true (or false). For it is an immediate consequence of the logical form of the statement that everything that happens has a cause that it is not merely unfalsifiable but also unverifiable. Suppose that there is something which appears to have no cause. One can never definitively rule out the possibility that it does but that one has not yet detected it. The point is as simple as that.[4] Still, Honderich is quite right to insist on the point that the successes of quantum theory provide no very good reason to favour the view that determinism is definitely false over the highly plausible view that there is a lot that we don't know (and may never know) about how things work—in which case determinism may well be true. Even if quantum theory as currently formulated is incompatible with determinism, it certainly doesn't follow that determinism is false.[5] And it is worth noting how current developments in chaos theory provide a dramatic illustration of the way in which extremely simple deterministic determinants of the behaviour of systems can produce what looks like random behaviour.[6]

3 CONSCIOUSNESS

My problem with Honderich's account of consciousness can be quickly stated. 'Consciousness', he says, 'consists in general in [the] *interdependent existence of subject and content*' (p. 82). This interdependence is such that 'there can be no subject without a content, and no contents not in relation to a subject'.

To this it can be objected that exactly the same is true of a grammatical subject–predicate sentence, or a picture. This may seem like one of those sterile formal objections that philosophers specialize in, but I don't think it is. It may prompt the immediate reply that the notion of a subject is quite different in the two cases; a conscious subject is obviously not the same as a grammatical subject or the subject of a picture. But this reply threatens to reinforce the original objection, in so far as it suggests that the notion of a subject appealed to in the definition is already assumed to be the notion of a *conscious* subject; for if this is the case, an understanding of the nature of consciousness is simply presupposed by the definition.

I don't think there is much future in Honderich's definition. It seems that the best thing to do, when the question of what conscious experience is comes up, is simply

---

[3] He adds that determinist theories of the mind are superior to indeterminist theories of the mind, but this is potentially confusing, because by 'indeterminist theories of the mind' he does not just mean theories that postulate indeterministic factors in the operation of minds; he also means theories that postulate some kind of 'uncaused origination' of actions on the part of human agents.

[4] The statement is a 'universal-existential' statement; it is thus 'syntactically metaphysical', as the logical positivists used to say.

[5] Cf. J. S. Bell (1987: 160). Honderich has an excellent brief description and discussion of the 'two-slit' experiment on p. 312.

[6] For a good introduction to chaos theory, see Gleick 1987.

to point at it (so to speak); to say to others 'You know what it is (from your own case)'. Anyone who *is* conscious and capable of reading a philosophy book will know what is meant. This suggestion does not run up against the valid part of the objection to the idea of knowing what something is from one's own case. It is intended to be fully compatible with acceptance of the possibility that one's conscious experience is, qualitatively speaking, profoundly different from that of others. As I read him, one of Wittgenstein's most important valid points is precisely that you and I do not have to have the same experience of, say, the colour red (or pain), qualitatively speaking, in order for both of us to be able to know what red is, and mean the same thing by 'red' (or 'pain'). Similarly, you and I do not have to have even the same *general* sort of conscious experience, qualitatively speaking, in order for both of us to be able to know what conscious experience is, and mean the same thing by 'conscious experience'.[7]

Can one do nothing but point? Can one say nothing? Certainly one can say that for X to be conscious is for there to be something it is like to be X.[8] But this does not provide any sort of non-circular characterization of the nature of conscious experience, because there is something it is like to be a stone: to be a stone is to be like *this*, or like *this*, or like *that*. What one means, when one says that for X to be conscious is for there to be something it is like to be X, is that there is something it is like to be X, *experientially speaking*. But this last phrase simply reintroduces the notion of which one was hoping to give a non-circular account—the notion of conscious experience.

Consciousness can indeed be said to involve the 'interdependence of subject and content', as Honderich says. But when we consider this fact, I think we should not suppose that it is a truth only about self-conscious beings like our adult selves. It is a very fundamental truth, a truth about any being whatever that has conscious experience of any sort: experience entails a subject of experience. This must be granted whatever view one holds about the *nature* of the subject of experience. It is not a 'grammatical illusion', as some have said.[9] It is just a reflection of the simple point that experience is, necessarily, experience-*for*—experience for someone or something. This is as true for a new-born baby or a dog or a spider (if spiders have experience) as it is for us.

We may naturally think that in the case of new-born babies and spiders we do not have anything so grand as a Subject of Experience. But in a crucial sense we do—in just the sense in which it is true to say that all experience is necessarily experience-*for*-someone-or-something.[10] As Honderich says, 'a subject [is] one part of the linked

---

[7] Even if this is not a Wittgensteinian point, it is still an important point (it is arguable that Wittgenstein held the opposite view, and some read him to be saying that one does not have to have any phenomenally contentful sensory experience of red or pain at all, in order to know what red or pain is, or what 'red' or 'pain' means).

[8] Cf. Nagel 1979.

[9] But it is important to realize that it does not involve any sort of commitment to belief in the long-term diachronic continuity of subjects of experience.

[10] The claim that there must be a Subject of Experience expresses no more—and no less—than what is expressed by this necessary truth; but it expresses it in a useful way.

duality which is the nature of *any* [conscious] mental event' (pp. 146–7, my emphasis).

4   THE MIND–BRAIN OR PSYCHONEURAL RELATION

At some level—details aside—Honderich's account of the relation between conscious mental events and the brain must surely be close to the truth. (It is important to note that by 'mental events' he always means '*conscious* mental events'.) For it has, in a sense, a merely negative character. It indicates—schematically characterizes—the place in conceptual space where the mind–brain or conscious experience–brain relation must be found, by indicating where it cannot be found, given the constraints on any plausible account of it.

For example: any adequate account of the relation must adopt a fully realist attitude to conscious mental goings-on. They are real, as real as rabbits. And it must satisfy our (scientifically solid) intuitions about the 'intimacy' of the connection—the 'psychoneural intimacy', in Honderich's terms, between mental events and neural events. Again, it must allow for the fact that explanations of actions in terms of reasons (desires and beliefs) can be and often are simply *true*, in every sense in which explanations of physical events in the terms of physical science are simply true.[11] And it must do this in the face of the fact that actions and neural goings-on have full descriptions in 'purely' physical terms (terms which make no reference to the mental), given which it seems to be possible to give full explanations of their occurrence in 'purely' physical (non-mental) terms. And so on.

Honderich seems for the most part clear that he is not giving a genuinely positive account of the intrinsic nature of the conscious experience–brain relation, but only, as it were, of its abstract structure. At one point he does claim to have given 'a *complete answer* to the question of the nature of the psychoneural relation' (p. 169). But this seems to be a slip: on the whole he grants that this is impossible: 'the problem of the *nature* or *explanation* of psychoneural nomic correlation . . . remains insoluble' (p. 108); 'the problem of the ultimate nature or mechanism of connection between the mental and the neural [is] . . . still intractable' (p. 170, cf. p. 296).

This seems exactly right. It does seem that a negative account of the conscious experience–brain relation (an account that proceeds principally by saying what it is not, or by saying that it is the thing, *whatever its ultimate nature*, which fulfils the following conditions) is all that can be hoped for at present. And it does not seem implausible to suppose that we will never be able to understand the nature of the relation. We do not have, as yet, the remotest conception of how it is possible that a physical neural event should either 'realize' or 'be the basis of' or (to use Honderich's terms) be in nomic

---

[11] It should be noted that mental states like desires and beliefs, considered just as such, do not raise anything like the same sorts of problems as *conscious* mental states, states involving phenomenal feel. When desires and beliefs are considered apart from states which involve conscious entertainings of desires and beliefs, there is no more difficulty in understanding how the physical can 'realize' such states than there is in understanding how a chess computer can be constructed.

correlation with a conscious mental event, either in ourselves or in any other creature which is such that there is 'something it is like to be it', experientially speaking. There is absolutely nothing at all in current neurophysiology that looks like even so much as a first beginning on this problem.[12] There is absolutely nothing at all in our current scientifically informed conception of the nature of the physical that promises any sort of lead. Indeed the whole of our current scientifically informed conception of the nature of the physical militates powerfully against a solution to the problem.

The correct conclusion to draw from this, I think, is that there must be something quite fundamentally wrong or inadequate about our current conception of 'the physical'. We can know now that there must be something fundamentally inadequate or incomplete about our current conception of the physical precisely because of the problem it creates about the conscious experience–brain relation. (The only real alternative to saying this is to embrace dualism.) The descriptive-explanatory resources of our current conception of the physical simply fail to connect *in any way* with the phenomenon of the intrinsic qualitative or phenomenal character of conscious states.[13] Honderich suggests that a correct conception of the physical must not exclude the (conscious) mental. And this looks like the right thing to say. But, as things stand at present, it is a statement of faith, not something that advances our understanding in any way. For the fact remains that we have two fundamentally different descriptive-explanatory perspectives on things, and absolutely no idea of how they connect up. Our current conception of the 'intrinsic' nature of the physical does exclude the phenomena of conscious experience.

5   DETERMINISM, 'ORIGINATION', AND LIFE-HOPES

Having argued that determinism is conceptually viable in part I, and having affirmed and defended his belief that it is true in part II, Honderich moves on in part III to consider the consequences of this belief for our view of ourselves as rational, cognitive, social beings and agents. This part of *A Theory of Determinism* is much less clear than the other two, and I am not sure I have always understood it.

Honderich distinguishes four main areas of human life in which, he thinks, a properly worked out grasp of the truth of determinism would have significant consequences. (1) It would affect our attitude to our 'life-hopes' regarding our own futures and achievements; (2) it would affect our attitude to our knowledge claims; (3) it would affect our attitude to our relations to others; and (4) it would affect our attitude to issues of morality and moral responsibility, which concern both ourselves and others. Obviously enough, it would have these consequences principally because of the threat it poses to our ordinary conception of human free will.

---

[12] For some no doubt psychologically interesting reason, certain psychologists get rather angry when philosophers remind them of this fact.

[13] On this see McGinn 1989.

In each of the four cases, Honderich considers three main reactions to the consequences of determinism. (A) The reaction of *dismay*, dismay caused by the belief that many things that we hope or want to be true about ourselves cannot be true if determinism is true. (B) The reaction of *intransigence*, which involves the denial that determinism raises any real problem, and the rejection of the attitudes that make it seem as if it does: '[t]he defining feature of intransigence is the assertion . . . that determinism affects nothing—that it is true or can be true without anything changing' (p. 493). (C) The reaction of *affirmation*. This is a less rigid and ultimately more positive response than (B). It accepts that determinism does threaten and undermine certain desires and values that we have, but tries to cope with and profit from this knowledge. It 'involves our accepting a certain loss' (p. 493), and is 'the endeavour to give up certain attitudes, fundamentally the endeavour to accept the defeat of certain desires, by way of reflecting on the situation in which our success would put us. It is the endeavour to accommodate ourselves to what we can truly possess [given the truth of determinism], mainly by seeing its value' (p. 494).

I will concentrate on (1), the claim about 'life-hopes', because I fail to feel the force of (2), the idea that determinism poses a threat to our attitude to our knowledge claims, and because I agree with the general drift of Honderich's views about (3) and (4)—his views about the obvious and familiar problems which determinism poses for our ordinary view of moral responsibility, and hence for many aspects of our view of ourselves and others.

6 THE IMPOSSIBILITY OF 'TRUE' RESPONSIBILITY

First, however, I wish to argue that the threat that determinism poses for the heart of our ordinary conception of ourselves as truly free agents arises whether determinism is true or false.[14]

The basic point is an old one. According to our ordinary, strong conception of free will, free will entails *true moral responsibility*; and true moral responsibility entails being *truly deserving* of praise and blame (and punishment and reward) for our actions, in the strongest possible sense.

Perhaps the most graphic way to convey this conception of responsibility and desert is as follows: it is responsibility of such a kind that it makes *sense*, at least, to suppose that it might be just to punish those who have it with damnation in hell, or reward them with bliss in heaven. That is, given this conception of responsibility and desert, the idea that such punishment or reward might be appropriate makes perfect *sense* even if it is in fact part of a highly extravagant and distasteful myth.[15]

[14] I argue for this at some length in my book *Freedom and Belief*, Part I (esp. chs. 2 and 6).

[15] Those who find these religious notions grotesque may have difficulty in appreciating the way in which they make vivid the kind of true responsibility many people suppose themselves to have here on earth.

Less eschatologically, but otherwise similarly, the idea is this. One is possessed of true moral responsibility, and the fact that one is possessed of true moral responsibility entails that one is deserving of praise and blame (and punishment and reward) for one's actions irrespective of any considerations concerning any possible social (or other) utility of such praise and blame (or punishment or reward), simply because it is truly up to one what one does, in the strongest possible sense. One is the ultimate, buck-stopping originator of one's actions, in some sense which is certainly unavailable if determinism is true.

I will call the associated notion of desert 'true' desert, for ease of reference. The familiar point is that if determinism is true, then true desert, desert as ordinarily understood, is not possible. And free will and moral responsibility, which are most naturally defined in terms of such desert when one is seeking to characterize one crucial part of our ordinary understanding of them, are equally impossible. I do not think that anyone who reflects, and who has grasped the heart (if not the whole) of our ordinary understanding of free will and moral responsibility, can really disagree with this.[16]

But true-desert-entailing free will is equally impossible if determinism is false. Its falsity cannot help in any way to give us desert-entailing freedom. If some actions have indeterministic antecedents, that cannot make us responsible for them in such a way that we can be truly deserving of praise and blame for them. Similarly, if some of those features of our mental make-up which lead us to act in the way we do are not determined in us (say by heredity, upbringing and environment, and ultimately by events which occurred before our birth), but are partly or wholly the outcome of random events (present or past), that cannot help to make us truly deserving of praise and blame. *Mere indeterminism* (the falsity of determinism) is no help at all, if we are looking for true-desert-entailing freedom. What we would need for true-desert-entailing freedom (this is one way of putting it, at least) is not just indeterminism but true *self*-determination on the part of free agents.

To put the point very briefly: if we are to be truly deserving of praise and blame for our actions, then, since our intentional actions are necessarily a function of how we are, mentally, we must be truly responsible for how we are mentally, at least in certain vital respects. We must be genuine 'originators' of ourselves, and our natures, at least in certain respects. But the attempt to describe how we could possibly be true originators of ourselves in this way leads self-defeatingly to infinite regress (quite apart from being quite fantastically unrealistic): for even if one could somehow choose how to be, and then bring it about that one was that way, one would in order to do this already have to have existed prior to that choice, with a certain set of preferences about how to be, in the light of which one chose how to be. But then the question would arise: where did these preferences come from? Or were they just there, unchosen preferences for which one was not responsible? And so on.

---

[16] Criticism of this aspect of our ordinary understanding of the notion of moral responsibility is one thing; mere description of it is another.

This argument proceeds completely independently of any appeal to determinism or indeterminism, and if valid shows that true-desert-entailing freedom of will is provably impossible—impossible whether determinism is true or false.

Honderich sets out a fuller (but still abbreviated) version of this argument for the impossibility of true-desert-entailing free will or moral responsibility on pages 178–9 of his book.[17] He remarks that it would be 'alarming if true, in that it would make a good deal of this book, like a multitude of others, in one way otiose' (p. 178) and rejects it as too rapid. I do not understand his objections to it (on pp. 179–80), but I think he is quite right to be alarmed. For if the argument is valid, as I believe, then it is *completely unnecessary* to argue that determinism is true in order to argue that free will as ordinarily conceived is impossible, or in order to have good reason to go on to reflect on the consequences of this fact for our ordinary view of ourselves. And if this is so, the fundamental argument structure of *A Theory of Determinism*—(1) show that determinism is conceptually viable, (2) argue for its truth or probable truth, (3) consider its consequences for our view of ourselves as rational and social thinkers and agents—is seriously misconceived.

And yet there is a sense in which the damage is really quite superficial. For none of Honderich's three main argumentative projects is put in doubt. (1) and (2) can go ahead exactly as before; and the essential project of (3) can also go ahead, although many of the details of the argument will need to be altered or expanded. For as far as the essential project of (3) is concerned, it simply has to be allowed that the central task in (3) is not merely to consider the consequences of determinism, but to consider the consequences of the fact that, *whether determinism is true or false*, we cannot be ultimate originators of our actions in the way in which we ordinarily and unreflectively suppose that we can be—that is, in the true-desert, true-moral-responsibility entailing way.

Note that as soon as this point is conceded, as I think it should be, the force of any general conclusions reached is greatly increased: for they are no longer conditional on the unprovable truth of determinism. And this is clearly to the good. In fact, I suspect that anything of real importance to our view of ourselves as free, rational, social agents and knowers that can be shown to follow from the truth of determinism follows equally on the assumption that determinism is false; even though the truth of determinism may well have certain detailed consequences for our view of ourselves that the truth of indeterminism does not have.

7   AN ARGUMENT STRATEGY

One powerful argumentative strategy, in supporting this last claim, is as follows. Take any particular aspect of our view of ourselves as agents and knowers, etc. Suppose

---

[17] Quoting from my 1986: 28–9. I am puzzled by his claim that my view 'is in a way resolutely Compatibilist' (p. 478), because it is resolutely incompatibilist.

first, as Honderich does, that determinism is true, and ask what follows so far as that particular aspect is concerned. Suppose that what follows is that one has to give up certain features—cherished features, perhaps—of one's view of oneself and others.[18] So be it. Now ask whether it would really help if determinism were false, and there was objective indeterminism in nature. Ask if it would really allow us to retain belief in those aspects of our view of ourselves that appeared to be threatened by determinism.

So far as anything of importance is concerned, the answer, I believe, is that it would not. And this is principally because it could not give us true-desert-entailing responsibility for (or true 'origination' of) our actions of the sort we ordinarily if very vaguely suppose ourselves to have.[19]

It may be doubted that there is nothing of real importance that the present truth of determinism denies us, and that the present truth of indeterminism can give us. It may for example be said that determinism 'allows but one future' (p. 339), and that this is unsettling. We think our futures open, alterable, unfixed (p. 385), and this is important to us. Honderich thinks this gives us reason for wanting indeterminism to be true. But if determinism is true, now, are we really worse off in any important way?

I feel the pull of the thought that we are, but I think it is illusory. One very important point is this. Even if determinism is false, now, no one doubts that the world is at least massively regular in its behaviour. And this gives rise to a *Realism Constraint* on any postulation of indeterminism: any realistic postulation of indeterminism must suppose indeterminism to exist now and *as things are*; that is, with the world (the 'macro-world') behaving in the apparently deterministic way in which it does behave. It is no good saying that if determinism is false then something marvellous but very unlikely could very well happen, and that that is why it would be good if it were false. That would be utterly unrealistic, as Honderich realizes: even if determinism is false, one thing that is certain is that the world behaves very much as if it were true.

Let me apply the argumentative strategy mentioned above to one of the four things that Honderich believes to be threatened by determinism: our attitude to ourselves as knowers. The question is: why is determinism thought to pose a special threat? It is certainly true that if determinism is true, then we are determined to believe what we believe. But the key question immediately arises: will we be better off in any way

---

[18] This is to assume for the purposes of argument that we are capable of giving up many deeply cherished aspects of our ordinary conception of ourselves. In fact this is highly doubtful, and this is something of which, in general, Honderich takes far too little account. See P. F. Strawson 1962.

[19] Once one is clear on the point that indeterminism provides absolutely no sort of basis for belief in the possibility of (desert-entailing) 'origination' one is likely to have some difficulty with the terms of Honderich's discussion, since by 'indeterminism' he standardly means not just indeterminism, but 'indeterminism + some sort of "peculiar power" [p. 500] of true origination' (cf., e.g., p. 305).

This is perhaps the place to note that Honderich's definitions of compatibilism (ordinarily understood as 'free will is compatible with determinism') and incompatibilism (ordinarily understood as 'free will is not compatible with determinism') are rather unusual. This explains how he can hold that both are false without abandoning the law of excluded middle. In *Freedom and Belief* I argue that we are in some respects naturally compatibilist, and in other respects naturally incompatibilist, in our thought about freedom. Honderich agrees, and accordingly has both compatibilism and incompatibilism coming out false, by taking each of them to incorporate the claim that it fully represents most people's ordinary views on the matter.

at all if determinism is false, so that it is partly a matter of chance or random outcome that we believe what we believe? Will we be better at getting to truth, in this case? Will we be able to achieve certainty with respect to our beliefs in some way which is impossible if determinism is true? Will we be better at maths? No, no, and no. (Give me a deterministic pocket calculator any day.)

As usual, if determinism is a problem, it is very hard to see how the postulation of indeterminism can be supposed to help with it in any way at all. The old vague thought, I suppose, is that we want to be capable of reaching conclusions about what to believe 'on our own'. But what do we want to be governed by, in reaching our conclusions? We want above all to be sensitive to the way things are in such a way that we form true beliefs about the ways things are. On the whole we are quite good at this, and the theory of evolution gives a good account of why (and how) creatures that are good at forming true beliefs about their environment should come to exist. Such an account is entirely compatible with determinism.[20] So it is very hard, on reflection, to see why determinism is thought to threaten our view of ourselves as knowers. But even if determinism does pose some threat, there is a threat whether determinism is true or false.

8   THE UNHELPFULNESS OF INDETERMINISM (1)

Let me now try again to say in very general terms why I don't think that indeterminism gives us anything important that we want, or usefully diminishes any threat that determinism poses, although we may vaguely suppose that it does. Honderich is undoubtedly aware of most (if not all) of the points I propose to make—and this is something I would stress. The difference between us is that he doesn't draw the conclusion I draw: the conclusion that it is wrong to approach the central questions about the correctness or otherwise of our view of ourselves as free and responsible agents and knowers as if they were principally questions about the consequences of determinism for our view of ourselves.

Honderich might wish to object that he is not just generally concerned with what indeterminism can give us, but, more specifically, with what 'uncaused origination' can give us—where this is conceived of as something for which indeterminism is necessary but not sufficient. The notion of 'uncaused origination' is however highly unclear, and the general project of seeing what indeterminism can give us is a necessary part of seeing what 'uncaused origination' might be, and what it might be supposed to give us.

If determinism is false, then indeterministic occurrences can affect our lives. They may be (1) external: they may be in the world outside us. Or they may be (2) internal: they may be inside us in the sense of being in our bodies, or, more particularly, in our minds or brains. This is a rough division, but it will do. I will first very briefly consider possible indeterministic occurrences outside us, then possible indeterministic occurrences 'inside us' in the present sense of 'in our minds or brains'. Clearly, it

---

[20] 'Random' mutation, so called, is of course compatible with the truth of determinism.

will be indeterministic occurrences inside us that contribute to 'uncaused origination' if anything does, and which will therefore be thought to be particularly important.

If determinism is false, we may be affected by indeterministic or random occurrences outside us. Are we better off in this case than if we are affected only by occurrences which are part of the huge, complex, rich, and constantly surprising but ultimately entirely deterministic system of the world? I think not. Certainly one may be thwarted in some particular life-hope-involving project by some particular recurrent pattern of events outside one. And if one thinks that it is determined that this pattern will always be as it is, one's hopes of success in the project may be (and should be) destroyed. Indeed. But to derive hope that the pattern might next time not be repeated from the thought that determinism is or may be false would be deeply foolish. It would be to ignore the Realism Constraint: if the interruption of the pattern is not compatible with the laws of nature deterministically construed, it is quite unrealistic to hope for it. And if the interruption is compatible with the laws of nature deterministically construed, the truth of determinism poses no special threat, and is no special cause for regret.

It may be objected that the falsity of determinism is still good news in this case, because it does at least *increase the chances* of the interruption of the pattern. But, once again, this is foolish: any *realistic* assumption of the falsity of determinism has to acknowledge that this minute increase provides no grounds for any scintilla of reasonable hope that the pattern will be interrupted.

This is to leave aside the obvious further point that it would be entirely irrational to suppose that things would be more likely to go better for one, rather than worse, if determinism were false. And the point that if there were really *significant* indeterminism in the 'macro-world' (the Realism Constraint reminds us that there is not), then the main relevant effect this would have on one, as an agent pursuing goals, would be to increase the unpredictability of things in such a way that one's general efficacy as a planner and pursuer of projects would be diminished. Randomness of a sort that might be likely to buck a deterministic pattern which was hindering one (but which might equally give rise to something far worse than the pattern that was hindering one) would be purchased only at the cost of a diminution in one's effectiveness as a rational planner of action relying on the predictability of the world.[21]

So much, very briefly, for indeterminism outside one. What would indeterminism give one if it affected states or events inside one? (It is natural to think that this is the more important case.) It might either (i) change one's traits of character—the general way one was, mentally—and thereby have consequences for one's decisions, choices, actions, and achievements. Or it might perhaps (ii) affect one's decisions, choices, and actions directly, without first affecting the general way one was, mentally, or in respect of character. That is, events of decision, choice, and action might themselves be or crucially involve indeterministic events.

---

[21] To deny that there is in fact 'significant' indeterminism in the macro-world is not to deny that indeterminism of the sort postulated by certain contemporary subatomic physicists could conceivably have significant effects in the macro-world.

(i) This may perhaps seem promising at first—although one must always bear the Realism Constraint in mind. But does it really give one anything valuable? Well, suppose things have gone—or are going—badly for one. Suppose one feels trapped in a rut, or in what Freud called a *Wiederholungzwang*—a compulsion to repeat. One feels, perhaps, that one is the victim of some character defect *C*. And one has good (inductive) evidence that one is not going to be able to improve things. In this case, the thought that determinism is true may oppress one.

But would things be better if indeterminism were true? It seems not. The point is familiar. Suppose that determinism is true, and one is indeed determined to go on having *C*.[22] Clearly, if indeterminism instead is true, one may just lose *C*, and acquire *D*. But, given the Realism Constraint, it would be absurd to found any hopes on the utterly remote possibility that this might happen simply as a result of some random or indeterministic event, as Honderich is well aware.

Even if one ignores the Realism Constraint, and supposes there is significant indeterminism—call it *Unrealistic Indeterminism*—in the macro-world, things are no better. For why should things go well rather than badly in a world in which there is Unrealistic Indeterminism? Why on earth (which is where we are) should it bring about the particular change or changes one wants? In fact such a world is bound to be worse in at least one respect, for a reason already noted: whether determinism is true or false, one is usually able, by one's own actions and in accordance with one's wishes, to determine what happens to one in many respects, relying crucially on the predictability of the world. This reliance would be less justified in a world in which there was Unrealistic Indeterminism.

(ii) Now suppose again that there is Unrealistic Indeterminism, and that it affects one's decisions, choices, and actions directly (i.e. without affecting one's character or general mental traits). And suppose once again that one is in a situation in which it seems to one that one cannot achieve what one wants to achieve, given the way one is mentally or in respect of general character. Well, one now has the prospect that some of one's decisions and choices and actions may be uncaused events, which are not caused to be as they are by the way one is mentally. And so it seems that one (one?) may now possibly achieve what one wants to achieve if indeterminism is true, in a way which was impossible so long as determinism was true. But the same objection recurs:[23] the chances that merely random processes will produce the right decision or choice or course of action in one are infinitesimal. Thousands of other possibilities are equally likely. In this case, the operation of indeterministic factors is surely to be dreaded rather than desired.

It will be objected that this response ignores the Campbellian view of things.[24] According to this view, indeterminism does not open up thousands of possibilities.

---

[22] One is, among other things, determinedly such that one could not succeed in acquiring character trait *D* instead, perhaps by some strenuous psychotherapy.

[23] Along with the obvious objection that this sort of thing be any sort of basis for true responsibility.

[24] C. A. Campbell 1967.

It operates crucially in cases of conflict between what one most wants to do, *A*, and what one feels one ought to do, *B*. In such cases, causal constraints operate to ensure that there are really only two possibilities—*A* and *B*—so far as how one decides and acts is concerned. What the presence of indeterminism ensures is that one is not then determined to do what one does do.

Clearly this picture does avoid the objection stated in the last paragraph but one. But there is in turn a simple objection to it. Whatever 'uncaused origination' is supposed to be, it is supposed to be such that it makes true desert or true credit possible; that's the *point* of postulating it. But it seems absurd to suppose that one is truly responsible for one's decision and action, when facing a conflict between duty and desire, because what one then finally decides or does is causally undetermined. How can such indeterminism contribute in any way to one's ultimate responsibility for the decision or action?[25]

Perhaps the worst picture of these matters is the picture according to which indeterminism makes true origination possible because the Self can somehow control—channel or harness—indeterminism, in order to bring about what it wants or thinks best.[26] This picture often goes with dualism, and with the idea that the non-physical Soul or Self can intervene in an otherwise deterministic physical causal order. But, on its own, the postulation of such an interventionary Self furnishes no grounds at all for supposing either that there may be (1) 'uncaused origination', or that there can be (2) true responsibility in the sense of §6. As for (1): it provides no reason to think that the Soul's or Self's decisions about how to manipulate or buck physical causality are not themselves caused.[27] As for (2): even if one explicitly assumes that the non-physical Self's decisions *are* themselves uncaused, one runs into the old objection (§6.) that this provides no grounds for supposing that it is truly responsible for them in the sense of §6: if its uncaused decisions are in this case the right ones, this will be a matter of luck.

9   THE UNHELPFULNESS OF INDETERMINISM (2)

To return from the Campbell-inspired digression. It seems that there is no case in which the possible truth of indeterminism can improve our 'life-hopes', so far as the question of our ability to achieve what we want to achieve is concerned. It doesn't help whether it is internal or external. This seems to be clearly so when we submit to the Realism Constraint in our postulation of indeterminism. For then we have no reason, so far as all practical matters go (and hence so far as our hopes about our achievements go), not to treat the world as if it were in fact deterministic. And

---

[25] It appears to diminish it.

[26] Of course there is a sense in which we can 'originate' actions which is entirely compatible with determinism. By 'true' origination I mean origination of the sort which would make 'true' desert (§6) possible.

[27] In fact there may be no indeterminism at all, on this story. It may look as if there is indeterminism, from the physical point of view. But there may just be a more complicated form of determinism, one which involves the interaction of both physical and non-physical elements.

even when we postulate Unrealistic Indeterminism things are no better. For then we acquire uncertainty about the world without acquiring any reason to suppose that the indeterminism will in general go the way we want. And we have every reason to suppose that it will not in general go the way we want. For it is merely realistic, not pessimistic, to suppose that there are far more ways in which things can go wrong for us than ways in which things can go right; and indeterminism is not humanitarian.[28]

If indeterminism could really provide a basis for some kind of true-desert-entailing (or true-*credit*-creating) 'uncaused origination', there might be more to say on the subject, and some at least prima facie reason to prefer indeterminism to determinism. But it cannot provide any such basis (§6). Honderich is certainly right to say that a certain 'image' (good word to use) of ourselves as true, 'uncaused' *originators* of our actions is important to us, and he sees this image as being tied up, in some confused way, with our 'life-hopes'. But a little reflection shows that indeterminism can do nothing to support this image in any valuable way. The image of true-desert-entailing, true-credit-creating origination has to be given up whether determinism is true or false. (In practice, of course, it is almost impossible to give up.)

One natural objection to the idea that one's choices or actions may themselves be undetermined events is that if they are, then they are not really *one's own* choices or actions at all. This natural objection is, however, directly rejected by some philosophers, who say that although the event (of choice, say) is undetermined, it is precisely *your* choice that is undetermined. It happens in your head (or mind). You make a choice, and it is precisely that event—the event of *your* making a choice—that is undetermined. So here is a case in which you really are an uncaused originator of something. For you are 'host' to a choice; it is your choice (or 'choice'); and it has no causal antecedents.

Suppose we grant the possible appropriateness of this description of things. The objection to it is very simple. Like all other suggestions that appeal to indeterminism in order to defend freedom, it cannot help with the fundamental problem: how can the fact that a person's choice or action is uncaused in this way, rather than causally determined, in any way increase or strengthen the sense in which it is correct to say that he or she is responsible for the choice or action, relative to any determinism-compatible sense in which this is so? Imagine that the uncaused choice or action is not a good one, but a morally appalling one. Can the person be morally *more* blameworthy for it in this case than he or she would have been if it had resulted deterministically from (heredity-and-environment) determined character?

It seems to me that awareness of nearly all these points is explicit or implicit in Honderich's text. But I do not think he makes enough of them—and this is especially so in the case of the point that the image of true-desert-entailing, true-credit-creating origination has to be given up whether determinism is true or false. Of course one *can* consider the consequences of the impossibility of 'uncaused origination' within the highly restrictive framework generated by the assumption of the

---

[28] This objection is not to the point given the Campbellian picture of the role and scope of indeterminism; but even in that case we have no reason either to suppose that things will in general go the way we hope or to think that indeterminism can be any sort of foundation for responsibility.

truth of determinism. But if one is to approach the true centre of the question one must consider the consequences of the impossibility of such origination in the light of the fact that such origination is impossible *whether determinism is true or false*; and is therefore impossible *tout court*.

10   THE UNHELPFULNESS OF INDETERMINISM (3)

This said, it may be granted that there is a natural inclination to think that determinism is somehow worse than indeterminism. The thought (once again) is that if determinism is true then it is already determined whether or not I will die in this battle (Honderich's example on page 390), whereas if determinism is false it is not. Indeed. But whether determinism is true or false, what happens in the battle is in any case partly, and in many respects largely, a matter of the occurrence of factors beyond my control. And whether the occurrence of these factors is deterministic or partly indeterministic makes no real difference to me or my chances; whether for deterministic or partly indeterministic reasons, the enemy gunners will or will not fatally increase the angle of elevation of their gun; I will or will not tread on a mine, or trip in the track of a tank. I am not really better off, if it is not already determined whether or not I will die in battle. It is not as if my chances of survival are higher.[29] In some respects a life may be like a novel, which is not less enjoyable or surprising because it is already written down.

If one enjoys playing on a mechanical gambling machine (like a one-armed bandit) one's chances and pleasure are not improved if it is indeterministic. Nor are one's chances and pleasure reduced if it is not. If alternatively one plays a game of skill, one's chances and pleasure are not increased if one's talent and actions are indeterministically as they are; nor are one's chances and pleasure reduced if they are not.[30]

Consider a philosopher—perhaps a fiercely competitive philosopher— who believes in determinism, and who is playing an intense game of chess, when the thought occurs that determinism is true, and that everything that happens in the game is determined. This may cause a special *frisson*. But the thought that there may be entirely random inputs affecting the course of events isn't much more comfortable. (Is it more comfortable at all?) And now the other player has made a move. A response must be made. How could internal indeterminism help here? It would not improve one's powers of analysis.

[29] The Realism Constraint should also be borne in mind.

[30] Honderich suggests that determinism may 'do . . . us . . . hurt' not just (1) in subtracting origination from our world, but also (2) 'in ruling out what would be desirable, a world of *limited real uncertainty*' (p. 502). Against this it may be objected (1) that so far as 'origination' is concerned determinism excludes nothing that indeterminism permits, so that it does us no special hurt. (2) We have real and ineliminable uncertainty even if determinism is true; (epistemological) uncertainty does not depend on (ontological) indeterminacy. As Honderich says himself, 'it is very far from true that my world becomes in fact a predictable place by way of the truth of determinism' (p. 513). It might be that we wanted indeterminacy as well as real uncertainty. We might in any case *think* that we wanted indeterminacy as well as real uncertainty. But it is not at all clear that this belief survives much reflection.

In sum, it is an illusion to feel that if determinism is true then one is constrained or thwarted in some way which (a) affects one's life-hopes *with respect to any particular thing that one wants to achieve,* and which (b) is such that one would not be constrained or thwarted in that way if determinism were false. It is, perhaps, a potent illusion, but it is an illusion. 'Freedom' from 'subjection' to deterministic elements is just equal 'subjection' to indeterministic elements. It seems that what is wanted and imagined when the falsity of determinism is thought to be desirable is a certain kind of *control* over things which is neither facilitated nor even made possible by indeterminism.

To make this point is part of the response of 'intransigence', in Honderich's terms, but it can also be part of the response of 'affirmation'. And to understand it fully is to see that these responses are not to be thought of simply as responses to the consequences of *determinism,* but as responses to the fact that true origination, of the true-responsibility-creating kind we seem to want, is impossible in any case. I think that part III of *A Theory of Determinism* is flawed by its failure to confront this fact. And in a way quite unnecessarily: for, as remarked in §6, its essential project can be pursued without being tied to the issue of determinism.

11 'UNCAUSED ORIGINATION': WHY DO WE WANT IT?

There is another doubt which arises here. How far is a wish for true origination really bound up with our life-hopes anyway? Obviously it does not affect our hopes to win the Premium Bonds prize, or to live in peaceful times, or to avoid catching a personality-distorting disease. And a great many of our self-referential hopes about how our lives should go are of this general, non-action-related kind. Clearly a wish for true origination can only be relevant to those of our life-hopes that are hopes to achieve certain things by our own actions. It is only of these that Honderich says that an image of self as *uncaused originator* is 'indubitably . . . part of our life-hopes of a certain kind' (p. 391). But how far is this really true? Our thought is *very* vague here. And even if what Honderich says is true, it may be that when we—non-philosophers included—think a bit harder about what we want or believe, the image wavers and fades. Do we really want to be uncaused originators in this way? Does it really matter that much to our life-hopes?

In his book *Elbow Room* Dennett raises some serious doubts about whether the things we think we want, so far as free will (or 'uncaused origination') is concerned, are really worth wanting.[31] (There is a further connected question about whether we really want what we unreflectively think we want.) For even if determinism is true, and there is no 'uncaused origination', we can be and often are entirely free in the important and fully compatibilist sense of being able to do what we want or choose or decide or think right or best to do. We are often entirely free to pursue our life-hope-involving projects to the best of our abilities. And isn't this all that really matters, in

---

[31] The subtitle of his book is *The Varieties of Free Will Worth Wanting.*

the way of freedom of action, so far as our life-hopes about our own achievements are concerned, at least? What more could anyone reasonably want? Surely to be able to do (or attempt) what one wants or chooses to do (or attempt) is to have complete freedom of action, and all one could ask for so far as one's life-hopes are concerned? But this ability is compatible with determinism, and is in no way improved by the truth of indeterminism (either of the Realistic or of the Unrealistic sort).[32]

So even after we have granted (just for the sake of argument) that a capacity for 'uncaused origination' might be a real possibility, a question arises as to why one might want it. It is not as if a capacity for 'uncaused origination' is going to make one a faster runner, or a better thinker. In the next section I will suggest that the only plausible reason why people might want it, so far as their life-hopes were concerned, is an old and familiar one: it seems to be clearly necessary for true desert, or true responsibility in the sense of §6, and hence for true *credit* for one's achievements.

In fact the correct argumentative strategy at this point is to demand a detailed account of what 'uncaused origination' is supposed to be, because the attempt to describe it shows that it cannot exist in the way that we want, and that it is not made possible by the truth of indeterminism. Even to accept to talk as if 'uncaused origination' were a real possibility is to give too much away to the view being criticized—partly because the expression has a seductive and impressive ring to it.[33] Nevertheless I will do so—I will pursue one very loose and speculative line of thought about it without raising many of the objections that I think are appropriate.[34]

One potent idea behind the idea of 'uncaused origination' is perhaps that internal obstacles to achieving what one wants to achieve *will* be diminished. Consider a case in which one wants to be a different sort of person in some respect. One wants to change oneself and become F, because of desires and character traits G, H, and J, but feels one cannot, because of character traits K, L, and M. Then the idea is that if one is capable of 'uncaused origination', the K, L, and M factors can be overridden or disabled or ignored, while the G, H, and J factors operate.

But (once again) why should G, H, and J operate more than K, L, and M? Well (the vague thought presumably goes), because one *wants* them to. But this want is just another factor, N. And why should N operate rather than K, L, and M? Any reasons for thinking that one might be less hindered by bad determinants of one's actions and efforts if determinism were false seem to be equally good reasons for thinking that one might be less helped by good determinants of one's actions and efforts. If a capacity for 'uncaused origination' is a capacity for producing decisions or actions in which one is not caused to decide or act as one does by anything (anything other than oneself?), it seems that it is not much use to anyone.

Perhaps the old and murky thought is that the 'true self', with its given set of action-determining traits, is liberated (or more liberated) from internal constraints if

---

[32] Here I repeat or paraphrase the beginning of ch. 16 of *Freedom and Belief*.

[33] The only thing that is relatively clear about it is the *consequence* that its possession is meant to have: the consequence of being a free and responsible agent in the true-desert-entailing way described in §6.

[34] Discussed in *Freedom and Belief*, ch. 2.

'uncaused origination' is possible. But (1) this is very close to the unacceptable picture of the true self somehow *controlling* indeterministic or random elements in order to buck the otherwise deterministic order.[35] (2) This is not an idea of 'uncaused origination' of a sort that anyone believes themselves to possess here and now: for it is here presented precisely as something that would make things better than they are *if* it were possessed. (3) Connectedly, it ignores the Realism Constraint on the postulation of indeterminism, which supposes that any indeterminism that exists exists now and as things are, with people experiencing all the actual internal struggles and difficulties they do experience. (4) It does not really seem that there is 'uncaused origination' here at all. There are just people (seen now as 'true selves') who are acting in accordance with certain of their desires and preferences, their desires and preferences determining or affecting their actions (in a way compatible with determinism), and who are not hindered by certain other traits of character that they might otherwise have been hindered by if things had been different.

12   'LIFE-HOPES' AND TRUE RESPONSIBILITY

I suggest, then, that the only reason for wanting something that could conceivably be denoted by 'uncaused origination' which survives reflection is a very old and very familiar one: this 'uncaused origination' seems to be a necessary condition of the truth of many of our cherished beliefs about the reality of 'true' responsibility and desert, where these are conceived of in the strong sense sketched in §6. Thus, for example, such 'uncaused origination' seems to be a necessary condition of the truth of our belief in the appropriateness of praising achievements (or condemning wrongdoings) considered as things for which an individual *x* is *truly responsible in some ultimate way which is not possible if all x's achievements are ultimately a matter of luck* (luck in the widest sense—whether the luck of genetic inheritance and environmental influence, or the luck of random input). This, and only this, is the heart of the matter. Just as 'uncaused origination' is a necessary condition of true responsibility and true desert, so it is a necessary condition of 'true' credit for our achievements.

Let me try one more time to find some other motive for desiring 'uncaused origination', so far as 'life-hopes' are concerned. The best cases to look at are presumably cases where one hopes to achieve something difficult, something of the sort for which people are admired. But here, I suspect, there may be deep differences of outlook, depending on deep differences of temperament, mental style, size of 'ego', and so on. Rimbaud's life-hopes about artistic success and achievement did not depend on any sort of 'image of origination', but rather on hopes that his daemon or muse would be forthcoming. He had an entirely determinism-compatible (and self-as-uncaused-originator-*in*compatible) picture of such things. Talking of his processes of creation,

[35] Remember that even if this picture were acceptable it could not provide for true responsibility in the sense of §6 unless the self were somehow responsible for itself in a way which is impossible whether determinism is true or false.

he remarked that he was a mere 'spectator at the unfolding (or blossoming) of [his] thought: I watch it, I listen to it. . . . *I* am another'.[36] Such views are the rule rather than the exception among poets. What in the end does one do, when one tries to think and write and nothing comes? One sits and waits. One more or less vaguely pushes one's mind in the right direction, or re-reads one's previous sentence, and waits for something to *happen*. Then, if all goes well, something *comes* to one, *occurs* to one, *strikes* one. One *has* an idea. It is something *given*.[37]

More generally: many people's principal hope, when contemplating some future task, is that they will 'prove up to it'. Their life-hopes with respect to the task naturally incorporate the idea that they have a certain given (determined) measure of talent and determination, and they hope that it will prove to be enough. This is, I suggest, the normal thought. They may well wish to be more capable than they are. But to think that the existence of any kind of indeterminism could make this wish into a realistic hope is delusion.

These things being so, the idea that we often very much want to possess some capacity for 'uncaused origination' of action, when we contemplate our hopes of performing things which are difficult and worthy of achievement, may seem puzzling (unless it is simply because we want true credit to be possible). For one will not be more capable or more talented or do better if one is capable of 'uncaused origination'. The phrase may continue to echo suggestively in many people's minds, suggesting to them that if they had a capacity for uncaused origination they would be able to overcome obstacles that they feel they cannot at present overcome. One can only encourage such people to ask themselves once again how the existence of random events in the universe could realistically help with this.

I conclude that the only relatively clear reason for wanting 'uncaused origination' to be possible in one's own case, so far as life-hopes are concerned, seems to be the familiar one given above: it seems to be necessary *if* one wants to be capable of being truly responsible for—truly deserving of credit for—one's actions and achievements, in some ultimate way which is not possible if all one's achievements are ultimately a matter of luck in the widest sense (according to which all one's native endowments—one's talent, application, energy, etc.—plus or minus any random inputs that there might be to one's life, must ultimately be counted a matter of luck).[38]

I italicized the word 'if' in the previous paragraph, for here an aside seems appropriate. Individual temperamental differences are obviously important in this area of debate, and my appreciation of the issue may be weak because I find no trace of the

---

[36] Rimbaud 1871: 250.

[37] Although this is true of me, and well attested not only among poets but equally among scientists and musicians, perhaps it is less true of others.

[38] Gibbon is clear on this: 'When I contemplate the common lot of mortality, I must acknowledge that I have drawn a high prize in the lottery of life. . . . I am endowed with a cheerful temper, a moderate sensibility, and a natural disposition to repose rather than activity: some mischievous appetites and habits have perhaps been corrected by philosophy or time' (1789–90: 239).

want just mentioned (the want for true credit) in myself.[39] However, taken as a whole, my attitudes on such questions are dramatically inconsistent. For (a) I regard any gifts that I have, and anything good that I do, as a matter of pure good fortune; so that the idea that I deserve credit for them in some strong sense seems absurd. But (b) I find I do *not* regard others' achievements and good actions as pure good fortune, but feel admiration (and, where appropriate, gratitude) of a true-responsibility-presupposing kind. Furthermore, (c), I do *not* regard bad things that I do as mere bad luck, but have true-responsibility-presupposing attitudes to them (which may admittedly fade with time). Finally (d) I *do* naturally regard bad things that other people do as explicable in ways that make true-responsibility-presupposing blame inappropriate.[40] I suspect that this pattern may not be particularly uncommon.[41]

13 CONCLUSION

In sum, I can see the old and familiar point that 'uncaused origination' is necessary for true desert, but I cannot see how the desire for 'uncaused origination' (or belief in it) enters into our life-hopes except in so far as it is bound up with a belief in and desire for true desert and true credit. If it seems to do so, it is perhaps because it is deeply confused with other things, for example with the distinctly unmysterious desire and hope to be different from, or better than, or more talented or capable or strong-willed than one is; or with the desire for the world in general to be more easily changeable than it is.

I think, therefore, that there is an error of strategy in Honderich's discussion. He introduces the vague and potent notion of 'uncaused origination' and relies on our intuitive understanding of it in discussing the way in which it is threatened, as it surely is, by determinism. For some purposes this works fine. It is, however, arguable that the best way to pursue precisely the problems with which he is principally concerned in part III of *A Theory of Determinism* is to try to be very precise about exactly what is involved in the notion of 'uncaused origination'. But if one does this, one of the first things that is likely to emerge is a point which Honderich is unwilling to concede—that 'uncaused origination', in any sense in which we might reasonably want it, is no more available if determinism is false than if it is true; and, more generally,

---

[39] Honderich remarks (p. 510) that 'it is hardly possible to discuss our present subject without feeling uneasy . . . about falling into a kind of autobiographical reflection lacking a general relevance'. But it may be that all that can be of 'general relevance' in this area is some account of individual differences—some survey of the principal different types of individual attitude.

[40] (a) and (b) are on the face of it inconsistent, as are (a) and (c), and (c) and (d). It is worth noting that Mill, during his youthful depression, felt 'that it would be a blessing if the doctrine of necessity could be believed by all *quoad* the characters of others, and disbelieved in regard to their own' (1873: 102).

[41] Nietzsche would take a very dim view of it. Note that even if such a set of attitudes is perverse, it may disable a lot of bad emotions. Those who think it morally agreeable rather than perverse (however logically disgraceful) should bear in mind that those who possess it think of their possession of it as just a matter of luck—more good fortune, if that is indeed what it is.

that if determinism is really bad, then indeterminism is exactly as bad, so far as all really important aspects of our attitude to ourselves are concerned.

As remarked earlier, some people may find that the thought that determinism is true causes a special *frisson*, a certain peculiar gloom. But when one asks what the practical difference is between living in the richly unpredictable world we do live in if determinism is in fact true of it, and living in this world if indeterminism is in fact true of it, the answer seems to be 'None'. The sky, the sea, the trees are all the same in either case. And you and I are the same as we are in either case, for we are as we are in either case, with the abilities and defects that we have. And, crucially, 'true' responsibility (or true credit), in the sense described in §6, is impossible in either case—although most people take it for granted that such true responsibility is not only possible but actual, and will continue to take it for granted whatever philosophers conclude.

So I suggest that the main relevant consequence of belief in determinism[42] is that it may give rise to a certain *frisson* in some people. If these people also find it causes gloom, because it makes it so clear that we cannot be truly responsible for our actions in the way that we ordinarily suppose, they ought perhaps to reflect further on the fact that the falsity of determinism cannot help in any way. It cannot give us free will in the ordinary, strong incompatibilist sense.

---

[42] Not of determinism itself, for if it is true it has always been true.

15

Free Agents

1   INTRODUCTION

Are we free agents? It depends how you understand the word 'free'. In this paper I am going to take my bearings from the fundamental sense of the word in which we cannot be free agents in the absolute way we sometimes suppose because we cannot be *ultimately* (*morally*) *responsible* for our actions. I will express this by saying that we cannot be *U-free* agents. It does not follow from the fact that we cannot be U-free agents that we cannot have all the freedom of action we can reasonably want, for we can.

2   THE BASIC ARGUMENT

The short form of the argument that U-freedom is impossible is as follows.

(1) When you act, at a given time t, you do what you do, in the situation in which you find yourself at t, because of the way you are, at t.

(2) But if you do what you do at t because of the way you are at t, then in order to be ultimately (morally) responsible for what you do, at t (in order to be U-free, at t), you must be ultimately (morally) responsible for the way you are, at t, at least in certain fundamental, mental respects.

(3) But to be ultimately morally responsible for the way you are, at t, in certain fundamental mental respects, you'd have to be *causa sui* in those respects.

(4) But nothing can be ultimately *causa sui* in any respect at all (or if God can be, nothing else can be).

(5) So you can't be ultimately morally responsible for what you do—you can't be U-free.[1]

I call this the *Basic Argument* against U-freedom. Here is a variant.

(A) One cannot be *causa sui*—one cannot be the ultimate, originating cause of oneself.

(B) But one would have to be *causa sui*, at least in certain crucial mental respects, in order to be ultimately morally responsible for one's decisions and actions.

---

[1] The way you are when acting at t is a function of many things, including of course your experience of your situation (the reference to a particular time isn't necessary, but some find it helpful). It is not just or especially a matter of your character, and the argument has its full force even for those who question or reject the explanatory viability of the notion of character (see e.g. Harman 1999, 2000; Doris 2002).

(C) So one cannot be ultimately morally responsible for one's decisions or actions: one cannot be ultimately morally deserving of praise or blame for one's decisions or actions or one's character or indeed for anything else.

These are brief versions of the argument that U-freedom is impossible, and both premiss (3) in the first version and premiss (B) in the second can be questioned. While many think both are obviously true, others think they need argument. I have argued for both in other places,[2] and will take their soundness for granted in this paper. 'The *causa sui*', as Nietzsche says,

is the best self-contradiction that has been conceived so far; it is a sort of rape and perversion of logic. But the extravagant pride of man has managed to entangle itself profoundly and frightfully with just this nonsense. The desire for 'freedom of the will' in the superlative metaphysical sense, which still holds sway, unfortunately, in the minds of the half-educated; the desire to bear the entire and ultimate responsibility for one's actions oneself, and to absolve God, the world, ancestors, chance, and society involves nothing less than to be precisely this *causa sui* and, with more than Baron Münchhausen's audacity, to pull oneself up into existence by the hair, out of the swamps of nothingness . . .[3]

3   CAUSA SUI

U-freedom is impossible because one of its necessary conditions—being *causa sui*, at least in certain respects[4]—is unfulfillable. But the fact that U-freedom is impossible does not prevent us from enquiring into its conditions—into what it would take to be a U-free agent. We can specify the conditions of impossible things. We can say what something has to be like to be a round square: it has to be an equiangular, equilateral, rectilinear, quadrilateral closed plane figure every point on the periphery of which is equidistant from a single point within it. It is because we know the content of the concept ROUND SQUARE[5] that we know that there cannot be such a thing, and the same is true of the notion of U-freedom: we couldn't know that U-freedom was impossible unless we not only knew at least one necessary condition of U-freedom, but also knew that that necessary condition—the *causa sui* condition—was unfulfillable.[6]

So we may enquire into the conditions of an impossible thing, and that is what I want to do in this paper. Suspending judgement on the question whether it is actually impossible for a thing to be *causa sui*, I want to try to state sufficient conditions of U-freedom, reworking my previous attempt to do this in Part III of my book *Freedom and Belief* (1986).

---

[2] See e.g. Strawson 1986: ch. 2, 2001 and Essay 13. (2) may also be questioned, of course; see Strawson 1986: 29.

[3] Nietzsche 1886: §21.

[4] I will usually take the qualification 'at least in certain respects' for granted.

[5] I use small capitals for names of concepts.

[6] Some say that statements or concepts that are self-contradictory are meaningless, but this cannot be right, because meaningfulness is a necessary condition of contradictoriness.

—Surely a conviction so strong and so central to our conception of ourselves must at least have an intelligible possibility as its object![7]

I think the content of the notion of U-freedom or ultimate responsibility can be vividly characterized, and is in that sense perfectly—fully—intelligible, even though it turns out not to be a coherent possibility.

One dramatic way to characterize it is by reference to the story of heaven and hell. Ultimate moral responsibility is responsibility of such a kind that, if we have it, it *makes sense* to propose that it could be just to punish some of us with torment in hell and reward others with bliss in heaven. It makes sense because what we do is absolutely up to us. I stress 'makes sense' because one doesn't have to believe in the story of heaven and hell in order to understand the notion of ultimate responsibility that it is used to illustrate. Nor does one have to believe in the story of heaven and hell in order to believe in ultimate responsibility; many atheists have believed in ultimate responsibility.

A less dramatic but equally effective way of characterizing ultimate responsibility is this: ultimate responsibility exists if and only if punishment and reward can be truly just and fair without having any pragmatic justification.[8]

Many philosophers set their primary focus on the notion of a U-free *action*, rather on the general notion of U-freedom or U-free *agenthood*. There is, however, an important sense in which the task of giving a general account of free *agenthood* is strictly prior to the task of giving a general account of free *action*. This is certainly so in the case of standard compatibilist accounts of free action that define freedom of action simply as the absence of certain sorts of constraints on action, for if one defines freedom in this way by reference to action one needs an account of free agenthood, that is, an account of what sort of thing is capable of genuine free action when suitably free from constraint. Stones, after all, are not subject to any of the constraints standardly proposed as restrictions on free action by compatibilists (they are not kleptomaniacs, they do not suffer from OCD, they do not have first-order wants that they do not want to have), but they are not *ipso facto* capable of free action. So all fully spelt out compatibilist *Constraint* theories of free action have to give an account of free agenthood. They cannot simply say that freedom is freedom from some specified set of constraints.

It may seem easy to specify what it takes to be a U-free agent: all it requires is that one be

[0] *causa sui*

and that one be

[1] an agent.[9]

On this view, an agent's being *causa sui* is not only necessary for it to be a U-free agent but also sufficient. So once one has an account of what it is to be an agent all

---

[7] Cf. Nagel 1987: 6.   [8] Cf. Strawson 1998: 748–9.

[9] In this paper I will restrict attention to agents that are capable of intentional action, and when I speak of acts or actions I will mean intentional actions (obviously chemical agents are not agents in this sense; nor are economic climates that are agents of change).

one has to do is to analyse, as far as one can, what is involved in being *causa sui*. And here there seems to be little to say. To be the cause of oneself is to be the cause of oneself. The notion CAUSA SUI has nothing hidden about it. If it feels obscure, that is only because it is so evidently paradoxical. The feeling of obscurity does not show that the concept CAUSA SUI does not come clear before the mind (the feeling may stem principally from the fact that the notion presents vividly as something impossible, but without the obvious visualizable impossibility of ROUND SQUARE).

On this view, then, the analysis of U-free agenthood is quickly done, once we know what it is for something to be an agent: we just add [0] to [1]. But it is not so simple, for three reasons. First, we need to take account of the fact that when we are concerned with U-freedom we are necessarily concerned with what it might be for something to be *causa sui* with respect to, and so radically responsible for, certain of its *mental* characteristics. Thus suppose we have a good account of what it is to be an agent. It's not as if adding a completely general account of what it is to be *causa sui* ('It's really quite simple . . . in the case of stones, for example, it's just for the stone to be—truly—the origin or creator of itself') will leave us with nothing more to say about what it is to be a U-free agent. For the way of being *causa sui* that concerns us will essentially involve complicated mental things like the capacity to reflect on the content of one's own character traits and preferences in such a way as to choose among them.

Second, it would be helpful to have some further account of what it is to be an agent, for in the present context being *causa sui* is merely the differentia that distinguishes U-free agents from all those other members of the species *agent* that are not U-free agents.

Third, it is not clear that being *causa sui* and being an agent are sufficient for being a U-free agent, even if they are necessary. In *Freedom and Belief* I argued that even if one were an agent, and even if one were *causa sui* in the right kind of way, one might still not be a U-free agent.[10] Thomas Nagel and Ingmar Persson disputed this claim in their reviews of *Freedom and Belief*,[11] and I will consider their objections in §16 below.

4 AGENTHOOD

I take it that a dog—*Fido*—is capable of performing intentional actions for reasons, and is therefore an agent in the present sense. But no one I know thinks that Fido can be a U-free agent in the way that many think human beings can be. No one believes that Fido can be ultimately responsible for what he does in such a way as to be (without any sort of qualification) fully morally deserving of praise or blame for his actions. It seems, then, that we need an account of what we share with dogs that makes both species agents, followed by an account of what it is that differentiates us from dogs in such a way that our candidacy for U-freedom survives when theirs lapses.

---

[10] Strawson 1986: Part III.   [11] Nagel 1987: 5–6; Persson 1987: 66.

So what is it to be an agent? I will be brief and take it that one is an agent if and only if one is

[2] capable of forming beliefs of certain sorts

[3] capable of having desires (pro-attitudes) of certain sorts

[4] capable of self-change (e.g. self-movement)

[5] capable of practical reasoning (in a realistically inclusive sense in which dogs and one-year-old children are capable of practical reasoning).

Some may say that this list of conditions contains redundancy, others may say that it states only necessary conditions, not sufficient conditions (even after it has been allowed that a being can be an agent, an entity capable of performing intentional actions, even if it never actually acts). Others again may say that it is circular, because [5] already relies on an understanding of the notion of an agent. [5] certainly needs further careful exposition, and there is a great deal to say about all these conditions,[12] but here I will take a general understanding of what they involve for granted. Readers may insert their own preferred account of what is minimally sufficient for being an agent (a being capable of intentional action) at this point. No one, I hope, will want to say that dogs, dolphins, and one-year-old infants are not really capable of intentional action.

5 SELF-CONSCIOUSNESS

The question is now this: if conditions [1]–[5] state what agenthood is,[13] what has to be added to them to get U-freedom? It seems clear that something must be added, given that dogs and human infants fulfil these conditions but are not U-free agents.

Well, [0], the *causa sui* condition, is presumably crucial, and this creates a difficulty, because if we want to test the effect of adding [0] to the minimal case in which [1]–[5] are fulfilled we have to suppose, very artificially, that at some point in their (individual) pasts dogs and infants have the sophisticated capacities necessary for becoming *causa sui* in the required way (for example, the capacity to reflect on the content of one's own character traits and preferences in such a way as to choose among them) although they revert, after becoming *causa sui*, to being things that evidently do not have such capacities.

Let us nevertheless suppose this for the sake of argument.[14] Are dogs and infants, if *causa sui*, then U-free agents? Are [0]–[5] sufficient for U-freedom? One may well think not; one may feel that there is some other crucial missing condition. And there seems to be a leading candidate, the condition that one be

---

[12] The beliefs and desires must be such as to link up in a certain way in the mind of the putative agent.

[13] [1] does no work.

[14] Some may think this is all too fantastic to be about what really concerns us when we think about the problem of free will. I think, on the contrary, that it is crucial to understand that we are led to exactly such places when we think seriously about the problem.

[6] fully and explicitly self-conscious.

Surely any truly U-free agent must be able to explicitly grasp or apprehend itself *as* itself, in the way distinctive of and definitive of self-consciousness, in thinking about itself and its actions—in a way that (we take it) dogs and infants cannot?

It's far from clear why [6] should be thought to make the crucial difference, when it comes to something so momentous as U-freedom, but many think it can and does. They think that adding [6] self-consciousness to [1]–[5] is enough to secure U-freedom, or at least full moral responsibility, quite independently of [0]. To be a U-free agent, they may say, is just to be a genuinely self-conscious agent, for a self-conscious agent can really know what it's doing and that it is itself doing what it's doing. [6], they may say, renders [0], the problematic (unfulfillable) *causa sui* condition, completely unnecessary:

—That's right. The capacity for fully explicit self-conscious deliberation in a situation of choice—the capacity to be explicitly aware of oneself as facing choices and engaging in processes of reasoning about what to do—suffices by itself to constitute one as a U-free agent in the strongest possible sense; whatever else is or is not the case. *Causa sui* be blowed; one's full self-conscious awareness of oneself and one's situation when one chooses simply annihilates any supposed consequences of the fact that one neither is nor can be *causa sui*. The mere fact of one's self-conscious presence in the situation of choice confers U-freedom on one, and obviously so. One may in the final analysis be wholly constituted as the sort of person one is by factors for which one is not and cannot be in any way ultimately responsible, but the threat that this fact is supposed to pose to one's claim to U-freedom is simply vapourized by the fact of one's fully self-conscious awareness of one's situation.

I think this view has considerable power and attractiveness. I think it correctly describes one of the substructures of our deep *belief* in U-freedom. But I'm sure that it is not an account of anything that could really *constitute* U-freedom, because it ignores [0], the *causa sui* condition.

What about the converse view that [0], being *causa sui*, renders [6], being self-conscious, unnecessary? On this view, if Fido could be *causa sui* in the required way he would *ipso facto* be a U-free agent in every sense in which we are, and whatever else was or was not the case. If Fido once brought it about that he was the way he was, mentally, in the relevant respects, at some strangely lucid time in his past, then he would now be a U-free agent, even though he is not—no longer—not self-conscious.

Does anyone believe that self-consciousness is not necessary for true freedom? Persson does not explicitly endorse such a view, but he does raise a doubt about whether 'common sense in its judgements of desert and its adoption of reactive attitudes' requires self-consciousness on the part of the agent judged.[15]

There is a quick reply to this, already touched on. It seems clear that the *causa sui* requirement that is supposed to be necessary for U-freedom cannot possibly be fulfilled by an unself-conscious creature. For to fulfil it one must at some time have consciously and explicitly decided on a way to be, mentally, in certain respects,

---

[15] 1987: 65.

and (roughly) one must then have acted on that decision with success, and have intentionally brought it about that one is the way one is, mentally, in the relevant respects.[16] But it is not possible to do this in the required way without being self-conscious, if only because one must grasp that the mental features one contemplates are one's own. So fulfilment of [0], the relevant *causa sui* condition, requires fulfilment of [6], the self-consciousness condition, and cannot render it unnecessary.

The reply to this reply has also been touched on. Suppose that a self-conscious being, C, has done everything needed to be *causa sui*: it has intentionally brought it about that it is the way it is, mentally, in the relevant respects; it has set up its own practical-moral constitution in such a way it is indeed wholly responsible for that constitution, and in such a way that we judge it to be ultimately morally responsible for what it does. Now, suddenly, C loses all capacity for self-consciousness, while continuing to be a complex agent (C, we may suppose, is a cousin of *Nemo*, a being who is by definition as much like an ordinary adult human being as it is possible to be without being self-conscious).[17] Does this mean that suddenly C is no longer a U-free agent at all, no longer ultimately morally responsible for what it does? Anyone who thinks self-consciousness is necessary for U-freedom will think so, and I agree, partly for reasons still to come; but Perssonian common sense may think it far from obvious.

I will return to this idea when considering Nagel's objection to a different but related case. For the moment I will assume that [6], self-consciousness, is at least necessary for U-freedom, in addition to [1]–[5], the basic conditions of agency.

6 STRUCTURALISM AND ATTITUDINALISM

Many agree that self-consciousness is necessary for U-freedom, even if they want nothing to do with the *causa sui* condition; they think it necessary for genuine moral responsibility whether or not genuine moral responsibility requires *causa-sui*-involving U-freedom. And they not only think that self-consciousness is the crucial difference between dogs and ourselves, when it comes to the question of U-freedom (or to the question of *causa-sui*-free moral responsibility), or at least that it is *one* crucial difference between dogs and ourselves. They also think, much more generally, that whatever the final analysis of U-freedom turns out to be, U-freedom is and must be simply a matter of having a certain sort of (suitably complex or sophisticated) agentive-cognitive make-up or *agentive structure* that can be fully described, for all the purposes of the free will issue, in very general functional-capacity terms like [1]–[6] above.

I will call this position the *Agent-Structuralist* position—the *Structuralist* position, for short. It is I think both natural and attractive, but I am going to argue that it is incorrect, and that there are among the conditions of U-freedom conditions that require that the agent possess certain experiential or as I will say *attitudinal* properties

---

[16] See e.g. Strawson 1986: 28–9, 1998: 746.   [17] See Strawson 1986: 19–20.

over and above any *agent-structural* properties that are necessary for U-freedom.[18] This makes me an *Attitudinalist*, as opposed to a Structuralist, in a sense that I will explain.

Structuralists can scoop up all the conditions so far considered. They can include [0], the *causa sui* condition, in the set of agent-structural conditions along with all the conditions of self-conscious agenthood. They can treat it as just one more general agent-structural condition. It's true that it is a condition of a different sort from the conditions of self-conscious agenthood already stated ([1] to [6]) in as much as it is not a requirement that one have some enduring functional capacity but rather a requirement that one's overall motivational structure have been generated in a certain way. But Attitudinalists can simply give the *causa sui* condition to the Structuralists, allowing it to count as just one more agent-structural condition in addition to the conditions of self-conscious agenthood, while continuing to insist that agent-structural conditions can never be enough for U-freedom, and that further distinctively attitudinal conditions must be added to any proposed set of agent-structural conditions.

Structuralists may also propose to include the requirement that one be

[99] subject to determinism

or alternatively

[98] not subject to determinism

among the general agent-structural conditions of U-freedom, and once again Attitudinalists need not object.[19] They can allow conditions like [99] or [98] to be counted as agent-structural conditions in the largest sense (they are clearly not attitudinal conditions). They can also, perhaps, agree that either [99] or [98] is necessary for U-freedom—although they are just as likely to think that neither is (I am going to leave [98] and [99] out of account in what follows). But throughout all this they will continue to insist that no set of agent-structural conditions can ever be enough for U-freedom—not even when [0], the *causa sui* condition, has been included in the set of agent-structural conditions—because attitudinal conditions are also required.

The Attitudinalists think that the Structuralists are failing to treat the problem of free will with sufficient generality. The Structuralists, they think, are not sufficiently aware of how bleak and weird and intuitively unfree creatures that fulfil all the conditions so far mentioned—[0]–[6] ± [98] or [99]—might be; Structuralists profess to be thinking about the conditions of U-freedom in an entirely general way, but they are not sufficiently aware of how many special features of ordinary human beings they are taking for granted and presupposing. The Attitudinalists hold that some of these features, properly examined, turn out to be conditions of U-freedom, attitudinal conditions that are irreducible to agent-structural conditions.

---

[18] Frankfurt's requirement that a free agent must be capable of forming second-order volitions (Frankfurt 1971) is a straightforward agent-structural condition on the present view of things, and can be included in the list of conditions of U-freedom by any agent-structuralists who wish to do so.

[19] Several compatibilists have favoured [99] (see for example Hobart 1934), and all incompatibilist libertarians have favoured [98]. There is a presumption that [0] is incompatible with [99] unless the agent in question is God or the universe, and many red herrings lie this way.

7 THE BELIEF-IN-U-FREEDOM CONDITION

What might these attitudinal conditions be? One proposal is that

[10] believing one is a U-free agent

—conceiving oneself as a U-free agent, experiencing oneself as U-free, figuring oneself as U-free—is itself a condition of being U-free. On this view, U-freedom is not just a matter of possessing certain agent-structural capacities. A U-free agent must also see or experience itself, think or conceive of itself, in a certain specific way. It must have a certain attitude to itself and its agency. It must fulfil the attitudinal *belief-in-U-freedom* condition. (In what follows 'belief in U-freedom' refers only to a creature's belief in *its own* U-freedom.)

What does this amount to? The first thing to say, perhaps, is that it is not strictly necessary to figure oneself as a specifically *moral* agent, or have any grasp of the notion of morality at all, in order to fulfil the belief-in-U-freedom condition. We (human beings) ordinarily associate the idea of U-freedom closely with moral issues—to such an extent that we may think that to have a sense of oneself as U-free is necessarily to have some grasp of moral matters.[20] But this is not so. Self-conscious agents that face difficult life-determining choices while lacking any sort of conception of morality can have a sense of U-freedom—of radical, absolute, buck-stopping *up-to-me-ness* in choice and action—that is just as powerful as any sense of U-freedom grounded primarily in experience of moral requirements. They can fulfil the belief-in-U-freedom condition just as resoundingly as we do.[21]

—Perhaps, perhaps not. But what is there to back the idea that belief in U-freedom might be a condition of U-freedom?

Well, suppose an agent *a* fulfils all possible agent-structural conditions of U-freedom. It performs an action and is in no way physically or psychologically constrained in any of the ways standardly cited in (for example) compatibilist constraint theories of freedom. Suppose we know all this, and believe that U-freedom is possible, and take it that *a* has performed a U-free action. Then we discover that it really has *no sort* of conception of itself *as* a U-free agent, no sense that it is a U-free agent. Can we still hold it to be truly a U-free agent? Put yourself in *a*'s shoes: you act, when you do, with no sense of yourself as a U-free agent. You have no sense whatever of yourself as something that can be ultimately, radically responsible for what you do. Is a life spent like that the life of a U-free agent, something that can be ultimately responsible for what it does, morally deserving *without any sort of qualification* of praise or blame or punishment or reward for its actions? I don't think so.

---

[20] Kant (1788: 4; Ak. 5. 4) took our knowledge of the moral law to be proof that we were U-free agents—to be the means by which we could know with certainty that we were U-free—even though we could not understand how U-freedom was possible.

[21] See e.g. Strawson 1998: 746. I will take it that a sense of things being truly or radically up to one is the same as, or sufficient for, a sense of oneself as U-free.

Let 'B(a, p)' represent '*a* believes that *p*', and let 'Fa' represent '*a* is U-free'. The belief-in-U-freedom condition states that

$$[Fa \rightarrow B[a, Fa]]$$

—that if you are U-free then you believe you are—and that this is so because believing you are U-free is partly *constitutive* of being U-free, and not, say, because being U-free is a property that is necessarily epistemically evident, like being in intense pain. It seems paradoxical because it appears to offend against a very basic (even if not exceptionless) epistemic principle, the *principle of independence* of belief and thing believed.[22] Suppose *a* has an ordinary factual belief *p*.[23] If *p* is true then it is true in virtue of the obtaining of some state of affairs S_1. Obviously. The principle of independence states that the state of affairs of *a*'s having *p*—call this S_2—cannot itself be part of S_1. If *a* has *p* and *p* is true in virtue of S_1 then S_1 cannot include or involve S_2. S_2, *a*'s having *p*, cannot itself be among the truth-conditions of *p*. In general, a true belief must be supposed to be a representation of some state of affairs essentially other than itself; it must be supposed to be something which can always in principle be subtracted from the world in a way that leaves its object—the state of affairs it is a belief about—untouched.

There are, certainly, cases which appear to contravene the principle of independence: it is arguable that one makes a promise, or a knight move, or asserts that *p*, or obeys an order to do *x*, or enters into a contract, only if one believes one does; it is arguable that one is fashionable, or chic, only if one believes one is.[24] These seem to be properties of which it is true to say that there is some kind of *awareness condition* on possessing them. Roughly, it seems that you have to be aware that you have the property in order for it to be true that you have the property. And this awareness cannot be a standard matter of your coming to form the belief that you have the property as a consequence of the fact that you have it, because the awareness appears to be (partly) constitutive of your actually having the property.[25] These properties, however, are all properties that one has only by virtue of participating in some conventional activity or other, and it seems that we can give a satisfactory explanation of their existence by reference to the existence of the relevant conventions. But the case of U-freedom, we suppose, is not like that at all. If U-freedom is real, it is certainly not real because of the holding of some convention, human or otherwise.[26]

---

[22] The converse form of the general claim, $[B[a, \phi a] \rightarrow \phi a]$, is also interesting.

[23] Here '*p*' refers to *a*'s actual mental state of belief (or actually entertained thought) rather than merely to the content of *a*'s belief or thought considered independently of *a*'s mental state. I take it that thoughts or beliefs considered as actual features of the world can be true or false just as statements can be.

[24] I believe that this is not true of entering into a contract, given UK law. For other cases see Strawson 1986: 200–25 (for the case of the 'Mystery Draw', in which believing you are a winner is a necessary condition of being a winner, see pp. 207–11).

[25] See further Strawson 1986: 201, 303–4.

[26] Are there any clear non-conventional cases? Suppose I think (believe) that *this very thought (belief) is puzzling*—this mental particular, call it *q*, the 'token' thought (belief) I am now entertaining. In this case *q* is the thought (belief) *that q is puzzling*; that is its content. So *q* is a true thought (belief) (if and) only if *q* is puzzling. So that in virtue of which *q* is true

This issue can seem very puzzling, but I am going to leave it here for the moment. I am going to put [10], the belief-in-U-freedom condition, on hold in order to ask whether there are any other attitudinal conditions of U-freedom. And to do this I need to go back before going forward.

8 THE ABILITY-TO-CHOOSE CONDITION

In §4 I offered a base set of agent-structural conditions on U-freedom. A U-free agent must obviously be [1] an agent, and must therefore be [2] capable of forming beliefs of certain sorts, [3] capable of having desires or pro-attitudes, [4] capable of self-movement or self-change, [5] capable of practical reasoning. I took it that dogs and humans have all these properties in common, and were on a par in so far as possession of the basic property of agenthood was concerned. But it may now be said that the base set of conditions of agenthood—genuine intentional agenthood—is incomplete. It must be supplemented by the condition that one be

[7] (genuinely) able to choose

that is, genuinely able to entertain and decide between alternative courses of action; for [2]–[5] do not by themselves guarantee this.

Is this true? It depends on how one understands [5], the practical reasoning condition: on one natural view the capacity for practical reasoning already involves being able to choose in this way. But one can also allow that [2]–[5] do not or may not guarantee possession of the ability to choose, and add in [7] as an extra (agent-structural) condition. I will take the second course, because there is no harm in having redundancy in the list of conditions of U-freedom, given that the aim is only to state sufficient conditions.

The basic conditions of genuine agenthood now read as follows. B is an agent if and only if B is

[2] capable of forming beliefs of certain sorts

[3] capable of having desires or pro-attitudes

[4] capable of self-movement (self-change)

[5] capable of practical reasoning

[7] (genuinely) able to choose.

All conditions of agenthood, including the new *ability-to-choose* condition, are a fortiori conditions of U-freedom, and I take it that Fido can fulfil all of them.[27]

---

is not fully specifiable independently of mention of *q* itself. This does seem perfectly possible, and not in any deep way paradoxical, but it is entirely unlike the supposed case of U-freedom. Crucially, it is not a case in which the claim is that to have a property you have to believe you have it.

[27] It seems clear that dogs, not to mention other unself-conscious beings like Nemo, can be said to make choices. For some further considerations in support of this, see Strawson 1986: 141–5.

9 *RICH* ABILITY TO CHOOSE

We do not, however, think that Fido is a serious candidate for being a U-free agent, by comparison with ourselves; and when we ask what makes the difference it is very natural to think that one crucial thing he lacks is

[6] full self-consciousness

as defined in §5. Some, as remarked, think that self-consciousness makes all the difference—they think it suffices all by itself to make us U-free where Fido is not and cannot be U-free. Others like myself doubt that self-consciousness alone can make such a dramatic difference; but there are a number of things that can be said in support of its importance. The intuitive case for its necessity was put on p. 364, and the introduction of the ability-to-choose condition suggests a different way of conveying its importance. For it may now be said that the problem with Fido and other unself-conscious beings like Nemo (p. 365) is that they cannot *really* choose between alternatives—not in the strongest sense, not in the way that we can—, and that this is so precisely because they are not fully self-conscious. Part of *what it is* to choose between alternatives in the full sense of the notion of choice is to be aware (believe) that you are able to choose, and to be aware of this in a fully self-conscious manner. In which case [6], self-consciousness, is a necessary condition of [7], unalloyed or full ability to choose; so that while we can be truly able to choose, dogs can't be. On this view, fully self-conscious awareness of oneself as able to choose when in a situation of choice doesn't make the difference between ability to choose and ability to choose U-freely. Rather, it makes the difference between being (genuinely or fully) able to choose and not being (genuinely or fully) able to choose at all.

Well, this can perhaps seem a natural thing to say—although it appears to contravene the principle of independence just as clearly as the paradoxical belief-in-U-freedom condition does.[28] In fact I think it equally natural to say that Fido—and if not Fido then Nemo—can genuinely choose between alternatives, but for expository purposes (and because redundancy doesn't matter when one is attempting to state sufficient conditions) I am going to allow that

[8] *rich* ability to choose

is something more than that ability to choose, now reclassified as

[7] *basic* (genuine) ability to choose

that unself-conscious creatures may be supposed to have; noting that [8] presupposes

[6] self-consciousness

---

[28] It takes time and care to lay out the case fully. On one view, one can't take it that the notion of a situation of choice is independently available in the way I assume here, because one's being in a situation of choice is itself constituted partly by one's sense that this is so. I pursue these complications with great but perhaps overexcited ardour in Strawson 1986: ch. 14.

since rich ability to choose is precisely the capacity to be fully self-consciously aware of oneself grasped *as* oneself as able to choose when choosing. But it does not simply follow, from the fact that one is self-conscious and has basic ability to choose, that one has rich ability to choose, for it is at least conceivable that one's self-consciousness may never turn itself in that direction (as it were). So [7] and [6] do not strictly entail [8], and [8] needs to be listed as an independent and separate condition.

Is [8] an agent-structural condition or an attitudinal one? It doesn't matter much how one classifies it. Some may hold that it is best treated as an attitudinal condition because it does not really increase the agent's agentive capacities in any way: all it adds to what is already the case, agent-structurally speaking, is awareness that what is the case is the case; and ability to choose and self-consciousness are already in the set of agent-structural conditions. Others, however, may think that it is best seen as an agent-structural condition, in as much as it genuinely enriches the overall agentive-cognitive complexity of the agent. I think there are worthwhile arguments on both sides, but here I am going to treat [8] rich ability to choose (self-consciousness-illuminated ability to choose) as a further agent-structural condition of U-freedom, because I want to concede as much as possible to the Structuralists in order to highlight the force of the Attitudinalists' claim that there must also be allowed to be attitudinal conditions of U-freedom.

Is rich ability to choose really necessary for U-freedom? If you already think that it is enough to be an agent and fulfil the *causa sui* condition you may doubt this (in a Perssonian spirit). But it does seem plausible that we would not judge a being to be a U-free agent—capable of being ultimately responsible for what it does in such a way that it can be, without any sort of qualification, morally deserving of praise or blame or punishment or reward for its actions—if it was not even capable of being fully self-consciously aware of itself as able to choose when choosing. So I hope you will go along with conditions [8] (and [6]), at least for the moment.

So this is how things stand. [1]–[5]+[7] give the base set of conditions of agenthood. And if you agree that merely being an agent and being *causa sui* are not enough for U-freedom then you will probably also agree that [6] and [8], self-consciousness and rich ability to choose, are also necessary for genuine U-freedom.[29] So the present proposed set of conditions of U-freedom consists of [1]–[5]+[7], the base set of conditions of agenthood, [6], full self-consciousness, [8], rich ability to choose, and [0], the *causa sui* condition: [0]-[8]. The question is: Is this enough? Do we also need [10], the belief-in-U-freedom condition?

10 STOLIDUS

Well, one question—an interesting question—is whether [8] already *entails* [10] believing you are a U-free agent.

---

[29] Once again it doesn't matter much if they are not necessary, since we are only trying to state sufficient conditions of U-freedom.

Perhaps to be richly able to choose, fully self-consciously aware of oneself as choosing when choosing, is *necessarily* to have the sense that it is truly or radically *up to one* what one chooses—in a way that simply amounts to believing you are a U-free agent. Perhaps an agent that has rich ability to choose is *bound* to experience itself as U-free, when choosing, and is therefore (on one reading of Sartre) bound to *be* U-free, when choosing. On this view, there is a crucial, overpowering sense in which such a being, fully self-conscious as it is, *can know inescapably what it is doing, in the moment of choice or action*, in such a way that it is for that reason (alone)—and inevitably, whether it likes it or not—U-free in fact.[30] (It is a sense in which Fido and Nemo, not being self-conscious, do not and cannot know what they are doing.)

Is this right? I don't think so. I don't think [8] entails [10]. I am now going to present some cases in support of this claim, and in order to do so I'm going to put aside the unfulfillable *causi sui* condition, because it makes no difference to the cases.

Consider *Stolidus*. Stolidus is a being of extremely limited conception, a very blinkered personage, an agent who comes to be fully self-conscious while remaining very stunted in his general conception of things, including in particular his conception of his own agency. Stolidus is emotionally very dull, mentally very sluggish.[31] He is, certainly, able to choose between two things X and Y in the way that Fido and Nemo can, and he can (being self-conscious) come to be fully self-consciously aware of himself as able to choose between X and Y in a particular situation of choice. And he standardly does come to be so aware of himself; he has rich ability to choose. But he need not thereby figure himself as U-free, either in the moment of choice and action or in general; this self-conception is not forced on him; he need not fulfil the belief-in-U-freedom condition.

He is, in a particular situation of choice, fully self-consciously aware of himself as now able to choose between X and Y; he is aware that he will very shortly opt for and actually perform either X or Y. But it does not follow that his thought must—*ipso facto*—be informed by any sense that it is *radically up to him* which he does. Aware of all that he is aware of, he need not and does not turn round upon himself and figure himself as U-free. And he doesn't. He simply lacks this view of things.

Well, this is surely possible. But I think it can be hard to see. It is natural for us, human beings, to think that any genuine, fully self-conscious, explicit sense of oneself as able to choose, when choosing, *just is* a sense that things are radically up to one, and so *just is* a sense of oneself as U-free. And yet I think it is a mistake. One might restate the point by saying that although Stolidus goes essentially beyond any unself-conscious (Fido-like or Nemo-like) form of awareness of choice, in being fully self-consciously aware of himself as now able to choose between X and Y, still the able-to-chooseness part of the content of his state of awareness may remain in essentials like Fido's. It is simply not the case that the able-to-chooseness part of the content of a

---

[30] In its strongest form this line of thought dismisses the *causa sui* condition as superfluous (and metaphysically preposterous), but for the moment we may suppose that the being in question does also fulfil the (unfulfillable) *causa sui* condition.

[31] Stolidus' actions are ordinarily of small importance, his thought is mostly concerned with the more or less immediate present. He moves through time inside a shell of self-concerned, short-term aims. But these things are not necessary features of the case.

state of awareness of choice *must* transmute into 'truly-up-to-me-ness'—into belief in U-freedom—just by coming into the light of self-consciousness. Belief in U-freedom (experience of oneself as U-free) essentially involves a further perspective, a further *attitude* to what is going on, a further way of thinking of oneself that Stolidus does not have. And it is—I propose—*essentially* more than the fullest and most explicit possible self-conscious awareness or conception of oneself as something that is able to choose what to do; whether this conception is a general standing conception one has of what sort of thing one is, or an explicit and occurrent apprehension of what sort of thing one is in the moment of choice. And it is not any sort of agent-structural condition.

I think our saturated familiarity with our own case, our tendency to think that any sense of self must be like our own, causes us to elide, and not to notice, a transition. The natural thought is this: 'If I am truly fully aware, now, that I am able to choose what to do, surely I *ipso facto* have the experience that what I do is truly up to me, that I am truly (and inescapably) a U-free agent in this situation? Surely there is no further basic content to my experience of myself as U-free than my full awareness of myself as truly, fully, able to choose?'

Stolidus suggests that this is not so. He makes the point by virtue of his extremely limited outlook. *Moira*, the 'true no-U-freedom theorist', will make the same point, later, by virtue of her unusually inclusive outlook. But I want to delay her entry for the moment in order to ask whether there are any other attitudinal conditions of U-freedom that we need to take into account before attempting to face up to the paradoxical belief-in-U-freedom condition.

11   THEORIA

I think there are. Consider *Theoria*,[32] the spectator subject, who fails to be a U-free agent because of her overall emotional attitude or identificatory relation to her agency. She fulfils all the agent-structural conditions on U-freedom listed so far,[33] but there is something fatally amiss in her attitude to herself as an agent. She is detached from her motivation in some curious way. She acts, and for reasons that she can give, but it is as if it is not really she who desires, decides, and acts, but rather as if her desires and beliefs work it out among themselves beneath her disengaged, spectatorial, inward gaze.

Theoria resembles Camus's *étranger* at his most detached.[34] She is somehow disengaged from life, including her own. When *l'étranger*, Meursault, alludes to one of his own desires, it is half as if he were recounting a fact about a feature of the world which is extraneous to him, for he—what he most truly is—seems to be just the detached reporting self. The desire seems to be something that affects his life rather in the way that things external to one, details of one's surroundings, do. And yet it is still his desire—it is no one else's. It is, one might say, something he apprehends before it is

---

[32] From θεωρειν, to be a spectator at the games.   [33] [1]–[8]; [0] has been put aside.
[34] Camus 1942.

something he feels, but that it is his is part of what he apprehends. There is no defect in his self-consciousness.

The same is true of Theoria. She has no strong particular sense of herself as a decision-making, self-governing agent. She doesn't really see herself as the decider and rational planner of action. Or rather, she does, for there is no defect in her self-consciousness—her ability to grasp herself as herself—considered as a cognitive capacity, and she is after all aware of practical-rational calculations going on in her; but she does so only in some spectatorial manner. She doesn't feel herself to be an agent in the definite, vivid, participatory way in which we do. She has no real sense of expressing herself in action, no sense (such as we ordinarily have) of having a will that issues in action in such a way that one is responsible for and in some way committed to what one does. She is aware that her actions are actions executed by a body that is hers, and motivated by reasons correctly identifiable as hers—they are certainly no one else's, and they do in fact motivate this her body. She is able to give reasons why she did something, as we do—'I wanted X and believed doing Y was the best way to obtain X, given Z'; and it remains correct to say that she decides to do Y. No one else does, and she is a single psychophysical thing, and she is not schizophrenic. And yet there is something vital missing in the way she wants X, and in her attitude to what are correctly identifiable as her projects and actions. She never has the experience of participatory involvement in the mental stages of action-production that we can have—the experience underlying the sense that it is really I who decide and am responsible for my actions. And this seems to matter a great deal, when freedom, or at least U-freedom, is in question. Unlike us, she doesn't feel herself to be the decider and animator of action, and it seems that she thereby fails to be the decider and animator of action in the right kind of way for her to be a U-free agent. She is not 'identified' with the process. She is more like someone who watches an action-producing process—her own—from an internal point of view. There is something wrong with her attitude, her affective relation, to herself, so that although she is a self-conscious agent, she is not a U-free agent.[35]

Imagine a woman who, although she remains outwardly normal and goes about her business, has entered into an acute state of 'existential' crisis, or accidie, or, more particularly, depersonalization or aboulia. Imagine someone for whom life has lost its point, and who acts merely mechanically in some sense, although outwardly normal, continuing to execute complicated and calculated actions, continuing with her job, for example. To us, ignorant of her inner condition, her actions seem to be performed by a normally free and responsible agent. But this appearance is—I propose—illusory.

Constraint theorists may say that Theoria has as good a claim to be a U-free agent as any of us—she fulfils all the agent-structural conditions on U-freedom—and

---

[35] On Frankfurt's theory of freedom it might be thought that Theoria could be ruled out on agent-structural grounds—on the grounds that she could not form 'second-order volitions', i.e. desires that other, first-order desires that she had should (be such as to) move her to action. But she can have (the capacity to form) such second-order desires, in just the sense in which she can have first-order desires; the problem is that she will be spectatorially detached from them as well.

that the reason she is not actually free in her actions is that she has a psychological condition that counts as a freedom-removing constraint. But this is not the right way to see her. In my story, Theoria is an alien creature, and her experience of agency is normal among her kind—the Theoreticals. The Theoreticals, like ourselves, have just one of the many possible kinds of experience of self, agency, and life available to beings that fulfil the agent-structural conditions on U-freedom.

I conclude that if and in so far as we judge Theoria's kind of experience of agency to be insufficient for, incompatible with, U-freedom—and I think we should, even if she fulfils the *causa sui* condition—we place an attitudinal condition on freedom, a condition whose fulfilment involves something essentially more than whatever is involved in fulfilling the agent-structural conditions. What should I call it? The *integration* condition?[36] The *non-alienation* condition? I will call it the *engagement* condition: one must be

[11] engaged

if one is to be a U-free agent. In her detachment Theoria fails the engagement condition. If complete lack of any such sense of engagement could be decisively established in a human being (here it is *ex hypothesi*) it might suffice even in a court of law to absolve from responsibility.

Let me repeat the point that the Theoreticals' experience of agency is merely different from, and in no way inferior to, or somehow incorrect relative to, our own. It cannot be held to involve some form of psychological constraint just because it is different in this way. What Theoria's case shows, I suggest, is that there can be fully self-conscious agents as complex as we are who cannot be said to be U-free agents simply on account of the character of their experiential attitude to themselves and their agency. It looks as if Theoria will also fail the belief-in-U-freedom condition, but I do not think one has to show this in order to say what it is about her precludes her being a U-free agent in spite of fulfilling all the agent-structural conditions.

The general conclusion is that U-freedom *cannot* consist merely in the fulfilment of some set of agent-structural conditions: it cannot consist in the possession of some perhaps as yet undiscovered set of maximally action-enabling cognitive and practical capacities. For we also require a certain attitude to self and agency, an experiential disposition which it is very hard to specify precisely in a positive way, but which Theoria at any rate does not have.

12   THE NATURAL EPICTETANS

Suppose we accept [11], engagement, as an attitudinal condition on U-freedom, a condition that must be added to any plausible set of agent-structural conditions. And suppose we put aside the controversial belief-in-U-freedom condition. The question is then whether the engagement condition is the only attitudinal condition that is needed.

---

[36] I called it this in *Freedom and Belief*.

Imagine an enormously congenial world inhabited by a race of gifted, active creatures. They fulfil all the agent-structural conditions of U-freedom so far proposed, and the (attitudinal) engagement condition. What is unusual about them is that they are never undecided in any way. They are fully—richly—able to choose, but they never hesitate at all about what to do. They never ponder alternatives, although they are perfectly well aware of them. They never consciously deliberate about which ends to pursue or about how to pursue them (they have no need to) and always succeed in doing what they want to do.

These are the *Natural Epictetans*—never failing, never disappointed in their congenial world, always able to do what they want to do because always wanting to do only what they are able to do.[37] Their experience is radically unlike ours. But they are not like Theoria. The strangeness of their experience (relative to ours) does not derive from a failure to fulfil the engagement condition.

The Natural Epictetans take decisions—they are agents responding variously to circumstances in complex ways, beings who actually act—but they are never undecided. Decision is not something they ever apply themselves to in any way. It is not something they live through or dwell on or notice as such. Decision does not issue from previous indecision. It is not a resolution or conclusion of anything. Perhaps their world is much less complicated than ours, but it need not be.[38] Their deciding is in any case effortlessly smooth. They never wonder or worry 'Which (action) shall I perform?'.[39] Given their capacities, they are always capable of acting otherwise than they do in fact act, and they are fully capable of the thought 'I could do otherwise'. Any natural Epictetan can fully understand a story in which it is faced with a button, and knows that pushing or not pushing it in the next twenty seconds will lead to very different results. But we may suppose that they never in fact think such a thought as 'I could do otherwise'. And if some of them, musing philosophically, were to think it, it would have no energy for them, no relations with the notion or experience of difficult choice; for they do not know what it is to face or make such choices. It would in effect have no more import for them than either 'I have such and such capabilities' or 'I might have been, or wanted, otherwise'.

The Natural Epictetans, then, can never be frustrated. They are never in a situation in which they think 'I could have done A (could do A), if it had not been (were not) the case that C' with a sense of external constraint or hindrance. If a natural Epictetan were to encounter constraint or hindrance, in spite of the fabulous congeniality of its world, so that it found itself unable to do what it had until that moment wanted to

---

[37] Epictetus enjoins one to adapt one's desires to one's circumstances, so that one is never frustrated by them.

[38] They may be extraordinarily intelligent, and find the complexity simple. If God existed, and were an agent, his experience of agency might be like a Natural Epictetan's.

[39] A creature that was never undecided as to what to do might experience freedom = unhinderedness of action in unconstrained circumstances solely as a result of the contrast afforded to such free = unhindered action by experience of hindering constraints in other circumstances. And if it lacked the immediate Epictetan reflex it might experience hindrance in doing what it wanted to do and think 'I could do (have done) A if it were not (had not been) for C'. It might even reason as follows: 'Since I cannot do A, I will do B'; or again, thinking ahead, 'If I cannot do A, I will do B'. But, thinking these things and these things only, it need never have any sense of U-freedom at all.

do, then it would by virtue of the *immediate Epictetan reflex* always immediately cease to want to do what it found itself unable to do.

External *constraint* is one thing; *indecision* is even more important. The Natural Epictetans are never in a situation in which they might think 'I could do A, and I could do B, and I can't do both, so which shall I do?'. They are fully capable of thinking such a thing, cognitively speaking, but they never do so in fact, given the automatic natural Epictetan nature of their volition.

In one way, then, they enjoy all the freedom that it is possible for any being to have. And yet there seems to be a sense in which they are not U-free agents at all because they do not know what U-freedom is. They seem, with respect to the freedom they enjoy, like creatures that have ears but live in a soundless world. Such creatures experience total silence—they hear it in the sense that we can be said to hear it—but we feel that they do not know what silence is. And if they do not know what it is then there is a sense in which they do not and cannot experience it as we who know noise can and do. In the same way, sighted creatures living in a lightless world may have no concept of darkness. Living in a uniformly blue world, with no differences of shade resulting from shadow or distance, they may have no concept of blue or of other colours.

But what do these cases show? If one takes two things A and B (such as freedom and lack of freedom) which contrast in such a way that there is either A or B but not both, the complete lack of B should not have as consequence that there is no A. On the contrary; there is nothing but A. What may lack in such a case, however, is any experience of the contrast between A and B. And this may lead, as above, to lack of any explicit awareness or conception of either A or B.

But why should lack of explicit awareness of A be supposed to have as a consequence lack of A itself, as lack of any sense or conception of U-freedom seems to have as a consequence lack of U-freedom itself? Well, that is the question. But it does seem to be so. (Compare the sense in which Adam and Eve, when innocent, were not and could not be good.) I do not think one can simply say that the Natural Epictetans are in fact U-free agents, and that their coming to know this would be a standard case of a belief being formed in such a way as to represent or reflect an already existing belief-independent fact. That does not seem true to how things are. There seems to be a sense in which the Natural Epictetans are not U-free agents at all, precisely because—it is natural to put it in this paradoxical way—they don't have a proper grasp of the fact that they are. Even when we put aside the strong (*causa sui* requiring) notion of U-freedom for some weaker notion of freedom we may feel that their sense of freedom lacks some essential contrastive grounding, either in the form of experience of constraint, coercion and inability, or, quite differently, and more importantly, in the form of experience of indecision, of having to make difficult choices between alternatives. Certainly the Epictetans know that they are fully free agents in the compatibilist sense: they are utterly unconstrained and fully self-conscious and do what they want to do and know they do. But if it is claimed that they are in these conditions bound to figure themselves as U-free, this is far from clear. If there is any sense in which they experience themselves as U-free, I think it will be like the sense in which the inhabitants of the silent world experience their world as a silent world.

It may again be suggested that they must at least be able to *conceive* of doing otherwise, of constraint, and even of experiencing indecision; whereas the inhabitants of the silent world cannot conceive of noise at all. It may be suggested that ability to conceive of the possibility of indecision, and indeed of choice-out-of-indecision, or at least grasp of the notion of options being open to one, is *essentially constitutive* of (and so entailed by) rich ability to choose, which the Natural Epictetans possess by hypothesis. But one may grant this, for the purpose of argument. For it is not plausible that mere possession of the ability to conceive of difficult choice or indecision without any actual experience of it—nor even any actual thought about the possibility of it—is bound to precipitate belief in U-freedom of the kind we appear to require of genuinely U-free agents. Having no natural occasion, the Natural Epictetans may never formulate the possibility of indecision. They are not speculative creatures. They are without anxiety. Never having had conflicting desires, never having experienced indecision, an Epictetan never deploys its general conception of itself as capable of doing many different things in the thought that it is now able to do other than what it is now about to do in such a way as to encounter the strong, immediate sense of open choice that is so central to our lives.

In fact it is not particularly important whether an Epictetan ever actually entertains any thought of indecision, or of the possibility of doing otherwise. What is important is whether it ever dwells on such things, whether they ever matter to it in a certain way. And it is a consequence of the description of their case that this does not happen. The Natural Epictetans know they produce the actions they produce, they know they are causally responsible for them in that sense, but still they lack any sense of themselves as *U-free* in their actions. Agency, for them, is something like what it is like for us when we are involved in doing something that we entirely unproblematically want to do, and that there is only one way of doing, and that we can do without any difficulty; something that involves performing a long sequence of simple intentional actions with regard to which we have no sort of thought that there might be alternative ways of doing them. Here there can be a strange resistlessness, no consciousness of choice or indecision.

The proposal, then, is that the Natural Epictetans aren't U-free agents although they are fully self-conscious, engaged agents: they can't be U-free agents—even if they fulfil the *causa sui* condition—because they have no sense of what U-freedom is. They fail to fulfil condition [10], the belief in freedom condition; they fail to figure themselves as U-free.[40] Some may say that to be free in such a way that one doesn't even know that one is is the truest freedom of all: 'the sense of liberty is a message read between the lines of constraint. Real liberty is as transparent, as odourless and tasteless, as water'.[41] This is a good thought, but the other thought seems to remain undiminished: to have no sense of U-freedom at all is not to be a U-free agent.

---

[40] They may even have second-order desires, and what Frankfurt calls second-order volitions—desires that their first-order desires be such that they move or will or would move them to act, all of which are effortlessly satisfied.

[41] Frayn 1974: §85.

Here a further point comes into play. If U-freedom requires being *causa sui*, and if being *causa sui* is impossible, then U-freedom is impossible. So any belief that one is a U-free agent is false. Now it seems that nearly all human beings do believe they are U-free agents (although many philosophers try to pretend otherwise); and it may be that they—we—can hardly help this. But it would be very surprising indeed if *all possible* self-conscious agents that had rich ability to choose—all possible self-conscious agents that were able to choose and knew it—were by that fact alone compelled to believe that they possessed such U-freedom. For it would be very surprising if all possible self-conscious agents, however intelligent and knowledgeable they were, were compelled to believe something demonstrably false. It may be that belief in U-freedom is a necessary condition of U-freedom even if U-freedom is demonstrably impossible (being round is a necessary condition of being a round square), and even if any belief in U-freedom is demonstrably false. Stranger things have been the case. But one point about Theoria and the Natural Epictetans that must now be registered is that whatever their defects—whatever we may think they lack when we compare them with ourselves—it is most unclear that failure to have a false belief is ever a defect.

There is perhaps a connection here with accounts of spiritually advanced states of mind, and, more particularly, accounts of what the experience of choice and agency is like in such circumstances. Krishnamurti puts it as follows:

You do not choose, you do not decide when you see things very clearly; then you act [in a way which] which is not the action of will. . . . Only the unintelligent mind exercises choice in life. . . . A truly intelligent [spiritually advanced] man can have no choice, because his mind can be aware of what is true, and can thus only choose the path of truth. It simply cannot have choice. Only the unintelligent mind has free will.[42]

Saul Bellow has a related thought:

In the next realm, where things are clearer, clarity eats into freedom. We are free on earth because of cloudiness, because of error, because of marvellous limitation. . . . [43]

—Surely such clarity and such intelligence, which presumably rule out belief in U-freedom, must bring U-freedom with them if anything does? And if so, belief in U-freedom isn't after all a necessary condition of U-freedom.

The trouble is that nothing brings U-freedom with it, because U-freedom is impossible. The highest forms of Krishnamurtian intelligence will indeed rule out belief in U-freedom, because they will involve clear understanding that U-freedom is impossible.[44] But this will not show that belief in U-freedom is not a necessary condition of U-freedom.

[42] Krishnamurti, quoted in Lutyens (1983: 33, 204). In a similar vein, perhaps, Spinoza remarks that 'God . . . cannot be said . . . to act from freedom of the will' (1675: pt. 1, prop. 32, coroll. 1).

[43] 1977: 140. I do not think that Spinoza disagrees when he says that freedom is consciousness of necessity, although he is considering a somewhat different conception of freedom. See S. Hampshire 1972: 198 ff.

[44] A stage on the way to Nietzsche's *amor fati*.

Einstein backs up Krishnamurti and Bellow, judging that 'a Being endowed with higher insight and more perfect intelligence, watching man and his doings, would smile about man's illusion that he was acting according to his own free will'.[45] The basic argument that U-freedom is impossible is entirely a priori, but there are also extremely strong a posteriori reasons for thinking it impossible. It seems unavoidable if Einstein's theory of special relativity is anything like correct, for example—a point that has received little discussion in recent debate about free will.

13   INDECISION

Suppose it granted that the Natural Epictetans are not U-free agents. The question, then, is what they lack. 'Well, they cannot be genuine U-free agents because they do not figure themselves as U-free—they fail [10], the belief-in-U-freedom condition.' Fine, but I want to continue to put aside the belief-in-U-freedom condition for the moment. Is there anything else they lack? Is there anything that would tip them over into fulfilling the belief-in-U-freedom condition?

I do not think there is; but the best candidate, perhaps, is this. If one asks about the deep sources of belief in U-freedom, experience of *indecision* seems, as remarked, far more important than experience of *constraint* or hindrance. Suppose, contrary to hypothesis, that the Natural Epictetans experience constraint, and have thoughts of the form 'I could have done A, if it had not been for C.' Suppose further that the experience of such constraint serves as a contrastive foil against which other, unconstrained actions are experienced by them as free—as free = unhindered. This doesn't advance them much, I think, for what they may still lack in this case is any sort of experience of indecision, of difficult choice. It is that that promises most powerfully to give rise to experience of things as radically 'up to one'.[46]

14   MOIRA

No doubt—but the question is now this. Is vivid experience of indecision sufficient for belief in U-freedom? Does it compel belief in U-freedom? The answer, I think, is No. When we picture an agent that is fully self-conscious, engaged, richly (fully self-consciously) able to choose, and that is currently experiencing itself as vividly, even agonizingly, undecided as to what to do, we may wonder how it can fail to figure itself as U-free, as able to choose U-freely. It is at this point that we have to reckon

---

[45] Einstein 1931. For an excellent presentation of the a-posteriori point see Putnam 1967. Lockwood (2005: ch. 3) effectively rebuts Putnam's critics.

[46] Although it seems that it is precisely because they lack any sort of experience of indecision that the natural Epictetans fail to figure themselves as U-free, it would be very implausible to suggest that it is actually *impossible* to have a sense of oneself as U-free if one does not experience indecision. There is nothing incoherent about the *neo-Epictetans*, who are exactly like the natural Epictetans—they never actually experience indecision—except precisely for the fact that they do experience themselves as U-free.

with *Moira*, who is a *true no-U-freedom theorist*. Moira sees that U-freedom requires being *causa sui*, she sees that being *causa sui* is impossible, and she lives in the full light of this understanding—in spite of being an agent who makes difficult choices and acts in the world.[47]

Moira is fully self-conscious and she is fully engaged. Experience of desires of the kind that the engagement condition guarantees, and a strong interest in their fulfilment, are not incompatible with true—lived—espousal of the no-U-freedom position. And we can put her, too, in front of a button in such a way that she cannot fail to be aware that she faces a choice. But she is so deeply intimate with the thought that everything that she is is ultimately not self-determined that she has no sort of sense of herself as U-free when facing the momentous button—as U-free to choose in such a way as to be ultimately morally responsible for her choice—, although she now knows that she is able to choose what to do. She may well find herself calculating consequences and very uncertain what to do, but she is not compelled by this into any sense of herself as U-free in a way she knows to be impossible.

One might say that Moira is a sophisticated fatalist.[48] I think that it is extremely hard for us to imagine what it is like to be her. It requires a conception of things that is way outside the normal human range (even if not unattainable by human beings). And yet I think that it must be allowed that she could exist, and that rich ability to choose cannot in and of itself necessitate belief in U-freedom. There is, after all, a clear sense in which U-freedom is demonstrably impossible, and it would—as remarked—be very strange if it were metaphysically impossible for there to be an agent that was, like Moira, both able to comprehend this impossibility and able to grasp that it was in a situation in which it was able to choose.

This is really the only argument that can be given for Moira's possibility, but it is perhaps enough. Here as so often in philosophy argument seems to be no substitute for imagination directed onto a given description.

Some may still think that [1]–[8]+[11], rich, fully engaged ability to choose, must simply amount to [10], belief in U-freedom: that the conviction of U-freedom really must be inescapable in these circumstances in the way Sartre supposed. It is very natural to think this, and yet I think it is unwarranted.[49] If in the present case we cannot see the gap between [8] and [10] it may be because we can't imagine a human being who is a true no-U-freedom theorist like Moira but is in other respects—including

---

[47] Her sisters—Pepromene, Eimarmene, and Chreousa—are *true* or *genuine incompatibilist determinists* of the kind discussed in *Freedom and Belief* (281–4). They make the present point as well as Moira, but their position depends on a belief—in determinism—that could be false.

[48] Naive fatalism holds that there is no point in deliberating or in doing anything because everything is predetermined (or is the will of God) in such a way that nothing you can do can change how things will be. It is false because one's doings and deliberations can change things, being themselves real parts of the (possibly deterministic) causal process. Sophisticated fatalism doesn't make this mistake. It consists in the attempt (or is the result of a successful attempt) to comprehend fully the fact that one is not and cannot be ultimately self-determined or self-determining. It seems, though, that if one is an ordinary human being, one simply cannot attain the perspective of sophisticated fatalism in one's daily life.

[49] This, perhaps, is the true—rarely acknowledged—heart of the philosophical problem of free will.

internal phenomenological respects—normal. But it is not surprising that we cannot imagine this, because it is impossible: if Moira is human, she is not normal at all. Either we must suppose that her sense of self is not recognizably human, or we must suppose that it has dissolved away entirely. The first supposition would seem to be a reasonable one, for she is a self-conscious, embodied being, and can have an unexceptionable grasp of the simple truth that she is a single thing in the world, in addition to possessing that self-presence of mind, normal in the self-conscious, that involves a sense of oneself as something that is somehow single just *qua* mental. But, granted that she does have a sense of self, this cannot be supposed to fall within the range of the recognizably human. A basic sense of oneself as U-free when unconstrained, as possessed of radical 'up-to-me-ness', seems indissociable from the ordinary, sane and sober adult human sense of self, and Moira's sense of self is not like that at all. It cannot be, given the nature of her experience of choice and agency: she has no trace of belief in U-freedom.

The line between rich ability to choose and experience of oneself as U-free may appear a fine one in a book written for human beings, and by one, for we may be unable to see the distinction easily, and may have difficulty in employing the device of sympathetic identification to the case. But in a book written for creatures of some other planet, perfectly fatal creatures of a deeply deterministical persuasion, the difficulty might rather be to explain how any apparently intelligent race could suppose the line between having and believing oneself to have rich ability to choose (a property widely instantiated, both on Earth and on this other planet) and believing oneself to be a U-free agent (an impossible property) could be thought to be a fine one.

Even this may be hard for us to accept, for there remains something very powerful about the Kantian or quasi-Kantian idea that *any* rational agent that is fully self-consciously conscious of being able to choose cannot but suppose itself to be a U-free agent by reason of that consciousness alone. But, having considered Stolidus, Theoria and the Theoreticals, Meursault and his variants, the Natural Epictetans, Moira and her sisters, I submit that this idea is nevertheless wrong. And for all that I have painted Moira as not recognizably human, I don't suppose Einstein differed much from her in respect of his attitude to free will.

15   MAXIMAL ABILITY TO CHOOSE

—All right. Rich ability to choose as so far defined[50] may not be sufficient for belief in U-freedom, but you have not yet described the fullest form of ability to choose: *maximal* ability to choose. Maximal ability to choose is indeed sufficient for belief in U-freedom, and it involves something more than rich ability to choose as currently defined. For it involves *a certain sort of active deployment of the concept of choice*. It emerges as something more than rich ability to choose precisely when someone like you goes in for thought-experiments designed to track the minimal case, as here.

---

[50] 'The capacity to be fully self-consciously aware of oneself grasped *as* oneself as able to choose when choosing'.

Maximal ability to choose is nothing special or mysterious. It's a widely possessed property. The trouble with Stolidus and the Natural Epictetans is that they don't really have—deploy—the concept of choice at all, and therefore do not have maximal ability to choose. As for Moira, either she too doesn't have it, or she is not what she claims to be: it is *impossible* for a being that genuinely possesses and deploys the concept of choice to be a true no-U-freedom theorist. Fully to possess and deploy the concept of choice is necessarily to have something more than that full-consciousness-on-the-point-of-action-of-the-fact-of-facing-action-alternatives that has been allowed to Stolidus and his more enlightened companions. If the concept of choice is properly active in experience of rich ability to choose then rich ability to choose is maximal ability to choose—which amounts to belief in U-freedom. The concept of choice adds to the minimal fully self-conscious option-facing awareness allowed even to Stolidus the *essentially* belief-in-U-freedom-involving idea that *I* can (and do—and must) *pick* the option I favour, that what happens lies in my hands, is truly up to me, and so on. It is given in the very concept of choice. So you need to add

[9] maximal ability to choose

to

[8] rich ability to choose

as a condition of U-freedom—or simply replace [8] by [9]. And then you must take account of the fact that fulfilling [9] is sufficient for fulfilling [10], the belief-in-U-freedom condition.'

To which the reply is that Moira certainly has and deploys the concept of choice. She blocks the claim that [9] entails [10] in any form in which it does not beg the question by simply building belief in U-freedom into any possession of the concept of choice that is allowed to count as 'full' or 'genuine'.

—Your assertion that she is possible, possessing [9] and lacking [10], also begs the question.

Well, but I am fond of her; and she is backed by the thought that being *causa sui* is provably impossible, and that it is very hard to believe that it could be metaphysically impossible that any (finite) self-conscious rational agent should believe—live—the truth.

   The first reply, then, is simply that Moira as described does fulfil condition [9], but not condition [10]. The second, more determined reply is that it still seems wrong to say that anything at all is lacking, intellectually or cognitively speaking, even in Stolidus's case, so far as possession of the concept of choice is concerned. His self-conscious awareness that he faces options is his being aware that he (*he*) has action-alternatives. He knows what it is to act, and that he can act. He knows, in sum, that he is able to choose between different courses of action. If we still think he lacks something this is probably because we blend the concept of choice with affective or non-cognitive elements that make it hard for us to see that he has all that is cognitively necessary, so far as possession of the concept of choice is concerned. We build an attitudinal element into what we claim to be a merely agent-structural condition.

   The same goes for the Natural Epictetans, whatever the resistlessness of their agency. We can put them all—Stolidus, Moira, Theoria, the Natural Epictetans—in front of the momentous button. They are intellectually fully aware of the nature of the situation. It is just that they do not live it in anything like the way we do. They experience being able to choose, and in a fully self-conscious manner, but they do not experience themselves as U-free. But this (as remarked) can hardly be a defect, since U-freedom is impossible.

16   IS BELIEF IN U-FREEDOM REALLY A CONDITION OF U-FREEDOM?

—But you put this impossibility to one side at the beginning of §10, before introducing Stolidus, and it is still to one side. So we may suppose, for purposes of argument, that all these creatures are in fact *causa sui* in the required way. In which case Moira is just wrong about the impossibility of being *causa sui*. She herself is in fact truly *causa sui*, although she believes she is not (she has no memory of having done whatever is necessary to being *causa sui*), and has, *ex hypothesi*, no sense of being U-free. Surely we must then hold her to *be* U-free. I will grant for the sake of argument that no unself-conscious creature is U-free even if it is appropriately *causa sui*; I will put aside Stolidus, Theoria, even, if you like, the resistless Natural Epictetans. But Moira— entirely self-aware, engaged, maximally able to choose and *causa sui* . . . surely she is indeed U-free, ultimately morally responsible, without any qualification whatever, for her actions? She has, by hypothesis, no sense or belief that she is U-free. But how can she not simply be wrong, in this case?

This, in effect, is the objection Nagel raised in 1987. After summarizing my position—that if a man never really experienced or believed himself to be U-free then even if all the other conditions of U-freedom were met (including the *causa sui* condition), he would still not be U-free and would not be truly or ultimately responsible—he objects to it as follows:

this is a difficult claim to assess, since it involves a counter-possible conditional: but it doesn't seem right to me. If true responsibility [U-freedom] were possible, couldn't someone be deceived (even self-deceived) about whether he had it? Couldn't he act with the illusion that all this was just happening to him, while actually it was his doing, and he was fully responsible for [U-free in] a choice which saved or failed to save ten other people from torture?[51]

In reply, note first that this description somewhat misrepresents the case, for in not believing that one is U-free one does not think that what is happening when one acts is 'just happening' to one. One is, like Moira, fully aware when acting, that it is indeed oneself that is doing what is being done and that one is performing an intentional action; it is just that one feels oneself to be entirely clear on the point that it is not possible to be ultimately morally responsible for what one does. Now one is in fact wrong about this, given the present 'counter-possible' hypothesis, and in that sense

---

[51] 1987: 5–6; Persson 1987 has a similar doubt. The example of torture is used in *Freedom and Belief* (p. 103) in an attempt to dramatize the idea that there are situations in which one could not possibly fail to feel U-free.

one is under an illusion, but one's illusion is not that one's action is 'just happening' to one.

This, though, is a minor misunderstanding, and the core of Nagel's question is simply this:

Couldn't this person act with the conviction that he is not U-free, not able to be ultimately morally responsible for what he does, while actually being *causa sui* and so U-free in his choices and actions?

I have said No. If he really has no sense at all of being U-free, then he cannot be U-free, even if he is *causa sui*. But I am not sure what to say if you disagree. Here we are reaching the end of argument, and it may be best to stop. But we can perhaps expose a little more structure by considering one more addition to the proposed set of conditions of U-freedom—which state, so far, that to be U-free one must be

[0] *causa sui*

[1] an agent

[2] capable of forming beliefs

[3] capable of having desires (pro-attitudes)

[4] capable of self-movement (self-change)

[5] capable of practical reasoning (in the inclusive sense noted on p. 363)

[6] fully self-conscious

[7] possessed of *basic* ability to choose (p. 369)

[8] possessed of *rich* ability to choose (p. 370)

[9] possessed of *maximal* ability to choose (p. 382)

[10] possessed of the belief or sense that one is U-free

[11] engaged (in the special sense defined on pp. 373–5).

Consider, then, the proposal that one must be

[12] possessed of the conception of U-freedom

whether or not one applies it to oneself and thereby fulfils condition [10].[52] [12] is entailed by [10],[53] but does not entail it, so we can consider a Moira who fulfils [12] but not [10], and a Moira who fulfils neither [10] nor [12].

The point of doing so is simply that some may be prepared to allow that [12] may be a condition of U-freedom, while denying, with Nagel, that [10] is. If Moira fulfils [12] but not [10], they may say, the error she makes about herself, in failing to recognize that she possesses a property of which she has a perfectly good grasp, simply does not remove her from the company of the U-free. Even if she has no sort of belief that she is U-free, she is nonetheless capable of being ultimately morally responsible—without any qualification whatever—for what she does, given that she fulfils

---

[52] To possess the conception of U-freedom is not to have thought the notion through in such a way as to see that it is impossible. One may possibly have done this but few of those who actually possess it have done so.

[53] Just as [2]–[7], at least, are entailed by [1].

[12]. But if she fails [12], and a fortiori [10]—if she has no sort of conception of U-freedom, and a fortiori no belief that she herself is U-free—then even if she is *causa sui* she cannot really be counted among the company of the U-free.

You may be wondering why [12] on its own should make such a difference. I sympathize—and although I'm prepared for the sake of argument to let [12] classify as a merely cognitive requirement, a merely agent-structural condition of U-freedom, it is arguable that the cognitively most powerful minds won't actually be able to understand the conception of U-freedom that is in question (for them it will be as difficult as visualizing a round square is for us). Which leads me to wonder whether grasp of the conception isn't essentially partly an attitudinal matter, in some covert way, and not a merely cognitive matter.[54]

17 CONCLUSION

What should one make of all this? I'm really not sure. I find I still hold the view I formed in 1979. I think there are ineliminable attitudinal conditions on U-freedom in addition to structural conditions and, in particular, that if anything is truly U-free then this is essentially partly because it believes it is. One is U-free, if one is, partly because one sees oneself and one's action in a certain way—as U-free. The proposal is that this is an outright metaphysical condition of U-freedom, a constitutive condition of U-freedom, although it is an attitudinal condition, and a paradoxical one at that, given that it offends against the principle of independence.[55] U-freedom is not just a matter of certain practical capacities, on this view. A U-free agent must see or conceive itself in a certain specific way, and its seeing itself in this way is not a necessary consequence of its possession of any set of abilities or capacities or attitudes that does not include this way of seeing itself.[56]

---

[54] A final proposal might be that one must not only have a general, standing sense that one is U-free, but must also be [13] capable of having one's outlook animated or informed by an explicit sense of oneself as U-free when choosing or acting; this must in fact be one's standard condition, when engaging in choice or actions of moment. [13] is triggered by the possibility, so far left open, that a being might fulfil [10] in general while being somehow incapable of having any trace of any explicit thought of itself as U-free in the moment of choice or action.

[55] p. 368. For a suggestion about how to avoid contravention of the principle of independence see Strawson 1986: ch. 15.

[56] I'm most grateful to Gideon Yaffe for sending me written comments on this paper after I was unable to present it at the Werkmeister Conference on Causation and Free Will at Florida State University in January 2002.

16

Realism and Causation

Philosophers have sought to combine two things: (1) realism with respect to the existence of an 'external', physical, 'mind-independent' world, and (2) a 'Regularity' theory of what causation is, considered as an entirely mind-independent phenomenon in that world. I will call the combination of (1) and (2) *Regularity Realism*, and will argue that even if Regularity Realism does not entail any actual contradiction, it is implausible in the very highest degree: realism with respect to the external world rationally requires the adoption, in some no doubt philosophically developed version, of the ordinary, common-sense view of what causation is, in that world.

This may be thought to be obvious. It is worth arguing for only if there are indeed Regularity Realists. (Hume is certainly not a straightforward Regularity Realist.) The assumption that there are Regularity Realists is therefore the principal justification for this paper. Two views about this assumption seem to be current. One is that the Regularity theory is still the orthodoxy among analytic philosophers, most of whom are also realists about the external world. The other is that there is widespread dissatisfaction with the Regularity theory.

A third view is that philosophy is littered with unsuccessful attempts to say exactly what is wrong with the Regularity view. One can but try. I begin with brief sketches of the two views of causation just mentioned, the Regularity view and the common-sense view.

1

According to the basic Regularity theory of causation, causation is something which does indeed exist in the world. It is something 'in the objects', in Hume's phrase.[1] But

I am grateful to Paul Snowdon for comments on a version of this paper, as I am to Simon Blackburn, who drew my attention to D. M. Armstrong's book *What is a Law of Nature?* For comments on a later version I am grateful to Neil Cooper and Colin McGinn. When citing Hume's *Enquiry* I give the Selby-Bigge page reference followed by the Beauchamp page reference (e.g. '3/57'); in the case of the *Treatise*, the Selby-Bigge page reference followed similarly by the Norton page reference. This paper is not, however, concerned with the details of Hume's position.

[1] Here I take Hume to mean what we ordinarily mean by 'object', although it is important to remember that he sometimes treats 'object' as interchangeable with 'perception'. On the whole, the phrase 'object-involving event' is a good alternative to Hume's use of the word 'object' as it occurs in, say, his 'philosophical' definitions of causation in §1.3.14 of the *Treatise* (170/114, 172/115), and I will sometimes use this phrase in what follows.

it is, in itself, nothing more than regular succession. To say that one object-involving event A caused another object-involving event B is simply to say that B succeeded A (and was 'spatiotemporally contiguous' to A) and that events of type A are regularly and indeed always succeeded by (contiguous) events of type B.[2] That is all that causation is, considered as something that exists in the mind-independent world. But, while causation is nothing more than such regularity, it is also nothing less. Causation is something real, and regularities of succession actually *constitute* causation as it is in the objects. As A. J. Ayer says, expounding the Regularity theory, 'in nature one thing just happens after another'. This is all that causation is, in so far as it is anything at all *in the objects*. Anything else that we wish to say about causation has its place 'only in our imaginative arrangements and extensions of these primary facts'.[3]

Such a Regularity theory of causation—one could loosely express it as the view that there is no 'because' in nature—stands in strong contrast with our ordinary view. And I take it that it is our (science-enriched) ordinary view of causation that provides the basis at least for the main philosophical rival to the Regularity view, which I shall call the 'Producing Causation' view, and of which I shall offer two versions.

According to the first, causation is something which does indeed exist in the world, and it exists because there exist constant, *objective forces*—the 'fundamental forces' postulated by physics, say—which govern the way objects behave and interact. Such forces are part of the nature of things, as scientists know, and objects behave as they do because of the nature of these forces.[4] To say that one object-involving event A caused another object-involving event B is to say that, given the existence and the nature of the forces informing and governing the objects involved in A and B, the occurrence of A (i) produced or gave rise to or brought about and (ii) necessitated the occurrence of B.[5]

The second version is similar but simpler, in as much as it makes no explicit mention of the notion of objective forces: to say that one object-involving event A caused another object-involving event B is simply to say that A (i) produced or gave rise to

---

[2] Cf. A. J. Ayer, 1973: 179. Hume's famous definition of causation 'in the objects' runs as follows: 'we may define a CAUSE to be 'an object precedent and contiguous to another, and where all the objects resembling the former are placed in like relations of precedency and contiguity to those objects, that resemble the latter' (1739–40: 170). I shall regularly bracket or omit mention of the 'spatiotemporal contiguity' condition: given the present purpose, nothing much hangs on anyone's attitude to it.

[3] Ayer, op. cit.: 183. This could be called the *Simple* version of the Regularity theory—although it just *is* the Regularity theory, in so far as it is a theory that makes a straightforward ontological claim about what causation actually is, in the world. In itself, it involves no epistemological doctrine about what we can know, although Hume, for one, was much concerned with this epistemological question (and although empiricist epistemological considerations were undoubtedly what led him to formulate the Regularity theory in the way he did). Below I will consider some arguably more cautious versions of the Regularity theory. They do not affect the main argument. As J. L. Mackie says, 'the crucial question [for the Regularity theory] is to what extent . . . regularities . . . constitute causation as it is in the objects' (1974: 80).

[4] Even if current physical theory about the fundamental forces (the gravitational, the strong, and the electroweak) is open to improvement in its details, it is nonetheless theory about ('relationally' about) the real forces existing in nature, on the present view.

[5] The word 'govern' is of course a metaphor. I shall try to provide a supporting context in §4, where the use of the notion of forces will be defended further.

or brought about and (ii) necessitated the occurrence of B: each object has a certain intrinsic nature or constitution, and it is in virtue of objects having the intrinsic natures or constitutions that they do have that they do act and react, and cannot but act and react, in the regular ways in which they do.

On the whole I shall adopt the more controversial terminology of the first version; but in §4 I shall suggest that in effect the two versions come to the same thing, so that the terminology of objective forces is avoidable.

Having chosen the notion of objective forces as a central problematic notion in terms of which to characterize and develop our ordinary notion of causation, I will avoid other forms of words popular in 'non-Humean' accounts as far as possible. In particular, I will avoid speaking of 'natural necessity', or of 'laws of nature' (understood in a strong, non-Regularity-theory sense), or of the 'causal powers' of objects. It is very difficult to keep control of these rival terminologies. But here the notion of objective forces is being understood in such a way that accounts of causation given in terms of these other notions may be supposed to reduce naturally to the account in terms of forces. For example: (1) if objects have *causal powers*, they have the powers they do wholly in virtue of the nature of the forces informing (and so governing) the matter of which they are constituted. (2) Given that there are *natural necessities*, or *laws of nature* understood in a strong, non-Regularity sense, they are as they are entirely because the objective forces that inform and govern all matter are as they are. (3) In yet another idiom: the phrase 'objective forces' is taken to be suitable as a name for that in which the existence of any *de re* physical necessities consists.

Objective forces, then, are taken to be the fundamental fact when it comes to causation. On this view, it makes no sense to speak of forces as themselves governed by laws; rather, there are any laws there are because there are the forces there are. The existence, constancy, and particular nature and strength of these forces are part of the ultimate given; they are basic, not-further-explicable facts about how things are.

Both the versions of the 'Producing Causation' view may be found vague. Hume teaches us to think that phrases like 'necessitate', 'produce', and 'give rise to', are all equal in their failure to illuminate the nature of causation. I do not think that they are damagingly vague, in fact. They are good words for what most people think goes on in those cases that are agreed on all sides to be cases of causation. But even if they are vague, they suffice, here, to distinguish the Producing Causation view from the Regularity view that is at present under consideration, because Regularity theorists clearly reject the view that part of what it is for A to cause B is for A to produce or give rise to or necessitate B.

Regularity theorists may deny this—at least in part. They may claim to give a perfectly good sense to the first two phrases, 'produce' and 'give rise to'. But they cannot deny that they are not using these phrases in the ordinary way. For according to the Regularity theory, the objective fact of A's causing B is *wholly described* when it is said B succeeds (and is contiguous to) A and that events of type B regularly and indeed always succeed (contiguous) events of type A: no more needs to be said. But—succession is not the same thing as production: (1), 'A was (contiguously) succeeded by B', says a great deal less than (2), 'A produced B'. And to add (3), 'Events of type A are regularly and indeed always succeeded by (contiguous) events of type B', to (1) does not close the gap between (1) and (2) at all. This is a simple fact about English. Regularity theorists may claim that they can legitimately speak of one thing 'producing' or 'giving rise to' another just as they can legitimately speak of one thing 'causing' another. But one can concede their claim with respect to 'cause', taking 'cause' as a neutral philosophical word whose availability to all parties allows the dispute about what causation is to begin in the first place, and reject it in the case of 'produce' and 'give rise to', insisting on the ordinary meaning of these phrases. This is what I am doing here.

According to the Regularity view, then, to say that A caused B is certainly not to say that A produced or gave rise to B, as the Producing Causation view says, let alone to say that A necessitated B. So the two views stand in fundamental contrast. They stand in contrast even when considered without reference to the notion of necessitation, about which I shall say little more. The contrast has been heightened here by the inclusion in the Producing Causation view of reference to forces conceived as objective phenomena whose existence is part of what constitutes the existence of causation in the world. Given this inclusion, 'the Producing Causation view' may henceforth be taken to be short for 'the objective-force Producing Causation view'.[6]

2

So much for the two views of causation, the Regularity view and the (objective-force) Producing Causation view. I shall now argue for the untenability of Regularity Realism—the combination of the Regularity theory of causation with realism with respect to the external world.

In doing so, I will assume that Regularity Realism is at least a coherent view. In fact, however, this is seriously questionable, given an ordinary understanding of external-world realism according to which it involves belief in the existence of space-occupying objects. For it is arguable (1) that acceptance of the basic conception of material objects that are cohabitants of a single space rationally (if not logically) requires acceptance of the idea that these objects *affect* or *modify* or can affect or modify each other in certain ways; (2) that if anything is to constitute causation in this world of objects, then these events or processes of affecting and modifying must be held to be part at least of what constitutes it; (3) that therefore a Regularity theory of causation cannot possibly be true of such a world, because nothing ever *really* causally affects or modifies anything else strictly speaking, according to the Regularity theory of what causation is: we may allow ourselves to *speak* of things affecting or modifying each other, on the Regularity view, but all there really are, so far as *causation* is concerned, are (mere) relations of (contiguity and) succession between object-involving events.

This is an argument to the effect that Regularity Realism is unobviously incoherent. I think some such argument is probably correct, and will try to develop one in §4.

---

[6] Note that the Producing Causation view does not exclude the possibility of indeterministic occurrences. It does not entail the view that everything has a cause. It is simply a view about what causation is, in so far as some things are correctly said to be instances of causation.

For purposes of discussion, however, I will assume that Regularity Realism is at least a coherent view.

3

Regularity Realism's main opponent is *Producing Causation Realism*—the view that combines realism with respect to the physical world with a common-sense-based Producing Causation view of causation. I will use the word 'Realism' on its own, and capitalized, as short for what Regularity Realism and Producing Causation Realism have in common—realism with respect to the physical world: understanding this in the ordinary way as the view that there is a realm of 'external' or 'mind-independent' physical objects situated in space by which we are affected and of which we accordingly have experience and about which we accordingly think and talk.[7]

I shall not here consider *Regularity Idealism*, which combines a Regularity theory of causation with some sort of idealist—or phenomenalist—view of objects. It is however extremely plausible to say that the only natural home of a Regularity theory is within some sort of idealist or phenomenalist theory, and, conversely, that if one is an idealist, or phenomenalist, then the Regularity view is in fact the correct or best view for one to take of what causation is in the objects—given what one understands by 'object'. But this needs a separate argument.

4

The notions of things *affecting* or *modifying* one another, and of one thing (or event) *producing* or *bringing about* another, are perhaps the most basic components of the ordinary notion of causation. To hold the Producing Causation view is at least to hold that such relations really do hold between individual objects or object-involving events. And to claim that the holding of such relations is an essential part of what causation consists in is already to have adopted an irreducibly non-Regularity-theory point of view (§2).[8]

---

[7] There are many possible varieties of realism with respect to the external world. Such realism does not in fact have to commit itself on the question of whether we have *experience* of the real world. Nor does it necessarily involve belief in the existence of *objects*, let alone objects of the 'middle-sized dry goods' sort. Nor, perhaps, does it have to involve belief in *space*. Here I am concerned only with its most common form; I am not concerned with 'scientific' realism.

[8] There is a sense in which Regularity theorists do not conceive causation as a real relation that can hold between two individual object-involving events A and B at all: for on their view, one cannot specify that in which the causal relation between A and B consists without going beyond the particular portion of reality that consists of A and B and their relations at the time at which A is said to cause B, and making reference to *sets* of relations (actual or possible) between object-involving events of *types* A and B. Cf. D. M. Armstrong 1983: 39–40, 102; and Saul A. Kripke 1982: 67–8.

But why go further? Why introduce reference to such allegedly dubious things as objective forces? Simply because nothing in the meaning of the relation-specifying words 'affect', 'modify' and 'produce' rules out the possibility that these relations could hold between objects and object-involving events in the world without there being any *regularity* in the world's behaviour, let alone any exceptionless regularity. If causation were just production, affecting, and so on, then it seems that there could in theory be causation without any regularity.

It is this—the fact that any adequate account of causation must capture the fact that causes are 'regular in their operation'—that forces one to introduce *some* further feature into one's picture of that in which the existence of Producing Causation consists. It is this that leads one from the relative safety of postulating relations of affecting, modification, and production between objects and object-involving events, to postulating the existence of things like objective forces—forces which are (as it were) inherent in the nature and texture of things, like the tension in a spring, and in virtue of whose existence the ways in which objects and events affect, modify or produce each other are constant and regular. Here I shall take it that any adequate philosophical development of our ordinary view of causation has to say something on the subject of what it is about the world that makes it regular in its behaviour, and that introduction of the notion of objective forces is as good (and as scientifically natural) a way as any of doing so.

According to the objective-force Producing Causation view, then, for one object-involving event A to cause another, B, is for A to (1) *produce* or *bring about* B, the objects involved in A (2) *affecting* or *modifying* the objects involved in B, in accordance with (3) the *objective forces* which govern them. But the question still remains. What are these forces, and this governing? Philosophers commonly hold the postulation of things like objective forces to be deeply suspect, both epistemologically and (therefore) metaphysically, though it rarely or never occurs to scientists to doubt their existence. And so it seems that they require further defence.

In fact, it is sufficient for the purposes of the main argument of this paper to take the notion of forces for granted as an element of our ordinary (science-influenced) view of causation. For the principal objection to Regularity Realism does not depend on or flow from any detailed account of what objective forces might be. Indeed it appears to hold good even if no detailed account of them can be given at all (this is argued in §9). And this is an important point about the overall strategy of this paper. The main aim is a negative one. It is to argue that Realists cannot be Regularity theorists. And it seems that this aim can be accomplished without offering any positive non-Regularity-theory account of what causation might be. Nevertheless I shall now attempt a brief elucidatory account of the notion of objective forces on behalf of the Producing Causation Realists. According to this account, Realists have only to examine the notion of *matter* in order to see that to postulate the existence of matter and its properties is already to postulate the existence of objective forces, in the present sense.

1. There is a danger, when trying to give an account of what forces might be, of adopting a natural but highly misleading picture of the world according to which there are (on the one hand) *objects*, possessed of certain intrinsic properties, yet in

themselves inert and static, which are governed in their behaviour by *forces* (on the other hand) that are entirely external to them.

2. This bad, *separatist* picture fosters the prejudice that the propertied objects, the things one can see and feel, are somehow more real than the forces, dubious intangibles.[9]

3. In fact, however, the objects cannot be fully described apart from the forces.[10] Forces may seem less real, more abstract, more like mere explanatory *posits*, than objects and matter. But this is a superficial view. Matter and the forces that partly constitute its nature just do not come apart like this.

4. Indeed when one talks about objective forces one is (according to the present account) really just talking about matter and its intrinsic nature or properties in a certain kind of way. *The existence of forces is nothing over and above the existence of matter and its fundamental properties.* The way we naturally think about these questions may make this claim seem implausible. But according to the present view its truth is a simple consequence of taking proper account of the *temporality* of matter.

Matter, as ordinarily conceived, is essentially something that persists through time. And it is ordinarily supposed to possess certain unchanging fundamental properties as it persists through time; it is, in other words, supposed to have a certain persisting, intrinsic, stable *nature*, as it persists through time. But to postulate such non-coincidentally stable, continuant, propertied matter, as all ordinary Realists ordinarily do, is (in effect) already to have postulated the existence of forces whose existence is part of the mode of existence of matter and its properties. For what (as it were) holds matter together, as something with a (constant) nature, from instant to instant? What maintains it as something that remains qualitatively similar from instant to instant? The answer cannot be, 'Nothing at all'. For then the transtemporal qualitative similarity or stability is entirely coincidental, and matter cannot after all be said to possess a (more or less) stable, persisting intrinsic *nature*.[11] So the answer must be, 'Something'. And the present suggestion is that the phrase 'objective forces' is as good a name as any for whatever that something is. No one will deny that the notion of possessing properties is necessary to the notion of matter's having a certain nature *at* a time; but the notion of forces governing or inherent in matter is equally necessary to the notion of matter's having a certain nature *through* time.[12]

---

[9] Philosophers who reject this picture when it is described to them in this way may nonetheless operate with it as a background when discussing causation.

[10] To define what an atom is adequately, for example, is to describe it as being constituted of particles which are in turn defined partly by reference to the fact that they are governed by certain fundamental forces (the strong, the gravitational, and the electroweak).

[11] For this notion of coincidence see further §9 and n32. This notion of the stability of matter is of course compatible with the fact that there is intense activity and variation from moment to moment at the molecular, atomic, and subatomic levels.

[12] The question is not only 'What maintains things composed of elementary particles through time?' ('What holds them together?'), but also 'What underwrites the persistence (let alone the sameness of behaviour) of elementary particles, as such?'. The second question might seem to call

In effect, then, to suppose that matter has certain intrinsic, non-coincidentally transtemporally stable properties just is to suppose that there are objective forces. So, since Realists do ordinarily assume that matter has such properties, they in effect also assume the existence of objective forces. To temporalize the ordinary (and Realist) conception of matter-and-its-properties in the simple but necessary way described above—to *dynamicize* the ordinary, unreflective, *static* conception of matter and its properties—just is to admit the notion of objective forces. Indeed, given the temporal nature of matter, postulating forces is really exactly as uncontroversial as saying that matter has properties.

At the very least, talk of forces is much less suspect, metaphysically or ontologically, than it usually appears, given the usual separatist view of the relation between objects and forces.[13] It seems that strong reasons for talking of forces flow directly from extremely general metaphysical considerations about how one may best conceive of the ultimate nature of reality, *given* that one is a straightforward realist with respect to matter and objects. The point is such a simple one that its import is perhaps not readily apparent.

Realists accept without hesitation the idea that matter has a certain basic, essentially unchanging, not-further-explicable nature or constitution. They accept that it *just is* this way, and not that way. Exactly the same attitude is appropriate in the case of the fundamental forces that structure each atom, each proton, each electron. They just are like this, and not like that. Part of what it is for matter-in-time to have the real, particular, not-further-explicable nature that it has just is for it to be structured (and hence governed) by the particular forces that it is structured (and governed) by. (Intuitively, the physicists' claim that *mass* and *energy* can be transformed into each other seems to lend support to the view that *matter* and *forces* are not really distinct phenomena at all. But the present argument is independent of this suggestion.)

This account of the nature of matter-in-time can be extended in an obvious way into an account of how forces govern the *interactions* of matter (the following is no doubt too simple, but it gives the general idea): (1) the way parts or parcels of matter (objects) interact is (of course) a function of how they affect and modify each other. (2) The way in which they affect and modify each other is (of course) a function of what properties they have. Hence (3) the way in which they interact is governed by objective forces. For (4) to talk of such forces is simply to talk in one way of what it

---

for some further notion than that of objective forces—some notion like 'fundamental modes of persistence or continuance' (cf. Mackie's discussion of the notion of a 'form of persistence', op. cit.: 218 ff.). Both these questions connect with difficult issues in the philosophy of physics (perhaps talk of 'matter' must in the end reduce to talk of 'fields', or 'distributions of energy'). Here I will continue to present the general argument just in terms of the notion of forces.

[13] An analogy could be drawn between the relations between the absolute theory of space and the relational theory of space, on the one hand, and, on the other hand, (1) the separatist picture of forces as structuring principles of the universe that exist independently of objects, and (2) the current view that for forces to exist is simply part of what it is for propertied matter-in-time to exist.

is for the objects to have the temporally persisting properties that they do have. It is part of what it is to take seriously the Realist assumption that temporally continuant objects have continuously temporally persisting properties or natures.

To use the word 'force' at all may be to risk rapid dismissal from some philosophers. Perhaps those who are inclined to react in this way should carefully compare their attitude to the word 'force' when doing philosophy with their attitude to it when reading about (say) fundamental physics. Certainly they should bear in mind how tightly the notion of force has here been tied to the notion of matter: the word 'force' simply gives clear (blunt) expression to a notion whose intelligibility (and indeed applicability) one is effectively committed to recognizing, given that one is an ordinary Realist about matter. Look up at your surroundings, persisting through time.

Nevertheless, Realists who cannot stomach forces can restrict themselves to speaking merely of 'the nature of matter-in-time', or something of the sort, compatibly with the conclusions of this section. In the end it is simply matter-in-time that is in question; it is matter-in-time that is the given, the ultimate not-further-explicable fact, the best candidate for the necessary mystery.[14] To talk explicitly of objective forces after having rejected the bad separatist picture of the relation between matter and forces is just to give a certain natural characterization of an ineliminable aspect of the concept of matter-in-time.

If this is on the right lines, straightforward realism about physical objects and their properties requires acceptance of the notion of forces. The notion of temporally persisting* matter (or of objects with a certain stable and persisting nature) simply depends on the notion of forces.[15] It is only fixation on a picture of matter that presents it non-temporally as static stuff, grasped as it is at a given instant, that allows us to suppose that this is not so. This account of forces therefore amounts to a certain kind of 'Unobvious Incoherence' argument against Regularity Realism, in so far as Regularity Realism cannot admit the existence of such forces.[16]

[14] That there is necessarily a mystery in the existence of the world follows from the fact that all explanations come to an end.

* Note added in 2007. I have changed 'perduring' to 'persisting' here and in one other place. When I wrote this paper I did not know about the special use of 'perduring' adopted by some philosophers when contrasting 'three-dimensionalist' as opposed to 'four-dimensionalist' views of the existence of objects in time.

[15] Note that acceptance of this view does not force one to reject inductive scepticism with respect to predictions of future events. For to claim (1) that to postulate the existence of propertied matter-in-time (as a Realist) is already to postulate the existence of objective forces is not necessarily to claim (2) that it must be supposed that such forces (let alone exactly the same forces) must always continue to hold sway in the future. Perhaps there is an anti-universe that will some day disrupt our own universe.

[16] Clearly, Regularity Realism cannot admit that there are objective forces, but maintain that their holding sway or operation is no part of causation. If there are forces, then their holding sway or operation has to be counted as part of what constitutes causation.

The principal objection to Regularity Realism is still to come, however, and does not rely on this particular account of forces. Indeed it will henceforth be assumed, for the sake of the argument of the rest of this paper, that to posit the existence of objects in the ordinary Realist way is *not* already to commit oneself to granting the existence of something like objective forces, and that therefore a coherent Regularity account of the interactions of such objects is at least a possibility.

5

Whether or not Realism is true, our experience has the character of being experience of a world that is highly regular in its behaviour. The question arises naturally: *Why* does our experience have this regular character? I will first consider the Producing Causation Realists' answer to the question, and then the Regularity Realists' answer. (The Regularity Idealists' answer is discussed briefly in note 27.)

The Producing Causation Realists' answer, of course, is that our experiences have the character of being experiences of a world that is highly regular in its behaviour because the genuinely externally existing world of which they are experiences is governed by constant, objective forces: it is a world in which objective-force Producing Causation exists over and above mere succession, and mere regularities of succession. One's experience has a regular character because it is experience of a world in which particular object-involving events do not merely stand in relations of contiguity and succession, but produce or give rise to one another in accordance with the constant forces that inform and govern and indeed constitute objects (or: in accordance with the nature of matter-in-time). Perhaps we cannot prove that this is so, or that such forces exist. (We cannot prove that Realism is true, or that objects exist.) But it may well be so—most people believe it is.

This, the Producing Causation Realists' answer to the question 'Why does our experience of the world have the character of being experience of a world that is highly regular in its behaviour?', may be thought to be profoundly unillumin-ating (especially by adherents of the Regularity theory). It may be objected that even if the notion of objective forces is an *intelligible* one, still, to posit the exist-ence of such forces in order to explain the regularity of the interactions of objects is to make a claim that is completely vacuous, since it is both unverifiable and unfalsifiable.

Producing Causation Realists may be prepared to agree that it is unverifiable and unfalsifiable, while denying that it is vacuous. They may be prepared to agree that there is a sense in which all the evidence we can ever have for the existence of (objective-force) Producing Causation consists in experience of regularities of succession. They may agree with Hume that regularity of succession is all we can ever *know* of causation. But they can then lay stress on the word 'evidence', as just used. Regularity of succession is indeed, and precisely, *evidence* for the exist-ence of objective-force Producing Causation. It is not what *constitutes* causation, as Regularity theorists claim. In fact, experience of regularity of succession is evid-ence for the existence of objective forces in rather the same way as experience as a whole is evidence for the existence of an external world of objects. It is, perhaps, not conclusive evidence. But anyone who says that to posit the existence of object-ive forces is a vacuous step may well have to grant that to posit the existence of an external world is an equally vacuous step. But it is not a vacuous step. The claim that there is an external world (of tables and chairs, etc.) is a substantive claim.[17] It could be true. It could be false. And the claim that there are objective forces is arguably in the same case (it is argued in §8). Regularity Realists cannot say that espousing a Regularity theory of causation is just good empiricist epistemological hygiene—not going beyond the evidence, or 'meaning-empiricism', or some such thing. For in this sense of 'going beyond the evidence' it is arguable that they have, in being realists about an external world of objects, already gone far beyond the (sensory) evidence. A fortiori, they have granted the possible legitimacy of moves of this sort.

It may not be provable that there are objective forces, then. But *if* Realism is true, and if there is an external world of objects of which we have experience, as is at present assumed to be the case, then it is (to put it mildly) overwhelmingly likely that there are. For suppose the contrary: Realism is true, and there is an external world of objects that is highly regular in its behaviour, but there are no forces at all governing what goes on in this external world. ('In nature one thing just hap-pens after another.') There are all those mind-independent physical objects knock-ing about out there completely independently of us, persisting and interacting, and nothing—*nothing*—governs or orders the ways in which they do this. And yet they persist and interact in a highly regular fashion. How can this be so? It is really rather extraordinary. For, *ex hypothesi*, nothing constrains them to behave and interact in a way that exhibits any order or regularity at all.

This extremely simple point about the absurdity of adopting realism about mater-ial objects without at the same time adopting some sort of objective-force Produ-cing Causation view is the main objection to Regularity Realism.[18] It is sometimes objected to Hume that he cannot as a Regularity theorist distinguish between a causal sequence and an 'outrageous run of luck'. But it seems that Realists who espouse the Simple version of the Regularity theory that is at present under consideration are even worse off. For it seems that they assert positively that all causation actually *is* an out-rageous run of luck.[19]

[17] Here I am in direct disagreement with positivists like Carnap. See his 'Pseudoproblems in Philosophy' (1928: 334).

[18] Here I agree with John Foster (1982–3: 87–101, esp. §11), and with D. M. Armstrong (1983, cf. e.g. ch. 4, §§1, 2, 5). Armstrong presents his argument in terms of laws of nature (which he conceives of as complex mind-independent entities, relations of necessitation between universals) rather than in terms of objective forces: inference to such laws, he says, is inference to the best explanation of the regularity of the world's behaviour.

[19] It is no good protesting that Regularity theorists do at least hold that there are laws of nature. For, as Armstrong points out, there is a sense in which Regularity theorists take laws of nature to be 'cosmic coincidences' (op. cit. p. 161, and cf. pp. 40–1). And it remains true, given a Regularity theory of laws, that all there actually is in the world, so far as causation is concerned, is regular succession. There is nothing about the world that makes it a regular world. Cf. also W. Kneale 1949: esp. 70–103, and n29 below.

6

So much for Producing Causation Realism. It assumes we have experience of mind-independent objects, and it has an extremely simple explanation of why these objects appear to us to be law-governed: they appear to be law-governed because they really are governed by constant, objective forces; for these forces to hold sway is part of what it is for matter-in-time to exist.

This explanation is of a highly general sort (indeed it could not be more general), and it does not, of course, explain why any particular thing happens as it does. But it is not vacuous. The best way to see this is to contrast Producing Causation Realism's account of the world with Regularity Realism's account.

Regularity Realism agrees with Producing Causation Realism that our experiences have the character of being experiences of complex patterns of regular succession in an external world; and it agrees that the reason why this is so is that things in the world really do exemplify such complex patterns of regular succession in their behaviour. But it denies that the reason why our experiences are experiences of complex patterns of regular succession is that the things they are experiences of are governed by something like objective forces whose existence is not simply identical with, but in some sense underlies, and gives rise to, the regularity of succession. For, it says, there is nothing more to causation than the bare, ground-floor, not-further-explicable fact of regular succession (see note 16).

The trouble is that this makes the regular succession completely astonishing, as already remarked: all those totally unprincipled physical objects on the loose out there, interacting in seemingly perfectly law-governed ways—and for no reason at all. For no reason at all: there is no objective state of things, out there in the world, that is the reason why they do so. It is not just that we do not and cannot know either that there is or that there is not some objective reason why they behave in this way. Regularity Realism goes further. In effect, it asserts positively that there is no reason why. For it asserts that all there is, objectively, so far as causation is concerned, is just regular succession: there is no real 'because' in nature. Regular succession is all. (Reasons for thinking that this may not be Hume's view are given in note 36.)

Now it is true that all explanations must come to an end. But some stopping points are vastly preferable to others. Given Realism (object realism), the phenomenon of (observable) regularity is not in itself a tolerable stopping point. It demands a reason, a ground.[20] Objective forces are a possible stopping point. The fundamental forces, and their particular strength, we can accept—together with Planck's constant, the charge on the electron, and so on—as features of how things just are in a not further explicable way.[21]

---

[20] This is not simply to push the problem back to *un*observable regularities: even if we and the world were so constituted that (a) there was nothing unobservable by us, and (b) we could somehow know that this was so, regularity would still demand an objective reason or ground.

[21] We can then say that given how things are—given that there are the particular objective forces there are—certain things are *in fact* (as a matter of contingent fact) necessary: naturally necessary. (In order to prove that the natural necessities that do in fact obtain, necessarily obtain, one would

It does not follow, from the fact that explanation comes to an end, that there is no 'because' in nature.

7

As described in §6, Regularity Realism seems an extraordinary view. What produces it? I think it arises from a deep (but not irresolvable) tension that exists between the two individually admirable philosophical motives that together produce the Regularity Realists' position—empiricism and realism. This tension, which has arguably been the main motor of philosophical dispute for at least the last 250 years, arises because *realism*, as traditionally conceived, tends to make claims about what things exist that 'go beyond' all available evidence for their truth, according to traditional *empiricism*'s conception of evidence. I will argue that the oddity of Regularity Realism lies in the fact that it accepts the full realist commitment with respect to objects, and then attempts to avoid it, at least partially, with respect to causation, for empiricism-inspired reasons that are inappropriate given its realism with respect to objects.[22]

The tendency of empiricism, unchecked, is always anti-realist; it has a strong tendency to degenerate into some form of verificationism: to treat the question of what there is (and even the question of what we can—intelligibly—talk about) as the same question as the question of what we can find out, or know for certain; to reduce questions of metaphysics and ontology to questions of epistemology. Empiricists who wish to maintain a basic commitment to realism have therefore to protect this commitment against the anti-realist inclinations of their empiricism.

This commitment to realism brings with it a commitment to the possibility of verification-transcendent facts; to the possibility of the existence of unknowable things (unknowable by us, at least); to the idea that certain things may just be the case although one cannot (ever) discover or prove that they are.[23] It keeps epistemology

have to give an a priori proof that a material universe could not have differed from the one we inhabit in any possible respect. I assume such a proof is not possible.)

[22] A certain confusion about what regularity is may also be one of the things that helps to make Regularity Realism seem like a possible position. This confusion is to be found at one (and perhaps only one) point in Mackie's book *The Cement of the Universe*. He writes that 'the crucial . . . question is to what extent . . . complex regularities . . . constitute causation as it is in the objects. It is undeniable that we ordinarily suppose . . . that there are . . . regularities *underlying* . . . many of the sequences that we take to be causal' (p. 80, my emphasis). But, first, a regularity cannot be said to underlie a *single* causal sequence A–B; all that can be said is that a single causal sequence A–B forms part of a regularity—i.e., part of an extended sequence S of single A–B sequences. Nor, second, can a regularity be said to *underlie* an *extended* sequence S of single A–B sequences. The regularity lies wholly in the regularity of S itself (i.e. there are no A-not-B sequences), and has no further existence as something that underlies S. It just *is* the regularity of S itself; it cannot be said to underlie S in such a way that it might be invoked in order to explain it. (To talk of regularity as underlying causal sequences is to try to reap the benefits of a Producing Causation theory while ostensibly sticking to a Regularity theory.)

[23] Realism has many varieties in this careful age, and this characterization of the realist commitment may be thought to obliterate important distinctions (e.g. between 'semantic' and 'ontological' realism). But I take it to be true by definition of any interesting form of (ontological) realism of the kind that is at present of concern.

well apart from metaphysics and ontology. It allows one to say—for example—that even if regularities of succession are all that we ever know of causation (as well as all we need to know), yet they are not all that there are; and to insist (against certain varieties of 'linguistic' or 'meaning' empiricism) that regularities of succession are not all that we really talk about, or *can* (intelligibly) talk about, when we talk about causation—any more than sense-data, or experiences, are all that we really talk about, or can (intelligibly) talk about, when we talk about objects.

8

This last parallel—between ordinary talk about causation and ordinary talk about objects—is a revealing one. It is worth developing further, for although there is a difference between the two cases, there is also an important similarity. I shall proceed in a fairly rough fashion, ignoring a number of possible qualifications.

The difference is this. Those who make the (broadly speaking phenomenalist) claim that there is a sense in which sense-data are all that we really talk about or can talk about when we purport to talk about objects (conceived in the ordinary way as things in the external, mind-independent world) deny any ultimate non-mental reference at all to such talk. And this is not necessarily so in the causation case. For those who say that regularities of succession are all that we really talk about or can talk about when we purport to talk about causation (conceived in the ordinary way as something in the mind-independent world) *may* be (a) phenomenalists, and so deny any non-mental reference to talk of causation, just as they do to talk of objects. But they may equally be (b) Realists (object realists); in which case they will grant that we talk about something non-mental, in such a case—objective regularities of succession in the mind-independent world—and simply deny that we talk about anything more than such regularities.

Here the relevant case is (b), because we are concerned with Regularity Realism. And the present point is this: even if one only considers those Regularity theorists who are Realists about objects, there is still a revealing parallel between their Regularity-theory attitude to talk about causation, and the phenomenalist attitude to talk about objects. For, as Regularity theorists, Regularity Realists hold that in asserting the existence of causation, conceived in the ordinary way, there is a clear sense in which we 'go beyond' a body of evidence taken as given. Exactly similarly, phenomenalists hold that in asserting the existence of objects, conceived in the ordinary way, we 'go beyond' a body of evidence taken as given. The parallelism of attitude is complete although in the one case (the case of the phenomenalistic understanding of object talk) the evidence taken as given consists merely of our experience, while in the other case (the case of the Regularity-theory understanding of causation talk) the evidence taken as given consists of objective regularities of succession conceived as existing in the mind-independent world.*

---

* This paragraph differs slightly from the originally published version.

It is this parallel that I want to examine further, by considering two questions and two broadly speaking Humean answers:

(Q1) Why do we believe that there are physical objects—objects conceived of in the ordinary way?
(A1) Because of the 'constancy and coherence' of our experiences—on account of the particular patterns that they form together.

(Q2) Why do we believe that there is Producing Causation—causation in the ordinary strong sense of the word?
(A2) Because of the order and regularity of our experiences—on account of the particular patterns of regular succession that they form together.

Consider now four claims commonly made in response to (A2)—in response to the claim that we believe in Producing Causation (simply) because of our experience of regular succession.

(C1) Well then, that's all that causation really is, in itself—regular succession.

(C2) 'Regular succession' is all that you can really mean by the word 'causation'; for otherwise you go inadmissibly beyond the evidence (actual or possible).

(C3) The claim that Producing Causation exists (or that objective forces exist) is unintelligible.

(C4) You cannot know that Producing Causation exists (or that objective forces exist).

These claims are all familiar. But consider the corresponding responses to (A1)—responses to the claim that we believe in objects (simply) on account of the coherent patterns our experiences form together:

(O1) Well then, that's all that objects really are, in themselves—patterns of experiences.

(O2) 'A pattern of experiences' (or of sense-data, or a collection of ideas) is all that you can really mean by 'object', for otherwise you go inadmissibly beyond the evidence.

(O3) The claim that objects (as ordinarily conceived) exist is unintelligible.

(O4) You cannot know that objects (as ordinarily conceived) exist.

Now Regularity Realists standardly reject all of (O1)–(O4), as Realists—object realists.[24] And the nature of the parallel between (C1)–(C4) and (O1)–(O4) strongly suggests that *if* one rejects (O1)–(O3) on Realist grounds, then two things follow:

(i) that although one does not *ipso facto* have reason to reject (C1), that is, the Regularity view, one is no longer in any good position to cite an empiricism-motivated

---

[24] In fact they do not have to reject (O4); one can be a Realist and grant that Realism is not provably true (in fact a properly worked out Realism must grant this). So (O4) and (C4) are not really at issue here, except in so far as part of the present point is that (C4) is not more defensible than (O4).

concern for parsimony of assumption and ontological commitment, or for not 'going beyond the evidence', as a sufficient reason for accepting (C1);

(ii) that one does have reason to reject (C2)–(C3), because the sorts of ways in which (C2)–(C3) are standardly justified are simply incompatible with one's Realism.
(ii) suggests that anyone who asserts that talk of Producing Causation or objective forces is *unintelligible* may in the end be hard put to it to say why talk of objects (as ordinarily conceived) is not similarly unintelligible. And this constitutes one argument against Regularity Realists, who may be inclined to invoke unintelligibility in the causation case while claiming to find no such difficulty in the object case.[25]

(i) does not in itself provide any positive reason why Realists should *reject* (C1), the Regularity view. So I shall now try to expand the very simple argument given in §5 for the claim that a commitment to realism does indeed create powerful reasons for rejecting (C1) in favour of some form of the objective-force Producing Causation view.

9

Why so? Because Realism creates an overriding theoretical need to suppose that there is something, in the real world which it postulates, which is *the reason why* the objects in that world behave regularly.[26] It creates a theoretical need to connect the regularity of the world's proceedings to features of the world that are not themselves the feature of regularity. One does not have to be able to say in any detail what these features are, or what the connection is; one can even hold, on Humean grounds, that this cannot be done. One just has to hold that there are such features, and such a connection; not on grounds of logical consistency, but, ultimately, just on grounds of minimal theoretical plausibility.[27] For it seems that to deny that there are such features, and such a connection, is, as already remarked, to assert that it is, *within and on the terms of the external world whose reality one proclaims*, an objective fact that the world's regularity of behaviour is a purely chance matter. It is not just to assert that we cannot

---

[25] The discussion of the close relation between the notion of objective forces and the notion of propertied matter-in-time in §4 constitutes another such argument, in as much as it argues (perhaps contrary to some very deep prejudices) that one cannot employ the latter notion without acquiescing in some version of the former notion.

[26] Here again I am in sympathy with Armstrong and Foster (op. cit.), both of whom argue that one is rationally obliged to 'infer to the best explanation' of the world's regularity, and hence to postulate something like objective forces, or 'forms of (objective) natural necessity' (Foster 1982b: 90), or 'laws of nature' conceived as complex mind-independent entities (Armstrong, pp. 7–8, 172). Unlike them, however, I am not specifically concerned to combat inductive scepticism.

[27] Berkeleian and phenomenalistic idealists, by contrast, do not need to endorse the supposition that there is some feature of the world of objects that is the reason why it is regular, given how they define 'world' and 'object'. Berkeley does give a reason for the regularity of the world of objects (or 'objects'), but he gives it in terms of something—God—that exists outside that world. It is reasonable to demand of atheistic phenomenalists that they too should give some reason for the regularity of their world of objects; and it is hard to guess what they will say; but again they will not have to give it in terms of something internal to that same world (or 'world').

know that the regularity is not a purely chance matter. It is to assert positively that it is a purely chance matter: that is, it is to assert positively that there is nothing about the world that makes it a regular world; it just is a regular world.

But this, in effect, is precisely what Regularity Realism says. To assert that regularity is all there is to causation in the real world is to assert positively that the world has no fundamental features F which are of such a kind that it has the feature of being regular in its behaviour *because* it has F. It is to assert positively that the regularity obtains by pure chance (i.e. for no reason), within and on the terms of the world of which it is a feature. It is to postulate a vast objective coincidence. And this is unacceptable.[28]

Regularity Realists cannot avoid this objection by saying that they do not hold the Regularity theory as a positive theory of what causation actually is in the objects, but only as an ontologically non-committal theory, motivated by epistemological caution, about the correct way for us human beings to think and talk philosophically about causation 'in the objects'. For they have already committed themselves to a real and regular world of objects, and they have to face the consequences. If they want to avoid saying that the regularity is, on the terms of that world, just a vast coincidence, then they must grant that some further theoretical step can correctly be taken, *however unspecific*, which traces the existence of the regularity to some further feature of reality that is not itself the regularity.[29]

However unspecific: in a way, 'the objective-force Producing Causation view' is really no more than a useful name for the view that one must as a Realist grant that this step can be taken. As such, it need not offer any positive description of what non-Regularity-theory causation is like. It can insist that we are as Realists rationally obliged to posit that objective-force Producing Causation exists, as something distinct from regularity, while agreeing with Hume that we cannot have any experience of it that is distinct from our experience of regularity.[30]

It will be objected that to try to make the existence of regularity comprehensible in this way, by asserting that there is objective-force Producing Causation, is simply to replace one candidate for being the ground-floor, not-further-explicable fact about causation with another, and is not to make any real progress. (It is, vacuously, to posit one extra thing, or kind of thing, without deriving any real explanatory benefit from

---

[28] Cf. n16. Suppose objects behaved completely randomly (apart from the considerable non-randomness that is already involved in their being persisting objects at all), and that we had despite this somehow managed to evolve in such a way as to have self-conscious experience of the sort we do have, and to employ concepts of an objective world. There is a clear sense in which we would not under such conditions need to suppose that there was any *reason why* things happened as they did, in the way that we do, given that things happen in the regular way they do (and given that we are Realists).

[29] The version of the Regularity theory entailed by the Ramsey-Braithwaite-Lewis 'systematic theory of laws' (for a brief statement see Armstrong, op. cit.: 66–73) provides no answer to this point. Note that the present claim is not so much that one is rationally obliged to make an 'inference to the best explanation' of regularity in the world of objects, as that one is rationally obliged not to insist on a vast objective coincidence.

[30] It can also disagree with Hume on this last point.

In 'Causality and Determination', G. E. M. Anscombe makes the point that there is a sense in which we do directly perceive Producing Causation (and experience forces) in witnessing and undergoing such things as knocks, pushes and pulls, and so on (1971: 68f.)

it at all. It is to claim to explain the world's property of regularity of behaviour in terms of a regular-behaviour-producing feature.) But to say this—to make this *virtus dormitiva* kind of objection—is to miss the present point, which is not really concerned with *explanatory progress* at all, but rather with a certain kind of theoretical coherence. We do not have to be able to give an explanation of regularity that is not open to the *virtus dormitiva* objection; the point is simply that we have (as Realists) to accept that there is, in the real world, some real reason why objects behave regularly in the way that they do.[31] Regularity Realism says that there is no reason at all why there is regularity in the world. And it has to say this, because if there were any feature of the physical world, considered just as such, that could correctly be said to be the *reason why* there was regularity, then that feature could *ipso facto* correctly be said to *be* causation understood in some essentially non-Regularity-theory way as something other than regularity. And so it seems that Regularity Realists have to treat the world's regularity as a vast objective coincidence.[32]

It will be objected that there is still an absolutely fundamental difference between postulating objects and postulating objective forces or Producing Causation: objects are directly observable, forces are not; one can quite simply see and touch objects, and one cannot similarly see and touch forces or Producing Causation. This objection is perhaps irresistibly natural. But if the foregoing is right it turns out to have no real weight at all.[33]

10

Some Regularity Realists may still reject the conclusion. They may claim that all they are saying, in espousing a Regularity theory of causation on empiricist principles,

---

[31] See further §11. All explanations must come to an end, but 'the Regularity theory . . . gives up much too soon' (Armstrong, op. cit.: 159). It may be said: if you say that *objects* are regular in their behaviour because there are objective forces, the question about regularity just re-arises: 'Why are *forces* regular in their operation?' On the present view the following sorts of answer to this question are appropriate: 'They just are—such is their nature' (or, equally, 'Such is the nature of matter' see §4); or 'Asking this question is a bit like asking why matter is extended' (see §1). The essential point remains unaffected: there cannot be just regularity; one is rationally obliged to suppose that there is something in the world that is not itself regularity—and perhaps one can simply call this 'matter', rather than 'forces'—that is, given its nature, the reason for this regularity.

[32] There is of course nothing like the same implausibility in postulating that (a) a *single event* (like the 'Big Bang' or a subatomic event) is a chance occurrence, as there is in postulating that (b) the regular behaviour of the whole universe for billions of years is a chance occurrence (the present argument is not just an invocation of the Principle of Sufficient Reason). Doubts may be raised about the sense of the notion of chance or coincidence when talking of the whole history of the universe. But for present purposes the notion is sufficiently well defined by the example: a clear case of the postulation of a vast objective coincidence is the claim that (b) above is something for which there is, objectively, no reason at all.

[33] It can also be challenged directly; see n30 above. Recall also the argument about the connection between the notions of objects and forces given in §4; and the point, made in n15, that the present argument is not directly concerned to challenge inductive scepticism about the future (the claim is not that we can now either sense or legitimately postulate something that will guarantee us certain knowledge of the future).

is (roughly) that regular succession is all that the word 'cause' can really mean, as a word that has genuine application to the external, mind-independent world, given the nature of our experience of that world (and, equally, the circumstances of our learning of the word 'cause'). One could call this the *Meaning* version of the Regularity theory. But if one is a real Realist then this supposedly more non-committal position is not really distinct from the Simple or full-blooded 'regularity constitutes causation' position. For to be a Realist about the external world, and then to say (roughly) that regular succession is all that the word 'cause' can really *mean*, or refer to, as applied to that world, just is to say that this is all that causation can really *be*, in that world. So it is not only the Simple version of the Regularity theory, according to which causation is 'in the objects', and regularity actually *constitutes* causation as it is in the objects, that cannot be combined with Realism. The Meaning version does no better.

The same goes for the *Appropriate Ascription* version, according to which all one has to say, or indeed can properly say, about the word 'causation' and its cognates, is just that they are words that it is 'appropriate to ascribe' in certain experiential circumstances. On this view, any further questions about the ultimate reality or onto-logical or metaphysical status of what one is talking about (in this case causation) can and should be dismissed as without substance, or at least as without philosoph-ical importance.[34] But *Realists* cannot reasonably adopt the Appropriate Ascription approach in the present case, because they have already gone beyond the epistemo-logical prophylaxis of such an approach in a crucial respect. They do not make the 'appropriate ascription' move in the case of objects. They are fully ontologically or metaphysically committed to objects, and this has clear consequences for what other views they can reasonably hold. It is true that the Appropriate Ascription version of the Regularity theory is *logically* compatible with Realism; and unlike the Simple ver-sion it does not positively deny the existence of objective forces or Producing Caus-ation, in such a way as to turn the objective regularities of the world into a cosmic coincidence. But in taking the apparently much more moderate line of simply deny-ing that any further question needs to be raised about whether or not there is any reason for the objective phenomenon of regularity of succession, it is ultimately as unsatisfactory as the Simple version of the Regularity theory, when combined with Realism.

The reason for this is familiar. For the Realist, the objects we talk about are fully mind-independent—truly out there. They are as they are, out there, and, given the way they are, some statements are simply true of them, others are simply false. In par-ticular, the statement 'There is some reason why they behave regularly in the way that they do' is either true or false (whether or not we can ever find out which is immaterial).[35] So Realists cannot reasonably adopt the Appropriate Ascription ver-sion of the Regularity theory, which simply hedges on the issue of truth. Their Real-ism effectively commits them to accepting that there is an answer—either 'Yes' or 'No'—to the question 'Is there some reason why objects behave regularly in the way

[34] The Appropriate Ascription version is of course related to the Meaning version.
[35] See n23.

that they do?' But the only plausible answer for them to give, as Realists, is 'Yes' (§9). And the only plausible *general* answer for them to give to the next question that arises, namely, 'Well then, why is there this regularity of behaviour?', is: 'Because there is Producing Causation; *that is,* causation conceived as something that is real and that is, whatever exactly it consists in, something other than (mere) regularity.' Or, more particularly: 'Because there are objective forces, forces that are as real as matter itself—being, indeed, part of what constitutes the nature of matter-in-time.'[36]

It seems, then, that the Appropriate Ascription theorist's supposedly intermediate position is simply an illusion. The wish to occupy some such position is the product of two highly natural desires: the desire to be a robust realist (especially about objects) and the desire to be a rigorous and ontologically sober empiricist (especially about causation). But it is not a tenable position. It involves a failure to think through the consequences of robust realism (about objects) for rigorous empiricism (generally considered).[37]

Regularity Realists may finally object to the Producing Causation view by asking 'What difference does it make?', and claiming that the answer to this question is 'No difference at all.'

Suppose that this is the right answer, and that the predictions and expectations of holders of the Regularity theory view and holders of the Producing Causation view are identical—so that people who abandon either view for the other one have no reason at all to change their practices or expectations as a result. No objection to the Producing Causation view can be based on this fact. For it does not follow from the fact that the evidential import of two views is the same that there is no difference between them. One might as well say that there is no difference between (Lockean) realism and (Berkeleian) idealism. Excessive empiricists, and pragmatists who do not take the notion of truth very seriously, think that it does follow. They refuse to see that there can *be* a difference that fails to *make* a difference—an evidential difference, that is. But Regularity theorists certainly cannot take this line. For they insist that their view is correct, and that the Producing Causation view is wrong, *although* the

---

[36] Hume's position is complex, and perhaps not entirely consistent. But I doubt whether the Hume who wrote the *Enquiry* would have disagreed with the argument of this paper, or at least with its conclusion. His official position is of course sceptical with respect to the existence of the external world; cf. *Enquiry* §12.1 (152–3/114–15), *Treatise* §1.3.5 (84/59). Often, however, he writes in an apparently straightforwardly Realist way; and when he does so he appears to espouse a full-blooded Producing Causation view. The following quotation from the *Enquiry* is entirely typical of Hume in his Realist frame of mind: 'The scenes of the universe are continually shifting, and one object follows another in an uninterrupted succession; but the power or force, which actuates the whole machine, is entirely concealed from us, and never discovers itself in any of the sensible qualities of body' (63–4/51). On this view 'the power or force which actuates the whole machine', and whose existence is the reason why things happen in regular ways, is certainly real, although we can never know anything about its nature. It is something over and above regular succession, and there is regular succession *because* there is this '[actuating] power or force'. There are dozens of similar apparently straightforwardly referring uses of expressions like 'power', 'energy', 'force' to be found in his writings, e.g. in *Enquiry* §4 and §7 (30/27, 33/29, 63/51, 67/54, 70/55–6, 72/57, 74/58, 77/60–1).

[37] I think this argument, which traces an untenable position to an unresolved clash between realism and empiricism, can be generalized to good effect in several other areas of philosophy—especially the philosophy of mind (cf. the spectacle of behaviourism and its philosophical derivatives).

two views have the same evidential import. They set up their view in specific opposition to the Producing Causation view. So they can hardly appeal to the 'It makes no difference' point in defence of their view against the Producing Causation view.

Regularity theorists would also be unwise to press the *virtus dormitiva* objection to the Producing Causation view considered in §9—the objection that to posit Producing Causation as in some way *explanatory* of regularity is exactly parallel to positing a *virtus dormitiva* as explanatory of the fact that opium induces sleep. According to this objection, positing Producing Causation amounts to no more than the vacuous positing of a regularity-producing feature as the reason why there is regularity, since we can give no independent description of Producing Causation, no description of it that is independent of its alleged effect, observable regularity.

In fact, however, this objection works against the Regularity theorist. For, given the terms of the parallel, the (Simple) Regularity theorist is insisting that there is no reason at all why opium induces sleep: it just does, and that's that. And this, we suppose, is plain false. The Producing Causation theorist, on the other hand, is saying that there is a reason why opium produces sleep. It induces sleep because it has a *virtus dormitiva*: that is, because it has certain intrinsic (objective-force-involving) properties which are such that it has this effect. Now this remark may not be very helpful, but it is, we suppose, certainly true.

In conclusion: two main arguments have been put forward for the view that Regularity Realism is indefensible, and that realism about objects rationally requires realism about something like Producing Causation or objective forces. According to the first, one cannot even make proper sense of (1) the ordinary Realist notion of objects without reference to (2) the notion of something like objective forces; the two notions are indissolubly connected. It follows that those who deny that we can avail ourselves of (2) are mistaken in thinking that we can nevertheless avail ourselves of (1). If (2) is ultimately unintelligible, then so is (1). But there is no question of Realists' giving up (1). So, somehow or other, they must accommodate (2). On this view, Regularity Realism is unobviously incoherent.

According to the second argument, even if Regularity Realism is not incoherent, Realists are rationally obliged to posit the existence of something like objective forces simply in order to forestall the charge of grotesque theoretical implausibility.

The conclusion seems plain. Those who are unwilling to forsake the Regularity theory of causation must pay the price: they must renounce the (real) world. But even when they have done so, they will still face the question of why we have experience, and of why it is regular in character.[38]

---

[38] '*That* there are or have been regularities, for whatever reason, is an established fact of science.... *Why* there have been regularities is an obscure question, for it is hard to see what would count as an answer (W. V. Quine 1969: 126). Perhaps so. But it is still a real question. And if one does not answer 'There is some reason why', one must answer 'There is (or may be) no reason why', and embrace the 'coincidentalism' described above. Wouldn't 'a nothing ... serve just as well as a something about which nothing could be said'? (L. Wittgenstein 1953: §304.) On the present view, even if it were true that one could say nothing about objective forces, the correct Realist answer to this last question would still be 'No' in their case.

17

The Contingent Reality of Natural Necessity

Nicholas Everitt's objection to my discussion of the regularity theory of causation is a common one. I think it misses the point, but the point it misses is in a way a delicate one, and hard to express, and the general worry he expresses is a natural one. For that reason it is important, and its importance is reflected in the fact that it is very difficult to find a satisfyingly substantive way of stating the difference between regularity theories of causation and non-regularity theories of causation. I have had no new ideas about how to do this since I wrote Essay 16 (1987) and *The Secret Connexion* (1989b), but I will restate some of the ideas in the former, and in chapters 8 and 22 of the latter, in order to try to answer Everitt, who considers only chapter 5.

1

My principal doubt about Everitt's type of objection is this. Is it going to have the consequence that the regularity theory of causation is an a priori truth? I assume that most philosophers would agree that the regularity theory of causation is not an a priori truth, and that any objection to an attempt to state a non-regularity theory of causation which had the consequence that the regularity theory of causation was an a priori truth would be unsatisfactory. I may be wrong in making this assumption: it may be that some defenders of the regularity theory of causation would not mind if their account of things had the consequence that the regularity theory was an a priori truth. But it would be very good to get this fact out into the open, if it is a fact.

Everitt's objection divides into two parts, which he calls (a) and (b) (p. 206). He is right that (a) is beside the point, and I will concentrate on (b), or rather on the general objection of which (b) is one particular expression. In talking of explanation he sets up the issue in terms I tried to avoid, but the basic point is nevertheless usefully summarized, again in terms of explanation, in the entry on the cosmological argument in Flew's *A Dictionary of Philosophy*, where it is observed that any attempt

to explain why things are as they are must always ultimately be made in terms of general facts that are not, and cannot be, further explained. So why should the existence of the Universe, and perhaps the fact that it has whatever fundamental regularities it does have, not be accepted as the fundamentals, requiring no further explanation? (1979: 74)

This is a reply to a paper by Nicholas Everitt called 'Strawson on Laws and Regularities' (1991).

Going into a little more detail, I think one can state Everitt's final argument against my position as follows. (1) Either there is no ultimate explanation (or reason) for how things are, or there is. (2) To suppose that there is an ultimate explanation (or reason) for how things are is to suppose that some sort of 'ontological argument' can be used to show that what exists necessarily exists (perhaps by showing that there is something which necessarily existed in the past, whose existence necessitated, and explains, the existence of what now exists). (3) All such ontological arguments are hopeless. (4) So we have to accept that there is no ultimate explanation or reason for how things are.

But I am prepared to accept that ontological arguments are hopeless, and that there can be no ultimate explanation for how things are. So why is it thought that this undermines my objection to the regularity theory of causation?

Perhaps the idea that it does comes to this:

—You (G. S.) accuse the regularity theory of causation of being grossly implausible in claiming that the regularity of the behaviour of the universe has been, for fifteen billion years, a fluke, a matter of complete chance. And yet you are prepared to grant that there can be no ultimate explanation for anything. But to grant that there can be no ultimate explanation for anything is presumably to grant that everything is ultimately a fluke or a matter of complete chance—including, presumably, the regularity of the universe.

Most of us don't want to say that there is a reason for everything. We don't want to invoke the Principle of Sufficient Reason (according to which there is a reason for everything), and we know explanations come to an end. Nor do we want to employ ontological arguments to the effect that something that exists in the world necessarily exists. Most of us don't want to say that about anything. And so we seem obliged to hold that, ultimately, there is no reason for anything, and a fortiori, no ultimate reason why the world is regular in the particular way that it is.

You propose *the nature of matter* as the reason why the world is regular in the partic-ular way that it is (1989b: 90, 224–5). But those who do this face the question why the nature of matter is constant or regular in the way that it is. And if they give a reason R1 why the nature of matter is constant and regular in the way that it is, they will be asked why whatever is invoked in R1 is constant and regular in its underwriting of the constancy and regularity of the nature of matter. And if they give a reason R2 why whatever is invoked in R1 is constant and regular in its underwriting of the constancy and regularity of the nature of matter, they will be asked why whatever is invoked in R2 is constant and regular in its underwriting of the constancy and regularity of whatever is invoked in R1. The only way to stop this regress, short of an ontological argument, is to answer, at some point, 'That's just the way things are.'

In reply: I'm happy to say 'That's just the way things are' at some point. If someone asks why the nature of matter is as it is, I will say 'That's just the way things are', agreeing with Hume's spokesman Philo in his *Dialogues Concerning Natural Religion*. Philo asks the fundamental question: 'How could things have been as they are, were there not an original, inherent Principle of Order somewhere . . . ?' (1779: 174). He knows explanations come to an end, and accordingly says 'Why not stop at the mater-ial World?' (p. 161), when seeking to stop the regress of demands for explanation. For as he says, it may well be that 'such is the Nature of material Objects . . . that they are all originally possessed of a *Faculty* of Order and Proportion' (p. 163). He suggests that 'were the inmost Essence of things laid open to us, we should then discover a Scene, of which, at present, we can have no Idea'. For 'we should clearly see, that it was absolutely impossible for them, in the smallest article, ever to admit of any other Disposition.' (pp. 174–5)

It may yet be asked how I can say 'That's just the way things are.' It may be said that to give this answer is to concede that regularity is an ultimate fact, not further explicable in terms of something which is a reason for it. And since the 'That's just the way things are' answer must be given at some point, it seems regularity must be an ultimate fact, not only not further explicable in any way, but also something for which there is, objectively, no reason. But to say this is to say that the regularity theory of causation must be true. And we reach this conclusion from our armchairs. So the regularity theory of causation is after all an a priori truth.

It is, however, a trivial point that all explanations come to an end. It would be very odd if it followed from this that the regularity theory of causation must be true. Ultimately we must stop giving reasons and say 'This is just how things are.' But this does not commit us to the necessary truth of the regularity theory of causation. It does not commit us to the view that there is, objectively, *in the nature of things as they currently exist*, no reason why they are regular in the way that they are—so that their regularity of behaviour from moment to moment to moment is, in some inescapable sense, a continuous fluke. For the matter which is 'just how things are' is: matter with a nature given which it cannot but behave as it does; matter whose nature is such that there is, as an ultimately *contingent* matter of fact, such a thing as 'natural necessity'.

And this, of course, is how things are. And so I am entirely happy to accept that there may be a sense in which it is, in Everitt's terms, 'flukish that the universe should contain precisely [the] set of basic substances' that it does (1991: 208). This is meant to be his final objection to my position, but I simply accept it, in so far as I accept the story of the Big Bang, and the coherence of the (admittedly difficult) idea that the Big Bang is itself something for which there was no reason at all.

2

In the end, the whole thing comes down to the old question of whether one is prepared to accept the idea that there is or could be such a thing as natural necessity. Many empiricists and positivists cannot bear the idea of natural necessity. Even this late in the century, they are tempted to say that the idea of natural necessity is 'unintelligible', meaning not just that we cannot fully understand it even if it exists, but that it is incoherent in some way, so that it cannot exist. They think that we cannot genuinely suppose that something exists unless we can say what would count as observing it, or at least as having good evidence for its existence. And they think that the regularity of the world does not count as (good but, of course, logically inconclusive) evidence for the existence of natural necessity, but only as (conclusive) evidence for the existence of regularity. In fact, they turn the regularity theory of causation into an a priori truth in their own inimitable way, by endorsing a theory of meaning according to which no attempt to state a rival theory of causation, that is, a non-regularity theory of causation, can count as properly meaningful. But I am still assuming that any account of things that turns the regularity theory of causation into an a priori truth is *ipso facto* vitiated.

Let me restate the point. Even if it is true that ultimately there is not only no humanly attainable *explanation* of the existence of the universe, but also no *reason* for the existence of the universe, it just does not follow that everything that happens is ultimately a matter of chance, any more than it follows that a man is a bastard if his parents are. For what could possibly come into existence, by chance, is, precisely, some inherently non-chancy stuff—matter—something whose nature is such that it cannot but be regular in its behaviour—something that is, by its nature, *constitutionally* regular in its behaviour. And that, of course, is what we've got in this universe, however it came to exist.

At the risk (worth while I think) of seeming to move confusingly close to the regularity view, one might express this position as follows. Reality is constitutionally regular. To say that reality is *constitutionally* regular is *not* to say that it *just is* regular. For it is true of an objectively utterly random (and therefore not constitutionally regular) world which is flukishly identical to our world in respect of its regularity properties that it *just is* regular. So to assert that regularity is constitutionally regular is to reject the regularity theory utterly. For it is to assert that there is something about the nature of reality in virtue of which it is regular in the way that it is: *so that the mere fact of its regularity isn't the only fact there is, so far as the question of what causation is is concerned.* The point may seem fine to some but the italicized phrase denies the heart of the regularity theory.[1]

3

Explanations come to an end, philosophical arguments go on for ever. I sympathize with Quine when he says

> *That* there have been regularities, for whatever reason, is an established fact of science... *Why* there have been regularities is an obscure question, for it is hard to see what would count as an answer. (1969: 126)[2]

In these terms, the present position can be expressed as follows. We may grant for the sake of argument that the universe came into existence with the Big Bang, and that the Big Bang was not merely something of which we can give no explanation, but something for which there was, objectively, no reason. Now, however, the universe is in existence, and it has (we may assume) been running in a regular way ever since it came into existence. Let's suppose that Quine is right to say that it is hard to see what

---

[1] Cf. Strawson 1989b: 225–6, and for some more exotic difficulties with the notion of regularity, p. 29, and p. 227 n.

[2] In fact one can think that 'natural necessity' is a very good answer, while respecting the positivism that finds it hard to know what such an answer amounts to.

could count as an answer to the question of why there have been regularities. It is nevertheless a real question. And if the right answer to it is not 'There is some reason why, *given the nature of what came into existence in the Big Bang*', then the right answer to it is 'There is no reason why, *given the nature of what came into existence in the Big Bang*.' Perhaps my adherence to the non-regularity view of causation amounts to this: I cannot accept the second answer, and so I accept the first.

18

David Hume: Objects and Power

1

Many people think that Hume[1] holds a straightforward 'regularity' theory of causation, according to which causation is nothing more than regular succession or constant conjunction. 'If Hume is right', Saul Kripke says, then 'even if God were to look at [two causally related] events, he would discern nothing relating them other than that one succeeds the other.'[2] 'Hume's conclusion', according to Roger Woolhouse, is 'that so far as the external objects which are causes and effects are concerned there is only constant conjunction'; so far as the 'operations of natural bodies' are concerned, 'regularity and constant conjunction are all that exist'.[3] Even now, Barry Stroud thinks that Hume's view is that 'all that ever happens in the world independently of minds is that one thing succeeds another and resembles other instances that followed similar antecedents'.[4] I will call this the standard view. I will argue that it is wrong, and that Hume believes in causal power, or 'natural necessity', or 'Causation', as I will sometimes call it.[5]

2

If you want to know what Hume thought about causation, you have to give priority to his first *Enquiry*, which begins as follows:

When I cite a work I give the original publication date, while the page reference is to the edition listed in the bibliography.

[1] In quoting Hume I refer to the first *Enquiry*, the *Treatise*, the *Dialogues*, the *Correspondence*, and the *Letter from a gentleman* as 'E', 'T', 'D', 'C', and 'L', respectively, followed by page numbers. I treat the *New Letters of David Hume* as volume three of the two-volume *Correspondence*. In the case of the *Enquiry* I give the Selby-Bigge page reference followed by the Beauchamp page reference (e.g. '3/57'); in the case of the *Treatise*, the Selby-Bigge page reference followed similarly by the Norton page reference. When quoting I mark my emphases by italics, and the author's by bold italics.

[2] Kripke 1982: 67. According to the regularity theory of causation (and ignoring certain complications), a particular event of type A (say A1) is the cause of a particular event of type B (say B1) if and only if A1 is prior to and spatiotemporally contiguous with B1, and all events of type A are prior to and spatiotemporally contiguous with events of type B. Causation is just regular succession: 'in nature one thing just happens after another' (Ayer 1973: 183).

[3] Woolhouse 1988: 149–50.　　　　[4] 2000: 11.

[5] Two recent critics of the 'standard' view are Wright 1983 and forthcoming, and Craig 1987: ch. 2. Cf. also Kemp Smith 1941: 396–402.

Most of the principles, and reasonings, contained in this volume, were published in a work in three volumes, called *A Treatise of Human Nature*: a work which the author projected before he left college, and which he wrote and published not long after. But not finding it successful, he was sensible of his error in going to the press too early, and he cast the whole anew in the following pieces, where some negligences in his former reasoning and more in the expression, are, he hopes, corrected. Yet several writers, who have honoured the author's philosophy with answers, have taken care to direct all their batteries against the juvenile work, which the author never acknowledged, and have affected to triumph in any advantages, which, they imagined, they had obtained over it: *a practice very contrary to all rules of candour and fair-dealing, and a strong instance of those polemical artifices, which a bigotted zeal thinks itself authorized to employ.* Henceforth, the author desires, that the following pieces *may alone be regarded as containing his philosophical sentiments and principles* (E2/1).

These are strong words for Hume, and they express hurt. Responding anonymously in 1745 to an early attack on the *Treatise*, he described the quotations from the *Treatise* given by his 'accuser'—which read like a summary of what many for most of the twentieth century regarded as Hume's essential views—as 'maimed excerpts' (L3) selected with 'a degree of unfairness which appears to me altogether astonishing' (L20). The accuser (probably William Wishart) used Hume's words, but 'pervert[ed] them and misrepresent[ed] them in the grossest way in the world' (C3: 15).

Hume's public response was to write the *Enquiry* (1748). He wrote it to counteract the misinterpretation of the *Treatise*, and to correct certain mistakes: 'The philosophical principles are the same in both: but I was carried away by the heat of youth and invention to publish too precipitately. . . . I have repented my haste a hundred, and a hundred times' (C1: 158). 'I . . . acknowledge . . . a very great mistake in conduct, viz my publishing at all the Treatise of Human Nature. . . . Above all, the positive air, which prevails in that book, and which may be imputed to the ardor of youth, so much displeases me, that I have not patience to review it' (C1: 187).[6] He expected a much better reception for the *Enquiry*, in which 'the same doctrines [are] better illustrated and expressed'—a striking remark when one is trying to establish Hume's views about causation, given that all the main support for the view that Hume was an outright regularity theorist derives from the *Treatise*, and vanishes in the *Enquiry*.

'But allow me to tell you, that I never asserted so absurd a proposition, as *that anything might arise without a cause*: I only maintained, that our certainty of the falsehood of that proposition proceeded neither from intuition nor demonstration; but from another source' (C1: 187). Hume was irritated by the suggestion that he thought otherwise—that he was 'denying the truth of [a] proposition, which indeed *a man must have lost all common sense to doubt of*' (L22). He would have been equally irritated by the allegation that he asserted that regular succession is all there is to causation. The most direct proof of this is given on pp. 435 below.

---

[6] This remark about the 'positive air' is particularly poignant when one considers those who persist in thinking that Hume held an outright ontological 'bundle theory of the self'. The principal 'negligences in . . . expression' that Hume finds in his *Treatise* and regrets in his Advertisement to the *Enquiry* are doubtless his phrasings of epistemological points in a dramatically ontological idiom (see Craig 1987: ch. 2 §5).

In asking that the *Enquiry* alone should 'be regarded as containing his philosophical sentiments and principles', Hume lays a clear obligation on us. We can read the *Enquiry* back into the *Treatise*, when trying to understand his considered view; we can't go the other way. Everything in the *Treatise* that is or appears incompatible with the *Enquiry* must be discarded. Nothing in the *Treatise* can legitimately be used to throw light on any passage in the *Enquiry* unless two conditions are fulfilled: the passage in the *Enquiry* must be unclear (this is not often the case), and the passage from the *Treatise* must not be incompatible with anything in the *Enquiry* that is not in dispute. Even when a passage from the *Treatise* is called in evidence, its claim to make a contribution to interpretation must be weak when compared with competing claims from passages in the *Enquiry* other than the passage under consideration.

If we also respect Hume's insistence that 'the philosophical principles are the same in both' the *Treatise* and the *Enquiry*, we have a further obligation. In order to understand the *Treatise*—in order, in particular, to avoid being misled by the dramatic and polemical exaggerations of the 'ardor of youth'—we must read the *Enquiry* back into the *Treatise* wherever possible, and give it priority. For it was written to correct the misunderstanding of the *Treatise*.

Nearly all present-day commentators ignore this obligation, and many of them have their exegetical principles exactly the wrong way round.[7] Hume deserves sympathy, for it is bad to be attacked for views one never held, and worse to be praised and famous for holding them.[8] I know of no greater abuse of an author in the history of philosophy.[9] Many love the *Treatise* because they love argument, and this is understandable; many excellent philosophers are condemned to the lower divisions in philosophy because, consciously or not, they are more attached to cleverness and argument than truth. Hume is not among them, however, and no one can avoid the obligations described in the preceding paragraph. It cannot be plausibly argued that there is early Hume and late Hume, that they are importantly different, and that each deserves study in his own right. Hume was at work on the *Treatise*-clarifying *Enquiry* within five years of the publication of the *Treatise* and probably earlier, and (once again) was most insistent that the philosophical principles are the same in both. We have no reason to judge him to be self-deceived on this matter.[10]

3

When Hume talks of 'objects' he usually means genuinely external objects, in a sense to be explained further below. Sometimes, however, he only means to refer to mental

---

[7] Year after year, the Oxford University Examination Decrees for the History of Philosophy from Descartes to Kant specify that Hume is to be studied in connection with the *Treatise*; no mention is made of the *Enquiry*. A proposal to include the *Enquiry* was rejected by the Oxford Sub-Faculty of Philosophy in 1999.

[8] It is bad to be praised for holding views one never held even when they are right, but worse when they are absurd.

[9] Perhaps the near-exclusive focus on the *Groundwork of the Metaphysic of Morals*, in the discussion of Kant's moral philosophy, is a comparable case.

[10] See Buckle 1999a and 1999b for some excellent recent work on this issue.

occurrences, or what he calls 'perceptions', and it may be suggested that this is always so: that he only means to refer to the 'immediate', mental objects of experience, in talking of objects. This suggestion is worth mentioning, because if it were correct it would be easy to understand why Hume might wish to adopt a regularity theory about causation in the 'objects'.[11] But it is not correct—Hume didn't mean to refer only to mental occurrences or perceptions, and when I use the word 'object' I will mean what he usually meant in the contexts with which I will be concerned: objects that are genuinely non-mental things, things that exist independently of our minds.[12]

I will argue for this soon. For the moment I will take it for granted, because it allows me to state the main objection to the standard view of Hume. It is that the standard view fails to distinguish clearly between two fundamentally different notions, one ontological, the other epistemological. It fails to distinguish sufficiently between the ontological notion of causation as it *is* 'in the objects', and the epistemological notion of causation so far as we *know* about it in the objects.[13] But this distinction is crucial. In the end Hume's regularity theory of causation is only a theory about causation so far as as we can know about it in the objects, not about causation as it is in the objects. As far as causation as it is in the objects is concerned, Hume believes in Causation.

In other words: the 'standard' view confuses Hume's epistemological claim

(E) All we can ever know of causation is regular succession

with the positive ontological claim

(O) All that causation actually is, in the objects, is regular succession.

It moves, catastrophically, from the former to the latter. The former is arguably true. The latter is fantastically implausible. It is 'absurd', as Hume would have put it.[14]

Although (E) and (O) are clearly distinct, Hume sometimes abbreviates his main claims, in the *Treatise*, in such a way that he seems to slide from (E) to (O), propelled by his theory of ideas or meaning. In these cases, the passage from the merely

---

[11] This point is discussed in Strawson 1989: 45–6 and Appendix A, 'Cartoon-film Causation'. On this view, Hume agrees with Berkeley about what causation is, considered as a phenomenon in the physical world, but puts things differently.

[12] Hume sometimes means events when he talks of objects. When this is so, the present claim is that he means events that involve genuinely external, mind-independent objects, not merely mental events. In *The Secret Connexion* (ch. 22.2) I point out that Hume's belief in causal power does not depend on belief in external objects, although they go naturally together. On the general question of Hume's use of the word 'object', see Grene (1994).

[13] Cf. Mackie 1974: ch. 1 and Craig 1987: ch. 2 §§4 and 5.

[14] In fact nothing in the present account of Hume hangs on the claim that the regularity theory is absurd (see e.g. Armstrong 1983; Foster 1982b; Strawson 1987, 1989: chs. 5, 8, 22), but I take it to be obvious that there is more to causation than regularity (it is equally obvious that this can't be conclusively proved). The Regularity view is very like dogmatic phenomenalism: to suppose that regularity is all there is to causation is like supposing that objects consist merely of perceptions (actual or possible). It is a delicate matter to find the best way of saying what causation involves, over and above regularity; but there is a fundamental respect in which one has already said enough when one has granted that matter has a certain nature.

epistemological claim (E) to the ontological claim (O) appears to be made via the semantic claim

(S) All we can legitimately *manage to mean* by expressions like 'causation in the objects' is regular succession.

The transition is made as follows. (1) (E) is true. (2) If (E) is true, (S) is true (that's strict empiricism for you). (3) If (S) is true, (O) is true. Hence (4) (O) is true. Why does (O) follow from (S)? Because, given (S), when the phrase 'causation in the objects' comes out of our mouths or pens, or occurs in our thought, it inevitably just means regular succession. So (O) causation in the objects—here is the phrase, meaning 'regular succession'—just is regular succession. After all, regular succession is regular succession.[15]

I am going to reject this view of the consequences of Hume's theory of ideas (or theory of meaningfulness). Let me raise an initial doubt. Suppose there were good grounds for thinking that Hume's theory of ideas did license the (very strange) move from (E) to (O) via (S)—and hence licensed the claim that all we can suppose a thing to be is what we can detect or experience or know of it, simply because we cannot manage to mean anything more than what we can detect or experience or know of it, when we think or talk about it. Even if this were so, the following decisive objection to attributing (O) to Hume would remain: (O), the claim that causation is definitely nothing but regular succession, and that there is definitely no such thing as Causation, makes a positive ontological assertion about the ultimate nature of reality. It is therefore violently at odds with Hume's scepticism—his scepticism with respect to knowledge claims about what we can know to exist, *or know not to exist*, in reality. As a strict sceptic with respect to knowledge claims about the nature of reality Hume does not make positive claims about what definitely does exist (apart from mental occurrences or 'perceptions', whose existence he rightly takes as certain). But, equally clearly, he does not make positive claims about what definitely (or knowably) does not exist. For such claims are equally unwarranted, from the sceptical point of view. Ignorance, as he says, is never a 'good reason for rejecting any thing' (E73/57). This point about Hume's scepticism is enough to refute any attribution of (O) to him.

4

The following objection may be put. As a strict sceptic with respect to knowledge claims, Hume will not claim that we can know that there is definitely nothing like Causation in reality. Equally, though, he will not claim that there definitely is something like Causation in reality.

This is true. It requires us to take note of the distinction between knowledge and belief. Those who think that Hume is a straightforward regularity theorist with

---

[15] The same type of invalid argument can be made if one replaces 'causation' and 'regular succession' with 'external objects' and 'perceptions' respectively, or with 'the self' and 'a series of perceptions' respectively.

respect to causation standardly suppose that he makes a *knowledge* claim on the question, claiming that causation is definitely just regular succession, and that therefore there is definitely nothing like Causation. Such a knowledge claim is ruled out by his scepticism. The *belief* that there is some such thing as Causation is not ruled out, however. Scepticism can acknowledge the naturalness of this belief, and grant that it may well be something like the truth; it will merely insist that although we believe it, we cannot prove it to be true.

Some think that Hume cannot even admit to *believing* in the existence of anything like Causation, given his scepticism. I will discuss the motivation for this view in §§5 and 6. For the moment it suffices to say that Hume is not a Pyrrhonist.[16] This objection fails to take account of his doctrine of 'natural belief', according to which we have certain natural beliefs (for example in the existence of external objects) which we find it practically impossible to give up. Scepticism of the Humean kind does not say that these beliefs are definitely not true, or unintelligible, or utterly contentless (see §6). Genuine *belief* in the existence of X is fully compatible with strict scepticism with regard to *knowledge* claims about the existence of X.[17]

In fact Hume never really questions the idea that there is Causation—something in virtue of which reality is regular in the way that it is. Following Newton, he repeatedly insists on the epistemological claim that we know nothing of the ultimate nature of Causation. 'The power or force, which actuates the whole machine . . . of the universe . . . is entirely concealed from us' (E63/51), and 'experience only teaches us, how one event constantly follows another; without instructing us in the secret connexion, which binds them together, and renders them inseparable' (E66/53). We cannot know the nature of Causation—of the 'because something is, something else must be' relation (Kant 1781–7: A235/B288). But to say that is not to doubt that Causation exists.

5

These quotations seem very clear. But it may now be objected that Hume can't mean what he says. He can't mean what he says because he holds that the idea of causation as something more than regular succession—the idea of Causation—is completely *unintelligible*. What's more, he says the same about the notion of 'external objects'.

The fact that he said the same about the notion of external objects may, however, be part of the solution, not part of the problem. I will now approach the general issue of Hume's attitude to questions of meaning and intelligibility by defending the view that he was committed to the intelligibility of the realist conception of objects. This commitment is obvious in the *Enquiry*, and also in the *Treatise*, but some doubt it, believing that Hume is some sort of idealist about objects, and is forced to be so by a theory of meaning which entails that talk of external objects is unintelligible.

[16] 'I am not such a sceptic as you may, perhaps, imagine' (C1: 186).
[17] See Kemp Smith 1941: 62–8, and ch. 21.

The central point is simple. When present-day philosophers say that something is unintelligible they mean that it is incoherent and cannot exist. But Hume—with Locke, Berkeley, and many others—uses the word 'unintelligible' in the literal sense, which survives in the standard non-philosophical use of the word—as when we say that a message is unintelligible, meaning simply that we cannot understand it, although it exists ('Ni chredai Hume nad yw achosiaeth yn ddim ond cyd-ddigwyddiad rheolaidd'). When Hume says that something is unintelligible, then, he means that we cannot understand it. In particular, he means that we cannot form an idea of it, or term for it, that has any positive descriptive content on the terms of the theory of ideas. To say this, however, is not to say that we cannot refer to it, or that the notion of it is incoherent.

Hume's position on this matter is like Locke's position with respect to the 'real essence' of gold. Locke takes it that the real essence of gold is completely unknown to us. This leads him to say that in so far as the word 'gold' carries a 'tacit reference to the real essence' of gold, as it does in common use, it has '*no signification at all*, being put for somewhat, whereof we have no idea at all'.[18] In other words, the word 'gold' is *completely meaningless*—it lacks any positive descriptive content on the terms of the theory of ideas—in so far as it is taken to refer to the unknown real essence of gold. And yet it does so refer, as Locke concedes. We can perfectly well talk about the real essence of gold and take it to exist.

Berkeley makes a similar move when he proposes that the term 'notion' be used as a 'term for things that cannot be understood'. It is, he says, 'absurd for any man to argue against the existence of [a] thing, from his having no direct and positive notion of it'. It is only where 'we have not even a relative notion of it' that we 'employ words to no manner of purpose, without any design or signification whatever'. But 'many things, for anything I know, may exist, whereof neither I nor any other man has or can have any idea or notion whatsoever'.[19] This is Berkeley speaking.

Kant makes a similar move. On the one hand, he says that the categories, which include the concept of cause, 'have only an empirical use, and have *no meaning whatever* when not applied to objects of possible experience'. On the other hand, he says that 'in *thinking*', and a fortiori in intelligible—hence contentful, hence mean-ingful—thinking, 'the categories are not limited by the conditions of our sensible intuition, but have an unlimited field. It is only *knowledge* of what we think . . . that requires intuition.'[20]

The point is routine in Hume's time. He continually stresses the fact that there may be aspects of reality of which we can form no positively descriptive conception on the terms of the theory of ideas, and in which are in that sense wholly unintelligible by us. This is an integral part of his scepticism. It is, in fact, an integral part of any sound philosophy.

---

[18] Cf. Locke (1689–1700:3.10.19), and Mackie (1976: 93–100).

[19] 1721: §23; 1713:177, 184.

[20] Kant 1781–7, A696/B724 (cf. also A239–40/B298–9); B166n (cf. also A253–4/B309). Kant gives a clear indication of what he means by the word 'meaning' in the phrase 'no meaning whatever' on A241/B300: when the categories are not applied to what is given in sensible intuition, he says, 'all meaning, *that is, all reference to the object*, falls away'.

The claim about Hume may still be doubted. So I will consider what happens in the *Treatise* when Hume explicitly considers the thought that talk of realist external objects is 'unintelligible', given his theory of ideas.[21]

6

Speaking of the notion of external objects, Hume says that it is 'impossible for us so much as to conceive or form an idea of any thing *specifically different* from ideas and impressions' (T67/49). By 'specifically different' he means 'of a different species or kind'; so his claim is that we cannot form any idea of anything which is of an entirely different species or kind from ideas and (sensory) impressions. Why not? Because the content of our ideas is entirely derived or copied from our impressions, and such impression-copy content can never amount to a genuine representation of something entirely different from impressions. But this means it can never amount to a genuine representation of an external object. For an external object is by hypothesis an essentially non-mental thing, and is *obviously* of an entirely different species from an essentially mental thing like an impression and an idea.[22]

Hume, then, seems to be saying that we can never conceive of or form any idea of such a thing as an external object. But he goes straight on to grant that we can after all form some sort of conception of external objects:

> The farthest we can go towards a conception of external objects, when [they are] suppos'd specifically different from our perceptions, is to form a *relative* idea of them, without pretending to *comprehend* the related objects. (T68/49)

This is the farthest we can go; external objects are 'incomprehensible'; we have only a 'relative' idea of them. But a relative idea of X is not no idea at all. An everyday example of a case in which one has a referentially efficacious, but in a sense contentless and hence merely 'relative', idea of something X is the idea one has of something when one can refer to it only as, say, 'whatever it was that caused this appalling mess'. In this case, one may have no positive conception of the nature of X.[23]

In the case of Causation, our merely relative idea of it is 'that in reality in virtue of which reality is regular in the way that it is'; or, in Hume's terms, it is 'the power or force, which actuates the whole machine . . . of the universe' (E63/51) and on which

---

[21] At this point the argument becomes a bit more complicated. The direct argument that Hume believes in Causation starts in §7, and does not depend on the details of the next section.

[22] Here I put aside an important complication. It has to do with Hume's attitude to Locke's 'resemblance' theory. Briefly, if the Lockean account of the resemblance between primary qualities of objects and ideas of primary qualities is at all defensible, then it is arguable that objects are *not* entirely (qualitatively) different from perceptions, even though they are indeed of an entirely different *species* or kind. On this view, ideas of primary qualities really can give us some genuine idea of what external objects are like; they render them at least partly 'intelligible'. Hume's final position on Locke's claim is one of agnosticism (E153/114). See Wright 1983: ch. 2.

[23] Except, perhaps, the thought that it is a physical phenomenon. But who knows? Maybe it isn't even a physical phenomenon.

the 'regular course and succession of objects totally depends' (E55/45). It is 'that circumstance in the cause, which gives it a connexion with its effect' (E77/60), 'that very circumstance in the cause, by which it is enabled to produce the effect' (E67–8/54). Or—to quote the *Treatise* rather than the *Enquiry*—it is that which is in fact the 'reason of the conjunction' of any two objects (T93/65). This description suffices to pick Causation out in such a way that we can go on to refer to it while having no descriptively contentful conception of its nature on the terms of the theory of ideas.

Many quotations from Hume's *Dialogues* can also be called in support. The dialogue form raises certain problems of interpretation, but there is no doubt that Philo represents Hume's views.[24] Many still proceed as if the *Dialogues*—Hume's most carefully composed work of philosophy, and arguably his 'greatest work of metaphysics'[25]—simply does not count when it comes to understanding Hume's views. They seem to be viscerally incapable of admitting that quotation from the *Dialogues* has the same weight as quotation from the *Enquiry* and the *Treatise*, and have in consequence no hope of getting Hume right. They cannot hear Hume speaking as Philo when he says

'Tis observed by arithmeticians, that the products of 9 compose always 9 or some lesser product of 9, if you add together all the characters, of which any of the former products are composed. Thus, of 18, 27, 36, which are products of 9, you make 9 by adding 1 to 8, 2 to 7, 3 to 6. Thus 369, is a product also of nine; and if you add 3, 6, and 9, you make 18, a lesser product of 9. To a superficial observer, so wonderful a regularity may be admir'd as the effect either of chance, or design; but a skilful algebraist immediately concludes it to be the work of necessity, and demonstrates, that it must for ever result from the nature of these numbers. Is it not probable, I ask, that the whole economy of the universe is conducted by a like necessity, though no human algebra can furnish a key which solves the difficulty? And instead of admiring the order of natural beings, may it not happen that, could we penetrate into the intimate nature of bodies, we should clearly see why it was absolutely impossible, they could ever admit of any other disposition? (D191)

Let me return to the discussion of objects in the *Treatise*. Hume writes that:

we may *suppose*, but never can *conceive* a specific difference betwixt an object and an impression. (T241/158)

This contrast is important. It occurs at several other points in the *Treatise* (e.g. T68/49, already quoted), and the idea behind it, expressed in one way or another, is routine in Hume's time. Anything that is to count as a genuine *conception* of something must be descriptively contentful on the terms of the theory of ideas: it must have directly impression-based, impression-copy content. By contrast, a supposition that something exists or is the case can be a genuine *supposition*, genuinely about something, and hence intelligible in our present-day sense, without being contentful (or

[24] Cf. Essay 19: §8.
[25] Wright 1995: 350. Some think that Hume attacked all metaphysics. In fact he considers his own work in the first part of the *Treatise* and in the first *Enquiry* to be metaphysics (as Kant observes (1783: 6)), and remarks, in his essay 'Of the Rise and Progress of the Arts and Sciences', that metaphysics is one of the four principal 'branches of science. Mathematics and natural science . . . are not half so valuable' (1741–2: 126).

meaningful or intelligible) on the terms of the theory of ideas. So the natural supposition that there are external objects 'specifically different from perceptions' is an intelligible one in our sense, and may well be true. All that follows from the theory of ideas is that we cannot form any well-founded descriptively contentful conception of external objects.[26]

Here as elsewhere Hume respects the principles of his scepticism, which prohibit the claim that we can know that there *isn't* anything to which the merely 'relative' idea of objects realistically conceived might relate or refer. Hume grants that there may be such external objects, firmly believes that there are, and merely insists that there will always remain a sense in which their nature is 'perfectly inexplicable' by us (T84/59).[27] The conclusion of the famous discussion of objects in 1. 4. 2 of the *Treatise* is not that there are no external objects, or that the notion of such things is incoherent—that is, unintelligible in our strong, modern sense. On the contrary. In the penultimate paragraph Hume remarks that he began his discussion of objects by 'premising, that we ought to have an implicit faith' in our natural, sense-and-imagination based belief in external objects (T217/144). He concludes that this is indeed what we ought to do, announcing in the final paragraph that he will proceed upon the 'supposition . . . [that] there is both an external and an internal world' (T218/144).

His conclusion, then, is certainly not that there are no external objects. Nor is it that the idea of external objects is incoherent (unintelligible in our strong modern sense). He has two main points, of which the first is that we can supply no decent rational foundation or justification for the belief that there are external objects: 'By what argument can it be proved, that the perceptions of the mind must be caused by external objects, entirely different from them, though resembling them . . .?' (E152–3/114). It cannot be proved, he says. For 'it is a question of fact, whether the perceptions of the senses be produced by [such] external objects, resembling them', and if we ask 'how shall this question be determined?', the answer is 'By experience surely; as all other questions of a like nature. But here experience is, and must be entirely silent' (E153/114).

In other words: it is either true or false that there are external objects, but we cannot know which. A fortiori, the supposition—and natural belief—that there are external objects is intelligible, and hence meaningful. Hume himself takes it that it is true, for the belief that it is true is part of natural belief.

His second point is that there is nonetheless something profoundly problematic, incomplete, misleading—defective, relative, inadequate, inaccurate, imprecise, imperfect, vulgar, loose, uncertain, confused, indistinct, 'fiction'-involving (see for example T267/174, T218/144, T160/108, T639/47, T234/153, E67n/154n, E76/60, E77n/60n)—about any conception of external objects (or Causation) that

---

[26] More precisely: we cannot do this unless Locke's resemblance claim is defensible in some form; and this too we cannot know. See n22. For a recent development of the point, see Craig 1987: ch. 2. See also Wright 2000.

[27] Either partly or wholly inexplicable, depending on the defensibility of Locke's resemblance claim. See, once again, n22.

purports to be anything more than a merely 'relative' notion of external objects. This view is a consequence of his theory of ideas, and the question he faces is then this: 'What exactly is the content of natural beliefs featuring defective conceptions of this sort?' He doesn't answer this question in any detail, however. It is a question which tormented many in the twentieth century, but it was not one about which Hume felt he needed to say any more. The point he insists on is that we are deluded if we think we have any sort of complete, adequate, accurate, precise, perfect, philosophical, tight, certain, distinct, legitimately sense-based conception of external objects (or Causation).

Suppose for a moment that the standard view is right to claim that Hume thinks that the idea of external objects has no content at all, and indeed can have no content. The argument about causation that was given in §3 can be rerun for objects as follows: (1) All we can ever know or observe of external objects are perceptions. (2) So (given standard meaning-empiricist principles) all we can legitimately manage to mean by expressions like 'external object' (or 'table', or 'chair') are perceptions. (3) So the statement that external objects are nothing but perceptions must be true—because when the phrase 'external objects' is used, it inevitably just means perceptions. Hence (4) phenomenalism is true: outright ontological phenomenalism, the view that external, physical objects are definitely—yea provably—nothing more than perceptions. Do not suppose that the conclusion can be tamely stated as 'Even if something other than perceptions exists, we can't manage to mean this "something".' On the present view, the quoted sentence is already a kind of nonsense, because the phrase 'something other than perceptions' cannot really manage to refer to something other than perceptions in the way it purports to do.

Fortunately, this is not Hume's view. It is, he says, a straightforward '*question of fact*, whether the perceptions of the senses be produced by *external objects . . . entirely different from them*' (E153/114). This is very clear. Or consider the *Treatise* again: 'we may well suppose in general' that physical objects are different from perceptions; there is no problem with this. The problem is that it is 'impossible for us *distinctly* to conceive' this (T218/144).

Certainly Hume says things that admit the interpretation I am rejecting. He wrote the *Treatise* in the 'ardor of youth'. He was tempted into provocative expressions he regretted (Hume CI: 187, E2/1). Even in the *Treatise*, however, he followed Locke and Berkeley (and many others) and anticipated Kant (and many others) in making the essential move, distinguishing between what we can suppose and what we can conceive in such a way as to allow that language can intelligibly be supposed to refer to something of which we have (and can have) no impression-copy-contentful idea.

Simon Blackburn has argued that little weight can be placed on the fact that Hume makes a distinction between what we can suppose and what we can conceive, because Hume himself does not make much of it.[28] But we could grant, for purposes of argument, that Hume does not make much of the distinction—although he relies on it constantly. We could grant that Hume, in the *Treatise*, in the iconoclastic ardour of youth, sees the necessity of making the distinction between what we can suppose

[28] 1990: 261–3.

and what we can conceive as somewhat *annoying*. The fact remains that it is something that he finds himself obliged to record, in the course of his sceptical progress. He duly does so, clearly and unambiguously.[29] It is, as remarked, a routine distinction, utterly indispensable in any serious empiricist enterprise. It immediately blocks the disastrous argument from (1) to (4) set out on the previous page, and Hume takes it for granted in the *Enquiry*, which omits nearly all the technicalities of the *Treatise*. He take it, in particular, and to repeat, that it is a straightforward although undecidable 'question of fact, whether the perceptions of the senses be produced by external objects . . . entirely different from them, though resembling them (if that be possible)'.[30]

It is a very simple point. Hume has to grant that thought and language can reach beyond perceptions in such a way that the thought that something other than perceptions exists can be allowed to be intelligible and possibly true. For if he does not do this, then, once again, he is condemned to dogmatic metaphysics; to outright ontological idealism; to the view that the statement 'Perceptions are all that exist' is *provably true*. He is landed with a form of metaphysical certainty that he cannot possibly tolerate, as a sceptic who denies the possibility of attaining knowledge about the ultimate nature of reality (other than perceptions). This is the first, crucial component of what John Wright calls his 'sceptical realism'. The second is simply his endorsement of certain 'natural beliefs'. He really does believe that external objects exist, and that Causation exists (see §§7–11 below).

Blackburn claims that it is an 'error of taste to make sceptical realism a fundamental factor in the interpretation of Hume' (op. cit. pp. 259, 267), but this is back to front. It is a grave error of taste and judgement to think that a philosopher of Hume's sceptical profundity could have failed to adopt a sceptical realist attitude. Blackburn's claim (p. 262) that Hume dismisses the 'supposes' versus 'conceives' distinction out of hand is not supported by the text he quotes from the *Treatise*, and is controverted both by Hume's announcement (on the same page) that he will proceed on the supposition that 'there is both an external and an internal world' (T218/144), and by his earlier declaration that the existence of body is something 'which we must take for granted' (T187/125), and by his practice throughout the *Treatise* and the *Enquiry*.

Blackburn is also wrong to claim that he quotes 'the two major passages' in which the suppose/conceive distinction features, 'with enough surrounding context to matter' (p. 261). For he omits Hume's most striking employment of the distinction:

Since we may suppose, but never can conceive a specific difference betwixt an object and impression; any conclusion we form concerning the connexion and repugnance of impressions, will not be known certainly to be applicable to objects. (T241/158)

Here Hume is stating that the relations we discover on the basis of our impressions cannot be known to apply to real objects. His closing use of the word 'objects' is

---

[29] Note his equally clear statement, when arguing that we can have no idea of Causation, that he is 'indeed, ready to allow, that there may be several qualities both in material and in immaterial objects, with which we are utterly unacquainted' (T168/113): the realm of existence does not necessarily cease where the realm of words or positively contentful conceptions ceases.

[30] In the last seven words of this quotation Hume adverts to the point discussed in n22.

straightforwardly realist, and the clause 'will not be known certainly' adds the scepticism to the realism. He goes on to say that although we cannot have certainty, we can 'by an irregular kind of reasoning from experience, discover a connexion betwixt objects, which extends not to impressions' (T242/158). No one who acknowledges no distinction between objects and perceptions can say this.[31]

Blackburn's claim (p. 262) that Hume 'affirms idealism' when he says that 'we never really advance a step beyond ourselves' in our conceptions (T67/49) is also false. It turns Hume into a metaphysician of exactly the sort that he was not. At this point Hume is making a routine empiricist epistemological claim about the limits of knowledge and understanding. He is directly echoing Locke when he wrote 'It seems probable to me, that the simple Ideas we receive from Sensation and Reflection, are the Boundaries of our Thoughts; beyond which, the Mind, whatever efforts it may make, is not able to advance one jot' (*Essay*, 2.23.20). And Locke—that great and paradigmatic realist—was not affirming idealism.

All in all, Hume handles this issue in just the right way. He travels to the frontier of the absurd thesis about meaning (the thesis that leads to mad metaphysical phenomenalism) in accordance with his empiricist theory of ideas. Then he stops, acknowledging, correctly, that it is intelligible to suppose that things other than perceptions exist, and expressing with great force the point that we can have no (certain) knowledge of their nature:

As long as we confine our speculations to *the appearances* of objects to our senses, without entering into disquisitions concerning *their real nature and operations*, we are safe from all difficulties . . . . If [however] we carry our enquiry beyond the appearances of objects to the senses, I am afraid, that most of our conclusions will be full of scepticism and uncertainty.[32]

These are the sentiments of a sceptical realist (and follower of Newton) who relies on the distinction between 'supposing' and 'conceiving' and is far from affirming idealism.

One useful thought for those who doubt that Hume generally writes as a sceptical realist is as follows: he repeatedly distinguishes between the 'sensible qualities' of objects, on the one hand, and the objects themselves and their 'secret' or unknown nature or internal structure, on the other hand. Whenever he does so, he is *ipso facto* thinking of objects in a realist fashion as something more than perceptions (as something more than idealist or phenomenalist objects). For he holds that there is nothing hidden or unknown in perceptions: unlike genuine external bodies, perceptions have no unobservable ontic backsides or innards: 'The perceptions of the mind', he says, 'are perfectly known', whereas 'the essence and composition of external bodies are . . . obscure' (T366/237). It follows that bodies cannot be perceptions, on Hume's view. For nothing can be both perfectly known and obscure.

I will now begin on the direct argument—it is little more than an argument by quotation—that Hume believes in Causation, after first briefly stating his view

---

[31] Craig (1987: 124–5) and Wright (2000) have good discussions of this passage.

[32] T638–9/46–7n. This is a note Hume added in order to try to correct misunderstanding of the text. Note the restraint of 'most' and the mildness of 'scepticism and uncertainty'.

about the nature of our idea of Causation, and describing an apparent tension in his thought.

7

The result of applying Hume's theory of ideas to the idea of Causation is clear: we have no idea of it at all, conceived of as something in the world of physical objects. Why not? Because we can form no positively descriptively contentful conception of it. Why not? Because we can form a descriptively contentful conception of something only out of impression-copy content, and there is no impression of Causation to be found in or derived from objects. Why not? Because all we ever actually observe is regular succession, one thing following another.

It follows that no term like 'power' or 'force' can ever really *manage to mean* anything in the world, on the terms of the theory of ideas. It cannot pick up descriptively on anything in the world. It can only manage to pick up descriptively on something in the mind: the feeling of determination in the mind which we come to experience on being confronted with regular succession in the world. For this, according to Hume, is the impression-source from which our actual idea of power or Causation is derived.[33]

It has been widely believed that Hume went on from the epistemological claim that we have no idea of Causation to the outright ontological claim that there is nothing like Causation, and that causation is nothing but regular succession. And it is true that Hume's empiricist theory of ideas, strictly and literally interpreted, creates some pressure on him to put things in this way (cf. §3). But this pressure is comfortably offset by his scepticism and realism—which one might equally well call his deep philosophical common sense—as I will shortly show by quotation. The strict and literal interpretation of Hume's theory of meaning is not Hume's interpretation,[34] and in fact he takes it for granted that there is Causation.

There is certainly a tension in Hume's expression of his thought: he uses terms like 'power' and 'force' in a way that is arguably ruled out by his theory of ideas. If we call such terms 'Causation' terms—terms that purport to refer to Causation, that is, to causation conceived of as something essentially more than regular succession—we can state the tension as follows: Hume holds that no Causation term can manage to 'positively-contentfully' mean anything like Causation. And yet he allows in practice that they can manage to mean something like Causation, at least in the sense of genuinely *referring* to it.

Well, this is at most a tension; it is not an inconsistency. The appearance of tension arises because our understanding of words like 'meaning' and 'unintelligible' is not the same as Hume's. There is obviously no difficulty in the idea that we may successfully use a term to refer to something which has some manifestation in our experience,

---

[33] Cf. E75/59 (and T165/111). On E67n/54n, Hume remarks that the experience of effort we have in pushing and pulling things (e.g.) also enters into the 'vulgar . . . idea of power'. Cf. also E78 n/61 n.

[34] Cf. Craig 1987: ch. 2.

even though we have no positive conception of its nature, over and above the thought that it is something and has the manifestation that it has (cf. §5). The idea that we can do such a thing is correct and indispensable. (It is even more obvious that we can refer to something when we only have an 'inadequate' or 'imperfect' idea of it.)

8

I have claimed that Hume grants that Causation terms may reach out referentially to refer to Causation in the world, just as terms purporting to refer to external objects may reach out to external objects, and I will now try to show that he consistently uses Causation terms like 'power' and 'force' in a straightforwardly referring way. He assumes that Causation exists: it is that on which the 'regular . . . succession of objects *totally depends*' (E55/45); it is 'the *reason* of the conjunction' that we observe between two (types) of objects (T93/65). He takes it for granted that there must be something about the world in virtue of which the world is regular. The idea that there might be nothing—the 'Humean' view—is not a candidate for consideration. The point he cherishes and wants to drive home, spectacularly contrary to the orthodoxy of his time, is simply that we have no positive descriptive conception of the nature of causal power.[35]

On page 30/27 of the *Enquiry*, Hume writes that

no philosopher, who is rational and modest, has ever pretended to assign *the ultimate cause* of any natural operation, or to show distinctly the action of *that power, which produces* any single effect in the universe.

Following Newton, here as elsewhere, he goes on to say that we can greatly simplify our account of the laws of nature, reducing it to a 'few general causes',

but as to *the causes of these general causes*, we should in vain attempt their discovery. . . . These *ultimate springs and principles* are totally shut up from human curiosity and enquiry.

But they certainly exist.

This natural reading is doubted by those who think that all Hume's apparently referring uses of Causation terms are really ironic, but they ignore his admiration for Newton. There is, furthermore, a serious difficulty in the idea that a book written specifically in order to clarify misunderstanding should be loaded with irony in such a way as to be deeply misleading.

On page 33/29–30, Hume writes that

---

[35] The worst reason for attributing the 'Humean' view to Hume is probably the one considered in n40 below. Note that the word 'depends', in the quotation from E55/45, cannot be supposed to indicate any sort of causal dependence. The way in which regular succession depends on powers and forces may be supposed to be something like the way the properties of a substance like mercury are held to depend on its property of having a certain atomic structure. The crucial idea is simply that there is something in the nature of things in virtue of which things are regular in the way they are, something which is therefore not just the fact of the regularity itself. One could put the point by saying that regular succession is a manifestation or aspect of Causation, and depends on it in that sense.

It is allowed on all hands that there is no known connexion between the sensible qualities and *the secret powers* [of bodies],

for nature

conceals from us those *powers and principles on which the influence of. . . objects entirely depends.*

And on pages 63–4/51 he writes that

The scenes of the universe are continually shifting, and one object follows another in an unin-terrupted succession; but *the power or force, which actuates the whole machine*, is entirely con-cealed from us, and never discovers itself in any of the sensible qualities of body.

Speaking as Philo, he says

Chance has no place, on any hypothesis, sceptical or religious. Everything is surely governed by steady, inviolable laws. And were the inmost essence of things laid open to us, we should then discover a scene, of which, at present, we can have no idea. Instead of admiring the order of natural beings, we should clearly see, that it was absolutely impossible for them, in the smallest article, ever to admit of any other disposition. (D174)

Some have suggested that when Hume talks of secret or concealed powers or forces, all he really means are constant conjunctions, or objects, that are too small to be detec-ted.[36] But even if this interpretation were thought to have some plausibility for the plural uses of terms like 'power' and 'force', it would have none for the more com-mon singular uses. When someone speaks of the 'power or force, which actuates the whole machine . . . of the universe', and says that it is 'entirely concealed' from us, it is very implausible to suppose that all he really means are all those hundreds of constant conjunctions that are too small to be seen.[37]

On pages 37–8/32 of the *Enquiry*, after speaking of

our natural state of ignorance with regard to the power and influence of all objects,

Hume goes on to give an argument against the appeal to past experience in justify-ing induction that makes essential use of the idea that causal power exists. Although particular experiences of objects at particular times may indeed show us

that those particular objects, at that particular time, were endowed with . . . *powers and forces,*

---

[36] Cf. e.g. Broackes 1993: 100–1; Winkler 1991: §1.

[37] Cf. Strawson 1989: ch. 18. At this point the following objection may be made: 'Hume talks as if Causation exists for ease of exposition. He grants its existence to his opponents for the sake of argument, so that he can then shoot home his epistemological point that even if it does exist we can know nothing about its nature. But he doesn't really believe in it at all.' This view is not strictly refutable, because it denies outright the relevance and force of all the direct evidence against it; but there is no reason to believe it. There is no reason to claim that a sceptic and follower of Newton like Hume holds that there is definitely nothing about reality in virtue of which it is regular in the way that it is, so that its regularity is an objective fluke from moment to moment. There isn't even any reason to claim that he believes that there *may* be nothing about reality in virtue of which it is regular in the way that it is, so that the regularity *may* be an objective fluke from moment to moment. Hume certainly insists that we can't know whether the 'original, inherent principle of order [lies] in thought or in matter', but he is clear on the point that there is some such principle of order, and that 'chance has no place, on any hypothesis' (D174).

still, he says, we can never be sure that the objects in question will continue to have just those same powers in the future. The reason why induction cannot be justified by appeal to past experience, therefore, is precisely that

the secret nature [of bodies], and consequently all their effects and influence, may change

—between now and the next time we observe them. So the reason why induction is not rationally justifiable by appeal to past experience is certainly not that there isn't really any power governing bodies. It is not that bodies do not really have any secret nature or powers governing their effects and influence, so that anything might happen. On the contrary. Bodies do have a secret nature which determines their effects and influence. The trouble with appeals to past experience is simply that past experience can never provide a guarantee that the secret nature of bodies will not change in the future, bringing change in their effects and influence.[38]

This clarifies something that is obvious on reflection but often misunderstood: there is *no special link between inductive scepticism and the regularity theory of causation.* The argument for inductive scepticism just quoted appeals essentially to Causation.

9

When things go normally, Hume says, ordinary people suppose that they perceive

the very force or energy of the cause, by which it is connected with its effect. (E69/55)

They only feel the need to invoke some invisible unperceived power or principle when something happens which they think of as extraordinary. But philosophers do better, for they can see that

even in the most familiar events, *the energy of the cause* is . . . unintelligible. (E70/55)

They realize, that is, that we have no positive conception of its ultimate nature in any case at all—although it certainly exists. Going on to talk of the Occasionalists, Hume sets out their view

that the true and direct principle of every effect is not any power or force in nature, but a volition of the Supreme Being. (E70/56)

He strongly implies that he finds their view absurd, and ill-motivated even on religious grounds. More important for present purposes, however, is the methodological argument he presents against them. First, he observes that it is precisely their acknowledgement of our ignorance of power or energy in objects that leads them to 'rob nature, of every power', and attribute all power to God. Next, he observes that it is awareness of 'the same ignorance' that then leads them to rob the human mind

---

[38] Blackburn thinks that I invoke fundamental physical forces 'to soothe away inductive vertigo' (1990: 266), but I have no wish to do this. Nothing could do it, as Hume's argument shows (cf. Strawson 1989: 113). Blackburn is equally wrong to think that I want a 'straitjacket' (cf. op. cit. pp. 264–8), something that can give certainty about the future (see Essay 17).

too of power, and to 'assert that the Deity is [also] the immediate cause of the union
between soul and body', for example, when we act.

He then grants that they are right about our ignorance in these departments: we
are indeed

totally ignorant of the power on which depends the mutual operation of bodies (E70/56),

(although there must of course be some such thing); and we are

no less ignorant of that power on which depends the operation of mind on body, or of body
on mind (E70/56),

(although of course there must be some such thing). But if it is acknowledgement of
our ignorance that leads the Occasionalists to attribute all power to God, then they
should realize that our ignorance of any power that might be attributed to God is
equally complete:

We are ignorant, it is true, of *the manner in which bodies operate on each other*: Their *force or
energy* is entirely incomprehensible: But are we not equally ignorant of the manner or force by
which . . . seven the supreme mind operates either on itself or on body? (E71/57)

Yes, he answers, and goes on to make a remark that again appears to suffice to refute
the standard view of Hume:

Were our ignorance, therefore, a good reason for rejecting any thing, we should be led [to
deny] . . . all energy in the Supreme Being as much as in the grossest matter. We . . . comprehend as little the operations of the one as of the other. (E72–3/57)

Here things are very clear. Our ignorance is not a good reason for rejecting the possible existence of anything. This quotation refutes the view that he can be supposed
to be positively denying the existence of Causation, in going on at such length about
how we are ignorant of it.

Hume continues with a distinction between what we *mean* and what there *is* which
clearly illustrates that the tension described on p. 428 is unproblematic for him: 'when
we talk of gravity,' he says,

we *mean* certain effects, without ever comprehending *that active power* [i.e. gravity itself]
(E73n/58n)

—which nonetheless exists. And Newton famously agrees: 'the cause of Gravity . . . I
do not pretend to know'.[39] In a general comment on his account of forces in Definition VIII of his *Principia* (1687), he says that he intends 'only to give a mathematical
notion of those forces, without considering *their physical causes and seats*', and that he
considers certain 'forces not physically, but mathematically: wherefore the reader is
not to imagine that by those words ['attraction', 'impulse', or 'propensity towards a
centre'] I anywhere take upon me to define the kind, or the manner of any action, *the
causes or the physical reason thereof*, or that I attribute *forces, in a true and physical sense*,
to certain centres'. Newton is quite clear that we have a merely relative idea of such

39 1692–3: 3.240.

forces: we can have no knowledge of their nature beyond the knowledge we have of their observable manifestations.

10

On page 74/58 of the *Enquiry* a famous passage occurs which may at first seem to support the standard view. Hume claims that when we step back from our ordinary belief that we can observe power or necessary connexion in the objects, we realize that the belief is not correct, and that the truth of our epistemic situation, critically assessed, is as follows:

All events seem entirely loose and separate. One event follows another; but we never can observe any tie between them. They seem *conjoined*, but never *connected*. And as we can have no idea of any thing which never appeared to our outward sense or inward sentiment, the necessary conclusion *seems* to be that we have no idea of connexion or power at all, and that these words are absolutely without any meaning....

It follows, according to him, that

when we say ... that one object is connected with another, we *mean only* that they have acquired a connexion in our thought ... a conclusion which is somewhat extraordinary, but which seems founded on sufficient evidence. (E76/59)

In other words, we try to talk about the real force or energy in the world, but these words, in our use, only manage to (positively-contentfully) mean their impression-source: that is, a feeling of determination in the mind, derived from experience of regular succession or constant conjunction.

But Hume does not say that regular succession is all that causation is. Once again, his point is that this is all we can know or comprehend of causation. He admits that it seems 'somewhat extraordinary' that when we talk of causal connection between two objects we do not really manage to mean the real causal connection between them (which of course exists), but mean only that they have acquired a connection in our thought on account of having been observed to be constantly conjoined. But he doesn't take this as grounds for any sort of ontological assertion that this is all that causation (really) is, but rather as an occasion for an epistemological remark about the *profound limitations on the human capacity to grasp the nature of reality*:

what stronger instance can be produced of the surprising ignorance and weakness of the understanding than the present [one]? (E76/60)

That is, in our unreflective moments (or excessively exalted philosophical moments) we are pretty sure we know about causal power in the objects if we know about anything. But in fact human understanding is so restricted that it cannot even 'comprehend' the nature of causal power, in so far as it involves something more than observable regular succession. The 'somewhat extraordinary' conclusion, then, is not that there is really no such thing as Causation. That would certainly be an extraordinary conclusion, but I don't think that it ever crossed

Hume's mind.[40] His point is this: it is truly extraordinary that despite the fact that causal power is all pervasive, governing our thoughts and actions and our world in all respects, still human understanding is utterly incapable of grasping its true nature in any way. That's how limited we are:

Our thoughts and enquiries are . . . every moment employed about this relation. Yet so imperfect are the ideas which we form concerning it, that it is impossible to give any just definition of cause, except what is drawn from something extraneous and foreign to it. (E76)

It concerns us at every moment, and yet we cannot grasp its true nature at all. This purely epistemological point is what the philosophers Hume was arguing against could not believe.[41]

11

The view that Hume's point is epistemological is further confirmed by what he goes on to say about his two 'definitions' of cause. When he says that 'the ideas which we form concerning' cause are

so imperfect . . ., that it is impossible to give any just definition of cause, except what is drawn from something extraneous and foreign to it (E76/60),

he is referring to the two definitions that immediately follow, which specify the content that the idea of cause has given its impression sources: they tell us what we can legitimately manage to mean, on the terms of the theory of ideas, when we talk about causes. The first defines causation as constant conjunction or regular succession and the second defines it in terms of a feeling of determination in the mind (E76–7/60,

---

[40] It is an elementary error to suppose that Hume's frequent remarks to the effect that 'any thing may produce any thing' (e.g. T173/116, E164/122) provide any support for the claim that he considered the idea that there might be no such thing as Causation. The view he is endorsing, in making such remarks, is simply this: that so far as *reason* (or a-priori thought) is concerned, there is no *logical* contradiction in the idea that any one thing may produce any other thing, however disparate the two things may seem to us. This view is correct, and is entirely compatible with the view (which he also holds) that given the way things actually are in reality (considered independently of anything that reason has to say about it), nothing can possibly happen any differently from the way it does happen. Consider the quotation from the *Dialogues* on p. 423.

[41] 'When a man speaks as do others, that does not always signify that he is of their opinion. But when he positively says the opposite of what is commonly said, though he might say it only once, we have reason to judge that it is his view' (Malebranche 1674–5: 672–3). Broackes (1993) cites this passage as support for the standard view of Hume, and is right to think that Hume is saying the opposite of what is commonly said: for Hume is saying that we have no (legitimate) positive conception of the nature of causation. He is not, however, saying what the standard view has him say; *that* idea hasn't occurred to him, and the claim that the Malebranche quotation supports the standard view is scuppered by the points made in §2 above. It must also be offset by two true remarks of Kant's: 'many historians of philosophy, with all their intended praise, . . . attribute mere nonsense . . . to past philosophers. They are incapable of recognizing, beyond what the philosophers actually said, what they really meant to say' (1790: 160). 'If we take single passages, torn from their context, and compare them with one another, contradictions are not likely to be lacking, especially in a work that is written with any freedom of expression . . .; but they are easily resolved by those who have mastered the idea of the whole' (1787: Bxliv).

T170/114, 172/115–16), but both are held to be imperfect because they cannot representationally encompass causation or power 'as it is in itself' (E77n/60n). They can define it only by reference to something other than itself.

An enormous amount has been written about the content of the two definitions, but here I am concerned only with Hume's view of what they achieve: his view that it is actually impossible for us to give anything other than an 'imperfect' definition of cause. Some deny that Hume thinks his definitions are imperfect, pointing out that in the *Treatise* he says that they are 'exact' and 'precise' (T169/114). But we can allow this (though both these words disappear from the corresponding passage in the *Enquiry*). We can allow that he thinks his definitions are 'just', or as just as any definitions of cause can be (E76/60, T170/114). For the present point is then this: Hume says that the definitions are imperfect *in spite of* the fact that he thinks they are entirely exact, precise, and just. So what can he mean by 'imperfect'?

He is very clear about it. He means that the definitions do not really capture the true nature of causation at all. The trouble is that

we cannot remedy this inconvenience, or attain any more perfect definition, which may point out *that circumstance in the cause, which gives it a connexion with its effect.* (E77/60)

The trouble, in other words, is that although there is something about the cause-event in virtue of which it is connected with its effect, in any particular case, we cannot form any genuine descriptively contentful conception of it, on the terms of the theory of ideas.

Note that this quotation suffices by itself to refute the view that Hume held a regularity theory of causation. For if causation in the objects were just regular succession or constant conjunction, there would be *no inconvenience or imperfection in the first definition at all.* And in giving the first definition, we could hardly be said to be in the position of finding it 'impossible to give any just definition of cause, except what is drawn from something extraneous and foreign to it'.[42]

Some may say that all that Hume means, when he says that one has to refer to circumstances foreign to the cause, is that one has to go beyond the individual cause-event considered on its own: one has to mention the effect-event, and other events of the same type as the cause-event and effect-event, and even the human mind. But let us suppose that this is at least part of what he meant.[43] The present point retains its full force. For Hume says that the definitions are imperfect specifically because they cannot 'point out that circumstance in the cause, which [actually] gives it a connexion with its effect' (E77/60; cp. E67–8/54). There is something about the cause itself which the definitions cannot capture or represent: they leave out the essential thing. The imperfection in question is the imperfection that definitions have when they do not fully capture the nature of the thing that they are meant to be definitions of. We can't give a perfect definition of cause because of our ignorance of its

---

[42] Many still reject the present interpretation of Hume, but none of them has made any sort of reply to this point. (I discuss the strongest prima-facie evidence for the opposite view of Hume in Strawson 1989: chs. 14–15.)

[43] Cf. Wright 2000.

nature. All we can encompass in our definition are its observable manifestations—its regular-succession manifestations (first definition), and the feelings of necessity or determination or habits of inference in the mind to which these give rise (second definition).

There has been a lot of speculation about the differences between Hume's use of the word 'definition' and our present-day use,[44] and in this context Edmund Burke's remarks about definition are illuminating, for they were made in 1757, nine years after the publication of the first edition of the first *Enquiry*, in a work which Hume read.[45] 'When we define', Burke writes,

we seem in danger of circumscribing nature within the bounds of our own notions, which we often ... form out of a limited and partial consideration of the object before us, instead of extending our ideas to take in all that nature comprehends, according to her manner of combining.... A definition may be very exact, and yet go but a very little way towards inform-ing us of the nature of the thing defined.[46]

Here, I propose, Burke uses 'definition' in exactly the same way as Hume. So too Priestley in 1778:

A *definition* of any particular thing ... cannot be anything more than an enumeration of its known properties.[47]

A definition of a natural phenomenon, as opposed to a definition of a geometrical figure, records human understanding's best take on that phenomenon. As such, it may be very 'exact' and 'precise' (T169/114) while also being very 'imperfect', 'lim-ited and partial' in its representation of the nature of the phenomenon defined.[48]

Hume restates his position as follows:

If we examine the operations of body, and the productions of effects from their causes, we shall find that all our faculties can never carry us farther in our knowledge of [the] relation [of cause and effect] than *barely* to observe that particular objects are *constantly conjoin'd* together [cf. the first definition], and that the mind is carried, by a *customary transition*, from the appear-ance of one to the belief of the other [cf. the second definition]. (E92/70)

That is, all we can get to know of causation is the content of the two imperfect defin-itions. That is, we can't get very far. We can 'barely' (merely) observe this much. So these two definitions do not say what causation actually is; they just express all we know of it. And

---

[44] Craig has a good discussion of differences between Hume's use of 'definition' and ours (1987: ch. 2 §4).

[45] He called it 'a very pretty treatise' (C3: 51).   [46] 1757: 12.   [47] Priestley 1778: 34.

[48] The practice is not restricted to the eighteenth century. Russell uses 'define' in exactly the Hume/Burke sense when discussing the nature of matter: 'all that we ought to assume is series of groups of events, connected by discoverable laws. These series we may *define* as "matter". Whether there *is* matter in any other sense, no one can tell' (1927b: 93). Russell makes it very clear that to give a definition is not to make an ontological declaration. Compare also Eddington's remark that 'we know nothing about the intrinsic nature of space, and so it is quite easy to conceive it satisfactorily' (1928: 51); it is in this sense that Hume's definitions of cause are exact and satis-factory.

this conclusion concerning human ignorance [is] the result of the strictest scrutiny of this subject . . . . [W]e know nothing farther of causation . . . than *merely* the **constant conjunction** of objects, and the consequent *inference* of the mind from one to another. (E92/70)

The conclusion, then, is a conclusion about human ignorance. There is more to causation, but we are ignorant of it.[49]

12

Hume's principal targets are those philosophers (mechanists or mentalists) who think that they mean or know more than it is possible to mean or know; those who think that the intrinsic nature of causation is 'intelligible' (whether partly or wholly), and that they have some sort of genuine understanding of it. Hume thinks that it is dangerous to use words like 'power', 'force', and 'energy' without continual stress on our ignorance, for the use of these terms is likely to delude us into thinking that we do after all have some positively contentful or 'perfect' grasp of the nature of causation—a grasp that goes beyond what is given in experience of regular succession and the feeling of determination to which regular succession gives rise in human minds. This, just this, is, he insists, a mistake. Our best grasp of causation is very imperfect. We are ignorant of its nature. This ignorance is what has to be shown and argued for from all sides.

That's what Hume believed. At no point in the *Enquiry*, which must 'alone be regarded as containing his philosophical sentiments and principles', does he even hint at the thesis for which he is so unjustly famous: the thesis that all there is to causation in the world is regular succession; the thesis that there is (provably) nothing at all in the nature of things in virtue of which reality is regular in the way that it is, so that the regularity of the world is, from moment to moment, and knowably, an 'outrageous run of luck'.[50]

One might summarize the dispute about Hume as follows. Two things in Hume are incompatible: (1) the theory of ideas, strictly and literally interpreted, and (2) the

---

[49] Here again Hume follows Newton, who was criticized by Leibniz and Huygens—and even by Berkeley—for disrupting the existing mechanist world-picture by reintroducing 'inexplicable qualities' into nature. Blackburn calls some of these inexplicable qualities 'straitjacketing facts', and claims that Hume's attitude to them is 'contemptuous', but this is a mistake. Hume's contempt is for people who attempt to elaborate positive *theories* about the nature of these facts (cf. Blackburn op. cit. p. 268n). He has no contempt for the facts themselves, any more than Newton does.

[50] Reid loves criticizing Hume for adopting views contrary to common sense, and attacks him at length for denying that we can know a priori that 'every thing that begins to exist, must have a cause of its existence', but never criticizes him for holding a view apocalyptically contrary to common sense—the ontological regularity theory of causation. Why not? Because he reads Hume correctly, attributing to him the same view as Priestley: ' "a cause cannot be defined to be any thing, but *such previous circumstances as are constantly followed by a certain effect*, the constancy of the result making us conclude, that there must be a *sufficient reason, in the nature of things*, why it should be produced in those circumstances" . . . . This is Mr. Hume's definition [nb. definition] of a cause' (Reid 1788: 282, quoting Priestley). Cf. also T212/140 and the commentary on it in Strawson 1989: 166–7.

view that a straightforwardly realist view of objects and causation is at least coherent and intelligible ('it is a question of fact . . .' E153). Most people have argued that his adherence to (1) proves his rejection of (2), but this is the wrong way round. Hume's adherence to (2) proves his rejection of (1). And he not only thinks that a straightforwardly realist view of objects and causation is coherent and intelligible; he standardly takes it for granted that such a view is true.[51]

---

[51] This paper abridges, supplements, and adjusts arguments in *The Secret Connexion* (1989). I wrote it in 1992–3, and have made minor adjustments to it since then. Up to 1995 I tried to answer any objection that I came across and that seemed to me to need a reply; but publication has been long delayed and I have not been able to keep up (Winkler's enjoyable and influential 1991 paper raised no new objections, and it would have taken many pages to straighten out the tangles it contains). I would like to thank John Wright and Peter Millican for their comments, and audiences at Birmingham, Bristol, Cambridge, Lund, Oxford, and University College London.

19

Epistemology, Semantics, Ontology, and David Hume

In earlier times, it was . . . concluded that where the realm of words ceased, the realm of existence ceased also.

Nietzsche (1881: §115)

The question was not whether the concept of cause is correct . . . , for this Hume had never held in doubt; but whether it is thought a priori by reason.

Kant (1783: Preface)

1

Hume[1] mocked dogmatic metaphysicians who thought that they could achieve certainty in their conclusions about the ultimate nature of reality, and he was right to do so.

He was right to do so, but one can't get out of metaphysics altogether. For as soon as one admits that something exists—and one must do that—one has to admit that it has some (ultimate) nature or other. For to be is necessarily to be somehow or other (it is necessarily to have some nature or other). And as soon as one admits that what exists has some (ultimate) nature or other, one faces a choice. One can either hold that one knows what this (ultimate) nature is, and so endorse a particular metaphysical claim about the nature of reality. Or one can grant that one does not and perhaps cannot know what it is, or at least that one may—perhaps must—have an incomplete picture of it. The second option is the right one, but to deny the possiblity of knowledge is not to deny the existence of facts. Even if one holds that one does not and cannot know (or can only partially know) the nature of reality, one must grant

---

When I cite a work I give the original publication date, while the page reference is to the edition listed in the bibliography. This essay overlaps considerably with the previous essay.

[1] When quoting Hume I refer to the first *Enquiry*, the *Treatise*, the *Dialogues* and the *Correspondence* by the letters 'E', 'T', 'D' and 'C' respectively, followed by page numbers. In the case of the *Enquiry* I give the Selby-Bigge page reference followed by the Beauchamp page reference (e.g. '3/57'); in the case of the *Treatise*, the Selby-Bigge page reference followed similarly by the Norton page reference.

that it has a certain nature, and a fortiori that it is meaningful or intelligible to suppose that this is so. One must do this even if metaphysical speculation is fruitless. For, to repeat, something exists, and to exist—to be—is necessarily to be somehow or other: to have a certain nature.

Unsurprisingly, Hume knows this. It is unsurprising that he knows it because it is obvious. His considered position on the question of propositions about the ultimate nature of reality is not that they are entirely meaningless.[2] It is that although they may be meaningful, they are radically undecidable. It is because they are radically undecidable that they are a waste of time, and that arguments for them are mere 'sophistry and illusion' (E165/123). It is not because they are entirely meaningless or incoherent.

In the *Enquiry* he puts the point by asking a rhetorical question:

By what argument can it be proved, that the perceptions of the mind must be caused [as Locke supposes] by external objects, entirely different from them, though resembling them (if that be possible) and could not arise either from the energy of the mind itself [as the solipsist supposes], or from the suggestion of some invisible and unknown spirit [as in Berkeley's view], or from some other cause still more unknown [as in Kant's view]? (E152–3/114)

His answer is that it cannot be proved by any argument. 'It is', he says,

a question of fact, whether the perceptions of the senses be produced by external objects, resembling them.

That is, it is either true or false. It could be true. And so it is certainly meaningful. But it is radically undecidable. For

how shall this question be determined? By experience surely; as all other questions of a like nature. But here experience is, and must be entirely silent.[3]

2

The great flight from metaphysics culminated in twentieth-century verificationist positivism. But twentieth-century verificationist positivists did not escape from metaphysics. For even they granted that sense-data certainly exist—just as Hume granted that perceptions certainly exist. If verificationist positivists had gone on to say that sense-data are definitely all that exist, they would have adopted a patently metaphysical position—one of the most remarkable on record. And the same would have been

---

[2] In talking of his considered position I mean his position as clarified in the *Enquiry*, which he prefaces with the request that it 'alone be regarded as containing his philosophical sentiments and principles' (E2/1). See Strawson Essay 18: §2.

[3] E153/114. Note that Hume's assertion that it is a question of fact whether the perceptions of the senses are caused by external objects is categorical. It is not qualified by the doubt he has just expressed about whether anything like Locke's *resemblance* claim (his claim that our ideas of primary qualities like extension and motion resemble or correctly depict primary qualities as they actually are in objects) could ever be true. See further Wright 1983: ch. 2; Strawson 1989: 50 n, 51 n.

true of Hume, if he had adopted the view that perceptions (i.e. experiential episodes) are definitely all that exist. He did, in effect, consider this view.[4] But he did not, of course, endorse it, for he was a sceptic. He held, correctly, that we cannot hope to know what the truth is, so far as the ultimate nature of non-mental reality is concerned.

It can seem that verificationist positivists are obliged by their theory of meaning to say that sense-data are all that exist. In that case, their theory of meaning turns them into dogmatic metaphysicians. That can't be what they want. So what else can they say? They can say instead that sense-data are all that we can *know* to exist. They can allow that it is, after all, not actually meaningless or incoherent to suppose that other things may exist, things of which we have no conception, things, perhaps, of which we can have no conception. But if they admit this in general—and they must, if they are remotely sensible—, then they must be prepared to grant that in the particular case of sense-data, too, there may possibly be more to them and their existence than we know, or can know.

So they face the following choice. Either

(1) sense-data are mere contents with no hidden nature or backside or cause—

a views that risks turning into a form of radical metaphysical idealism. Or

(2) sense-data are not mere contents with no hidden nature or backside or cause, and there is something more to them and their existence—

in which case some other unknown and indeed unknowable metaphysical possibility is realized.

One can accept the first view or the second. Either way one is metaphysically committed. One can say that one does not know which of the two views is true, although one of them must be. In this case too, one must grant that there are metaphysical matters of fact. It is an illusion—ludicrous but widely endorsed—to suppose that considerations about meaning can exempt one from granting this. I'll develop the point by returning to Hume.

3

Hume either holds

(A) perceptions are definitely all that exist in reality—

one of the most remarkable dogmatic metaphysical positions on record—or

(B) there may be something more than perceptions, we cannot know that there is not something more, we naturally believe that there is something more, and it is certainly not entirely meaningless, or unintelligible, or incoherent, to suppose that there is something more

---

[4] Cf. e.g. T233/153, T634/399. Hume argues that perceptions could be self-subsistent substances, in so far as the notion of substance is intelligible at all; in which case they could exist without any other substances existing.

or something stronger than (B), that is, the negation of (A),

(C) something other than perceptions definitely exists in reality.

In his writings taken as a whole he generally takes it for granted that (C) is true—that perceptions are not all that exist in reality. He is repeatedly dismissive of the idea that perceptions are or might be all that exist. He says, for example, that the idea that physical objects do not have a continued existence independent of our perceptions 'has been peculiar to a few extravagant sceptics; who . . . maintained that opinion in words only, and were never able to bring themselves sincerely to believe it'.[5]

It is true that, on the official terms of his theory of ideas, Hume thinks that we cannot really get at the something-more-than-perceptions in thought or language—because we can't form any idea of it that has positive representational content ('impression'-based representational content, in Hume's terms). But we can certainly suppose, in a general way, that the something-more-than-perceptions exists. Thus, for example, 'we may well suppose in general' that physical objects are different from (and over and above) perceptions: there is nothing illegitimate about doing this, on Hume's view. The only problem is that it is 'impossible for us distinctly [nb. distinctly] to conceive' this (T218/144).

These quotations come from the *Treatise*, and Hume is also clear on this point in the *Enquiry*. So far as our perceptions are concerned, it is, he says, a straightforward 'question of fact' (E153/114) whether one particular theory which postulates something more than perceptions is true or false.

Some think that Hume should not have said this, given his theory of ideas, strictly construed. But he did say it, with very great clarity, at a crucial point in his definitive statement of his 'philosophical principles'. So if it is true that he should not have said it, given his theory of ideas, then this constitutes a powerful proof that he recognized limits on the validity of his theory of ideas.

Is it true that he should not have said it, given his theory of ideas? Well, he certainly does seem to hold that we cannot form any positive, descriptively specific (impression-copy-based) idea of the 'something more than perceptions' on the terms of his theory of ideas.[6] This, however, does not prevent him from allowing that we can suppose 'something more than perceptions' to *exist*, without contravening the rules of his theory of ideas. If one adopts an empiricist approach at all, one will wish to say that the concept SOMETHING is derived from perceptions in some way. It will nonetheless remain what it is—an idea whose semantic point is to be entirely unspecific. And all that Hume has to allow, in order to say that the idea of something more than perceptions does have respectable content on the terms of his theory of ideas, and is not contradictory in so far as it does have content, is that the entirely unspecific idea of *something*, or equivalently of *something that exists*, does not inevitably refer only to perceptions, and specifically to perceptions, given its source.

---

[5] T214/142; cf. also T227–8/150; and T366/237.
[6] Unless something like the Lockean resemblance claim can be made out. See n3 and the reference there.

Does he allow this? Of course. No thoughtful sceptic can do otherwise. Perhaps the young Hume of the *Treatise*, following the radical empiricist thought to its intoxicating root, was tempted by the view that even the entirely unspecific idea of *something* can only ever refer to perceptions, given its etiology.[7] But he says a great deal that is incompatible with this view, in the *Treatise*, and in the *Enquiry* he is admirably blunt, in the passage which has already been quoted twice: 'It is', he says, 'a question of fact, whether the perceptions of the senses be produced by external objects . . . entirely different from them, though resembling them.'[8]

Consider, also, his remark that 'no man that reflects, ever doubted, that . . . perceptions' of the sort 'we consider, when we say, *this house* and *that tree*', are 'nothing but . . . fleeting copies or representations of other existences, which remain uniform and independent' of our perceptions (E152/114). This quotation immediately refutes two views about Hume. It refutes the common view that he thinks that physical objects are really nothing but our mental perceptions. But we can simply give that point away, for what is much more important for present purposes is that it refutes the common view that he thinks that it is completely unintelligible to suppose that physical objects are anything more than our mental perceptions. The same goes for his remark, in the *Treatise*, that 'the perceptions of the mind are perfectly known', whereas 'the essence and composition of external bodies are . . . obscure'.[9]

4

In the last section I considered three possible views about perceptions. I will now briefly consider the parallel views about causation. Hume either holds that

(A′) regular succession is definitely all there is to causation, in reality

or that

(B′) there may be something more than regular succession, we cannot know that there is not something more, we naturally believe that there is something more, and it is certainly not entirely meaningless or unintelligible or incoherent to suppose that there is something more

or something stronger than (B′), that is, the negation of (A′), namely

(C′) something more than regular succession definitely exists in reality, so far as the phenomenon of causation is concerned.

Once again, on the official terms of his theory of ideas, Hume thinks that when we consider the nature of causation in so far as it is or may be something more

---

[7] Some may cite the claim he makes when discussing the nature of belief in the Appendix to the *Treatise*: 'we have no abstract idea of existence, distinguishable and separable from the idea of particular objects' (T623/396). But this quotation, considered in context, does not support the extreme view.

[8] E153/114. I feel it appropriate that this paper should have a faintly liturgical quality.

[9] T366/237; cf. also the passage from T218/144 quoted above; and many others.

than regular succession, we cannot satisfactorily get at or comprehend the something more in thought or language, because we can't form any idea of it that has positive (or impression-based) representational content. But we can certainly suppose that it exists. Hume is clear on this point. He takes it for granted that the something more does exist, and is merely concerned to stress the point that we cannot know its nature, in opposition to the majority of his contemporaries, who were convinced that we could.[10]

In one rather beautiful sentence Hume remarks that

the scenes of the universe are continually shifting, and one object follows another in an uninterrupted succession; but the power or force, which actuates the whole machine, is entirely concealed from us, and never discovers itself in any of the sensible qualities of body. (E63–4/51)

Here his view seems clear: 'the power or force which [actually] actuates the whole machine . . . of the universe' certainly exists, but its nature is entirely concealed from us in so far as it is something more than or other than regular succession.

5

I will return to causation in §7, and make some remarks about Hume's two definitions of cause. For the moment, I will continue with some more general observations.

Consider the thesis that there may be aspects of reality that are completely unintelligible by us (i.e. ununderstandable by us or incomprehensible to us). Barest common sense—not to mention a minimum degree of modesty or sceptical reserve—requires us to grant the truth of this thesis. But some people appear to think that Hume the sceptic is denying it. This is because they think that he is using the word 'unintelligible' in the strong modern philosophical sense, according to which to say that something X is unintelligible is to say that the idea of X is in fact incoherent, and hence that X cannot exist. On this view, when Hume says that the existence of anything other than perceptions is unintelligible, he is saying that only perceptions exist and can exist.

Hume certainly does not mean this by the word 'unintelligible'. He uses the word in the more natural and literal way, which survives today as the standard non-philosophical use of the word—as when we say that a message is unintelligible, meaning simply that we cannot understand it, although it exists.

The evidence that Hume used the word 'unintelligible' in this second, milder sense is overwhelming, for if he had used it in the standard modern philosophical way then he would have been a dogmatic metaphysician who held that only perceptions exist and can exist. What is more, he would have reached this full blown ontological conclusion—that only perceptions exist—first by arguing that perceptions are all we can

---

[10] Many of them—including the older Newton—thought that causal power had to involve mental volition of some sort.

know, and second by arguing that they are all that we can think (about) or mean. On this view, Hume takes it that absolute metaphysical certainty about the ultimate nature of reality is not difficult to achieve. It is not a matter of 'sophistry and illusion' (E165/123) after all. It's really easy.

This is the line of argument I discussed in chapter 3 of *The Secret Connexion*. You are supposed to be able to get from an epistemological claim to a metaphysical/ontological claim via a semantic claim.[11] In the case of the regularity theory of causation, the argument goes like this:

(E) All we can ever know or observe of causation in the objects is regular succession.

But if so, then, given standard meaning-empiricist principles,

(S) All we can legitimately manage to mean by expressions like 'causation in the objects' is regular succession.

But if this is so, then the statement

(O) All that causation actually is, in the objects, is regular succession

must be true.

Why? Because, given (S), the semantic claim, when the phrase 'causation in the objects' occurs, inevitably just means regular succession. So (O) causation in the objects—here is the phrase occurring, inevitably meaning 'regular succession', whatever else I like to think it means—just is regular succession. After all, regular succession is regular succession.[12]

It is helpful to rerun this argument for the case of 'external' or physical objects.

(E′) All we can ever know or observe of physical objects are perceptions.

But if so, then, given standard meaning-empiricist principles,

(S′) All we can legitimately manage to mean by expressions like 'physical object' or 'table' or 'chair' are perceptions (actual or possible).

But if so, then the statement

(O′) All that physical objects actually are, are perceptions.

must be true.

Why? Because, given the semantic claim (S′), when the phrase 'physical objects' occurs, it inevitably just means perceptions. So (O′) physical objects—here is the phrase occurring, inevitably meaning 'perceptions', whatever else I like to think it means—just are perceptions. After all, perceptions are perceptions.

So phenomenalism is true. Not just mild methodological phenomenalism, but mad metaphysical phenomenalism: the view that physical objects are definitely nothing

---

[11] It is arguable that the popularity of this idea, or something close to it, is the key to nearly everything that is wrong in the last 300 years of philosophy. Compare Carnap 1950.

[12] As a whole, the argument goes like this. (1) (E) is true. (2) If (E) is true, (S) is true. (3) If (S) is true, (O) is true, given the meaning of the words it contains: it's a tautology. (4) Hence (O) is true.

more than perceptions or sense-data. Or, in other terms, the view that statements about physical objects reduce without any loss of semantic or ontological import to statements about sense-data. On this view, even if something other than perceptions exists, we can't 'manage to mean' this something. Except that this way of putting it won't do at all. For the sentence 'On this view, even if something other than perceptions exists, we can't "manage to mean" this something' is actually nonsense. It's nonsense because the phrase 'if something other than perceptions exists' cannot really contain the reference to something other than perceptions that it purports to contain.

This is not Hume's view. For it is, as he said, 'a question of fact, whether the perceptions of the senses be produced by external objects . . . entirely different from them' (E153/114). And here he means external objects that are not themselves perceptions, but are, as he says, 'entirely different from' perceptions, and 'produce' perceptions. Remember what he says in the *Treatise*: 'we may well suppose in general' that physical objects are different from perceptions; there is no problem with this. The problem is that it is 'impossible for us *distinctly* to conceive' of this (T218/144; my emphasis).

It is arguable that Hume also said things in the *Treatise* that invite the interpretation I'm rejecting. He was, when he wrote that great book, lit up by what he later called the 'ardor of youth' and by the intense and dubious pleasures of philosophical iconoclasm. But even in the *Treatise* he made the essential move already mentioned; the move that allows that language can intelligibly be supposed to refer to something of which we have (and can have) no impression-based idea or conception. He distinguished between what we can suppose and what we can conceive.[13] A genuine *conception* of something must have impression-based representational content. A *supposition*, by contrast, can be genuinely about something even if it lacks impression-based representational content, and is therefore a merely 'relative' idea.[14]

The distinction between supposing and conceiving, and the notion of a relative idea, can be appealed to in the following way. Consider your perceptions of tables, chairs, and so on. As a sceptic, you have no idea what gives rise to them or produces them, but you suppose that something—call it 'X'—does, and you may very well be right. Clearly you can refer to and think about X simply as 'whatever causes these perceptions'. Here you have a merely relative idea of X. You have no positive idea of its nature, no impression-based conception of it. You can't even be certain that it exists. You know of it only indirectly, by its supposed relation to something you do have direct experience of—your perceptions. Here you 'suppose an external universe', as we all do (E151/113), without claiming to have any certain knowledge of its nature.

Some have objected that little weight can be placed on the fact that Hume makes a distinction between what we can suppose and what we can conceive, because Hume

---

[13] Cf. e.g. T67–8/49, 218/144, 241/158, E151–3/113–15. As far as I know, the importance of this point was first made clear by John Wright (1983: 106–7) and Edward Craig (1987: 123–4).

[14] Suppose you go to your room and find a peculiar mess. You have absolutely no idea what caused it, but you suppose, reasonably, that something did. Call this something 'X'. Clearly you can refer to and think about X simply as 'whatever caused this mess'. Here you have a merely relative idea of X.

himself does not make much of it.[15] This, however, is a non sequitur. It could be granted, for present purposes, that Hume does not make much of the distinction (although he relies on it constantly). It could even be granted that Hume, in the ardour of youth, sees the necessity of making the distinction between what we can suppose and what we can conceive as somewhat annoying. The fact remains that it is something that he finds himself obliged to record, in the course of his sceptical progress. He duly does so, and he does so clearly and unambiguously.[16] He handles the issue just as he should. He pushes to the edge of the wild thesis, the thesis that leads to mad metaphysical phenomenalism, in accordance with the empiricist theory of meaning, and then draws back in just the right way, acknowledging that it is intelligible to suppose that things other than perceptions exist.

It is clear, after all, that this acknowledgement is a necessary part of his philosophy. He has to grant that thought and language can reach beyond perceptions in such a way that the thought that something other than perceptions exists can be allowed to be intelligible and possibly true. For if he does not do this, then (once again) he is condemned to dogmatic metaphysics. He is committed to the view that the statement 'All that exist are perceptions' is provably true! He is landed with a form of metaphysical certainty that he cannot possibly tolerate, as a rigorous, strictly non-committal sceptic who correctly denies the possibility of attaining final knowledge about the ultimate nature of (non-mental) reality.

It cannot be right to attribute such a view to Hume. It turns him into an extravagant fanatic, of the sort that he often scolded, in his interpretation of the demands of empiricism. It turns him into someone who thinks metaphysical certainty is cheap—someone who thinks that one can infer necessary non-existence from (necessary) ignorance.

Only a fool would do such a thing, and Hume explicitly denies the validity of the inference in his reply to the Cartesian Occasionalists in the *Enquiry*. The Occasionalists think that we have to attribute all power to God because we are ignorant of the nature of causal power in the world—'totally ignorant of the power on which depends the mutual operation of bodies', and 'no less ignorant of that power on which depends the operation of mind on body, or of body on mind' (E70/56). Hume fully agrees with them, but he points out that our ignorance does not stop there. For we are, he observes, equally ignorant of the 'manner or force by which . . . even the supreme mind, operates either on itself or on body' (E72/57). And then he makes the obvious, necessary move:

Were our ignorance, therefore, a good reason for rejecting anything, we should be led into that principle of denying all energy in the Supreme Being as much as in the grossest matter (E72–3–57.)

---

[15] Cf. e.g. Blackburn (1990). For some criticisms of Blackburn, see Essay 18: §6.

[16] Compare his statement, when arguing that we can have no idea of causation in objects, that he is 'indeed, ready to allow, that there may be several qualities both in material and in immaterial objects, with which we are utterly unacquainted' (T168/113). Here too Hume is clear that the realm of existence does not cease where the realm of words or positively contentful conceptions ceases.

Here Hume states a basic principle of consistent scepticism, annihilating the Occasionalists' argument in passing: he says that ignorance—even necessary ignorance—is not a good reason for denying the possible existence of anything. As Hume knows, any sane philosopher must allow that it is comprehensible that there should be things that are incomprehensible and unknowable by us. One cannot infer non-existence from ignorance. One cannot infer non-existence from unintelligibility.

Even the good Berkeley agrees: 'many things, for anything I know, may exist, whereof neither I nor any other man can have any idea or notion whatsoever'.[17]

6

The same applies in the case of Hume's discussion of causation. One cannot infer non-existence from ignorance or unintelligibility. Like Kant (like any philosopher who has not gone overboard), Hume grants, in practice, that contentful thoughts about matters of fact can extend beyond the bounds of sense, even though we cannot attain any certain knowledge of what (if anything) lies beyond the bounds of sense.[18] He grants this even though he is faced with a considerable problem about the exact nature or content of such thoughts, given his meaning-empiricism. His meaning-empiricism obliges him to say that there is something seriously problematic, incomplete, or misleading—defective, relative, inadequate, inccurate, imprecise, imperfect, vulgar, loose, uncertain, confused, indistinct, 'fiction'-involving (cf. e.g. T267/174, T218/144, T160/108, T639/47, E67n/54n, E67/60, E77n/60n)—about the content of any such thoughts. Note, though, that this is not to deny that they have content. To say that a thought or belief is imprecise or involves a fiction, for example, is automatically to imply that it has content of some sort.[19]

In its most extreme form, meaning-empiricism is obliged to say that these thoughts have absolutely no content at all, in so far as they purport to be about something other than what is immediately given in the content of experience. This is not Hume's view. He grants (once again) that it is, at the very least, intelligible to suppose that there exists something other than perceptions. His scepticism and his deep philosophical common sense combine to fix him in this view. Just as realism entails scepticism, so scepticism entails at least this amount of speculative realism.[20] This he knows.

---

[17] *Third Dialogue* (1713: 184).

[18] Cf. Kant (1781–7: B166 n): 'in our *thinking* the categories [e.g. of cause and substance] are not limited by the conditions of our sensible intuition, but have an unlimited field. It is only *knowledge* of what we think . . . that requires intuition'.

[19] Hume is struck by the thought that attempts to reach beyond perceptions, e.g. in expressing the supposition that there are external objects, must somehow still use impression-based contents, given the terms of his theory of ideas. Cf. e.g. T218/144 (lines 6–11/19–23), 241/158 (lines 20–4/21–4). It is worth adding that Hume's use of the word 'fiction' is not necessarily pejorative: see Strawson 1989: 55, n36.

[20] Cf. e.g. Strawson 1989: 120, n4.

7

I want to reinforce this point by considering Hume's two 'definitions' of cause. In *The Secret Connexion* I argued that the only natural reading of the discussion of causation in the *Enquiry* is that Hume's primary point is epistemological, not ontological.[21] It is clear who he is targeting: all those of his contemporaries who wrongly think that they know more about Causation than it is possible to know, and that they have some sort of genuine understanding of its ultimate or intrinsic nature. Hume wants to prove to them that they are wrong. He wants to prove that we are completely ignorant of the nature of causation in so far as it involves something more than regular succession. This ignorance is what has to be shown and argued for from all sides, in Hume's view. It has to be argued for because it is very hard to see and very surprising, for philosophers and ordinary people alike. Why is it so surprising? Because 'our thoughts and enquiries are ... every moment, employed about' the relation of cause and effect (E76/60). The point is not only that our practical thoughts, as we negotiate the world, are saturated with causal assumptions, expectations, predictions, speculations, and so on. It is also that we take ourselves to have direct understanding of the nature of causation in experiencing pushes and pulls, impacts, pressures, weights, and so on.

The view that Hume's point is purely epistemological is evident from his discussion of his two 'definitions' of cause. He begins by saying that 'the ideas which we form concerning' cause are

so imperfect ... , that it is impossible to give any just definition of cause, except what is drawn from something extraneous and foreign to it. (E76/60)

And here he is referring to the two 'definitions' of cause which immediately follow. These definitions are held to be imperfect because they cannot representationally encompass causation or power 'as it is in itself' (E77n/60–1n), but can define it only by reference to what is 'extraneous and foreign' to it.

For present purposes, the content of the two definitions doesn't matter. What matters is Hume's view of their status as definitions—his emphatically stated view that it is actually *impossible* for us to give anything other than an imperfect definition of cause. Roughly speaking, the two definitions provide an account of the content of the idea of cause we human beings actually possess, given the idea's basic impression-sources. They give information about all we can really descriptively mean, according to the theory of ideas, when we talk about causes. But Hume holds that although the two definitions do do this, they are seriously imperfect, as definitions. They do not really capture the true nature of causation at all.

Why not? Because both of them are 'drawn from something foreign to the cause'. And

---

[21] For a similar view, see e.g. Wright 1983; Craig 1987. This section reformulates Strawson 1989: ch. 21 and closely parallels Essay 18: §10.

we cannot remedy this inconvenience, or attain any more perfect definition, which may point out that circumstance in the cause, which gives it a connexion with its effect. (E77/60)

There is of course something about the cause-event in virtue of which it is connected with its effect, contrary to the so-called 'Humean' regularity theory of causation; but, simply, we do not and cannot know what it is, or give any positively descriptive characterization of it.

Clearly, if causation in reality were just regular succession (a matter of priority, contiguity, and constant conjunction), there would be no inconvenience or imperfection in the first definition at all. It would be an absolutely perfect definition. And, in giving the first definition, we could hardly be said to be in the position of finding it 'impossible to give any just definition of cause, except what is drawn from something extraneous and foreign to it'. This point destroys the once standard view of Hume.

Some may say that all that Hume means, when he says that one has to refer to circumstances foreign to the cause, is that one has to go beyond the individual cause-event considered on its own: one has to mention the effect-event, and other events of the same type as the cause-event and effect-event, and even the human mind (something which is clearly extraneous and foreign to a causal interaction between billiard-balls). So let us suppose that this is at least part of what he meant.[22] The present point retains its full force. For Hume says that the definitions are imperfect specifically because they cannot 'point out that circumstance in the cause, which [actually] gives it a connexion with its effect' (E77, picking up on a phrase in E67–8). That is, there is something about the cause itself which the definitions cannot capture or represent: they leave out the essential thing. What is the imperfection that Hume is referring to? It is the imperfection that definitions have when they do not fully capture the nature of the thing that they are meant to be definitions of. We can't give a perfect definition of cause because of our ignorance of its nature. All we can encompass in our definition are its observable manifestations—its regular-succession manifestations, and the feelings of necessity or determination (or habits of inference) in the mind to which these give rise.

There has been a lot of discussion of possible differences between Hume's use of the word 'definition' and our present-day use, but a key witness has been ignored. Edmund Burke's remarks on the notion of definition are particularly valuable for having been made in 1757, nine years after the publication of the first edition of the *Enquiry*. 'When we define', he writes,

we seem in danger of circumscribing nature within the bounds of our own notions, which we often . . . form out of a limited and partial consideration of the object before us, instead of extending our ideas to take in all that nature comprehends, according to her manner of combining . . . . [A] definition may be very exact, and yet go but a very little way towards informing us of the nature of the thing defined. (1757: 12)

Here, I propose, Burke uses the term 'definition' in exactly the same way as Hume. A definition of a natural phenomenon, as opposed to a definition of a geometrical

---

[22] Cf. Wright 2000.

figure, simply records human understanding's best take on that phenomenon. As such, it may be very 'imperfect', 'limited and partial' in its representation of the nature of the phenomenon. It may very well fail to constitute an exhaustive specification of the nature of the phenomenon. Newton takes exactly the same line in his *Principia*.[23]

8

Hume was a sceptic. As a sceptic he would not have claimed to know for certain that there was causal power or objective necessity in the universe. He did, as a sceptic, and in the wake of Berkeley, consider the metaphysical possibility that there might be no physical objects as ordinarily conceived of. But I don't think he ever even considered the metaphysical possibility that is the equivalent, in the case of causation, of the metaphysical possibility that there might be no physical objects as ordinarily conceived of: that is, the possibility that the whole order of the world might be, as it were, a continuous fluke; or, in other words, the possibility that the regularity theory of causation might be true as an ontological doctrine. It is, after all, a far more bizarre idea than the idealist idea that objects might be nothing but perceptions. For even if objects are nothing but perceptions, their orderly behaviour stands as much in need of explanation as it does if they are physical objects as ordinarily conceived.[24]

Consider some remarks by Philo, Hume's spokesman in the *Dialogues*:

How could things have been as they are, were there not an original, inherent principle of order somewhere, in thought or in matter? . . . Chance has no place on any hypothesis, sceptical or religious. Everything is surely governed by steady, inviolable laws. And were the inmost essence of things laid open to us, we should then discover a scene, of which, at present, we can have no idea. Instead of admiring the order of natural beings, we should clearly see, that it was absolutely impossible for them, in the smallest article, ever to admit of any other disposition. (D174–5)

'Tis observed by arithmeticians, that the products of 9 compose always 9 or some lesser product of 9, if you add together all the characters, of which any of the former products are composed. Thus, of 18, 27, 36, which are products of 9, you make 9 by adding 1 to 8, 2 to 7, 3 to 6. Thus 369, is a product also of nine; and if you add 3, 6, and 9, you make 18, a lesser product of 9. To a superficial observer, so wonderful a regularity may be admir'd as the effect either of chance, or design; but a skillful algebraist immediately concludes it to be the work of necessity, and demonstrates, that it must for ever result from the nature of these numbers. Is it not probable, I ask, that the whole economy of the universe is conducted by a like necessity . . . ? And instead of admiring the order of natural beings, may it not happen, that, could we penetrate into the intimate nature of bodies, we should clearly see why it was absolutely impossible, they could ever admit of any other disposition? (D191)

---

[23] Cf. e.g. Definition VIII, discussed in Essay 18: 432; see also p. 436. For further discussion of the status of the two definitions, see especially Craig 1987: 102–9.

[24] Cf. Strawson 1989: 219–20.

These are not the views of a regularity theorist. They are Hume's views, dramatically presented and too little known.[25]

Some say that it cannot be proved that Philo is Hume's spokesman, but we have all the proof we need. Philo is the representative sceptic. No one denies that he is the best candidate. In a letter Hume imagines Gilbert Elliot and himself writing a dialogue together; he casts Elliot as Cleanthes, and says of himself 'I should have taken on me the character of Philo, in the Dialogue, which you'll own I could have supported naturally enough' (C1: 154). In another letter he wrote 'In every dialogue, no more than one person can be supposed to represent the author' (C1: 173).

There are perhaps two main reasons why the identification of Hume with Philo has been disputed. The first is that the clever mischief of Philo's apparent concession that there is a god (in Part 12 of the *Dialogues*) has been widely misunderstood. Hume was certainly an agnostic, and he was certainly an atheist with respect to the Christian God as standardly defined, but there is nothing that he cannot accept in Philo's brilliant argument in Part 12.[26]

The second main reason why the identification of Philo with Hume has been found uncomfortable is that Philo talks in a realist fashion about natural or objective necessity, while granting that its nature is unknowable. But on the present view, this confirms the acceptability of the identification, rather than constituting an objection to it. Philo, like Hume, believes in the existence of some principle of order given which the universe is regular in the way that it is, while holding that we know nothing about its ultimate nature.

Let us try the contrary hypothesis: that Philo is not Hume, and Hume really does hold the view that causation is nothing but regularity. A bewildering question arises: Why does Hume allow Philo to assume the intelligibility (and assert the truth) of some form of objective necessity thesis without any challenge? If Hume really holds (and particularly cherishes) the view that causation is nothing but constant conjunction or regular succession, why doesn't he ever put any of his arguments for this view into anyone's mouth in the *Dialogues*, even where the context invites it . . . ?

It cannot be countered that the *Dialogues* is marginal to Hume's main work in philosophy (this is sometimes assumed to be the case, in the wake of a tradition of interpretation that cannot accommodate the *Dialogues*). For it is, if anything, the jewel at the centre, uniquely brilliant in itself and particularly treasured by Hume. Shortly before he died he wrote to his publisher about the *Dialogues*: 'Some of my friends flatter me, that it is the best thing I ever wrote' (C2: 323).

It should be added that it is not a late work, as some suppose. He began work on it in 1749, shortly after the first edition of the *Enquiry* was published in 1748. He

---

[25] Here Hume has abandoned his ardent-youth endorsement (on T166/112) of a wild, Wittgensteinian global subjectivism about necessity while retaining the idea (also to be found on T166/112) that natural necessity is like mathematical necessity. On this interesting matter see Strawson 1989: 156–60.

[26] Philo's long speech beginning 'All men of sound reason . . .' is particularly relevant: D217–19. Here his understanding of the deity turns out—as he explicitly says—to include nothing that any atheist can possibly wish to disagree with (it also constitutes a further affirmation of causal realism).

reworked it at various times, was too cautious to publish it during his life, but took particular care to ensure that it would be published after his death.

9

I have noted the parallel between the strict empiricist approach to physical objects and the strict empiricist approach to causation, and have argued that Hume cannot be arguing for the thesis that there is definitely no such thing as causation as ordinarily conceived of. He is certainly not arguing the parallel thesis for objects, and claiming that objects definitely do not exist in so far as they are supposed to be different from perceptions. In the case of objects, he is working out the sceptical arguments and establishing the limits to knowledge. We should not suppose that he is doing something completely different in the case of causation, pursuing a positive metaphysical programme and arguing that causation is definitely just constant conjunction. Both in the case of causation and in the case of objects he is working out the sceptical arguments and establishing the limits to knowledge. Placed in historical context, his scepticism with respect to knowledge of objects is relatively familiar, while his scepticism with respect to knowledge of causation is more original although not unanticipated.

Many have thought that Hume argues from epistemology to semantics to ontology—from 'can't know X' to 'can't mean X' to 'X does not (and cannot) exist'. He doesn't. Many have thought that it is a good line of argument. It isn't. Some think that it is the cornerstone of rigorous empiricism. It isn't. The problem is not merely that it is an invalid form of argument. That's a relatively minor defect, if one is trying to be a radical empiricist. The major defect is that it leads, as I have argued, to gross immodesty, false certainty, and mad metaphysics.

10

I will end with a thought about Wittgenstein. Those who think that Hume positively endorses some sort of idealism about objects, and some sort of regularity thesis about causation, are rather like those who think that Wittgenstein denies the reality of the sensation of pain. Consider the result of substituting 'regular succession' for 'pain-behaviour', and 'causation' for 'sensation', in §304 of Wittgenstein's *Philosophical Investigations*. Wittgenstein's imaginary interlocutor speaks first:

But you will surely admit that there is a difference between regular succession accompanied by [or involving] causation and regular succession without any causation?
Admit it? What greater difference could there be?
And yet you again and again reach the conclusion that the causation itself is a *nothing*.
Not at all. . . . The conclusion was only that a nothing would serve just as well as a something about which nothing could be said.

It seems to me that Wittgenstein is muddled as compared with Hume (whom Wittgenstein once said he could not read, because he—Hume—was so muddled). Nevertheless this passage, with these substitutions, expresses part of Hume's view rather well.

One may also substitute 'external object' for 'sensation':

And yet you again and again reach the conclusion that the external object itself is a *nothing*.
Not at all. . . . The conclusion was only that a nothing would serve just as well as a something about which nothing could be said.

The same thoughts apply.[27]

---

[27] Ellipsis is dangerous in commentary on Wittgenstein. In full the final response runs as follows: 'Not at all. It is not a *something*, but it is not a *nothing* either! The conclusion was only that a nothing would serve just as well as a something about which nothing could be said.' The omitted sentence is a rhetorically dramatic contradiction—that's why it ends with an exclamation mark—and the basic claim is given by the following sentence: 'the conclusion was *only* that a nothing would serve just as well as a something about which nothing could be said'. One could gloss the contradictory sentence by saying that its claim is that pain-sensation (or causation or external objects) is not a something of which one can give any positively descriptive account in (public) language (or: on the terms of the theory of ideas).

Bibliography

Algarotti, F. (1737/1739) *Sir Isaac Newton's Philosophy Explain'd For the Use of the Ladies*, trans. Elizabeth Carter (London: E. Cave).

Annas, J. (1984) 'Personal Love and Kantian Ethics in *Effi Briest*', in *Philosophy and Literature* 8: 15–31.

Aristotle (*c.*330 BCE/1953) *Nichomachean Ethics*, trans. J. A. K. Thomson (London: Allen & Unwin).

—— (*c.*340 BCE/1936) *De Anima*, trans. W. S. Hett (Cambridge, MA: Harvard University Press).

Armstrong, D. M. (1980/1997) 'Against "Ostrich Nominalism"', in *Properties*, ed. D. H. Mellor and A. Oliver (Oxford: Oxford University Press).

—— (1983) *What is a Law of Nature?* (Cambridge: Cambridge University Press).

Arnauld, A. (1641/1985) 'Fourth Set of Objections', in *The Philosophical Writings of Descartes*, vol. 2, trans. J. Cottingham *et al.* (Cambridge: Cambridge University Press).

—— (1683/1990) *On True and False Ideas*, trans. with an introduction by Stephen Gaukroger (Manchester: Manchester University Press).

Attridge, J. (2004) Letter to the *Times Literary Supplement*, December 10.

Auden, W. H. (1940) 'Heavy Date', in *Another Time* (New York: Random House).

Audi, R. (1999) 'Doxastic Voluntarism and the Ethics of Belief', *Facta Philosophica* 1: 87–109.

Austin, J. L (1956/1961) 'Ifs and Cans', *Philosophical Papers*, ed. J. O. Urmson and G. J. Warnock (Oxford: Clarendon Press).

Ayer, A. J. (1973) *The Central Questions of Philosophy* (London: Penguin).

Ayers, M. R. (1991) *Locke*, vol. 1 (London: Routledge).

Baddeley, A. (1994) 'The remembered self and the enacted self', in *The remembering self: construction and accuracy in the self-narrative*, edited by U. Neisser & R. Fivush (Cambridge: Cambridge University Press).

Baker, N. (1991) *U and I* (New York: Random House).

Bell, J. S. (1964) 'On the Einstein Podolsky Rosen Paradox', *Physics* 1: 195–200.

—— (1987) *Speakable and Unspeakable in Quantum Mechanics* (Cambridge: Cambridge University Press).

Bellow, S. (1977) *Humboldt's Gift* (Harmondsworth: Penguin).

Berkeley, G. (1710/1975) *Principles of Human Knowledge*, in *Philosophical Works*, ed. M. R. Ayers (London: Dent).

—— (1713/1975) *Three Dialogues*, in *Philosophical Works*, ed. M. R. Ayers (London: Dent).

—— (1721/1975) *De motu*, in *Philosophical Works*, ed. M. R. Ayers (London: Dent).

Bickhard, M. H. (2003) 'Process and Emergence: Normative Function and Representation', in *Process Theories: Crossdisciplinary Studies in Dynamic Categories*, ed. J. Seibt (Dordrecht: Kluwer Academic).

Blackburn, S. (1990/2002) 'Hume and Thick Connexions', in *Hume's Enquiry Concerning Human Understanding*, ed. P. Millican (Oxford: Oxford University Press).

Blattner, W. (1999) *Heidegger's Temporal Idealism* (Cambridge: Cambridge University Press).

Block, N. (1978) 'Troubles with Functionalism', in *Minnesota Studies in the Philosophy of Science* 9 261–325.

Blumenfeld, L. (2003) *Revenge: a Story of Hope* (New York: Washington Square Press).

Brewer, M. W. (1995) 'Compulsion by Reason', in *Proceedings of the Aristotelian Society*, supp. vol. 69: 237–53.

Brewer, W. F. (1988) 'Memory for randomly sampled autobiographical events', in *Remembering Reconsidered: Ecological and traditional approaches to the study of memory* edited by U. Neisser & E. Winograd (Cambridge: Cambridge University Press).

Broackes. J. (1993) 'Did Hume hold a Regularity Theory of Causation?', in *British Journal for the History of Philosophy*, 1: 99–114.

Broad, C. D. (1925) *The Mind and Its Place in Nature* (London: Routledge & Kegan Paul).

Bruner, J. (1987) 'Life as Narrative', *Social Research* **54**: 11–32.

_____ (1990) *Acts of Meaning* (Cambridge, Mass: Harvard University Press).

_____ (1994) 'The "remembered" self', in *The remembering self*, edited by U. Neisser and R. Fivush (Cambridge: Cambridge University Press).

Buckle, S. (1999a) 'Hume's Biography and Hume's Philosophy: "My Own Life" and *An Enquiry concerning Human Understanding*', in *Australian Journal of Philosophy* 77: 1–25.

_____ (1999b) 'British Sceptical Realism: A Fresh Look at the British Tradition', in *European Journal of Philosophy* 7: 1–29.

Burge, T. (1998) 'Reason and the First Person', in *Knowing Our Own Minds*, ed. C. Wright, B. C. Smith, and C. MacDonald (Oxford: Oxford University Press).

Burke, E. (1757/1990) *A Philosophical Enquiry into the Origin of our Ideas of the Sublime and Beautiful*, ed. Adam Phillips (Oxford: Oxford University Press).

Campbell, C. A. (1957) 'Has the Self "Free Will"?', in C. A. Campbell, *On Selfhood and Godhood* (London: Allen & Unwin).

_____ (1967) 'In Defence of Free Will', in *In Defence of Free Will* (London: Allen & Unwin).

Campbell, J. (1994) *Past, Space, and Self* (Cambridge, Mass: MIT Press).

Camus, A. (1942/1982) *The Outsider*, trans. J. Laredo (London: Hamish Hamilton).

Carnap, R. (1928/1967) 'Pseudoproblems in Philosophy', in *The Logical Structure of the World and Pseudoproblems in Philosophy* (London: Routledge & Kegan Paul).

_____ (1950) 'Empiricism, Semantics, and Ontology', in R. Carnap, *Meaning and Reference*.

_____ (1956) *Meaning and Reference* (Chicago: University of Chicago Press).

Carr, E. H. (1961) *What Is History?* (London: Macmillan).

Cassam, A.-Q. A. (ed.) (1994) *Self-Knowledge* (Oxford: Oxford University Press).

_____ (1997) *Self and World* (Oxford: Clarendon Press).

Castañeda, H.-N. (1966) 'On the Phenomeno-Logic of the I', in *Self-Knowledge*, ed. A.-Q. A. Cassam (Oxford: Oxford University Press).

Chalmers, D. (1995) 'Facing up to the Problem of Consciousness', *Journal of Consciousness Studies* 2: 200–19.

_____ (1996) *The Conscious Mind* (New York: Oxford University Press).

_____ (1997) 'Moving Forward on the Problem of Consciousness' in *Explaining Consciousness: the Hard Problem*, ed. J. Shear (Cambridge, Mass: MIT Press).

_____ and Clark, A. (1998) 'The Extended Mind', *Analysis* 58: 7–19.

Chomsky, N. (1968) *Language and Mind* (New York: Harcourt, Brace & World).

_____ (1986) *Barriers* (Cambridge, Mass: MIT Press).

_____ (1988) *Language and Problems of Knowledge* (Cambridge, Mass: MIT Press).

_____ (1992) 'Language and Interpretation', in *Inference, Explanation and other Philosophical Frustrations*, ed. J. Earman (Berkeley: University of California Press).

_____ (1993) 'Explaining Language Use', *Philosophical Topics* 20: 205–31.

_____ (1994) 'Naturalism and Dualism in the Study of Language', *International Journal of Philosophical Studies* 2: 181–209.

_____ (1995) 'Language and Nature', *Mind* 104: 1–60.

_____ (1996) *Powers and Prospects* (London: Pluto).

_____ (1998) 'Comments: Galen Strawson's *Mental Reality*', *Philosophy and Phenomenological Research* 58: 437–41.

Churchland, P. M. (1995) *The Engine of Reason, the Seat of the Soul* (Cambridge, Mass: MIT Press).

Clark, A. (2001) *Mindware—An Introduction to the Philosophy of Cognitive Science* (Oxford: Oxford University Press).

Clarke, D. (2003) *Descartes's Theory of Mind* (Oxford: Oxford University Press).

Conan Doyle, A. (1890) 'The Sign of Four' (London: Spencer Blacket).

Connolly, C. (1944/45) *The Unquiet Grave: A Word Cycle by Palinurus* rev. edn. (London: Curwen Press).

Conze, E. (1963/1967) 'Buddhist Philosophy and its European Parallels', in E. Conze, *Thirty Years of Buddhist Studies* (Oxford: Cassirer).

Copeland, D. (1992/1996) *Generation X* (London: Abacus).

Cottingham, J. (2002) 'Descartes and the Voluntariness of Belief', *Monist* 85: 343–60.

Craig, E. J. (1987) *The Mind of God and the Works of Man* (Oxford: Oxford University Press).

Crane, T. and Mellor, D. H. (1990) 'There Is No Question Of Physicalism', *Mind* 99: 185–206.

Davidson, D. (1971) 'Agency', in *Agent, Action, and Reason*, ed. R. Binkley *et al.* (Toronto: University of Toronto Press).

Davies, P. (2001) 'Liquid Space', *New Scientist*, 3 November.

Dawkins, R. (1982) *The Extended Phenotype* (Oxford: W. H. Freeman).

_____ (1986) *The Blind Watchmaker* (London: Longman).

Debiec J., LeDoux, J., and Nader, K. (2002) 'Cellular and Systems Reconsolidation in the Hippocampus' *Neuron* 36(3): 527–538.

Demopoulos, W., and Friedman, M. (1985) 'Critical Notice: Bertrand Russell's *The Analysis of Matter* and its Historical Context and Contemporary Interest', *Philosophy of Science* 52: 621–39.

Dennett, D. (1971) 'Intentional Systems', *Journal of Philosophy* 68: 87–106.

_____ (1981) 'True Believers: The Intentional Strategy and Why It Works', in *Scientific Explanation*, ed. A. F. Heath (Oxford: Oxford University Press).

_____ (1988) 'Why everyone is a novelist' *Times Literary Supplement* 16–22 September.

_____ (1998) 'Quining Qualia', in *Consciousness in Contemporary Science*, ed. E. Bisiach and A. Marcel (Oxford: Clarendon Press).

_____ (1991a) *Consciousness Explained* (Boston: Little, Brown).

_____ (1991b) 'Real Patterns', *Journal of Philosophy* 88: 27–51.

_____ (2001) 'Are We Explaining Consciousness Yet?', *Cognition* 79: 221–37.

Descartes, R. (1618–28/1985) *Rules for the Direction of the Mind* in *The Philosophical Writings of Descartes*, vol. 1, trans. J. Cottingham *et al.* (Cambridge: Cambridge University Press).

_____ (1637/1985) *Discourse on the Method* in *Philosophical Writings of Descartes*, vols. 1, trans. J. Cottingham *et al.* (Cambridge: Cambridge University Press).

_____ (1645–6/1991) Letter to an Unknown Recipient, *The Correspondence* in *The Philosophical Writings of Descartes*, vol. 3, trans. A. Kenny *et al.* (Cambridge: Cambridge University Press).

_____ (1649/1985) *The Passions of the Soul* in *The Philosophical Writings of Descartes*, vol. 1, trans. J. Cottingham *et al.* (Cambridge: Cambridge University Press).

_____ (1985) *The Philosophical Writings of Descartes*, vol. 1 and 2, trans. J. Cottingham *et al.* (Cambridge: Cambridge University Press).

Deutsch. D. (1997) *The Fabric of Reality* (Harmondsworth: Penguin).

Dickinson, E. (1870/1971) 'Letter to Mrs Holland', in *Emily Dickinson: Selected Letters*, ed. T. H. Johnson (Cambridge, MA: Belknap Press).

Doris, J. (2002) *Lack of Character: Personality and Moral Behavior* (Cambridge: Cambridge University Press).

Dretske, F. (1985) 'Misrepresentation', in *Belief: Form, Content, Function*, ed. R. Bogdan (Oxford: Oxford University Press).

_____ (1988) *Explaining Behavior* (Cambridge, Mass: MIT Press).

_____ (1995) *Naturalizing the Mind* (Cambridge, Mass: MIT Press).

Eddington, A. (1928) *The Nature of The Physical World* (New York: Macmillan).

Einstein, A. (1931) 'About Free Will', in *The Golden Book of Tagore: A Homage to Rabindranath Tagore from India and the World in Celebration of His Seventieth Birthday*, ed. Ramananda Chatterjee (Calcutta: Golden Book Committee).

Eliot, G. (1860/1960) *The Mill on the Floss* (Harmondsworth: Penguin).

_____ (1871–2/1970) *Middlemarch* (Harmondsworth: Penguin).

Evans, G. (1973/1985) 'The Causal Theory of Names', in *Collected Papers* (Oxford: Clarendon Press).

_____ (1980/1985) 'Things Without the Mind', in *Collected Papers* (Oxford: Clarendon Press).

_____ (1982) *The Varieties of Reference* (Oxford: Oxford University Press).

Everitt, N. (1991) 'Strawson on Laws and Regularities', *Analysis* 51 206–8.

Flanagan, O. (1992) *Varieties of Moral Personality* (Cambridge, Mass: Harvard University Press).

Flew, A. (1979) (ed.) *A Dictionary of Philosophy* (London: Macmillan).

Fodor, J. (1981) 'The Present Status of the Innateness Controversy', in J. Fodor, *RePresentations* (Brighton: Harvester).

_____ (1989) 'The Persistence of the Attitudes,' in *Psychosemantics* (Cambridge, Mass: MIT Press).

_____ (1998) *Concepts* (Oxford: Oxford University Press).

_____ (2000) *The Mind Doesn't Work That Way* (Cambridge, Mass: MIT Press).

_____ and Lepore, E. (1994) 'What Is The Connection Principle?', *Philosophy and Phenomenological Research* 54: 837–45.

Ford, F. Madox (1924/1989) *Joseph Conrad, A Personal Remembrance* (New York: Ecco Press).

Foster, J. (1982a) *The Case for Idealism* (London: Routledge).

_____ (1982b) 'Induction, Explanation, and Natural Necessity', in *Proceedings of the Aristotelian Society* 83: 87–101.

Frankfurt, H. (1969) 'Alternate Possibilities and Moral Responsibility', *Journal of Philosophy* 66: 828–39.

_____ (1971) 'Freedom of the Will and the Concept of a Person, *Journal of Philosophy* 68: 5–20.

_____ (1975) 'Three Concepts of Free Actions', *Proceedings of the Aristotelian Society Supplementary Volume* 49: 113–25.

_____ (1988) *The Importance of What We Care About* (Cambridge: Cambridge University Press).

Frayn, M. (1974) *Constructions* (London: Wildwood).

Frege, G. (1918/1967) 'The Thought: A Logical Inquiry', in *Philosophical Logic*, ed. P. F. Strawson (Oxford: Oxford University Press).

Garrett, D. (1997) *Cognition and Commitment in Hume's Philosophy* (Oxford: Oxford University Press).

Gazzaniga, M. (1998) *The Mind's Past* (California: California University Press).

Gazzaniga, M. (1998b) 'The Neural Platonist', *Journal of Consciousness Studies* 5: 706–17.

Gerrans, P. (2000) 'Refining the Explanation of Cotard's Delusion', in *Pathologies of Belief,* ed. M. Coltheart and M. Davies (Oxford and Malden, Mass: Blackwell).

Gibbon, E. (1789–90/1900) *Memoirs of My Life and Other Writings*, ed. G. Hill (London: Birkbeck).

Gide, A. (1891) *Traité du Narcisse* (Paris).

Gleick, J. (1987) *Chaos* (London: Heinemann).

Glover, J. (1970) *Responsibility* (London: Routledge & Kegan Paul).

Goff, P. (2006) 'Experiences don't Sum', in *Consciousness and its Place in Nature*, ed. A. Freeman (Thorverton: Imprint Academic).

Gorky, M. (1913–23/2001) *Autobiography*, translated by Isidor Schneider (Amsterdam, The Netherlands: Fredonia Books).

Greene, B. (2004) *The Fabric of the Cosmos* (New York: Knopf).

Grene, M. (1994) 'The Objects of Hume's *Treatise*', *Hume Studies* 20: 163–77.

Grote, J. (1865) *Exploratio Philosophica Part 1: Rough Notes on Modern Intellectual Science* (Cambridge: Cambridge University Press).

Gulick, R. van (2001) 'Reduction, Emergence and Other Recent Options on the Mind-Body Problem: A Philosophical Overview', in *Journal of Consciousness Studies* 8: 1–34.

Hampshire, S. (1972) 'Spinoza and the Idea of Freedom', in *Freedom of Mind* (Oxford: Oxford University Press).

Harman, G. (1998) 'Intentionality', in *A Companion to Cognitive Science*, ed. W. Bechtel and G. Graham (Oxford: Blackwell).

_____ (1999) 'Moral Philosophy meets Social Psychology: Virtue Ethics and the Fundamental Attribution Error', in *Proceedings of the Aristotelian Society* 99: 315–31.

_____ (2000) 'The Nonexistence of Character Traits', in *Proceedings of the Aristotelian Society* 100: 223–6.

Harré, R., and Madden, E. H. (1975) *Causal Powers: A Theory of Natural Necessity* (Oxford: Blackwell).

Heidegger, M. (1927/1962) *Being and Time*, trans. J. Macquarrie and E. Robinson (Oxford: Blackwell).

Hemingway, E. (1929) *A Farwell to Arms* (London: Cape).

Hirsch, E. (1986) 'Metaphysical Necessity and Conceptual Truth', *Midwest Studies* 11: 243–56.

Hirst, W. (1994) 'The remembered self in amnesics', in *The remembering self*, edited by U. Neisser and R. Fivush (Cambridge: Cambridge University Press).

Hobart, R. E. (1934) 'Free Will as Involving Determinism and Inconceivable without It', *Mind* 43: 1–27.

Hobbes, T. (1651/1996) *Leviathan*, ed. R. Tuck (Cambridge: Cambridge University Press).

Hodgson, S. (1870) *The Theory of Practice: An Ethical Enquiry in Two Books* (London: Longmans, Green, Reader, and Dyer).

Hoffman, R. E. (1986) 'Verbal Hallucinations and Language Production Processes in Schizophrenia', *Behavioral and Brain Sciences* 9: 503.

Holmes, R. (1989) *Coleridge—Early Visions* (London: HarperCollins).

Honderich, T. (1988) *A Theory of Determinism: The Mind, Neuroscience, and Life-Hopes* (Oxford: Clarendon Press).

Hubbard, E. (1909) article in *Philistine*.

Hume, D. (1932) *The Letters of David Hume*, ed. J. Y. T. Greig (Oxford: Clarendon Press).

_____ (1739–40/1978) *A Treatise of Human Nature*, ed. L. A Selby-Bigge and P.H. Nidditch (Oxford: Clarendon Press).

Hume, D. (1739–40/2000) *A Treatise of Human Nature*, ed. D. F. Norton and M. Norton (Oxford: Clarendon Press).

—— (1741–2/1985) *Essays* (Indianapolis: Liberty Classics).

—— (1745/1967) *A Letter from a Gentleman to his Friend in Edinburgh*, ed. E. C. Mossner and J. V. Price (Edinburgh: Edinburgh University Press).

—— (1748/1975) Enquiries concerning Human Understanding and concerning the Principles of Morals, ed. L. A Selby-Bigge (Oxford: Clarendon Press).

—— (1748/1999) *Enquiry Concerning Human Understanding*, ed. T. L. Beauchamp (Oxford: Clarendon Press).

—— (1779/1947) *Hume's Dialogues Concerning Natural Religion*, 2nd edn., ed. N. Kemp Smith (Edinburgh: Nelson).

—— (1779/1993) *Hume's Dialogues Concerning Natural Religion*, ed. J. C. A. Gaskin (Oxford: Oxford University Press).

—— (1978) *New Letters of David Hume*, ed. R. Klibansky and J. V. Price (Oxford: Clarendon Press).

Humphrey, N. (1983) 'The Colour Currency of Nature', in *Consciousness Regained* (Oxford: Oxford University Press).

Isham, C., and Butterfield, J. (2000) 'Some Possible roles for Topos Theory in Quantum Theory and Quantum Gravity', *Foundations of Physics* 30: 1707–35.

Jackson, F. (1994) 'Metaphysics by Possible Cases', *Monist* 77.1: 93–110.

—— (1998) *From Metaphysics to Ethics* (Oxford: Clarendon Press).

James, H. (1864–1915/1999) *Henry James: A Life in Letters*, ed. P. Horne (London: Penguin).

James, W. (1890/1950) *The Principles of Psychology* (New York: Dover).

—— (1904a/1912) 'Does Consciousness Exist?', in W. James, *Essays in Radical Empiricism* (London: Longmans, Green and Co).

—— (1904b/1996) 'A World of Pure Experience', in W. James, *Essays in Radical Empiricism* (Lincoln, Nebraska: University of Nebraska Press).

—— (1909/1996) *A Pluralistic Universe* (Lincoln, Nebraska: University of Nebraska Press).

Johnston, M. (1992) 'How to Speak of the Colors', *Philosophical Studies* 68: 221–63.

—— (2003) 'Parts and Principles of Unity', in *Handbook of Contemporary Philosophy* (Oxford: Oxford University Press).

Joyce J. (1922/1986) *Ulysses* (Harmondsworth: Penguin).

Juvenal (*c.*100 CE/1970) *The Sixteen Satires* (London: Penguin).

Kane, R. (1989) 'Two Kinds of Incompatibilism', *Philosophy and Phenomenological Research* 50: 219–54.

—— (1996) *The Significance of Free Will* (New York: Oxford University Press).

Kant, I. (1781–7/1889) *Critique of Pure Reason*, ed. E. Adickes (Berlin: Mayer and Müller).

—— (1781–7/1996) *Critique of Pure Reason*, trans. W. S. Pluhar (Indianapolis: Hackett).

—— (1781–7/1933) *Critique of Pure Reason*, trans. N. Kemp Smith (London: Macmillan).

—— (1783/1953) *Prolegomena*, trans. P. G. Lucas (Manchester: Manchester University Press).

—— (1785/1960) *Fundamental Principles of the Metaphysic of Morals*, trans. T. K. Abbott 1960 (Indianapolis: Bobbs-Merrill).

—— (1785/1964) *Groundwork of the Metaphysic of Morals*, trans. H. J. Paton (New York: Harper & Row).

—— (1788/1956) *Critique of Practical Reason*, trans. L. White Beck (Indianapolis, Bobbs-Merrill).

—— (1790/1973) 'On a Discovery', in *The Kant-Eberhard Controversy*, trans. H. Allison (Baltimore, MD: Johns Hopkins University Press).

____ (1793/1960) *Religion within the Limits of Reason Alone*, trans. T. M. Greene and H. H. Hudson (New York: Harper & Row).

____ (1993) *Opus postumum*, trans. E. Förster and M. Rosen (Cambridge: Cambridge University Press).

Kemp Smith, N. (1941) *The Philosophy of David Hume* (London: Macmillan).

Kneale, W. (1949) *Probability and Induction* (Oxford: Clarendon Press).

Kripke, S. (1972/1980) *Naming and Necessity* (Oxford: Basil Blackwell).

____ (1982) *Wittgenstein on Rules and Private Language* (Oxford: Basil Blackwell).

Ladyman, J. (1998) 'What is Structural Realism?', *Stud. Hist. Phil. Sci.* 29: 409–24.

La Mettrie, J. (1747/1996) 'Machine Man', in *Machine Man and Other Writings*, ed. and trans. A. Thomson (Cambridge: Cambridge University Press).

Lampinen, J., Odegard, T., and Leding, J. (2004) 'Diachronic Disunity', in *The Self and Memory*, ed. D. Beike *et al.* (New York: Psychology Press).

Lange, F. A. (1865/1925) *The History of Materialism*, trans. E. C. Thomas, intro. Bertrand Russell (London: Routledge & Kegan Paul).

Lehrer, K. (1989) *Reid* (London: Routledge).

Leibniz, G. (1686/1988) *Discourse on Metaphysics*, trans. R. Martin, D. Niall, and S. Brown (Manchester: Manchester University Press).

____ (1720/1965) *Monadology and Other Philosophical Essays*, trans. P. and A. M. Schrecker (Indianapolis: Bobbs-Merrill).

Lewis, D. (1983) 'Introduction', in D. Lewis, *Philosophical Papers*, vol. 2 (Oxford: Oxford University Press).

____ (1994) 'Reduction of Mind', in *A Companion to the Philosophy of Mind*, ed. S. Guttenplan (Oxford: Blackwell).

____ (1999) 'Introduction', in D. Lewis, *Papers in Metaphysics and Epistemology* (Cambridge: Cambridge University Press).

____ and Langton, R. (1996/1999) 'Defining "Intrinsic" ', in D. Lewis, *Papers in Metaphysics and Epistemology* (Cambridge: Cambridge University Press).

Libet, B. (1985) 'Unconscious Cerebral Initiative and the Role of Conscious Will in Voluntary Action', *Behavioral and Brain Sciences* 8: 529–66.

____ (1987) 'Are the Mental Experiences of Will and Self-Control Significant for the Performance of a Voluntary Act?', *Behavioral and Brain Sciences* 10: 783–6.

____ (1989) 'The Timing of a Subjective Experience', *Behavioral and Brain Sciences* 12: 183.

____ (1999) 'Do We Have Free Will?', *Journal of Consciousness Studies* 6: 47–57.

Loar, B. (2003) 'Phenomenal Intentionality as the Basis of Mental Content', in *Reflections and Replies: Essays on the philosophy of Tyler Burge*, ed. Martin Hahn and Bjorn Ramberg (Cambridge, Mass: MIT Press).

Locke, J. (1689–1700/1975) *An Essay Concerning Human Understanding*, ed. P. Nidditch (Oxford: Clarendon Press).

____ (1696–9/1964) 'The Correspondence with Stillingfleet', in *An Essay Concerning Human Understanding*, ed. and abrid. A. D. Woozley (London: Collins).

Lockwood, M. (1981) 'What *Was* Russell's Neutral Monism?', *Midwest Studies in Philosophy* 6: 143–158.

____ (1989) *Mind, Brain, and the Quantum* (Oxford: Blackwell).

____ (1993) 'The Grain Problem', in *Objections to Physicalism*, ed. H. Robinson (Oxford: Clarendon Press).

____ (1996) " Many Minds' Interpretation of Quantum Mechanics', *Brit. J. Phil. Sci.* 47: 159–88.

____ (2005) *The Labyrinth of Time* (Oxford: Oxford University Press).

Loux, M. (2002) *Metaphysics: a Contemporary Introduction*, 2nd edn. (London: Routledge).

Lutyens, M. (1983) *Krishnamurti: the Years of Fulfilment* (London: John Murray).

Lycan, W. (1996) *Consciousness and Experience* (Cambridge, Mass: MIT Press).

McCauley, R. N. (1988) 'Walking in our own footsteps: Autobiographical memory and reconstruction' in *Remembering Reconsidered: Ecological and traditional approaches to the study of memory* edited by U. Neisser & E. Winograd (Cambridge: Cambridge University Press).

McCrone, J. (2003) *New Scientist*, May 3.

McDowell, J. (1979) 'Virtue and Reason', *Monist* 62: 331.

—— (1994) *Mind and World* (Cambridge, Mass: Harvard University Press).

—— (1998a) 'Having the World in View: Lecture One', *Journal of Philosophy* 95: 431.

—— (1998b) 'Précis of *Mind and World*', *Philosophy and Phenomenological Research* 58: 365.

McGinn, C. (1982) *The Character of Mind* (Oxford: Oxford University Press).

—— (1983) *The Subjective View* (Oxford: Clarendon Press).

—— (1989/1991) 'Can We Solve the Mind-Body Problem?', in C. McGinn, *The Problem of Consciousness* (Oxford: Blackwell).

—— (1995) 'Consciousness and Space', *Journal of Consciousness Studies* 2: 221–30.

MacIntyre, A. (1981) *After Virtue* (London: Duckworth).

MacKay, D. (1960) 'On the Logical Indeterminacy of a Free Choice', *Mind* 69: 31–40.

Mackie, J. L. (1974) *The Cement of the Universe* (Oxford: Clarendon Press).

—— (1976) *Problems from Locke* (Oxford: Clarendon Press).

McLaughlin, B. (1992) 'The Rise and Fall of British Emergentism', in *Emergence or Reduction? Essays on the Prospects of Nonreductive Physicalism* ed. A Beckermann, A. H. Flohr, and J. Kim (Berlin: Walter de Gruyter).

—— (2002) 'Colour, Consciousness, and Colour Consciousness', in *Consciousness: New Essays*, ed. Quentin Smith (Oxford: Oxford University Press).

Malamud, B. (1979) *Dubin's Lives* (New York: Farrar Straus & Giroux).

Malebranche, N. (1674–5/1980) *The Search After Truth*, trans. T. M. Lennon and P. J. Olscamp (Ohio: Ohio State University Press).

Maxwell, G. (1978) 'Rigid Designators and Mind-Brain Identity', in *Perception and Cognition: Issues in the Foundations of Psychology*, ed. C. Wade Savage (Minneapolis: University of Minnesota Press).

Mele, A. (1995) *Autonomous Agents: From Self-Control to Autonomy* (New York: Oxford University Press).

Mele, A. (2005) 'Decisions, Intentions, Urges, and Free Will: Why Libet has not Shown what he Says he Has', in *Explanation and Causation: Topics in Contemporary Philosophy*, ed. J. Campbell, M. O'Rourke and D. Shier (Cambridge, Mass: MIT Press).

Merleau-Ponty, M. (1945/1962) *The Phenomenology of Perception*, trans. Colin Smith (London: Routledge & Kegan Paul).

Mill, J. S. (1873/1971) *Autobiography* (Oxford: Oxford University Press).

Montaigne, M. de (1563–92/1991) *The Complete Essays*, trans. M. A. Screech (London: Penguin).

Moore, G. E. (1905–6/1922) 'The Nature and Reality of Objects of Perception', in G. E. Moore, *Philosophical Studies* (London: Routledge).

Murdoch, I. (1970) *The Sovereignty of Good* (London: Routledge & Kegan Paul).

Nagarjuna (*c*.150/1995) *The Fundamental Wisdom of the Middle Way*, trans. and comm. J. Garfield (Albany, NY: SUNY Press).

Nagel, T. (1974) 'Panpsychism', *Philosophical Review* 53.

_____ (1979) 'What Is It Like To Be a Bat?', in *Mortal Questions* (Cambridge: Cambridge University Press).

_____ (1986) *The View from Nowhere* (New York: Oxford University Press).

_____ (1987) 'Is that You, James?', *London Review of Books* 9, 1 Oct.

_____ (1998) 'Conceiving the Impossible and the Mind-Body Problem', *Philosophy* 73: 337–52.

Neisser, U. (1981) 'John Dean's memory: a case study' in *Cognition* 9: 1–22.

Newton, I. (1687/1934) *Principia*, trans. A. Motte and F. Cajori (Berkeley: University of California Press).

_____ (1692–3/1959–1977) *Correspondence*, ed. H. W. Turnbull *et al.* (Cambridge: Cambridge University Press).

Nida-Rümelin, M. (1996) 'Pseudonormal Vision: An Actual Case of Qualia Inversion?', *Philosophical Studies* 82: 145–57.

Nietzsche, F. (1881/1997) *Daybreak*, trans. R. Hollingdale (Cambridge: Cambridge University Press).

_____ (1885–8/2003) *Writings from the Late Notebooks* (Cambridge: Cambridge University Press).

_____ (1886) *Beyond Good and Evil (Jenseits von Gut und Böse)* (Leipzig: Naumann).

_____ (1887/1994) *On the Genealogy of Morals* (Cambridge: Cambridge University Press).

Norretranders, T. (1991/1998) *The User Illusion: Cutting Consciousness Down To Size* (London: Penguin).

Novalis (1802) *Heinrich von Ofterdingen*, ed. F. Schlegel (Berlin).

Papineau, D. (1987) *Reality and Representation* (Oxford: Blackwell).

Pascal, B. (*c.*1640–62/1965) *Pensées* rev. edn., trans. A. J. Krailsheimer (London: Penguin).

_____ (1656–7/2004) *Provincial Letters*, in *Thoughts, Letters and Minor Works* (Whitefish, Mont: Kessinger Publishing).

Peacocke, C. (1983) *Sense and Content* (Oxford: Clarendon Press).

_____ (1999) *Being Known* (Oxford: Clarendon Press).

Perry, J. (1979/1994) 'The Problem of the Essential Indexical', in *Self-Knowledge*, ed. A.-Q. A. Cassam (Oxford: Oxford University Press).

Persson, I. (1987) 'Review of *Freedom and Belief*, by Galen Strawson', *Theoria* 53: 59–67.

Pessoa, F. (1914/1998) *Fernando Pessoa & Co., Selected Poems*, edited and translated by Richard Zenith (New York: Grove Press).

Pettit, P. and McDowell, J. (1986) 'Introduction', in *Subject, Thought, and Context* ed. P. Pettit and J. McDowell (Oxford: Oxford University Press).

Philo of Alexandria (20–50/1929–62) *Collected Works*, trans. F. H. Colson and G. H. Whitaker (Cambridge, Mass: Harvard University Press).

Pillemer, D. (1998) *Momentous Events, Vivid Memories: How Unforgettable Moments Help Us Understand the Meaning of Our Lives* Cambridge, MA: Harvard University Press.

Pitt, D. (2004) 'The Phenomenology of Cognition, or What is it Like to Think That *p*?', *Philosophy and Phenomenological Research* 69/1: 1–36.

Plutarch (*c.*100 CE/1939) 'On Tranquillity of Mind' in Plutarch, *Moralia* VI, trans. W. C. Helmbold (Cambridge, Mass: Harvard University Press).

Pöppel, E. (1978) 'Time Perception', in *Handbook of Sensory Physiology*, vol. 8, ed. R. Held *et al.* (New York: Springer).

Priestley, J. (1777/1818) *Disquisitions Relating to Matter and Spirit*, in *The Theological and Miscellaneous Works of Joseph Priestley*, vol. 3, ed. J. T. Rutt (London).

_____ (1777/1965) *Priestley's Writings on Philosophy, Science and Politics*, ed. J. A Passmore (New York: Collier).

Priestley, J. and Price, R. (1778/1819) *A Free Discussion of the Doctrines of Materialism, and Philosophical Necessity*, in *The Theological and Miscellaneous Works of Joseph Priestley*, vol. 4, ed. J. T. Rutt (London).

Prior, A. (*c*.1967/1997) 'A Statement of Temporal Realism', in *Logic and Reality: Essays on the Legacy of Arthur Prior*, ed. B. J. Copeland (Oxford: Oxford University Press).

Pullman, B. (1998) *The Atom In The History Of Human Thought* (New York: Oxford University Press).

Putnam, H. (1967) 'Time and Physical Geometry', *Journal of Philosophy* 64: 240–7.

Quine, W. V. (1951/1961) 'Two Dogmas of Empiricism', in W. V Quine, *From a Logical Point of View*, 2nd edn. (New York: Harper & Row).

—— (1969) 'Natural Kinds', in W. V Quine, *Ontological Relativity and Other Essays* (New York: Columbia University Press).

Ramsey, F. (1925/1997) 'Universals', in *Properties*, ed. D. H. Mellor and A. Oliver (Oxford: Oxford University Press).

Rees, G. (1960) *A Bundle of Sensations* (London: Chatto & Windus).

Regius, H. (1647/1985) *An Account of the Human Mind, or Rational Soul, which explains what it is and what it can be*, in *The Philosophical Writings of Descartes*, vol. 1, trans. by J. Cottingham *et al.* (Cambridge: Cambridge University Press).

Reid, T. (1764/1970) *Inquiry into the Human Mind*, ed. T. Duggan (Chicago: University of Chicago Press).

—— (1788/1969) *Essays on the Active Powers of the Human Mind* (Cambridge, Mass: MIT Press).

Ricoeur, P. (1990/1992) 'Personal Identity and Narrative Identity', in P. Ricoeur, *Oneself as Another*, trans. Kathleen Blamey (Chicago: Chicago University Press).

Rilke, R. M. (1910/1983) *The Notebooks of Malte Laurids Brigge*, trans. Stephen Mitchell (New York: Random House).

Rimbaud, A. (1871/1972) *Oeuvres complètes* (Paris: Gallimard).

Rosch, E. (1997) 'Mindfulness Meditation and the Private (?) Self', in *The Conceptual Self in Context: Culture, Experience, Self-understanding*, ed. U. Neisser and R. Fivush (Cambridge: Cambridge University Press).

Rosenthal, D. (1986/1991) 'Two Concepts of Consciousness', in *The Nature of Mind* (New York: Oxford University Press).

—— (1991) (ed.) *The Nature of Mind* (New York: Oxford University Press).

Ross, M. (1989). 'Relation of implicit theories to the construction of personal histories' *Psychological Review* **96**: 341–357.

Rotter, J. B. (1966) 'Generalized Expectancies for Internal Versus External Control of Reinforcement', *Psychological Monographs* 80.

Ruhnau, E. (1995) 'Time Gestalt and the Observer', in *Conscious Experience*. ed T. Metzinger (Thorverton: Imprint Academic).

Russell, B. (1912/1959) *The Problems of Philosophy* (Oxford: Oxford University Press).

—— (1925) 'Introduction' in F. A. Lange, *The History of Materialism*, trans. E. C. Thomas (London: Routledge & Kegan Paul).

—— (1927a/1992a) *The Analysis of Matter* (London: Routledge).

—— (1927b/1992b) *An Outline of Philosophy* (London: Routledge).

—— (1948/1992c) *Human Knowledge: Its Scope And Limits* (London: Routledge).

Russell, B. (1956/1995) 'Mind and Matter', in *Portraits from Memory* (Nottingham: Spokesman).

—— (1967–9/1978) *Autobiography* (London: Allen & Unwin).

Ryle, G. (1949) *The Concept of Mind* (Harmondsworth: Penguin).

Sacks, O. (1985) *The Man Who Mistook His Wife For A Hat* (London: Duckworth).

Sartre, J.-P. (1938/1996) *La nausée* (Paris: Gallimard).

—— (1943/1969) *Being and Nothingness*, trans. H. E. Barnes (London: Methuen).

—— (1948) *Existentialism and Humanism*, trans. P. Mairet (London: Methuen).

Saunders, S., and Brown, H. (1991) *The Philosophy of Vacuum* (Oxford: Clarendon Press).

Schacht, R. (1983) *Nietzsche* (London: Routledge & Kegan Paul).

Schechtman, M. (1996) *The Constitution of Selves* (Ithaca: Cornell University Press).

Schiffer, S. (1987) *Remnants of Meaning* (Cambridge, Mass: Bradford/MIT Press).

Schopenhauer, A. (1819/1969) *The World as Will and Representation*, vol. 1, trans. E. J. F. Payne (New York: Dover).

Scoville, W. B., and Milner, B. (1957) 'Loss of recent memory after bilateral hippocampal lesions', *Journal of Neurology, Neurosurgery, and Psychiatry* 20: 11–21.

Seager, W. (1995) 'Consciousness, Information, and Panpsychism', in *Explaining Consciousness: the Hard Problem*, ed. J. Shear (Cambridge, Mass: MIT Press).

Searle, J. (1992) *The Rediscovery of the Mind* (Cambridge, Mass: Bradford/MIT Press).

Sellars, W. (1956–63/1997) *Empiricism and The Philosophy of Mind*, intro. R. Rorty (Cambridge: Mass: MIT Press).

Shaftesbury, Earl of (1698–1712/1900) 'Philosophical Regimen', in *The Life, Unpublished Letters, and Philosophical Regimen of Anthony, Earl of Shaftesbury*, edited by B. Rand (New York: Macmillan).

Shoemaker, S. (1970) 'Persons and their Pasts', *American Philosophical Quarterly* 7: 269–85.

—— (1982/1984) 'The Inverted Spectrum', in *Identity, Cause, and Mind* (Cambridge: Cambridge University Press).

—— (1990/1996) 'First-person Access', in *The First-Person Perspective and Other Essays* (Cambridge: Cambridge University Press).

—— (1999) 'Self, Body, and Coincidence', *Proceedings of the Aristotelian Society* 73: 287–306.

Siewert, C. (1998) *The Significance of Consciousness* (Princeton, NJ: Princeton University Press).

—— (2002) 'Consciousness and Intentionality', *Stanford Encyclopedia of Philosophy*, http://plato.stanford.edu.

Smilansky, S. (1994) 'The Ethical Advantages of Hard Determinism', *Philosophy and Phenomenological Research* 54: 355–63.

Smolin, L. (1997) *The Life of the Cosmos* (London: Weidenfeld & Nicolson).

Sommers, T. (2005) *Beyond Freedom and Resentment: An Error Theory of Free Will and Moral Responsibility* (PhD Thesis, Duke University).

—— (2007) 'The Objective Attitude', *Philosophical Quarterly* 57: 321–342.

Spelke, E. (1994) 'Initial knowledge: six suggestions', *Cognition* 50: 431–55.

—— (1990) 'Principles of Object Perception', *Cognitive Science* 14: 29–56.

—— and Hermer, L. (1996) 'Early Cognitive development: Objects and Space', in *Perceptual and Cognitive Development*, ed. R. Gelman, T. Kit-Fong *et al.* (San Diego: Academic Press).

Spinoza, B. (1675/1985) *The Collected Works of Spinoza*, trans. E. Curley (Princeton, NJ: Princeton University Press).

—— (1675/1985) *Ethics*, trans. E. Curley (Princeton, NJ: Princeton University Press).

Steward, H. (1997) *The Ontology of Mind* (Oxford: Clarendon Press).

Stoljar, D. (2006) *Ignorance and Imagination: The Epistemic Origin of the Problem of Consciousness* (Oxford: Oxford University Press).

Stone, J. (1988) 'Parfit and the Buddha: Why There Are No People', *Philosophy and Phenomenological Research* 48: 519–32.

Stone, J. (2005) 'Why There Still Are No People', *Philosophy and Phenomenological Research* 70: 174–92.

Strawson, G. (1986) *Freedom and Belief* (Oxford: Clarendon Press).

—— (1987) 'Realism and Causation', *Philosophical Quarterly* 37: 253–77. [Essay 16]

—— (1989a) 'Red and "Red"', *Synthese* 78/2: 193–232. [Essay 4]

—— (1989b) *The Secret Connexion* (Oxford: Clarendon Press).

—— (1989c) 'Consciousness, Free Will, and the Unimportance of Determinism', *Inquiry* 32: 3–000. [Essay 14]

—— (1990) 'What's so Good about Reid?', *London Review of Books* 12.4: 14–15.

—— (1991) 'The Contingent Reality of Natural Necessity', *Analysis* 51: 209–13. [Essay 17]

—— (1994a) 'The Impossibility of Moral Responsibility', *Philosophical Studies* 75:5–24. [Essay 13]

—— (1994b) *Mental Reality* (Cambridge, Mass: MIT Press).

—— (1997) ' "The Self" ', *Journal of Consciousness Studies* 4: 405–28.

—— (1998a) 'Free Will', in *The Routledge Encyclopedia of Philosophy*, ed. E. Craig (London: Routledge).

—— (1998b) 'Précis of *Mental Reality* and replies to Noam Chomsky, Pierre Jacob, Michael Smith, and Paul Snowdon', Symposium on *Mental Reality, Philosophy and Phenomenological Research* 58: 433–35, 461–86.

—— (1999a) 'The Self and the Sesmet', *Journal of Consciousness Studies* 6: 99–135.

—— (1999b) 'Realistic Materialist Monism', in *Towards a Science of Consciousness III*, ed. S. Hameroff, A. Kaszniak and D. Chalmers (Cambridge, Mass: MIT Press), 23–32.

—— (1999c) 'The Sense of the Self', in *From Soul to Self*, ed. M. James and C. Crabbe (London: Routledge).

—— (2000) 'Epistemology, Semantics, Ontology, and David Hume', *Facta Philosophica* 1: 113–31. [Essay 19]

—— (2000/2002) 'David Hume: Objects and Power', in *The New Hume Debate*, ed. R. Read and K. Richman (London: Routledge) and *Reading Hume on Human Understanding*, ed. P. Millican (Oxford: Oxford University Press). [Essay 18]

—— (2000) 'The Unhelpfulness of Indeterminism', *Philosophy and Phenomenological Research* 60: 149–156.

—— (2001a) 'Hume on Himself', in *Essays in Practical Philosophy: From Action to Values*, ed. D. Egonsson *et al.* (Aldershot: Ashgate Press), 69–94.

—— (2001b) 'The Bounds of Freedom', in *The Oxford Handbook on Free Will*, ed. R. Kane (Oxford: Oxford University Press), 441–60.

—— (2002a) 'Knowledge of the World', *Philosophical Issues* 12. [Essay 3, revised and renamed]

—— (2002b) 'Postscript to 'The Self'', in *Personal Identity*, ed. R. Martin and J. Barresi (New York: Blackwell), 363–70.

—— (2003a) 'Real Materialism', in *Chomsky and his Critics*, ed. L. Antony and N. Hornstein (Oxford: Blackwell). [Essay 1]

—— (2003b) 'What is the Relation between an Experience, the Subject of the Experience, and the Content of the Experience?', *Philosophical Issues* 13: 279–315. [Essay 6, revised]

—— (2004) 'Real Intentionality', *Phenomenology and the Cognitive Sciences* 3. [Essay 11, revised]

—— (2005) 'Intentionality and Experience: Terminological Preliminaries', in *Phenomenology and Philosophy of Mind*, ed. D. Smith and A. Thomasson (Oxford/New York: Oxford University Press), 41–66. [Essay 10]

—— (2006a) 'Why Physicalism entails Panpsychism', in *Consciousness and its Place in Nature*, ed. A. Freeman (Thorverton: Imprint Academic), 3–31. [Essay 2]

Strawson, G. (2006b) 'Reply to Commentators, with a Celebration of Descartes', in *Consciousness and its Place in Nature*, ed. A. Freeman (Thorverton: Imprint Academic), 184–280.

—— (2008) 'The Identity of the Categorical and the Dispositional', *Analysis* 68/4.

—— (2009) *Selves: An Essay in Revisionary Metaphysics* (Oxford: Clarendon Press).

—— (in preparation a) *The Evident Connexion: Mind, Self and David Hume* (Oxford: Clarendon Press).

—— (in preparation b) *Locke on Personal Identity* (Princeton, NJ: Princeton University Press).

—— (in preparation c) *Life in Time* (Oxford: Oxford University Press).

—— (in preparation d) *Intentionality!*

Strawson, P. F. (1959) *Individuals* (London: Methuen).

—— (1966) *The Bounds of Sense* (London: Methuen).

—— (1979) 'Perception and its Objects', in *Perception and Identity*, ed. G. F. MacDonald (London: Macmillan).

—— (1980) 'Replies', in *Philosophical Subjects*, ed. Z. van Straaten (Oxford: Clarendon Press).

—— (1995) 'Reply to Cassam', in *The Philosophy of P. F. Strawson*, ed. P. K. Sen and R. R. Verma (Delhi: Indian Council of Philosophical Research).

Stroud, B. (2000) *The Quest for Reality* (New York: Oxford University Press).

Stump, E. and Kretzmann, N. (1996) 'God's Knowledge', in *The Rationality of Belief and the Plurality of Faith*, ed. T. D. Senor (Ithaca, NY: Cornell), 94–124.

Swann, W. B. (1990) 'To be adored or to be known: the interplay of self-enhancement and self-verification' in *Handbook of motivation and cognition: Foundations of social behavior*, edited by R. M. Sorrentino, & E. T. Higgins, volume 2 (New York: Guilford).

Taylor, C. (1989) *Sources of the Self* (Cambridge: Cambridge University Press).

Toland, J. (1704) *Letters to Serena* (London).

Trefil, J. (1997) *Are We Unique? A Scientist Explores the Unparalleled Intelligence of the Human Mind* (New York: Wiley).

Tucker, A. (1765–1774/1834) *The Light of Nature Pursued* (London: Tegg and Son).

Tye, M. (1995) *Ten Problems of Consciousness* (Cambridge, Mass: MIT Press).

Updike, J. (1989) *Self-Consciousness* (London: Deutsch).

Uus, U. (1994) *Blindness of Modern Science* (Tartu: Tartu Observatory).

Van Fraassen, B. (1980) *The Scientific Image* (Oxford: Clarendon Press).

Van Inwagen, P. (1989) 'When Is the Will Free?', *Philosophical Perspectives* 3: 399–422.

Velarde, M. G., and Normand, C. (1980) 'Convection', *Scientific American* 243: 92–108.

Wagenaar, W. (1994) 'Is memory self-serving?', in *The remembering self: construction and accuracy in the self-narrative*, edited by U. Neisser & R. Fivush (Cambridge: Cambridge University Press).

Wallas, G. (1926) *The Art of Thought* (New York: Harcourt Brace).

Warnock G. (1971) *The Object of Morality* (London: Methuen).

Wegner, D. M. (2002) *The Illusion of Conscious Will* (Cambridge, Mass: MIT Press).

—— and Wheatley, T. (1999) 'Apparent Mental Causation: Sources of the Experience of Will', *American Psychologist* 54: 480–92.

Weinberg, S. (1997) 'Before the Big Bang', *New York Review of Books*, 12 June (New York).

Westphal, J. (1986) 'White', *Mind* 95: 311–28.

Wiggins, D. (1970) 'Freedom, Knowledge, Belief and Causality', in G. Vesey (ed.) *Knowledge and Necessity* (London: Macmillan).

Wilkes K. (1998) 'ΓΝΩΘΙ ΣΕΑΥΤΟΝ (Know Thyself)', *Journal of Consciousness Studies* 5: 153–65.

Williams, B. (1978) *Descartes: The Project of Pure Enquiry* (Harmondsworth: Penguin).

Winkler, K. (1991) 'The New Hume', *Philosophical Review* 100: 541–79.

Wittgenstein, L. (1922/1961) *Tractatus Logico-Philosophicus*, trans. B. McGuinness and D. F. Pears (London: Routledge).

—— (1914–51: 1980) *Culture and Value* (Oxford: Blackwell).

—— (1953) *Philosophical Investigations*, trans. G. E. M. Anscombe (Oxford: Blackwell).

Woolhouse, R. (1988) *The Empiricists* (Oxford: Oxford University Press).

Worrall, J. (1989) 'Structural Realism: The Best of Both Worlds?', *Dialectica* 43: 99–124.

Wright, John P. (1983) *The Sceptical Realism of David Hume* (Manchester: Manchester University Press).

—— (1995) 'Critical Review of *Hume's Theory of Consciousness*, by Wayne Waxman', *Hume Studies* 21: 344–50.

—— (2000) 'Hume's Causal Realism: Recovering a Traditional Interpretation', in *The New Hume: For and Against Realist Readings of Hume on Causation*, ed. R. Read and K. Richman (London: Routledge, UCL Press).

Wundt, W. (1874/1911) *Principles of Physiological Psychology*, trans. E. B. Titchener (New York: Macmillan).

Yeats, W. B. (1933/1950) 'Vacillation' from *The Winding Stair and Other Poems* in *Selected Poems* (London: Macmillan).

Index

This index does not cite every occurrence of every listed term or topic. Page numbers in bold indicate the place at which an entry is introduced or defined, or the main place at which it is discussed.